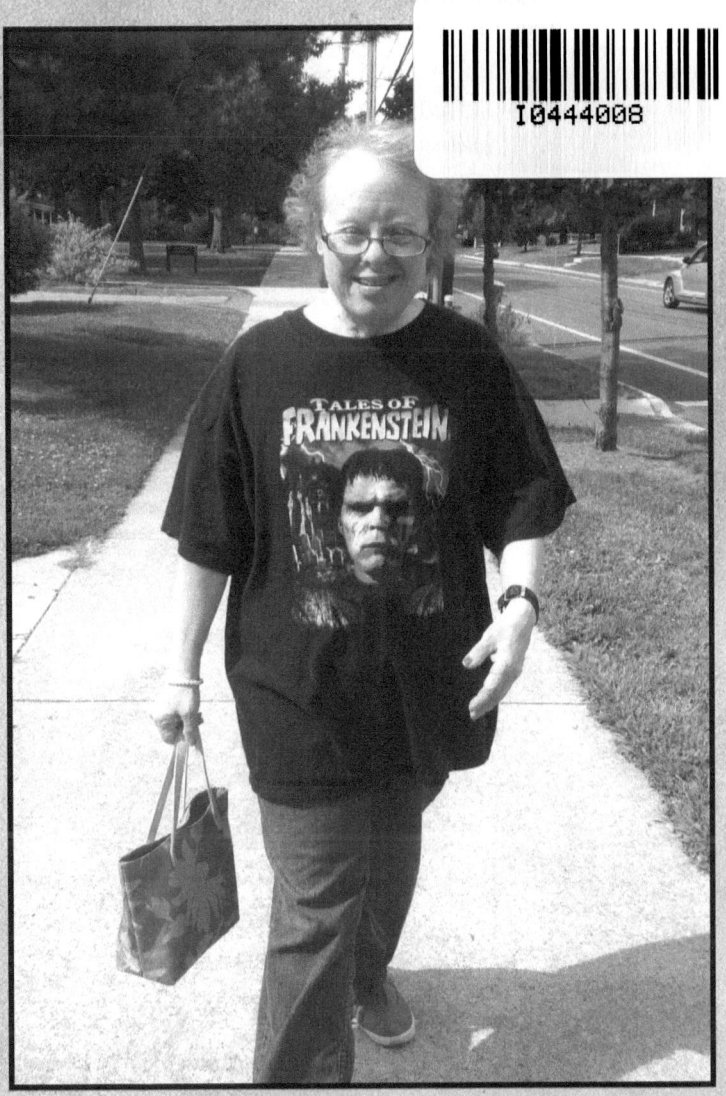

This issue is dedicated to my late sister Heather, who was truly my muse and "partner-in-crime" when it came to everything monster (and *Monster!*)-related. Our family grew up surrounded by overstuffed bookshelves, immersed and awash in esoterica: art, folklore, the occult, zoology/cryptozoology, movie memorabilia, comic books, Asian culture, plus a dizzying array of literary volumes covering theological and mythological iconography (etc., etc). So it was a given that the modern mythology of Creature Features would become an everyday thing to a couple of Monster Kids like Heather and myself. She passed away in 2017, and I sorely miss—and always shall—her joyous outlook on such things as life, *kaiju*, Harry Potter, music, God and monsters... heck, you name it!

MONSTER!

Issue 33 • Spring 2018

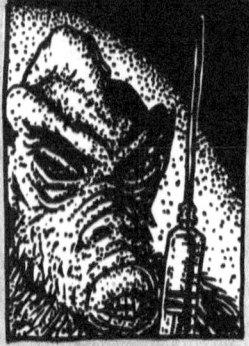

Editorializing! 4
  |- Oscar® Meets The Horny Fish-Monster
Monster! Mail 7
  |- Reader Letters, Art Contributions & Whatnot

Cover Articles:

The Mummy in Australia 11
  [with Endnotes on p.33]

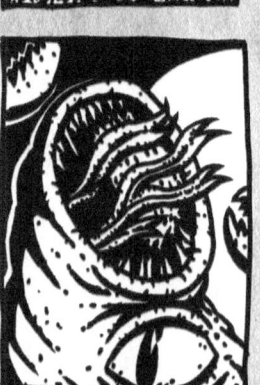

Inside *The Outer Limits*: 35
Interviews with *OL* Alumni Harlan Ellison
& Robert Culp
    |- Ellison 38
    |- Culp 51

Channel of Darkness: 70
Doctor Who & the BBC's Gothic Horrors of
the 1970s *[Part 1] [with Endnotes on p.92]*

Other Unique, Exclusive Features:

National Kid: 97
The "Superman" of Japan
(ナショナルキッド / *Nashonaru Kiddo*)

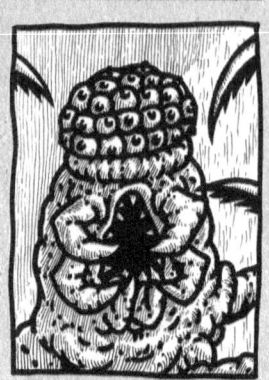

Anarchy & Monsters: 127
The Brett Piper Interview (Parts 2 & 3 [of 6])

Monster Magazines That Time Forgot: 182
Poster Mags
    |- Interview: Dez Skinn 195

Vishal Furia's *Lapachhapi*: 201
A Real Game-Changer for Indian
Horror Cinema! *[Article/Director Interview]*

Return of My Monster Movie Marathon Diary: ... 207
Godzilla A Go-Go!

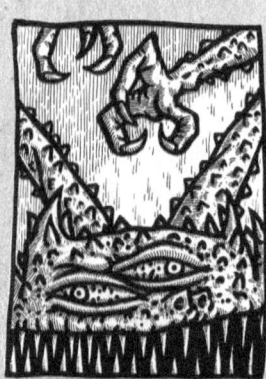

Monster! Roadshow: 235
Recently Discovered 8mm Footage
Makes a Monkey Out of *M*!

[Sidebar] Goin' Ape Over Mighty Joe Young; ... 240
or, even a Giant Gorilla Can't
Make a Monkey Out of *Monster!*

Art by Heather™	248
Creature Feature Reviews	250
Keys to the *House*: Turning Experimentation into Expression!	307
Musings on *The Mummy* (2017)	322
He Who Laughs Last: A Tribute to the Late, Great George A. Romero (1940-2017)	327
M! Movie Checklist: Video availability listings	333
Midnight Snacks *[New Feature!]* Bonus *M!* "Mini" Reviews	349

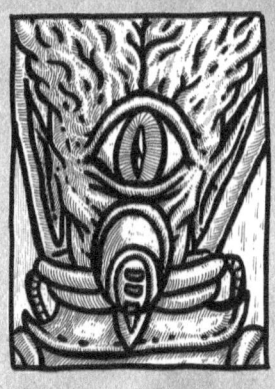

Front & Rear Cover Art: C. Michael Hall's tribute to The Mummy, *Dr. Who* and *The Outer Limits*!
Contents Pages (& p.10) Art: Marcio Costa

Other Original Art Contributions:
Heather Paxton (pp.248-249), Alex Wald (pp.96, 108, 115), Andy Ross (p.256), Allen K. (Koszowski [p.8])

Contributing Writers: Daniel Best, Dana Marie Andra, Dan Ross, Stephen Jilks, Stephen R. Bissette, Christos Mouroukis, Troy Howarth, John Harrison, Neil D'Silva, Michael Hauss, Dennis Capicik, Martín Núñez, Mark Nelson, Jeff Goodhartz, Sebastien "Seb" Godin, Andy Ross, Eric Messina, Les Moore, Mongo McGillicutty, Tim Paxton, and Steve Fenton

Brian Harris, Publisher/Il Padrone
Tony Strauss, Edit-Fiend/Proofreader

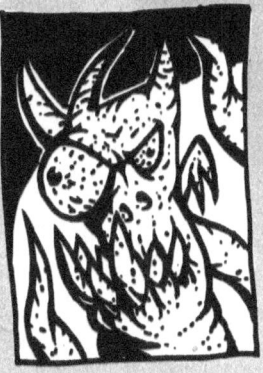

Heather Paxton
Inspiration Source

Timothy Paxton
Editor, Publisher & Design Demon

Steve Fenton
Editor, Image/Info-Wrangler & Co-Proofreader

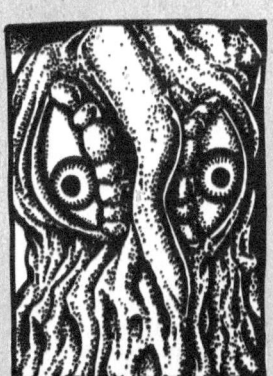

MONSTER! is published erratically. Subscriptions are NOT available. © 2018 WK Books, unless otherwise noted. All rights reserved. No part of this publication may be reproduced, distributed, or transmitted in any form or by any means, including photocopying, recording, or other electronic or mechanical methods, without the prior written permission of the publisher, except in the case of brief quotations embodied in critical reviews and certain other noncommercial uses permitted by copyright law. For permission requests, write to the publisher: "Attention: Permissions Coordinator," at: Tim Paxton, Saucerman Site Studios, 26 W. Vine St., Oberlin, OH 44074 • kronoscope@oberlin.net.

MONSTER! contains photos, drawings, and illustrations included for the purpose of criticism and documentation. All pictures copyrighted by respective authors, production companies, and/or copyright holders.

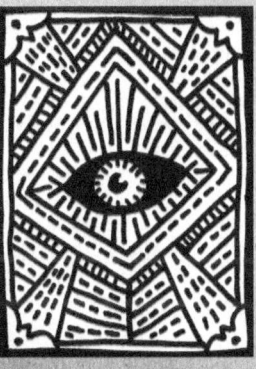

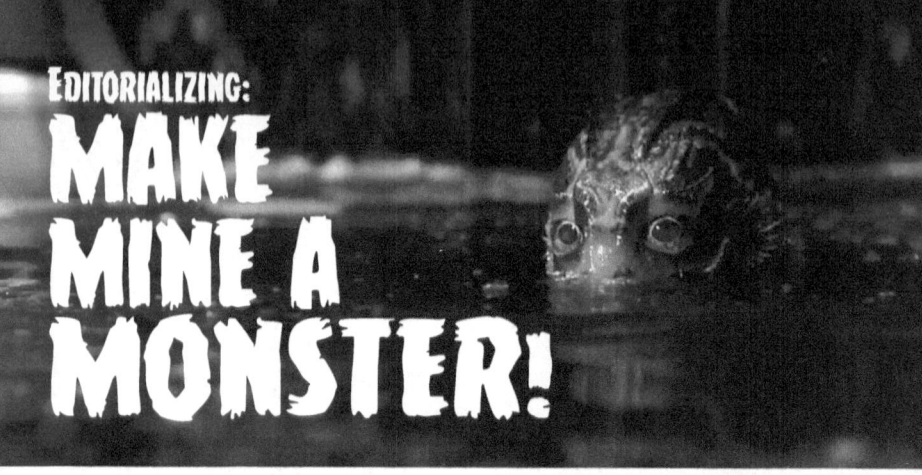

EDITORIALIZING:
MAKE MINE A MONSTER!

I must admit I dozed-off into a sound snooze right before the Oscars ceremony began back in February. Frankly, I've had little interest in the way-overhyped program since that time close to a quarter-century ago when Martin Landau won his well-deserved Best Supporting Actor award for Tim Burton's **ED WOOD** (1994), only to have his anticlimactic acceptance speech after winning a statue for his memorable role—be it largely played for broad caricature or not—of Béla Lugosi in that film was abruptly cut short by intrusive music before Landau could even properly thank those who spiritually shared in his win; not to mention maybe—just *maybe!*—say something nice about Lugosi (an actor who has been largely long-forgotten by Hollywood, if not fandom's "monster kid" generation) along the way. But no such luck. *Booh!*

After awaking the morning after that Sunday night a few months back, I made myself a pot of coffee, settled down to breakfast and turned-on my laptop to catch up on the morning news… Imagine my pleasant surprise when I learned that Guillermo del Toro's **THE SHAPE OF WATER** had not only won the Oscar for both Best Picture and Best Director, but also scored statues for Best Original Score and Best Production Design too, plus was nominated for no less than *nine* more besides (including for Best Cinematography and Best Film Editing, albeit nothing for its superlative visual FX work).

For a monster movie, of all things! Yes indeed, a genre that has never won big at the Oscars before did so for 2017. There are likely nitpickers who would argue that **THE SHAPE OF WA-TER** is either more of a sci-fi film or a fantastical romance, and *not* an all-out monster movie. Well, okay, you're entitled to your opinion … but there's a honking great *gillman* at the center of its plot, and that constitutes more than enough of a monster to suit Yours Truly! I was stunned. Sure, fantasy/SF films have been nominated for Best Picture in the past (my favorite 'longshots' being Neill Blomkamp's alien [i.e., "prawn"]-and-robot-filled **DISTRICT 9** in 2009—which was only nominated for several awards [four in total, including Best Picture] rather than actually winning any, but close enough—and George Miller's action-packed 2015 dystopian post-apocalyptic actioner **MAD MAX: FURY ROAD**, amassing a 'six-pack' of Oscars out of a half-score noms). Further back in time, Peter Jackson's critter-crammed third *LotR* franchise entry **RETURN OF THE KING** (2003) waddled home with fully *eleven* wins (!)—Best Picture included—as did a psycho killer-themed horror film (1991's **SILENCE OF THE LAMBS**, which was awarded a ten statuettes)… But an honest-to-gods *monster* movie?! Now *that's* a real precedent-setter, and hopefully a game-changer too.

At the 46th Academy Awards in 1974, William Friedkin's '73 blockbuster occult shocker **THE EXORCIST** (see also pp.76-77) was nominated in ten categories, including Best Picture. It is historically important for being the first horror movie ever to receive a nomination in that category, and this singularly influential—not to mention HUGELY controversial—demonic/spiritual possession film helped greatly in reshaping/redefining genre cinema virtually the world over, even in non-primarily-Christian countries. Almost *all* the output of India's horror industry [cinematic or otherwise] is roughly based on it in at least some way![1] Despite not winning either Best Picture or Best Director (etc.), **THE EXORCIST** nevertheless did garner a deuce of awards for Best Adapted Screenplay (by the source novel's author, William Peter Blatty) and Best Sound Mixing (its audio mix being one of the keystones in the film's dramatic effectiveness), but maybe

---

[1] Much of this subgenre was covered in *Weng's Chop* #10.

it was considered just too *terrifying*—and possibly blasphemous/sacrilegious by some?—to ultimately win the top honors (also including Best Actress [Ellen Burstyn], Best Supporting Actress [Linda Blair] and Best Supporting Actor [Jason Miller]). took the back seat to both George Roy Hill's period crime dramedy **THE STING** and an infamous onstage streaker/scene-stealer about whom unflappable Oscars host David Niven drolly quipped, "Well, ladies and gentlemen, that was almost *bound* to happen! *[For those younger readers who may not be familiar with the term, "streaking" (i.e., running around in the nude in public) was a popular antiestablishment/antiauthoritarian craze back in the '70s – TP.]* The Brit wit shortly went on to add, "But isn't it fascinating to think that probably the only laugh that man will ever get in his life is by stripping-off and showing his 'shortcomings'?" (!). But I digress!

At this point I must admit I have *never* been an avid follower of the Academy Awards, so excuse me while I dig around for some information...

The earliest horror film ever to win at the Oscars was the 1931 **DR. JEKYLL AND MR. HYDE**, a pre-Code production directed by Rouben Mamoulian, for which Fredric March won Best Actor[2]; this comes as no surprise if you've seen his powerhouse performance in the film. For the most part, over the next 90-odd years, if they won any awards at all, Fantasy and its sister genres Horror and Science Fiction largely took home the gold for what you would expect: Best Makeup is a given, in most cases (**AN AMERICAN WEREWOLF IN LONDON** [1981], Cronenberg's **THE FLY** [1986], **HARRY AND THE HENDERSONS** [1987], **MEN IN BLACK** [1997], **PAN'S LABYRINTH** [2006], etc.), Best Costume, Best Visual Effects (**ALIENS** [1986]), Cinematography, Sound Effects, Art Direction, et cetera.[3] Only rarely did a horror or monster movie make it into the Top Four categories, although there were a few post-Fredric March examples to be had: Ruth Gordon won Best Supporting Actress for Roman Polanski's monster infant-in-the-making thriller **ROSEMARY'S BABY** (1968), while Natalie Portman also did as a bonkers ballerina in Darren

Aronofsky's psychological horror entry **BLACK SWAN** (2008), and **THE SILENCE OF THE LAMBS** (1991) took home statuettes for Best Picture, Best Director (Jonathan Demme), Best Actor in a Leading Role (Anthony Hopkins), Best Actress in a Leading Role (Jodie Foster), and Best Adapted Screenplay (by Ted Tally).

But a *monster* movie taking home the prize for Best Picture? Now *that* was sure something to wake up to!

Could this signal the start of some kind of lasting trend, I wonder? Are the Academy finally starting to wake up and smell the coffee? If so, hopefully there'll be no more fluffy trivialities like **SHAKESPEARE IN LOVE** (1998) taking home the award for Best Picture![4] **THE SHAPE OF WATER** is every bit as romantic as John Madden's '98 commercial hit, it just approaches its material in a, uh, somewhat *different* manner (to say the least!). Might a sequel be in the works? Let's hope not, as I felt that the film ended perfectly well as it was, without any need for a continuation. Not that del Toro is much known for doing sequels anyway, so the odds of it happening are slim to virtually nil.

****

On a different, more somber note, as for this issue of *Monster!* being over a year late... Well, 2017 was a very tough one indeed for me, as my sister and long-time movie *compadre* Heather Paxton passed away in June from what I suspect was an Alzheimer's-related illness. For those who are not aware of just how majorly Heather had factored into my life for the past dozen years or so prior to that tragic loss, allow me to expand a little bit on our history and how it related directly to my publishing endeavors. Heather was afflicted with what some physicians would call a severe case of Down's Syndrome. Although she could not really function normally in our society as an independent individual, she was very much a Paxton through and through nevertheless. Monsters were her *passion* and, like myself, she could personally relate to their unique 'otherness' (as you might expect, her being so obviously different from most so-called 'normal' folk herself, both in a physical and mental sense). She

---

2 Well, March actually shared with Wallace Beery in **THE CHAMP** in one of the only six (6) ties ever recorded at the Academy Awards. So, technically, it *wasn't* a hands-down/totally-in-the-bag win for horror, by any means, but it was a good start.

3 A typical, although fine, example is Francis Ford Coppola's hoopla-laden **BRAM STOKER'S DRACULA** which won for Best Costume Design, Best Sound Editing, and Best Makeup in 1994. Another example would be the lavish-but-dull 1943 version of **THE PHANTOM OF THE OPERA**, which won for Best Cinematography and Best Art Direction, albeit for the opera-house nonsense rather than for anything to do with horror.

4 As it did in 1998, and that really threw me. It was an only-okay romantic comedy period piece; granted there wasn't much else in the running other than for Spielberg's WW2 epic **SAVING PRIVATE RYAN**. As for horror or monster movies that year, they were pretty thin on the ground as well. Seriously, Bill Condon's **GODS AND MONSTERS** rightfully *should* have won Best Picture, but it wasn't even nominated. The film did walk away with Best Adapted Screenplay by Bill Condon (from Christopher Bram's 1995 novel *Father of Frankenstein*), though, so that was something, at least.

drew them, collected magazines, comics, books, movies and music about them, and—much to her delight—she even had a book published that showcased her lifelong love of God and Monsters. Being her primary caregiver for a number of years, I spent a great deal of time with Heather while I was in the process of writing articles and doing design/layout work on *Weng's Chop* and *Monster!* in-between working on other publishing projects on the side. Her passing was exceedingly tough on me, understandably enough, and I miss her intensely, that was how strong the bond between us was (still is, and always will be).

That said, various other 'real world' personal factors—not just in regards to me but for the rest of the *WC/M!* posse too—were also responsible for delays in this ish's publication. However, when all is said and done, we trust that this 370something-page whopper of an issue will more than make up for our overlong stretch of 'downtime'. While I haven't really contributed anything to this issue other than its design aspect *[Which is a BIG contribution, pardner. We couldn't do it without ya! Your spiritual presence is also always very much appreciated. – SF]*, I will be back as-per-usual tackling Indian monster movie material come next issue. Till then, I hope you enjoy this issue. (If not, you can always just use it for a doorstop!) |- **Tim P.**

LAME 'LEGALESE' BULLSHIT" (a.k.a. "THE FINE PRINT IN BLOCK CAPS")

Hopefully without coming across as either dickish or combative in any way here, I'd like to with the utmost civility stress that our readers and/or contributors should kindly be advised, starting now and henceforth (as heretofore, without us ever actually 'officially/formally' stipulating as such prior to this) that "ANY AND ALL OPINIONS EXPRESSED ABOUT ANYTHING WHATSOEVER IN *MONSTER!* ARE NOT NECESSARILY THOSE OF EITHER THE PUBLISHERS, EDITORS OR CONTRIBUTORS, NOR MAYBE EVEN ANY OF THEIR FAMILY MEMBERS AND FRIENDS OR DOGS AND CATS EITHER… (but then again, some—or even many, for that matter—just *might* be. But we'll never know, will we?!" Yes indeed, me being, I proudly and unapologetically confess right to the bitter end, a 1,000,000% Free Speech Absolutist (something which is becoming rarer than tits on a bull or gold-capped hen's teeth these days, so it seems)—there, I said it!—I am all for (did I mention 1,000,000% already?) people—as in anyone and everyone, *without exception*—freely and openly expressing their views either verbally or in print (etc.) in any way, shape or form they see fit. Free Speech is without question one of the *true*, crucial bastions/cornerstones of very Civilization itself, regardless of whichever culture, and it is being gradually eroded, and sometimes even swiftly stifled virtually the world over right now.

Thanks largely to the current Orwellian climate of would-be thought control by The Establishment (the phony-baloney corporate/state-controlled mainstream media very much included), I have lately become rabidly non-PC to the point of overkill, and I'm afraid ya gonna have ta *KILL* me to stop me voicing my opinions (whether asked-for or otherwise) if I feel a need to say something. Because I utterly REFUSE to be silenced by ANYONE (I *dare* ya ta try! ☺), and I freely encourage EVERYONE, bar none, regardless of their belief system(s), to do likewise themselves until death. IMO, humanity seriously needs to jolt itself back to a semblance of normalcy in a big way ASAP, and virtually the **ONLY** way to properly achieve anything even close to that is by re-embracing long-held Age of Enlightenment standards of freedom of expression, most especially here in the Western Hemisphere, but just about everywhere else besides too.

That said, Tim and I definitely do discourage our valued contributors—not that they've been doing so, mind you—from engaging in any sort of overt political soapboxing within the frameworks of their articles or other writings published herein. Although we are all for contribs unabashedly expressing their views on subjects other than the various forms of monster-related pop culture we cover if they choose to, so long as they don't overdo it and we the editors believe it fits the context of whatever piece it appears in and they aren't simply spewing it forth in a self-indulgent torrent… you know, kinda like I'm doing right now! Like Tim has said to me more than once, that kind of thing should be kept to writers' personal blogs rather than us using-up (I hesitate to say 'wasting') our valued physical pages on it, which can always be better filled by something more on-point, we feel. That said, cussing (if needs be) and smutty talk (within reason), is totally acceptable to us. All we ask is that people don't overdo it (too much), and that writers exercise due discretion at such times as they might wish to get a bit raunchier than the norm so as not to risk dragging *Monster!* too far down into the gutter. Rest assured that the ONLY time a contributor's work will be altered (if any) is for *purely editorial* (i.e., aesthetic) purposes, *NOT* on censorial grounds in regards to any perceived 'objectionable' content, cuz that's entirely in the mind's eye of the beholder, so what constitutes it can vary drastically from person to person, as we all well know. Regardless of the specific content, if we decide that part of it simply doesn't 'fit' our format or 'image' (such as it is) and sticks out like a sore thumb from the rest of a piece and the zine as a whole, we may have to give it the chop, I'm afraid; but *only* on those grounds, not arbitrarily as we see fit.

Anyway, even though I think that self-censorship is one of the very *worst* kinds—but *only* when we do it for other people's sake for whatever reason, not independently by ourselves if we have genuine second thoughts about an idea and opt to modify our words accordingly—it's time for me to STFU now (don't all cheer at once! ☺ [*YAAAAAAYYYY!!!*]).

Sincerely Yours,
Steve F.

PS. I give you my word here and now that I will NEVER get so self-indulgently 'political' on you EVER again in this mag. If you wanna know the truth, I absotively positulety HATE wasting my valuable creative time on politics/politicians, and I really do think our TLC-saturated pages are put to much better use by us all sticking strictly to talking about one of our lifelong pop-cultural loves… **MONSTER MOVIES!!!**

*(Oh, and one last thing: *Godzilla for President of the World!* [Insert extra-LOUD "Big G"-style war-roar here.] Now *there's* a kind of global ruler I'd gladly bow down before. All hail the godzilarchy/kaijocracy!)

MONSTER! Mail

c/o Saucerman Site Studios, 26 West Vine Street, Oberlin, OH USA • kronoscope@oberlin.net

From actor George Stover (in response to our Don Dohler article and interview with him in *Monster!* #31 [November 2016]):

Thanks for the mag, Tim!
Really enjoyed it. This is certainly THE Don Dohler issue, what with all the coverage of him, me and the movies!! I don't get much "ink" anymore in this Internet age, so it's nice to be on paper again. Tell me, is "Les Moore" a pen name? I can't find him here on Facebook. I'd like to ask him if he can steer me in the direction of getting those foreign versions of **THE ALIEN FACTOR** and **NIGHTBEAST** for my collection.
Best, George

Hey George, it was our pleasure! The entire creature crew here at Monster! *all love Don's work, so we'll gladly publish anything we can about his films, and your interview was both informative and entertaining. As for those foreign titles you inquired about: man, would I ever love to have those myself! I'm sure they're out there somewhere, and if we ever come across any VHS tapes or DVDs of* **NIGHTBEAST** *or* **THE ALIEN FACTOR**, *I will let you know. ~ Tim P.*

Hey George: Steve F. here. Do excuse our belated response, but Thanks Muchly for your kind response to the issue, as well as for originally consenting to do the interview in the first place! We were more than happy to give yourself and the late Mr. Dohler some "ink"; it's not as if

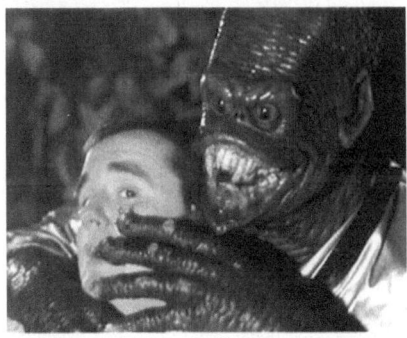

The toothsome titular critter of Don Dohler's **NIGHTBEAST** (1982, USA) seems to be getting way too touchy-feely with Geo. Stover in this shot. But not to worry, it isn't like it wants to impregnate him with an alien fetus or anything, just rip his head off, is all

you're both not fully deserving of every drop! As for your inquiry in regards to the elusive Les Moore, we must confess that the guy is quite the enigma, even to us. (Unlike our mascot Mongo McGillicutty, who's absolutely no mystery to anyone but himself!) Mr. Moore—whom we can only assume uses a pseudonym for the simple reason that he forwards his M! *contributions to us via highly secretive means in order to remain as anonymous as possible—informs us that he will definitely be looking into your request about those foreign editions of yours and Don's movies, and will get back to us as soon as possible about*

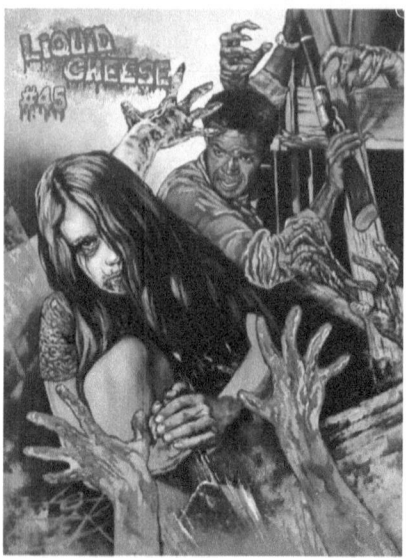

Liquid Cheese #45

Monster! #32 and the absolutely wonderful layout. In its balance of stylistic brio and easy-on-the-eyes readability, in its scrupulous attention to detail (as in, to name but one example, the rigorous execution of your house style of title formatting), and in the sheer mind-boggling scope of a 360-page issue, it is truly a knockout achievement.

I make no pretensions to any sort of professional expertise in this area, but I am often called upon to assist with the assembly of my workplace's internal publication, so I have some distant idea of just how much work it takes to make an end product look and feel as effortlessly done as yours does. And when you consider just how full-to-bursting it is with photos and graphics of every sort, the accomplishment of bringing that all together in as aesthetically pleasing a final package as you have—well, I thought it merited a tip of the hat!
Kudos!
John Moran

it. Thing is, the flighty bugger has a habit of taking-off to parts unknown for whoever-knows-how-long of a time at a stretch without notice, so there's no telling when he'll get around to it. Rest assured that we shall keep you posted if he ever turns anything up, though! ☺ *(Come to think of it, perhaps we might even run a special entry all about the video availability of Don's canon in the Vid Info pages for* M! *#34.)*

On Aug 14, 2017, at 8:48 PM, John Moran <john_moran51@comcast.net> wrote:

Ever since the tragic demise of *Video Watchdog* became imminent, I've been sampling a wide spectrum of genre & cult movie magazines in the hopes of filling that *'Dog*-sized hole, and I just had to take two seconds to drop you a line regarding

Hey John, thanks for the kind words about our li'l publication. Monster! *has undergone some heavy reconstruction over the past year-and-a-half, and at times it felt as if we might be set to go-under for keeps. But thanks to our steadfast, patient posse of contributors for this and past issues, Steve and I will keep on grinding-out new and exciting projects...albeit maybe not as regularly nor frequently as we have done in the past. [But small press publishing is in our blood and what we live for, John, so there ain't no stopping us now!* ☺ *– SF.] As for the 'look' of our zine, it's kinda funny about* M!*'s layout and design elements. The latest issue of Dave Kosanke's essential fanzine* Liquid Cheese *(#45, available from* http://liquidcheesefanzine.storenvy.com/products*) contained a 'flashback' review of* Photo Fiends, *my ancient first attempt as a teenager at emulating* Famous Monsters. *It's been almost* 40 years *(!!!) since the three issues of* PF *were*

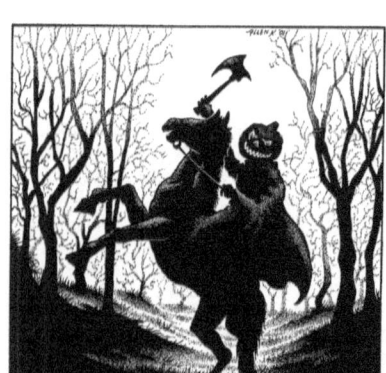

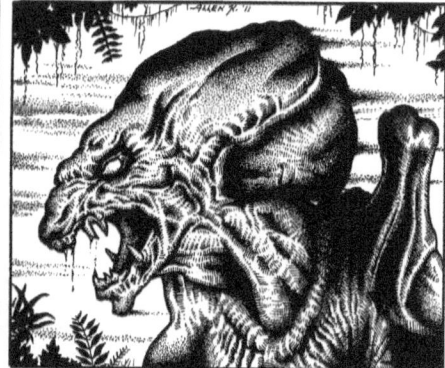

Editorial and Monster! Mail

published and, looking back at its plain, straightforward design, not a whole lot has changed in my zines in that respect. ~ Tim P. [I beg to differ, pard! *PF* was waaay sweeter on the eyeballs than most other amateur zines were back then—and offset-printed on glossy paper to boot, yet!—and *M!* (as well as every other print project I work on with you, our books included) is a total *beaut*, as anyone with an eye for artistry/aesthetics can plainly see by the present beautifully-designed/maximum TLC ish we've co-created! (OK, self-indulgent horn-tooting over!) – SF.]

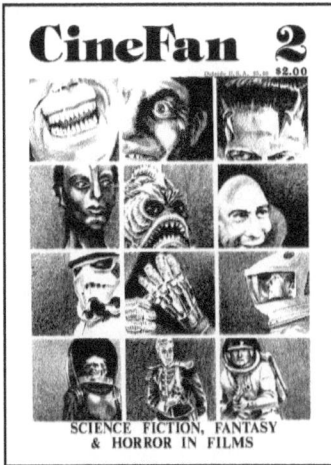

Dear Mr. Paxton,
I have just discovered *Monster!* and I love it. I am a World Fantasy award-winning artist who has been published in many horror/fantasy/SF books and magazines, both film and fiction-related. I love monsters. So your magazine is right up my artistic alley. I have tons of unpublished art here, both black and white and in color, that I would be happy to let you use for free except for a copy or two of any issue that they might be used in. The latest issue I have is #27. Are you still publishing? I am attaching a couple of pieces so you can see my type of work and which you can use if you think they would fit. These have not appeared anywhere yet. I can send many more for consideration. I am fairly well-known in the Lovecraftian art field.

So, thanks for such a great magazine. I hope to hear from you.
My Best,
Allen Koszowski

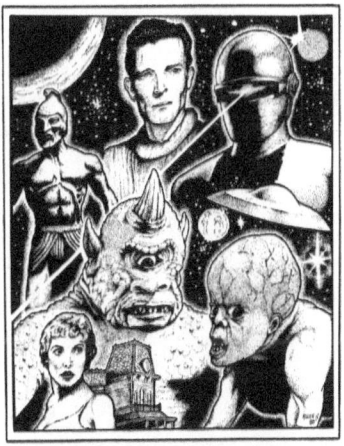

Hey Allen, it's been a lo-o-o-o-ong *time, but this is actually the* second *letter I've gotten from you over the past, um, few decades! Dating from the mid-1980s, said missive is now no doubt buried somewhere amidst my sprawling and decidedly disorganized fanzine collection, tucked away inside my copy of* Dementia #1 (1986), *one of the many zines for which you did the cover art. I have been a fan of your masterful artwork since my days of collecting HPL fanzines and chapbooks, many of which bore your cover designs. I am always up for putting out another special HPL-inspired issue of* Monster!, *and when that happens, we will definitely be in touch; which isn't to say we won't gladly run other works of yours in the interim! ~ Tim P.*

Hey Allen: Steve F. here. I just wanted to say that we really appreciate your offer of trading us artwork for copies of M! and we're all-for the idea. I'm very familiar with your fabulous draftsmanship from any number of fanzines, including Midnight Marquee, Wet Paint *and* Cinefan *(etc. [see 3 pics at right this page]), so it was quite the honor indeed to have you contact us from out of the blue. Here's hoping we can collaborate with you in the near future. Methinks we're long-overdue for another Lovecraft-themed issue, and you'd be an ideal fit for it!*

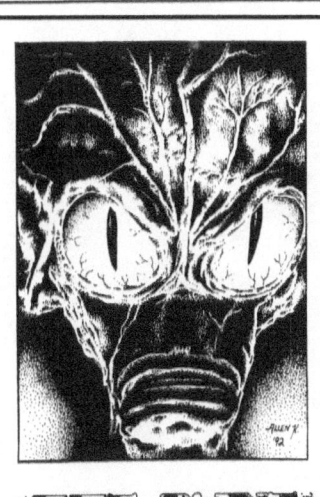

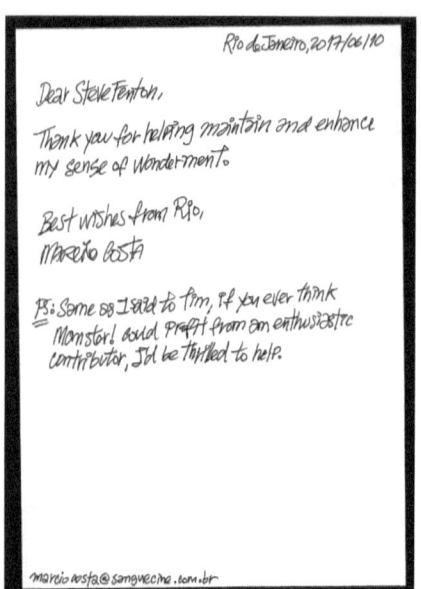
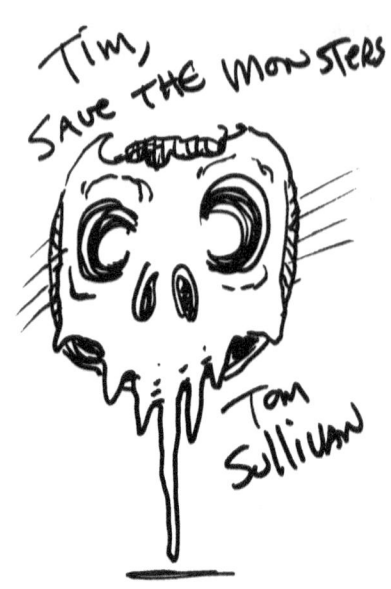

Hey Marcio, we'd love to have you contribute some more artwork to the mag, and thanks for your kind offer to do so. If you feel up to doing some spot illustrations for us that pertain to specific movies (or other subjects we're covering), that would be great, but you can also even send us random drawings on our main theme, if you wish. By the way, we still have that lovely Yokai Monsters spot illo you sent us a while back on file, and we can definitely find a place for it in a future ish! But by all means send us anything else you think might fit too. Your bold, high-contrast B&W style drawings reproduce so well in a monochromatic mag like ours, and they pop right off the page! |- Steve F.

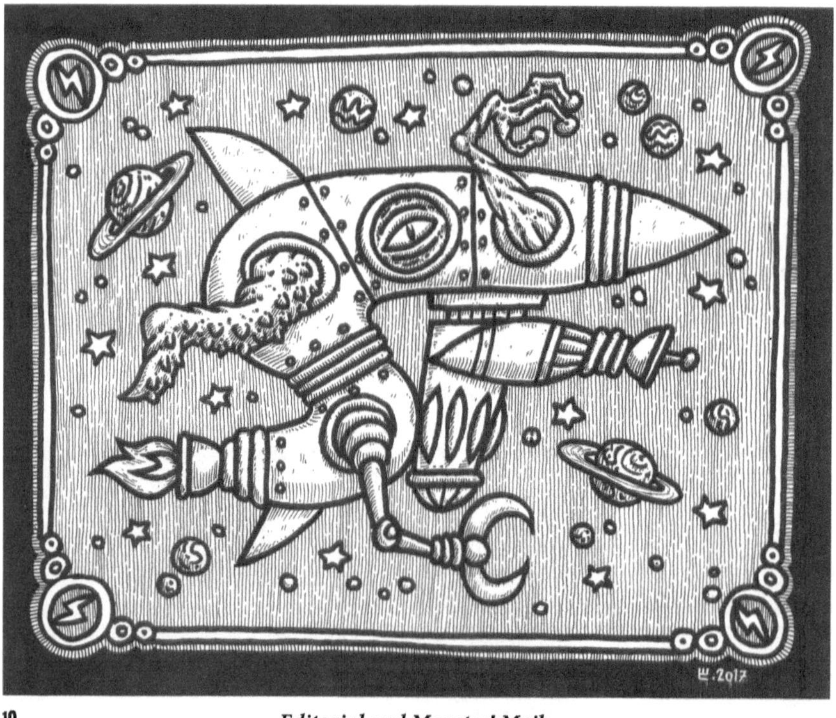

THE MUMMY IN AUSTRALIA

by Daniel Best

[with Endnotes on p.33; indicated in the article text by numbers given in bolded superscript]

Introductory Note: This article deals only with Universal Pictures' initial sextet of *Mummy* entries, not the studio's only-slimly-connected "Second Wave" and "Third Wave" 'reboots' of the franchise; although it does also cover Hammer Films' series, the first of which was officially sanctioned by Universal.

****

Out of all the monsters that Universal Studios unleashed Down Under, almost none had as much longevity as The Mummy did. When other monsters fell by the wayside after the national 1948 horror film ban here in Australia, mummy movies were still required viewing at the cinemas, mainly for children. Their short running times (usually about an hour) made them irresistible for exhibitors wanting to package two films, plus newsreels and cartoons on a Saturday morning or afternoon, and the cheap thrills that they brought were harmless enough. More importantly, unlike Dracula or Frankenstein, The Mummy could be pointed to as an educational tool. Universal's handling of Egyptology and life after death resulted in more than one eager child, and even adults, seeking-out books and actually learning something new from it. In later years, the movies became regular fixtures at drive-ins, repackaged for midnight horror multi-bills. Even a horrific murder in 1944 which was blamed on **THE MUMMY'S GHOST** didn't diminish the franchise's appeal amongst the more youthful consumer demographic.

And, in a twist that is still a mystery in itself, Hammer Films' 1959 reworking of **THE MUMMY** became one of the few genuine horror movies to get released during the blanket ban of such fare in Australia, and it was quite possibly the first Christopher Lee/Peter Cushing co-starring horror ever released when it hit the drive-in circuit here in 1961.

The success of the first Mummy movie owed a lot to the discovery of King Tutankhamen's tomb by Howard Carter in 1922. Australia, taking its lead from England, was a nation fascinated by exploration and discovery, and Carter's find was headline news here, as elsewhere. The supposed 'curse' of King Tut's Tomb only added to the exotic appeal and mystery. People were enthralled by the sights of pyramids, golden coffins and death-masks, and previously unknown boy kings. If ever a country was suited for a movie about Egypt's walking dead, it was Australia!

****

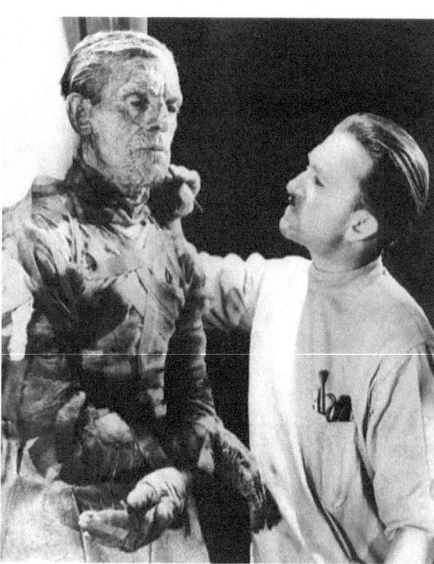

Top Left: In full Ardath Bey getup on the set of **MUMMY** '32, "Karloff the Uncanny" calmly peruses the script. **Top Right:** Makeup artist Jack P. Pierce's wrinkled, wizened (to quote the contemporaneous trade paper *Hollywood Filmograph*) "masterpiece of facial adornment" on the actor went far in expressing not just Imhotep's innate chronological ancientness, but all the subtle nuances of his very soul itself, too

1933: THE MUMMY

In 1932, Universal Pictures knew they were onto a winner with horror films. Both **DRACULA** and **FRANKENSTEIN** (both 1931, USA) had been incredible successes for the studio, making household names out of their respective stars, Béla Lugosi and Boris Karloff. As Universal scrambled for new material, Egypt, the concept of reincarnation and mummies were fresh in the public's eye, buoyed by the discovery (and plunder!) of the boy king Tutankhamen, and the supposed curse that had been placed upon his tomb.

To that end, Carl Laemmle, Jr. commissioned a script from John L. Balderston[1]—who, while working as a foreign correspondent for *The New York Times*, had actually reported on the unsealing of King Tut's tomb back in '22—that would exploit those themes and, in doing so, create an all-new horror sensation for the public.

Once the script was ready, Universal began to hire-on those personnel who would bring the film to life. Directing the movie was the renowned cinematographer, Karl Freund,[2] who had made his name in Weimar Germany working on such silent classics as Paul Wegener's **THE GOLEM** (*Der Golem, wie er in die Welt kam*, 1920), F.W. Murnau's **THE HEAD OF JANUS** (*Der Januskopf*, 1920) and Fritz Lang's **METROPOLIS** (1927). Freund had moved to America in 1930 and remained there, working on **DRACULA**, for which he contributed greatly to the overall mood of the film. He would round-out his career working as a cameraman again, on the television show *I Love Lucy*.

Moving on to casting **THE MUMMY**, there was really only *one* choice to play the title role—Boris Karloff.[3] Unlike the paler-skinned Eastern European Béla Lugosi,[4] although a Britisher, Karloff already *looked* Egyptian. This Middle Eastern hue came from his naturally swarthy complexion, which is now attributed to his Indian heritage[5] (over the course of his career, the actor played more than one Indian character, of both the Eastern and American kind, as well as Asians from the Orient too). Karloff never officially confirmed, nor denied, this part of his heritage in his lifetime, instead referring to his skin tones as his natural 'tan', and then blaming that on the California sun.

Karloff was born in England, but his mother, Eliza, was born in Bombay,[6] India, to an Indian mother. A popular theory of the time was that Karloff himself was the illegitimate offspring of Eliza and an unknown Indian sailor, adopted into the Pratt family as their own. The claims of illegitimacy were never proven though, so Karloff remained a Pratt, albeit one with a quarter Indian blood.

It is worth noting that, over the years, much debate has been made about which man, Karloff or Lugosi, was the better actor, and why Karloff thrived in motion pictures, whereas Lugosi suffered. Putting aside the argument over their acting abilities, it becomes clear why Karloff's star continued to rise while Lugosi's stagnated: *language*, pure and simple.

No matter how good of an actor he was, how versatile and attractive he might have been, the Hungarian-born Lugosi never quite mastered the English language, and neither could he lose his accent, nor did he ever have any desire to do so. However the British private school system-reared Karloff,[7] could slip into an assortment of different accents with ease and, despite a slight lisp, was as articulate as anyone in the industry. While Karloff could easily pass as an Egyptian (or one of any Asiatic race, for that matter) with only a minimum of makeup due to his skin-tone and linguistic skills, Lugosi would have clearly had to struggle and would require hours in the makeup chair on a daily basis, just to get his skin

[Continued on p.16]

pigmentation correct; not to mention the special ethnic accent which, without training and heavy rehearsal, he would never be able to master. And the proud Lugosi flatly *would not* train or work at changing his natural manner of speech an iota.

In summary, Karloff was believable in his versatility. Lugosi was not.

This is not to say that Karloff could have acted as well or better in every role that Lugosi took, or vice versa, or that either man was a better technical thespian than the other. It's hard to imagine how **DRACULA** would have turned out with Karloff in the title role. The role, that of an Eastern European prince, was a perfect fit for Lugosi, and his accent really added to—and enhanced—the film's credibility. If nothing else, **DRACULA** with Boris Karloff instead would have been *very* different indeed, and possibly nowhere near as successful. What we do know is that, when Lugosi played Frankenstein's

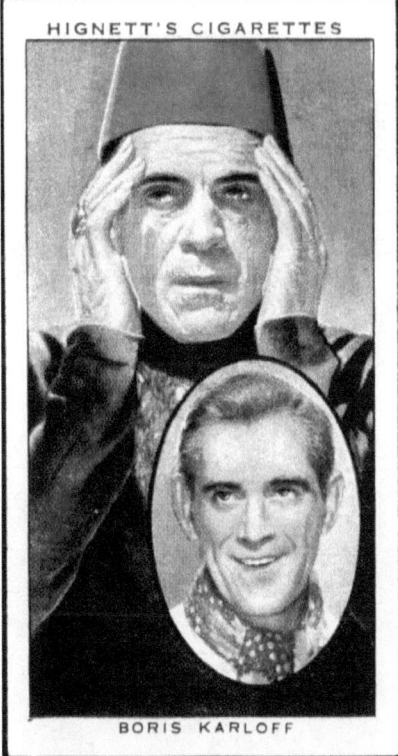

Card #27 in the Brit tobacco company Hignett's 1938 cigarette card series "Actors – Natural & Character Studies" depicted Karloff as both 'himself' and in-character for/ as **MUMMY** '32. **Next 2 Pages:** The film's Austrian—not *Australian!*— program

Die Mumie

(Der Mann vor 3000 Jahren)

Regie: KARL FREUND

In den Hauptrollen:
Boris Karloff, Zita Johann und **David Manners**

Fabrikat:
Universal Pictures Corporation, New York

Verleih für Österreich:
Universal Pictures Ges. m. b. H., Wien VII.

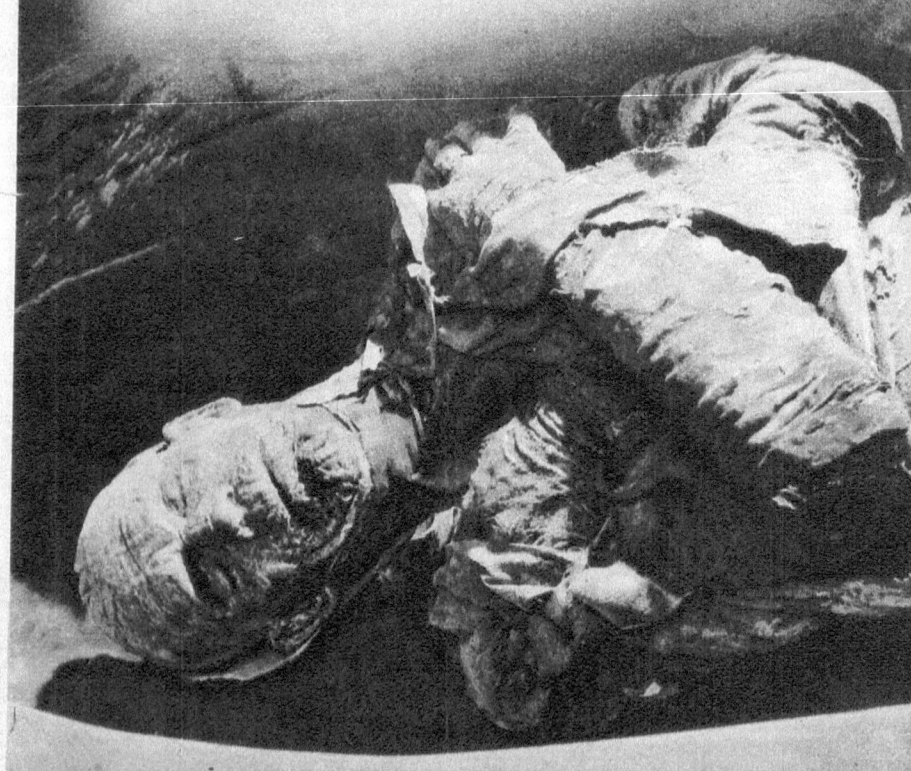

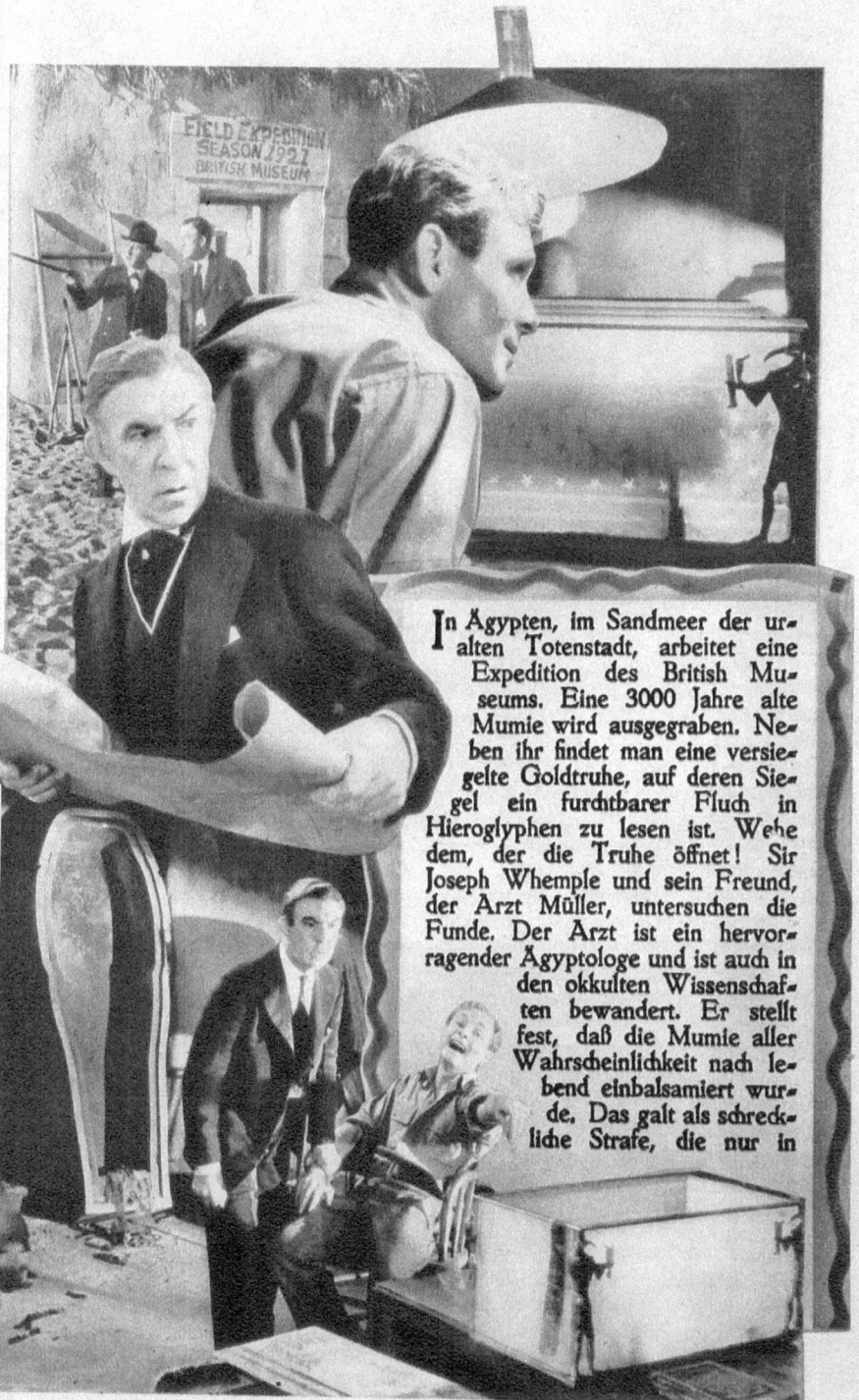

In Ägypten, im Sandmeer der uralten Totenstadt, arbeitet eine Expedition des British Museums. Eine 3000 Jahre alte Mumie wird ausgegraben. Neben ihr findet man eine versiegelte Goldtruhe, auf deren Siegel ein furchtbarer Fluch in Hieroglyphen zu lesen ist. Wehe dem, der die Truhe öffnet! Sir Joseph Whemple und sein Freund, der Arzt Müller, untersuchen die Funde. Der Arzt ist ein hervorragender Ägyptologe und ist auch in den okkulten Wissenschaften bewandert. Er stellt fest, daß die Mumie aller Wahrscheinlichkeit nach lebend einbalsamiert wurde. Das galt als schreckliche Strafe, die nur in

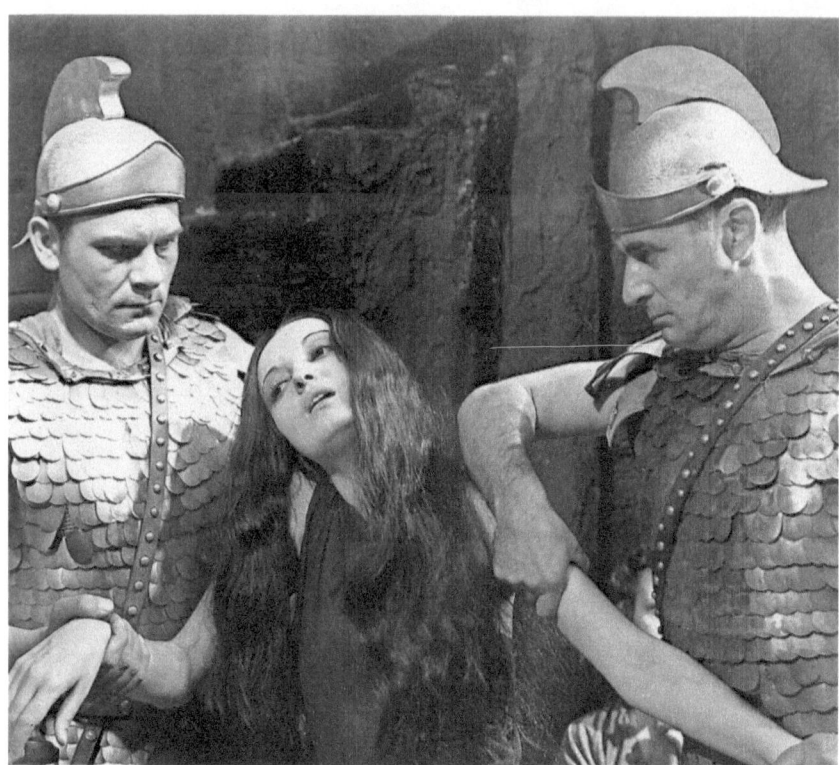

Monster (just the once in **FRANKENSTEIN MEETS THE WOLF MAN** [1943, USA, D: Roy William Neill]—one of the only times, if not the only time, when the two actors each performed the same character—Lugosi's portrayal was nowhere near as effective as Karloff's.

Others in **THE MUMMY**'s roster of players included two cast members from Universal's **DRACULA**: these in the forms of Edward Van Sloan, who had brought the role of Van Helsing to life (as well as working with Karloff on **FRANKENSTEIN**), and David Manners, who was a perfect casting choice for Jonathan Harker's part. Joining the trio in the female lead role was a relative newcomer to film, Zita Johann.[8] The movie was made with relative ease, without any major issues, other than the usual discomfort to Karloff, this time when he was fully made-up as the mummy in Jack P. Pierce's makeup.[9] The finished film was ready to be released in America in 1932, while an Australian premiere was planned for early '33. It was then that the film hit a snag, which saw it used as a 'bargaining chip' in a long-running dispute between American film studios and Australian exhibitors.

The latter had long been rallying against the former's practice of "block booking" movies in Australian picture houses. In 1931, the Fox Film Corporation acquired a controlling share in Hoyts, the largest cinema chain in Australia, and were unfairly focusing on the circulation of their own films at the expense of everyone else's. Other studios, including Universal, were also adhering to what was known as block booking (a.k.a. the contract system). This system was a simple one: in order to survive, exhibitors were 'encouraged' to make bookings which required them to accept *all* of a studio's output over a given period, this in order to be allowed access to 'better' films featuring popular stars or subjects. These bookings included films not-yet-seen, or, in some cases, even yet-to-be-made. While this practice guaranteed that an exhibitor would be assured of getting box-office hits, they also had to take on average—and, in many cases, *below*-average— product which would not normally even have been brought over, let alone actually received screenings. The successes of hit movies were supposed to offset the poor receipts of the dross, but this wasn't always the case.

By 1932, Australian film studios began to complain that block booking had the negative effect of squeezing-out Australian- and English-produced films from local cinemas. To this end, exhibitors from the cinema chains joined forces with the Australian studios to form a new company, General Theatres Corporation, to first protest, and then fight back against, the would-be monopolistic American studios. The fighting strategy was simple: exhibitors would *not* accept any more block bookings.

The ensuing battle was dubbed "the Film Wars" by the media. By January 1933, major chain cinemas, due to a lack of new product, began to close their doors to the public, with the exception of chains such as the Mayfair, which showed British films on an almost exclusive basis and, ironically, smaller, mostly independent, cinemas who weren't beholden to the block booking system for their livelihood. Each week saw more theatre employees being laid off. Opposing this were the independent cinemas, those located in suburban and country locations, which, with their own association representing them in the form of the Motion Pictures Exhibitors Association (MPEA), weren't tied-into block bookings, and were screaming for a resolution to the pressing problem. Knowing that such a resolution was in everybody's best interests, the American studios began agreeing to terms, with the notable exception of MGM, who had struck a deal with the Fuller's Theatre chain, and saw no reason to renege on it.

As January rolled on, the dispute continued. By the second week into the New Year, Universal had made an attempt to break the deadlock. Using its Australian representative, Universal made contact with independent theatre owners via the MPEA and offered to deal with them directly. In this way, suburban and country cinemas would get the latest movies before the capital cities did. Two of the movies being offered were **THE MUMMY** and yet another eagerly-awaited Karloff suspense/horror, James Whale's **THE OLD DARK HOUSE** (1932, USA).

Universal knew it held the high cards. **THE MUMMY** had opened in America in December of '32, and, by the third week of January '33, it was showing all over the country to solid houses. Reviews for the film were generally excellent, and the box-office interest was even better. One new Karloff film was great, two new Karloff films was something to be grabbed immediately! Independent theatres, claimed the MPEA, were outside any conflict between the studios and the General Theatres Corporation and, furthermore, the MPEA had long been disgruntled with the terms under which films were parceled-out to non-urban cinemas. The MPEA accepted the Universal offer.

But what Universal knew, and had not passed onto the MPEA, was that **THE MUMMY** wasn't

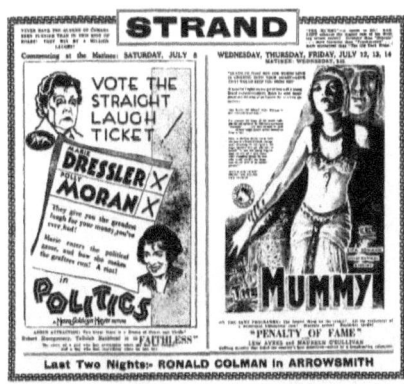

Above: Australian newspaper ad. **Preceding Page:** Ziva Rodann in one of the 'reincarnation' scenes that was cut from **M '32**

doing anywhere near the same blockbuster business in America as similar horror movies such as **DRACULA** were, with the former's ticket sales dropping-off markedly in some cities, if maintaining a steady holding pattern in others.

The offer by Universal couldn't have come at a worse time for the General Theatres Corporation. Their negotiations with MGM promptly collapsed as they continued to argue strength through unity. The MPEA didn't see things that way, and made moves to accept the Universal offer, thus bypassing the usual chain of command. In doing so, and responding to threats from the General Theatres Corporation, the MPEA also made contact with then-Prime Minister Joseph Lyons to ask for his direct intervention in the dispute. Three days after the MPEA informed Universal that it wanted their films, the Film War fizzled-out. While both sides made concessions, neither side really won. Block booking would continue, but the difference was that the entirety of a studio's output was now no longer required to be accepted by exhibitors, who could pick and choose. The General Theatres Corporation also called for an official Government inquiry into the practice of block bookings, but that would take months, if not years, to happen and, until such a time as the rules were changed, it would be business as usual.

Finally **THE MUMMY** was ready for release. Advance screenings were held in all major cities in late February, and photos of Karloff in his Imhotep makeup began to appear in newspapers. "If you want to look interesting when you grow older, make more faces now", Karloff was quoted as saying.[10] The same newspapers were reporting that Karloff's ghoulish appearance wasn't all due to makeup. "Karloff can distort the muscles

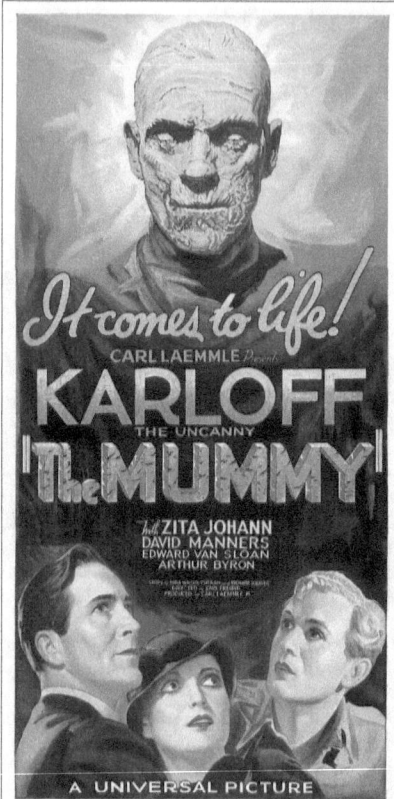

This ultra-rare US insert poster for **M '32** is part of the Kirk "Metallica" Hammett collection; its art is attributed to Karoly Grosz

THE MUMMY was released nationally on March 16th, 1933. Unusually for an American film of the period, it hit city cinemas in all Australian states on the same weekend, which had been the plan of Universal Australia all along. The supporting feature came in the form of a Slim Summerville/Zasu Pitts comedy, **WHAT A LIFE**.

Local posters and advertising for the film differed from their American counterparts. In Australia, the emphasis was placed on Ms. Johann, shown standing in a seductive pose with Karloff's head looming behind her. David Manners was in both advertisements as well. In one he is seen in a passionate kiss with Johann, the other has him gazing up at her. A third, rarely-seen advertisement used a still of Johann from the movie, with Karloff nowhere to be seen.

Not a single advertisement or poster showed Karloff in his full mummy makeup, though, as Universal was saving that big reveal for the film proper.

Yes, the studio had struck gold once again! Reviews heaped praise on Karloff, with many claiming that his portrayal was even better than his star turn in **FRANKENSTEIN**. Johann was labelled "exotic", and big things were predicted for her. Further descriptions said the film was eerie and the acting excellent.[13] The critics' generally favorable responses to the movie were summarized by a two-line review in *Table Talk*: *Karloff's best. The weird story of an Egyptian high priest, who comes back to life, has some truly thrilling moments.*[14]

of his face in any manner and control them in any particular position for a reasonable length of time", reported *The Sun*, "and in his 'Mummy' make-up he divided his face, not according to its exterior appearance, but according to the muscles, into segments and 'columns,' accentuating the effect with grease paint and color."[11]

The first reviews of **THE MUMMY** were positive. "This mummy, which is supposed to waken back to modern life, is magnificently played by Boris Karloff," wrote an unnamed critic in *Smith's Weekly*. "He makes his part the most shuddersome we have seen outside the fields of nightmare, and completely dominates the film."[12]

Also appearing in newspapers were photos of Zita Johann. Her stunning beauty was fodder for the gossip and film columns, and she was often described as being 'strangely fascinating'. Also singled-out was Freund's direction and cinematography, with the film being praised for its usage of shadows and darkness to convey a suitable mood.

THE MUMMY proved to be incredibly popular with public, and was still being screened repeatedly well into the '30s, and even on into the '40s too. It would have appeared that, at this stage, neither Karloff nor Universal Films could put a foot wrong, and the public eagerly awaited the inevitable sequel to arrive, starring the magnificent "Karloff the Uncanny"…

…As it happens, they would be waiting a *LONG* time!

1941: THE MUMMY'S HAND

It took no less than *eight* years before the next instalment in Universal's *Mummy* series saw release in Australia, by which time Karloff had long since moved on. His 'replacement' was a comparatively unknown actor, Tom Tyler, who was best-known for westerns. Despite this substitution, critics were still looking for any remaining trace elements of Karloff in the film,

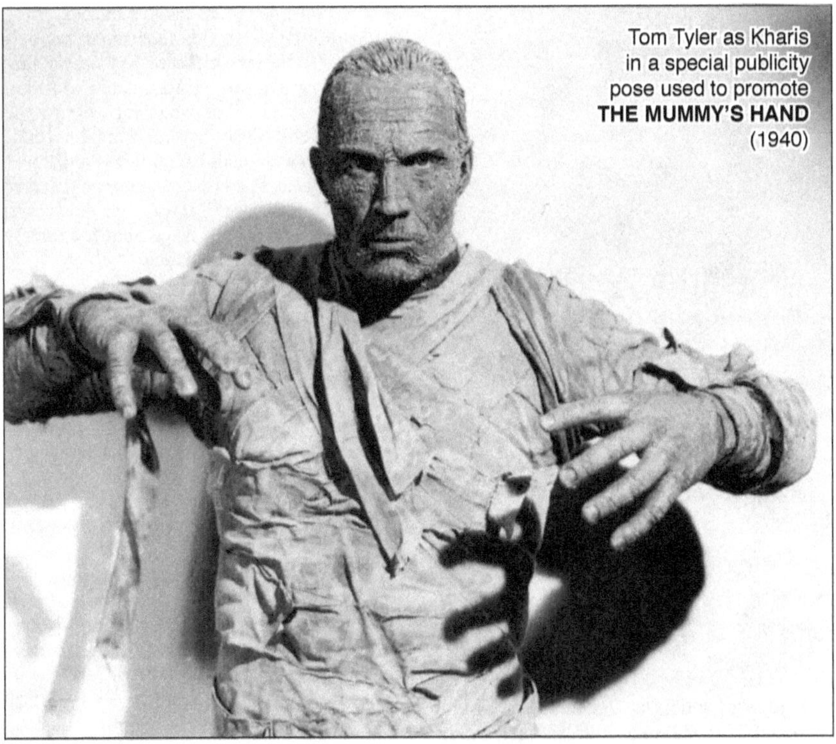

Tom Tyler as Kharis in a special publicity pose used to promote **THE MUMMY'S HAND** (1940)

and were left feeling disappointed when they couldn't find any.

As Karloff had been replaced, so had the mummy himself. Now called Kharis,[15] he was brought back to life by the application of special herbs and sent out to kill on command. In Western Australia, the movie was described as "eerie"[16], as had been **MUMMY** '32 by some critics. Best of all, the new movie was promoted with the following memorable tagline: *"Frankenstein was a sissy compared with **THE MUMMY'S HAND**!"*

South African-born comedic character actor Cecil Kellaway[17] was an object of interest for Australian audiences. Kellaway had moved to Australia in 1921 and performed on the stage for the J.C. Williamson firm. *[Incidentally, said theatrical company figures prominently in Daniel Best's excellent book,* Australian Gothic: The Untold Story of the 1929-'31 Dracula *Stage Tour "Down Under"(WK Books, 2017), which contains a greatly-expanded, heavily-illustrated new version of a pair of articles which formerly appeared here in* Monster! *–SF.]* Kellaway had made the transition from stage to film while in Australia, finally leaving for America in the late 1930s. There were more than enough people seeing **THE MUMMY'S HAND** who not only remembered Kellaway from the stage, but considered him to be an Australian, if not by birth, then certainly by 'adoption'. Advertising for **THE MUMMY'S HAND** placed Kellaway's name above the title, giving him fourth billing.

The Sun, in its review, went one further, stating that, "Best that **THE MUMMY'S HAND** has to offer is a tipsy act by Cecil Kellaway."[18]

Other than for Kellaway's contributions, the critics savaged the film, offering-up reviews which praised the overall feel of the film ("eerie") while nonetheless tearing it to shreds, mainly because it wasn't as good as its predecessor. *The Sunday Sun* found the whole film amusing, as evidenced by their own review:

When Princess Ananka was buried, Karis [sic]*, her Egyptian adorer (played by Tom Tyler),*

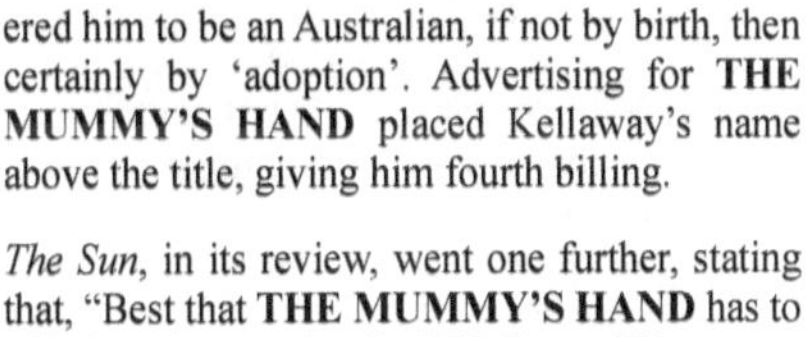

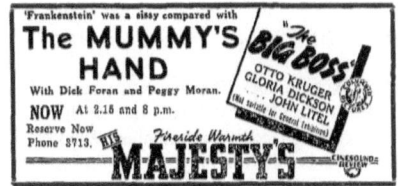

Australian newspaper ad: *"Frankenstein was a sissy compared with **THE MUMMY'S HAND**!"*

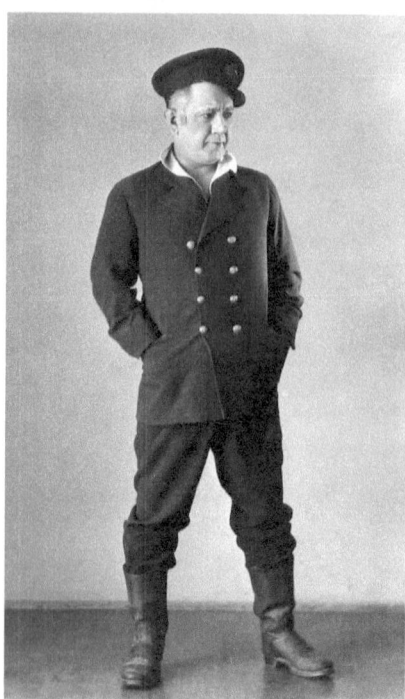

Comic relief specialist Cecil Lauriston Kellaway (1890-1973) in J.C. Williamson's play *Turned Up*, circa 1929. The actor's jovial, loveable performance as "The Great Solvani" in **THE MUMMY'S HAND** constitutes a goodly chunk of its entertainment value

on to do such decent business at the box office, the *Smith's* critic changed their mind, but only to a point. The saving grace? Kellaway! "Best performance is given by Australian Cecil Kellaway. Why hasn't Hollywood yet woken up to this actor's ability? He makes this film something more than a mere midnight thriller. For the rest, the cast is able, the thrills laid on with a trowel, the result satisfactory."[21] It was a good review, if inaccurate; as has been noted above, Kellaway was actually from South Africa.

Poor reviews aside, **THE MUMMY'S HAND** proved popular enough with audiences to earn an extended run in most cities, beginning in New South Wales in January 1941, after which it toured around the country, ending in South Australia in October of that year. After getting its 'second wind', so to speak, regional newspaper critics were a lot kinder to it than before.

1942: THE MUMMY'S TOMB

With World War II then raging at full force elsewhere, Australia was facing a very real and present danger of being invaded in 1942. Imperial Japanese forces had bombed Darwin (in the Northern Territory), dropping more bombs and killing more people in a single raid on February 19th, 1942, than they had at Pearl Harbor, Hawaii just a couple of months before on December 7th, 1941. Darwin had been ordered evacuated and, in response to the attack, the Menzies Government had drafted plans, known as the Brisbane Line, which would see the northernmost areas of the country abandoned and handed-over to invading forces should they arrive on Australian soil. The incoming Government, led by John Curtin, rejected this defense and called upon all Australians to take up arms and fight, as opposed to being sent to Europe, India or Africa to fight for the British. The young country was at war, both with a foreign agent and (at times) with itself as American troops were brought in to help hold the line, causing friction. This friction culminated with the infamous Battle of Brisbane, which saw Australians, both civilians and members of the armed forces, engaged in a running riot with American servicemen, resulting in one death and several injuries. Despite the censors' best efforts to keep this incident quiet, news spread.

was buried with her—alive. Sorcery by the high priests of Ananka's tomb prevented death from claiming him. So Karis [sic] had insomnia per the thousand years, ready to become a monster of revenge should the tomb be desecrated. That's why Prof. Petrie (Charles Trowbridge), bone-hunter Banning (Dick Foran) and his sweetheart Marta (Peg Moran) stir up a little hell of horror when they do ravage the tomb. Karis [sic], a dreadful sight in his clammy wrappings, gets up from his sarcophagus (scream here, girls), proceeds to strangle members of the party and finally carries Marta off to his Master, the High Priest of the Tomb (Ed. Ciannelli).

Verdict: Don't be mum. Yell your loudest.[19]

Meanwhile, *Smith's Weekly* ran two separate reviews of the film at different times. Their first impression of **HAND** was scathing: "Muddled in writing and clumsy in production. Altogether an inferior chiller and will not appeal to [the] average adult."[20]

A few months later, after the movie had gone

An American soldier named Eddie Leonski had landed in Melbourne on February 2nd, 1942. During his short time in the country, he murdered three women, becoming known as "The Brown-out Strangler", due to his tendency to strangle his victims during night-time periods when the lighting was low. Leonski was caught and handed over to the United States Army, whereafter he was court-martialed and summarily executed on November 9th that year.[22]

Into this mix of confusion, fear and upheaval, horror films kept on coming, but their impact was fading somewhat as they became more mere escapist entertainment rather than the true horrors they once were. But still they came. Only now they were competing with newsreels showcasing the *real* horrors of the world in the form of the war right on Australians' doorsteps.

If the prime selling point in Australia for **THE MUMMY** had been Boris Karloff, and Cecil Kellaway for **THE MUMMY'S HAND**, then for **THE MUMMY'S TOMB**, it was Lon Chaney, Jr. Still fresh and a hot commodity from his star turn as the title character in George Waggner's lycanthropy hit **THE WOLF MAN** (1941, USA), Chaney was the virtual heir apparent to both his father's and Boris Karloff's legacies. As one exhibitor put it: *"Lon Chaney, Jun., now quite renowned for his blood-chilling roles, appears at the Grand tonight in **THE MUMMY'S TOMB**, probably the most awesome of his pictures."*[23]

This time there was a far shorter wait for the next *Mummy* film, as **THE MUMMY'S HAND** was still in cinemas when **THE MUMMY'S TOMB** premiered. Unlike the previous entries in the series, **TOMB** was paired-up with other films, usually a popular western or war film, in order to get people in through the doors. Part of this double-billing tactic was due to the film's length—or rather, *lack* thereof. Whereas 1932's founding entry **THE MUMMY** had run for 73 minutes, and could be paired with a short, newsreels and a cartoon or two, **TOMB** ran for a scant single hour, so it wasn't anywhere near long enough to be billed on its own. From now on, every *Mummy* movie released in Australia would be on the bottom end of a double bill.

As for **TOMB**, it got excellent reviews with Chaney and, of all people, makeup artist Jack Pierce, being singled-out for praise. In Pierce's case, his praise was long overdue, as reviewers had made honorable mention of his skills in making-up Karloff ten years previously, while making the point that Chaney's mask appeared to be rubber. Rubber mask or not, Chaney's performance was hailed as being his best yet in a horror film, even if the plot was recycled.

"The vogue of the horror film", wrote the critic in *The Voice*, "although somewhat diminished, still continues to hold its own. **THE MUMMY'S TOMB** is the latest creation to enter the field of entertainment. The idea of an ancient Egyptian mummy, kept alive for thousands of years, is certainly a fantastic one."[24]

The film had a staggered release around Australia, supported, for the most part, by the usual Cisco Kid western. It began its run in Western Australia in December 1942, moved to Tasmania, and then went around the country, ending in South Australia in July 1944, the month after D-Day.

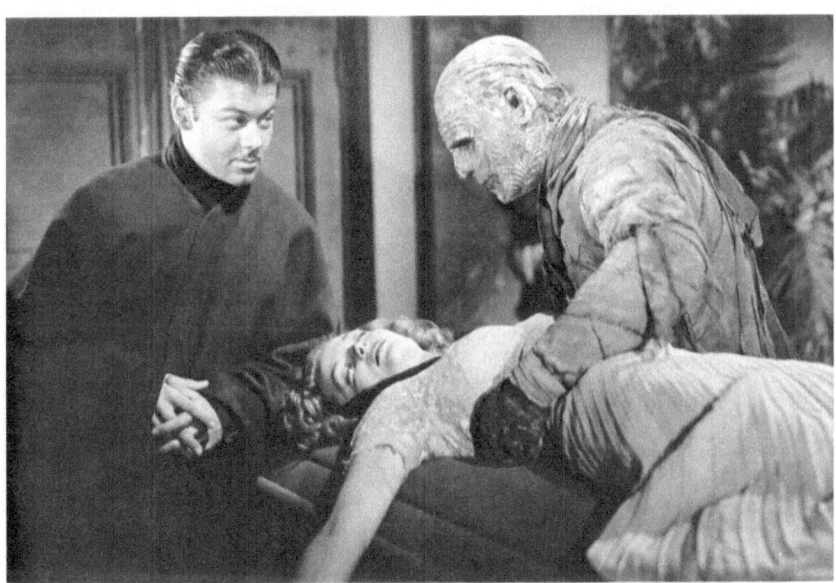

Altar Boys: Turhan Bey and Lon Chaney, Jr. place Elyse Knox on a pedestal in **THE MUMMY'S TOMB** (1942)

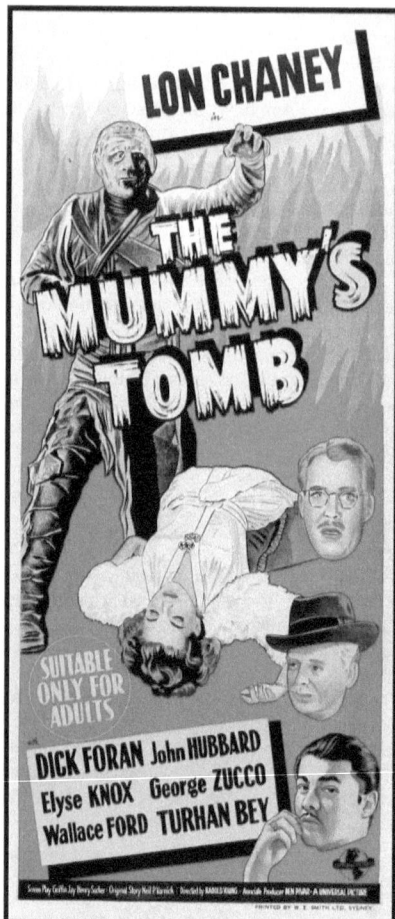

Australian daybill poster

1944: Rape, Murder and THE MUMMY'S GHOST

Two years after **TOMB**, **THE MUMMY'S GHOST** hit cinemas. By now audiences were used to the sight of Kharis on the screen, and the thrills weren't as vivid as they once were. The short running time—and the *Mummy* movies were getting shorter with each entry—meant that, once again, the movie couldn't be released as a standalone feature. So, as with **TOMB**, it was paired with westerns, in this case a Charles Starrett one, **RIDING WEST**. The lack of previews saw critics writing only the barest, most basic of 'reviews' sight-unseen, based solely upon the publicity materials that Universal had sent them and, in some cases, the plot synopses of the previous two series entries. For most reviewers, it was business as usual: grave-robbers steal a mummy, Kharis comes back to life, kills people, is destroyed. Wash, rinse and repeat! **GHOST** would see Chaney returning as Kharis, and his performance was given glowing reviews, despite the limited acting required for the role, for which Pierce's makeup did much of the work (which was one of the primary reasons why the actor reputedly so strongly disliked playing it).

However, it was a screening of **GHOST** that would end in tragedy, and thus thereafter negatively mark the movie in Australia for rest of the 1940s, as the horror movie that 'caused' a murder.

Two horror movies were at Melbourne cinemas in the first week of October 1944. Robert Siodmak's **SON OF DRACULA** (1943, USA) was on at Oakleigh, while **THE MUMMY'S GHOST** was being shown twice a day at the Liberty on Lygon Street, East Brunswick. Both movies were products of Universal Studios and both featured Lon Chaney, Jr. in their title roles. Neither movie had attracted all that much attention, other than **SON OF DRACULA** getting placed upon *The Catholic Weekly*'s "AO" list, and the films were being quietly shuffled around the suburbs as part of double bills, with comedies and minor dramas as the second features on the card.

On October 4th, Ronald Morgan, a 24-year-old returned soldier with an intellectual disability, hopped on the tram and went to see **THE MUMMY'S GHOST**, just one of a few dozen people who would see it on a typical Spring day in Melbourne. What set Morgan apart from the rest was what he did next…

Morgan emerged from the movie, caught the tram back to Moonee Ponds, where he lived, and, when passing-by Janice Baul, a bright 7-year-old on her way home from school, he kidnapped her. Morgan dragged her into his house, where he bashed her head in with the jagged end of an exploded mortar shell from his time in the Army. He removed her clothing and sexually assaulted her, then dragged her body out into a nearby alleyway, assaulted her again, then left her for dead.

Baul was subsequently found, barely alive, and rushed to the Children's Hospital. Sadly, she never regained consciousness, and died from her severe wounds two days later.

As Morgan had been seen by witnesses talking to Baul, police quickly arrested him. While in custody, he made a full confession, stating that he'd gone to the movies (i.e., **THE MUMMY'S GHOST**) and was strongly affected by the images that he had seen. He'd been moving in a daze since walking out of the cinema, and had no memory beyond his arrival at home, upon which he read a newspaper and promptly blacked-out. The next thing he knew, Baul was in his lounge room, so he hit her in the head. He then panicked and dumped both she and her clothing. He didn't admit to the sexual assaults, but didn't deny them either. The charge of carnal knowledge and abuse was quietly withdrawn, and the murder charge pursued.

Despite his crime, Morgan's background was a sad one. He suffered from an undiagnosed intellectual disability from birth, but, as diagnoses of such disabilities weren't common, or even recognized as being a disability at all in that era, he was classified as a lunatic. As a child in South Australia, he tended to wander off from home, leading his parents to admitting him to a Salvation Army receiving home. In short, his disability had resulted in him being abandoned by his family and institutionalized. When his family moved to Melbourne, they took him with them, only to promptly place him into another receiving home for care. By now Morgan was tired of being locked-up, so he promptly escaped. He was captured, sent back and officially certified as insane. He escaped again in 1940, and this time enlisted in the Australian Imperial Force (AIF). It didn't take long for the army to realize he had problems, so they discharged him, again officially certifying him as insane and sending him to yet another receiving home. Once again he escaped and, as was becoming habit, he re-enlisted in the service, although it is unknown if he did so under his own name or used a pseudonym. It didn't matter to the army, and they promptly sent him off into battle, a situation that he was woefully inadequate to cope with. By 1943 he'd been found out, was certified insane for the *third* time, and again discharged from the military. This was how he'd ended-up in Moonee Ponds, unemployed, unsupported and alone.

The jury was faced with a difficult decision: was Morgan responsible for his actions? Doctors testified from the dock that, while he knew what he had done was wrong from a legal standpoint, morally speaking Morgan had no idea what he had done wrong. Nevertheless, the jury had no choice but to find him guilty and, despite their pleas for mercy, Morgan was sentenced to death. But everything was not as it appeared. Morgan *did* have serious issues, and these issues would come back to haunt the children of Victoria in years to come.

His sentence was commuted to life without parole upon appeal, and Morgan remained in jail until he was eventually released in 1969. His story didn't end there, though. Once released, he couldn't control his urges and was arrested, charged and convicted for committing fifteen sexual offences upon girls under the age of 10 years. He was

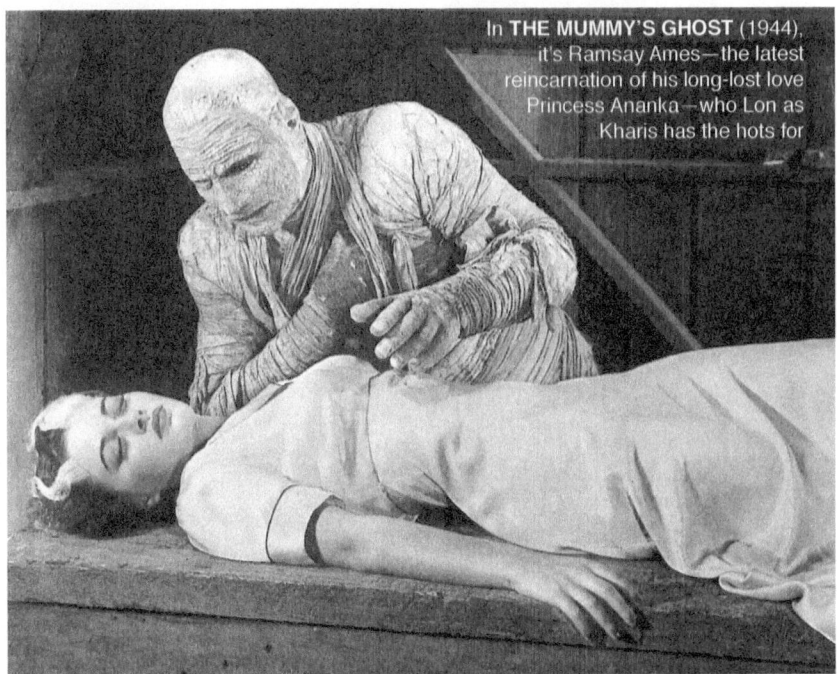

In **THE MUMMY'S GHOST** (1944), it's Ramsay Ames—the latest reincarnation of his long-lost love Princess Ananka—who Lon as Kharis has the hots for

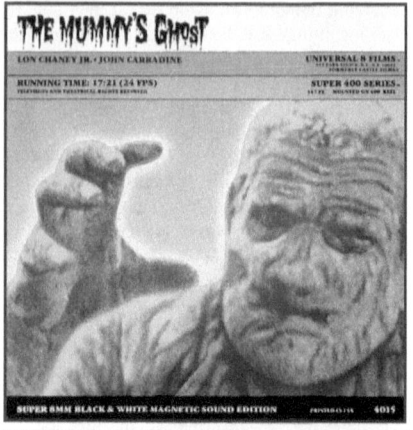

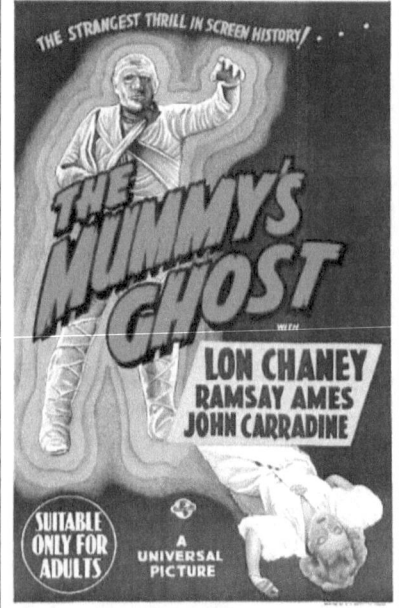

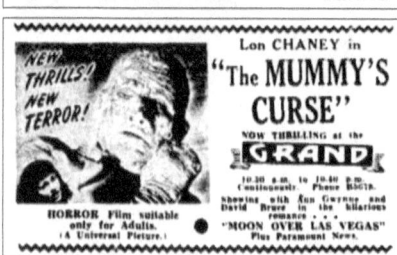

Top to Bottom: Kharis looks rather constipated on this US 8mm film box; an Australian one-sheet poster; and a very teensy-weensy ad for the final Kharis film that appeared in a local Aussie newspaper

handed another ten-year sentence, to be served on top of the 17 years he now owed the parole board for his early release. In 1976, he was gaoled for another 36 years. He won the right to appeal his sentence in 1989, but remained incarcerated, earning the dubious distinction of becoming Victoria's longest-serving prisoner ever.

So, however indirectly, you could say that **THE MUMMY'S GHOST** and Lon Chaney, Jr. had claimed a life! Ironically, only twenty years before, **THE HUNCHBACK OF NOTRE DAME** (1923, USA, D: Wallace Worsley), starring Chaney's father, had also been linked to a tragic death. The connection between the murder and the horror movie was reported in the newspapers, but not to the extent that it could have been. Universal Australia were very keen to keep the connection out of the media, if only to not have one of their horror films so intimately connected with a all-too-genuine real-life horror.

With World War II then still in full force, and the crimes of Eddie Leonski still fresh in people's minds, the connection between Morgan and his mental state was of greater interest. Another reason for the relative quietness of the case in the media was due to the Army's negligence in allowing Morgan to not only serve in the first place before getting discharged, but then actually allowing him to *re*-enlist, even though his official record clearly stated that he was legally insane.

In the end, it mattered not. Morgan was quickly forgotten as the war entered its last months. **THE MUMMY'S GHOST** was eventually paired-up with other horror films and released in the "Horror Show" series, the tragedy of poor little Janice Baul's brutal sexual violation and murder was forgotten by all, barring her family and the police officers who worked on the case.

1945: THE MUMMY'S CURSE

The last entry in Universal's original *Mummy* series hit Australian cinemas in April of 1945, to a largely disinterested audience. With the by-now-standard running time of an hour, as with its predecessors, the movie was never considered to be a stand-alone feature, and it was quickly double-billed with comedies, musicals or the ever-popular westerns.

Unlike the earlier instalments, the reviews for **CURSE** were harsh, reflecting the fact that, once again, the plot was merely recycled from the **MUMMY** '32. *The Voice* in Tasmania gave the film two stars, rating the actors' performances, including Chaney's, as being fair, and gave the impression that, if one had seen the Karloff

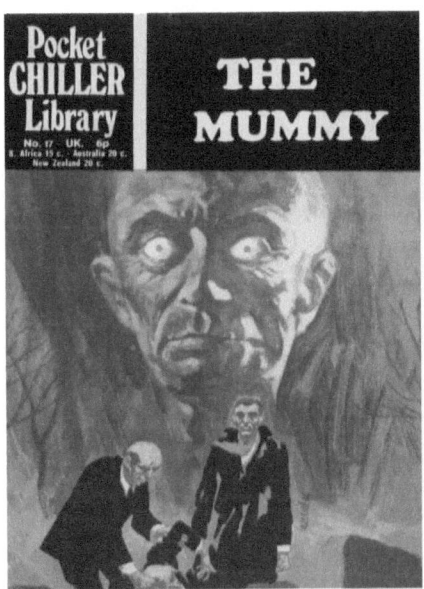
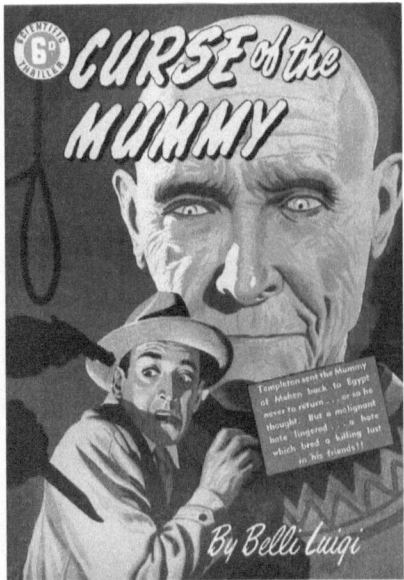
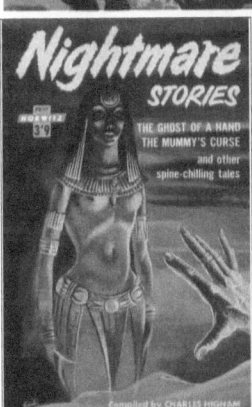
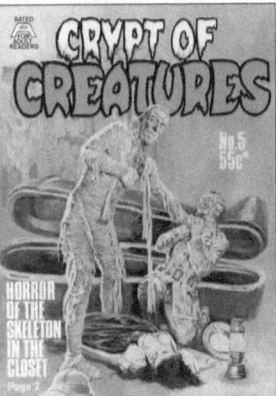
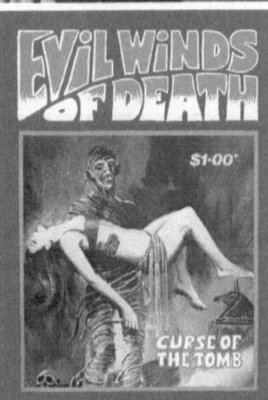
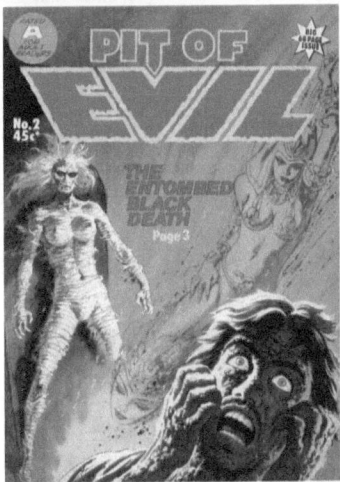

An Assortment of Australian 'Mummy'-Themed Pulp Paperbacks & Comic Magazine Covers: The novel at top right by Belli Luigi dates from the late 1940s, while the short story anthology at center far left is from 1962. The mid/late-'70s digest periodical at top left is actually of British origin, but it was also available for sale in Australasia at some outlets. The three early '70s Aussie comics mags depicted at dead-center, above right and directly at left were all put out by the Gredown publishing house, a famous and prolific Australian company with which this article's author Daniel Best is highly familiar (why not visit his blog 20th Century Danny Boy @ ohdannyboy.blogspot.ca)

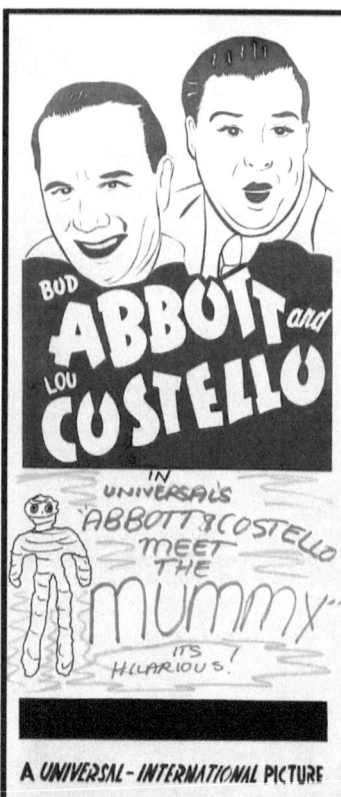

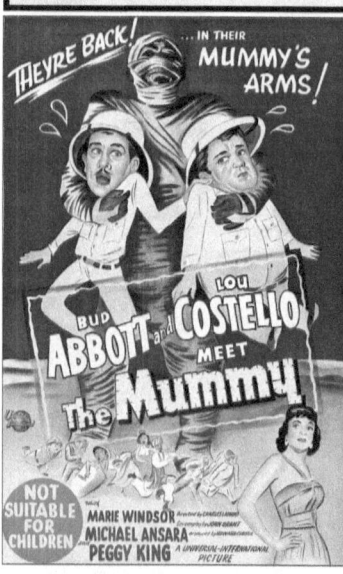

Top: The title on this stock Australian daybill poster is hand-written in colored magic markers! **Above:** The film's Aussie one-sheet

original, then there was no real need to see this one. The critic for *The Western Herald* (in New South Wales) was crueler in his review, claiming that "Sergeant Mike", the lead canine in the supporting feature, performed better than **CURSE**'s human cast!

In Adelaide, a Charlie Starrett western was paired with the movie, and the reviews were decent, with the film's more scary moments being described as genuinely chilling.

However, it'd all been seen and done before—and better—and the public knew it. Each capital city ran the film for a week, after which time **CURSE** was parceled-out to the suburbs and country areas for the rest of the run. In most country areas, the film was chosen as the supporting feature for the likes of **THE GHOST OF FRANKENSTEIN** (1942), **THE SPIDER WOMAN** (1943) and **HOUSE OF FRANKENSTEIN** (1944), that latter feature illustrating that a movie with a *lot* of monsters made for better entertainment than one with just a single monster. **HOUSE** also proved that, when it came to monsters, Universal were pinning their highest hopes on "The Big Three": Frankenstein's Monster, Dracula and The Wolf Man. The Mummy was no longer a going concern.

CURSE began its run in Sydney in April 1945, lasting for a week, after which time it was quietly sent out around the country, for hit-and-run one-week bookings, finishing-up its run in Adelaide in March 1946. New life was breathed into the movie—as well as a few others, too—when horror movies received mass-releases in August of 1947. **CURSE** and **TOMB** were two of the films selected, along with **THE WOLF MAN** (1941), **THE GHOST OF FRANKENSTEIN** (1942), **FRANKENSTEIN MEETS THE WOLF MAN** and **SON OF DRACULA** (both 1943), as well as the non-Universal John Carradine vehicle **REVENGE OF THE ZOMBIES** (1943, D: Steve Sekely). The movies were then placed into theatres with advertising targeted at children on school holidays. Upon entry into the cinema, kids were given headache powders and told that their lives were now insured for £1000—something that they no doubt got a real kick out of hearing![25] Parents and the media were horrified at the thought of children as young as 12 (*GASP! SHOCK! HORROR!*) being allowed to watch such films, but this was proof that what had once been horrific back in the 1930s was now no more than cheap-thrill entertainment for 'modern' (i.e., late '40s) kids.

The Universal *Mummy* series was at an end... for now!

1955: ABBOTT AND COSTELLO MEET THE MUMMY

By the mid-'50s, like virtually all of Universal's classic monsters by then, The Mummy was totally played-out, so its meet-up with Abbott and Costello was inevitable. The old Universal horrors were now dusted-off each and every school holiday season for reruns at the cinemas, targeted squarely at children. In just over twenty years, what had once been objects of sheer terror for adults were now comedy fodder for the kiddies, providing cheap thrills for a generation still recovering from the real horrors of World War II. Keeping apace of the times, new monsters were emerging: the likes of giant ants and spiders, mutated lizards and other oversized beasts were now the order of the day. The Atomic Age was here!

As for The Mummy, he was now just a boob, a foil, a plaything for Bud Abbott and Lou Costello to toy with and make a mockery of. What had once captivated people's imagination, fascinating them with Egyptology and such concepts as reincarnation, was now reduced to just a joke…and not a very *good* one at that. Kharis was now renamed "Klaris" *[sic!]* and was played by veteran stuntman Eddie Parker, who had doubled for Chaney in the earlier *Mummy* movies as well as doing the lion's share of the work for Lugosi in **FRANKENSTEIN MEETS THE WOLF MAN**. The employment was steady for Eddie (whose face nobody ever saw), and he went through his paces striking all the standard, now-clichéd mummy poses, grunting on cue when required. Parker was a professional, he was being paid in a time of uncertainty and, by now, the mummy makeup was limited to a one-piece over-the-head mask and full-length body-suit (with a zipper up the back!), but it was incredibly unlikely that anybody would ever recognize him anyway, and they might even just assume it was ol' Lon, Jr. in the suit, business as usual.

Yes indeed, it was a far cry from the headier days of Karloff, Freund, Johann, Manners & Co., and it showed.

The film was one of the last movies the comic duo ever made. Their routine was becoming tired and old hat with the public, but the kids lapped it up. They started in film in 1940 with **ONE NIGHT IN THE TROPICS** and, before the decade was out, had racked-up a total of 25 films, all with the same formula. Lou would mess things up, Bud would bash and browbeat him, things would get better, and Lou would end up on top, much to the amusement of Bud. Wash, rinse and repeat!

MEET THE MUMMY was the 11th film the duo made in the 1950s, and they were fast coming to their end. Reviews of the movie were just as tepid as the film itself: "You can imagine the mirth-making scrapes A and C get themselves into when they slip into the crypt of old King Tut"[26]… "Much the same slapstick as before"[27]… And those were two of the *better* notices!

Critics from *The Western Herald* didn't even bother watching the movie; they went and saw **STALAG 17** (1953, USA,

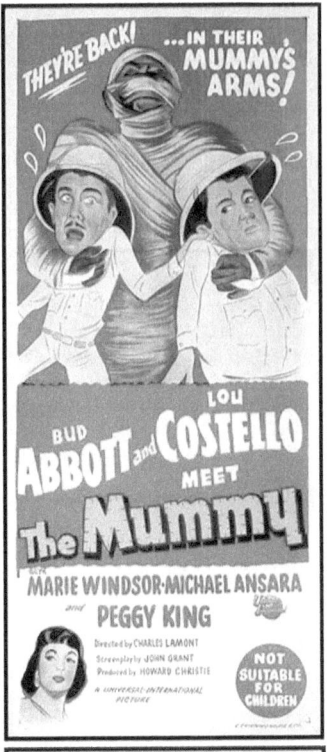

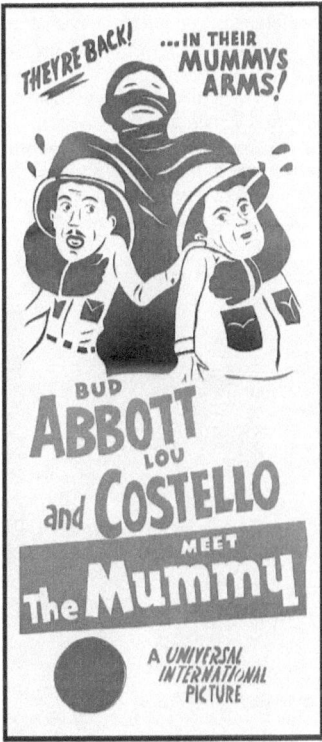

Right: A pair of alternate Australian daybill posters for **A&CMTM**, the one at top a lithograph, the bottom one a screen print; artists unknown

D: Billy Wilder) instead. All wasn't lost, as it was pointed out that it was the 40th film that the duo had made together, after all. Even that claim was wrong: the critic was off by four.

A&CMTM quickly fell to the bottom of the bill, supporting the likes of **FOXFIRE** (1955, USA, D: Joseph Pevney), a Jeff Chandler and Jane Russell potboiler. The film suffered the same fate as most of the A&C 'horror' team-ups in that it was released under more than one title, including simply **MEET THE MUMMY**, *sans* its stars' names. Whatever the title, though, the film proved popular with children, and it remained in cinemas as a support feature for other films until the end of the decade. Inevitably it eventually popped-up on television where, much like all of A&C's output, it became a popular regular Saturday afternoon feature, so that was something at least.

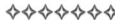

It truly was the end of the line for the Universal Monsters. The cast of the original 1932 **MUMMY** had different fates over the years. In '55, the year that **ABBOTT AND COSTELLO MEET THE MUMMY** was released, the principal players of **MUMMY '32** could be found variously scattered all across the planet. Boris Karloff was busy, as always, taking on virtually every job he was offered, working on television, in film, and doing voiceovers for children's records.

Zita Johann, the mysterious beauty who had played the heroine in Universal's originating mummy outing, had since retired from stage and screen and was teaching acting to people with learning disabilities. She would be lured out of retirement to appear in one more (truly forgettable) horror movie, **RAIDERS OF THE LIVING DEAD**, in 1986. It was her final film.

Karl Freund moved back into cinematography, winning an Academy Award for his work on MGM's **THE GOOD EARTH** (1937, D: Sidney Franklin), and being nominated twice more.[28] When Bud and Lou met The Mummy, Freund was working as a cameraman on the hit sitcom *I Love Lucy*. Having conquered cinema as a medium, introducing such innovations as the tracking shot, Freund switched to television for, as he said, the challenge of it. The steady paycheck was also a bonus.

David Manners, who had played John *[sic!]* Harker in Lugosi's **DRACULA**, as well as the male lead in **THE MUMMY**, had retired from the screen in 1936 and went to live the quiet life with his partner, Bill Mercer. He wrote novels and painted.

Edward Van Sloan, who appeared in **DRACULA** (as Van Helsing), **FRANKENSTEIN** *and* **THE MUMMY**, had also retired from the screen and stage. At the age of 73, he felt he deserved the rest.

Producer Carl Laemmle, Jr., the son of Universal's founder Carl Laemmle, was also retired, but not voluntarily. Upon being ousted from the company following a hostile takeover in 1936, he retired to his mansion in Beverly Hills, where he lived his life as a recluse, haunted by the ghosts of his past. He was washed-up before he'd reached 30, and now, not yet 50 years old, his best days were behind him.

Even Bud and Lou didn't last for long after **MEET THE MUMMY**. It was their penultimate film. They made one more film as a duo, **DANCE WITH ME, HENRY** (1956, USA, D: Charles T. Barton), which bombed big-time at the box office before Lou, tired of Bud's drinking, dumped him and went out on his own. Lou Costello flew solo for but one more film, Sidney Miller's 1959

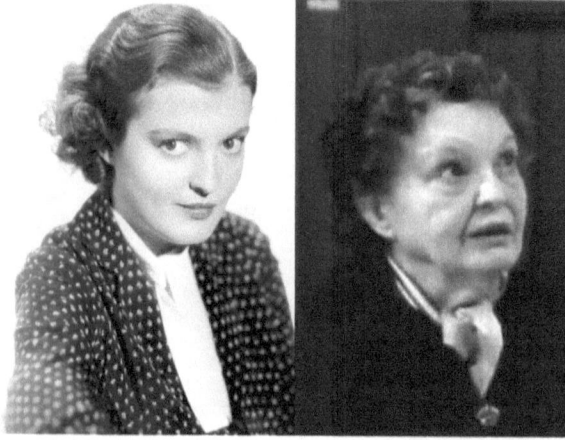

Zita Johann, who had played the heroine in **MUMMY '32**, would be lured out of retirement to appear in one more horror movie, **RAIDERS OF THE LIVING DEAD**, in 1986. It was her final film 'giant woman' farce **THE 30 FOOT BRIDE OF CANDY ROCK**, dying of a heart attack earlier that same year; as a consequence, it was released posthumously, some five months after his death. Bud Abbott hung on long enough to see their films enjoy a revival during the '60s and early '70s, before himself passing away in 1974.

Imhotep, Kharis or Klaris—whatever people wanted to call him—had suffered the same fate. As a screen character, he was 23 years old by 1955, and his glory days were already more than a decade in the past by the time he terrorized Abbott and Costello (or was it vice versa?!). When last seen, he was propping-up a bar in Egypt while Bud and Lou ran about like idiots, performing pratfalls, hitting one another and generally taking the mickey out of him. It was a sad, and ignoble, way to lay The Mummy to rest, for sure.

But Imhotep wasn't totally dead, not yet. As it had taken an Englishman to bring him to life in 1932, so it would take another Englishman to breathe new life into the character; an Englishman every bit as versatile as Karloff named Christopher Lee. However, but for a stroke of good fortune, that Universal-approved 'reboot' of their moldering *Mummy* franchise was in danger of getting banned in Australia...

1960: THE MUMMY – Hammer Avoids The Horror Ban

Despite the ongoing ban on horror films, such movies sometimes did manage to slip through the censors' nets under the guise of suspense thrillers, dramas, and science fiction. One of the few true horror films which succeeded in getting past the Australian censor and gaining a release was Hammer Films' and Terence Fisher's **THE MUMMY** (1959, UK). This featured Christopher Lee in the title role, along with his frequent co-star Peter Cushing, who was then just becoming known for his television work in this country, and was still fondly remembered for his part in the 1948 Old Vic tour.

Hammer had dabbled with a number of genres, from science fiction (e.g., Val Guest's **THE QUATERMASS XPERIMENT** [a.k.a. **THE CREEPING UNKNOWN**, 1955, UK]) to action, light comedy and straight drama. The studio entered into the horror stakes with a bang in 1957 with Fisher's **THE CURSE OF FRANKENSTEIN** (1957, UK) and its likewise Fisher-directed '58 follow-up, an adaptation of Stoker's *Dracula* (retitled [as it had also been in America] **THE HORROR OF DRACULA** in Austra-

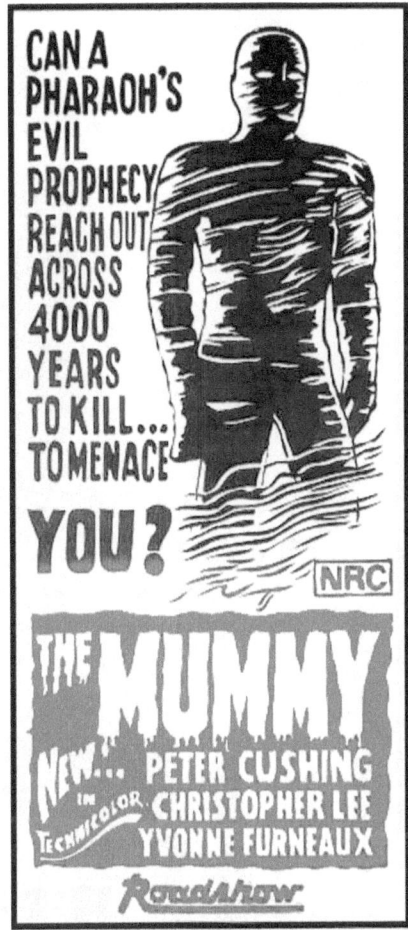

Two-tone (i.e., dark blue and vivid red) screen-printed Australian daybill for Hammer's Universal-approved '59 'reimagining' of the 1932 classic

lia, when it was finally first released here in the early 1970s). Both these international box-office smashes featured Lee and Cushing, and it was the role of Dracula that would see Lee typecast much in the same manner that Béla Lugosi had been some 27 years previously. Unlike Lugosi, though, Lee would eventually break free of The Lord of Vampires' grip thanks to the sheer volume and diversity of his output, coupled with his staunch refusal to perform the role beyond the early 1970s.

Hammer Films was everything that Universal, RKO, MGM and Paramount were never able to be, due to the restrictions placed upon them by American censors. Hammer horrors were colorful, packed with sex (or at least sexiness), blood and gore. Indeed, in their later productions, it

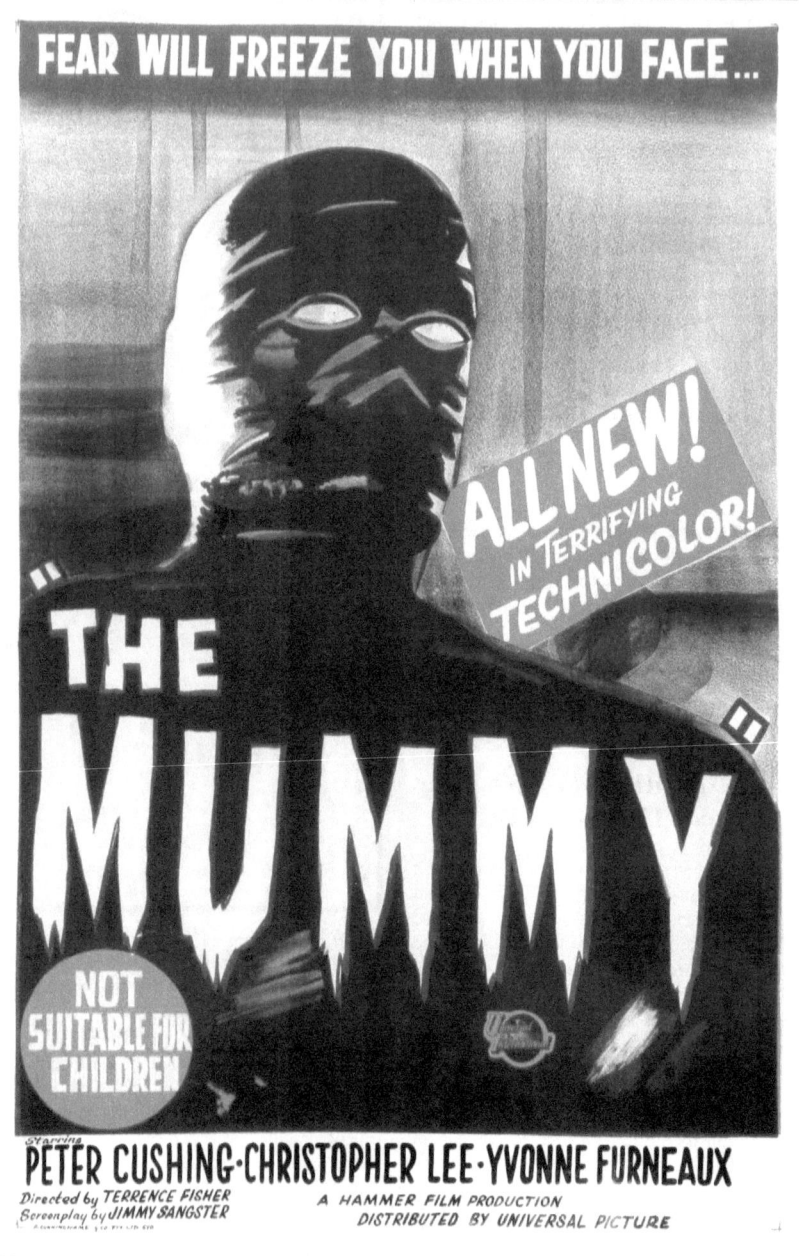

Lithographed Australian one-sheet poster for **MUMMY** '59

wasn't unusual to see just as many bare female breasts in a Hammer film as there was graphic blood and guts.

While some Hammer product was being released in Australia, their horror fare was rejected outright, often purely going by title alone. A mere mention of the dreaded words "Dracula", "Frankenstein" or "Werewolf" might be all it took for the Chief Censor to issue a ban without actually even bothering to screen a film beforehand. If Hammer's Australian distributors were hoping that the release of **THE MUMMY** here in May 1960 would open-up the floodgates of horror to the Australian cinema-going public, it was about to find out that the situation would mostly remain strictly business-as-usual, however.

Just how **MUMMY '59** succeeded in slipping past the censor unnoticed remains a mystery. It is clearly, beyond any shadow of a doubt, a genuine horror film and, unlike Jack Arnold's **CREATURE FROM THE BLACK LAGOON** (1954, USA), displayed not even any token traces of science fiction, nor could it be classified as just a plain old thriller either. Its classification was that of a mystery/suspense film, and it was given an "A" rating—meaning for adults only—and its advertising made it clear that the movie was not suitable for children.

Critics savaged the film, but they didn't shy-away from labeling it a horror movie, even if they did fail to appreciate it being the first such film released here since the ban of 1948. Wrote one,

"This Technicolor piece has all the familiar ingredients of mummyism; archaeologists in cotton suits; a mysterious Egyptologist in a red fez who spends most of the time chanting to a hawk-beaked God; an intrepid young man (capably played by Peter Cushing); the young man's beautiful wife, who at the climax is conveniently left unattended so that the mummy can march away with her; and, of course, the mummy itself, a fabulous creation in tattered grey bandages. It is quite necessary, too, to have a quota of sceptical detectives, as well as some gibbering pubfolk. Theoretically this adds to the drama of the final hunt, even though it's really Christopher Lee under the bandages. It is, to coin a phrase, mummybo-jumbo."[29]

No matter what the reviews said, **THE MUMMY** was the very first authentic Hammer Horror to be released in Australia, featuring one of the classic monsters from the Universal pantheon, and the public ate it up. It quickly settled into the drive-in circuit and became an annual feature for New Year's Eve horror marathons and Midnight Horror shows across the country. In cinemas it was often paired with a classic Universal (for some reason, Universal's 1944 'monster mash' **HOUSE OF FRANKENSTEIN** was typically selected) and ran at suburban and art-house cinemas throughout the 1960s.

Despite Hammer's success in getting **MUMMY '59** released in Australia, none of the sequels would be shown here until the ban was lifted in 1969, and even then it would take time for those movies to hit the screens. Released elsewhere in 1964, Michael Carreras' **THE CURSE OF THE MUMMY'S TOMB** wasn't released in Austra-

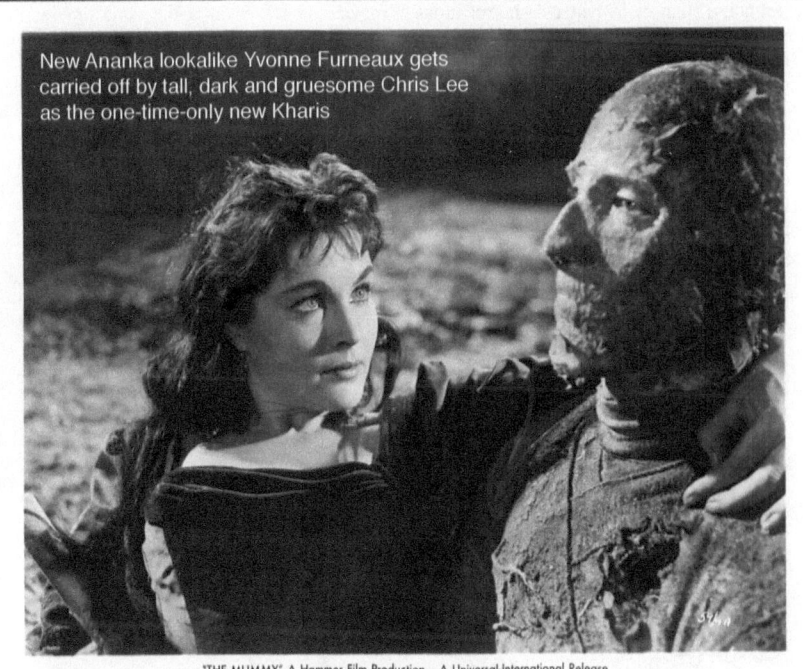

New Ananka lookalike Yvonne Furneaux gets carried off by tall, dark and gruesome Chris Lee as the one-time-only new Kharis

"THE MUMMY" A Hammer Film Production — A Universal-International Release

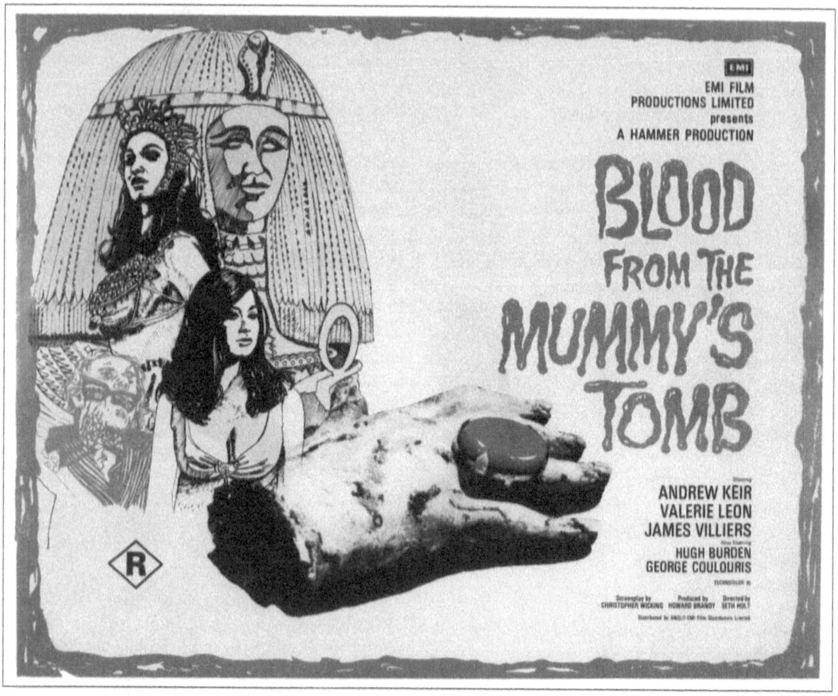

Australian title lobby card, art unsigned

lia until 1973, when it became an instant hit at drive-ins. If it reached cinema screens, it was as an 'art-house' film or as part of a horror movie marathon. John Gilling's **THE MUMMY'S SHROUD** came next. Released worldwide in 1967, although actually the third Hammer *Mummy* movie, it was only the second one yet to be released in Australia, appearing in cinemas in November 1970. The fourth and final series entry, Seth Holt's and Michael Carreras' **BLOOD FROM THE MUMMY'S TOMB** (1971, UK) was released Down Under in June 1972. As with most of Hammer's releases in the 1970s, it went straight to smaller cinemas and drive-ins. At one point it was possible to see Hammer's *Mummy* movies on television at the same time as they were playing at the cinema.

Even worse was that all the Hammer *Mummy* movies suffered at the hands of the censors. The films were brutally cut, and it would take until the rise of home video in the early 1980s before Australians at long last got to see the full, uncut versions.

But it was worth the wait!

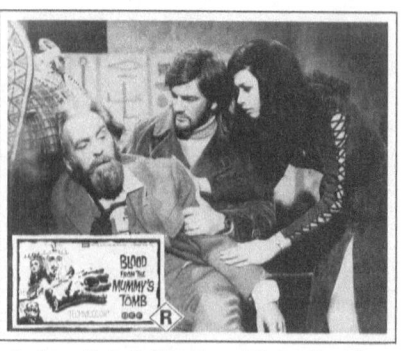

Andrew Keir *[left]* replaced Peter Cushing on **BFTMT** shortly into production; Australian lobby card

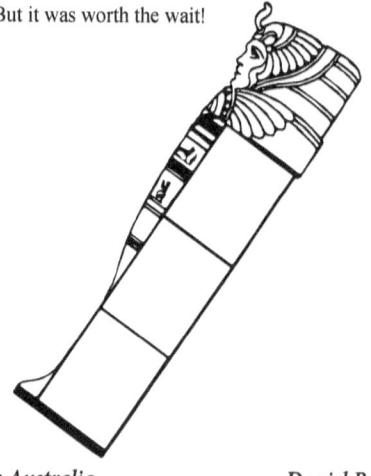

ENDNOTES

1. Balderston, a noted playwright, wrote the original script for the stage production of *Dracula* (which provided the basis for the '31 Lugosi film adaptation **DRACULA**), along with an early treatment for Whale/Karloff's first *Frankenstein* film, whose script was adapted from Balderston's composition. His post-Universal credits include **THE MAN WHO CHANGED HIS MIND** (a.k.a. **THE MAN WHO LIVED AGAIN**, 1936, UK, D: Robert Stevenson), also starring Karloff, as well as **THE PRISONER OF ZENDA** (1937, USA, D: John Cromwell) and **GASLIGHT** (1944, USA, D: George Cukor). He was nominated for the Academy Award twice, but failed to win.

2. Born Karl Freund on January 16th, 1890, in Dvůr Králové (Königinhof), Bohemia, in the Austro-Hungarian Empire, he began working in film in 1905 at the age of just 15. He died in Santa Monica, California on May 3rd, 1969.

3. Born William Henry Pratt on November 23rd, 1887, in Camberwell, London, England. He died in Midhurst, Sussex, England on February 2nd, 1969, just three months prior to Karl Freund's death.

4. Born Béla Ferenc Dezső Blaskó on October 20th, 1882, Lugosi was originally from the town of Lugos, Kingdom of Hungary, Austria-Hungary (now Lugoj, Romania). He died in Los Angeles, California on August 16th, 1956.

5. There was a good reason for Karloff's silence about his Anglo-Indian heritage – prejudice. Anglo-Indians were, at that time, considered to be half-castes, and thus regarded as inferior to so-called 'normal' Anglos or English people. It's the same reason why Merle Oberon, also an Anglo-Indian, born in Bombay, would always insist that she was Tasmanian by birth, even though no records ever existed of her being born there.

6. Now known as Mumbai.

7. Karloff was born into privilege. The son of a diplomat, he was sent to private schools, leading him to King's College, London, where he studied to enter the British Government's Consular Service, but he dropped-out of University in 1909.

8. Born Elisabeth Johann on July 14th, 1904 near Temesvar, Hungary (now Timisoara, Romania). She died in Nyack, New York on September 20th, 1993.

9. Reports stated that he passed-out due to the bandages and makeup covering every part of his body, literally suffocating him.

10. "Make More Faces", *The Sun* (New South Wales [NSW]), February 12th, 1933.

11. *Ibid.*

12. "The Mummy", *Smith's Weekly* (NSW), February 18th, 1933.

13. *The News* (South Australia [SA]), May 8th, 1933.

14. "The Mummy", *Table Talk* (Victoria [VIC]), March 16th, 1933.

15. Also erroneously referred to as both "Karis" and "Claris" in Australian newspapers.

16. "Eerie Horror Film", *The Sunday Times* (Western Australia [WA]), February 23rd, 1941.

17. Cecil Lauriston Kellaway was born on August 22nd, 1890 (the IMDb claims 1893). He died in Hollywood on February 28th, 1973.

18. "Films of the Week", *The Sun* (NSW), February 3rd, 1941.

19. *The Sunday Sun* (NSW), February 2nd, 1941.

20. "Box Office Prophecies", *Smith's Weekly* (NSW), November 30th, 1940.

21. "The Mummy's Hand", *Smith's Weekly* (NSW), February 8th, 1941.

22. "Leonski Hanged – Murderer of Three Women", *The Age* (VIC), November 10th, 1942.

23. *The Daily News* (WA), December 4th, 1942.

24. *His Majesty's Voice* (Tasmania [TAS]). March 20th, 1943.

25. "Horrors Enliven School Holidays", *The Sun* (NSW), August 21st, 1947.

26. "What's On in Town", *The Mirror* (WA), January 21st, 1956.

27. P. and C. Council Reviews, *The Canberra Times* (Australian Capital Territory [ACT]), February 4th, 1956.

28. In 1941, Freund was Oscar-nominated for a pair of MGM productions, **THE CHOCOLATE SOLDIER** and **BLOSSOMS IN THE DUST**. He didn't win for either.

29. "The Mummy", *Sydney Morning Herald* (NSW), May 1st, 1960.

MONSTER!'S SPRING SUPERNATURAL STUNNER

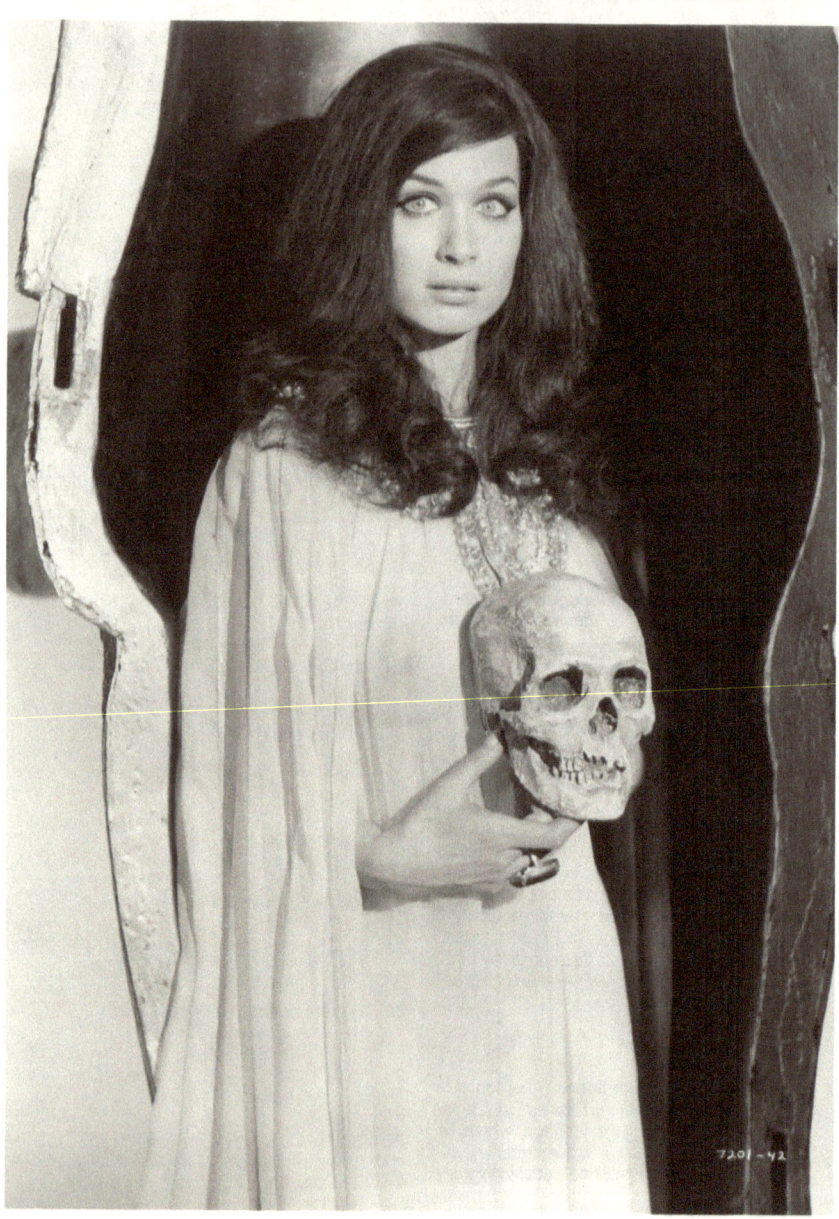

Voluptuous Hammer Glamour gal Valerie Leon would be considered one sexy—to use the popular Aussie colloquialism—'sheila' (a.k.a. chick), be it either "Down Under" or "Up Over"… and anywhere else in-between, for that matter. Here she can be seen striking an alluring pose (showing subtle hints of, um, areola in the process!), not for a distaff version of *Hamlet* about to launch into her big "Alas, poor Yorick!" spiel, but for **BLOOD FROM THE MUMMY'S TOMB** (1971). Yes indeed, she's enough to—*ahem*—'warm the cockles' of any self-respecting, red-blooded, er, mummy's heart! ☺

INSIDE THE OUTER LIMITS
Interviews with OL Alumni
Harlan Ellison & Robert Culp
by Dana Marie Andra

Growing up in the age of 'Sixties television meant feasting from a menu loaded with the likes of The Wild, Wild West, The Twilight Zone, One Step Beyond, The Avengers, The Prisoner, Batman, The Green Hornet, The Fugitive, The Addams Family, My Favorite Martian, *etc.; but, aside from* The Munsters, *there were few, if any, monsters to be found anywhere on the TV landscape. Movie theater audiences had been thrilled and chilled by monsters, gothic horror and science fiction for decades, but television was then still in its early days, and testing the boundaries of what audiences wanted and what was possible.* Famous Monsters of Filmland *magazine celebrated the world of monsters and made us hunger for them, but TV doled them out only in increments, late at night and on weekends, leaving it up to local programs featuring horror hosts like Vampira, Zacherley and M.T. Graves to introduce young viewers to classic and not-so-classic films from the '30s, '40s and '50s, from* **FRANKENSTEIN** *(1931) and* **KING KONG** *(1933) to* **THE GIANT CLAW** *(1957) and* **THE CRAWLING EYE** *(1958).*

This was especially true in 1963, when the TV schedule was dominated by comedies, westerns, detectives, and variety shows. That all changed, however, on September 16th, 1963, when The Outer Limits *premiered on ABC. Promos for the show suggested it would be unlike anything else ever seen before on television and, from the very first episode, the program delivered what it promised.*

I was only 7 years old in 1963, and I was initially drawn to the show by the promise of monsters, which I'd already come to love, thanks to an older boy who lived across the street from me. His room was filled with monster magazines, beautifully-painted Aurora monster model kits, and 8mm Castle Films' monster home movies, sparking my lifelong love of monsters. So when *The Outer Limits* came along, the monsters were the hook, but it was the stories, aided by the music of Dominic Frontiere, that gave the monsters substance, and really made them matter. Profoundly affecting was the third episode, "The Architects of Fear." Starring Robert Culp and Geraldine Brooks; it told the story of a man turned into an alien as part of an ill-fated plan to compel mankind to unite against a common enemy. The idea of being turned into a thing from the planet Theta was horrifying enough, but it was made all the more tragic by the portrayal of his wife, left pregnant and alone by a mad plan gone awry. Culp disliked the design of the alien, calling it "pathetic," but some stations found it frightening enough to be censorable during its original broadcast; I, for one, found it uniquely unforgettable.

Robert Culp appeared in two more episodes before the series ended on January 16th, 1965: "Corpus Earthling", in which the aliens came in the form of sentient rocks, and the classic "Demon with a Glass Hand", written by Harlan Ellison (1934-), which (like Ellison's other script for the series, "Soldier") featured no monsters at all.

The Outer Limits lasted only a season-and-a-half, and many of the second season episodes lacked the energy and style of the first, but the series remains one of the best science fiction/gothic horror shows of all time, for reasons well beyond the monsters alone. The series was so darkly imagined, and the creative elements gelled with such a hauntingly visceral finesse, that its best episodes were imbued with the lasting qualities of beautifully-crafted nightmares. Over 50 years later, it defies comparison to any other series, and continues to inspire every attempt to create anything even remotely similar.

Memories of it remain so vivid in my own mind that I couldn't resist writing about it. My first article about *The Outer Limits* was for a 1996 issue of *Baby Boomer Collectibles*, talking about the series itself and all the peripherals it inspired—games, trading cards, comic books, soundtrack albums, etc.

The following year, I pitched an article idea to *Filmfax* magazine. My article for *Baby Boomer Collectibles* was about the series as a whole, but for *Filmfax*, I wanted to focus solely on the three episodes starring Robert Culp (1930-2010). *Filmfax* accepted the pitch, and my article, titled

Commercials and print ads prior to the series premiere intrigued fans of science fiction and horror alike

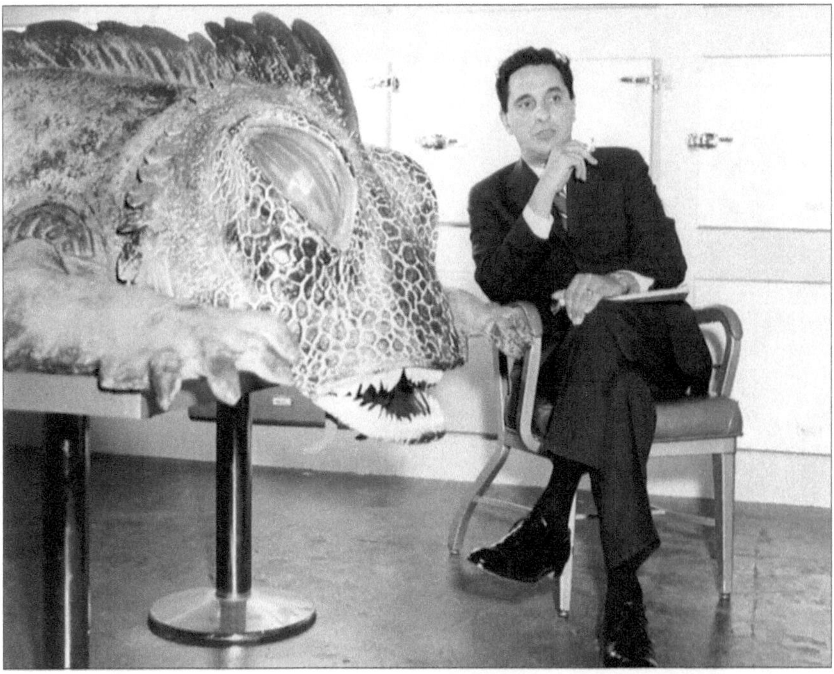

Joe Stefano with an Ichthyosaurus Mercurius from "Tourist Attraction"

"Robert Culp, Harlan Ellison and The Outer Limits" was the cover feature for issue #63-64. (My byline for both articles, by the way, was Mark Burbey, my name at the time that I wrote them.)

Before writing the piece for *Filmfax*, of course, I had to interview both Culp and Ellison. Robert Culp had long been one of my favorite actors, so I was very excited at the prospect of speaking with him, but as legend (and reality) would have it, Harlan Ellison can be very intimidating. I'd toyed with the idea of simply gleaning Ellison quotes from published sources, but when I approached Culp's agent to set up an interview, I was told I'd have to interview Ellison first.

Speaking with Culp was a genuine thrill. Hearing his distinctive voice coming over my phone was like stepping into an episode of *I Spy* or *The Greatest American Hero*! My conversation with Ellison went way better than expected, despite his answering the phone as if my call was a major interruption, and later giving me shit (and rightly so!) for not knowing who Reginald Rose was.

What follows are complete transcripts of those interviews. Both interviews cover working on their subjects' respective episodes, as well as other aspects of their long careers.

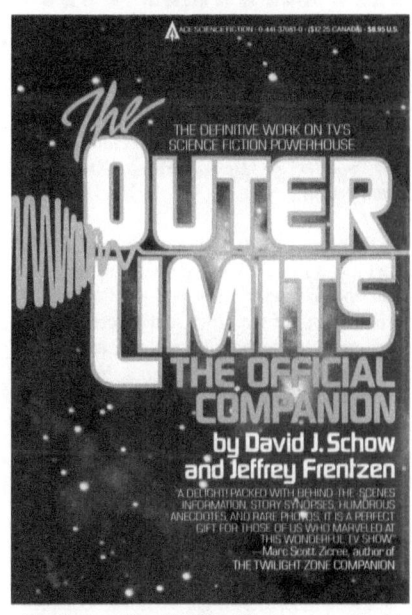

The first edition (1986) of the book by David J. Schow and Jeffrey Frentzen. A revised edition was published by usual record label GNP Crescendo in 1998. Both editions are now OOP, and Schow is currently working on a third edition

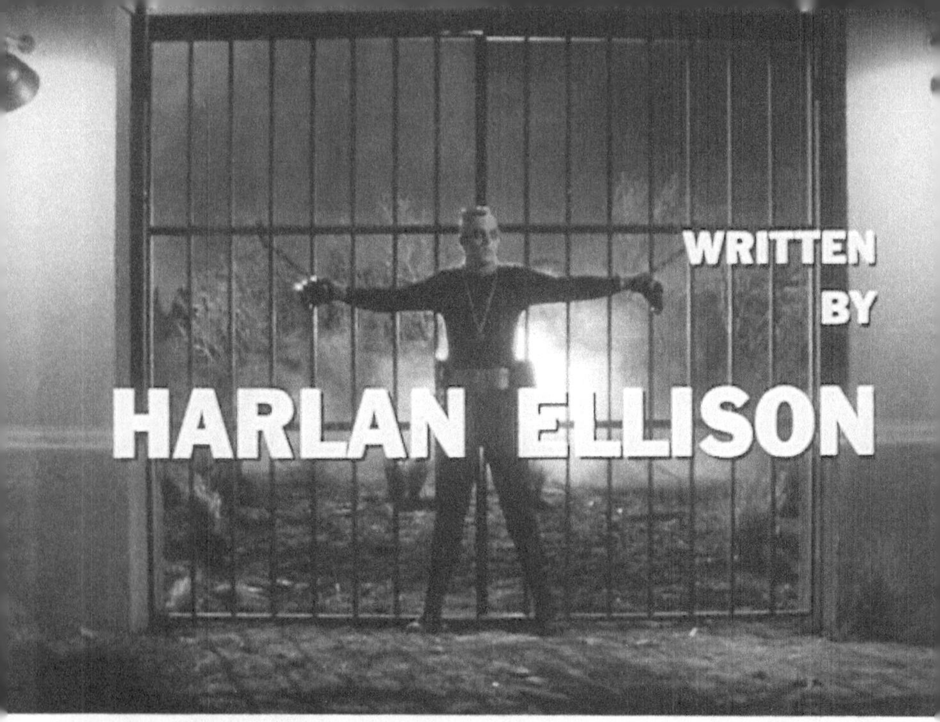

INTERVIEW WITH HARLAN ELLISON
(conducted on January 27th, 1997)

DANA MARIE ANDRA: You pitched some ideas to Joseph Stefano for **The Outer Limits**, *but didn't sell any for the first season. Were either "Soldier" or "Demon With a Glass Hand" among them?*

HARLAN ELLISON: I can't even remember what it was I pitched, but Stefano was very, very rude and, I wouldn't say bodily lifted me and threw me out of the office, but they were utterly uninterested in working with me at all. I had sufficient credentials at that point, in any case, having done *Burke's Law* and been quite popular with it. I'd been written-up in a whole bunch of magazines; it's very seldom that they single-out the writer on a television episode, particularly in those days. But, in fact, that had happened to me, and so virtually every show in town was trying to get me to write for them, and I liked the sound of what *The Outer Limits* was supposed to be. I can't remember if *Twilight Zone* was completely gone at that point *[it actually outlived OL by 8 months]*, but whatever it was I was not over there, so I figured *The Outer Limits* would be a good place to write some fantasy.

Well, when I went there, when they had their old

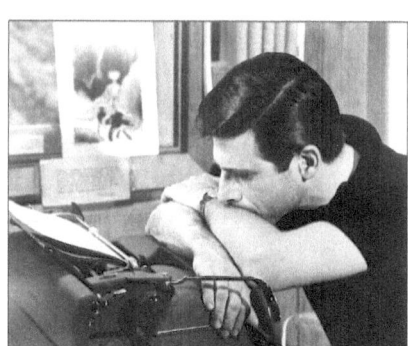

The Write Stuff: Counterculture wordslinger Ellison contemplates the dreaded blank sheet of paper

offices on Sunset Boulevard, right near the beginning of the Sunset Strip and just right at the edge of Beverly Hills, I remember very clearly going in and talking to Stefano, who was fairly arrogant and unpleasant. I think the reason he was upset with me was because I kept mentioning Robert Bloch who, of course, had written **PSYCHO** *[1960, USA]*, and Stefano was, at that point, trying to get everybody to believe that **PSYCHO** had come completely out of *his* head by way of Hitchcock. *[Stefano scripted the film adaptation from the novel by Bloch.]* He wasn't downplaying it and he wasn't denying it, but he certainly was not particularly pleased to hear somebody mention it. Since Bob Bloch was a very close friend of mine, this kind of thing, I think, put him off me. That's just my assumption. I'm woolgathering; it's pretty far-removed these days. But I think that's what it was, and he put the chill on and just dismissed me immediately, and I went away.

They did the first season, and nowadays people talk about it as if it was an icon. In those days, it was incredibly low-rated, and they got rid of Stefano and they got rid of the rest of the people who were involved: *[Leslie]* Stevens, Dominic Frontiere, all those people were canned by ABC, who just said "This series is a dog and it's costing us money, and we want to get rid of it." Well, they were going to bring in another series to replace it, but in truth, it was cheaper for them to keep *The Outer Limits*, because they owned a piece of it. They didn't have to share a lot of it with the studio; United Artists was doing it, and in those days, they weren't as big as they are now. They had very small studios on Sunset over in Hollywood, about three blocks past Hollywood and Vine, and because there was no money in the budget, everybody who had been involved—Villa Di Stefano Productions and Daystar and United Artists and ABC and Frontiere—they had kind of eased them out but given them a piece of the action. Everybody was taking money right off the top, so there was virtually nothing left to do any kind of production. As a consequence, the show was as good as it was in the second season because of the brains of two people: Ben Brady, who was the producer, and Seeleg Lester, who was the story editor. Seeleg had had a career in theater and in films, and so he knew how to make ends meet and how to stretch the dollar and how to build sets that were inexpensive.

[Note: *It's important to mention that the first season of* The Outer Limits *is generally considered by fans and critics to be superior to the second season, both in conception and execution. It's also important to note that* The Outer Limits Companion *by David J. Schow tells a somewhat different version of what happened at the conclusion of the first season. The series "closed out its first season with a 19.0 rating in an arena where a 16.0 (or better) was the baseline for renewal." ABC, however, wanted to move* The Outer Limits *to a different timeslot, one which Stefano felt would doom the show, so, as opposed to being fired, he "refused to continue as producer on the series if it was moved." The Outer Limits* Companion *is essential reading for anyone even remotely curious about this classic show.]*

HE: Also involved was Bobby (Robert) Justman, who subsequently went to work on *Star Trek*, and of course, that's how I wound up over on *Star Trek*. And Bobby Justman was, and still is, one of the cleverest production guys in the business. Bobby knew how to take a sow's ear and turn it into a Gucci bag, for Christ's sake. It was he who, I think—well, in any case, I can't remember quite how it was that I came to the show. I was approached; this was after the first season was over and I had seen it. I didn't have a whole hell of a lot of use for most of the shows they did the first season, because they were subscribing to an edict from ABC which was summarized as "let us see the bear on the beach." *[The "bear" referred to the prerequisite "monster of the week", as per the crew's "shop talk".]*

[Stefano and Leslie Stevens] were going to do a spin-off series of fantasy, and *[the pilot]* was the one in which the house is the clock—I can't remember the name of it [*"The Unknown"*]—but

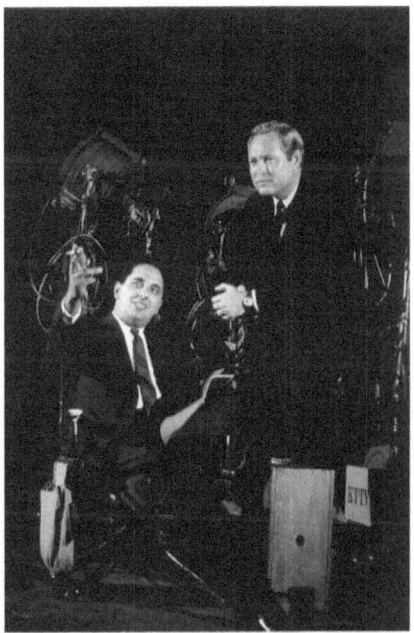

Writer-producer Joseph Stefano with series creator Leslie Stevens on the soundstage used for many Season One interior shots. (Photo by Gene Trindl for the March 21st, 1964 issue of *TV Guide*, courtesy of a blogpost by David J. Show @ wearecontrollingtransmission.blogspot.com)

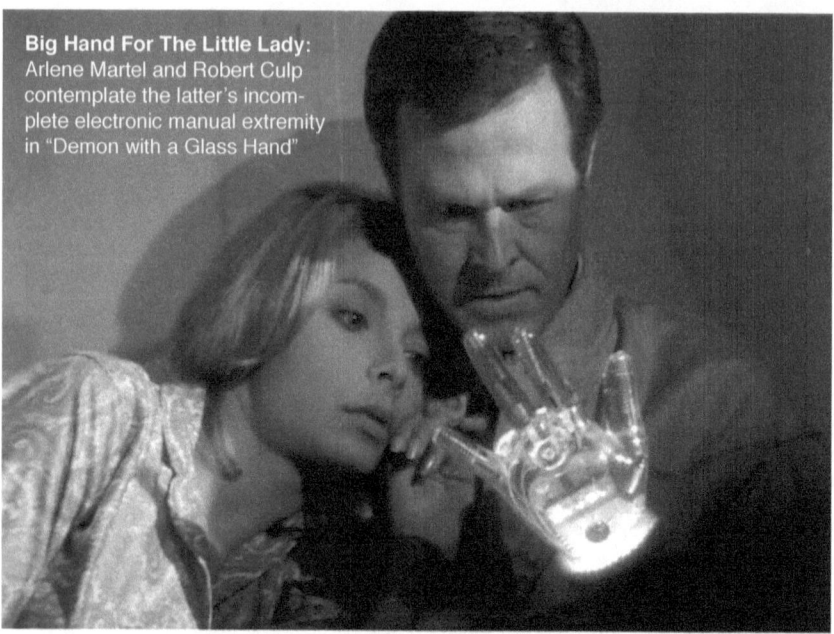

Big Hand For The Little Lady: Arlene Martel and Robert Culp contemplate the latter's incomplete electronic manual extremity in "Demon with a Glass Hand"

the production on that one, as you can probably tell, was about ten times greater than any of three episodes put together. But that pilot did not sell and they had to wind up using it as a segment on *The Outer Limits ["The Form of Things Unknown"]*. So that was pretty much the end of that, and I think Stefano got another movie gig at that point, so he sort of became an absentee landlord, and they were replaced by Brady and Lester.

DMA: At what point did you become involved in the second season?

HE: I really don't know how they came to find me. I wasn't that hard to find in those days, but what the actual mechanism was that I came to write for the show, I don't know. But

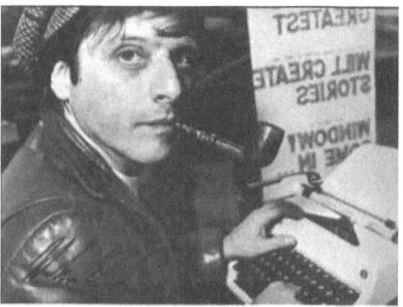

Ellison started writing in book store windows in the 1970s, to "show people it's a job ... like being a plumber or an electrician."

I came in and we hit it off immediately, and the story that I pitched to them was "Soldier," which was based on a short story of mine that had been published a few years earlier, and they liked it. I went to work on it and I got it done fairly quickly, and it did well for them, so I went forward with "Demon With a Glass Hand," which was an idea I'd had for a novel. I was going to write a novel, the title of which was *Obituary for an Instant*, and I had written maybe the first 110, 120 pages, and I got the call to work on *The Outer Limits*, and I had to sort of put it aside. Well, I didn't want to forget what the idea for the novel was, so I decided to write a short version of it, or use a section of the novel as the plot for "Demon With a Glass Hand."

The title, "Demon With a Glass Hand," was my way of adhering to the "bear on the beach" thing, by taking the metaphorical idea of an avenging demon and putting it in the title so that the "bear" would be in the title, but I wouldn't have to have a hideous monster. Well, I got screwed on that eventually, too, because the network demanded that the aliens look weird, and part of the plot, of course, was that they *didn't* look weird. They were supposed to be able to pass among us, because they didn't want to change time in any way, and people walking around with raccoon eyes, like "I'd rather fight than switch," would have been instantly obvious. But the network wanted it, so that's what they did to the aliens.

The treatment came out very, very well. It was a good story—the only problem was it would have cost about 180 million dollars to shoot! I've never published that particular treatment anywhere, but in it, at one point, two railroad engines collide and smash into each other. That alone would have used-up the entire budget for ABC that year, much less the show, and it was Bobby Justman who found the answer. One day we were talking about it, and we were going to have to junk it. By that time, I was very tight with those guys, and I brought in a number of other writers, including Robert Sheckley, who was going to do his famous story "Watchbird" for the show, but didn't. I brought in Denny O'Neil, who now does *Batman* at DC, and he's been the *Batman* editor for years. They were buddies of mine, and they were young guys then, and I brought them in, and they didn't actually wind up doing anything for the show, but it got me in very tight with Seeleg and Ben. We were sitting around one day in the office, talking about what the hell we're going to do with this story. Clearly it couldn't be shot the way I'd written it, and you've got to remember, I was still fairly young in the business at that time, and was unaware of what could and couldn't be done with special effects. But I learned so fast that subsequently, when I did *Star Trek* later, I was able to write all kinds of things that could have been done, and of course, weren't done, as you can tell from the book that I did, *The City on the Edge of Forever [1996]*.

So, we're sitting around and we're talking, and I got this epiphany, and it was an odd thought to have, but it was a thought that I got from a story Theodore Sturgeon had written, and the story was called "A Way of Thinking" *[1953]*. And this story was based on when Ted had been in the merchant marines. He was on a ship where they had a rod that had a cogwheel frozen on it, and people had been trying to pull this cog off the axle. Some guy on the ship said, "No, look at it backwards. It's all in a way of thinking." And he got a 50-pound maul or a 20-pound maul or whatever the hell it was, and he whacked the axle at the end and knocked the axle out of the cog. In other words, he did it backwards. Well, that bit of thinking had always stuck with me. I thought it was really a great way to look at the world; if you can't solve a problem doing it this way, stand it on its head and see if it'll work that way. And I suddenly said to them, "You know, *["Demon"]* is basically a chase." I had been very, very impressed with Ernest Lehman's script for **NORTH BY NORTHWEST** *[1959]*, which was a chase, and I suppose that's what influenced the original version of "Demon With a Glass Hand." And I said, "This story is just a chase, and a chase that's horizontal could equally well be a chase vertical if we could figure out a way to put it all in one building." And then I said, "What if the aliens erected a force field, if they trapped the guy inside to keep him there so he couldn't get away?" Bobby Justman said, "I know just the building," and he took me downtown to the Bradbury Building, which is the wonderful, art nouveau kind of building. Of course, everybody's seen it now; it's been in **BLADE RUNNER** *[1982]* and so many other movies. But at that time, it had only been in a couple of films; there was a detective series—I think it was the final year of *77 Sunset Strip*—Efrem Zimbalist, Jr. had his office in that building, so I knew the building quite well from seeing it. It was not as reclaimed and beautiful as

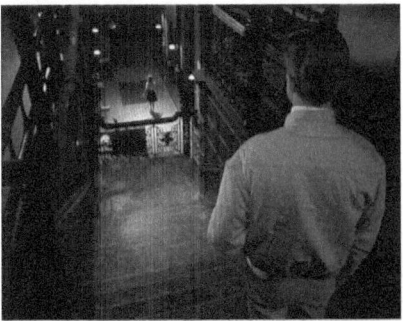

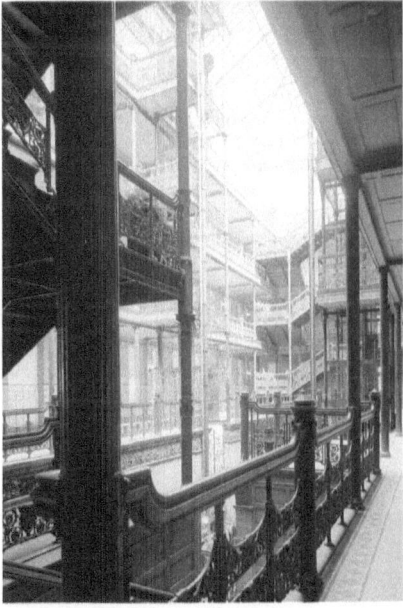

Top: The Bradbury Building made a unique physical backdrop for "Demon with a Glass Hand". **Above:** As it looks 'today' (photo by Jack Boucher)

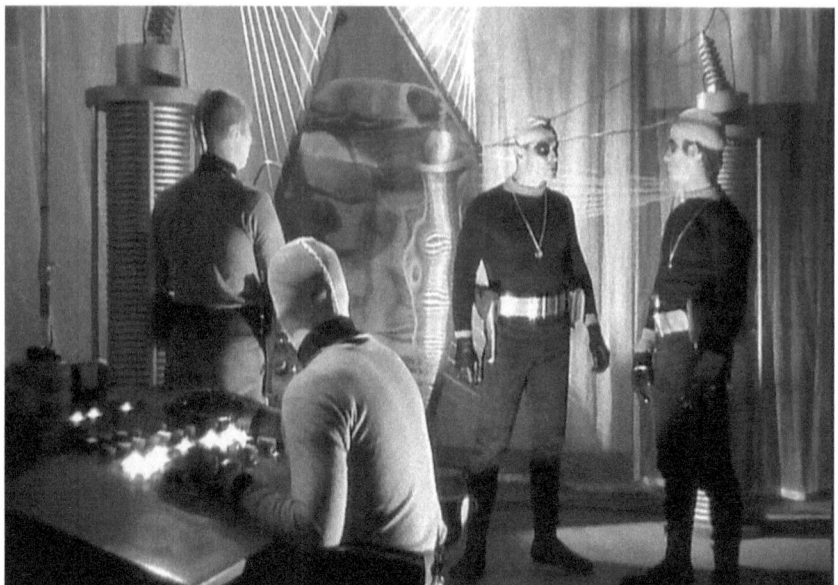

Robert Fortier (as Budge) is greeted by fellow-Kyben Rex Holman (as Battle) as he steps into our world through the time mirror

it is today; it was pretty rundown and ratty at that point, but nonetheless it had the beautiful points that it still has. The minute I looked at it, I said, "Yeah, this will do."

We went on a location examination, Bob and I, that went all the way from the roof—from the top of the building, where the water tower was, all the way to the sub-basements, where the sewers came in. In fact, I used all those things in the original script. A lot of it was dropped because they just didn't have the shooting time or the ability to get out and do it on the roof at night. But it was a natural for me, and I went back and I rewrote the script and made it all perfectly, interiorly logical that the characters couldn't get out. Of course, when it was shot, one of the great annoyances to me is that when Trent gets into the building, he comes up through the sewer; he comes up through a drain in the sub-basement. When he finally gets up onto the first floor, and the leader of the Kyben says, "Welcome, Mr. Trent. We're glad you're here. You're exactly where we want you to be. We lured you here. That's why you were able to get into the building, because, in fact, there's a force-bubble around the building and you'll never be able to get out." Well, he never questions that. He was downstairs on the first floor; all he had to do was run to the doors and reach outside and put his hand up against what would have been the glass facing that they would have put out there, and his hand would have vibrated against it, as he later did. Later on, he's upstairs in one of the dormers and he goes out and tries to get out on the ledge, and he does the "mime" thing of touching the barrier, but he didn't do it when he first got there, and that annoyed me because everything in the story, if not probable, was at least logical. People behaved in a way that was rational, but television always cuts that kind of stuff out. They say, "That isn't important. No one will notice." Well, of course, many people noticed, and worst of all, *I* noticed! But the show came out quite well.

DMA: During the writing and production of "Demon With a Glass Hand," did you encounter any of your usual creative conflicts with the network?

HE: No, not that I recall. They liked me and I liked them, and they trusted me. Once we had worked-out the problems of production, it went very, very, very smoothly. In fact, I was there the first night of shooting. They shot mostly at night, and that's when I met Bob Culp and we became enormously close friends, and have remained so to this day. In fact, I talked to him about a week or so ago about doing something on *Babylon 5*, but I think pilot season is coming up. He was offered a very, very good part on *Babylon 5* that would have entailed five different shows—three of them with voiceovers and two of them with him being a specially-created character. I had thought Bob wanted to do it, but when the time came, his agent said, "No, he's going to pass and wait for pilot season," which really dismayed me. This was only a couple of weeks ago.

But we've stayed very good friends, and the closest thing to a conflict that I had, and it wasn't *really* a conflict, was when I went on the set that first night and I met Byron Haskin *[director of "Demon with a Glass Hand"]*. I was still so gung-ho and so bright-eyed and bushy-tailed that I started explaining to him what I saw in this particular shot and that particular shot, and Byron Haskin, who was really one of the old, grizzled veterans of movies—I mean, he'd been around *forever*, and he was a wonderful man and a terrific director—he kind of looked at me, you know, and I can't remember his exact words, but they were, in essence, "Kid, get away, you're bothering me. This'll melt your ice cream cone. I'll do the job, just shut the fuck up and get away from me." He wasn't mean about it, but that's what it boiled down to. I was chagrined, of course, and I limped away into the shadows and watched the shooting that night, and I need not have worried, because his direction was gorgeous.

No, I had no conflicts with them. In those days, the only way you could stay alive writing television was if you did three shows at one time. The reason for that was because all the shows were buying at the same time. You would have the buying season, which was early in May through July and August, when they would start shooting for a September airdate. They had these cattle calls where you would go into a new show and you and maybe 100 or 200 freelance writers would be shown the pilot, either all at once in a theater, or, if it was at a studio, they would have a screening room and they'd take about 25 of you at a time and then everybody would subsequently make appointments to try to get into the show and beguile and outrage them with the plots and ideas you had so you could get a job. We'd have to do that with two or three shows, because in those days, a half-hour was maybe $2500, and I think an hour show was maybe five-grand, six-grand, something like that, and even though a dollar stretched a lot further in those days, nonetheless, you had to make most of your money in a three- or four-month period. The rest of the year you just sort of scuffled around and tried to get a movie or tried to get a pilot and stay alive. So, it meant that everybody was working on three shows at once and everybody was being yelled at, "Get your work in! Get your work in!" And "Demon" took me awhile to get finished.

They were already shooting "Soldier" while I was working on "Demon." They wanted to get as many scripts from me as they could, but I was involved in two or three other scripts at the time,

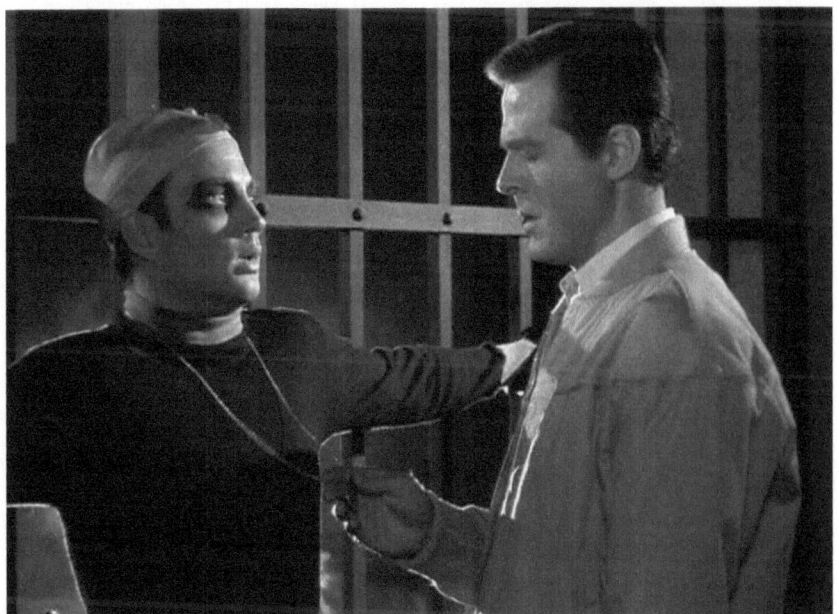

Culp as Trent interrogates Breech (Steve Harris) before removing the medallion that sends him hurtling back to the future

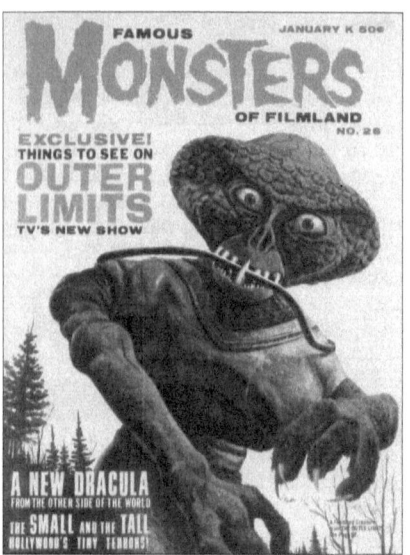

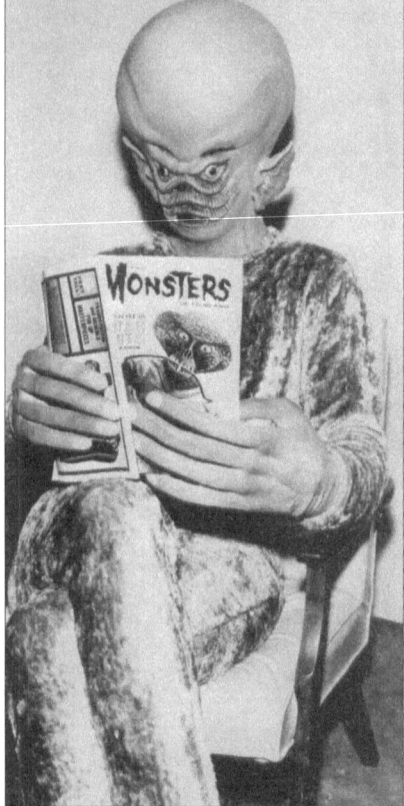

Top: *Famous Monsters* #26 (January 1964), featuring an interview with Joseph Stefano by Roger Elwood. The cover art is uncredited. **Above:** Wanted: More Readers Like ...

and so I was late getting my work done. Then there was the usual, "You're killing me! Where the hell's the script, Harlan?" kind of conversation, but there was never any rancor. I liked them, and I liked Seeleg enormously. I thought Seeleg was a bright man, and he was a kind man. And the nice thing about him, the reason there was probably very little rancor, was that because everybody else was clipping their, you know, what you would call the "vigorish". They were clipping their "vig" off the top of whatever small budget ABC had allocated for a segment. There was nobody watching. The network didn't give a shit; nobody really cared what we were doing, because they knew we weren't going to be on all that much longer. We were there just till ABC could find something that they thought could make them some money. And because nobody was watching, it really is a living example of what's wrong with this business, which is what Pauline Kael lamented as an art form that's run by businessmen. When no one was watching, when there was no big stake in it, they allowed us to do whatever we wanted, and as a result, we were able to use as much creativity as we had available in our brainpans, and do shows that, even today, hold up very, very, very well. They may not have the slickness and the technical gloss that is commonplace in television today, but boy, those shows really had a depth of story ingenuity and plot structure that was truly admirable. It was a holy and pleasant experience working on that show as a result. No, I don't recall any rancor. They didn't fuck with me, so there was no reason for rancor.

DMA: *Had you seen Robert Culp's previous two* Outer Limits *episodes—"Architects of Fear" and "Corpus Earthling"—by this time?*

HE: I'm not sure that I had seen his previous work on *Outer Limits*. I knew Culp's work very well from *I Spy*. *[Note:* I Spy *didn't actually premiere until eight months after the final episode of* The Outer Limits, *with filming of the initial pilot commencing in November 1964, one month after the airing of "Demon with a Glass Hand" on October 17th, 1964.]* I thought he was just a knockout actor, and it was, in fact, for him that I wrote the show. The part that was played by Arlene Martel was—I'm not sure anybody remembers this—but originally I had written that part for a black woman. It was supposed to be a black woman, and the network just, I mean, their hair stood on end, because—Christ! I think this was before the first big breakthrough when Dinah Shore kissed Harry Belafonte when he came on her variety show. That was the first time that a white woman had anything to do with a black man on television, even though *Star Trek* tries to pretend that it was Kirk and Uhura that did it. No, it was Dinah Shore and Harry Belafonte. It was still a fairly recent thing that Culp had been partnered with a black guy on *I Spy*. We're talking here the 'Fifties, for Christ's sake, and the 'Sixties, which was a period of utter repression in this country, and it was fairly *early* in the 'Sixties, so things weren't changed quite that much. They absolutely refused to allow me to do it as a black woman, and so I changed it and made her a Latina, which was the next step away from that heavy a controversy, but still it would kinda sorta make the point, and they, if you notice in the script, when Culp finds the door to go in, it says, "C. & E. Biros." Her name was Consuelo Losada, and her husband was Esteban Losada, but at the last minute the network said, "No, no, that's too Mexican. It's too Mexican. Don't do that. Make her Hungarian or something." So here's this woman named Consuelo Biros, and Esteban Biros, which makes no fucking sense at all, but it satisfied the network, and I was apoplectic about it.

It was not the first time I had been subject to the vagaries of the cupidity and cowardice of the network on anything that would even remotely smack of talking about the real world the way it was, and prejudice and bigotry, but it was a very annoying thing to happen to me. When I talked to Arlene Martel at the time, and Arlene Martel—her original name she had as an actress was Arlene Sax—and I think that was the name she had when I wrote the show, but by the time we got into it she was going under the name Arlene Martel. Arlene has changed her name a number of times for business reasons over the years. *[Note: Per Wikipedia, "Prior to 1964, she was frequently billed as Arline Sax, Arlene Sax or Tasha Martel.]* She and I talked at considerable length before the show, and I explained to her that it was supposed to be a black woman and then a Latina, and she said, "Well, let me see what I can do." And so, when she did it, of course she was blond, and there were not a lot of blond black women or blond Latinas at that point, so Arlene said, "Well, let me try and I'll do it with kind of a Spanish accent, and I'll do it with a babushka over my head; a bandana. I'll be able to try and capture some of that for you." I said, "Great," and that's exactly what she did. When you see her at first, she's wearing a kerchief over her head, which then later comes off. So, we lost the opportunity to do the first interracial kiss on television, which would have been a real sensation and which would have warmed the cockles of my little heart, but that's what happened. That was as close to any rancor as there was on the show, but that wasn't rancor with the production staff.

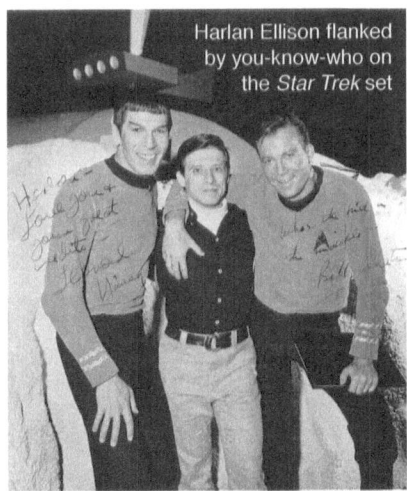

Harlan Ellison flanked by you-know-who on the *Star Trek* set

That was rancor with the network—what they call the "Standards and Practices" people.

DMA: Culp had a reputation on the Outer Limits **set as someone with many of his own creative ideas. What do you remember about Culp's approach and attitude during the shooting of "Demon with a Glass Hand?"**

HE: Well, oddly enough, I only met Bobby for a few minutes that first night. When I got there, I wanted to say hi to him because I had never met him, and here I'd written the show for him specifically, and they had told him I'd written the show

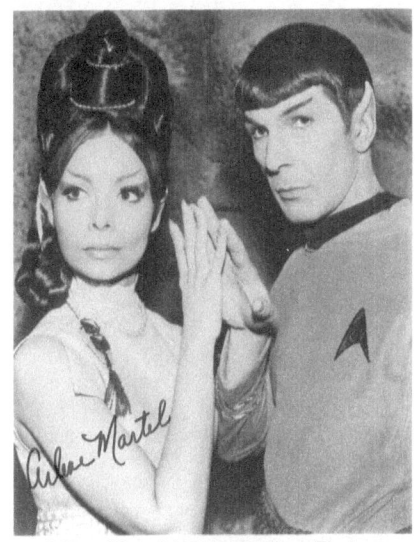

Arlene Martel (1936-2014) as T'pring, Spock's mate-to-be from *Trek*'s "Amok Time" episode

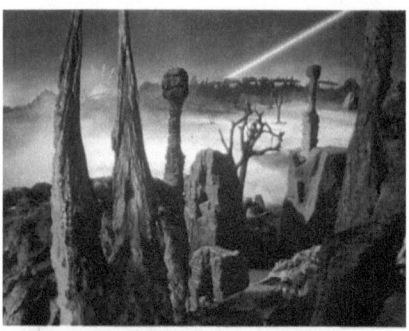

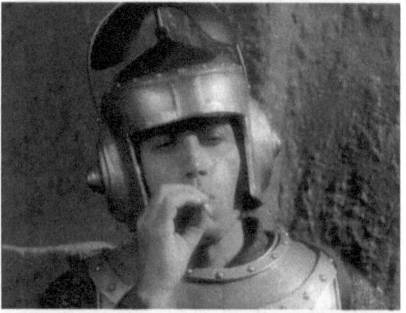

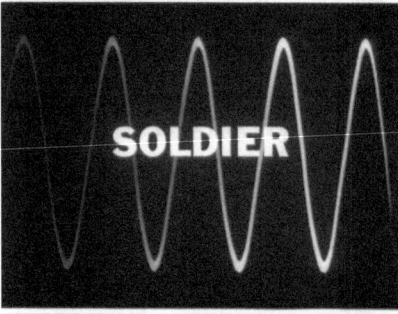

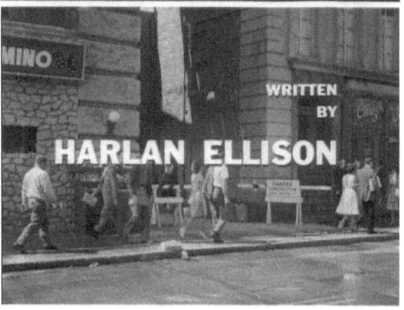

"Soldier" was the first story idea Harlan Ellison pitched to the producers of the second season of *The Outer Limits*. It starred Michael Ansara as Quarlo Clobregnny, a deeply-programmed soldier from the far future. 20 years later, the episode would provide partial inspiration for James Cameron's **THE TERMINATOR** (1984).

specifically for him, so he had said when I came down I should make myself known to him, and I said, "Where is he?" Somebody pointed up to, like, the third or fourth floor, and said, "He's up there somewhere." I went climbing up the stairs into the darkness, and there is a corner, with his, uh, they had these director's chairs and they had one with his name on it, and he was sitting in a corner reading, and he was reading a book on Pre-Columbian pottery. I remember that very distinctly, and I was enormously impressed, because he was very quiet, very soft-spoken. It was clear he didn't want to be bothered by anybody. That's why he was up there. He was getting away from the whole business end of it, and he said to me (the only thing I remember him actually saying)—I mean, he loved the part, he thought it was a terrific script—but he said, "I'm going to play this as if I were a ballet dancer."

And I thought, "*What?!* What does he mean?" Well, if you look at particularly the concluding scene of Act Two, where the hand tells him, "You have to die. The only way to save yourself is to die"—and he comes out from around the corner, and he starts walking down toward the camera. He's putting his feet one in front of the other, the same way a ballet dancer would. If you look at that scene, you'll see that he really *is*; he's got a very graceful way of doing it which I think gives the show a strange, ethereal quality, and gives *him* a strange, ethereal quality. I mean, don't forget, at that point you don't know that he's a robot, and yet there's something about him that is very alien, very strange, very odd. I think Bob found a way of showing that without doing the usual—what they call in acting circles "signifying"—where it's very broad and obvious what he's trying to do. So, he found a way of doing that, and that was what he said, that he was going to do it like a ballet dancer. Apart from that, we didn't have that much conversation that night, because shortly after, I made my great gaffe with Byron and sort of skulked off into the darkness myself to hide out so that I wouldn't be in anybody's way.

But subsequently Bobby and I got together and got to know each other so well, in fact, that when he was working with Sam Peckinpah, he invited me out to Malibu, and one of the most interesting nights of my life was spent in company with Bobby and Peckinpah and S. Lee Pogostin, the writer, and a blind flamenco guitarist. I was, at that point, dating a woman who was a *Playboy* "Playmate of the Month," and it was just a fascinating night, and that was only one of the subsequent nights that I spent in Bobby's company, and since that time, we've gotten together many, many times. Pogostin and Culp and Peckinpah were working on a picture called "SUMMER SOLDIERS," from an old expression about people who are only with you when things are good. They're called "summer soldiers" and "sunshine patriots". [Note: *The project was ultimately shelved due to conflicts between Peckinpah and Warner Brothers over the editing of* **THE WILD BUNCH** *(1969).*]

Those were interesting days. Bob and I discovered we had a couple of other things in common; we both collected Big Little Books, and both liked classical music, and we didn't go out and shoot pool every night, but we got together with some regularity, and we've just sort of stayed friends over the years.

DMA: One detail that I've always found distracting in this episode is when the glass hand is gloved, Trent seems able to move the fingers and actually grasp things with it.

HE: Yeah, yeah, I know exactly what you're saying. Well, don't forget, you're talking about a time, when, first of all, they didn't have the kind of special effects they have now. They didn't have the capacity for doing that kind of thing, and also, there was no budget! I mean, that show cost more than any other show in the second season. It was just a very expensive show, merely because it was so complex. It had a very broad story and a very long story and a lot of different sets, and it was amazing that they were able to bring it in on the budget that they did have. Yes, the thing that the hand is inflexible when he's got the mitten off, and absolutely flexible as a real hand when he's got it on—yeah, it's very distracting. But there's an infinitude more errors in it than that. For instance, the aliens all use contemporary weapons.

DMA: That was my next question!

HE: Kiddo, that's the network! That's the network. They didn't understand that aspect of the plot, and they didn't give a shit about it. Here they were spending all this money on the time-mirror and on sets, I mean, I wrote as many scenes as I possibly could for a limbo set, particularly the opening one where the Kyben is on the fence, or the teaser scene with the garbage cans. Those are all limbo sets. That's all they are. What you're seeing is what there is. They were shot on a sound stage with nothing else going on. We cut corners as much as we could. We used corner sets instead of full sets a number of times. We collapsed two or three scenes into one so that we wouldn't have to change locations, and even so, the network almost never consults the writer when they're doing these kinds of things. Neither the production people or the network people. They just go ahead and do it. If you say they have to have death-ray guns or lasers or blasters or whatever the fuck it is, they'll say, "Aw, just give him a .32 and let him go about his business." Well, as a consequence, there are inherent flaws in the way the show is run, but

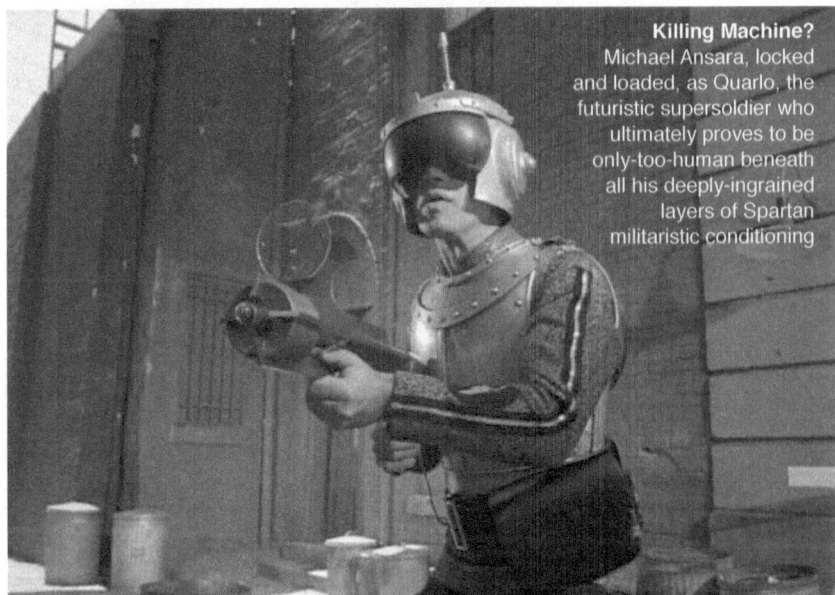

Killing Machine?
Michael Ansara, locked and loaded, as Quarlo, the futuristic supersoldier who ultimately proves to be only-too-human beneath all his deeply-ingrained layers of Spartan militaristic conditioning

oddly enough, they don't even bother me anymore. Maybe it's because I've seen them so many times, but this was one of the very first television shows that was put into the Archive of Popular History at, I think it's Oberlin College in Ohio, and I was invited to come to the dedication. The audience—now this is maybe 10, 12, 13, 14 years after it was done already—and it should have aged, and with the exception of the one line where Consuelo says, "I can't stand violence," well, in those days, that was a very funny line. People would laugh and the audience would laugh very hard. But other than that, everybody got into it very quickly and no one seemed to get the feeling that it had aged at all. And when I look at it now, I get the same feeling. There is a classic quality to it that I think is a product, not just of, you know, my ego will not permit me to think that my writing didn't have a whole hell of a lot to do with it, but beyond that, the direction and the acting are so good that I think the three aspects meld to produce what television can be when it's at its most inventive, and the days of doing that kind of work are long since passed. Nobody does that kind of thing anymore, because there's no market for it. Audiences don't want to see anthology shows. When I was subsequently on the revival of *The Twilight Zone*, we learned that the hard way. The show did very, very, very well, and among its demographic, we were like number one every Friday night. But audiences had been trained, as they have been even more today, to want to see the same characters week after week after week until they get tired of them and want them killed, which is the fickleness of the audience. And anthology shows just don't do it, because when we were on with *The Twilight Zone*, the same year *[1985]* was Spielberg's *Amazing Stories*, which also died. The only reason it stayed on any longer than our show did, and I think it was on maybe six or eight weeks longer, nothing more than that, was because they were spending a million dollars an episode, and we were spending far, far less than that. The only reason that they stayed on was because they had that kind of budget. Spielberg was willing to pump as much money into it as he needed to make it work. But we see now that anthology shows just will not make it, as anthology shows, *per se*. They've got to have an ongoing set of characters. The anthology series has pretty much moved over to cable, where they're doing these current *Outer Limits*. *[Note: The "reboot" of the show ran from 1995-2002.]*

DMA: In The Outer Limits Companion, B. Ritchie Payne [assistant to the producer on the original series] is quoted as saying that he arranged for you to see a rough cut of "Demon With a Glass Hand" and that you were very upset and wanted your name taken off the show...

HE: Yeah, probably. That happens a lot. I mean, it happened when they were doing the final *Twilight Zone* episodes in syndication and Joe Straczynski, who's my closest friend on *Babylon 5*, hired me to do a segment I wrote called, "Crazy as a Soup Sandwich." When they sent me the tape, I said, "It's awful, it's awful, take my name off it, I want my name taken off!" And I had already taken my name off a couple of things. Yes, I was very saddened by the inconsistencies (in "Demon with a Glass Hand"). For instance, I've mentioned a number of them to you already, but in the prologue, where the narrator is speaking, there was a typographical error when the mimeographing place did my script. So instead of the word being "Sumerian," in comes out "Sumerican," and everybody was so stupid, nobody said, "What the hell is 'Sumerican'?! Doesn't he mean 'Sumerian?'" They don't read these things. Actors don't read them, narrators don't read them, producers don't read them, the directors don't know—nobody seems to know, and all of a sudden, there it is. Now, if *I* had seen the dailies, if *I* had been invited to see the dailies, I would have caught it and I would have said, "No, no, no, my god, he's got to go back and dub in that line. We're going to have to loop in the word 'Sumerian.'" And here I am looking at it and here's "Sumerican," and then I see the guys with the raccoon eyes, and then they dropped-out the scene where Trent goes and checks the force-bubble, and I said, "My god, it's illogical. Can't you shoot that scene and stick it in?" Well, of course, they couldn't. They were way over-budget and they were finished, anyhow, so I was being a looney toon. So I said, "I hate it. Take my name off it." Well, Seeleg and Ben (Brady), and Bobby as a matter of fact, talked to me and they said, "Come on, yeah, it's got some flaws in it and it's not maybe the complete dream you had, but look how good it is." And I said, "Aww, all right," and I put my name back on it.

I don't think you'll find a piece of paper anywhere in which my name is not on that script. There are versions of my *Star Trek* script, and *Flying Nun* and various other shows, and *Voyage to the Bottom of the Sea*, where you'll find "Cordwainer Bird." But not that one. If I was pissed, I was pissed at what the network had done in editing it and censoring it. Not having seen the way they shot it, it was not the way the final shooting script was. They had done additional shooting scripts after the final, and they had changed Consuelo Lasada to Consuelo Biros, to this to that and the other thing, and though I knew about it, because I had talked with Arlene about it, I didn't realize how serious it was going to look to me. In those days—well, I guess I'm not much different now—but fuckin' with my art really gets me up on my hind legs.

DMA: Also in **The Outer Limits Companion,** *you said that Culp still wants to make "Demon with a Glass Hand" as a feature film, as the director. Any likelihood of this happening?*

HE: Well, we talk about it every once in a while. Nobody has come forward. No studio, no production company has actually come forward and said, "Let's make it." United Artists/MGM, who do the new *Outer Limits,* although they have remade a couple of the original shows, know better than to try to do mine. Because I've retained the rights to both of those pieces *[i.e., "Soldier" and "Demon with a Glass Hand"],* if they tried to remake them in one of their current-mode shows, they would go to their grave with my teeth in their throat. So, they're not going to do it. Every once in a while, every three or four years, someone will come and say," Gee, this ought to be remade, it's a great story" and "Isn't there a longer version?" and I say, "Yeah, there is. Parts of it are in the graphic novel *[1986],* which I'm not that wild about, either. Julie Schwartz at DC is a very close friend of mine and we wanted to do it, but even though I asked Marshall Rogers to do it, because I was enormously impressed by his work on *Batman* at the time, they didn't offer him enough money, and so he sort of phoned the job in, which I found pretty despicable, that an artist would do less than his best work because he wasn't getting the kind of money he wanted. I mean, whether you're getting stiffed or not on the money, you always create art on the same level of excellence, which is the outer limit, I suppose, of what you can do at that time. And for him not to do that because he wasn't getting as big a buck off it as he was supposed to get, I found really offensive and sad. So, the graphic novel is okay, but it ain't particularly memorable.

DMA: What's the current status of the "Demon" novel?

HE: Well, *"Obituary for an Instant"* is in the back file. The show came to take on a life of its own. That's happened to me a couple of times. For instance, *A Boy and His Dog [1969],* which is a small part of a very large novel which I've been working on for about 25 years, got a life of its own because it was published before the book came out and was an award-winner, and the same for "Demon." When "Demon" won the Writers' Guild Award, it became a huge icon and there was a sense of closure to it. I've retained the rest of the novel; I still have those 110-something pages, and they're pretty good, but the sense of wanting to write it is now long passed. I mean, we're talking, what year was that? Nineteen-sixty .... ?

DMA: ...Four. 1964.

HE: 1964, and here it is '97, for Christ's sake.

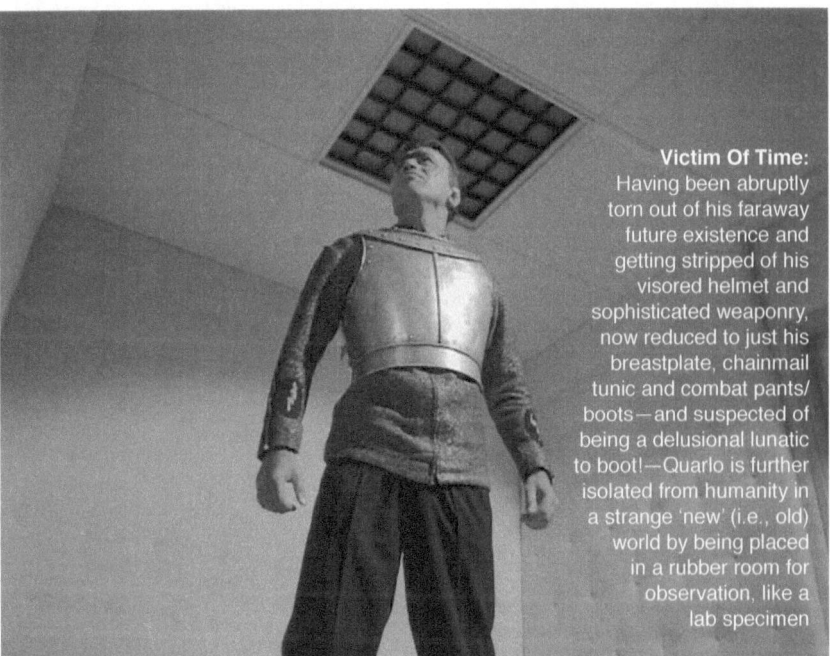

Victim Of Time: Having been abruptly torn out of his faraway future existence and getting stripped of his visored helmet and sophisticated weaponry, now reduced to just his breastplate, chainmail tunic and combat pants/boots—and suspected of being a delusional lunatic to boot!—Quarlo is further isolated from humanity in a strange 'new' (i.e., old) world by being placed in a rubber room for observation, like a lab specimen

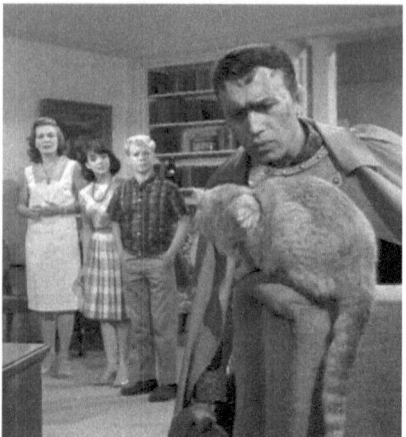

Quarlo attempts to converse with the family cat, believing it to be a telepath used for reconnaissance, as they are in 'his' future

I'll probably never get around to writing that novel. And I'm not sure it really needs to be written. The core of the story was what I used in the episode. There was a lot more to it. I had Trent living in our time, living on this planet for a long time and not knowing that he was a robot, and people around him being killed and butchered, and he can't figure out what the hell's going on, and eventually his memory is restored because the hand is put together. It was a good idea for its time, but I think the television show—it did it. It *did* it. You do an idea—I'm not one of those guys who writes sequels. I've never written a sequel to anything. The three *Boy and His Dog* stories that have appeared are all part of the same novel; they're not separate stories. They're different sections that have been published at different times. I've never written a sequel to any story and, until recently, when I did the CD-ROM game *I Have No Mouth and I Must Scream*, I had to rethink the story, and I came up with aspects of it that I didn't perceive were there, because I had written exactly what I wanted to write in that story. Well, the same goes for a thing like "Demon." "Demon" has been mined pretty well by me, and if I were to go back and try to do the novel, it might be interesting as a curiosity, but I don't think anything much more would be added to the story than what is there right now. The whole concept of this lonely, noble, courageous sort of "wandering Jew" that's carrying the entire human race around in his thoracic segment is kind of nice. It's kind of whole the way it is.

DMA: As someone who thinks a great deal of Robert Culp as both an actor and friend, is there anything special you'd like to add, as a summation of sorts?

HE: I suppose if I was going to say anything about Culp, one of the great evils that we live with today is the strange cultural amnesia that removes from notice and approbation anything older than fifteen minutes. The Gen X people, they worship Pauly Shore, and have never heard of Paul Muni. They think Sharon Stone is an icon, but they've never heard of Marta Toren. They will look at Sinbad as if he were John fuckin' Barrymore, and they'll forget about Culp. Culp has worked long and hard in the industry, and any show that he's in, he brings something wonderful to. He's a consummate actor and he's an intelligent actor. There's a smartness in what he does that I think the market no longer knows what to do with. The market now worships Chevy Chase falling on his face. Chevy Chase looks like Albert Schweitzer by comparison with Chris Farley, for Christ's sake! I think we've come to a very low state in entertainment, where boneheaded things like **INDEPENDENCE DAY** and **MISSION: IMPOSSIBLE**—which is just grotesque—can serve as moneymaking icons. The market becomes devalued and the Robert Culps and the Paddy Chayefskys and whoever all else, the Reginald Roses—the people who made television interesting at one time or another, those people had to go elsewhere. Paddy Chayefsky took a backseat to Reginald Rose. Reginald Rose was one of the other great writers of the golden age of television. And there are just an awful lot of actors and writers and producers and directors who have been aced-out by what is called contemporary television and contemporary film, and it's very sad. There is no honor in this industry, and a guy like Culp, who should be sitting very fat and pretty these days with plump roles to pick, is still scuffling and still working. So, I admire him. I think he's an absolutely admirable commendation for his art form.

DMA: I would have to absolutely agree. I thank you very much for your time. I appreciate it. •

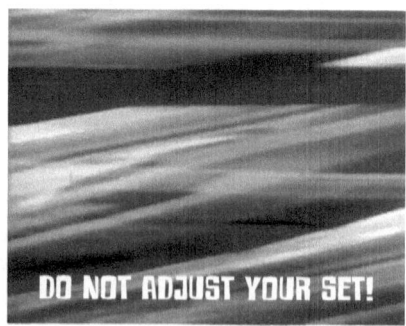

INTERVIEW WITH ROBERT CULP
(conducted on February 17th, 1997)

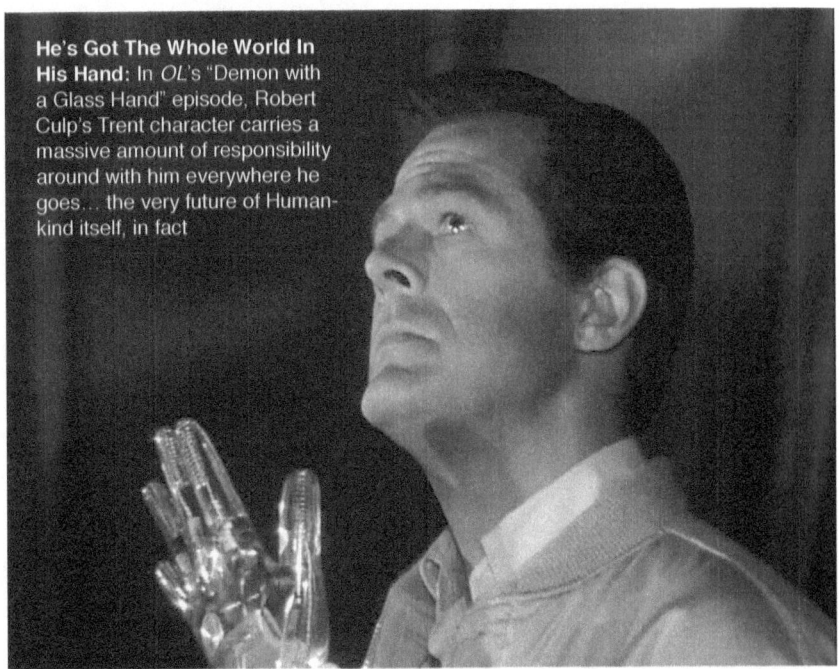

He's Got The Whole World In His Hand: In *OL*'s "Demon with a Glass Hand" episode, Robert Culp's Trent character carries a massive amount of responsibility around with him everywhere he goes... the very future of Humankind itself, in fact

DANA MARIE ANDRA: *Correct me if I'm wrong, but did you get your start in theatre at age twenty-one?*

ROBERT CULP: No, I started in the theatre at *fourteen*.

DMA: *At what point and how did you finally get into television and film?*

RC: This is very complicated, man, and it's going to take too long, and I don't want to go into this stuff. It's really ancient history. You can find it someplace. It's written down someplace.

DMA: *Okay...*

RC: I don't want to go into it all over again. Suffice it to say that my mother threw me into a little theatre group in Berkeley, California called the Berkeley Community Players when I was fourteen, in desperation because, as you can well imagine, I was a problem, in Berkeley, California in 1944. She wanted somebody, something to take my mind off whatever, and I just sort of went along with it, because I didn't understand what it was all about...until I stepped on stage the first time and hit the lights, and that was it. I knew what I was going to do. That was Berkeley, California, age fourteen. 1944.

From then on, my problem in life was to find a place to go, bearing in mind that I had to finish high school and college, where there was the most amount of theatre; where there were the largest number of potential productions on stage, and I went there. So after high school, I went from one college or university to another to find that spot, that niche, where there was the most amount of theatre, because I never stopped working for more than a week, ever. I worked on the stage steadily for 12 years, through amateur stuff on into a burst of radio; I got in on the last gasp of big-time radio in 1951, and I went to New York. I was given a ticket to come to New York. I wasn't quite finished with college, and I just got on a plane and never looked back. From then on, all my energies were in terms of Broadway and the theatre, and once in a while, just for money, there was this little thing called television, but it didn't amount to anything in those days. Nobody cared about it except the people who were in it, but there was money there, and God, I needed money to survive on. There wasn't very much money, but I met a guy who was a casting director then and was a casting director all his life. He became a lifelong friend. His name was Joe Scully. He came to my first job, on a thing called *You Are There [1953-1971]*, and I played a little bitty, tiny role, just one speech, speaking directly into the camera. I don't know if you've ever heard of *You Are There*, but it was a live show. The kinescopes that survive are lousy, but I've seen one recently. It was reshot on film. This particular one starred Paul Newman as Brutus, in "The Death of Socrates," and I played a Senator. Johnny Cassavetes, a whole bunch of guys you've heard of since; I can't remember everybody who was in it. A guy who went on to be a very famous Broadway director, Joseph Anthony, was in it, and we kind of got on pretty well. He cast me later in a play which was very important to me a few years later.

Mostly, all of my energies were devoted to the stage, and I never thought in the world I would ever come to that disgusting place called Hollywood. And then I had a hit with a play in 1956 and I won the first Obie for Best Actor of the Year ever given, for a play, *He Who Gets Slapped*. I played the role of "He". This is a minor, I repeat, *minor* Russian classic, a romantic tragedy, and it's a foolproof play. You can't miss with this play. I begged and pummeled and cajoled everybody I knew to get this part, and I finally got it, and I won the Obie and got all the reviews and the rest was history; I started to work. But I started to work in television. I also started to work on stage, but it's so slow compared to television. You rehearsed for a week, maybe two weeks, maybe three weeks if you're lucky, and you go and do the damn thing live, and it's over and there's a lot more money in it per day, I guess, whatever you want to call it, per week.

Among the things that happened was somebody asked me to come to Hollywood to do a thing called *Matinee Theater*, which was a live, one-hour show, every day. Every day at noon. It was like *The U.S. Steel Hour*, but it was one hour, every day, at noon, five days a week. I don't know how in the world this man did it; this little teeny-weeny man. His name escapes me at the moment; very handsome little man. Came to New York, cast some actors, I was one of them. I came out and I did one, and while I was waiting around to do another one that he cast me in, which was going to be in a couple of weeks, I got a call from the Morris office that represented me then to go over and meet these people at a (production company) called Four Star to do an episode of a half-hour television, black-and-white western called *Dick Powell's Zane Grey Theatre [1957-60]*. I went over there, met the guy,

he was nice, I liked him, he liked me, they cast me in this thing, I did the show, took three days to shoot it. Then I fiddled around, went up to San Francisco to see my mother and my grandparents; oh, and my dad. My dad was still alive then. He lived in Oakland (California); he was an attorney in Oakland.

I came back down to Los Angeles, there wasn't anything else immediately, I was ready to start a play, playing Kim Stanley's husband in an Arthur Lawrence play for Broadway. I mean, it was just big-time for me. It was the biggest thing that had ever happened. I went back, we were just getting started in this play, directed by the same guy, Joe Anthony, that I mentioned before, who I'd met earlier as an actor, and the Morris office said, "You can finish the play, but then you have to get on a plane to go to Hollywood, because you're going to do a series."

I said, "I am *not*. Are you crazy? I'm not going to Hollywood. Get outta here! I work on stage. I don't want to do TV."

And they said, "If you don't do it, you'll never work again. You'll have to go to England to get a job, because they'll blackball you."

I said, "Oh, man..." So finally I did go, and this thing was a pilot, and I didn't know it. This *Zane Grey Theatre* episode was actually a pilot for a television series called *Trackdown [1957-59]*. So I did that for two years and then started the grind. I've been there ever since.

Spring of '59, *Trackdown* was over with and I started on a year of unemployment. I didn't have a job for an entire year. I thought it was all over; might as well just go and do myself in. Finally, a little bit of time, I began to get little parts here and there, and started all over again. By the time **PT 109** *[1963]* came along, I was getting the highest price in town for people who were still doing guest stars on other people's television series. But it didn't do any good, because I didn't work that often, because I'd priced myself out of the market. So I did **PT 109, SUNDAY IN NEW YORK** *[1963, USA, D: Peter Tewksbury]* and **RHINO!** *[1964, USA, D: Ivan Tors]* almost back-to-back, and for all the good any one of them did me, I might as well have stayed in bed. Nothing happened.

I had children coming; I had a wife and two children, and another one on the way, and I had to do something, so I dreamed-up a pilot idea, I took it to Carl Reiner, he said, "I like your idea, but I'm not doing television this year, but I showed it to

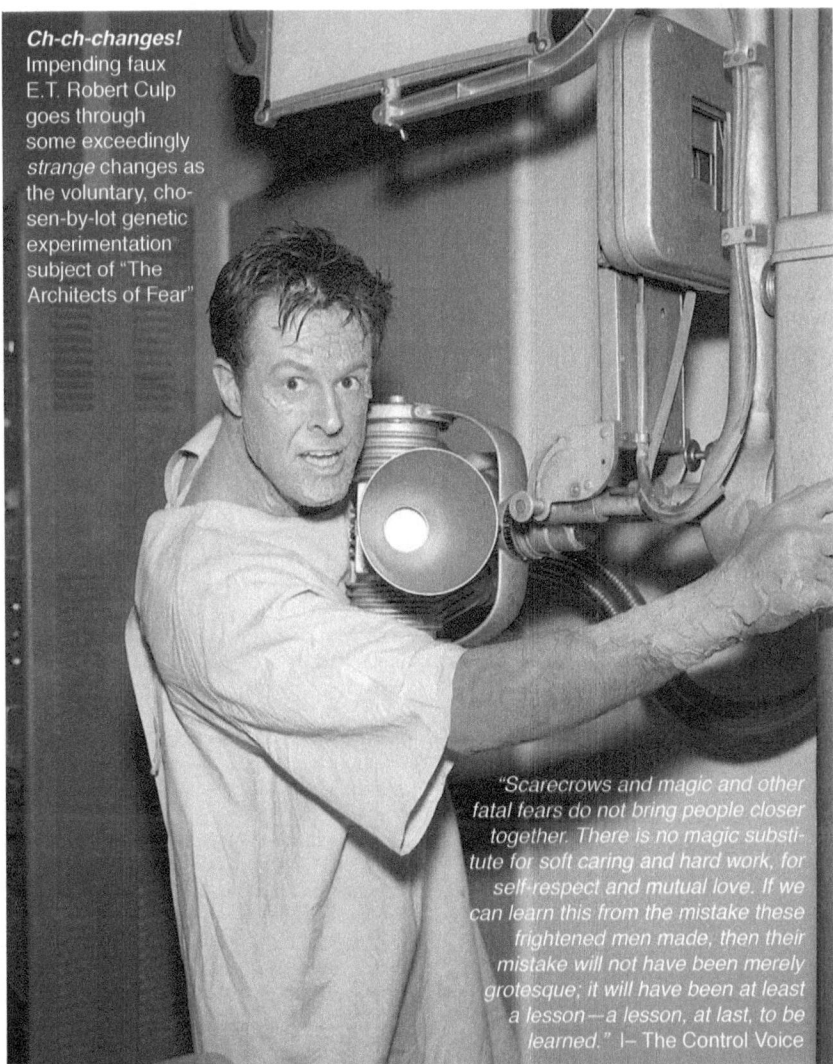

Ch-ch-changes! Impending faux E.T. Robert Culp goes through some exceedingly *strange* changes as the voluntary, chosen-by-lot genetic experimentation subject of "The Architects of Fear"

"Scarecrows and magic and other fatal fears do not bring people closer together. There is no magic substitute for soft caring and hard work, for self-respect and mutual love. If we can learn this from the mistake these frightened men made, then their mistake will not have been merely grotesque; it will have been at least a lesson—a lesson, at last, to be learned." I– The Control Voice

Sheldon Leonard. Why don't you go and talk to him?" So I did. He said, "I like your idea, but I like mine better." I said, "What's yours?" He said, "Two guys go around the world masquerading as a tennis bum and his trainer, and they're actually spies for the United States. Oh, and one of them is black." I said, "You're right. Yours is the better idea." So I waited for him for about three months, and that was *I Spy* [1965-68].

Now prior to this, in the last gasp of my, you know, sort of half-assed guest-stardom on television doing other people's television series, there was this thing called *Outer Limits*. It came into being at the right time for me, because it was one of the last anthologies. Anthologies had always been poison on television. They didn't get enough of an audience. Even *The Twilight Zone* struggled along, and struggled along for a few years to form the basis of its awards, but it never got quite the numbers they wanted to get. And that was the only one that was really hot stuff, except [Alfred] *Hitchcock* [*Presents, 1955-62*], which bore his name.

Now, the first one [i.e., Outer Limits] I was hired to do was "Architects of Fear." That was, like, the third episode, and here's a nice young man, skinny young man named Conrad Hall, D.P. on it. His first assistant is Bill Fraker, and the makeup man is Freddie Phillips. Fred Phillips is one of the great

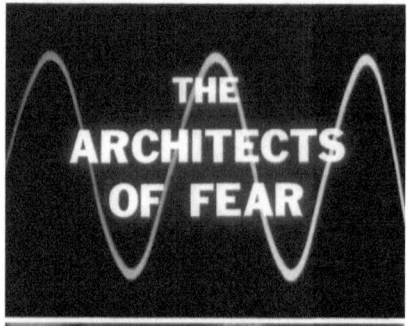

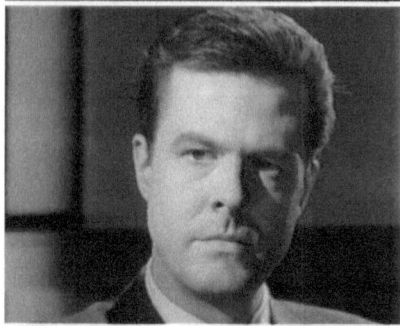

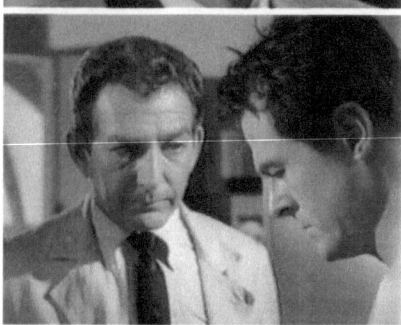

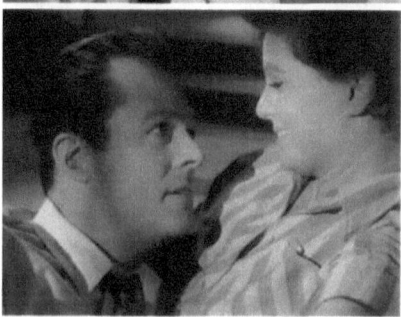

Written by Meyer Dolinsky (*Stoney Burke, Star Trek*) and directed by Byron Haskin (**THE WAR OF THE WORLDS**), "The Architects of Fear" co-starred Leonard Horn as Dr. Phillip Gainer, and Geraldine Brooks as Yvette Leighton. It's remembered as one of the most emotionally impactful and visually affecting episodes of the series

makeup-men of all time. I didn't know who these guys were. I had tunnel vision, and I was doing an awful lot of writing at the time, so I never did network very well in this business; you know, the "old boy" network which can support an entire career if you go out and make nice on folks. I never was very good on that, because I seemed to just not get out there and mix it up too well. I was too busy sitting at a desk, pounding on a typewriter. So, I did this first show. I got kind of turned-on by it. None of what we're talking about is literature, exactly, you know? It isn't what I started out to do in this form, the profession. I was supposed to be an actor, not a guy who frames performances in a split-second, and just gets the work on and does it, and you do the best you can and that's that. That's television, and still is. But it's there, it's money, I had a growing family to support, so I did it, and I kept thinking, "I'll get past this, I'll get past this. I'll go on to features, and the work will get more real."

And so, I did first "Architects of Fear," and the next thing I knew, it wasn't very long—a few months—but all of a sudden, along came "Demon with a Glass Hand" *[Note: Culp's second* Outer Limits *episode was actually "Corpus Earthling", which we clarify later in the interview.]* "Demon with a Glass Hand" was sort of a turning point for me, because I perceived how mysterious really good writing could be, for the big screen or television. It's very mysterious when it works. Sometimes it looks like it's going to work, and it doesn't, and I began to really zero in, seriously, on trying to figure out one from the other at the time. Obviously, Harlan Ellison and I became good friends off the episode, which I'm sure he's told you a great deal about. I'm sure he's told you his adventure picking-up his award a few years ago.

DMA: Which award was that?

RC: I don't know. It was an award that was given out to "Demon with a Glass Hand," and he had to wrestle these guys on the stage for it.

DMA: No, he didn't go over that one.

RC: That's a cool story. He found out that there was an award to be presented in an otherwise self-congratulatory event having to do with partially marketing and partially advertising. Anyway, the guys who make it all happen in terms of revenue for studios coming from video, okay? He goes over to Metro to receive the award. If the award's to be given out to anybody, there's nobody left, so he figures, well, they did ask him to be there—they said, "Oh yes, please be there"—and so he assumed that the award was going to be picked-up by him. Why not? There wasn't anybody else. When the award was announced, he started for the stage. He got to the stage, and out of the corner of his eyes he saw *three* other guys coming, that he'd never seen before. Young men. Young guys, guys who had sold this thing, and who had proven with the bookkeeping and the bookwork and all that stuff, that this was the single most financially successful one-hour episode ever made, ever, in the history of television. It made more money, dollars and cents, than any other one-hour show, ever. And that's what the award was about. But these guys had invented this category so that they could go up and get the award! They were just guys who worked for Metro! They had nothing to do with making the show. They just wanted an award. But there it was, and he started to argue with them on stage and there was a grab-fest going on over this dumb award. He got it, ran out, kept it, still got it. I think it's a great story. Real vintage Harlan Ellison.

DMA: **Indeed!** *When was this?*

RC: I don't know. About five years ago *[circa 1992].*

DMA: When you did "Architects of Fear," **The Outer Limits** *hadn't yet premiered on television. Did they show you the pilot?*

RC: No. In those days, they'd send you a script, and if you were sort of intrigued by it, or if they made you an offer financially that you couldn't refuse, you just took it. That was it and you hoped for the best, because there were an awful lot of slips between the cup and the lip, especially on television. Anything could go wrong with a perfectly good script. Although to tell you the truth, if you get a good episode script for a television series, an hour show, if it looks good on paper, a good journeyman director could bring in a very solid show, usually. It is not as dicey as going into a feature that looks better, and can still go on its ass for a lot of different reasons. But most of the directors who directed then and now are good, solid journeymen, and they know their profession, and they're not kids out of college, or they are not guys who are ordinarily writers who've never directed before, and so forth. Usually you get somebody who's solid, who's grounded, who knows all the rules of getting down in the trenches and making a movie. That was television, at least in those days.

DMA: Byron Haskin certainly had a solid background when he came to **The Outer Limits.** *In talking about this episode in* **The Outer Lim-**

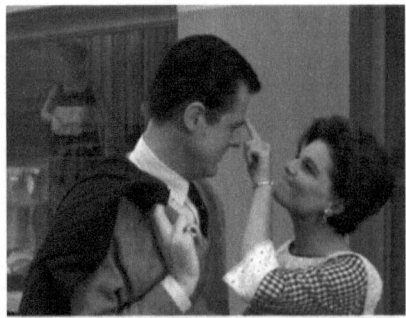

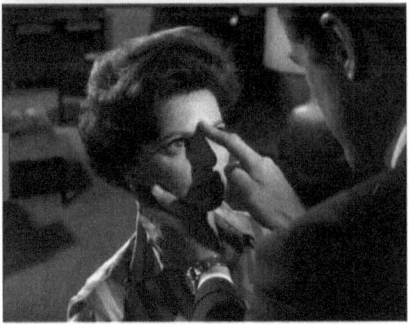

Allen Leighton (Culp) and his wife Yvette (Brooks) share a tender gesture—a sort of "mark against evil"—they use to quell their fears of the unknown and concerns of harm, a unifying thread that runs throughout the episode

its Companion, *he said, "Culp's middle name should have been 'Outer Limits'. Because he's a weirdo, of sorts. He wanted to make up his own camera angles, and use ideas that wouldn't have worked in a million years. I'd line-up a shot that would get us through and make the budget requirement, and meanwhile Culp would be hanging off some part of the ceiling on a rope, telling me his idea of an entrance would be better. His line was always, 'This would be a great way to play it!' but I never fell for that. We had our explosive moments over such things, but we got along."*

RC: Byron came on as sort of an honored guest. I had never heard of the guy. The only thing I think ... did he direct **THIS ISLAND EARTH**? *[1955]*

DMA: No, he did THE WAR OF THE WORLDS [1953].

RC: **WAR OF THE WORLDS**, that's right. **WAR OF THE WORLDS** is largely a stupid, boring movie, but there were some scenes in it that were pretty good. But the stuff that was

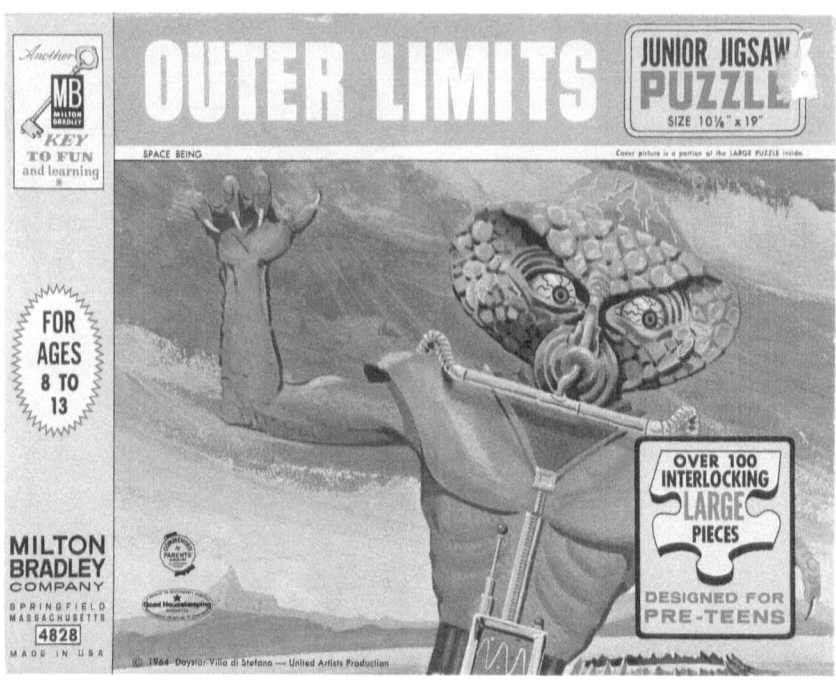

One of at least three colorful *Outer Limits* jigsaw puzzles produced by Milton Bradley in 1964

staged was crap. It was really unpardonable. All the rioting in the streets was about as believable, you know, as, well, I don't know what. It was terrible. So there hadn't really been very much science fiction that anybody could take seriously outside of **INVASION OF THE BODY SNATCHERS** *[1955]*, which worked because it was so simple. And Don Siegel happened to be a great director. He knew how to talk to people. Byron, on the other hand, had no idea how to talk to actors. He was just hoping for the best, and was a very jolly and charming man. I'm surprised at his take on whatever it was that went on between him and me. I don't remember that stuff at all.

DMA: That was from **The Outer Limits Companion**, *by David Schow. Have you not seen that?*

RC: No.

DMA: Those were the things Haskin said, and I was wondering what you thought about it...

RC: I thought he was kind of an adorable pixie. I never took him very seriously, but obviously he didn't take me seriously either.

DMA: He spoke of how you'd say, "This would be a great way to play this," and he would just shoot it the way he was going to shoot it anyway.

RC: Of course, and so he should. He's the director.

DMA: He also mentioned the blink of a scene in which you're in mid-transformation that you and Fred Phillips [makeup artist] put together, essentially on your own.

RC: I don't see how that's possible, frankly. If the director didn't want it in or didn't want to shoot it, didn't want to add it to his schedule of work for the day, which he's responsible for because it's going to slow him down or cramp his style at the end of the day, he wouldn't have done it. I don't understand that kind of question.

DMA: In the book, you had described how you and Fred Phillips had one day, during makeup, gone in and done this kind of mid-shot, and Haskin said it was done without his jurisdiction.

RC: I don't remember that. If it stuck in his memory, he's probably right, because it doesn't stick in my memory at all. I do remember that, in those days, the director was boss on the set, and it's beyond me how anybody could shoot anything, unless the producer wanted it shot, without the director's okay, especially when you've got Connie Hall and Billy Fraker standing there. I don't understand that at all.

However, did you ever hear the story about how that makeup...we're talking "Architects of Fear" now...how that makeup came about?

DMA: I'm not sure.

RC: I went to Fred Phillips, whom I'd never met before, before we started to shoot, probably the day before, and I said to him, you know, wringing my hands in frustration, "What the hell are we going to do? This is a major, major sequence. This is a zillion dollars on film. I mean, how the hell are we going to do this, this transformation, which is a process of surgery and shit that takes weeks and weeks and weeks. How are we going to do that?"

He said, "Well, we've got to start with something. We've got to be different from anything we've done before," which was not a big problem since this was the third or fourth show.

I said, "Well, what is the basic form of it? I mean, what have you worked out in your head?"

He said, "I haven't had time to work anything out in my head." He turned around and leaned down into one of those big barrels, you know, the big trash barrels that they have on the set? And he came up with a paper cup, and he said, "Let's start with this." And that's the way it began, and if you look at the makeup, if you can freeze on some of the frames, you'll see that at the core of it is this cone that's made of a paper cup. And I remember that he, we—he did the work, but we sort of, like, dreamed-it-up together. He did all of the work, but I added a few little notions of my own about what little I knew about anatomy and physics.

At the end, he gave me the makeup. I asked him, "Can I have the makeup, please?" He said, "What do you want with it? It's nothing. It's just gum and cotton. It's the same way they built Frankenstein, the original. Just gum and cotton, really, and a little bit of mortician's wax and some rubber tubes." I said, "Yeah, but I've got three boys at home. I want to scare the hell out of them." So I put the makeup on at home, and I came out into the front room, the kids were there, and I'm telling you, I had no idea it was going to be so awful. They all ran screaming from the room. Boy, I never did that again!

DMA: I can imagine. We've got a two-year-old, and I think he'd have a similar reaction.

RC: Yeah. If it's Daddy's voice and there's something wrong with Daddy, it's very frightening.

DMA: That was the scene, incidentally, that Haskin said was wasteful and that it had been done without his approval. From a viewer's point of view, however, that scene was a very important glimpse into the process, and it really added something that needed to be visualized.

RC: Well, now that you talk about it that way, maybe there was something to that. It might have been that we just argued about it and finally he agreed in desperation to shoot the fucking thing to shut me up. That's possible, and that's the way he dealt with it years afterwards. Because I knew as a writer—Haskin wasn't any writer, for Christ's sake, but I was. I was a seasoned writer already by then. I had written and sold things of my own by then and seen them produced, and they were pretty goddamned good, so I had a lot of confidence. I knew that you couldn't simply dissolve from the beginning to the end of that makeup

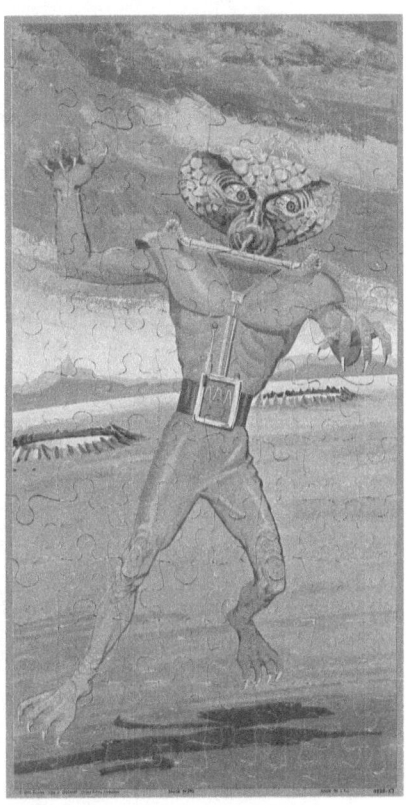

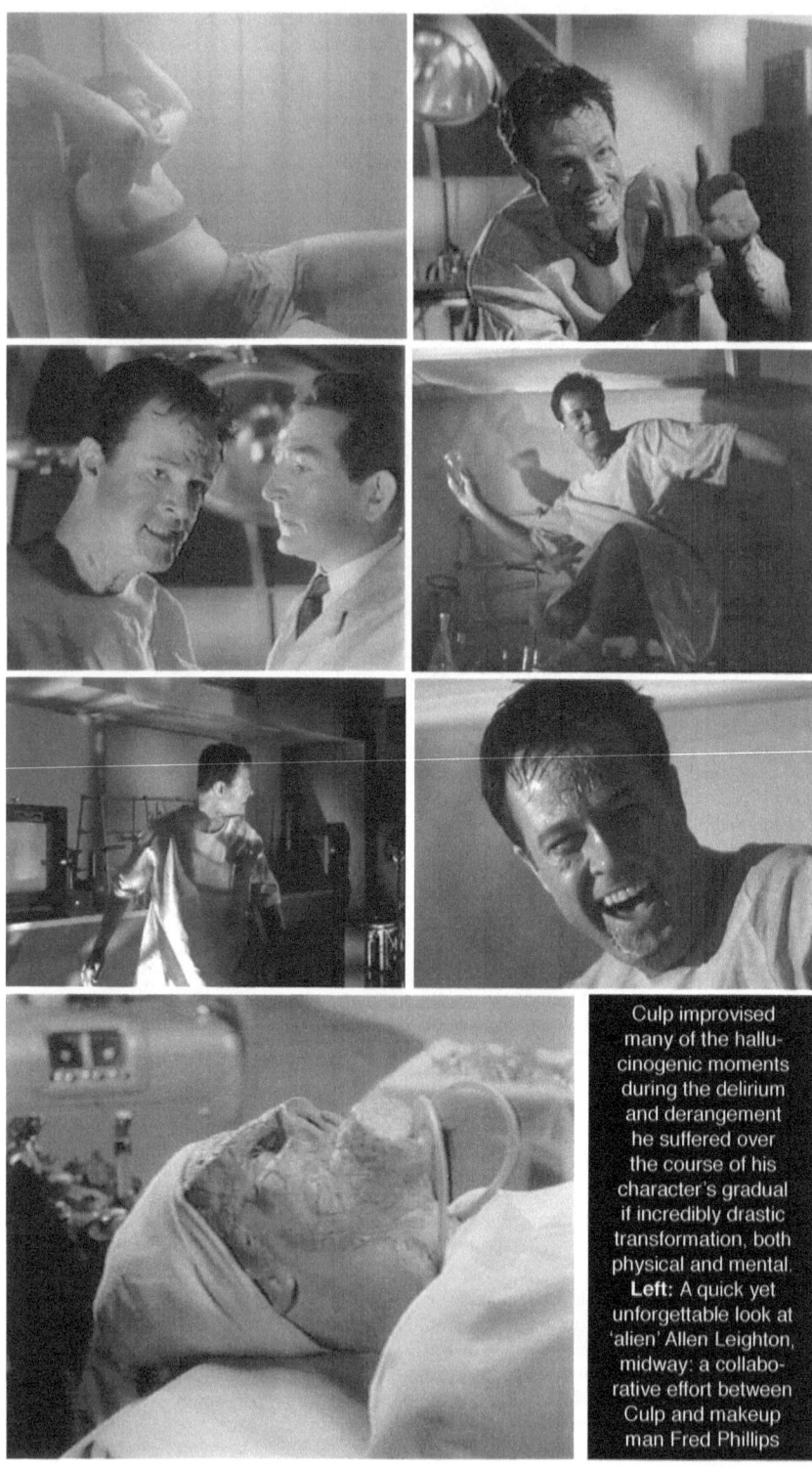

Culp improvised many of the hallucinogenic moments during the delirium and derangement he suffered over the course of his character's gradual if incredibly drastic transformation, both physical and mental.
Left: A quick yet unforgettable look at 'alien' Allen Leighton, midway: a collaborative effort between Culp and makeup man Fred Phillips

and have any notion of what this man was going through, unless you actually saw something. So I certainly would have insisted on a median scene if there wasn't anything there, a halfway mark for the surgical transition, which we didn't have time for, and we didn't have money for, and that may have been where the argument lay with Byron Haskin; he didn't think it was necessary.

DMA: There's a scene in the middle where you have a schizophrenic episode at the lab and start throwing things. Was that scripted, or did you just...?

RC: No, I just made it up.

DMA: The dialogue as well?

RC: Yeah, most of it. Most of the dialogue in a thing like that, you have to make it up. Whatever was there, it was indicated that he flips out, but that was about the size of it. "In this scene he flips out," then you sort of have to make it up as you go along. You keep shooting it until it gets believable, but we didn't have time for all that, so you'd better get it on the first couple of tries.

DMA: That was very powerful scene. I really liked it.

RC: Yeah. We had to block it, of course. The only time we'd ever blocked anything like that was in *I Spy*. In *I Spy*, I'd go and I would tell the cameraman to put the camera over there, and if you're not going to cover with a second camera, stay back for this until here and then you can move in. But otherwise, don't expect the same thing twice. We're not going to break the scene in two, because you can't break it up. We'll have to play it in a two-shot and a master, because we don't know what we're going to do next. Yeah, we can keep it physically so we're not going to step out of frame on you, but still, a lot of stuff worked that way in those days. It doesn't anymore. There was a lot more freedom in every way in those days than there is today.

DMA: Do you have any other special memories about making that particular episode?

Culp: "Architects of Fear," I've got to tell you, I thought when we made it that it was perilously close to a dreadful cartoon that wouldn't work, and I thought that the symbolism at the end, the means at the end where the creature silently does his number and the wife perceives that it's her husband in there, I said, "This may work or it may not, but we'd better make it a very strong,

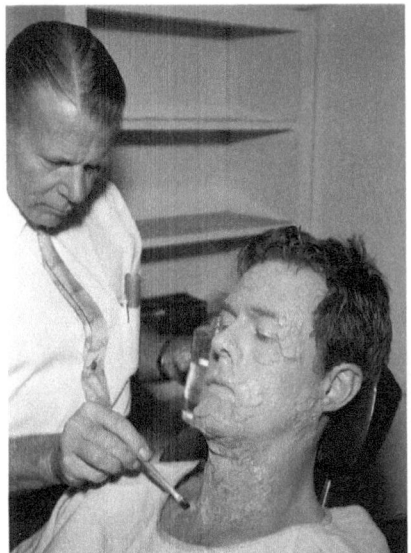

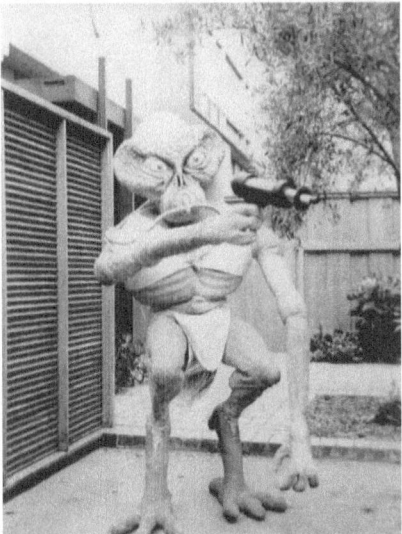

Top: Fred Phillips meticulously applies Thetan scales to Robert Culp. **Above:** Stuntman/acrobat Janos Prohashka brought the mock alien's costume to life

symbolic gesture, and there was some discussion about that, what it should be. Otherwise, I don't remember much of anything about it except I didn't have much faith in it, and—lo and behold—it worked pretty well. I *hated* the monster. I thought the monster was pathetic. The monster, I know you know, was played by Janos Prohashka, who was just a superb stuntman, and he was an artist, for God sakes. And he actually got himself up on those chicken legs, but you could

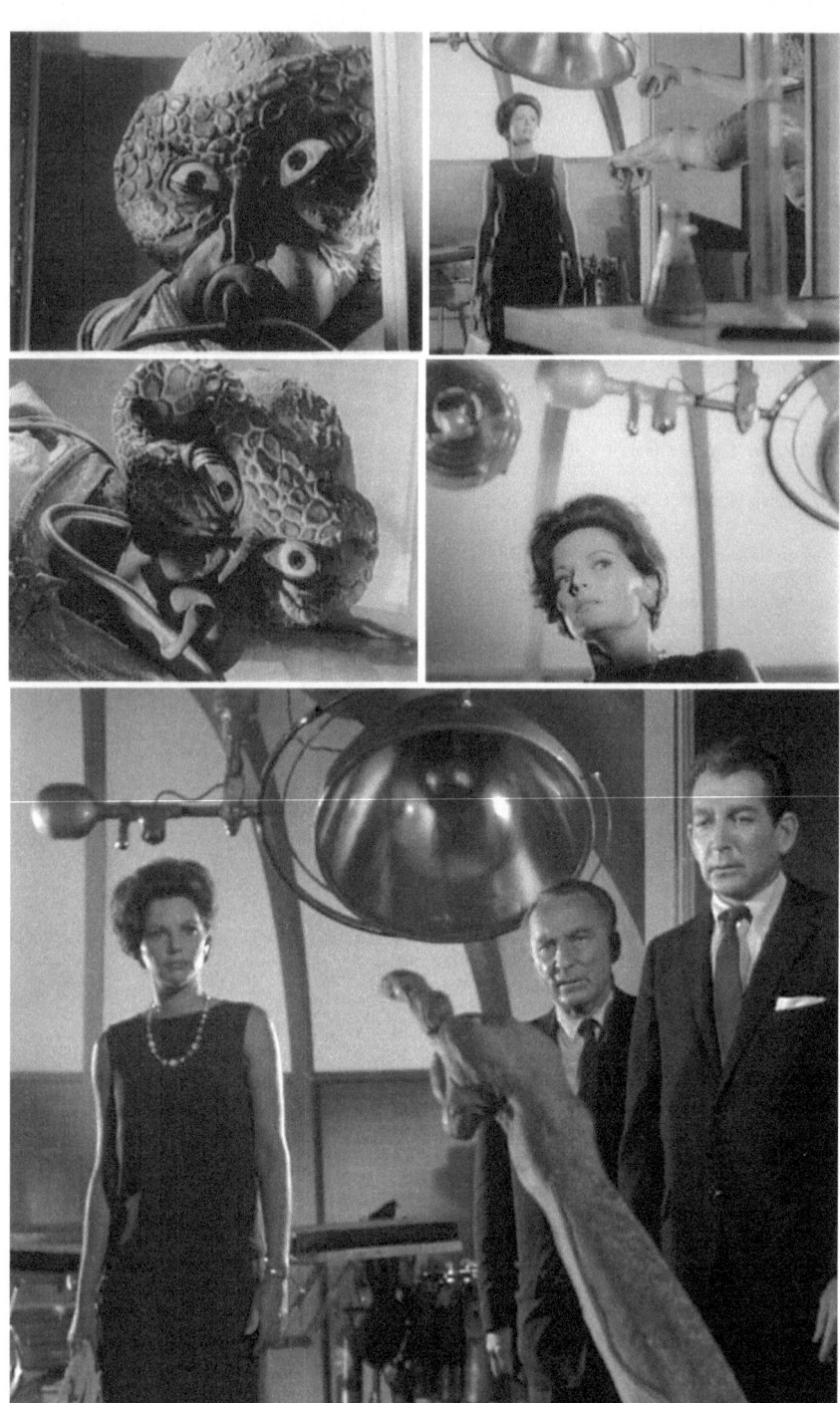

A wounded Allen Leighton makes his way back to the lab, the mission scuttled after his space craft goes off-course, and makes the reality of the situation known to his wife with one final "mark against evil"

never see them! You could never see them with the whole body, because the whole body was so crappy that you didn't *want* to see it! It was a big problem. He worked his ass off and, as hard as he worked, you couldn't see how good the work was that he did. And that was disappointing.

But mostly, people have a very fond memory of that show, or that particular episode of that show, but not like "Demon with a Glass Hand." "Demon" was different. "Demon" is in a class all by itself. "Demon" is one of those things that's like you caught lightning in a bottle. I was ready for it, Byron was ready for it, and Harlan had written a script that was ready for us. Despite the fact that when you look at it today, you say to yourself—you just can't help it—"Why are those assholes wearing those shower caps? Why do they have boot black around their eyes? What the fuck are they doing? That's silly!" Well, it *was* silly, but we had a license to be silly about that, because we didn't have any money and everybody knew it, so we just did what we could, but imagine trying to do that kind of shit today on The X-Files.

DMA: It wouldn't fly at all.

RC: You can't make it fly at all. But there was still that little bit of the 'Fifties left which allowed you, you know, they gave you a little license to be really shitty, and you got away with it.

DMA: I watched "Architects" just yesterday, and I've always felt that it's such a sad, sad story. Apart from the whole monster thing, it's a very sad story, with the husband and wife, she wants to have a baby—it's very touching.

RC: The groovy part, the part that makes the story work at all, is that he failed. He screwed-up and he failed, and it cost him his life. That part's kind of groovy. I hate it when, in the stories we have today, right always comes out right, and wrong always comes out wrong, and that's not the way life works. Writers were really trying in those days to address that issue, and nobody does that anymore. The same is true of "Demon," but in "Demon," when he makes his self-discovery of who and what he is, when he finally puts his hand together, he realizes that he is fallible even in his own terms, totally fallible and yet he has a job to do nevertheless. He has to go on. He has to survive. He has to survive and he has to go on because everything is at stake, like the race is at stake, but he's not ever going to be able to take any joy out of it. He just plods along, like the Golem, and that's cool. That's cool, but that's Harlan. That gets very large and it's worth a lot of thought. And that's Harlan.

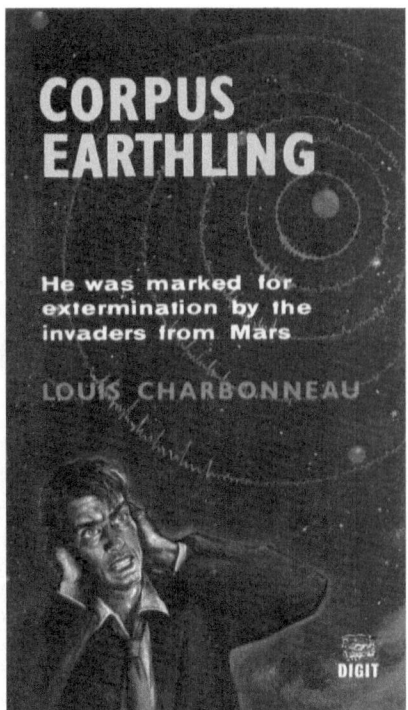

1963 British paperback edition of the OL episode's source novel; art unsigned

DMA: The second episode that you did, "Corpus Earthling"...

RC: That was the third one, wasn't it?

DMA: No, that came about two months after "Architects of Fear."

RC: Oh yeah? That was still in the first year, and what...? The other one came in the second year?

DMA: Exactly. "Demon" was part of the second season.

RC: I see. Well, I have no memory of that *[episode]* besides carrying Sal *[Salome]* Jens, who probably weighed more than I did, up and down those fuckin' stairs, out in front of the burning house so many times that I thought I'd drop her, I swear to god!

DMA: You mentioned that in The Companion, as well. That was a multiple-take shot?

RC: It went on and on. We did it over and over and over again, yeah. And mind you, I adore Sal Jens. I always have, but she's *not* little.

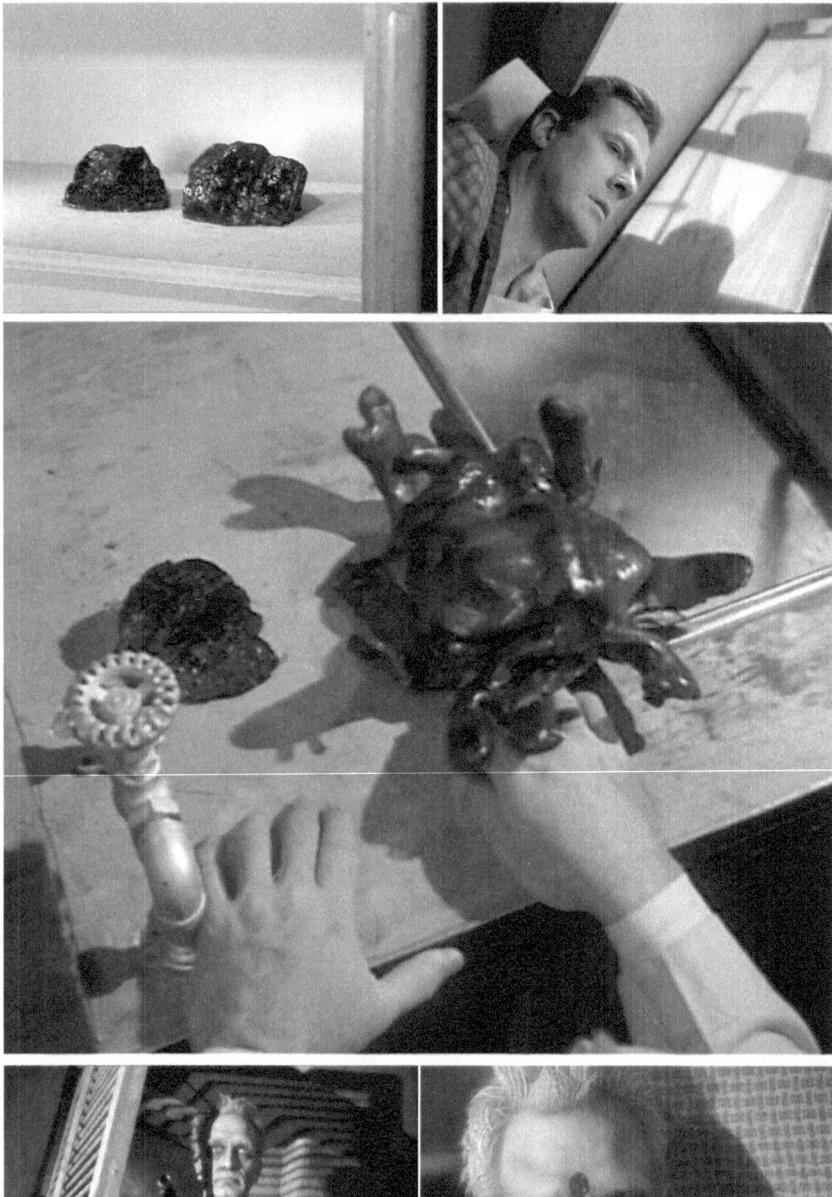

Rocks In His Head: Culp retained surprisingly few memories about making the highly-memorable episode "Corpus Earthling". Barry Atwater *[directly above, left and right]* co-starred with Salome Jens in this eerie tale of mind-controlling mineral alien parasites

DMA: The scene I really enjoyed in that episode is the one in which you describe this thing you're hearing in your head, and you're hesitant about sounding insane, but this voice has threatened to kill you. I've always liked your style, and the way you move, and that's one of the scenes where your style really shines through. But you have no other recollections of this episode?

RC: I have no memory of it at all, except, as I say, well, talking with Salome and trying to figure out what we're going to do with the next scene and the next scene and the next scene. Who directed that?

DMA: That was Gerd Oswald.

RC: Gerd Oswald! Nice fella. Nice fella. I liked him. No, you got me there, because I don't remember much of anything about it.

DMA: Where did they shoot the Mexico scenes?

RC: On the backlot, wherever they…where the hell…where was that shot?

DMA: Because it seemed like there was nothing around it.

RC: No, but you'd be surprised what you can find. It was probably out at Vasquez Rocks or someplace like that. I remember that it didn't seem like there was any high country around there, so it probably wasn't a backlot. What studio made that show?

DMA: United Artists.

RC: UA did it? UA wasn't even into TV. They just acquired the rights to it. It was probably MGM. [Note: *United Artist Television was formed January 1st, 1958, and MGM merged with UATV in 1981.*]

DMA: Ellison kept referring to UA when he was talking about "Demon."

RC: Well, I don't know where they used to shoot them, unless it was at Paramount. I can't recall. I think we probably went to someplace out in the valley, because there were lots of little ranches out there that rented-out by the day or by the week to television companies. I don't think it was out of Malibu. I think it must have been out in the valley.

DMA: So you have no other memories about

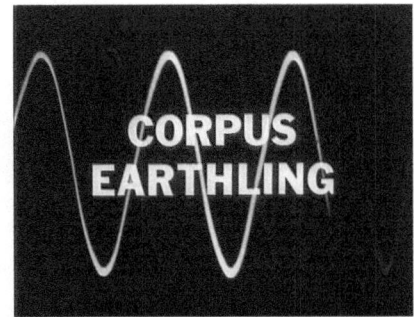

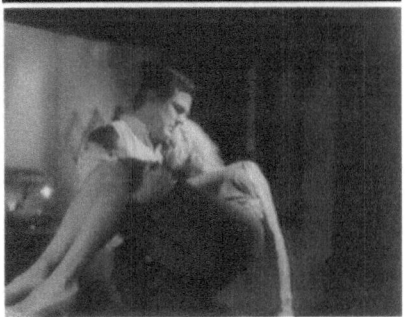

Most-memorable moment for Culp was carrying Salome Jens—"…who probably weighed more than *I* did!"—at the end of the episode

what went into your portrayal of Dr. Paul Cameron in "Corpus Earthling?"

RC: No, actually. Let me tell you—undoubtedly there was something else going on in my life and that was really like a phoner to me. I just don't recall it.

DMA: Ellison wrote "Demon With a Glass Hand" specifically with you in mind, playing Trent.

RC: Yeah, he told me that.

DMA: Did that help you in terms of writing to your strengths, or…?

RC: No, but obviously he had caught something, because everything in it was extremely easy for me to do. There was no reach at all. The physicality, which was considerable, came easily.

DMA: He said that you told him you were going to play it like a ballet dancer.

RC: Yeah.

DMA: How did you arrive at that idea?

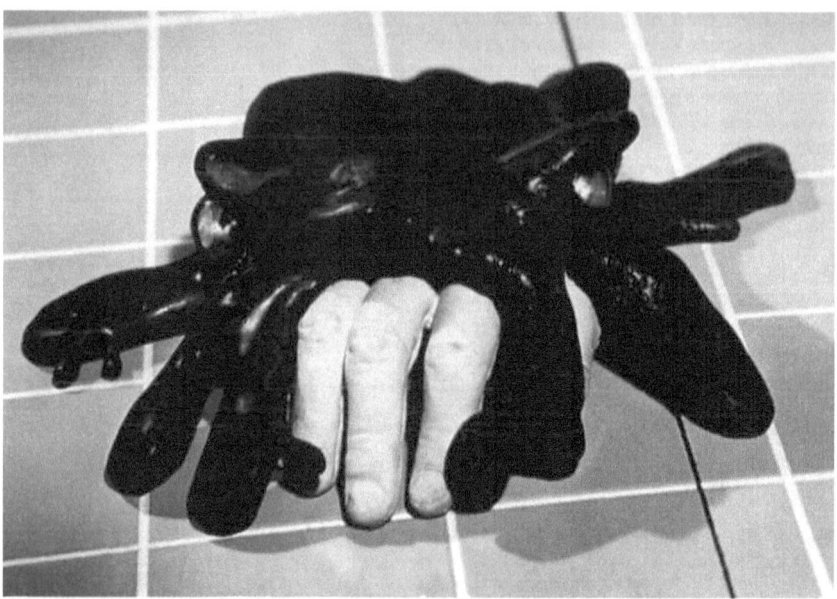

A realistic false hand was created by Project Unlimited for the parasitic possession scene in "CE", even though this shot doesn't actually appear in the episode

RC: Well, once I saw the... we didn't meet until the first night of shooting down at the Bradbury Building. The whole thing was shot at the Bradbury Building. All of it. I'd seen the set and I knew how the scenes were going to work from floor to floor, because I'd walked through some of it, enough of it, with Byron, to see that we start in the cellar and we go up to the roof, or the attic, whatever you want to call it. And I said this guy is going to be sort of like a sophisticated "Tarzan" in the trees, only it's in a building. He's going to have to be moving; I saw the guy kind of floating or flying or sailing, or anyway, moving. There had to be something—the guy was so low-key, so sort-of-ordinary and kind of an early action hero that there had to be something special about him, and I thought it had to be the way he moved. So I probably moved in that picture as I don't think I've done it anywhere else.

DMA: *One of the examples Ellison gave was when the hand told you that the only way to save yourself was to die, and when you're shot, you move your feet one in front of the other, like a ballet dancer would.*

RC: Oh, well I don't remember. You mean on the ground, when I'm laying down?

DMA: *No, when you're shot you're moving forward, one foot in front of the other, and then you fall.*

RC: Oh, well that's Harlan. He's a very colorful talker.

DMA: *Yes, he is. Ellison also mentioned being bothered by various changes, such as the "raccoon eyes" and the caps on their heads, et cetera, and he was thinking of taking his name off the episode, but that Ben Brady, Lester Seeleg, and you, helped talk him out of doing that.*

RC: I don't remember that, but I certainly would have made an effort. I'm sure I did if he said so. His memory is better than mine.

DMA: *One of the things that bothered me in "Demon," and Harlan mentioned this as well, was that the aliens used ordinary handguns, which didn't make any sense.*

RC: They did? I don't remember. Hey, listen, I'm not surprised. So many things didn't make any sense, man. And then, you know, when you really stop to think about it, why *would* they? They're in a different atmosphere, maybe their weapons don't work properly in this atmosphere, but handguns of this world do. I don't know. The point is, none of this stuff was ever explained, and you had to take tremendous license just to have the courage to go through with this.

DMA: *Another thing was with the glass hand. It seemed like when the glove was off, the hand seemed rigid and incapable of movement, and then when the glove was on, it seemed like a fully functional hand.*

RC: That always troubled me. I really always thought that it would have been possible to make a semi-rigid plastic hand that still had all the lights inside and all that shit, and nobody ever did. It didn't happen that way. At one point, I had thought I had talked Freddie or somebody into making a clear plastic cover, like a glove, but form-fitting. A form-fitting plastic glove that would be underneath the gray glove, and you could see it move in some shots. But then, the digits that were going to be photographed in close-up, would have to be somewhat like that, but it had already been built.

That's the other problem with trying to do stuff that is creatively effective. The only person who's in touch with what's actually going on is the guy who's responsible for the makeup. He's so busy all day, doing what he does, that he makes phone calls and gives instructions and expects them to be carried out, because it's got to be ready tomorrow, or next week. And it's a job that probably ought to take two months. There is no discussion. You just have to do it. When you get the prop in your hand and it doesn't work, you're fucked. You've got to figure out what to do about it, how to shoot it. So, it's amazing that things worked as well as they did, let alone what *didn't* work.

I'll give you a perfect example: I did a one-day, just for fun, on a thing called **SPY HARD** *[1996, USA, D: Rick Friedberg]*, on an airplane. I played this guy who, if you saw it, got his finger stuck in the tray table. And I said, "This is going to be interesting. I wonder how they've worked that out." But this is, you know, a 40-million-dollar picture, no problem, because they've got all the props, my God. I get there, and they've got a wet noodle piece of rubber for the tray table. I say, "What the fuck is this?" He says, "Well, we just have to attach it, see." I said, "Go ahead. Attach it." And it was *still* a wet noodle! I said, "How in hell am I supposed to work with this thing?" So we threw it out because it had been made without correct supervision, because it was a single sight-gag for X number of seconds only. So it didn't get the proper treatment, so we used a real one, mashed my fingers and gave me a neck ache the likes of which took me a whole month to get over, because I had to hold my foot up there to hold my fingers in. I was faking it, but I had to really pull hard on my fingers, and I pulled something in the back of my neck in the process. Anyway, that happens even today.

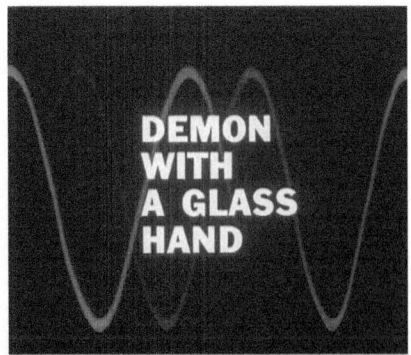

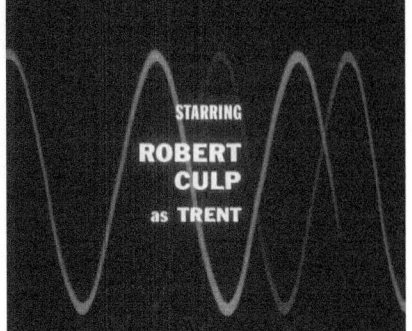

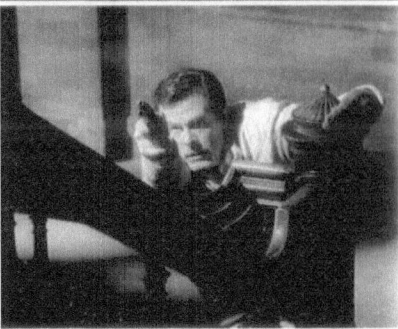

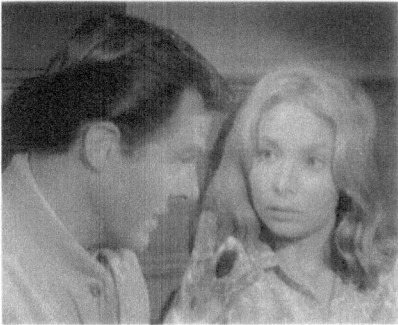

Top to Bottom: Opening titles; Culp as the mysterious Trent; and Arlene Martel (as Consuelo) watches an exchange between Trent and "The Hand", for which Culp himself provided the 'computerized' voice

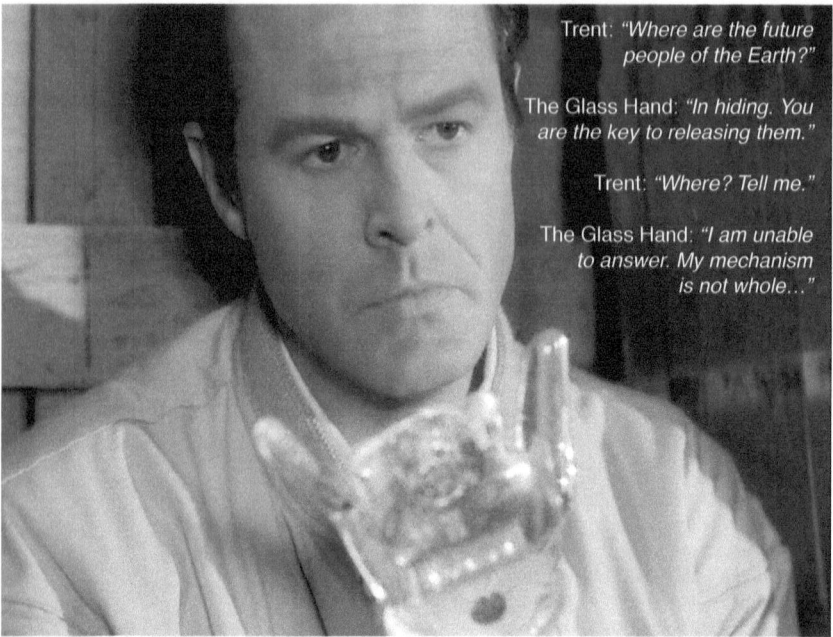

Trent: *"Where are the future people of the Earth?"*

The Glass Hand: *"In hiding. You are the key to releasing them."*

Trent: *"Where? Tell me."*

The Glass Hand: *"I am unable to answer. My mechanism is not whole..."*

DMA: So did you not see the finished glass hand until after principal shooting was finished?

RC: No, we used it in the show. I was in the shot with it.

DMA: Okay, then why didn't you hold your

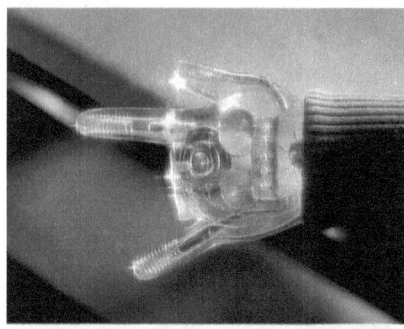

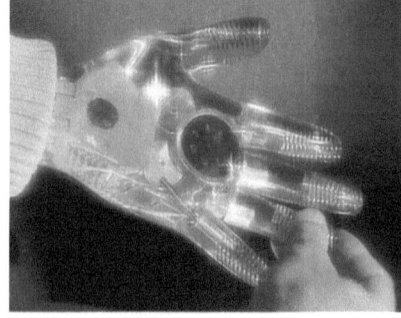

hand rigid so that when you had the glove on and were running around...?

RC: Because, *where* do you stop? I have to do all these stunts, I have to grab ahold of things—pipes, railings—I have to punch buttons, I have to punch guys, I have to hold guns—Jesus Christ!—where do you draw the line? So I said, "No, here's where I draw the line. When the glove is on, the hand is completely flexible. And for the rest of it, it isn't. Tough shit. I can't do anything about it. That's how I'm going to play the part." If they can't make the right prop, that's not my problem. It's their problem. Obviously it's Harlan's problem, too. I'm sorry about it, but I didn't do it. Sometimes you just have to take a little license.

DMA: In The Outer Limits Companion, *it's mentioned that you were, at that point, interested in directing a feature-length version of "Demon," and when I spoke with Harlan, he said that, every now and then, you'd both talk about it, but that nobody's coming forth with the money to do it. Would you still be interested in directing such a picture?*

RC: Absolutely. We have never talked about what the story ought to be—the expanded sto-

Left: Trent's 'digital' hand was a character in its own right, directing his actions in the pursuit of making itself complete ry—because the story that he has now, that we know, that's been committed to film, terrific as it is, is not enough of a story to make a movie out of. I've had a story in the back of my mind that I've never discussed with Harlan that I think is just a winner, but first of all, you've got to get somebody interested, because he's not going to work for nothing and I'm not going to work for nothing, and I'm sure as hell not going to do it on spec. Yeah, we tried a couple of times, and we never got close. We never even got into development.

DMA: Did Joseph Stefano ever come onto the set when you were shooting either "Architects of Fear" or "Corpus Earthling?"

RC: Joe? I don't know. He took a lot of pride in that show. He's a terrific guy. I don't know. He might have. I certainly knew Joe. He was a friend. I don't remember whether he was actually on the set or not. He was a busy man.

DMA: Other than the recent feature XTRO 3: WATCH THE SKIES [1995, USA, D: Harry Bromley Davenport], you haven't done very much science fiction, if any; unless you consider **The Greatest American Hero** *[1981-83] science fiction.*

RC: Well, *The Greatest American Hero* is kind of classic science fiction in its way, for television. I wrote one, which I directed, which brought the principals into direct contact with the little green guy, which had never been done before, and it worked out very well.

DMA: So there's no reason that you haven't done more science fiction, other than that none has been recently offered to you?

RC: I guess you can say nobody's offered me one to do, and my interests as a writer primarily have been in other fields, although I have just finished a fantasy fiction and a science fiction piece back-to-back, the last two things I wrote, which I'm trying to get on now. The science fiction piece is *huge*, a gigantic piece. Major-major-*major*. It's called *Snow Leopard*. The title of the other one is *Jack's Cat*. It's about a mysterious cat that turns out to be a goddess.

DMA: Ellison mentioned that he spent an evening in Malibu with you and Sam Peckinpah and S. Lee Pogostin, and that you were working on a film called "SUMMER SOLDIERS". What happened with that?

RC: Never got made. We were right at the edge of the greenlight, and Sam got in a fight with the studio on a personal basis and they cancelled the whole thing, and they still own it.

DMA: At the end of my conversation with Ellison, I asked him for an overall summary of you and your work, and he said, "Culp has worked long and hard in the industry, and any show that he's in, he brings something wonderful to. He's a consummate actor and he's an intelligent actor. There's a smartness in what he does that I think the market no

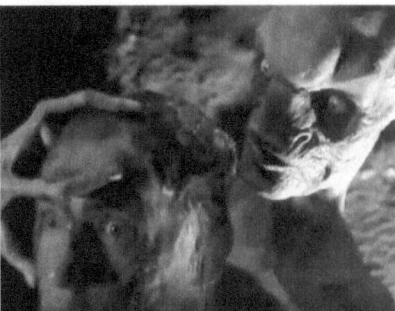

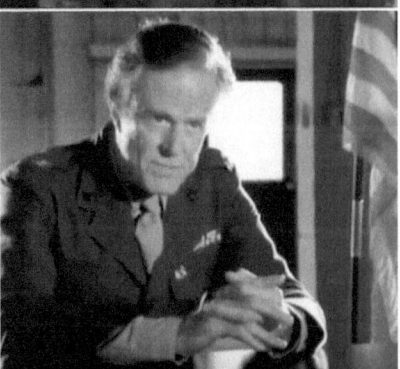

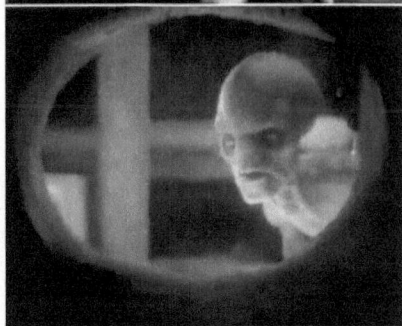

The less-than-stellar **XTRO 3: WATCH THE SKIES** (1995) featured Culp briefly in his final science fiction role, as Major Guardino longer knows what to do with." How would you respond to that?

RC: I don't know how to respond to that. I don't think it's accurate. It's a very nice thing to say, but I don't think it's really accurate.

DMA: *In what regard?*

RC: It's too complicated. I don't really want to go into it.

DMA: *What can we look forward to seeing you in next?*

RC: Well, mark this down and keep your eyes open for a project called "JOHN'S LAST JOB".

DMA: *Is that for television, or is it a movie?*

RC: A movie.

DMA: *Thank you so much for your time. It's been a pleasure.*

ENDNOTE:

Robert Culp went on to do a lot of episodic television work after this interview, including episodes of Diagnosis Murder, Chicago Hope, The Dead Zone, Robot Chicken, *and playing a recurring role on* Everybody Loves Raymond, *as well as doing numerous film and voiceover jobs, but none of the projects he mentions above (*Snow Leopard, Jack's Cat, *or* "JOHN'S LAST JOB"*) ever came to fruition; although, as of this writing, there was a blank page bearing that lattermost title on the IMDb, with no other information given, which may be in some way related (?). Culp left a lasting legacy of excellent work as an actor, writer and director, and will be long remembered for it. He passed away on March 24th, 2010.*

Harlan Ellison, meanwhile, continues to write and produce books, his most recent being Can & Can'tankerous, *a collection of previously uncollected short stories, published by Subterranean Press in 2015.*

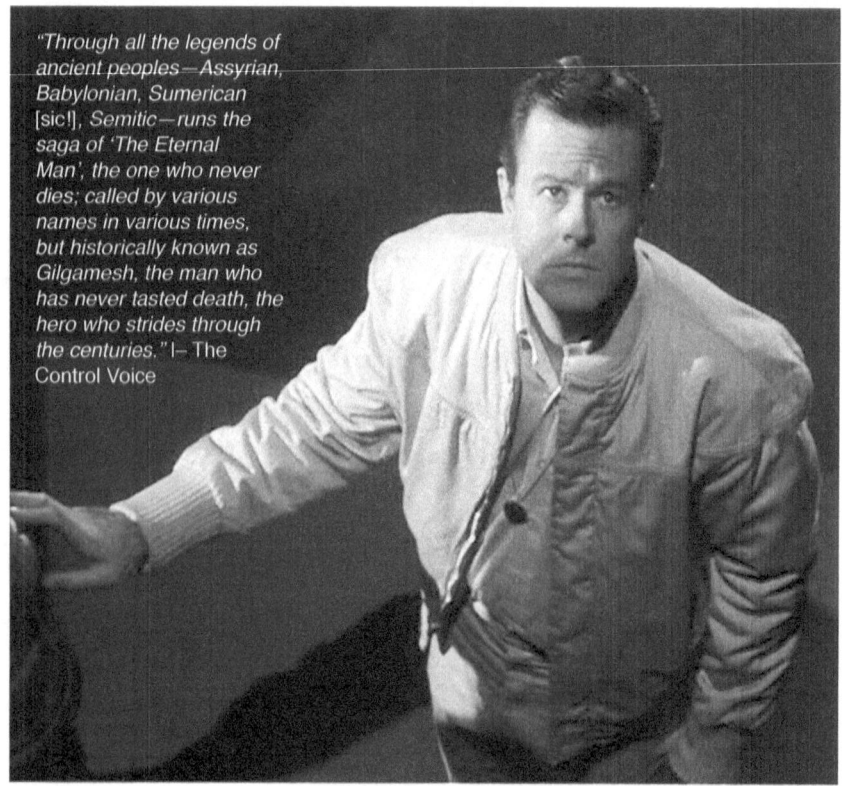

"Through all the legends of ancient peoples—Assyrian, Babylonian, Sumerican [sic!], Semitic—runs the saga of 'The Eternal Man', the one who never dies; called by various names in various times, but historically known as Gilgamesh, the man who has never tasted death, the hero who strides through the centuries." I– The Control Voice

FOR FURTHER STUDY, MAY WE SUGGEST:

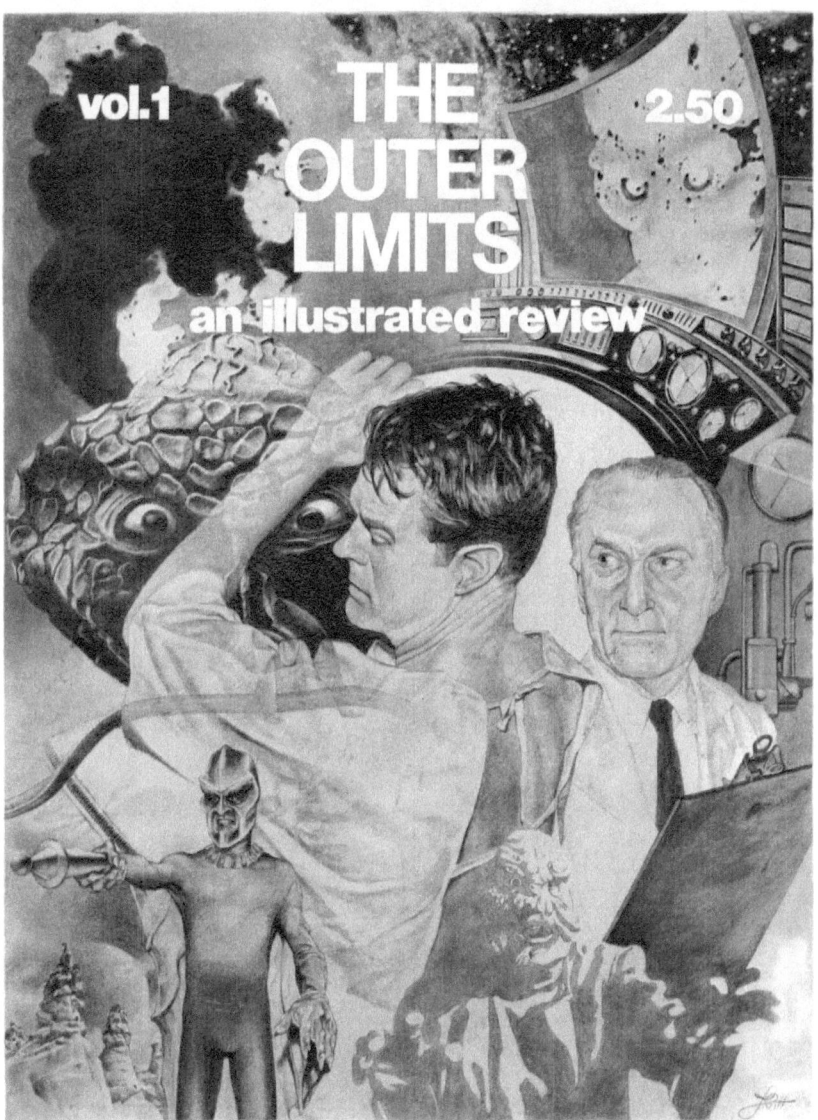

Above: The first volume (from May 1977) of Ted C. Rypel's two-volume paperbound OL fan tribute publication, whose central cover image (art by Joe Rutt) shows Robert Culp seemingly wrestling with his alien 'alter-ego' in "The Architects of Fear"; Volume 2 was published in May of '78. (Readers can see more about *The Outer Limits: an illustrated review* in particular and the show in general—both in its original and 1990s incarnations—at the weblog We Are Controlling Transmission [@ *http://wearecontrollingtransmission.blogspot.ca/2011/02/in-outer-limits-tavern-with-ted-c-rypel.html* and *wearecontrollingtransmission.blogspot.ca*, respectively])

Dana Marie Andra   Inside The Outer Limits

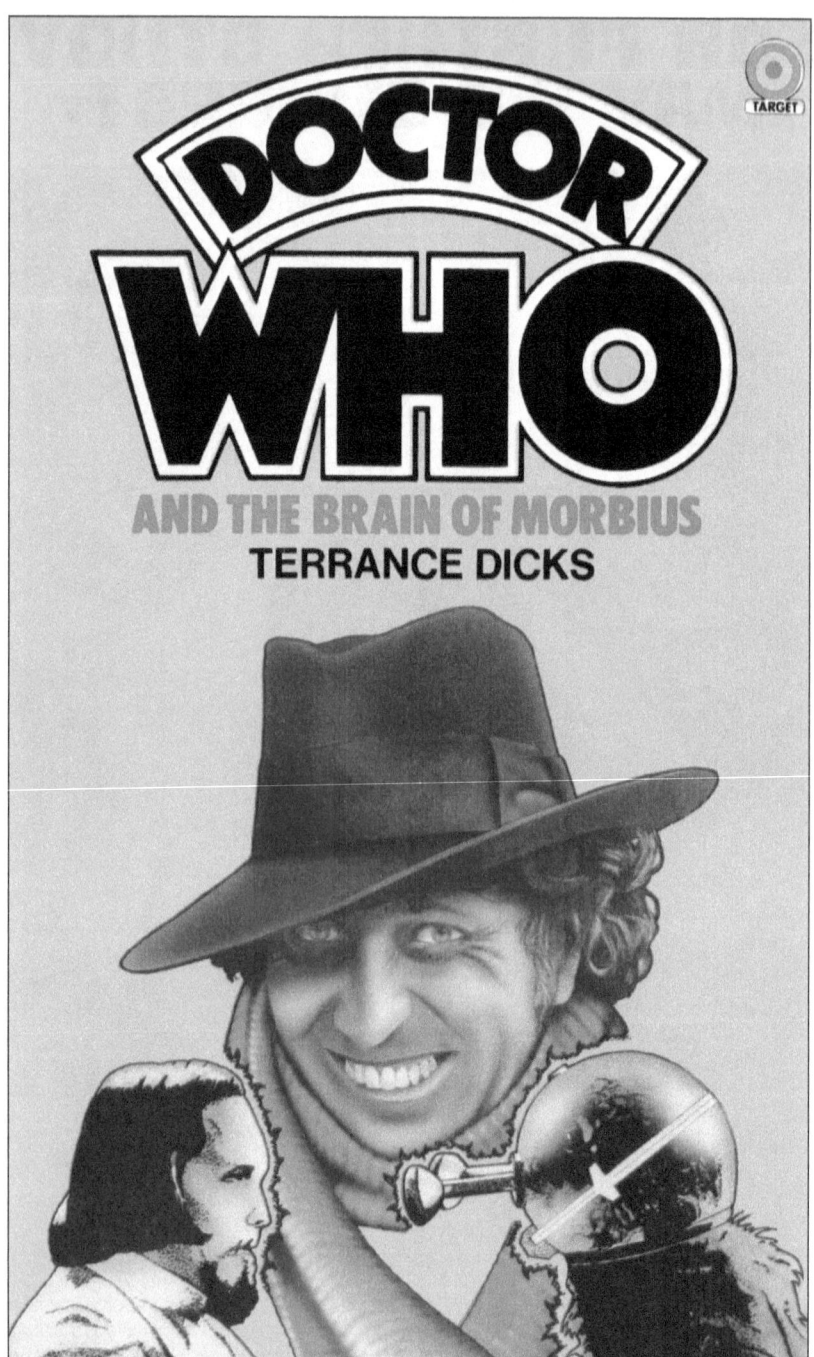

As per C. Michael Hall's fantabulous cover art to this issue, *Doctor Who*'s awesome 1976 adventure "The Brain of Morbius" (the cover of whose '78 Brit reprint edition of Target Books' tie-in novelization [art by Mike Little] is reproduced above) shall be covered by Stephen Jilks in our next ish. Be there or be squaresville, daddy-o!

CHANNEL OF DARKNESS
Doctor Who & the BBC's Gothic Horrors of the 1970s

(PART 1) by Stephen Jilks

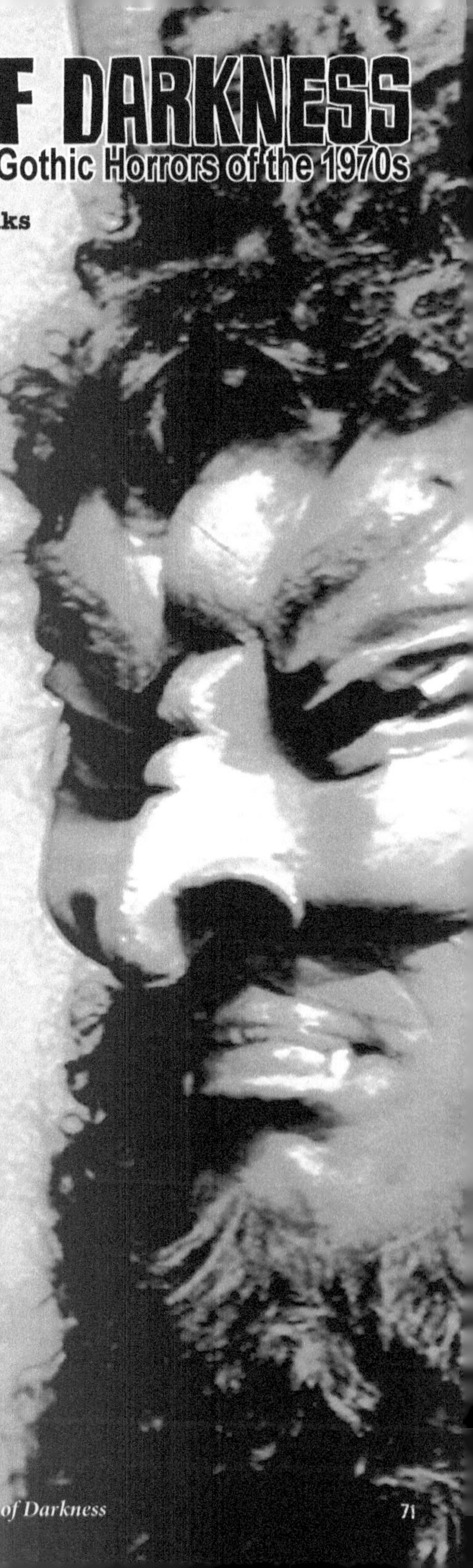

"Invention […] does not consist in creating out of a void, but out of chaos." |– Mary Shelley

"These anomalies are completely inexplicable!" |– A random scientist in an episode of the *Who* serial "Spearhead from Space" (1970)

Foreword: *At a time of much social and political upheaval, British Broadcasting Corporation television programming during the 'Seventies gave us a true Golden Age of Horror, if ever there was one. Playing-out against societal anxieties in regards to mass-manipulation/ brainwashing by Big Government and vast corporate conglomerates irresponsibly pushing out-of-control capitalism (etc.) to the detriment of the ecosystem amidst dark memories of imperialistic colonization and WWII, even hostile aliens from distant worlds—or sometimes other, more outright supernatural rather than paranormal beings—ruthlessly exploited both those in positions of authority and we common folks alike as helpless pawns to further their dark and invariably destructive agendas. Inevitably, many a literal rather than merely figurative monstrosity arose from out of the seething chaos during this highly fertile time for dramatic entertainment of a speculative-fictional nature. For which we can all be thankful!*

Along the way discussing such phenomenally successful, long-running series as Doctor Who *(1963–) and the annual* Ghost Story for Christmas *specials, exceptional stand-alone feature-length made-for-TV movies like* **THE STONE TAPE** *(1972) and* **COUNT DRACULA** *(1977), plus a whole lot more, this article takes an in-depth look at how the decade's telly terrors in Britain freely and wholeheartedly embraced The Gothic, as well as planting the seed/paving the way for the philosophical concept known as "Hauntology"…*

Introduction: The Shape of Things to Come | Molding BBC Terror

"C.S. Lewis meets H.G. Wells meets Father Christmas—that's the Doctor." |–Verity Lambert (Jessica Raine) in **AN ADVENTURE IN SPACE AND TIME** (2013)

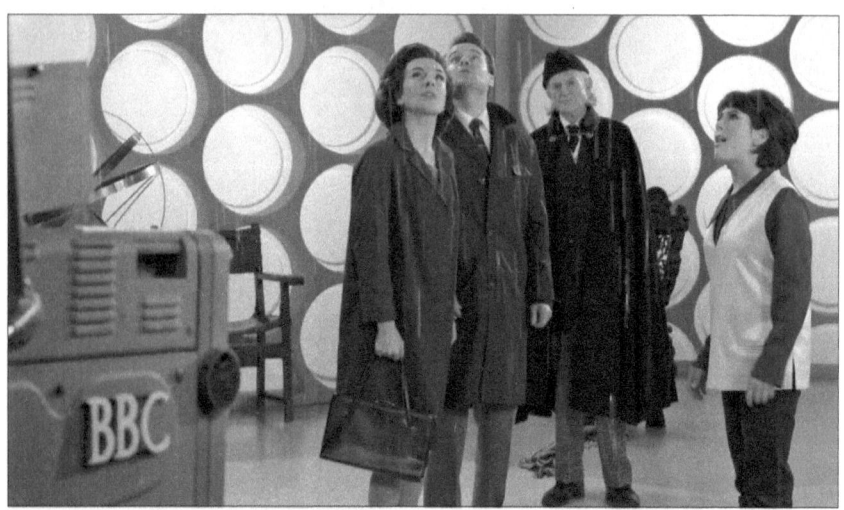

A faithful recreation of the first *Doctor Who* serial "The Dead Planet", as seen in the splendid BBC drama **AN ADVENTURE IN SPACE AND TIME** (2013)

In 1962, ITV (Independent Television) company ABC (Associated British Corporation) aired the science fiction anthology series *Out of This World*. Two years later, the creative force behind that series, Canadian writer-producer Sydney Newman (1917-1997), became head of the BBC (British Broadcasting System)'s fledgling drama department. Newman returned to the concept of the one-shot tale with *Out of the Unknown*, of which four series would feed the network's new sister channel BBC2 between 1965 and 1971.

For its final set of episodes, *Out of the Unknown* dropped its SF foundation to instead concentrate on themes of horror-fantasy; including Quatermass creator Nigel Kneale's *The Chopper* (airdate: June 16th, 1971), about a phantom motorcycle and its vengeful ghost rider *[see Endnote #1]*. By carrying-over this format, the BBC had planted the seed for the numerous more anthologies to come *[see Endnote #2]*. While they often prove popular with fans, such collections of self-contained/stand-alone stories/casts are typically known for their variable quality (a similar unevenness is inherent in sketch-comedy shows), yet their origins are held in high esteem, taking cues from the episodic structure of such Gothic novels as *The Monk* (1796) and *Melmoth the Wanderer* (1820), written by Matthew Gregory Lewis (1775-1818) and Charles Maturin (1782-1824) respectively.

In the early '60s, Newman also produced the *Pathfinders in Space* (1960-61) trilogy for Associated Television. These spaced-out science fantasies bridged the void between children's and adult television, but by its third serial *Pathfinders to Venus* ([1961] the second serial was entitled *Pathfinders to Mars*) the show had caved-in to pulpier genre expectations, with the likes of carnivorous plants and menacing pterodactyls added to the mix. As more plausible science was eroded into fantastical escapist fare, *Pathfinders* can be seen as more than merely a parallel for a certain future Time Lord...

Written by Mark Gatiss in commemoration of *Doctor Who*'s 50th Anniversary, the engrossing made-for-TV historical/biographical drama **AN ADVENTURE IN SPACE AND TIME** (airdate: November 22nd, 2013) reveals how Who's character nearly got exterminated for keeps after just four episodes. On the 22nd of November, 1963, John F. Kennedy was assassinated; the following day, *Doctor Who* debuted in its Saturday teatime slot, although many viewers were too distracted by the shocking news of JFK's assassination to watch the new show, while others couldn't even tune-in to anything at all because of a serious power outage.

But even before the now-more-than-half-century-old series premiered, there were tensions behind-the-scenes: Sydney Newman ordered a total reshoot of the debut episode to make it less scary and more child-friendly, and his decision to assign the BBC's first-ever female producer—in the form of pert mod partygoer Verity Lambert *[see Endnote #3]*—caused friction between the stuffy crew members. Subsequently syphoned-off to the depths of a lesser soundstage at Lime Grove Studio D, the team struggled to make the crudest of facilities and the oldest of cameras work in their favor. Adding to the crew's woes, even "The Doctor" himself, William Hartnell (1908-1975), was an aging, grumpy heavy drinker and smoker loaded with personal issues.

In the aforementioned 2013 docudrama, Verity (Jessica Raine) initially struggles to impress Newman (Brian Cox) with her handling of the project, but eventually wins him over with a newfound verve, loyally standing-by Hartnell (beautifully played by David Bradley, best-known as Argus Filch, the nasty caretaker of Hogwarts in the *Harry Potter* movie franchise) as he struggles with the jargon and the realization that his former "film star" credentials are now being played-out on a children's telly show. As Hartnell's memory steadily begins to decline, the actor becomes even more frustrated, angry and disorientated still, forcing Newman to abruptly let him go and then recast the lead role with a younger actor, Patrick Troughton ([1920-1987] briefly played in the movie by the highly dissimilar Reece Shearsmith). This drastic expediency which brought about the changing of *DW*'s lead actors fortuitously created the intriguing notion of the title character's ability to periodically regenerate in different human forms, and if Hartnell's health had not been only gradually deteriorating due to arteriosclerosis (hardening of the arteries) rather than a faster-acting disease, the legacy of *Doctor Who* could have been so much more abrupt. The success of the program, however, gathered momentum with the introduction of two of Who's most memorable foes: one bullishly determined for conquest and domination/subjugation of humanity, the other striving to take our very *souls* themselves from us…

Created by Terry Nation, the Daleks blend opposite extremes of menace: an impenetrably hard protective outer shell (or "mechanical exoskeleton", if you will), housing a seething, tentacled—if vulnerable—biological body within it. The most fundamental feature of the

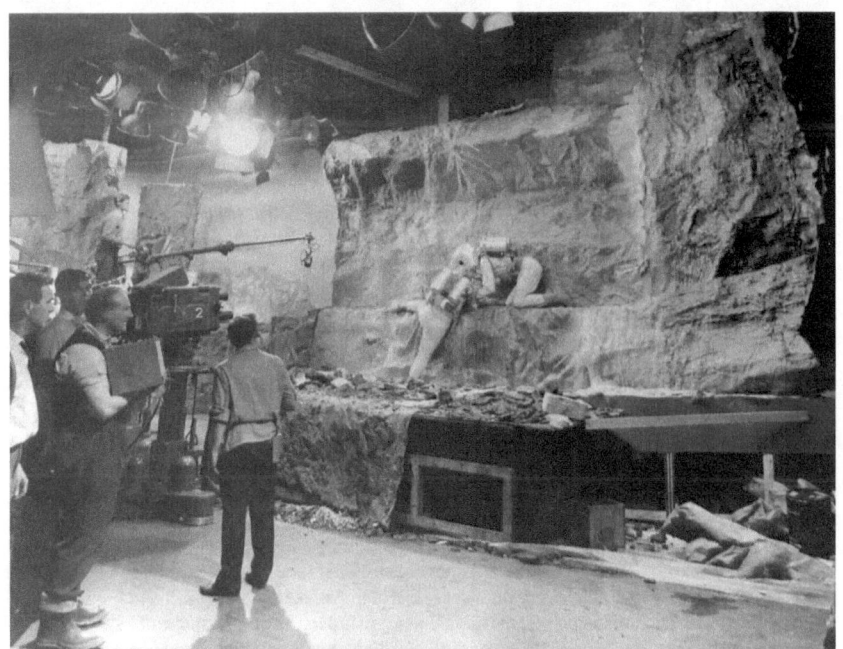

This rare on-set shot (*circa* 1960) from ITV/ABC's *Pathfinders in Space* illustrates both the cramped conditions and budgetary restraints under which the cast and crew were obliged to labor. As can be plainly seen by the short section of set before which the two spacesuited actors are performing, its edges barely even extend beyond the limits of the camera's frame! A similar state of affairs existed on early episodes of the BBC's *Doctor Who*, too

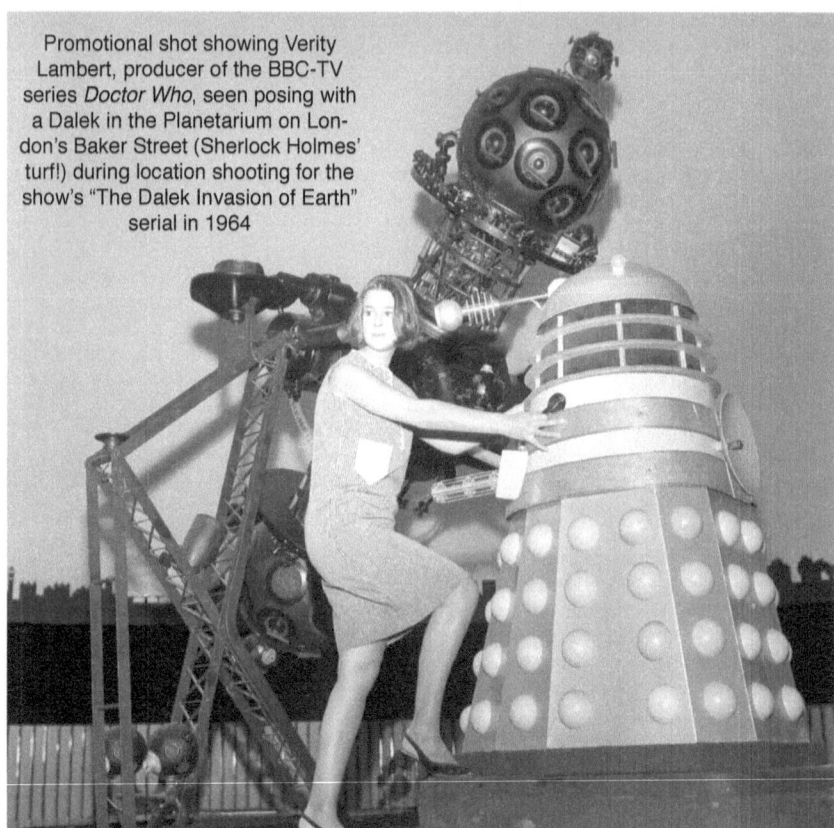

Promotional shot showing Verity Lambert, producer of the BBC-TV series *Doctor Who*, seen posing with a Dalek in the Planetarium on London's Baker Street (Sherlock Holmes' turf!) during location shooting for the show's "The Dalek Invasion of Earth" serial in 1964

"Borg"-like totalitarian Dalek culture is an unquestioned belief in their own superiority; other species are either to be killed-off outright immediately, or else become enslaved to then later be destroyed once they have served their purpose. In their debut story "The Daleks" (aired December 21st, 1963 to January 1st, 1964), the Daleks were portrayed as a warlike and paranoid yet at the same time complex race. In the later early *DW* serial "The Dalek Invasion of Earth" (aired November 21st to December 26th, 1964), the Doctor (Wm. Hartnell) must now face a full-blown galactic menace; this when the mechanized creatures aim to remove the Earth's core entirely and replace it with a powerful drive system with which to pilot our planet around the galaxy. More a "Dalek Invasion of the Home Counties" rather than the entire planet, the story is nevertheless still one of the most nihilistic and iconic in the Doctor's canon. This six-parter also signaled the start of the "Dalekmania" phenomenon *[see Endnote #4]*, but arguably may well have been the point where *Doctor Who* turned from a limited-run children's series with educational intent into a national institution.

"The Dalek Invasion of Earth"'s images of a shattered London are stark, and the collapse of civilization is portrayed much like an air raid during the Blitz by Hitler's Luftwaffe in the Second World War. To further expound/expand on this figurative WWII slant—*à la* what was envisioned much more literally in youthful English filmmakers' Kevin Brownlow's and Andrew Mollo's chillingly prophetic "alternate history" mockumentary / mockudrama **IT HAPPENED HERE** (subtitled **The Story of Hitler's England** [1965, UK]) from the same period—the story can even be read as a "*What if...?*" allegory of Nazi occupation, with its heroic resistance group evidently modeled on the patriotic partisans (such as France's brave and belligerent *Maquis*) who stubbornly resisted Hitler's invading Wehrmacht in occupied Europe. Indeed, the extra-sinister black Dalek presiding over the mining camp is even referred to as the "Commandant", while the extermination of all humans—the ultimate Holocaust—is the alien invaders' "final solution"; plus, as if to ensure that nobody misses the subtle symbolism involved, the Daleks actually raise their suck-er-tipped metallic "arms" in a *Sieg Heil*-style salute!

Even though the 1960s saw such technological/medical innovations as the pacemaker and spare part surgery, the notion of cybernetics was nothing new. In her novelette "No Woman Born" ([1944] first published in the December '44 edition of Street & Smith Publications, Inc.'s *Astounding Science Fiction* magazine, and oft-reprinted/translated ever since), American SF authoress Catherine Lucille "C.L." Moore (1911-1987) *[see Endnote #5]* tells of a famous dancer whose mind is transferred to a robot after her own human body is grievously burned in a theatre fire. This much-acclaimed and influential piece is considered one of the first fully-realized portrayals of cybernetic consciousness, a level which the Doctor's second-favorite (as in most-loved-to-hate) foes—the drone-like Cybermen—have rarely attained. "Our brains are just like yours, except that certain weaknesses have been removed... you call them *emotions*, do you not?" This is how the Cybermen are introduced in the *DW* serial "The Tenth Planet" (October 8th to October 29th, 1966). However, unlike "The Tenth Planet" and "The Moonbase" (aired February 11th to March 4th, 1967), wherein said mecha-men are pitched against no more than isolated pockets of humans, "The Tomb of the Cybermen" (aired September 2nd to September 23rd, 1967) was the first Cyber-story to exploit the real fear of total human-into-cyborg conversion. (Incidentally, the previous year in the second of AARU/Amicus Productions/British Lion's pair of spinoff *DW* theatrical features, **DALEKS – INVASION EARTH 2150 A.D.** [1966, UK, D: Gordon Flemyng]—which re-starred Peter Cushing as Doc for the second and final time—humans were similarly transformed into mindless/soulless automatons known as "Robomen" by the diabolical Dalek conquerors of our planet, with much the same dehumanizing result.)

Whether it be set in either the distant past or the far-flung future, serious science fiction typically addresses issues that are actually concerns of the contemporaneous present. As the Daleks and Cybermen have their origins in war-torn Europe and the advancement of medical technology, so too would *Doctor Who* update its topical themes and concerns during the chaotic 1970s. By the middle of that decade, relentless political gloom would manifest itself in a reevaluation—and regurgitation—of The Gothic...

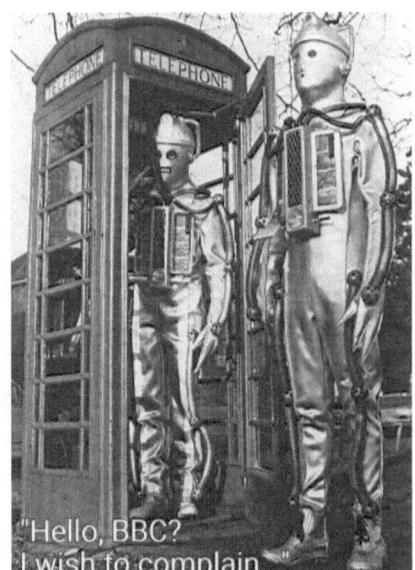

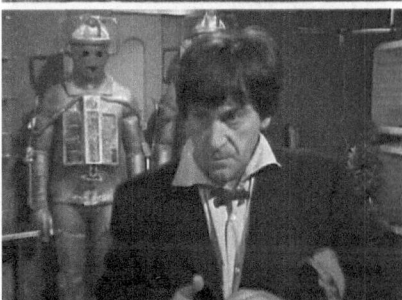

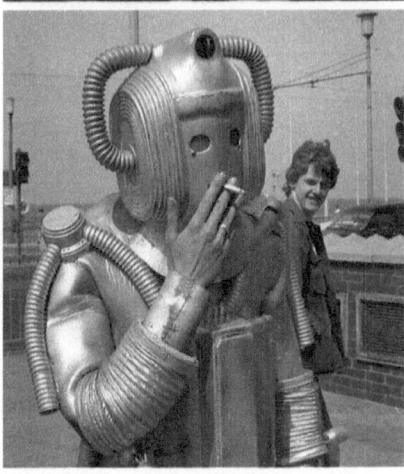

Top: Gag postcard. **Center:** Doc #2 Patrick Troughton in the Cybermen's clutches. **Above:** A Cyberman performer takes an on-set fag break during shooting of the 1968 *DW* serial "Invasion"

Part I:
From Satan to the Stars | The Horrors of 1969 Evaporate into Sci-Fi Cinema

"You know, a long time ago, being crazy meant something. Nowadays, everybody's crazy!" |– Charles Manson

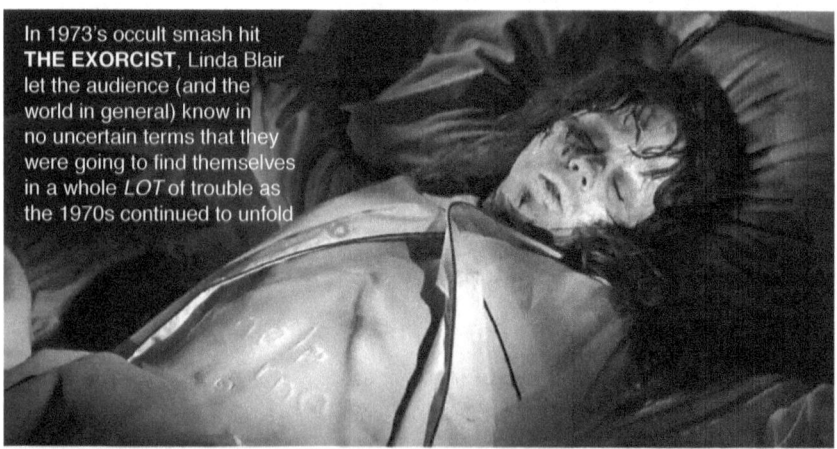

In 1973's occult smash hit **THE EXORCIST**, Linda Blair let the audience (and the world in general) know in no uncertain terms that they were going to find themselves in a whole *LOT* of trouble as the 1970s continued to unfold

The Counterculture mandate of the late 1960s—the "heightened consciousness" achieved through using psychedelic drugs—created profound shifts in perception. Austere visual entertainments within the so-called "Satanic 'Seventies" were actually instigated by sexual/sociopolitical changes back in the '60s, and the BBC's '70s terrors played-out upon a much larger canvas than before. After diabolically demented control freak Charles Manson and his brainwashed so-called "Family" mass-murdered no less than nine people during the summer of '69, the quasi-commune of socio/psychopathic yippies would become emblematic of macabre violence *[see Endnote #6]*, and thinly-veiled variations of both Manson and his sycophants' murderous exploits would appear in motion pictures (etc.) for years to come. One of the Manson cultists' victims—namely Sharon Tate, actress, model and the then-pregnant wife of Roman Polanski—became a bloodstained sentient force which, however horrifically and tragically, would infiltrate and become firmly ensconced into popular culture in perpetuity, for better or worse.

Then, in December '69, The Rolling Stones headlined what was to become a notorious free concert at Altamont Speedway in California. Woodstock—with its naïvely childlike, stoned-out messages of love and peace—had taken place less than four months previously, but Altamont signaled the end of the 1960s counterculture in a quagmire of bad trips and brutal violence. Captured in **GIMME SHELTER** (1970), the documentary co-directed by Albert and David Maysles and Charlotte Zwerin, this absorbing chronicle of the shambolic latter stages of The Stones' United States tour becomes more about an ill-fated moment in time rather than the actual music itself. Dubbed a "snuff" movie by Pauline Kael, this rockumentary begins with performances at Madison Square Garden showing Mick Jagger and company at an artistic high. But The Stones failed to understand how fragile the Woodstock spell could become when invoked too-hastily: the Altamont venue was still in doubt even a mere *day* before the concert's staging, and the resultant sanitary and medical facilities were woefully inadequate. By the time Jefferson Airplane took the stage, the struggles between the audience—stoned on bad acid and speed—and members of the Hell's Angels, hired as security, had become untenable. With 300,000 people thronged around a tiny stage, its surface inexplicably raised just four feet from the ground, and the bikers angrily bludgeoning at spectators with weighted pool cues, **GIMME SHELTER** contains little of the excitement of rock 'n' roll and a whole lot of real-world *horror*.

During the Stones' set, we witness an 18-year-old Black youth named Meredith Hunter being stabbed and beaten to death by the Angels some twenty feet or so from the stage. We see the blur of a gun in Hunter's hand; we see the glint of a knife guided by a biker as it hits its mark. With ever-mounting hostility, The Stones continue to play on in this arena of madness; the pale face of Jagger—freeze-framed in the Maysles' editing suite just as the credits are about to roll—speak far more than a mere thousand words of remorse *[see Endnote #7].*

During the same period, future convicted child rapist Roman Polanski's **ROSEMARY'S BABY** and Hammer's Dennis Wheatley novel-based **THE DEVIL RIDES OUT** (a.k.a. **THE DEVIL'S BRIDE** for its stateside release)—both released in 1968—would begin a new era of mainstream Satanic cinema (or "sinema," if you will). Then, after William Peter Blatty/William Friedkin's mega-smash **THE EXORCIST** took the world by storm in 1973, the major studios now viewed The Devil as even bigger business (i.e., in the name of Thee Holy Dollar). That said, his screen time in **ROSEMARY'S BABY** and **THE EXORCIST** is actually quite limited: an impregnation scene cameo in the former, and the appearance of Pazuzu the Assyrian demon in the latter. Rather, we are watching movies that embrace what might well be the Devil's works: such as paranoia, corrupted innocence and body horror. The spawn of Mia Farrow and the spiritual affliction of Linda Blair propelled the demon child and frayed family units of '70s cinema to form into the fatherly despair of Larry Cohen's **IT'S ALIVE** (1974), the titular telekinetic teenager of Brian De Palma's **CARRIE** (1976), and the painful divorce of David Cronenberg's **THE BROOD** (1979). With the release of **THE SHINING** (1980), Stanley Kubrick added to this downward spiral by reducing the family unit in the horror film to a place of little more than festering resentment.

Subsequent films in the *Exorcist* franchise themselves proved troublesome. When, in the original, Father Karras (Jason Miller) voluntarily absorbed Pazuzu into himself then jumped out the nearest window, it was the last clinical move in a franchise that really has nothing new to add. John Boorman's messy first sequel **EXORCIST II: THE HERETIC** (1977) is particularly overwhelmed by its mystical pomposity and derivative plot, starting the series' trend towards problematic, uneven productions and reshoots. Thankfully, however, series creator William Peter Blatty's own **THE EXORCIST III: LEGION** (1990) succeeded in stimulating a novel and eccentric take on things, as did the belated "prequels," Renny Harlin's **EXORCIST: THE BEGINNING** (2004) and Paul Schrader's showy/splashy **DOMINION: PREQUEL TO THE EXORCIST** (2005), which took things in a whole new direction (i.e., back into the past).

Religious gobbledygook in supernatural thrillers arguably reached its zenith in the '70s with Richard Donner's **THE OMEN** (1976, USA), starring Hollywood luminaries Gregory Peck and Lee Remick, but that film was also one of the first real horror movies to enjoy a really widespread (as in international) marketing campaign *[see Endnote #8].* As it happened, the Devil would rise to power, not within the world of politics, but rather via profit and advertising. In fact, the incredible box office returns of **THE OMEN** would enable Fox to complete George Lucas' escapist sci-fantasy **STAR WARS** (1977, USA).

A good part of the reason why the selling of Satan was so resolute in the decade is that a large majority of the stories purported to be based on "true-life" events, murder cases or ancient texts. This provided opportunities for a wide array of investigative media and exploitative tie-ins; **THE AMITYVILLE HORROR** (1979, USA, D: Stuart Rosenberg), in particular, groans under the weight of all the documentaries, lawsuits and counter-suits—and umpteen sequels/spinoffs/rip-offs—it has since launched, oftentimes thereafter sinking straight to the bottom of the barrel *[see Endnote #9].* As the 'Seventies developed, however, the successes of "feel-good" genre fare spearheaded by **STAR WARS** and Steven Spielberg's **CLOSE ENCOUNTERS OF THE THIRD KIND** (1977, USA) pretty much sounded the death knell for darker genres, at least as major going concerns at the box office. The whizzbang world of the escapist blockbuster was unchallenging, slick and clean, fomenting an optimism which reached-out to nothing less than the very stars themselves.

As America moved towards a blinkered would-be Utopia, '70s Britain toiled under heavy levels of unionization amid the "Winter of Discontent" of 1978-'79. James Callaghan's Labour government's policies for controlling inflation was the signing of their own death warrant, causing strikes by lorry drivers, hospital workers and waste disposal staff. Against the rise of Socialism and the defeat of then-Prime Minister Harold Wilson, the unions became more confident. The single most notorious action came from striking cemetery workers in Liverpool, who refused to bury dead bodies; at one point, more than *three-hundred* corpses piled-up in a cold storage depot, and Liverpool's City Council even went so far as discussing emergency plans for disposing of some of the increasingly-"overripe" corpses at sea. This nightmare scenario developed within a period of heavy snowfall (including blizzards), as the country suffered its worst weather for sixteen years. In a chilled Britain that couldn't even properly bury its dead, it was fitting that the BBC's programming should take on a decidedly *bleaker* tone...

Part II: Spearhead into the '70s | Turmoil Creates Flashes of Brilliance

"I find only freedom in the realms of eccentricity." |– David Bowie

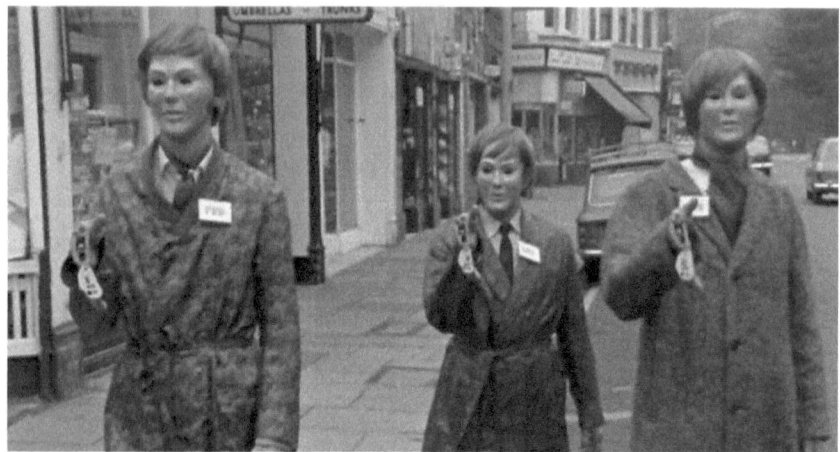

Auton Alert! Clothing store dummies come to unnatural life and kill as an alien intelligence's affinity with synthetics aids in its attempted conquest of humanity during the '70 *DW* serial "Spearhead from Space"

In the wake of the largely drug-enhanced optimism of the 1960s, Britain in the 1970s is, sadly enough, largely remembered for its economic disorder and IRA bombings. Television became champion over a British film industry virtually bereft of fresh ideas and funding; for example, the slow death of the formerly-flourishing Hammer Films during the first half of the decade can be linked to its failure to understand the dramatic cultural shift that late '60s/early-'70s cinema represented. Homegrown filmmakers such as the late Michael Reeves and Pete Walker—together with American independents George A. Romero, Tobe Hooper and Wes Craven—moved the horror genre into a whole new phase of emotional intensity and graphic violence that made Hammer's once-often-controversial output seem positively *quaint* by comparison.

Romero's pioneering, prototypical zombie shocker **NIGHT OF THE LIVING DEAD** (1968, USA) did for horror what Hammer had achieved a decade-plus earlier with Terence Fisher's **THE CURSE OF FRANKENSTEIN** (1957, UK): it made everything that came before it seem tame, lame and predictable by simple comparison. Romero's shot-in-monochrome, almost documentary-like film looked much like a newsreel, turning economy-of-necessity (such as resorting to using cheaper if by-then-passé B&W film stock) into stylistic/artistic value. Hammer, meanwhile, still largely stuck in a "same old/ same old" romantic Victorian Gothic world of vampires and mummies, conspicuously lacked any real direct connection to contemporary existence *[see Endnote #10]*.

In fact, the only "boom" movie genre of the day was the sex comedy. Existing in their own virtual parallel universe, Brit sexcoms are largely known for being unfunny—and perhaps worse still, un*sexy*—affairs, but they were for some reason fanatically popular with the paying punters. Essentially a "saucier" by-product of the *Carry On* craze, this lowbrow subgenre nevertheless thrived during the country's most troublesome cinematic period thanks to a pair of highly popular plot devices that require little in the way of budget for their effectiveness: female breasts! Also, let's not forget one of the cheapest "special effects" of all: slapstick, another primary ingredient of such farces.

Post-war affluence was fading fast, though then-Glam/Glitter Rock teenybopper superstar David Bowie's (1947-2016) dictum "One isn't totally what one has been conditioned to *think* one is" also illustrated a period of increasing individualism in the nation. Bowie's transformation into glam messiah Ziggy Stardust and such SF-tinged hit albums as *Aladdin Sane* (1973) and *Diamond Dogs* (1974) well captured the sweeping decadence of Britain, offering fans the only plausible escape route from bitter reality: FANTASY *[see Endnote #11]*.

****

If Terry Nation drew upon the totalitarian collectivism of Nazi Germany as inspiration (if that's the right term to use!) for the Daleks, writers of the Jon Pertwee *Doctor Who* era—having grown up in the aftermath of WWII—would lament the gradual but consistent loss of Empire. Now fearful of the colonization by citizens of its former imperialist glories, and with a military left humbled by the Suez Crisis, stories starring the "Third Doctor" (Pertwee being #3 in the Time Lord's lengthy lineage) had pompous politicians and overzealous generals being openly mocked for their reluctance to accept change and embrace the possibilities of an open world; in the seven-part *DW* serial "Doctor Who and the Silurians" (aired January 31st to March 3rd, 1970), for example, a race with a highly contentious prior claim to the Earth is systematically blown up.

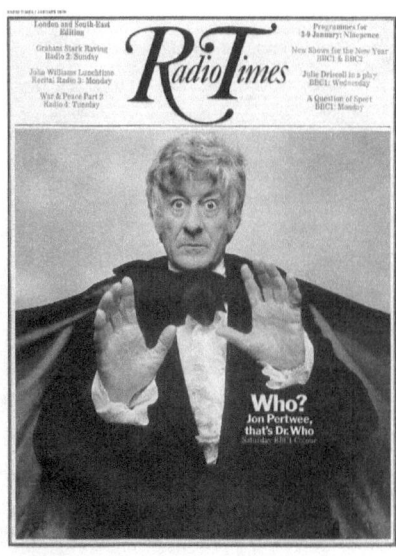

Coming right at the very cusp of the '70s, Jon Pertwee's (1919-1996) initial post-Patrick Troughton era adventure as his trademark fedora-, frilly shirt- and frockcoat-wearing version of The Doctor, entitled "Spearhead from Space" (aired January 3rd to 24th, 1970), was arguably the first *Who* to go for the jugular. Even though Pertwee was more known as a comedic actor—a talent which served him well as the ever-witty-to-a-fault Time Lord in the generally otherwise straight-faced series—he portrayed Who as a technology-orientated man of action, who was also not without his moments of wit and charm. (For instance, in one amusing scene during the '76 serial "The Green Death"

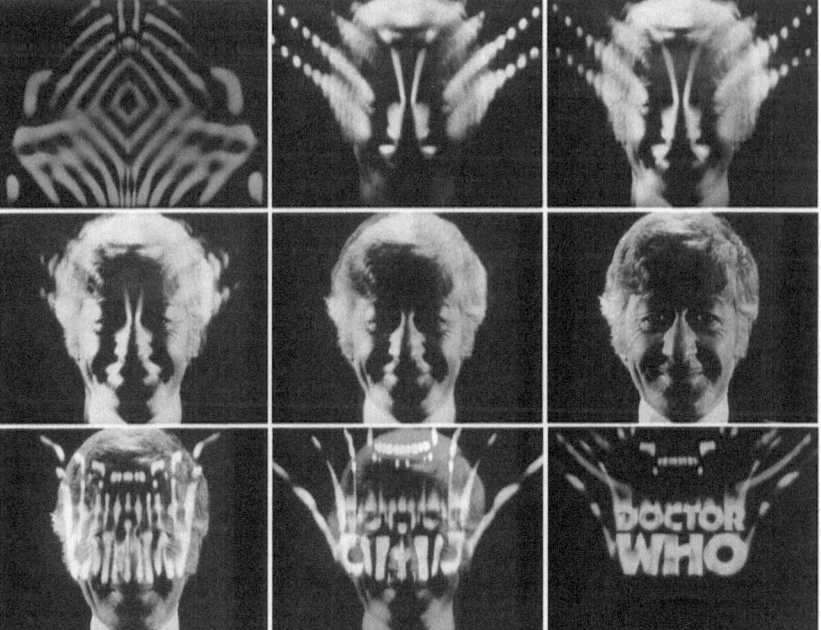

Top: Jon Pertwee is introduced to British telly fans in the January 3rd-9th, 1970 issue of The Beeb's weekly programming guide. **Above:** The new-fangled opening sequence for the Third Doctor's series, with Pertwee

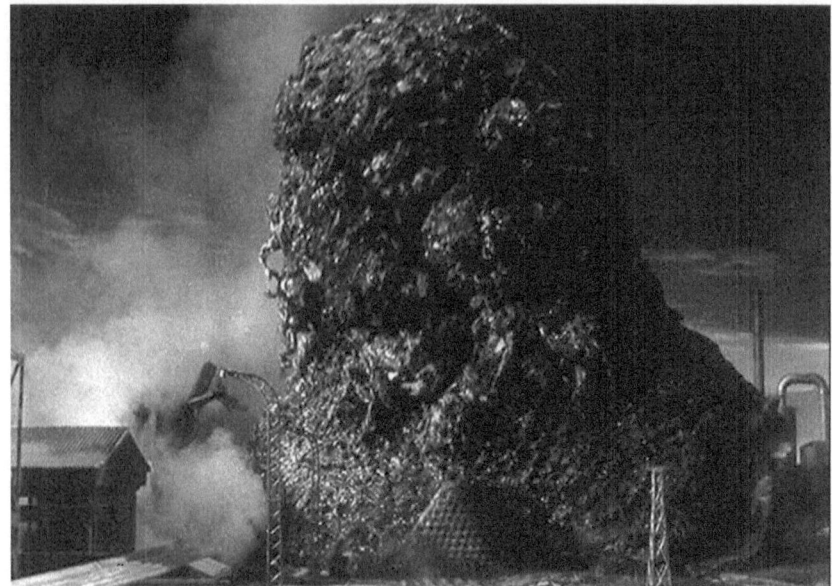

The first British *daikaiju* ever to stomp, slither and, um, hop across the screen.* A gigantic alien blob from the '57 Hammer film version of Nigel Kneale's '55 BBC-TV serial *Quatermass II*. (*That said, I guess we should also mention the earlier 'giant' iguana-as-"Nessie" from Milton Rosmer's **THE SECRET OF THE LOCH** [1934]!)

[further discussed below], the silver-haired ol' Doc cockily proclaims, "I'm quite *spry* for my age" before busting-out some inept if sprightly "Hai Karate"—allegedly aikido—moves on a group of overly-pushy corporate security goons [even if he is momentarily replaced by an all-too-obvious stunt double in a white "afro" wig!]. In the present "Spearhead" serial, the star's easily-spottable stand-in steps in once again to take over for a stunt scene when Who, speeding along on a motorbike—*sans* helmet, yet!—skids and drops said bike in a roadside ditch, landing on some grass rather than suffering any road-rash.) Pertwee remained in the role of Doc from '70 to '74, putting in a late-breaking "guest-starring" reappearance in the famous 20th Anniversary feature-length reunion special from the Peter "Dr. Who #5" Davison era entitled *The Five Doctors* (airdate: November 23rd, 1983).

The inaugural Pertwee serial "Spearhead from Space" would also foreshadow the kind of plagiarism yet to come (in this case, more than just shades of Nigel Kneale's teleserial *Quatermass II* [1955]), but this particular four-parter did at least introduce the creepily blank-faced, boiler-suited "doll people" known as Autons—which wouldn't have looked at all out of place onstage at a Devo concert ten years on!—and an all-new, grittier feel; why, even the special military organization U.N.I.T. (Unified Intelligence Taskforce [formerly United Nations Intelligence Taskforce]), at the start of their long integration, has blood-spots visible on one of their cracked windshields at one point. As the top-secret elite security force's staunchly dutiful and efficiently by-the-book leader Brigadier Lethbridge Stewart (Nicholas Courtney) at one point explains to an interested party (namely Ms. John as brainiac boffo boffin-babe Liz Shaw on their first meeting): "We deal with the *odd*. The unexplained. Anything on Earth...or even *beyond*". Why is it then that, no matter how many times The Brig and his lads (and lasses) have too-close encounters with weirdness and whatsits, whenever the next paranormal menace comes along, he seemingly initially remains just as skeptical of the existence of "things beyond human ken" as he was the very first time?!

"Spearhead" begins with new Who Pertwee's police callbox-shaped vehicle the TARDIS ("Time And Relative Dimensions In Space") touching-down on Earth—specifically, rural Essex—right in the middle of a believed "meteorite" shower, one which actually consists of around 50 hollow, glowing, globular objects (informally dubbed "thunderballs" by one character!) containing a non-physical composite being/collective intelligence called The Nestene

Consciousness ("All energy is a form of life!"). Arriving on our planet encased in a container made of material resembling our earthly plastic, this alien intelligence has an affinity for synthetics, and agent Channing (Hugh Burden) has infiltrated/usurped a lowly kiddies' doll-making sweatshop then converted it into a hi-tech factory under the ominous Auto Plastics corporate banner in order to mass-manufacture mannequin-like dead-spit if suspiciously waxy-complexioned facsimiles of powerful establishment and political figures (including a top-ranking British Army officer, Major General Scobie [Hamilton Dyce]). As a sideline, the AP co. also produces state-of-the-art plasticized figurines for display at Madame Tussauds' famed London Wax Museum ("There's nothing to be afraid of", says Who calmly. "They're only dummies...*I think*"). Yes, you guessed it: global invasion is the ultimate goal ("We are the Nestenes", proclaims Burden's alien-possessed Channing character during the final instalment's big expository reveal. "We have been colonizing other planets for a thousand-million years. Now we have come to colonize Earth"). Like ambulatory crash-test dummies, the fully-automated Autons silently and impassively—it's hard to show any emotion when your face is molded from immobile plastic!—go about their sinister business to the letter of the Nestenes' every command. Twin short-range blasts from poacher's wife Mrs. Seeley (Betty Bowden)'s shotgun or repeated shots from soldiers' rapid-firing SLRs don't even slow 'em down, let alone actually stop their advance...which is slow, steady and inexorable, rather akin to the advance of technology itself.

In addition to its opening nods to Kneale, whether intentionally or not, the scene wherein Seeley (Neil Wilson), a rabbit snare-setting yokel poacher, cautiously prods at a still-smoking newly-fallen mini-meteor in the woods with a stick recalls a similar famous one in **THE BLOB** (1958, USA) in which the film's initial monster victim, an old-timer played by Olin "Howlin" Howland, gets "blobbed" on the arm. Likewise evoking '50s American sci-fi, when one of the Nestenes' brain-controlled human thralls fearfully clutches at the back of his neck, you're half-expecting him to have a pulsating parasite affixed to it (*à la* those cerebrum-sucking "fuzzy slippers" in Bruno VeSota's **THE BRAIN EATERS** [1958, USA] or the hilarious cabbage-leaf "control creatures" in *SCTV*'s classic old "Zontar" sketches). After all, such developments were hardly unusual occurrences for '60s and '70s *Who*. Themes herein of dehumanization and

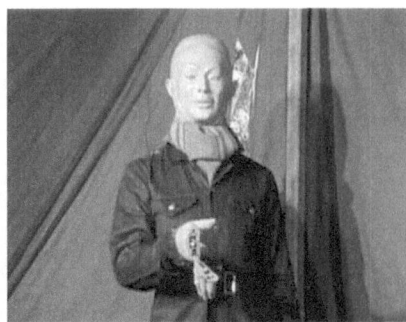

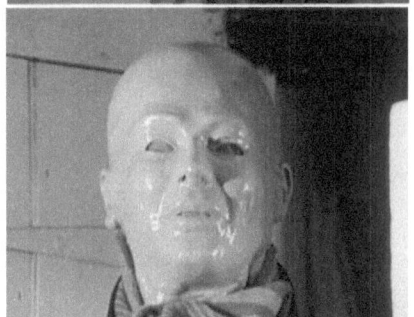

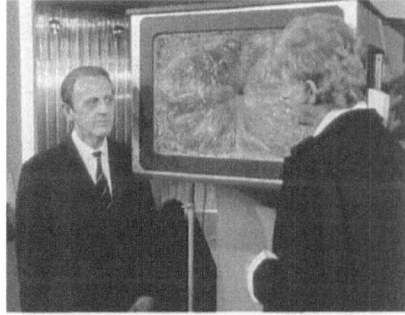

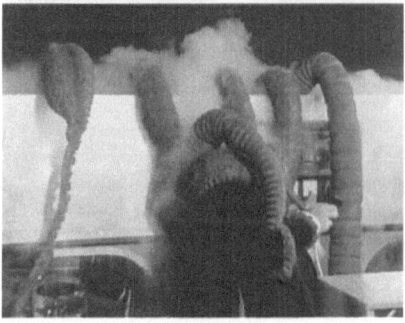

In "Spearhead from Space" (1970), plastic humanoid droids called Autons serve as the drones of a composite being/collective intelligence called The Nestene Consciousness, an—*ahem*—'anus'-like entity stored in a containment tank that ultimately transforms into a tentacled monstrosity in the serial's climactic episode

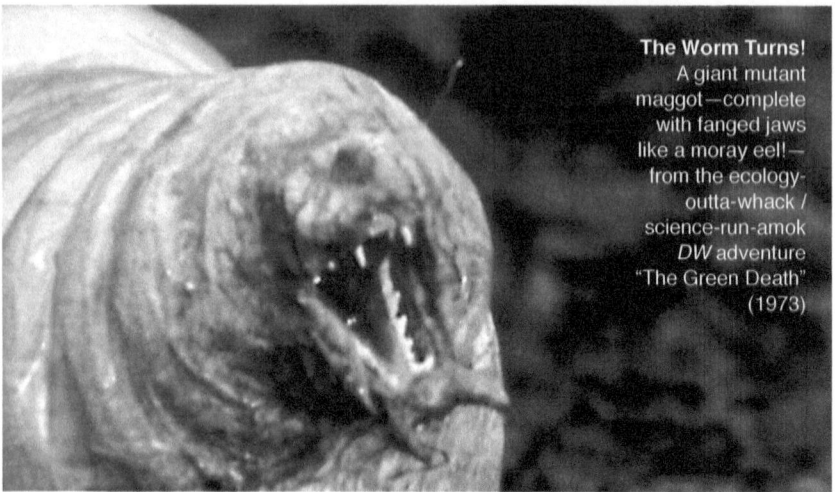

The Worm Turns! A giant mutant maggot—complete with fanged jaws like a moray eel!—from the ecology-outta-whack / science-run-amok *DW* adventure "The Green Death" (1973)

loss of individualism ("We have no individual identity", deadpans a Nestene zombie uncaringly) inevitably also harken back to McCarthyist era America and the likes of Don Siegel's **INVASION OF THE BODY SNATCHERS** (1955, USA) and the numerous similarly-themed dystopian SF scenarios that came after it. Another telltale clue as to the pronounced Hollywood influence on "Spearhead from Space" (etc.) are certain aspects of the Mme. Tussauds subplot; one scene of which clearly indirectly references a well-known revelatory moment from André de Toth's and Vincent Price's 3-D horror classic **HOUSE OF WAX** (1953); yet another touch of pure Science Fiction *Gothique*. Still another comes when, walking dead-like, the dormant army of Auton drone 'droids is collectively awakened from their urban clothing store window displays at daybreak—yes, it's the "Dawn of the Autons"!—to go on a "countrywide" (i.e., strictly localized and limited) people-culling spree, gunning citizens down *en masse* with the sneaky zappers hidden inside their forearms. A high-frequency sonic beam projector factors majorly into the grand finale, itself being yet another nostalgic throwback to a sci-fi B-flick from the Fabulous 'Fifties. Then, in a sudden unexpected and almost Lovecraftian moment (albeit a high-camp one), a bonus twist ending has feebly flailing, air-inflated latex tentacles—green ones, natch!—floppily besetting Who from out of the conspicuously anus-like (!?) Nestene Consciousness' containment tank and unsuccessfully attempting to throttle him. Ergo, talk about a highly memorable climax!

Interestingly enough, a mere month after "Spearhead" was aired, the BBC began transmitting *Doomwatch* (1970-72), a sobering set of cautionary tales that would last for three seasons. From the minds of Cyberman co-creators Gerry Davis (1930-1991) and Kit Pedler (1927-1981), the serial featured a Government-sponsored organization—led by Nobel Prize-winning Physicist Dr. Spencer Quist (John Paul)—which investigated ecological and technological dangers, hopefully for the betterment and preservation of both the environment and Mankind. One of the earliest examples of openly environmentally-conscious television, its audience was urged to ponder the dire consequences of the unregulated commercial exploitation of Earth's resources, a topic which is still very much a highly "hot-button" one to this day—if not even more so. *Doomwatch*'s "Department for the Observation and Measurement of Science" combated such menaces as super-intelligent man-eating rats, mind-destroying sound waves, toxic mutations and even a rogue plastic-eating virus (perhaps not such a bad thing at that!), although a final episode—exploring sexual permissiveness and its impact on human behavior—was banned outright. This story, contentiously entitled "Sex and Violence", courted controversy, not for its overall subject matter, but for a scene wherein footage of a real-life African execution was shown. Even though the program attempted to make the valid point—one which most well-adjusted people might (and indeed *should*) consider a total no-brainer—that watching *genuine* violence has a different effect on viewers than does fantasy violence, the episode was yanked by nervous executives regardless.

****

The beginning of the '70s not only stifled a hopeful future, but equality of the sexes was still a brooding, divisive issue, too. British feminists fought for their corner in a nation known for its "*Carry On*"-movie-style view of women, and this anger spilled-over during the 1970 Miss World contest at the Albert Hall, where *compère* Bob Hope fueled the flames by making a number of crass, non-PC comments *[Good for him! ☺ – SF.]*, and activists showered the stage with smoke and stink-bombs. Publications such as *Shrew* and *Spare Rib [see Endnote #12]* developed theoretical differences between socialist feminism and the more radical format and, as the decade continued to unfold, the liberation movement was addressing sexual stereotyping in education.

With the titular Time Lord exiled on a near-contemporary Earth, *Doctor Who* introduced a new female companion; although, rather than the fearfully shrieking/shrinking, constantly-threatened "damsel-in-distress" norm, Liz Shaw (Caroline John) was instead an independent, intellectually-disciplined scientist. Drafted to U.N.I.T. from prestigious Cambridge University, Shaw could comprehend the Doctor on a much more level footing than the shows' earlier heroines had done, but writer-producer Barry Letts ([1925-2009] sometimes jointly a.k.a. "Guy Leopold" in conjunction with series co-writer Robert Sloman), decided that she was just *too* intellectual to provide a proper dramatic balance…or perhaps "imbalance" might be a better term for it. Lasting for only a handful of serials, Shaw was either a character who was just too-far-ahead of the times—or perhaps merely one whom the writers found themselves struggling to relate to. The feministic traits of Doc's subsequent female sidekicks were very haphazard in '70s *Who*: Jo Grant (Katy Manning *[see Endnote #13]*) was a skittish, sometimes flighty but loyal junior U.N.I.T. operative; sassy, independent reporter Sarah Jane Smith (Elisabeth Sladen) regressed to damsel-in-distress fodder once more; leather-clad Leela (Louise Jameson)'s usual reflexes were to kill; and we had to wait for the first incarnation of Time Lady Romana (Mary Tamm) for the Doctor to have another scientific sparring partner on a par with aforementioned distaff boffin Ms. Shaw. Similarly, *Doomwatch* addressed accusations of sexism by enrolling Dr. Fay Chantry (Jean Trend) and Dr. Anne Tarrant (Elizabeth Weaver), although neither were exactly written as role models of independence.

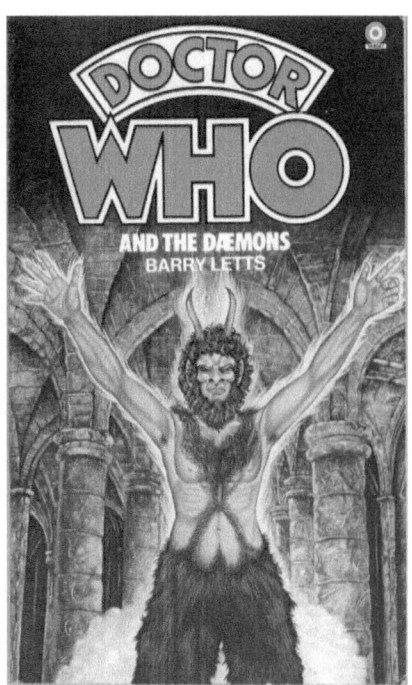

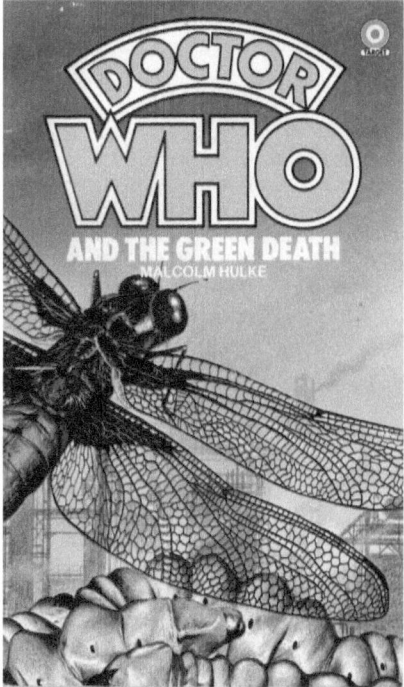

DW tie-in novelizations, with cover art by Andrew Skilleter *[top]* and Alun Hood *[above]*

Part III: The Pit of History | Ancient Diabolical Forces & Residual Hauntings

"Let's say it's a mass of data, waiting for a correct interpretation." |– Peter Brock (Michael Bryant) in **THE STONE TAPE** (1972)

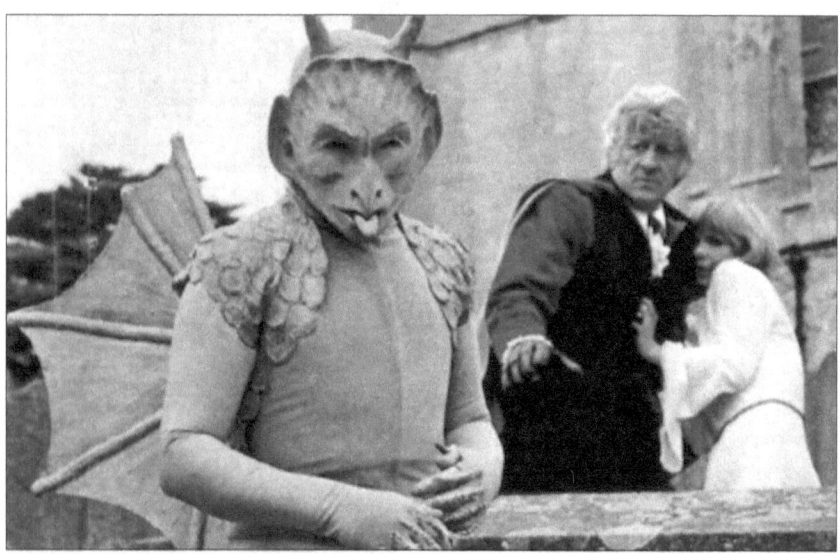

Promo still from the 1971 *Doctor Who* serial "The Dæmons", showing Jon Pertwee as Doc and Katy Manning as Jo recoiling in fright from Stanley Mason as the living stone gargoyle Bok

The Pertwee/U.N.I.T. era progressed by drawing on the works of Kneale quite liberally, if unofficially *[see Endnote #14]*, and the sulfur-'n'-brimstone-filled five-parter "The Dæmons" (aired May 22nd to June 19th, 1971) more than retreads already-well-trod *Quatermass and the Pit* (aired December 22nd, 1958 to January 26th, 1959) territory, as well as straying firmly onto tried-and-trusted Dennis Wheatley turf in the process. Despite its arguable shortcomings, it also stands as one of the very finest and funnest *DW* serials of the '70s nevertheless, for the large part.

The kickoff episode of this standout serial's quintet opens in classically atmospheric Gothic fashion, against the backdrop of a spooky old dark house during a nocturnal rainstorm amidst thunderclaps and lightning flashes, intercut with close-ups of such iconic occult symbols as an owl, a toad and a black cat's eyes. Yes indeed: a perfect milieu for ghoulies and ghosties and long-leggedy beasties and things that go bump in the night! "It really *is* the dawning of the Age of Aquarius", says Jo to the ever-scientifically skeptical Who early on. "Well, that means the occult…you know, the supernatural and all that magic biz". Who shortly goes on to pooh-pooh her ideas on the subject as "absurd", and much the same argument continues between various characters over the course of the serial.

For this one, popularly unpopular Whovian supervillain The Master (Roger Delgado)—posing as a bespectacled, not-so-reverend local country vicar named Mr. Magister, aided-and-abetted by his sycophantic sect of presumably defrocked deacons and vergers ([quote] "disciples") in monks' cassocks—employs black magic on a grand scale in an ambitious attempt to assimilate the immense powers of an eons-old evil entity known as Azal, whose essence is unleashed from an ancient (*circa* 800 B.C.) warrior chieftain's burial barrow known as the Devil's Hump at the ghost-and-witch-haunted village of Devil's End (shades of aforesaid *QatP*'s Hobbes End). Leading up to this, Ankh-wearing self-proclaimed white witch Miss Hawthorne ([Damaris Hayman] "I cast the runes!") vehemently opposes and protests Prof. Horner (Robin Wentworth)'s proposed opening of the long-sealed barrow, which is slated to happen at the stroke of midnight on the eve of the pre-Christian Celtic May Day festival known as Beltane ("…greatest occult festival of the year, bar Halloween", explains the prof.).

Hawthorne believes that such a desecration of the site will unleash "The Prince of Evil, The Dark One, The Horn-ed Beast" upon the world. Surprisingly enough, despite his earlier scornful remarks pertaining to the existence (or rather, *non*existence) of the supernatural, Doc believes that a cataclysmic cosmic catastrophe might well result on a global scale if the barrow-opening goes ahead as planned. (*DON'T do it!*)

Just as expected, all Hell breaks loose (or at least a goodly chunk of it anyway). Channeling Aleister "The Wickedest Man Alive [sic!]" Crowley's #1 Thelemic commandment, The Master commands his followers, "To do *my* will shall be the whole of the law!" Memorably enough, very much resembling a much-simplified version of one of the Stan Winston-created demonic denizens of Bill Norton's made-for-American-TV classic **GARGOYLES** (1972), the stone statue of a devilish, horned/winged blazing-red-eyed imp—one of Satan's servile elementals ("...creatures of The Devil")—comes to unnatural life and gains full mobility. Named Bok (quite possibly after Arkham House's master critter illustrator Hannes Bok?), this impish, diminutive, chalk-white living gargoyle is telepathically controlled by The Master and can shoot deadly sparks and hellfire from its talon-tips at will to dissuade—or outright evaporate!—foolhardy mortals who cross its path. Equally memorably, huge cloven hoofprints are sighted thereabouts from a helicopter, tracked clear across the moors by giant strides ("The animal that made these would have to be at least *thirty feet tall*!"). And not only that, but Devil's End is cut off from the outside world by some sort of impenetrable supernatural heat-shield/force-field (shades of the variations of such inexplicable invisible barriers seen in SF/monster movies like **VILLAGE OF THE DAMNED** [1960, UK, D: Wolf Rilla], **THE SLIME PEOPLE** [1963, USA, D: Robert Hutton] and **THE BUBBLE** [a.k.a. **FANTASTIC INVASION OF PLANET EARTH**, 1966, USA, D: Arch Oboler]). It is regular cast member Nick Courtney as Brigadier Lethbridge Stewart who accidentally discovers the presence of this unseen wall—actually a mushroom cap-shaped dome, a mile high and ten across—when, while using it as a pointer, he extends his swagger-stick ahead of him, only to have the end of it abruptly ignite like a sparkler on Guy Fawkes Night!

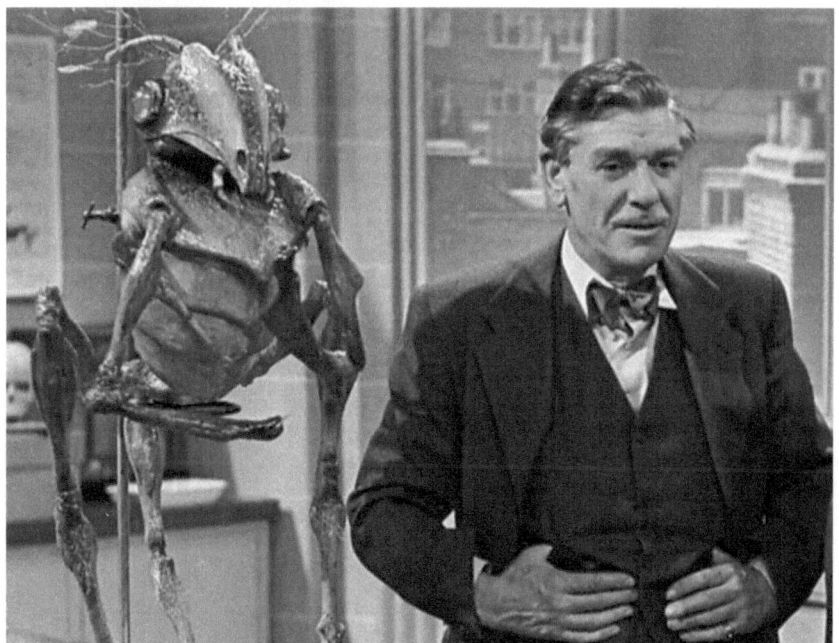

Nigel Kneale's Professor Quatermass (here played by André Morell) and one of the preserved "Martians" from the classic 1958-59 BBC-TV serial *Quatermass and the Pit*'s tale of ancient alien invasion and intervention in the development of the human race influenced more than a few *DW* plots, and also had an impact on both author Stephen King and filmmaker John Carpenter

Further adding to the whole Quatermassian feel that predominates, the BBC camera crew that is on-site to record the tomb's big-news unsealing remind us of the similar group—also from The Beeb—shooting a live documentary special at Westminster Abbey in the last act of Val Guest's exceptional **THE QUATERMASS XPERIMENT** (a.k.a. **THE CREEPING UNKNOWN**, 1955, UK). Evidently meant sarcastically in the current context, a burning bush is at one point seen on the Devil's End church grounds, having been instantaneously blasted into flames by a diabolic lightning bolt. A later sequence showing rustic Morris Dancers prancing round a Maypole leads into a scene that oddly faintly prefigures the climax to Robin Hardy's masterpiece **THE WICKER MAN** (1973, UK), this when The Doctor finds himself bound to said pole, accused as a witch ("Burn him! *Burn him!!*" chant the villagers every bit as avidly as the serfs in **MONTY PYTHON AND THE HOLY GRAIL** [1975, UK] do). In keeping with this subplot, early into the serial, Witchfinder General Matthew Hopkins' unhallowed name is heard mentioned in passing (the serial was largely shot on location in the village of Aldbourne in the South West county of Wiltshire, well within the range of Hopkins' old haunts).

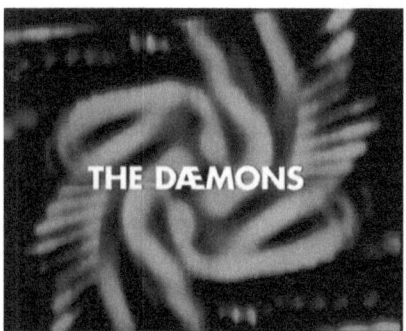

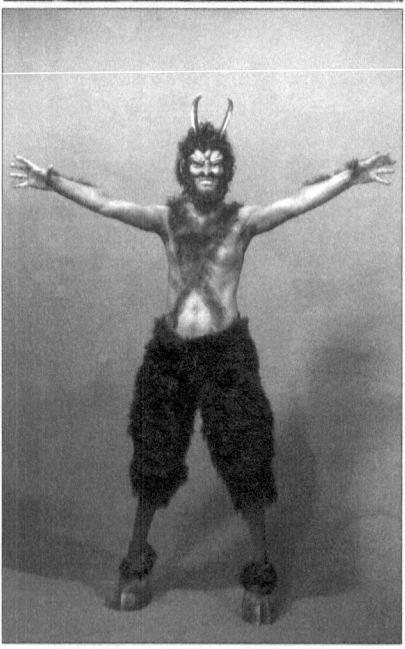

Top: Title card for the five-part 1971 *Doctor Who* serial "The Dæmons". **Above:** A promotional still of actor Stephen Thorne in full makeup as the Pan-like, devilish alien Azal

It isn't until the cliffhanger to the fourth and penultimate episode that we finally get to meet the "horn-ed" (that's how Miss Hawthorne pronounces it, in two distinct syllables), hirsute, hooved creature responsible for tracking-up the whole territory roundabout: namely the mighty Azal himself (Stephen Thorne)—a.k.a. Azael, The Fallen Angel—a towering, evilly guffawing, half-goat Pan-like figure, who is first seen rising to his full "30-foot" height c/o a crude Chroma key enlarging effect that's about as convincing as its baggy Fun Fur "goat legs" are; but then, when it comes to classic era *Who*, we never lower ourselves to nitpick in any serious manner about special effects failings, preferring to just suspend our disbelief and sit back and enjoy the show. After all, it's nitpickery like complaining about the lack of "realism" in the old school FX work which ultimately led to the kinds of way-overdone, computer-driven stuff (I hesitate to say "fluff") that's such an unnecessarily big part of modern-day *Who*, and which seemingly causes the quality of the show's scripts and stories to suffer for it. Better pantomimic theatricality and good writing than hackwork and technological overdose any day!

On that note, the story's overlying theme of technology and logical scientific reason versus paganistic magick and irrational superstition is established early on ("*Magic!*" – "*Science!* – *Magic!!*" goes one heated exchange between the witch and The Doctor), then further explored and expounded upon when it is revealed that many magical methods are in fact products of "psionic science". "*Science*, not sorcery", reiterates Dr. Who calmly to the overly-emotional Miss Hawthorne early into the fifth and final instalment. She believes that the psychokinetic energy generated by the more intense human emotions like fear and anger is what drives black magic; he in turn asserts that this type of

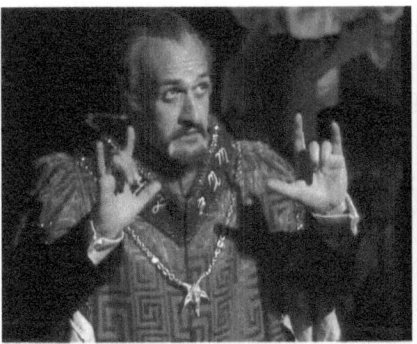 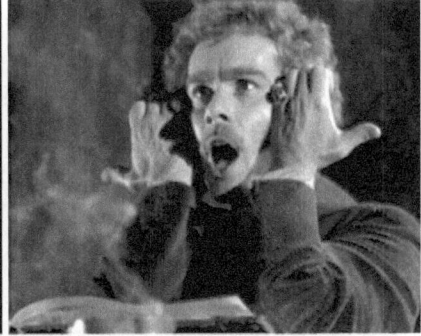

Demons...Therefore Aliens? The Master *[above left]* cries "Rise at my command! *Azal! Azal!! AZAL!!!*" and makes ritualistic hand gestures to call forth the devil-aliens in "The Dæmons"; while, in Daniel Haller's film **THE DUNWICH HORROR** (1970, USA), Dean Stockwell as Wilbur Whateley chants "*Yog Sogoth!*" in hopes of connecting with HPL's "Old Ones" using another form of hand symbol 'popularized' by Aleister Crowley in the 1920s

energy can be explained much more sensibly by scientific means. All the trappings of the occult, such as witches' sabbats, rune-castings and invocations, merely provide the needed catalyst that allows the psionic energy to flow between the worlds. One of many playful jabs at both science and superstition alike in "The Dæmons" comes when the feisty Miss Hawthorne, Dick Emery-style, hits a baddie with her handbag—which contains a heavy crystal ball that is ordinarily used for the purposes of seerism—and he drops on the spot like a sack of spuds. How's *that* for vulgarly demystifying an object that is regarded as sacred in some mystical circles!

ATTENTION: SPOILER ALERT! Piling still more paranormal possibilities atop the pile we've gotten already, the then (as now) highly-topical theme of ancient astronauts is raised when Dr. Who informs us that the Dæmons are actually extraterrestrial in origin and hail from Dæmos, a planet some 60,000 light years across the galaxy, having first come to Earth over 100,000 years ago "To help Homo Sapiens kick out Neanderthal Man", as Doc puts it; hence, the aliens are presented more as an in-some-ways almost benevolent—or at the very least impartial—race of superbeings that are far above such base human concerns as greed and power-mongering. The implication is that The Master represents a far darker malevolence than Azal and his Dæmons do, and that the latter are, as a consequence of their innately unchangeable nature, merely an entirely *a*moral (rather than merely *im*moral) race who do what they do out of no real sense of malice but for pure logic's sake, and it is actually the disgraced ex-Time Lord who is most at fault for attempting to harness and exploit their infinite power for his own selfish, nefarious ends. But, that said, from where we're standing, he definitely seems more like the lesser of two evils to us, for the simple reason that his own powers are so much more limited than theirs are, so his propensity for evildoing shrinks almost to insignificance next to that of the Dæmons themselves. After all, great evils have been committed based on so-called logic, so even the most logical beings aren't infallible, and who knows how they might misuse their powers? Some interesting moral dynamics do result as a consequence of this clash of moralities, though.

Naturally enough, The Doctor ultimately susses-out a solution involving a hastily jerrybuilt and consequently unstable device called a "diothermic energy exchanger" (Doc's obligatory pseudo-sciencey gobbledygook also includes "...EHF wideband width variable-phase oscillator with a negative feedback circuit tunable to the frequency of an air molecule..." [!]). As for the main villain of the piece, resplendent in his cleric's dog collar and scarlet ceremonial robes, the devilishly-goatee'd Delgado's always-memorable Master a.k.a. Magister ("Rise at my command! Azal! *Azal!! AZAL!!!*") is the absolute epitome of cultured but calculating, alluring evil. In one scene, the wacky wiccan Hawthorne woman—a spinster who is generally regarded as quite the kook by her neighbors—brandishes her ankh pendant at him like a crucifix at a vampire, without garnering even the slightest reaction; unlike how Bok the gargoyle reacts—in cringing, abject terror!—when Doc levels a piece of simple iron ("It's an old magical defense") at him, causing the creature to scarper pronto; a direct hit from

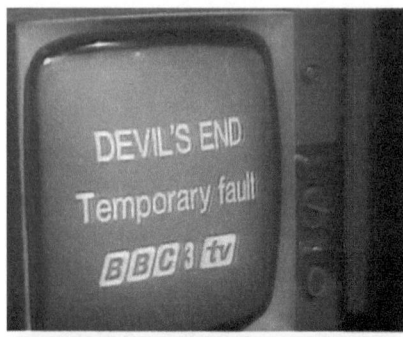

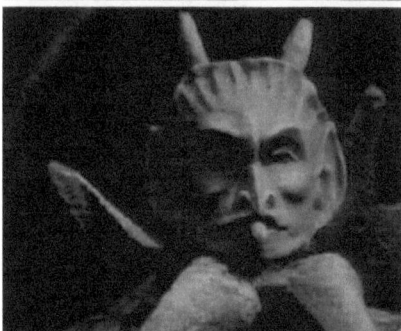

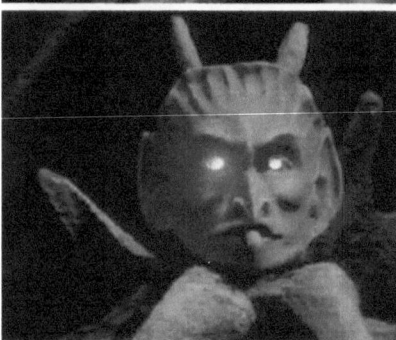

In 1971's "The Dæmons", somewhat reminiscent of Kneale's 1958 BBC serial (and subsequent '68 Hammer film) *Quatermass and the Pit*, live TV coverage is interrupted by paranormal activity. (Incidentally, the then-fictitious BBC 3 channel wasn't actually launched until February 2003!)

As you can probably tell from the above description of much of its contents, not only is this particular serial a bit needlessly overplotted at times, but it is also rather weakened by its somewhat too-simplistic, perfunctory denouement—i.e., Jo's valiant if to him illogical offer of self-sacrifice causes Azal to self-destruct—which, interestingly enough, thematically vaguely prefigures that to **THE EXORCIST** (1973), at least partially.

If being quite a bit less-complicated about it, some similar themes as those in "The Dæmons" were revisited for our next program to be discussed. Forming part of the third season of *Drama Playhouse*—the BBC's launching-pad for potential new series—*The Incredible Robert Baldick*'s failed pilot episode "Never Come Night" (airdate: October 6th, 1972) was Terry Nation's first completed work for The Beeb's drama department since his six episodes of The Daleks' "Master Plan" back in 1965. Directed by Cyril Coke, this promising if sadly never-commissioned series is a Victorian Gothic piece centering around the titular Baldick character (played by the prolific Robert Hardy, who appeared in Peter Sykes' occult thriller **DEMONS OF THE MIND** for Hammer that same year and had the year previous starred in The Beeb's effective M.R. James dramatization "The Stalls of Barchester" [airdate: December 24th, 1971]; the latter to be discussed in Part 2 of this article in *M!* #34). An egotistically eccentric Sherlockian detective/scientist who owns his very own steam locomotive with special armor-plated/bulletproof passenger carriages (complete with a built-in laboratory), Baldick also keeps an owl named Cosimo as a house-pet/mascot. A fusion of Sherlock Holmes and—*sort of!*—Carl Kolchak (one of the forerunners of *The X-Files*' Fox Mulder character played by David Duchovny, plus countless other "monster-hunters" since), Hardy plays Baldick with suffocatingly gung-ho gusto, but there are simply too many themes crammed into too-short a running time for them to jell into a satisfying whole. Elements of Victorian literature (e.g., dog-loyal assistants, windswept nights, etc.) and Gothic fiction (e.g., secrets in the woods, a ruined abbey, failed exorcism, unruly villagers, etc.) are further complicated by a twist involving an alien artefact; a sting-in-the-tail payoff that not only comes as a narrative anomaly but makes for an unnecessary *Quatermass*-style "resolution" to boot... without really resolving much of anything other than in the vaguest and most ambiguous fashion. Nice try though!

a U.N.I.T. bazooka subsequently proves to be a whole lot less effective against the irksome imp. Rather belatedly for such a self-appointed expert on such matters, Miss Hawthorne cottons-on that The Master's rather-too-obvious pseudonym is a word meaning the leader of a black magic coven; as the good Doctor subsequently deduces with no effort whatsoever, "*magister*" (as in the case of Hermann Hesse's epic mysticism/fantasy novel *Magister Ludi* [1931-43], a.k.a. *The Glass Bead Game*) is also Latin for... *Master!*

Squire Aldington (Reginald Marsh) and Reverend Elmstead (James Cossins) discover the badly-beaten corpse of a young woman in the reputedly haunted ruins of Duvel Woods Abbey, outside the village of Boardington. Consequently, Elmstead visits his friend Robert Baldick in hopes that the unconventional super-sleuth will assist him in solving this latest in a long line of murders (some 43 in all, "…always in terrifying circumstances") occurring in or around the abbey ("…local legend has it that the deaths go back into prehistory…"). Aided by his valet Thomas Wingham (Julian Holloway) and burly gamekeeper Caleb Selling (John Rhys-Davies, sporting HUGE, shaggy stick-on sideburns the size of ferrets!), Baldick delves into local parish records and discovers that the site of the abbey has long been associated with human sacrifice. Whilst they are excavating deeper within the crypt, fear and anxiety grips the group. Thomas falls down into a chamber below which is filled with human skeletal remains and pervaded by a palpable aura of absolute *evil* ("…like a physical presence in the place"). Baldick becomes convinced that the abbey contains an ethereal distillation of the terrors and phobias of all the people who have visited the enclosure ("We're fighting a primeval force"), and he later examines a strange object he retrieved from beneath the floor of the abbey: a small metal box ("Possibly from the past—or the *future*?") containing intricate electrical components and etched with indecipherable runic symbols.

Nation's stab at *Drama Playhouse* forms a trilogy of BBC Gothics, all broadcast within three months of each other, that were rooted in unusual prehistory. The anthology series *Dead of Night* ran for seven 50-minute episodes in 1972, although only three of these—"The Exorcism" (episode #1, aired November 5th, D: Don Taylor), "Return Flight" (episode #2, aired November 12th, D: Rodney Bennett) and "A Woman Sobbing" (episode #7, aired December 17th, D: Paul Ciappessoni)—are known to survive in the decimated BBC archives; one of the primary reasons for this being The Beeb's erstwhile habit of recycling videotape in order to cut down on costs. "The Exorcism" is a spook-story-as-social-commentary, which begins with Edmund (Edward Petherbridge) and his wife Rachel (Anna Cropper) showing Dan (Clive Swift) around their recently-renovated country cottage. As Dan's partner Margaret (Sylvia Kay) helps prepare their Christmas dinner, Rachel plays a clavichord, only to realize she has no idea what the tune she's playing is. The electricity abruptly cuts out, and the telephone also suddenly becomes inoperable. After digesting their meal, all four begin suffering

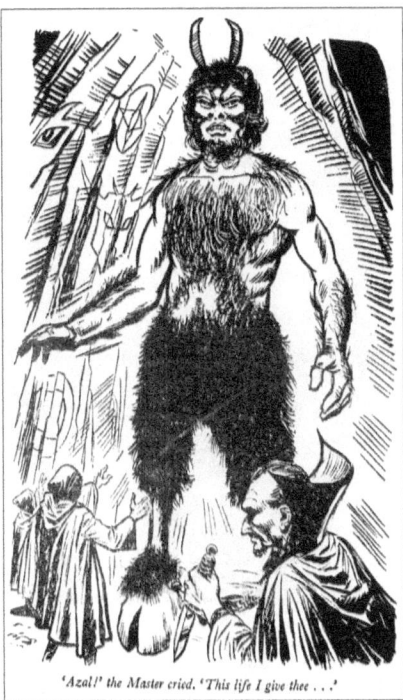

'Azal!' the Master cried. 'This life I give thee …'

The Master and his minions conjure up the alien "dæmons"; an illustration by Alan Willow from the novelization

from shooting pains; Dan finds that the main door of the place won't open, the windows can't be unlocked, and that the home's exterior has been inexplicably plunged into total darkness. Rachel falls into a trance, during which she relates the experiences of a woman whose husband was hanged whilst off trying to obtain food for she and their starving children, while the local squire and his family indulged heartily, oblivious to the poor family's fate. We learn that the wife locked herself and the children in their house to die from starvation, trusting that the very building itself would remember the great injustice done to her and her family by the callous gentry.

Later the same month that *Dead of Night*'s seventh and final episode "A Woman Sobbing" was broadcast, Nigel Kneale's made-for-TV feature **THE STONE TAPE** (aired on Christmas Day of '72 [D: Peter Sasdy]) would also feature supernatural manifestations of human trauma as its principal menace. Peter Brock, head of Ryan Electrics research (played by Michael Bryant, who gives a powerhouse performance), is working on innovating an entirely new recording medium that will revolutionize the industry and give their Japanese competitors

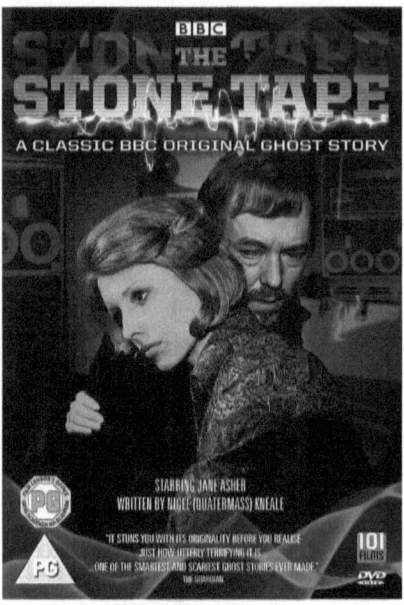

The 2013 UK DVD

a real run for their money. He and his select collectorate of scientists move into Taskerlands, a derelict Victorian mansion—built atop ancient Saxon foundations and containing a secret stairway leading nowhere, ominously enough—that has recently been renovated in order to act as their base of operations. Foreman Roy Collinson (played by seasoned Scottish actor Iain Cuthbertson, who a few months previous had ended his two-dozen episode run as London hoodlum Charlie Endell in the classic Brit kitchen sink/crime teledrama *Budgie* [1971-72], starring ex-rocker and teenybopper heartthrob Adam Faith in the now-iconic title role) says that the refurbishment of one of the rooms—intended to house the huge data banks of the facility's sophisticated computer system—remains uncompleted, as builders refuse to work there on the grounds that it is not only crawling with dry-rot (a.k.a. "creeping fungus" ["Even the *stone*'s got it!" exclaims Brock]) but, more especially, because it is also… *haunted*. While exploring the area, one of the research team, computer programmer Jill Greeley (Jane Asher, the former heroine of Roger Corman's **THE MASQUE OF THE RED DEATH** [1964, USA])—who is psychically sensitive and adeptly susceptible to sensing the paranormal ("I saw a *ghost*!")—experiences a paranormal vision of a screaming woman, who runs up the steps in the room, following which her ethereal apparition vanishes into thin air care of an entry-level Chroma key overlay/dissolve effect.

(*ATTENTION: SPOILER ALERT!* Skip down to the next paragraph to avoid them.) Upon inquiring among the local villagers, the scientific researchers learn that a young chambermaid named Louisa had died on the premises of Taskerlands after falling from said mysterious stairway, and Brock, who obsessively devotes himself, his team and all their hi-tech hardware to getting to the bottom of the mystery, comes to the eerie realization that the eponymous stone itself has somehow recorded and preserved images (when the "tape" [i.e., block of centuries-old Kentish ragstone] of the spectral visitation winds up getting accidentally wiped, this acts as a delicious metaphor for the BBC's aforementioned once-common practice of bulk-erasing video recordings of programs so as to reuse tapes and reduce expenses; an unfortunate practice which resulted in a substantial amount of programming being irretrievably lost, more's the pity). Thanks to her heightened degree of clairvoyance, the easily-spooked if staunchly resolute Jill concludes that the audiovisual imagery of the maid's death was masking a considerably more ancient recording ("…some deep-level record, *much older*; so old, and *shapeless*…") made by what Brock off-handedly describes as the "mineral medium", and she subsequently finds herself confronted by a seven-millennia-old malevolent presence ("…something *else*…") that is unleashed from the core of the living rock, which contains virtually limitless recorded memories, layered concentrically within it, like onion layers or the time-rings of a tree-trunk. The only-vaguely-seen, luminescent heavy-breathing/gurgling/whooshing monstrosities which Jill encounters in the dark, dank bowels of the haunted mansion are much akin to H.P. Lovecraft's "Old Ones" in essence, and there is very much a Lovecraftian tone to the entire affair. Having been supernaturally transported to a proto-Stonehenge, the clairvoyant falls to her death… but is she *actually* dead?

Kneale's stories typically involve conflicts that stem from some primal/primeval yearning, affecting the past, present, or future. **THE STONE TAPE**—which predates the thematically analogous **THE LEGEND OF HELL HOUSE** (1973, UK, D: John Hough) by just a few months—was one of the first dramatized stories to promulgate the hypothesis of residual haunting; that seemingly inexplicable ghostly entities may be explained in logical terms as "recordings" of past events made by the physical environments whereon they transpired *[see Endnote #15]*, to serve as lasting testimony for future generations. For what is ostensibly a ghost story, it primarily explores the actions and motivations of the *living*: how humans interact in such unusual situations—particularly in relation to such concerns as business and money—and whether indeed any live human presence is even required at the haunt site *at all*. **THE STONE TAPE** was much later remade by the BBC (in 2015), albeit for radio rather than television *[see Endnote #16]*.

Meanwhile, back in the '70s, *Doctor Who* offered its own brand of topical critiques. Telling of a backward planet's attempts to join a Galactic Federation, "The Curse of Peladon" (aired January 29th to February 19th, 1972) was a *DW* serial that would be decoded/decrypted for its commentary on the pros and cons of Britain's membership in the EEC (European Economic Community), later to become known as the EU (European Union). It is, however, "The Green Death" (aired May 19th to June 23rd, 1973) which lodges most in the memory with its ecological awareness ("It's time the world awoke to the alarm bell of pollution…!"). Here, The Doctor and Jo battle mutated insects and giant carnivorous maggots created by toxic waste in the contaminated Welsh coalmining village of Llanfairfach. The heroes of the piece are environmentalists and the villain is an unscrupulous capitalistic conglomerate called Global Chemicals—whose director of operations has been taken-over and used as its puppet/pawn by the super-computer acronymically known as BOSS ("Bimorphic Organizational Systems Supervisor") *[see Endnote #17]*.

As well as for the memorably icky monsters and its conscientious eco-biological concerns, "The Green Death" is also remembered for being Katy Manning as the Jo character's farewell show; this after she falls in love with a Nobel prizewinning young hotshot scientist named Professor Jones (Stewart Bevan) and decides to leave U.N.I.T. in order to accompany him on an expedition up the Amazon. What with accented actors uttering local colloquialisms like "Blodwyn", "boyo" and "mun" and indulging in clichéd banter about rugby, Welsh viewers may not be too flattered by their depiction onscreen, but the emotion-fraught parting of ways between Jo and The Doctor ("So, the fledgling flies the coop…") is like watching a true-life breakup occurring right on national television. Pertwee and Manning both speak in hushed, barely-audible voices, and you can tell that both actors were emotionally moved while filming the scene. The final images of The Doctor downing his drink before driving off in Bessie—his vintage Rolls Royce, personalized number plate: "WHO 1"; unequal parts flightless Chitty Chitty Bang Bang

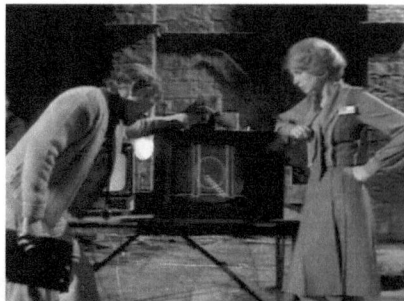

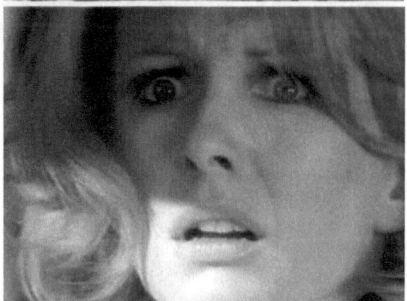

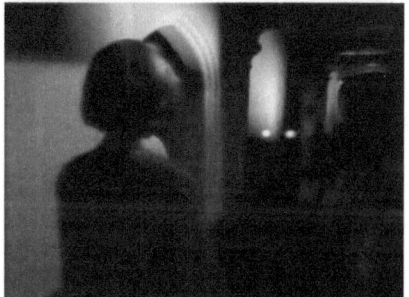

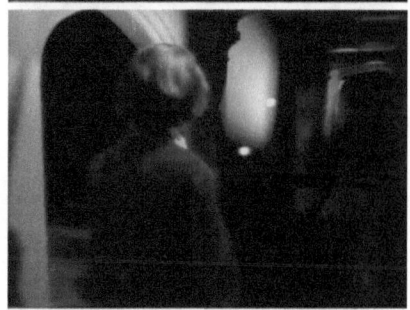

Paranormal activity meets scientific investigation in one of the spookiest moments of Nigel Kneale's BBC 2 Christmas special horror thriller **THE STONE TAPE** (D: Peter Sasdy). The science behind the terror has recently become more sound, as the phenomenon of "archaeoacoustics" has gained recognition in the scientific world. The producers of *Doctor Who* would later pay tribute to Kneale's story in the 2013 story "Hide"

and Herbie the Love Bug!—packs-in more raw sentiment than anything to be found in the *über-overkill* tradition of the modern-era show.

Mirroring Britain's institutional collapse was the first episode of Terry Nation's quirky "Death to the Daleks" (aired February 23rd to March 16th, 1974). Broadcast five days before the General Election defeat of Prime Minister Edward Heath amid the power cuts of the then-three-day-only week, there is something particularly resonant about a story which centers around a planet being drained of all its energy.

[End of Part 1. In Part 2, we continue with more '70s Who, plus discuss some of The Beeb's made-for-TV ghost stories and other Gothic horror productions – Eds.]

ENDNOTES:

1 While he never really regarded himself as a science fiction writer, Nigel Kneale (1922-2006) nonetheless painted cynical landscapes of our potential futures, and developed into a genuine seer (but then, SF, horror and fantasy literature are all popularly categorized under the umbrella heading of "speculative fiction", after all). This uncanny knack Kneale had for prediction included prophesying the disintegration/degeneration of broadcasting—as typified by trashy so-called "Reality TV"—all the way back in **THE YEAR OF THE SEX OLYMPICS** (airdate: July 29th, 1968). Kneale's arrival as a staff writer at the BBC

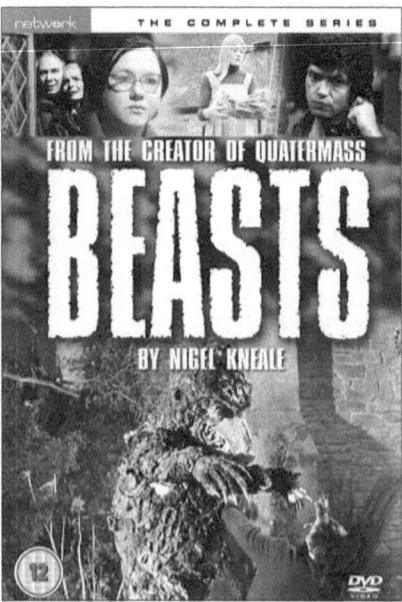

UK DVD cover for Nigel Kneale's six-episode ITV anthology series *Beasts* (1976), pretty much standard fare with paranormal animals being at the center of each episode... except for "The Dummy", which is about an actor playing a monster in a movie

coincided with television's post-Coronation ascension to mass public appeal, and as early drama was dominated by unambitious stage and literary adaptations, there is some justification in Mark Gatiss' claim that the writer virtually singlehandedly *invented* popular television.

2 Other BBC anthologies that started in the early '70s were *Menace* (1970, 1973) and *Leap in the Dark* (1973, 1975, 1977, 1980). The latter changed format as many times as its stories did; initially featuring paranormal documentaries, the middle seasons (presented by Colin Wilson) consisted of dramatized reenactments of events, before the final season morphed into original fiction dramas. *Play for Today* contributed tales of folk horror in "Robin Redbreast" (airdate; December 10th, 1970) and "A Photograph" (airdate; March 22nd, 1977), meta-fantasies like "Penda's Fen" (airdate; March 21st, 1974) and "Red Shift" (airdate; January 17th, 1978), plus "Vampires" (1979), a popular entry about three boys who, after watching Hammer/Terence Fisher's **DRACULA – PRINCE OF DARKNESS** (1966), begin believing that a man at a local cemetery is one of the undead.

3 Verity Lambert was a symbol of female advancement in the media. Lambert had the talent for creating interesting programs from few resources—perfect for The Beeb—and would later enjoy a long association with Thames Television and their Euston Films offshoot, where she would executive-produce the much-delayed miniseries *Quatermass* (aired October 24th to November 14th, 1979), starring John Mills in the title role. In 1985, she formed her own film company called Cinema Verity—a play on "*cinéma vérité*", the French term for filmic realism—which produced Fred Schepisi's **EVIL ANGELS (a.k.a. A CRY IN**

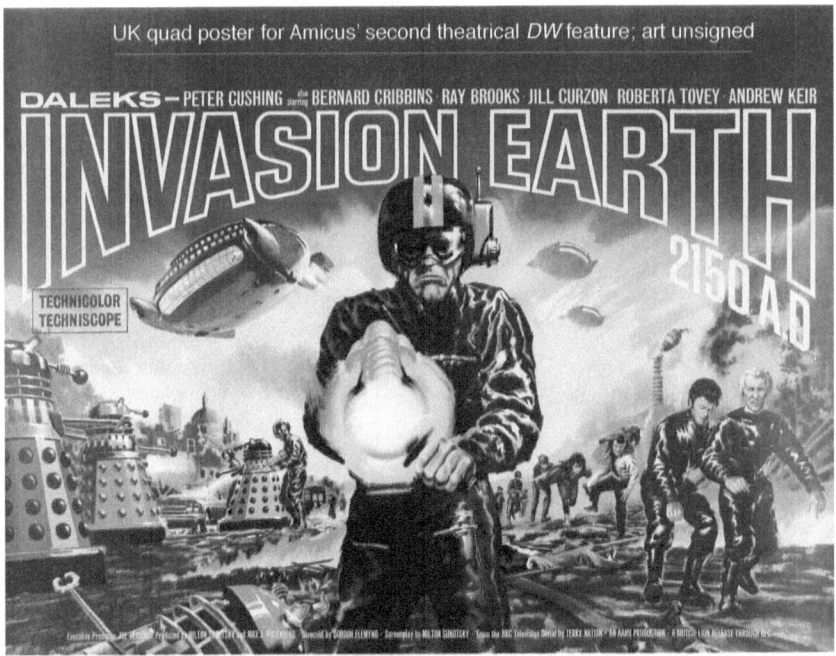

UK quad poster for Amicus' second theatrical *DW* feature; art unsigned

THE DARK, 1988, Australia/USA), starring Meryl Streep and Sam Neill, based on the infamous Azaria Chamberlain "dingo baby" case.

4 The Daleks basically created the merchandising arm of the BBC. Together with a whole cascade of toys, during the same period the hyper-aggressive robotoids also appeared in the two AARU/Amicus spinoff theatrical features, **DR. WHO AND THE DALEKS** (1965) and **DALEKS – INVASION EARTH 2150 A.D.** (1966), both starring Peter Cushing as a somewhat dottier-than-usual Doctor (the actor basically repeated much the same "dotty old duffer" routine a decade later for his role as Dr. Abner Perry in Amicus' subterranean monster fantasy **AT THE EARTH'S CORE** [1976]).

5 Catherine Lucille Moore's work paved the way for many other female speculative fiction writers. She and her first husband Henry Kuttner were prolific co-authors under their own names and male pseudonyms, and *No Woman Born* contains perceptions of beauty and femininity which are still all-too-relevant today. The writing is vivid and emotional, showing how Deirdre must relearn how to be (or perhaps to simply mimic) womanliness.

6 When Charles Manson and his followers moved to the Spahn Ranch in the San Fernando Valley, they founded their cult compound. The release of The Beatles' so-called "White Album" in 1968 triggered the cult's Helter Skelter murder spree—named after a famous track on said LP. Manson believed that the song prophesized an impending race war. According to him, this conflict would explode in the summer of 1969, when blacks would slaughter whites wholesale in a racial genocide; with his clan being spared this fate, as they would stay literally underground hiding-out in a city of gold in Death Valley.

7 In 2008, a former FBI agent asserted that some members of the Hell's Angels had conspired to murder Jagger in retribution for The Stones' lack of support for them following the infamous concert, and also for the negative portrayal of the Angels in the film. *[Like a gang of lawless thugs could be depicted as anything else but! – SF.]* The conspirators reportedly used a boat to approach a residence where Jagger was staying on Long Island, New York; the plot failing when the boat nearly got sunk by a storm.

8 During the same period, other stars also got embroiled into the enveloping fabric of this occultism/witchcraft "chic". Peter Fonda and Warren Oates encountered your archetypal black-robed devil worshipers in Jack Starrett's **RACE WITH THE DEVIL**

(1975), and that same year even Ernest Borgnine played a diabolist cult leader in Robert Fuest's **THE DEVIL'S RAIN**, whose congregation also included William Shatner and John Travolta (Borgnine would go on to play another crazed cult leader in Wes Craven's **DEADLY BLESSING** [1981, USA]). Burgess Meredith, Ava Gardner and Sylvia Miles would also immerse themselves in sinister supernatural shenanigans for Michael Winner's **THE SENTINEL** (1977, USA), which sparked some controversy for casting genuine deformed human extras as denizens of Hell come to Earth.

9 The whole Amityville charade began with Jay Anson's *The Amityville Horror: A True Story*, published in September 1977. Actually a hoax pulled by lawyer William Weber and George and Kathy Lutz, the truth has never so solidly stood in the way of a good story. Further sensationalized by Anson, details changed between reprinted editions, and flaws can be traced to erroneous household damage and fabricated police involvement. Even the Lutz's claim of demonic hoofprints in the snow would have been difficult to prove when weather records showed there had been no snowfall.

10 During Radio 4's *Houses of Horror* (2015), the astute observation is made that the difference between Hammer and their rival Amicus was that the latter's dour, modern-day settings were what remained after the former's big-bosomed damsels and mist-enveloped castles had evaporated from your romantic mind's eye. Amicus would fold in 1977, after reinventing itself for a triptych of family-oriented fantasy adventures (i.e., **THE LAND THAT TIME FORGOT** [1974], **AT THE EARTH'S CORE** [1976], and **THE PEOPLE THAT TIME FORGOT** [1977], all directed by Kevin Connor and starring Doug McClure), and classic-era Hammer finally concluded two years later with a largely uninspired remake of Hitchcock's **THE LADY VANISHES** (1979).

11 By 1976, Bowie's cocaine-fueled lifestyle would lead to an infamously wayward interview in *Playboy*, where he proclaimed himself "the only alternative for the Premier in England" through Fascism. In the piece, Bowie thanks drugs for "fucking him up nicely" and ultimately brands rock'n'roll as depressing, sterile and evil. Obliquely, in 1984, the musician was offered the role of Sharaz Jek in *Doctor Who*'s "The Caves of Androzani" serial (aired March 8th to 16th, 1984), only to decline because of touring commitments; the part was eventually filled by actor Christopher Gable instead.

12 So-called "Theoretical Liberation" publications such as *Spare Rib* developed the movement in a similar fashion to how the magazine itself was compiled. Founded by Rosie Boycott and Marsha Rowe, *Spare Rib* evolved with changes that included increasing current affairs coverage, becoming a work collective, and providing more direct dialogues with their readers.

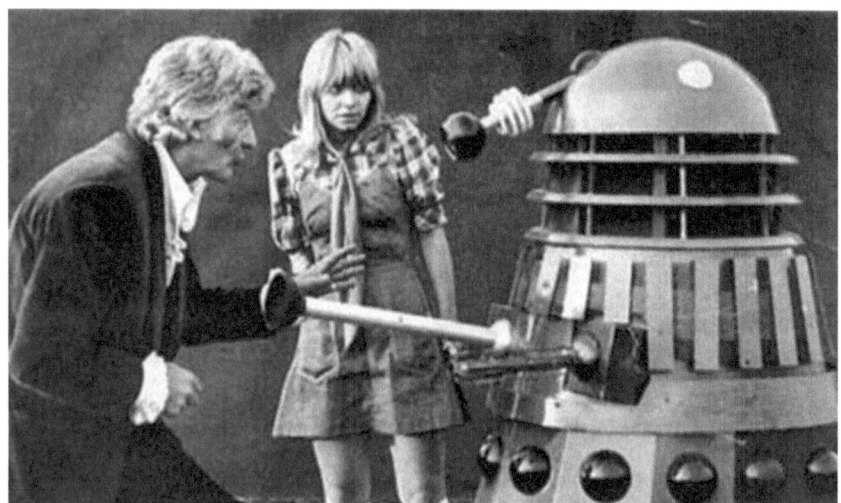

John Pertwee as The Doctor and Katy Manning as his companion Jo face off with one of the Daleks, the rogue Timelord's oldest foes

13 Manning would notoriously appear in *Girl Illustrated* Volume 8, #10 (September 1977) wrapped suggestively around a Dalek while wearing nothing but a pair of knee-boots (*"Exclusive! TV's Katy Strips"*). These boots were actually given to the actress by comedian Derek Nimmo as an opening night gift for her appearing opposite him in the West End farce *Why Not Stay for Breakfast?*). Further cashing-in, the actress also appeared tastefully quasi-nude in the British edition of *Penthouse*.

14 Nigel Kneale's disdain for *Doctor Who* has been well-documented because of its plethora of *Quatermass* "homages." But the writer's dislike can also be attributed to its perceived mistreatment of children, or as Kneale put it, "bombing the tinies with insinuations of doom and terror".

15 Kneale's teleplay popularized the theories of H.H. Price and Thomas Charles Lethbridge, who speculated that electrical mental impressions released during highly emotional or traumatic events can be "stored" in moist rocks and other items, and "replayed" under certain conditions.

16 Based on a new script by Matthew Graham and directed by usual movie director Peter Strickland (of **BERBERIAN SOUND STUDIO** [2012, UK] *et al*), on October 30th of 2015, BBC Radio 4 broadcast a new audio-only version of "The Stone Tape" as part of its *Fright Night* series for Halloween (double-billed with an all-new anglicized radio dramatization of Hideo Nakata's hit theatrical horror feature **RING** [リング / *Ringu*, 1998, Japan]). The cast for the new version of "Tape" included Romola Garai (in the Jill Greeley part), Julian Rhind-Tutt, Julian Barratt, as well as Jane Asher, star of the original TV version, this time playing Mrs. Greeley, the heroine's mother.

17 The opening scene of "The Green Death", in which Global Chemicals kingpin Stevens (Jerome Willis) stands before miners and brandishes a piece of paper while proclaiming about "wealth in our time" mimics Neville Chamberlain's famous "peace for our time" speech regarding the 1938 Munich Agreement.

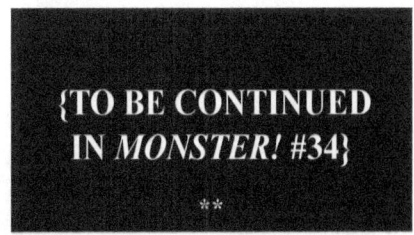

{TO BE CONTINUED IN *MONSTER!* #34}

**

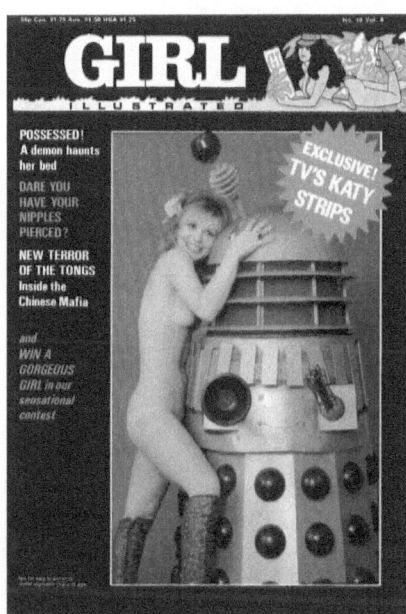
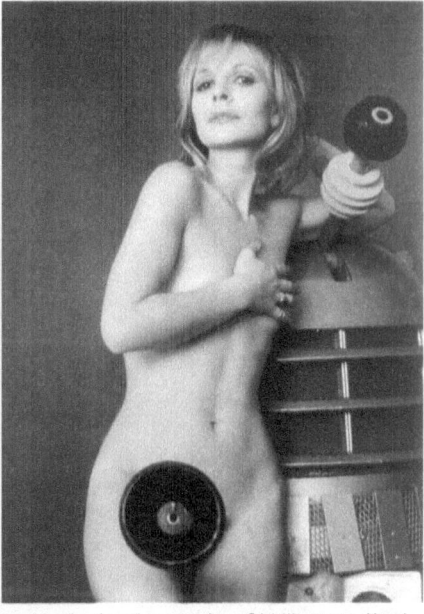

Katy "Jo Grant" Manning's chaste nudie spread in the local magazine *Girl Illustrated* had Brit fanboys all a-titter back in the 1970s!

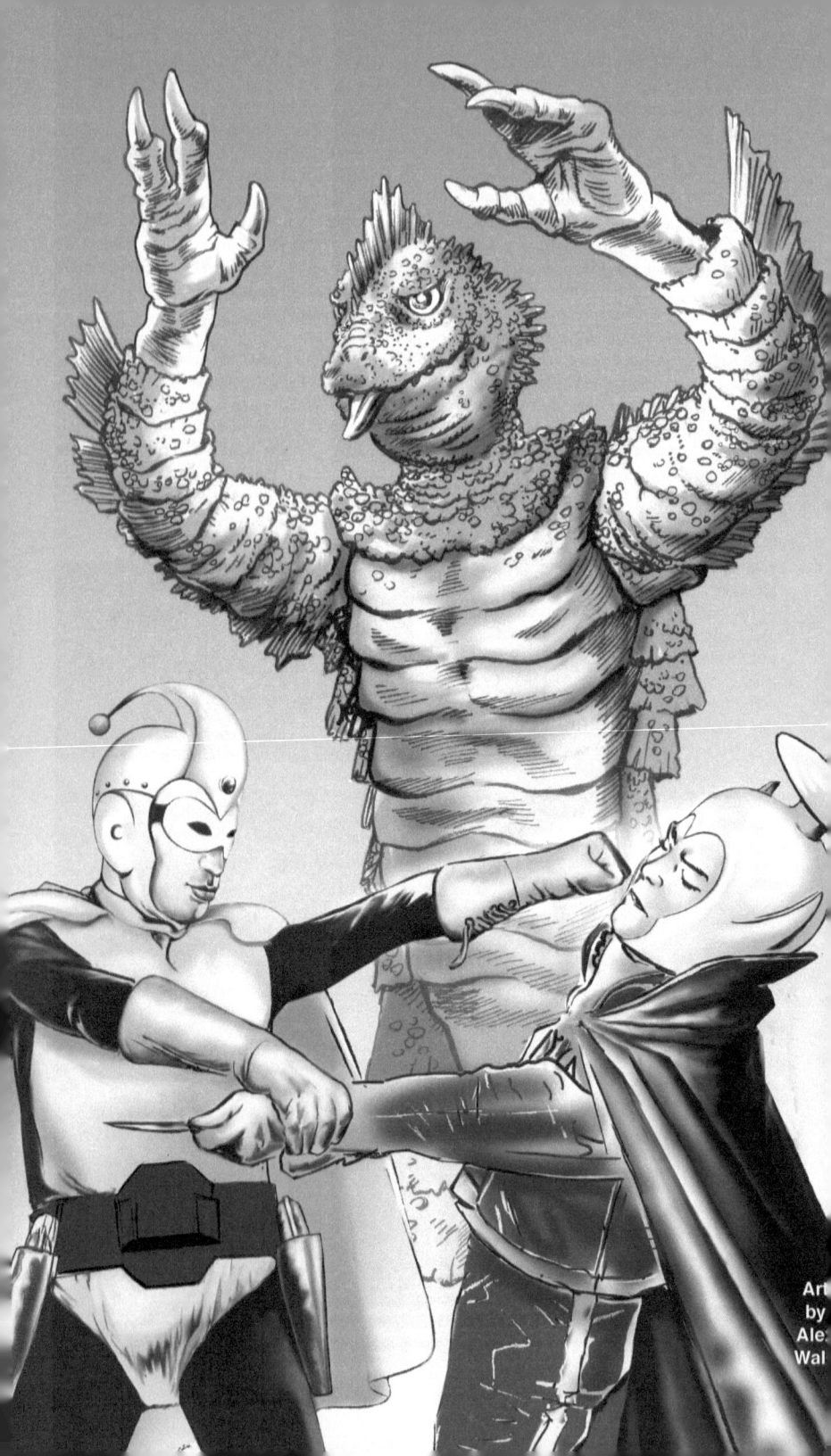

The "Superman" of Japan –
NATIONAL KID
(ナショナルキッド / *Nashonaru Kiddo*)

by Dan Ross

As the show's jaunty theme jingle tells us, *"He's faster than a jet aircraft! Stronger than the steel! The invincible knight of peace and justice... National Kid!"*

Yes, that's National Kid, *not* Superman...*a different super-strong alien visitor to Earth who helps defend we puny humans against invasions from both outer and inner space. Like more than one other Japanese TV program of the time,* National Kid *was inspired by George Reeves' American-made* Adventures of Superman *series (Warner Bros. Television Distribution, 1952-58). But unlike the other like-inspired programs and even* Superman *itself, the NK series, thanks to the strong sponsorship of Matsushita's National brand, had sufficient budget with which to create untoppable special effects, plus limitless amounts of unbridled imagination at its disposal besides.*

We'll dig into the effects, people, production and storylines of National Kid *shortly (pun intended), but first let's talk about...shorts...as in short pants...*

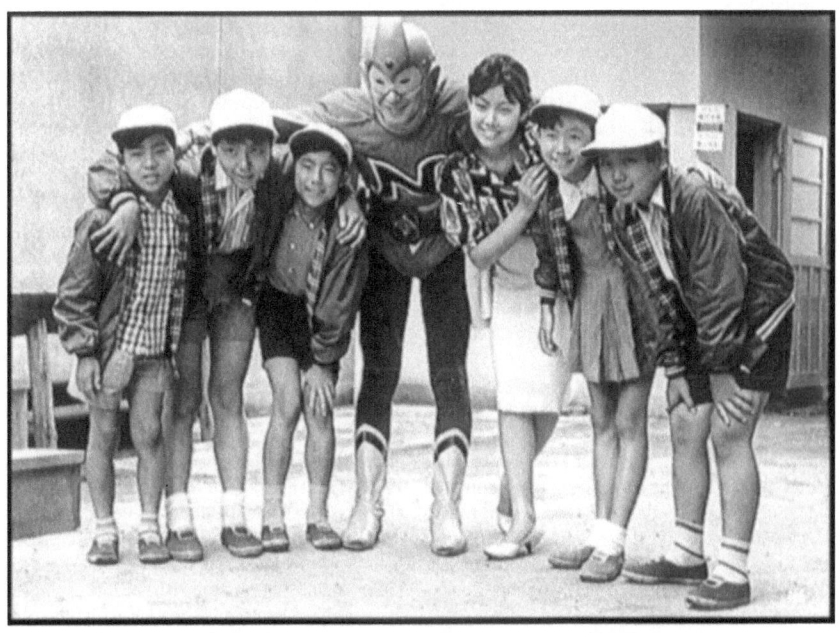

Super 7: National Kid and... *KIDS*! Our hero takes pause from his busy schedule for a photo-op with members of The Boys' (and Girls'!) Detective Club

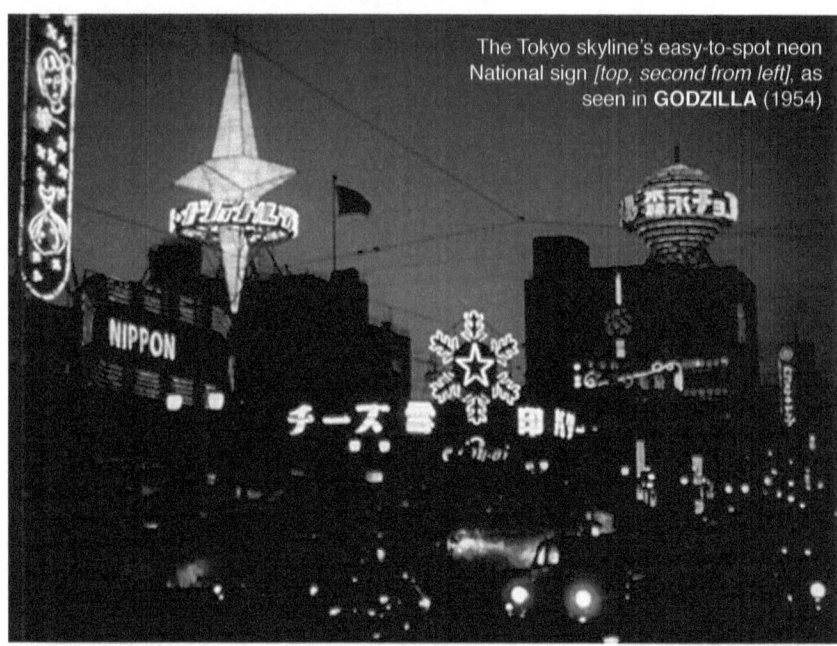

The Tokyo skyline's easy-to-spot neon National sign *[top, second from left]*, as seen in **GODZILLA** (1954)

Yeah, that's right: *SHORTS*! In the Japanese sci-fi hero *tokusatsu* ("special effects") shows from around this time period, the boys are all seen wearing (fairly) short shorts; not in any way "bootypants", you understand, but not exactly knee-length either. Why do I mention this? Upon occasion I've talked to people who thought this was a weird proclivity in such locally-produced movies as those in the *Starman* (1957-59) and *Prince of Space* (1958) series, and **INVASION OF THE NEPTUNE MEN** (宇宙快速船 / *Uchū Kaisokusen*, 1961, D: Koji Ota), *et cetera*. Well, it occurs in the TV shows too; possibly the first one, in 1960, being Fuji TV's *Boys' Detective Club* (少年探偵団/ *Shonen Tantei-dan*). That series was based on mystery writer Edogawa Rampo's eponymous series of novels for young adults, which ran from 1936 until 1962. But we'll come back to Rampo and his teen detectives later...

Shorts for men and boys appeared in a fashion magazine in 1945, and the new "look" took off like wildfire from there in Japan. They were sold off the racks at department stores, mainly in the big cities. Strangely, shorts became a sort of act of snobbery by the post-war *nouveau riche* urban fashionistas against their perceived social "lessers", with snooty rich kids in shorts looking down their long toffee-noses upon poor penniless country bumpkins with their unhip long pants. Eventually the prices leveled-out, and shorts went from an urban designer fashion fad in the late '40s and spread out into the countryside like wildfire during the '50s and '60s. All the 'cool' boys everywhere were now wearing shorts (while the girls *still* wore skirts!). So now you know. And don't be like those folks I've talked to who get all *freaky* about those boys in short-shorts, okay? Because we have them in spades on *National Kid*! Besides, if you lived through the 1970s in the US, you probably had a pair or two of very short gym shorts or cut-offs yourself. It was just a sign of the times. But enough of this fashion talk already!

To continue with our main topic, the Matsushita Electric Industrial Co., Ltd. (松下電器産業株式会社 / *Matsushita Denki Sangyō Kabushiki-gaisha*) started out in 1918 producing electric lamps for bicycles, and later expanded into electronics. In the 1950s they launched a new brand named Panasonic in order to hopefully become more accessible to the North American market, and eventually in Europe too. Years before the ubiquitous Panasonic line made its debut, though, in 1927 Matsushita started a brand called "National". This line manufactured radios, flashlights, televisions, rice-cookers, and hundreds of other household electrical appliances as well. Panasonic eventually arose from Matsushita trying to make inroads into the US market with their National brand, but there was already a different and well-established company called National in the

States, and that company wasn't interested in any brand-name confusion with a foreign competitor.

With the dawning of that world-altering decade the 1960s, the Age of Science was really churning in Japanese pop culture, especially in primary schools. Hence, Matsushita decided to cash-in on kids' ever-increasing interest in scientific matters. Who knew, maybe the kids of the day would grow up to become the engineers of tomorrow...perhaps even for Matsushita themselves? The company's idea was to engage with children through their 'kid-friendly' mascot (a tried-and-trusted sales tactic the world over to this day). They commissioned publishing giant Kodansha, Ltd. (株式会社講談社 / *Kabushiki-gaisha Kōdansha*) to create a manga drawn by Kazumine Daiji (一峰大二), who would later adapt many a *tokusatsu* series to the manga medium, including several *Ultraman* (ウルトラマン / *Urutoraman*) series, as well as *Denjin Zaborger* (電人ザボーガー / *Denjin Zabōgā*, a.k.a. "Electroid Zaborger"), *Tetsujin Tiger 7* (鉄人タイガーセブン / *Tetsujin Taigā Sebun*, a.k.a. "Iron Man Tiger 7"), *Nanairo Kamen* (七色仮面, a.k.a. "Seven Color Mask"), *Fuun Lion Maru* (風雲ライオン丸 / *Fūun Raionmaru*, a.k.a. "Storm Cloud Lion Maru") and *Mirāman* (ミラーマン, a.k.a. "Mirrorman").

Toei TV was commissioned to produce a science fiction drama based on Matsushita's 1955-created mascot National Kid; one which showcased plenty of cool, 'sciencey' gadgets. It's a baffling coincidence (!!!) that these gadgets were—each and every one of them—National-brand products that you could purchase at any local department store. In fact, out in the middle of Missouri, here in the U.S. of A., my Dad, a collector of all sorts of radios, TVs and cameras, had the very same "Magic Radio" model that National Kid gives to the Boys' Detective Club, which they use to call him in case of emergencies. That was the National T-11, six-transistor portable radio. The Kid's "Erolya" ray gun, meanwhile, was a National flashlight with a pistol-grip handle: or the "Kid-Flash," as it was labeled on the store shelves. Other such television and radio props peppered the series.

The creation of the mascot who wound up with both a manga and a TV series in order to promote National's brand was something I actually had a hard time finding any similar analog for in Western culture. Sure, there were the Geiko "Cavemen" that started out as one of the insurance agency's ongoing commercials, which got popular enough to have its own series, for a

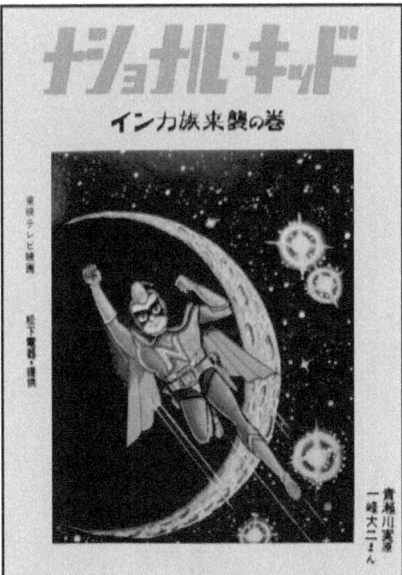

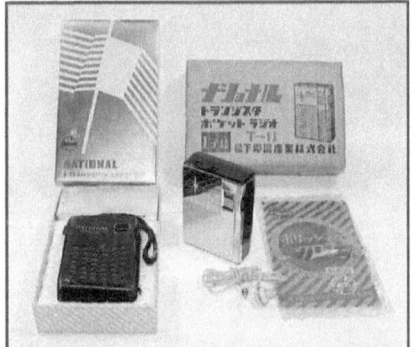

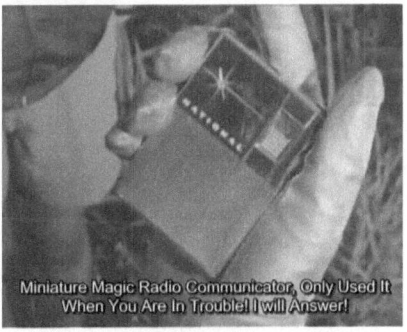

Top: *National Kid Volume 1*: "Invasion of the Incas" (Showa 35) manga. **Center:** National's "Magic Radio" in real life: the T-11, six-transistor radio. **Above:** The hi-tech transceiver that National Kid gives to the kids of the Boys' Detective Club in case of emergencies...and there are *plenty* of those!

Dan Ross　　　　National Kid • ナショナルキッド / *Nashonaru Kiddo*

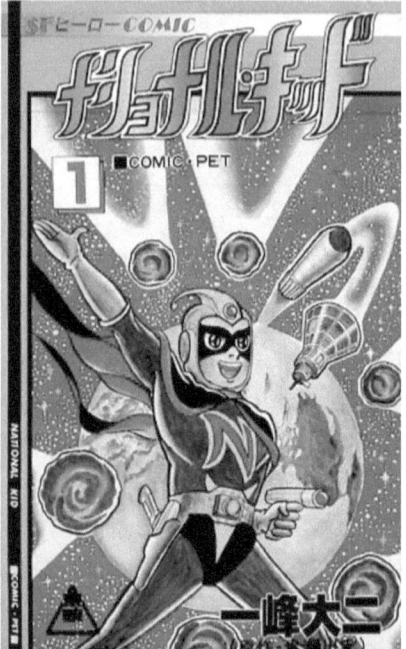

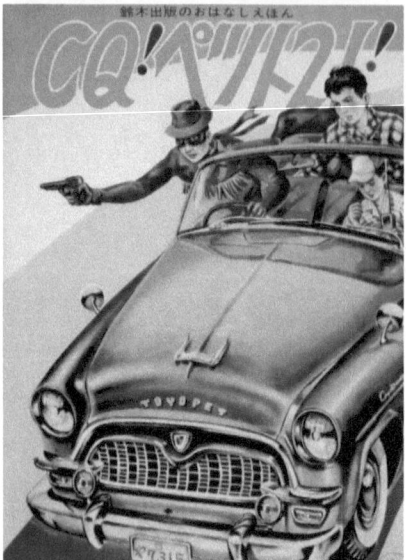

Top: *National Kid Volume 1* (art by Ichinagi Daiichi). **Above:** *CQ! PET 21!* (CQ! ペット 21!) tie-in kids' picture book, *circa* 1960

own, spawning oodles more spinoff merchandizing besides. That is perhaps the closest comparable marketing scheme to *National Kid*'s that I can think of. *NK* was a corporate mascot, which went beyond simple branding iconography and branched-off into television, comic books and other merchandise to help sell still *more* products.

In the world of Japanese brand name-based media properties, we can actually find a few others which closely relate to the *National Kid* marketing strategy. Senkosha's (producer of *Gekkō Kamen* a.k.a. Moonlight Mask [see *Monster! #32*, pp.40-67]) 1967 *tokusatsu* entry *Lightspeed Esper* (光速エスパー / *Kousoku Esupa*) was the mascot of Toshiba, starting in 1964. In 1966 it was adapted to manga by *Esper* designer Asano Riji, then later taken-over by legendary artist Leiji Matsumoto (of *Captain Harlock* [キャプテン・ハーロック / *Kyaputen Hārokku*], *Space Battleship Yamato* [宇宙戦艦ヤマト / *Uchū Senkan Yamato*], *Galaxy Express 999* [銀河鉄道999 (スリーナイン) / *Ginga Tetsudō Surī Nain*] *et al*). Following the manga, in '67 the TV series came about, all at the behest of Toshiba, who wanted to get their mascot as much air time as possible. Esper was the child of a couple of human scientists who were accidentally killed by aliens when the latter crash-landed on Earth. To in at least some way compensate, the mournful aliens took-over the parents' bodies in order to keep young Hikaru Azuma from being orphaned. The upside of this is that their alien super-intelligence was able to create a spacesuit for Hikaru which gave him superhuman powers of strength and flight through sea, air and space (a bit like Marvel's Iron Man). As Esper, he repelled the likes of alien invaders and rogue planets on collision courses with Earth. This planetary collision thing happened more than once, and in more than one such *tokusatsu* series at that…what's *up* with all those rogue planets zooming in out of deep space from every which way?!

Another instance involving a similar marketing strategy was the super-obscure—and now possibly lost—1960 series *CQ! PET 21!* (*CQ!* ペット 21!). The title of the show was literally the ham radio call-sign for "Black Mask" (no relation to the Jet Li movie character, needless to say!), a Green Hornet-like hero who bombs about in a Toyopet Crown convertible. In fact, almost all the cars seen in the show were of a Toyota make of some type, usually the latest models on the market, such as the RS 20 series Crown and the PT 20 Corona. This was a series sponsored by… you guessed it— *Toyota!* Some cross-pollination took place in *CQ*, as there was such an emphasis on ham radio usage

small while. But it wasn't originally intended as a TV series and the Caveman weren't company mascots (that would be the Geiko Gecko!). Then there's "The California Raisins", which were created to advertise the California Raisin Advisory Board and went on to have a cartoon show of their that it succeeded in boosting interest in radio communications; most of the blogs I've found relating to viewers watching the show tend to mention them buying ham radios as a result of it.

In 1954, during the early planning stages of adopting National Kid as a mascot, he had a couple of different names. He started off as Hyper Kid to specifically sell Hyper Dry Batteries. Super Kid was also suggested, because, as with the first televised Japanese *tokusatsu* hero, the aforementioned Gekkō Kamen, Kid was even-more-obviously inspired by the George Reeves version of Superman. Significantly more, in fact. In the end, National Kid was a super-strong alien from another galaxy, who could fly and whom bullets didn't affect, and he also had specific weaknesses to a Kryptonite-like element (a type of radiation called "Radiuex X"), which his enemies could and would utilize against him, thus weakening his powers considerably and rendering him easier to deal with. Plus he wore a spandex bodysuit, a cape *and* had a big red, curving stylized "N" emblazoned on his chest—which, not coincidentally, if it was turned sideways sorta-kinda looked quite a bit like a reversed "S" (for you-know-who!).

When Toei's television wing (東映テレビプロダクション / *Toei Terebi Purodakushon*) was brought onboard to produce the series, they hired seasoned movie industry veterans to be their showrunners. From Shintoho Co. Ltd. (新東宝株式会社 / *Shintōhō Kabushiki Kaisha*) producer Nosaka Kazuma (野坂和馬) and director Akasaka Nagiyoshi (赤坂長義), who had both previously worked on the *Starman* (スーパージャイアンツ / *Supa Giantsu*) movies, got the series started. In the special effects department, Jun Koike (小池淳) blazed a groundbreaking trail in televised effects work and also directed two-and-a-half of the show's final story arcs. This top trio hit the ground running, creating an ultra-high-quality program with effects that surpassed their *Superman* inspiration, and even exceeded those seem in Japan's own theatrical *Starman* (スーパージャイアンツ / *Sūpā Jaiantsu*, a.k.a. "Super Giant") movies. *[Speaking of which, we were hoping that the well-suited Mr. Ross might be up to tackling an article about said* tokusatsu *series for inclusion in a future issue of* Monster! *(Hint-hint! {Wink}. But no pressure you understand, though, Dan! ☺) – SF.]*

It helped that Matsushita threw hay-bales of

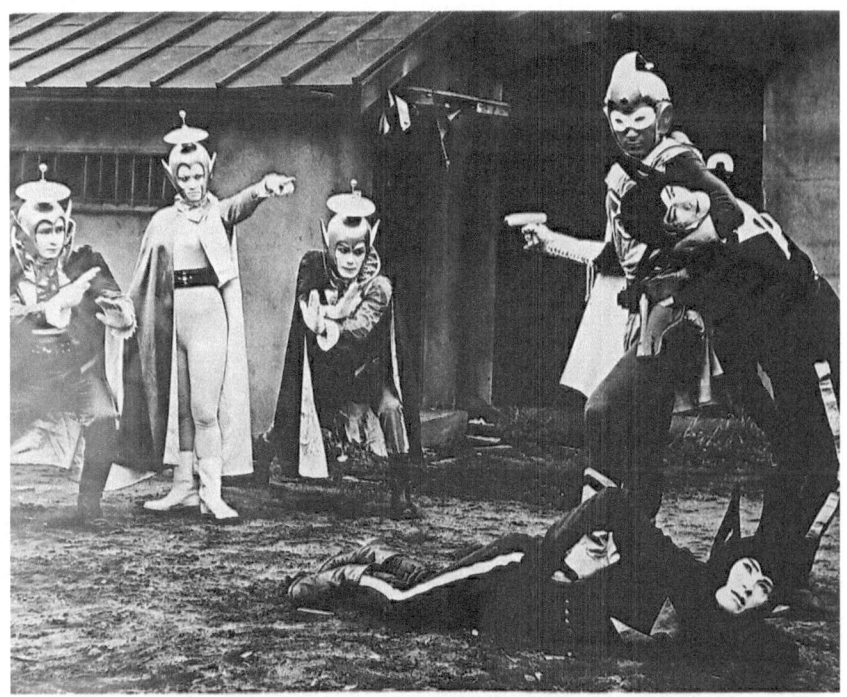

All In A Day's Work: National Kid was used to having a lot on his plate to deal with. Here he's got his hands—and feet!—full dealing with an alien villainess (Akutsu Katsuko) and her Inca Venusian minions. But does he look *worried* to you?! (Note the trusty "Kid Flash" pistol in his fist)

Dan Ross   National Kid • ナショナルキッド / *Nashonaru Kiddo*

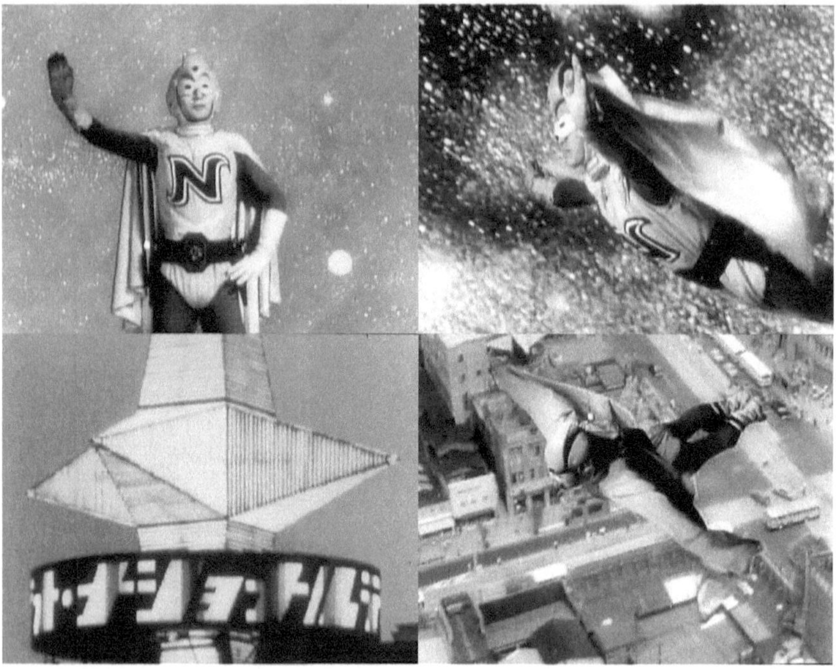

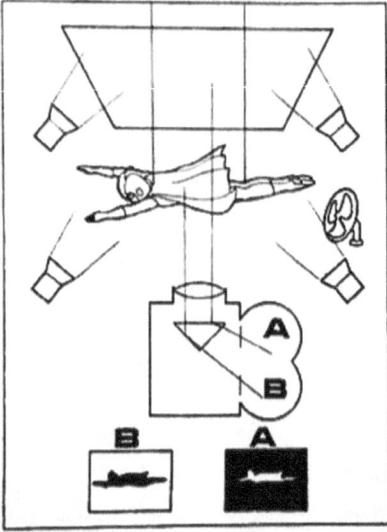

Top & Center Left: National Kid waves to his fans against a twinkly/sparkly star-field during the opening titles, and another shot of the National company's landmark neon sign. **Top Right & Center Right:** Two shots of our high-flying hero airborne, one in outer space, the other well within Earth's atmosphere. **Above:** A super-simplified diagram of NK's flying rig, from Japan's *Uchusen* magazine (Volume 4, 1980).

money at the project, with it being the most expensive series produced at the time, boasting a budget of ¥1.5-million (yen) per episode, while the average contemporary episode of a domestic Japanese television series was typically less than half to a mere third of that cost. So the increased production values were highly apparent.

The biggest deal the producers publicized with this new special effects show was the flying. The first story arc simply used rear-screen projection to pull-off their flying effects. Though it was quite well-done, the next story would instead utilize an innovative new adaptation of classic Hollywood camera technology. For this, the effects team rigged-up a camera to do an all-in-one, single-shot traveling matte process to composite National Kid and various flying aliens/spaceships onscreen against pre-filmed backgrounds. Because of my lack of Japanese *kanji* reading skills, I needed to parse-down the text and diagrams (from an article in *Uchusen* [宇宙船 / "Spaceship"; formerly known as *Space Magazine Uchusen*] Vol. 4, 1980), and gave that information to special effects industry veteran Jim Aupperle to decipher what exactly it was that Toei did to make this happen:

"It wasn't a sodium matte, which requires a very special prism. They weren't even using the Technicolor three-strip camera. The TV show

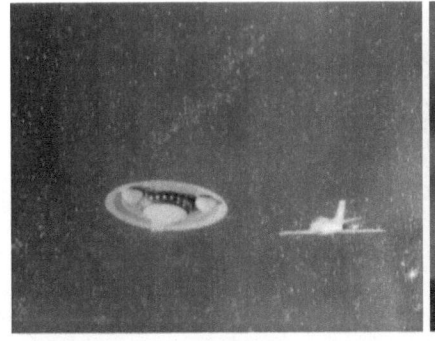
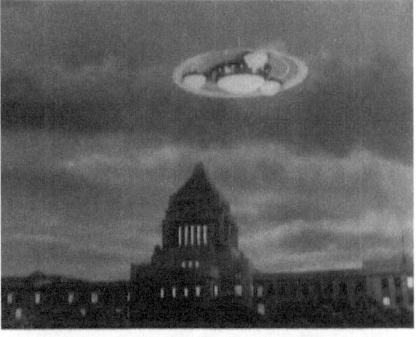

was in B&W, so color film was not even a consideration. They used an earlier two-color Technicolor camera, which was the color system throughout the 1920s silent films and into the early 1930s. That camera recorded only red and green through a prism and onto two strips of B&W film. Technicolor was able to get a very nice color combining the red and green (no blue), but since the TV show was in B&W, the National Kid *camera effects crew recorded the continuous-tone live-action on the red layer and the matte on the green layer. Very clever,* [I've] *never heard of anyone else using this..."*

A real in-camera traveling matte. This could likely be considered an early, analog version of the type of Chroma key process you see used in weather segments on the news.

Another standout achievement on *NK* was the superbly-blended background matte shots. Even more so than the flying effects, these matted-in backgrounds created a genuine sense of the fantastic. Multiple times throughout the show we see actors working within on-location scenery in the foreground, with some impressive object—such as a massive landed spaceship, say—visible in the background.

In other shots, such as flying saucers descending on Tokyo's National Diet Building (国会議事堂 / *Kokkai-gijidō*) or Paris, France's Arc de Triomphe, photographs of those landmarks were enlarged and used as flat (2-D), static backgrounds for the moving spaceship models to be superimposed upon. The lighting on the models was carefully adjusted so as to match the photos.

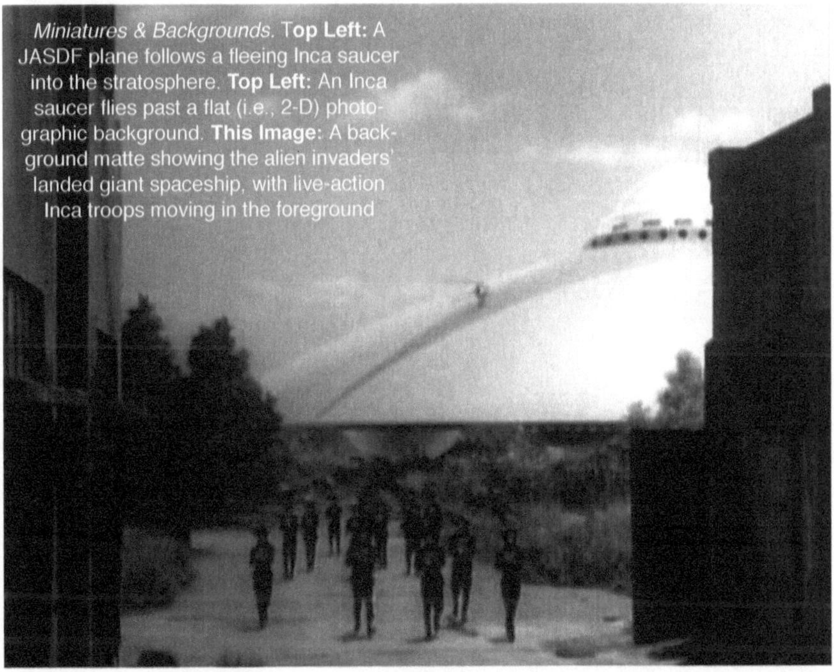

Miniatures & Backgrounds. **Top Left:** A JASDF plane follows a fleeing Inca saucer into the stratosphere. **Top Left:** An Inca saucer flies past a flat (i.e., 2-D) photographic background. **This Image:** A background matte showing the alien invaders' landed giant spaceship, with live-action Inca troops moving in the foreground

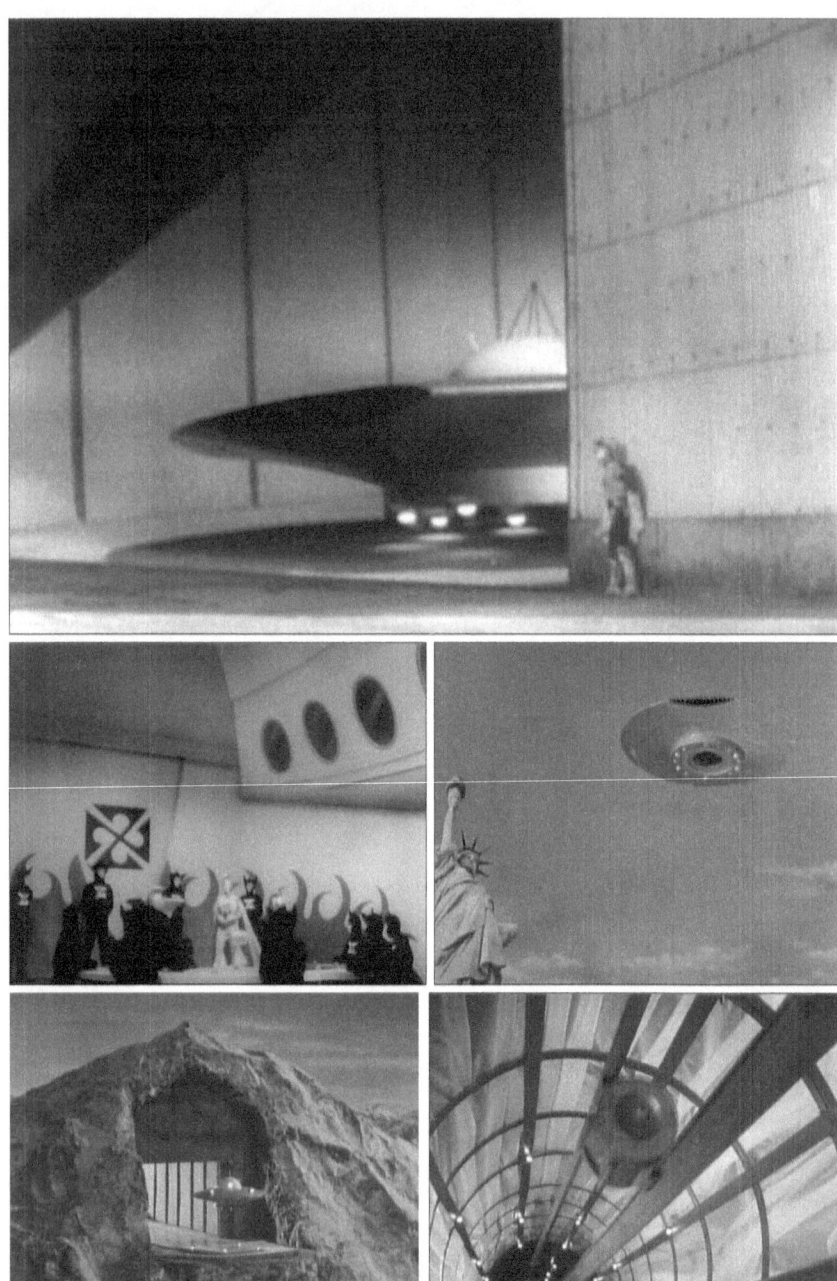

Top: An impressive matte shot showing a largescale set and full-size actor compositied with a background model saucer. **Center Left:** Spacious full-scale sets and mattes bring a real sense of size and scale to the Incas' mothership. **Center Right:** This evocative shot showing a Subterranean saucer flying past a famous foreign national monument resembles something right out of Harryhausen's **EARTH VS. THE FLYING SAUCERS** (1956). **Above Left:** The hidden entrance to the Subterraneans' lair. **Above Right:** Their hi-tech underground transportation tube sure is one handy way of zipping from A to B!

Rounding-out the stellar effects work was a whole battery of miniature sets, models, special props and costumes, the likes of which had never been seen on television before that time, and wouldn't be again for a good while afterwards. There were giant monsters (of both underwater and aboveground) varieties rampaging through miniaturized cities and subsea environments. In addition to various buildings rendered in miniature, we get an assortment of miniature spacecraft, steamships, submarines, automobiles, terrestrial military vehicles and jet planes, even an old sailing galleon, which included a full-scale mock-up of the deck used for shooting live-action scenes upon.

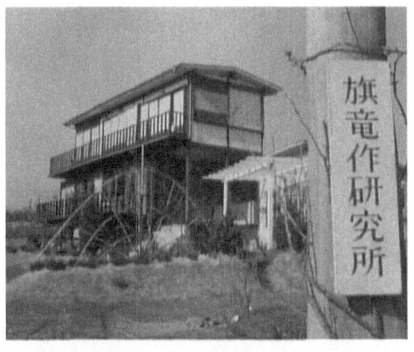

Notably, the spaceships were designed by the legendary Toru Narita (成田 亨), who made his mark working on **GODZILLA** (ゴジラ / *Gojira*, 1954) and other high-profile Toho *tokusatsu* movies. He would later work at Tsuburaya Pro (円谷プロダクション / *Tsuburaya Purodakushon*) creating monsters on various series, such as *Ultra-Q* (ウルトラQ / *Urutora Kyū*, 1965), *Ultraman* (ウルトラマン / *Urutoraman*, 1966), *Ultra Seven* (ウルトラセブン / *Urutora Sebun*, 1967) and *Mighty Jack* (マイティジャック / *Maiti Jakku*, 1968).

Additionally, there were large-scale sets of spaceship interiors and otherworldly cities constructed, as well as massive miniatures for other planets too. On Earth there were detailed miniature sets of rugged terrain, complete with twisting seaside roads and fantastical buildings. Altogether, it made for quite the impressive visual treat indeed!

In his foreword to the manga reprints of *National Kid*, novelist and fan guide author Yoshikazu Takeuchi (竹内 義和) points-out that it was intended for each chapter of the series to be dedicated to an enemy originating from a different elemental background: Earth, Sea and Sky...and—of course!—Space. The Venusian Incas were humanoid extraterrestrials who battled the JSDF and Kid in the skies over Japan; the Marine Devil Nelkon came from beneath the ocean; the Subterraneans

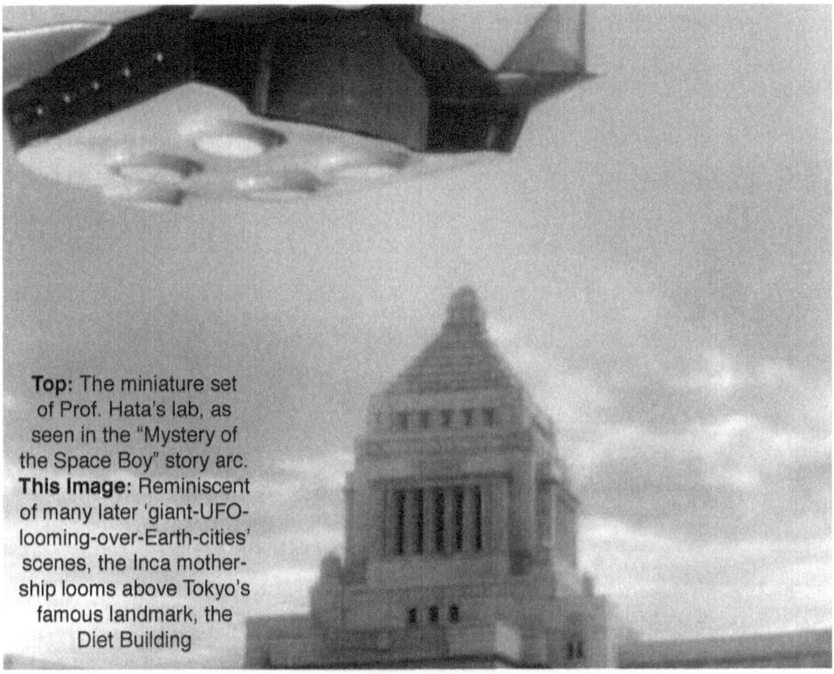

Top: The miniature set of Prof. Hata's lab, as seen in the "Mystery of the Space Boy" story arc. **This Image:** Reminiscent of many later 'giant-UFO-looming-over-Earth-cities' scenes, the Inca mothership looms above Tokyo's famous landmark, the Diet Building

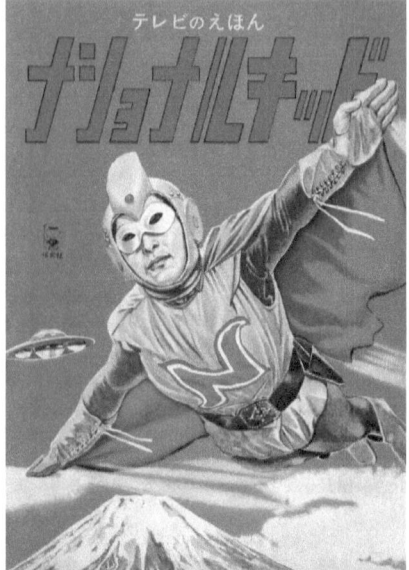

from under the Earth; and the extraterrestrial Zarokku, once again, hailed from outer space.

Along with visiting nature's elements, topical issues of the time were also addressed. The Venusians intent was to eradicate humanity because of our more-than-just-self-destructive species' reckless race towards nuclear armament, and for daring to turn our eye towards the stars and thus risk extending/expanding our kind beyond the boundaries of our own planet and thus risk jeopardizing life on others as well. Therefore, we are rightly regarded as a threat to spacefaring races of superior technological advancement and a heightened sense of what being 'civilized' truly means, much as we are in **THE DAY THE EARTH STOOD STILL** (both the 1951 and 2008 versions). While extraterrestrial emissary Klaatu gave we Earthlings fair advance warning and a chance to shape-up (if *not* ship-out), *NK*'s Venusians weren't having *any* of that pacifistic crap, and went straight for the kill right off the bat!

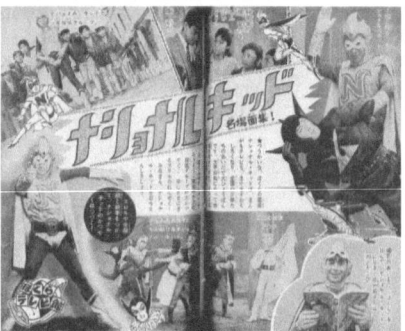

Also, the dangers of radiation are prevalent throughout the series. Like the oft-cited allegory of Godzilla representing the danger of atomic weapons, *National Kid*'s always-lurking radioactive dangers are a continual-if-subtle reminder of the metaphorical and literal fallout from the atom-bombings of Hiroshima and Nagasaki which put a horrible and inglorious end to Emperor Hirohito's megalomaniacal goals of Imperialist Japanese global conquest.

National Kid appeared on NET (株式会社日本教育テレビ / *Kabushiki-gaisha Nihon Kyōiku Terebi*)—now known as TV Asahi—from August 4th, 1960 until April 27th, 1961. Previous *tokusatsu* television shows by Toei were *Planet Prince* (遊星王子 / *Yūsei Ōji*, 1959), *Seven-Color Mask* (七色仮面 / *Nanairo Kamen*, 1959) and *Messenger of Allah* (アラーの使者 / *Ara no Shisha*, 1960).

The present series consists of 39 episodes, with four distinct story arcs. The entire run was fraught with turbulence, as storylines were either truncated or added-to depending on audience viewership, and suffered (or else were enhanced by) changes of director, as well as much of the juvenile cast, and even of the star of the show too.

The first story arc alone was intended to be 35 episodes, but due to low ratings and an early perception of the series as being unpopular, it was cut down to a mere thirteen episodes instead. The final story arc was set to run just five episodes. However, as the series gained in popularity, it was expanded-upon by another four episodes.

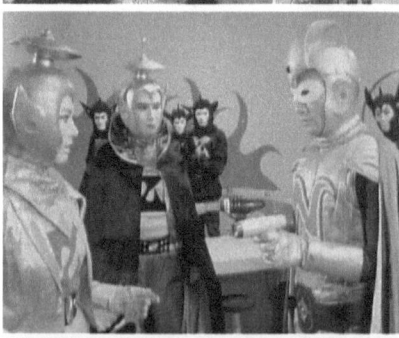

Top: One of the star attraction's home-grown *manga* volumes. **Center:** A period *National Kid* magazine spread. **Above:** During the "Attack of the Incas" story arc of the TV show, NK—his Kid Flash zapper firmly in hand!—inevitably faces-off against the villainous Venusian leaders at their hideout

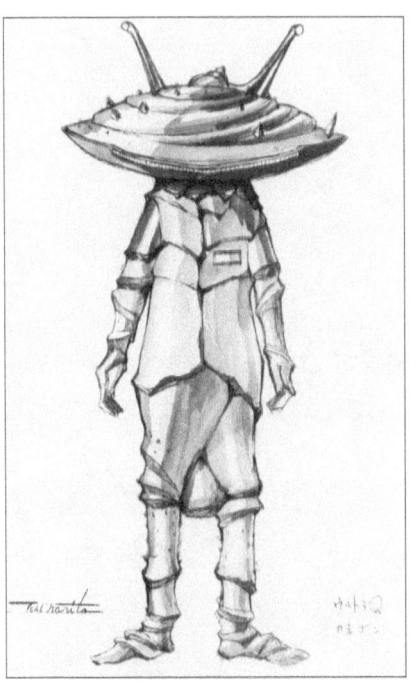
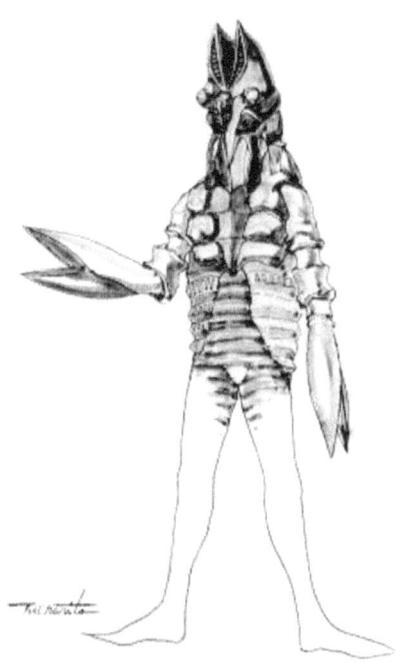
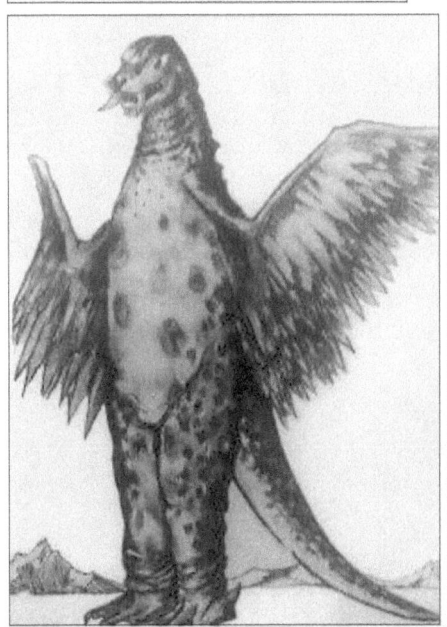
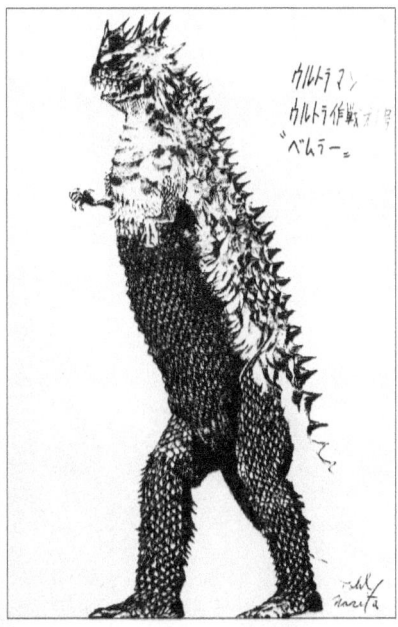

"Notably, the NK teleseries' spaceships were designed by the legendary Toru Narita (成田 亨), who made his mark working on **GODZILLA** (ゴジラ / *Gojira*, 1954) and other high-profile Toho tokusatsu movies." **This Page:** Narita's early conceptual sketches of various *kaijū* for later local TV shows. **Top Left:** The artist's rendition of Kanegon (カネゴン) for *Ultra Q* (ウルトラQ / *Urutora Kyū*). **Top Right:** Baltan (バルタン星人 / *Barutan Seijin*) for *Ultraman* (ウルトラマン / *Urutoraman*). **Above Left**: Peguila (ペギラ / *Pegira*) for *Ultra Q*. **Above Right**: Bemular a.k.a. Bemlar (ベムラー / *Bemurā*) for *Ultraman*

Dan Ross　　　National Kid • ナショナルキッド / *Nashonaru Kiddo*

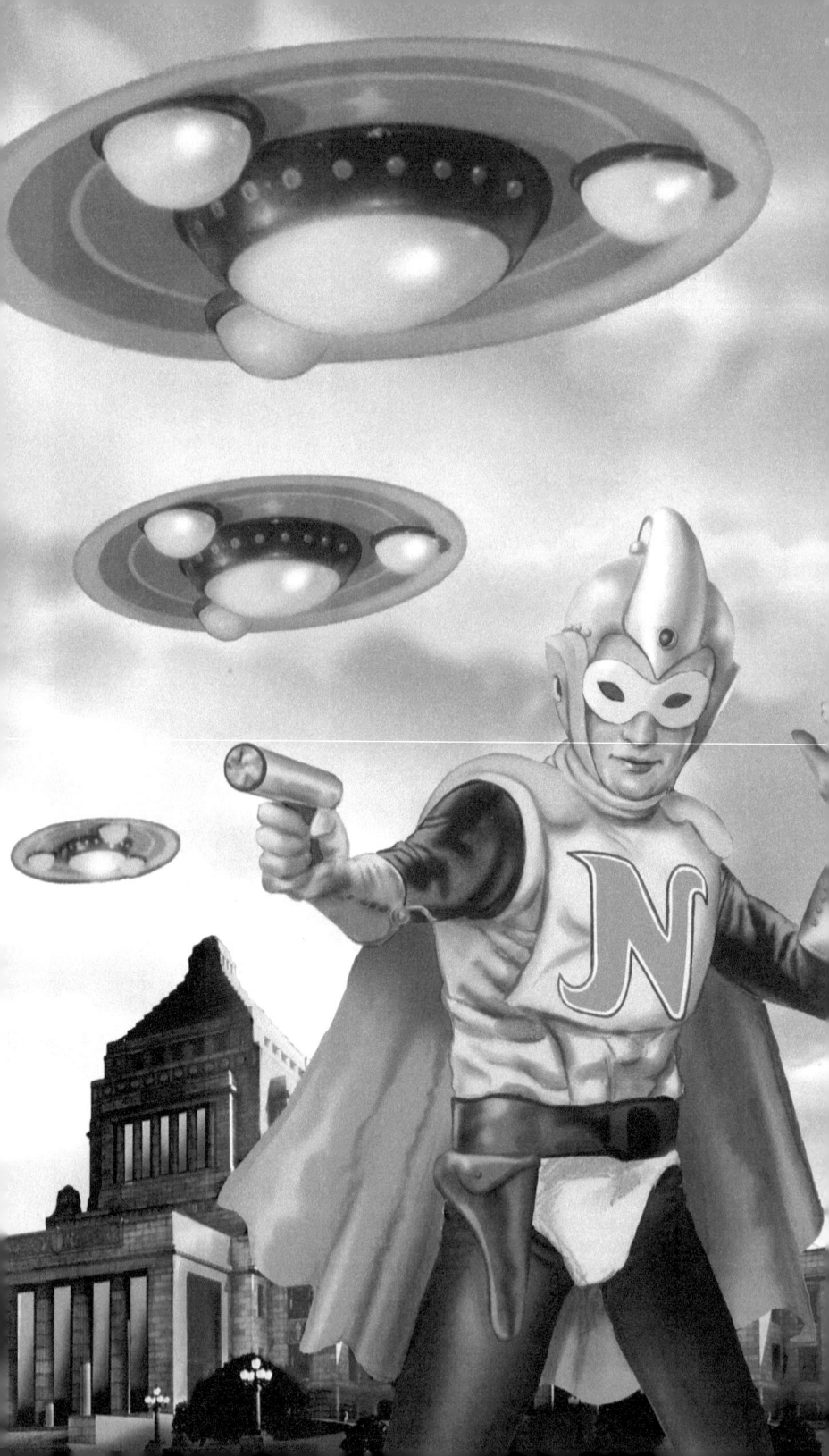

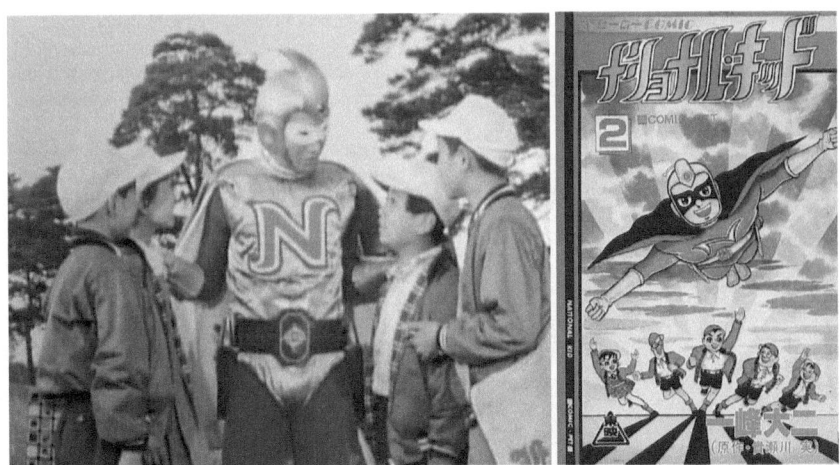

Above: The Kid and the kids of the BDC form a huddle to discuss their next plan of action, and the cover (art by Ichinagi Daiichi) to *National Kid Volume 2*

But due to the rollercoaster ride of the ratings, the instability of cast and crew and the extremely high production costs involved, it was decided to not continue things beyond the fourth story arc, and thus the series came to an end one episode short of hitting its fortieth.

While Akasaka Nagiyoshi directed the first story, effects director Jun Koike took over for most of the remaining production, with Norio Watanabe (渡辺成男) finishing-out directorial duties on the last four episodes of the series. Koike turned out to be the primary mover-'n'-shaker and heart of the show. Right from the beginning, a lot of the decisions about the direction of the production were left in his hands. It was his fascination with horror and mystery writer Edogawa Rampo (江戸川 乱歩)'s series of young adult-oriented adventures, *Boys' Detective Club* (少年探偵団 / *Shonen Tanteidan*), which introduced the similarly-named bunch of kids to *National Kid*. All the events of the series would revolve around this club of junior detectives (which, despite its name, included one or more girls at different times).

Rampo had two defining styles of writing within the 'hard-boiled' detective fiction genre, and he is primarily known worldwide for his darker, more adult-oriented novels and short stories, written in a style that is termed *Ero-Guro-Nansensu* ("Erotic, Grotesque Nonsense"). *Ero-guro* (エログロ) is a Japanese literary and media genre that emphasized eroticism and decadence. Many of Rampo's detective stories lived in this realm, which took standard mystery capers and pushed them over the line into fantasy and horror; dealing with crazed fetishes, and physical/sexual violence up to and including mutilation. I believe his darker subject matter could still shock and horrify even today's jaded audiences.

On the other hand, Rampo also wrote the juvenile-slanted, long-lived *Boys' Detective Club* (少年探偵団 / *Shōnen tantei dan*) series (totaling 26 books from 1936-1962), which dealt with a team of Hardy Boys-like teens getting into various adventures—and of course *mis*adventures!—that tended to veer-off into sci-fi or the outright supernatural. Detective Kogorō Akechi (明智 小五郎), who is featured in many of Rampo's *ero-*

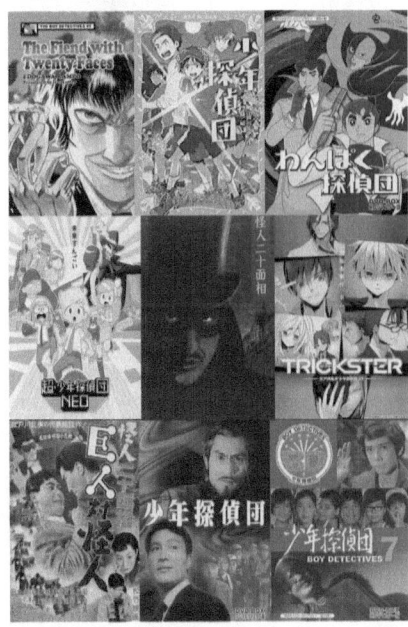

Dan Ross   National Kid • ナショナルキッド / Nashonaru Kiddo

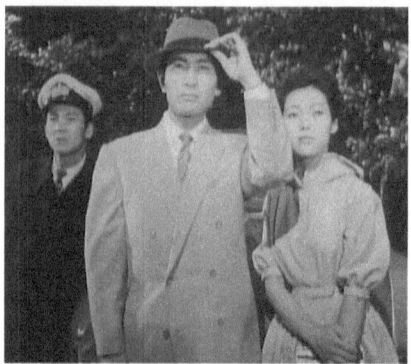

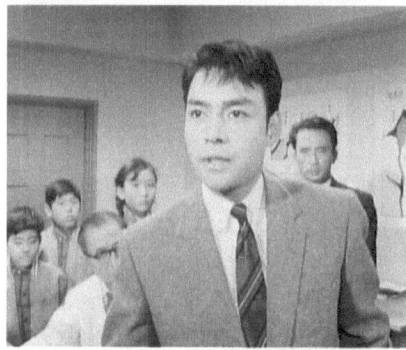

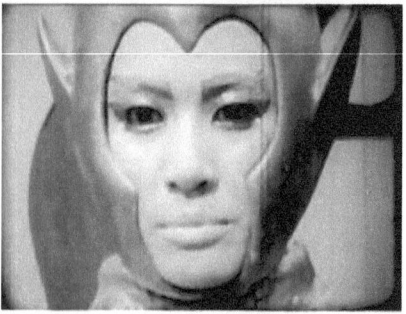

Goodies & Baddie! **Top:** Professor Hata #1, Kojima Ichiro. **Center:** Professor Hata #2, Tatsumi Hidetaro. **Above:** Akutsu Katsuko as the evil Inca Venusian 'matriarch'

thor Maurice Leblanc's Arsène Lupin character, with a whole lot of fellow Frenchmen Marcel Allain's and Pierre Souvestre's identity-switching supervillain Fantômas added for good measure).

In Japanese science fiction, detective, fantasy and horror genre films, television, comics and animation, there was and still is basically a whole cottage industry of adapting Rampo's teen sleuths, and in 2016 alone there were two completely different cartoon series adapting his stories.

On *National Kid*, Koike also experimented with the target age of the audience, lowering it from the teen/Junior High demographic for first story to younger elementary school-level in the second. As *NK*'s ratings rose, he 'aged-up' the demographic again, taking the opportunity to fold-in some of Rampo's trademark atmospheric spookiness in the process.

Kojima Ichiro (小島 一郎 [1924-1964]) starred as Ryusaku Hata (旗竜作) a.k.a. National Kid in the first two stories, to be replaced by Tatsumi Hidetaro (巽秀太郎 [1937-])—who had previously functioned as announcer on the show—for the final two. As the new director, Koike had remarked that Kojima was too thin and unhealthy-looking to be convincing in the part of the super-energetic/athletic hero. Soon after, Kojima transferred from Toei's TV division to their feature unit, where he immediately started working on film roles. In his stead, Tatsumi would take over for the rest of the series. After this, he would go on to act in a few movies, but primarily stuck with television in typical police and period dramas.

Ryusaku Hata (旗 流作) is a scientist, and the grandson of Professor Masakichi Hata, Director of the International Space Research Institute (incidentally, interestingly enough, a real-life Prof. Masakichi Hata, a former teacher at the Tokyo School of Fine Arts, who was still living at the time the show originally aired, is credited with designing the Imperial Japanese military's World War I Interallied Victory Medal, some 400,000 of which were minted and whose obverse depicted a relief of the Shinto warrior god Takemikazuchi [建御雷神], son of the deity Izanagi [いざなぎ]; there may or may not [?] be some connection between this particular Hata and the one in the TV show). In *NK*, Prof. Hata's grandson Ryusaku also 'moonlights' as tutor and mentor to the group of orphans who make up the Boys' Detective Group. In times of emergency, however, he disappears, then—within seconds after his alter-ego's disappearance—National Kid appears on the scene to save the day! (NK himself is in fact an alien

guro tales, makes frequent appearances in these young adult works, whose juvenile gumshoe protagonists are basically the 'Baker Street Irregulars' to Akechi's 'Sherlock Holmes'. It was not unusual throughout the series to see the boys run-up against some villainous cadre or other weird antagonist(s), or become embroiled in strange situations involving the likes of giant robotic beetles, an invisible man, flying saucers, haunted houses, atomic submarines along with Akechi's and the boys' nefarious arch-nemesis, known as "The Fiend with 20 Faces" (a master-of-disguise/crime in the 'gentleman thief' vein of French aufrom Andromeda who was sent to Earth to learn about human civilization, yet also functions as our champion/savior in the meantime.)

Obata Naoko (小畑尚子) is Ryusaku Hata's assistant, who also watches over the group of orphans, basically acting as their nanny of sorts. Ogura (nicknamed "Chaco") is played by adolescent actress Taichi Kiwako a.k.a. Shimura Taeko (太地喜和子 [1943-1992]), who had a highly prolific TV/movie career. Obata Yukio (小畑幸男) is Chaco's little brother, and the head of the Boys' Detective Group. He winds-up being played by three different actors throughout the run of the series. First played by Taku Fukushima (福島卓) in Parts 1 and 2, Koji Komori (小森甲二) in Part 3 and the first instalment of Part 4, and finally by Akira Asami (朝見朗) in the second half of Part 4. Other members of the Boys' Detective Group were similarly played by an array of different child actors throughout the series.

As is so typical of the format/formula, you can't have a masked vigilante hero show without some 'official' (and oftentimes overly-officious) representative of the legal establishment to fold into the mix. Detective Takeshi Takakura (高倉警部) from the Metropolitan Police Department relies on the intelligence and ingenuity of the Club to help him out on cases. Takakura is played by Koji Kawai (河合絋司), yet another actor who had an incredibly prolific career both in film and on television. Along with other *tokustatsu* shows such as *Kamen Rider* (仮面ライダー / *Kamen Raidā*), historical dramas, westerns, police stories, romance and several dozen more productions besides, he would play alongside Tatsumi Hidetaro (the second Ryusaku Hata/National Kid) in the long-running (from 1961-1977) TV crime drama series *Special Mobility Investigation Corps* (特別機動捜査隊 / *Tokubetsu kidō sōsa-tai*).

The dynamic of the *NK* story arcs tended to revolve around the boys and girl(s) looking for something fun and exciting to do and then unwittingly stumbling onto some insidious plot by aliens to do harm to the Earth. With their interest thus piqued, they would then snoop around and either get nabbed red-handed by or at least interfere to some degree in the would-be invaders/interlopers' plans. National Kid would invariably 'just happen' to show up in

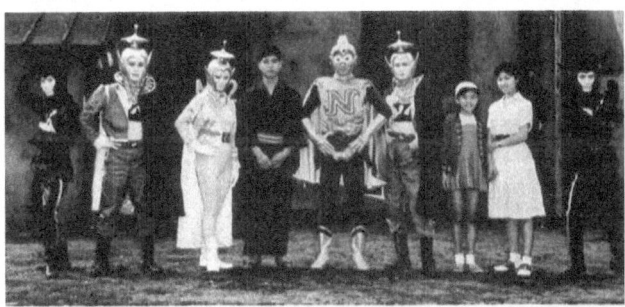
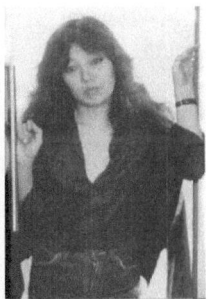
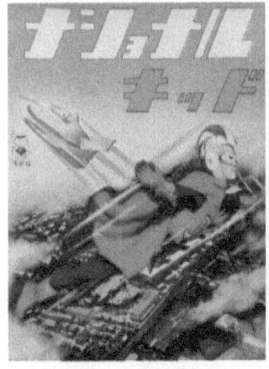
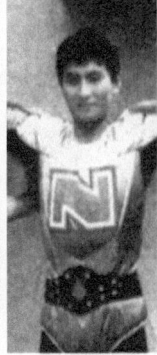
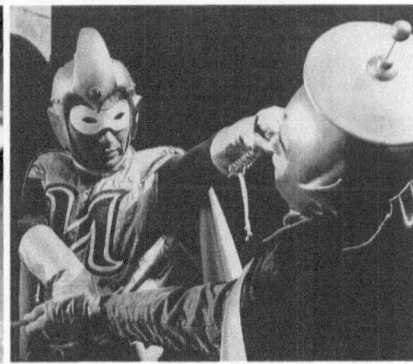

Clockwise, from Top Left: *National Kid*'s cast members line up for a group shot; actress Shimura "Chaco" Taeko later in her short life, *circa* the '70s (born in 1943, she died in 1992); NK much prefers to put his fist in a baddie's face rather than his foot in his own mouth; a rare 'unmasked' candid shot of NK #2 Kojima Ichiro in his costume, courtesy of the Japanese deep web; and a tie-in kiddies' book for the show

Dan Ross   National Kid • ナショナルキッド / *Nashonaru Kiddo*

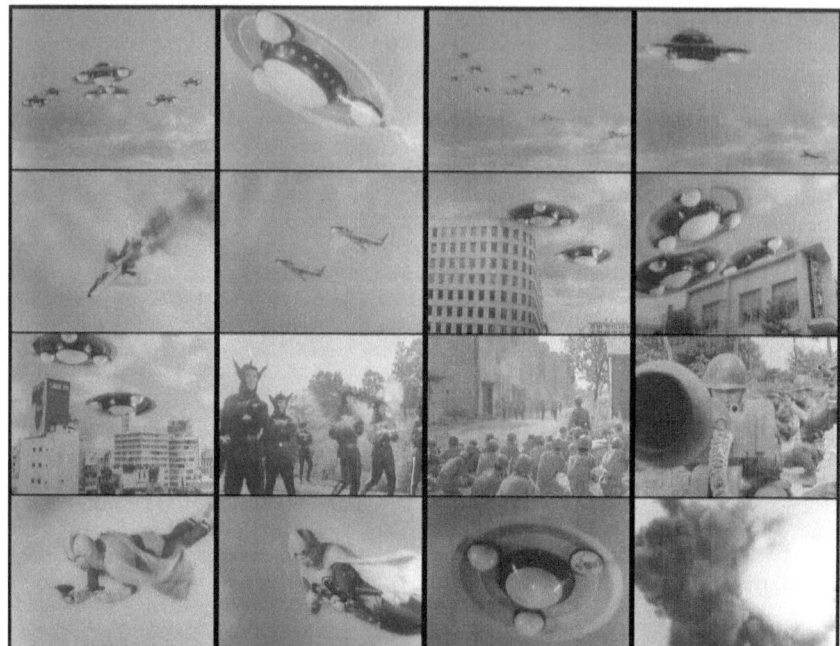

Above: This mad montage of random screen-captures well illustrates the spectacular fun to be had during the action-packed grand finale of *NK*'s 13-episode "Attack of the Incas" adventure

the proverbial nick of time to save them from the bad guys' dastardly machinations. A few episodes in, National Kid would present the group with the aforementioned "Magic Radio" so they could thereafter direct him to scenes of battle before they wind up getting themselves into any serious trouble. This gadget helped them out to some extent—for instance, in the first story it did help save them from being abducted to Venus—but typically they would wind up in some sort of extreme peril, no matter what.

The opening story is titled "Attack of the Incas", which forms the longest arc, at 13 episodes. The tone of the series is set right off the bat as the JASDF (Japan Air Self-Defense Force) has several jets out practicing maneuvers when they happen across—*you guessed it!*—a flying saucer. The squadron leader trails the craft until it rendezvous with a massive Venusian mothership in the upper reaches of the stratosphere. Sharp-eyed *tokusatsu* fans might spy this vessel in other series, as it was later repurposed by Toei for further use in both *Kikaida 01* (キカイダー01 / *Kikaidā Zero Wan* [1973-74]) and again later still by them in *Space Sheriff Gavin* (宇宙刑事ギャバン / *Uchū Keiji Gyaban* [1982-83]).

In *NK*, no sooner has it sighted the saucer's mothership than the pursuing jet is blown out of the sky by the giant UFO. In the aftermath of this attack, a meeting of Earth's foremost scientific specialists convene at Tokyo's aforementioned Diet Building to speculate on the hostile ship and its actions. Prof. Ryusaku Hata, who is knowledgeable about UFOs, is called in to give his opinion. During the meeting, the room's lights flash off and then back on, following which a message in an alien-looking script appears imprinted on the wall. Hata is able to recognize the writing as ancient Incan, and proceeds to translate a warning from "Abika" to not create nuclear weapons or venture out into space…or else. If humans continue on this recklessly foolhardy path of theirs, the Incans will destroy all of humanity!

The next scene introduces a group of three boys and a girl walking along a street towards Professor Hata's laboratory, all singing the *National Kid* theme song. How strangely 'meta' is that?! The kids pull-up short as they spy a highly suspicious-looking character skulking about in the bushes outside of Hata's residence ("He might be an Incan from Venus", surmises one). They then follow the lurker out into the back country, where it turns out he was leading the kids into

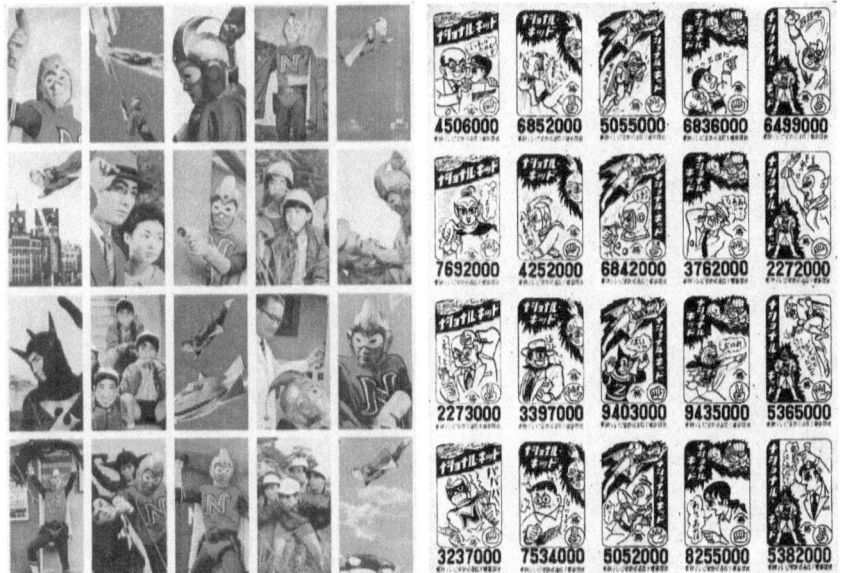

A montage of *National Kid* Menko cards, fronts and backs

a trap, and they walked right into it. He transforms from a seemingly normal-looking human into a Venusian! Then several more Venusians spring up, surrounding and capturing the kids. (The Venusian Incas are all dressed in head-to-toe black onesies, with a big white "Z" on their chests. They have large pointy ears reminiscent of a bat's, while their pallid faces appear through a skull-shaped opening in their get-ups' hoods.)

Back at his place, Hata has been waiting for the kids to show up, and finds it strange and worrisome that they are so late. When he goes out to look for them, he hears their plaintive wailings for help. So off Hata trots, and the next thing you know, National Kid is streaking through the air to their rescue! He fights and defeats the gang of Incas, who run off when they realize they are severely outclassed in the fighting department.

From here on out, it becomes a game of 4-D chess between the Venusian Incas, National Kid, the team of scientists and the Japanese Armed forces. A prestigious expert in astrobiology is kidnapped and brainwashed. In this altered state, he does his best to throw the other scientists, their government and the kids for a loop, providing the Incas with cover under which to (hopefully) execute their master plan to obliterate us. When that devious scheme gets thwarted by National Kid, the aliens resort to executing Plan B instead: this being to poison the Earth's entire water supply with a special type of radiation. To thwart this,

National Kid has to find the minerals which can be used to neutralize the atomic toxin. Plan C is all-out war, with a whole multitude of flying saucers attacking Japan. Both National Kid and the JASDF bring on a strong defense. This is a BIG effects showcase, featuring running air and land battles between jets, spaceships, and ground troops; lasting for about 15 minutes, which is a looooong time for one continuous block of *action*!

Once the problem of the Venusian Incas is all squared-away, Professor Hata takes his young wards on a deep-sea field trip in a bathysphere, during which they plumb the depths of the Japan Trench. While marveling at the ocean's flora and fauna, upon looking out of a porthole one of the boys catches a glimpse of what is seemingly a gigantic sea creature (reminiscent of an angler fish), with glowing eyes. And thus starts the nine-episode story arc "Deep Sea Devil Nelkon"…

Mere days after the Detective Group encounter that mysterious angler fish-like creature, ships along the nautical navigation lanes begin disappearing—including the very same bathysphere that Hata and the kids had only recently previously been aboard. Back at the laboratory, the girl Chaco is cutting-up a fish which the kids brought back from their expedition. Amazingly, as they look on, she discovers a small capsule inside the fish, which contains a note! It reads that the geological fault along the Japan Trench belongs to the ancient Coelacanth

Dan Ross   National Kid • ナショナルキッド / *Nashonaru Kiddo*

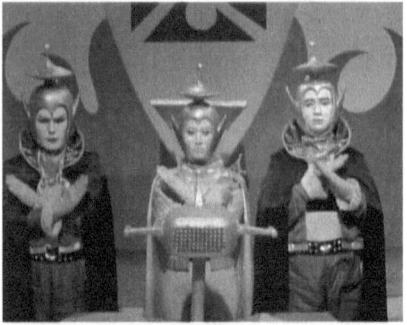
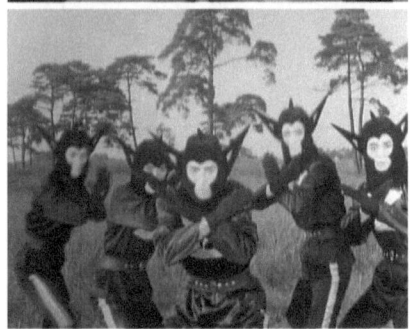
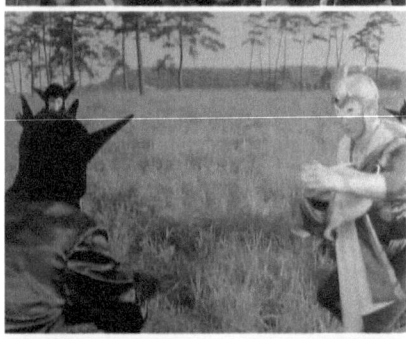
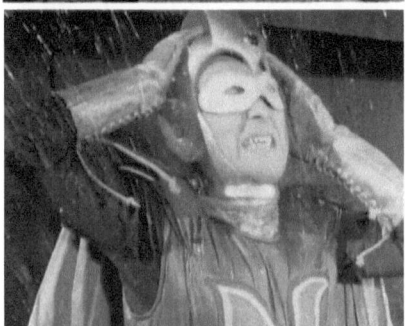

Top to Bottom: The inscrutably impassive Venusian leaders; pointy-eared Inca ninjas, ready to rumble; National Kid is more than willing to oblige 'em; but if he gets zapped by their dreaded Radieux X—his 'Kryptonite'—he's rendered helpless!

Empire, also warning that anyone who dares investigate the Trench shall become their enemies, and that the Coelacanth will declare war on the trespassers. So it seems that, be it inadvertently or not, Professor Hata and his kiddie crew are the ones who bring this trouble about.

It turns out that the disappearing ships are being sunk by the giant 'angler fish', which is in actuality a super-sophisticated submarine called "Guiltor" (ギルトール) that has been sent by the Coelacanth Empire to wreak havoc on the air-breathers above. Much like the previous story, it becomes a back-and-forth game of scientists being kidnapped, National Kid fighting to rescue them; the Boys' Detective Club alternately discovering secrets and getting into potentially deadly trouble.

There are several particularly nicely-done special effects set pieces in this story. At one point, Guiltor causes a tsunami at a seaside village. The villagers try to escape but are swept out to sea into the awaiting gaping maw of the killer submarine. This whole sequence is remarkably well produced. The miniature village hit by the waves isn't too hokey, and seems to be a quite large-scale set, while the process shot showing the floundering villagers desperately splashing about while trying to escape being swallowed-up by Guiltor in the background is seamless.

Another fun effects shot comes when the kids, in an inflatable raft, discover a ghost galleon. A major aspect of the visual oddity in these scenes is how seemingly way outside the standard sci-fi genre this 'supernatural' ghost ship seems to be, and it was probably included due to Koike wanting to insert more Rampo-like spooky elements into the series. More fitting to a horror show, the ship is a gnarly great hulk which seems to be haunted by *kitsunebi* (狐火), little ghostly "fox-fire lights" similar to will-o'-the-wisps (which are so commonly found in Asian folklore). There's also skeletons, spider-webs, crazily-tilting hallways; the whole spooky works.

The Coelacanth people are humanoid, having bodies reminiscent of the Creature from the Black Lagoon, with segmented, scaly appendages but topped with raptor-like, saurian heads. Typically they are clothed in black robes with pointy hats, like a virtual negative image of the Ku Klux Klan's garb. When needed—for instance, when there's fighting to be done—they pull the robes off to reveal their underlying ichthyic selves.

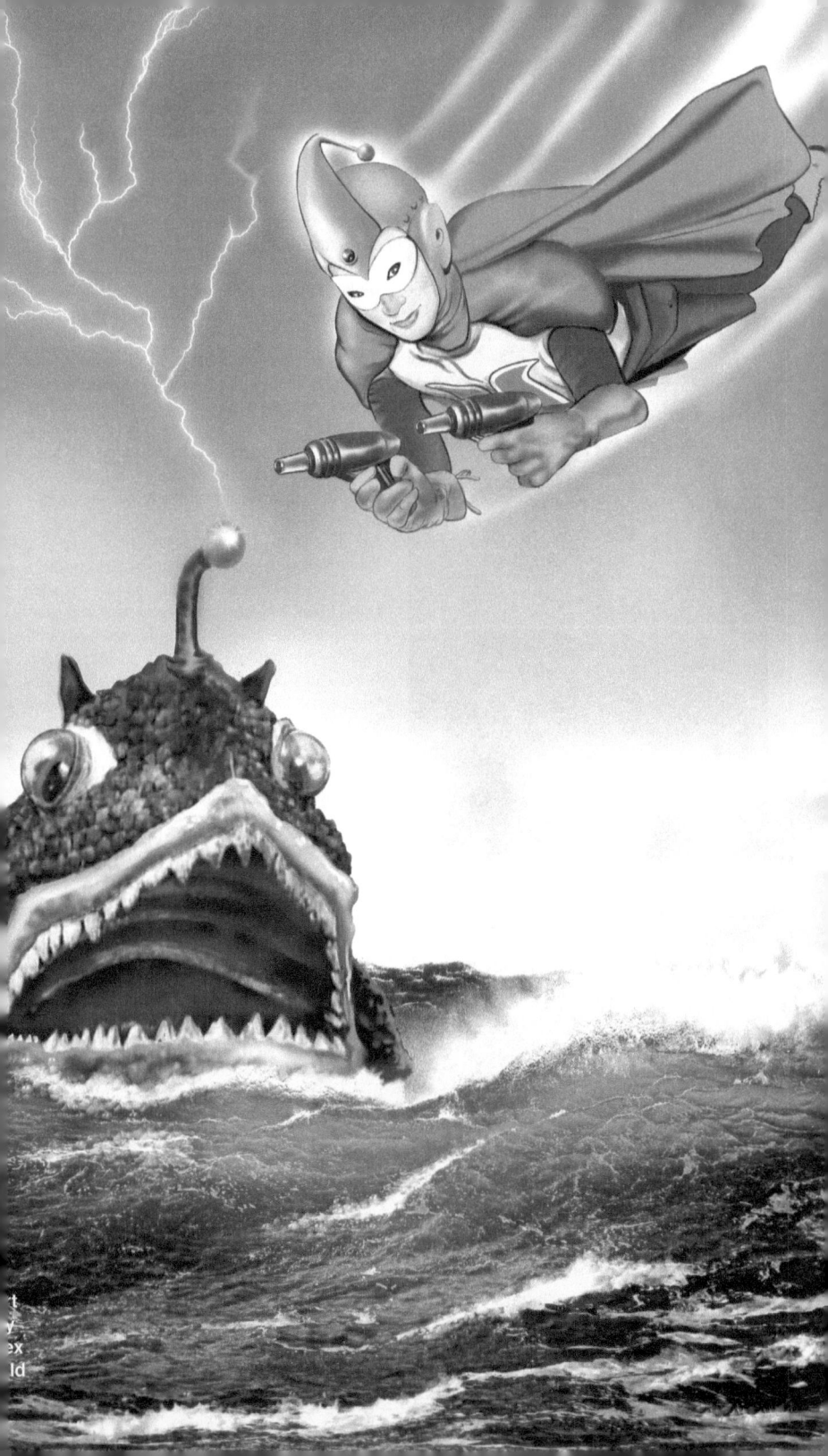

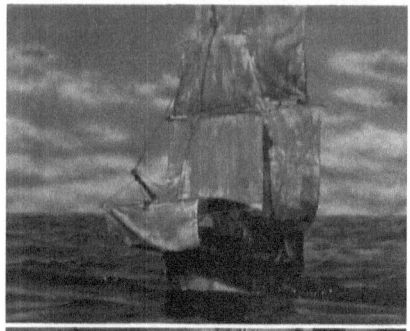

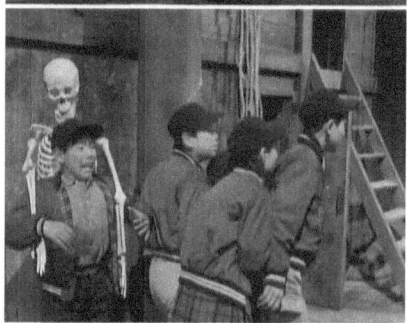

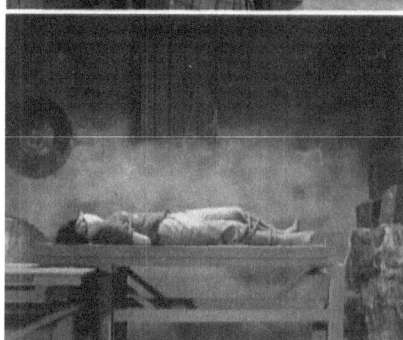

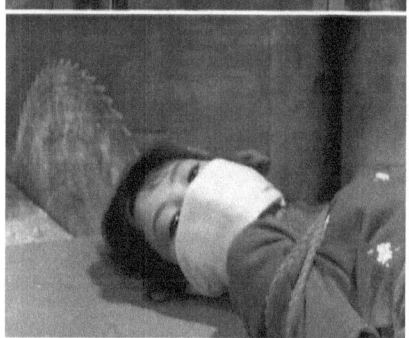

Top to Bottom: The haunted galleon from the "Deep Sea Devil Nelkon" arc; the gals 'n' guys of the BDC go aboard to investigate; resulting in a re-run-through of the hoary ol' cliffhanger with the bound 'n' gagged damsel-in-distress imperiled by a whirring circular table-saw

Personality-wise, there's not much to redeem the Coelacanths as they are—well—total *assholes* to everybody! While the Venusian Incas at least had a sense of duty to safeguard the galaxy, these fishy fiends take great joy in torturing, beating, and indiscriminately trying to slaughter everyone in their way. In fact, at one point they have a laugh amongst themselves about how dastardly they are! And speaking of "dastardly", there's even a scene with a 'damsel-in-distress' tied to a timber conveyor-belt leading to a large, woodcutting circular saw. Classic cliffhanger stuff, this!

The next caper, running eight episodes, is the "Underground Demon Castle". It's with this story that we find a new, more healthy-looking Professor Hata/National Kid, now played by Kojima Ichiro's fitter replacement, Hidetaro Tatsumi. We also first encounter an enemy that spans two storylines directly, and a third one indirectly...

At the end of the previous story ("Deep Sea Devil Nelkon"), the Coelacanth Empire is left to their own devices after being soundly defeated by National Kid and the Boys' Detective Group. But soon afterwards, the recently-trounced Coelacanths are attacked and their primary underwater cities destroyed by those known as Subterraneans. Knowing of his righteousness and benevolence, the undersea folk send out agents to seek help from National Kid.

The Subterranean Empire is a force even more vicious and conniving (no mean feat!) than the Coelacanths. They live deep in the bowels of the Earth, using an artificial sun to keep everything running. But their sun is fading, its power exhausted, you see. Therefore they feel the best move is to—*of course!*—conquer the surface dwellers, using a power source which is to be found only aboveground, in our domain. This power consists of two powerful elements which need to be combined in order to work. In the end, a rift opens between rival factions among the Subterraneans. Unable to reconcile their differences for the common good (i.e., bad), each faction has possession of one of the needed elements, yet with no way to combine them. Therefore, due to this stalemate/standoff situation, when National Kid chases one faction clear off the planet, the threat is conclusively ended.

Though they live within the Earth, the Subterraneans make extensive use of spacecraft (in the flying saucer vein) to get from place to place. They also have a battery of gigantic intergalactic vessels stored underground which could be used for military purposes and/or mass-exodus, if needs be. While the Inca Venusians had a fairly even-sided

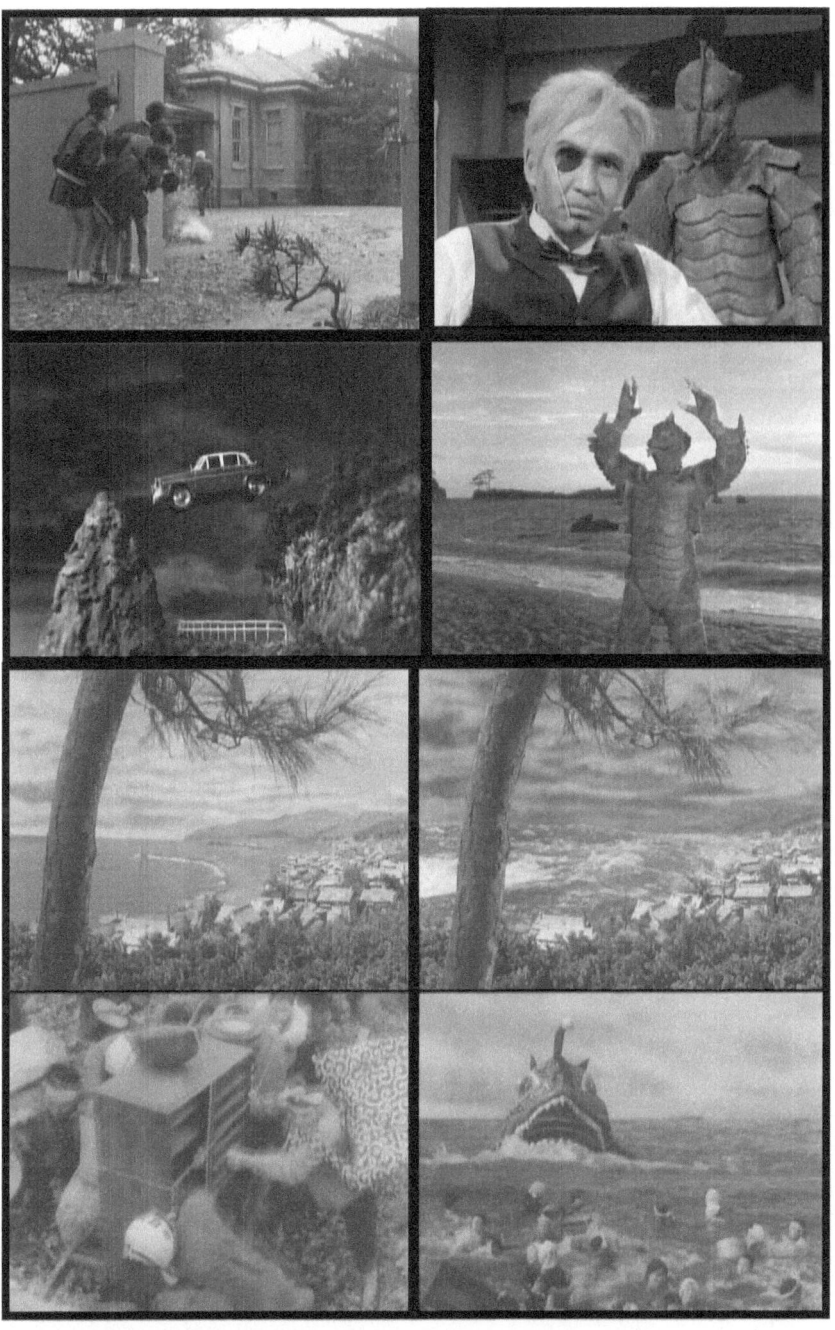

8 scenes from "Deep Sea Devil Nelkon". **Top Row:** The BDC peeking-in on a creepy professor who is in league with the fishy Coelacanth creatures. **2nd Row, Left:** Captive scientists are spirited away in a floating car! **2nd Row, Right:** A rubbery deep-sea Coelacanth critter comes ashore. **3rd & 4th Rows:** The fish-faced supersub Guiltor launches an aquatic attack on a coastal village by causing a tidal wave

Dan Ross *National Kid* • ナショナルキッド / *Nashonaru Kiddo*

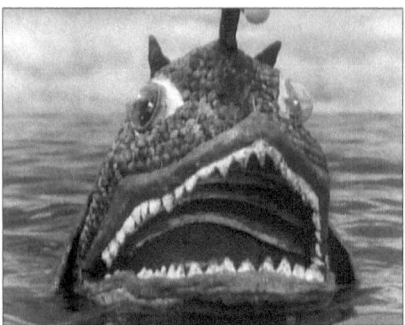

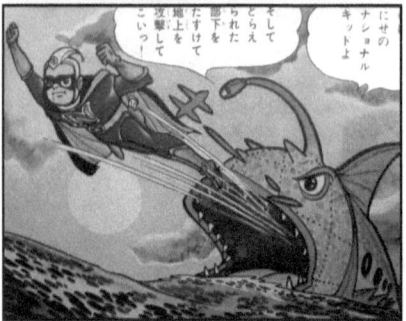

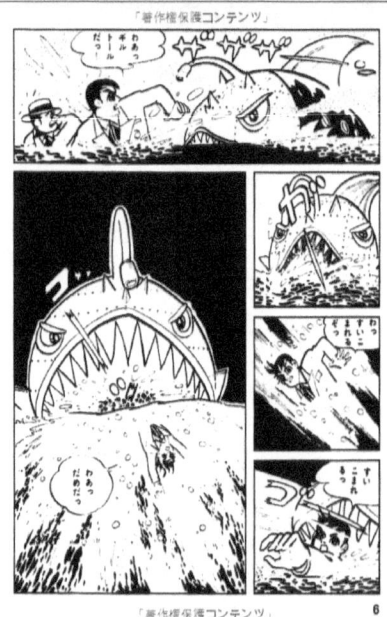

Top to Bottom: The ghastly monster submarine Guiltor surfaces from the Pacific depths; a *National Kid* manga panel showing the Coelacanths' dreaded angler fish-like submarine menacing our hero; and a page from *NK*'s 1961 Coelacanth manga

battle with Earthlings in the finale of their story, just *one* of the gigantic Subterranean ships lays waste to all of Earth's military might which took them on. Pretty impressive! These ships resemble a well-known multi-fuel-tank design popularized by acclaimed space/sci-fi painter Chesley Bonestell, designer Willy Ley and aerospace engineer Von Braun (first seen in the US magazine *Collier's* "Man will Conquer Space Soon" series). In 1958, the design was adapted into a highly popular plastic model kit manufactured by Lindberg called the "U.S. Moon Ship". The mold for that kit has been passed on to many companies over time, and it is still in production to this day, currently available from Round 2.

Despite their nasty natures, the Subterraneans themselves—human-like and with no alien make-up, just standardized neo-military-type jumpers and fezzes (!)—were not overly startling to look at. In the final instalment of the series, "Mystery of the Space Boy", we see President Gerstein (leader of the Subterraneans) and a cadre of his cronies escape to the distant planet Mazeran. There he informs the Mazerans that the Earth is a dangerous place full of violent, evil people who are getting close to achieving the means of space travel. It's a *bad* situation, and Gerstein could sure use some Mazeran help to subdue us uppity Earthlings. Being a thoughtful and fair-minded person, the leader of Mazeran dispatches his son Taro to walk among we humans to find out what the truth is…

Meanwhile, the Subterranean contingent on Earth get back to kidnapping and brainwashing officials and scientists. What better way to get their plans of reasserting their power over the surface world? At least in the *National Kid* universe, this seems to be 'Plan A1' for just about every extraterrestrial invader out there!

Unfortunately, while on his way to Earth from his home planet of Mazeran, Taro's ship is damaged and crashes, whereafter he is saved and befriended by the Boys' Detective Group. They show the alien emissary how good and compassionate humans are (or at least, *can be*), and Taro realizes that President Gerstein had been lying through his teeth to his father. When the Group returns to Taro's wreckage in order to salvage the communicator so he can warn his Dad of Gerstein's treachery, they are ambushed by the earthbound Subterraneans. During the resultant kafuffle, the long-range radio gets damaged, so the marooned Mazeranian is unable to contact Papa!

When the leader of Mazeran doesn't hear back from his son Taro, he assumes the worst: that Gerstein must have been telling the truth about us. So the attack is on! A joint fleet of Subter-

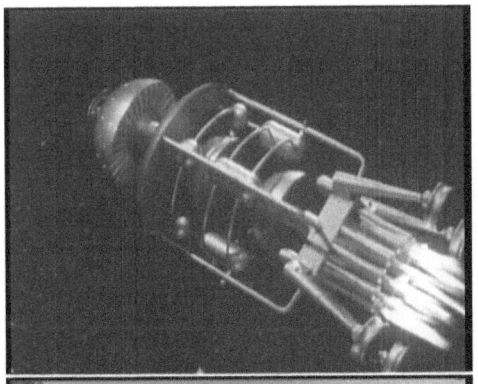
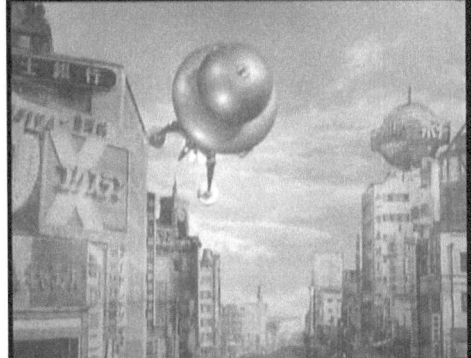
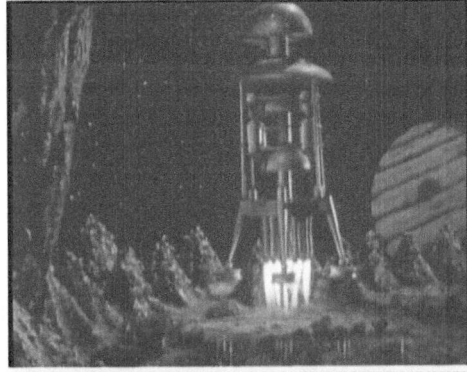
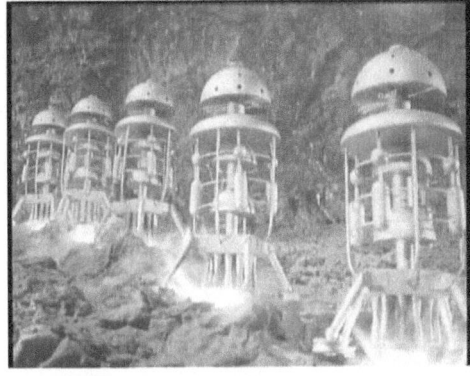
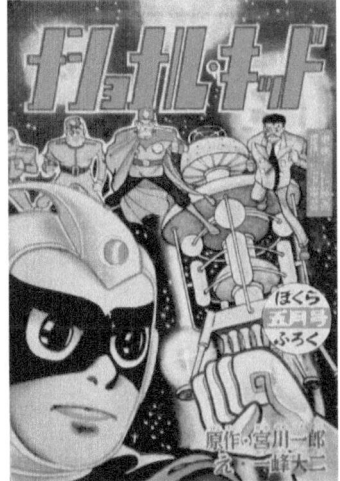
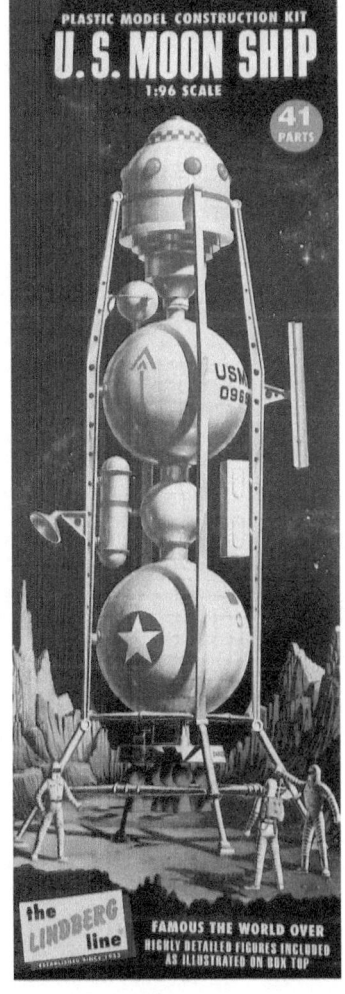

Dan Ross   National Kid • ナショナルキッド / Nashonaru Kiddo

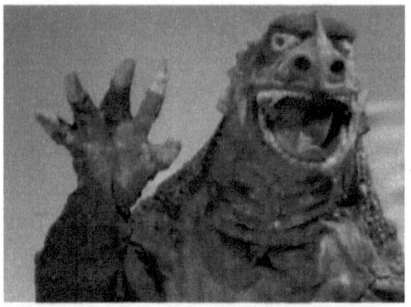
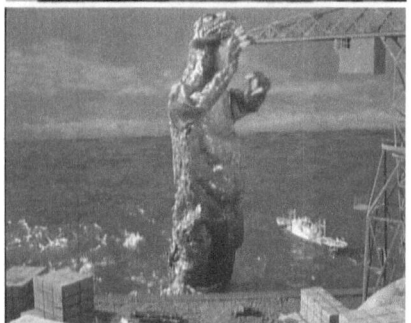
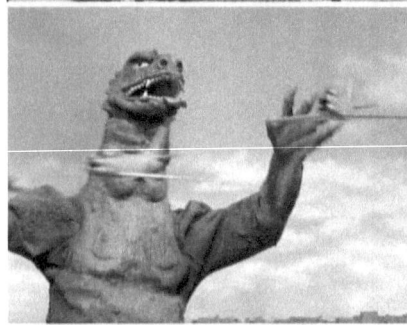
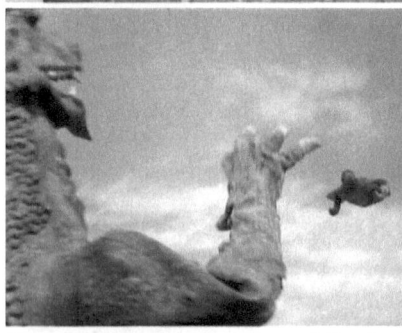

Top to Bottom: Looking ever-so-jolly, giant monster Gaplar a.k.a. Giabra (ギャプラ / *Gyapura*) waves howdy-doody in "Enigma of the Space Boy" (Episode #5). But don't be fooled by his lizardy grin for a second, cuz, like any other self-respecting *kaijū*, he really loves to bust shit up and can bat a jet fighter out of the air like it's a budgie!

anean and Mazeranian battleships descend on Earth. Just as both races launch their all-out attack on humankind, they come close enough for Taro to contact his father and set things straight. Angered by the betrayal, right in mid-attack, the Mazeran space force turns its might against the Subterraneans, destroying them once and for all.

Following a job well done, the Mazeranians head for home, but in order to *really* get to know humans better, Taro decides to hang out with the Boys' Detective Group for a while longer. Though the title of the story does not change, it is becomes a new story arc which now includes mysterious space-boy Taro among its protagonists.

While on a trip to a lighthouse, Taro and the Boys' Detective Group notice that out in the distance a strange glimmer is moving around in the ocean. Meanwhile Professor Hata is doing an aerial survey in the same area and he too sees the disturbance from above. Soon after the lighthouse is destroyed by an unseen force. Once again up in the survey plane Professor Hata spot daikaiju-sized lizard tracks leading away from the destruction.

It seems the denizens of the planet Zarock want to terraform Earth into a new swamp-world for themselves to dwell upon. Their first step, it goes without saying, is to pound we Earthlings into submission by unleashing the giant monster "Gaplar" (ギャプラ / *Gyapura*)—a monster that happens to be *invisible*! While the brilliant idea of a 'stealth' *kaijū* is pretty impressive, the truth of the matter is that the critter's suitmation costume wasn't actually completed until the final episode. Once constructed and therefore visible, one might see Gaplar on screen and think him related to the title monster of the 4-part Nippon/Fuji TV miniseries *Agon: Atomic Dragon* (幻の大怪獣アゴン / *Maboroshi no Daikaijū Agon* / "Giant Phantom Monster Agon", 1964), for they do look quite similar. Agon is a *wee* bit more detailed, but the two beasts share a similar profile.

Again we have a fake human agent of evil, the back-and-forth with the kids getting into/out of danger, National Kid indulging in fisticuffs with aliens, and so on. The Zarock people are basically human and also wear fezzes (!!) like the Subterraneans, but they have—*um*—long noses. In fact, they look an awful lot like the denizens of Krankor from *Prince of Space* (遊星王子 / *Yūsei Ōji*, a.k.a. "Planet Prince", 1959). The special effects *tour de force* this time around is our giant monster Gaplar, who, true to *kaijū* form, crushes a miniature city. Though the city itself isn't exactly spectacular-looking, it's not half bad considering the time and situation. It's used

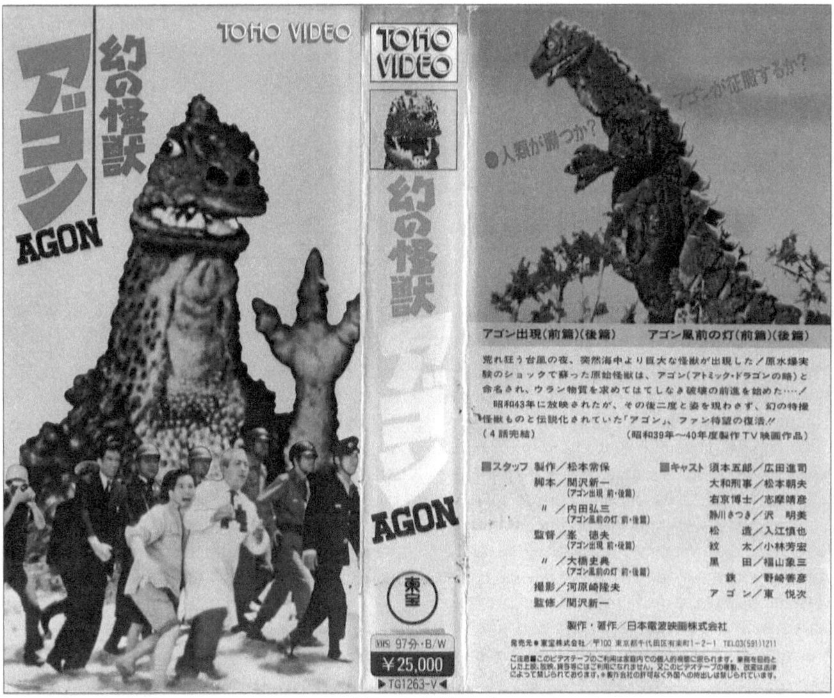

VHS sleeve for *Agon: Atomic Dragon* (幻の大怪獣アゴン) with titular kaiju rampaging away

only in the last episode of the series, after all the funds had been depleted on the (Hail Mary!) creation of the giant monster suit, which had remained sight-unseen until now. National Kid flies through the air fighting it with his trusty Erolya ray gun, that for the occasion has been specially-charged with something called "Radiation X", which the scientists have figured out will do-in this devilishly destructive monster but good.

Once this latest—and unfortunately, last—giant monstrous menace and the Zarockians have been defeated, National Kid reveals to all his allies (not that we didn't know already!) that he is in fact none other than Professor Hata—or is it the other way round?—and that he is also an alien from Andromeda. Feeling that his job is done for now, he flies off to return to his distant homeworld... for keeps, as it turned out.

Once the series ended, *National Kid* did not get any sort of push—be it a big one or otherwise—for international distribution. My research has turned up no other foreign exports of the show outside of Brazil, where it went on to become (and still is, to some extent) a cultural phenomenon, and there is still a sizeable Brazilian fanbase for it today. Multiple incarnations of VHS and DVD sets of the show have been distributed over the years, and it is now streamable on Netflix Brazil too. It's been seen in virtually constant televised reruns since making its Brazilian premiere, although it was taken off the air for a period during the '70s when it, along with *Superman* and any other "flying superhero shows", were yanked from circulation due to the censorious dictatorial regime which held sway at the time. Strangely, the state's directive was to protect the population from the scourge of poor moral values. Hmm...

National Kid's Brazilian debut was on RecordTV in São Paulo in 1964. It was distributed by Sato Co.

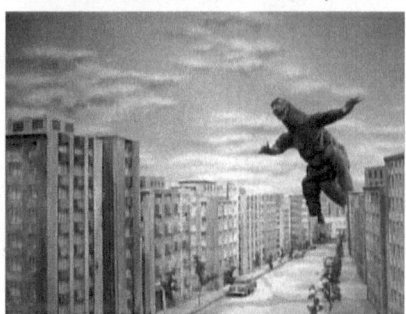

Giant monster Gaplar, who, true to *kaiju* form, goes on a city-smashing crusade

Dan Ross   National Kid • ナショナルキッド / *Nashonaru Kiddo*

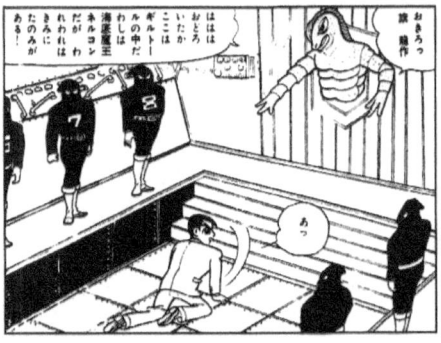
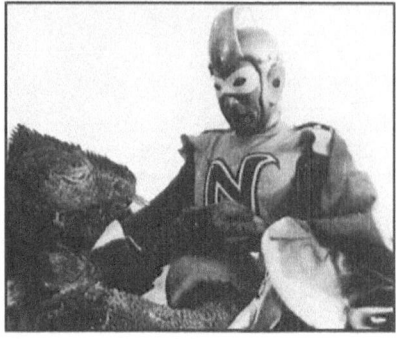

Ltd., with Portuguese dubbing via the International Academy of Cinema (AIC). After the resounding success of *NK*, the Sato Company also brought other popular Japanese shows to South America, such as the aforementioned *Ultraman*, *Jiraiya*, and many others. As for the current *tokusatsu* show under discussion, the original Portuguese dubs were destroyed in a fire at the RecordTV's studio sometime in the 1970s. New—and controversial—dubs were made in the 1990s; controversial because original fans felt these new dubs were less professionally-handled, and that within the dialog many of the familiar names got changed. Despite this, a company in Brazil released these newly-mixed dubs onto DVD several years before anyone in the show's nation of origin would.

Japan finally got around to restoring and releasing *National Kid* on DVD in 2015, but very little in the way of supplemental merchandise for the show has remained in production. Outside of some boutique garage kits from Japan and Brazil, there's no toys, figures, food or clothing lines. As of this writing, the only high-profile item still in production is a creepy-looking NK facemask which was highlighted and made famous in the manga and film series *20th Century Boys* (20世紀少年 / *Nijūseiki Shōnen*, 1999-2006). Though, oddly enough, Japan seems fairly indifferent to rediscovering this black-and-white gem, maybe one day we will see further iterations or merchandise from Brazil... so let's keep looking South and to the stars for more from National Kid!

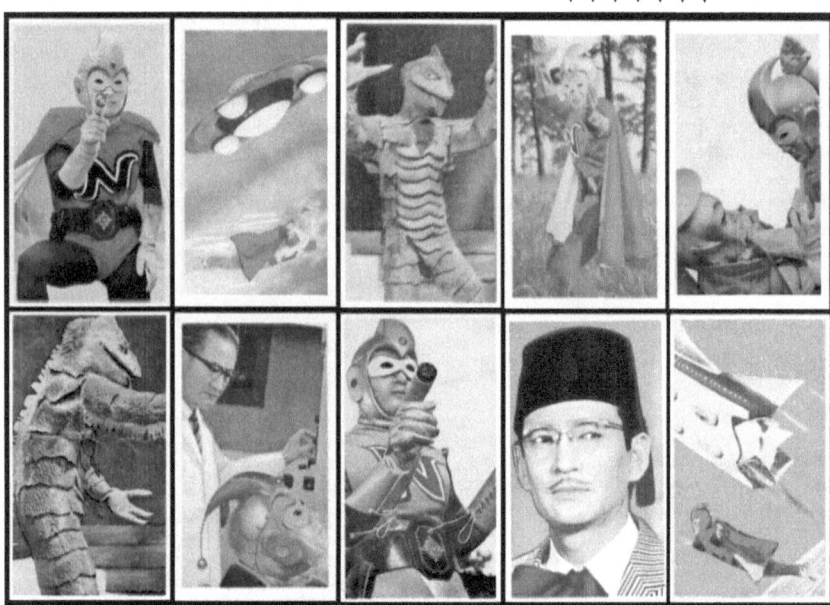

Top Left: Another panel from *National Kid*'s 1961 Coelacanth manga. **Top Right:** Another scene from the tele-version. **Above:** A mosaic more *NK* Menko cards

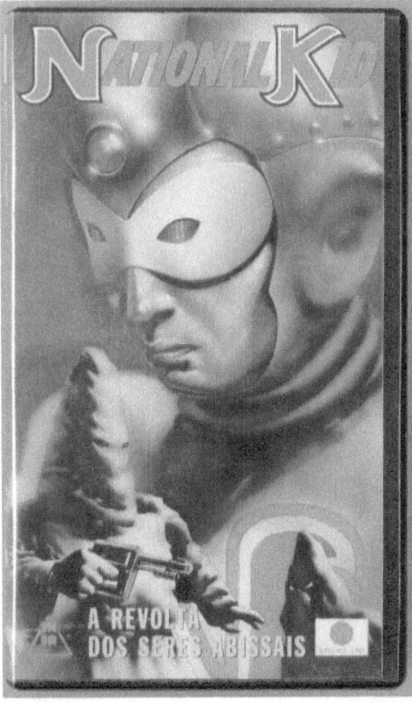 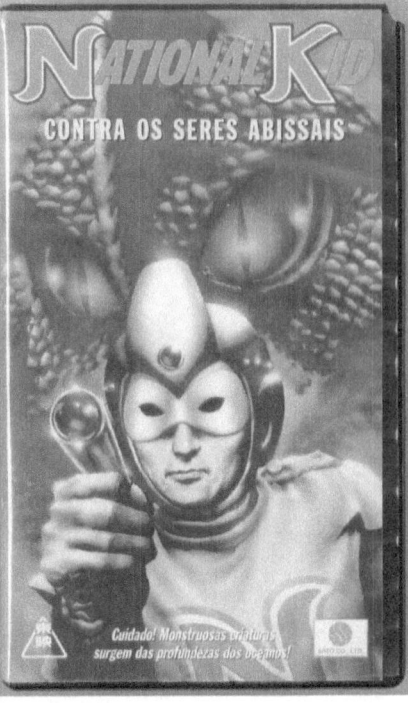

Above: The front covers to a pair of Portuguese-dubbed VHS releases from *NK*'s "Deep Sea Devil Nelkon" story arc—here respectively retitled *A revolta a dos seres Abissais* ("Revolt of the Abyssal Beings") and *Contra os seres Abissais* ("…versus the Abyssal Beings")—that were put out in Brazil in the '80s by Videolar de Amazónia / Sato Co., Ltd.; art unsigned

SPECIAL AUTHOR'S NOTE:

There were certain items which were difficult for me to parse on my own, and I would like to thank the following friends for their help:

Jim Aupperle is a visual effects and animation veteran who's been working in the movie biz since 1972. When confronted with a technical diagram and some broken-English translations I gave him, he was able to interpret what was going on to help make the article's description much easier to comprehend.

In order to describe certain nouns, *National Kid* uses a lot of *katakana* (the Japanese writing system used for transliterating foreign words) for what we might call 'technobabble', alien names and suchlike. I could not find an official English-language precedence for Westernizing some of these words, and the automatic machine translations I tried were all over the place. Therefore, I leaned-on professional translator Iyasu Adair Nagata at Twitter (@ *iyasuN*) for help in getting the nuance of some of these terms to sound correct and properly Westernized.

[*Editors' Note*: *Because Dan was considerate and diligent enough to include several additional paragraphs covering* National Kid's *home media information in some detail, we have included it in our Video Availability listings at the very back of this magazine.*]

Dan Ross   *National Kid* • ナショナルキッド / *Nashonaru Kiddo*

COOL STUFF

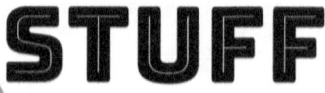

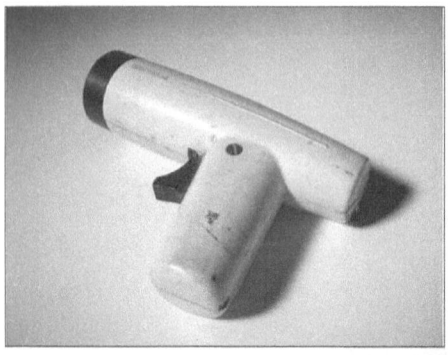

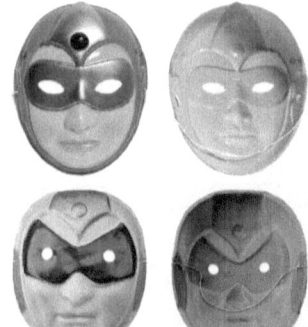

✧✧✧✧✧✧✧

Top: A promotional foldable die-cut *National Kid* mask given away free in electrical supply stores. **Above:** Pistol-grip NK flashlight, a.k.a. the "Kid Flash". **Above Right:** Frontal and rear views of a pair of mass-produced molded celluloid NK masks. **Right:** Flexi-disc, presumably of the show's theme song (?). **Below:** Detail of a promotional postcard printed with the theme's sheet-music and lyrics. **Below Right:** One of the, uh, *weirder* NK masks

✧✧✧✧✧✧✧

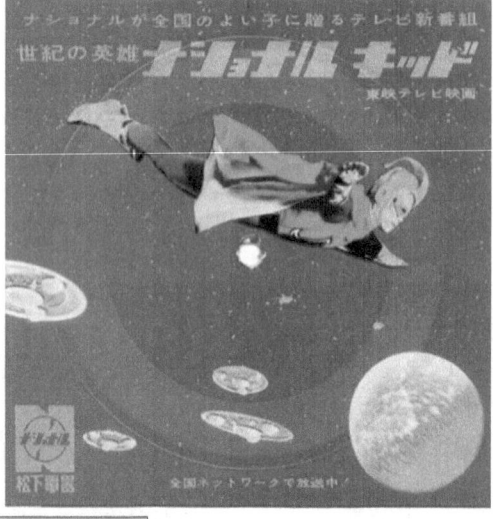

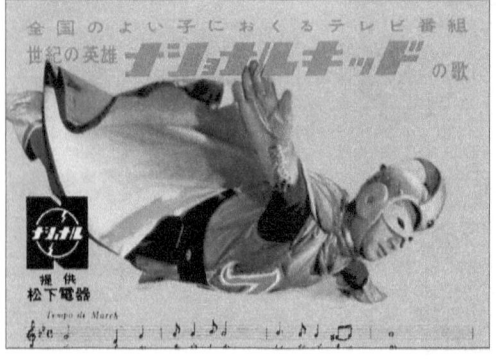

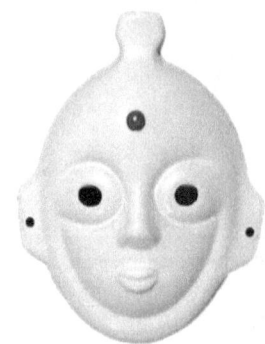

National Kid • ナショナルキッド / Nashonaru Kiddo   Dan Ross

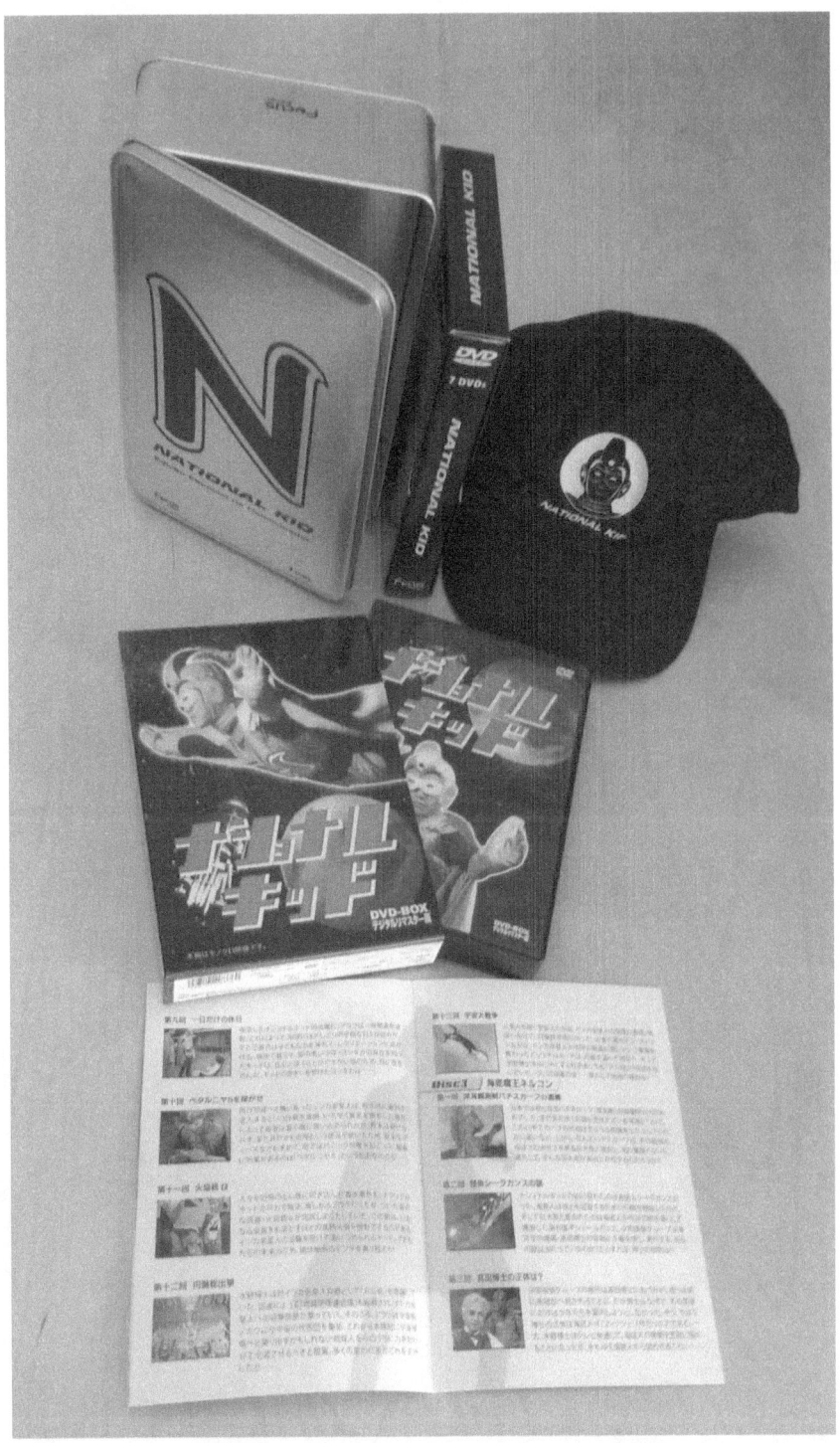

DVD box sets from Japan and Brazil; photo by Dan Ross

THE ECLECTIC COOL COLLECTION
WK BOOKS

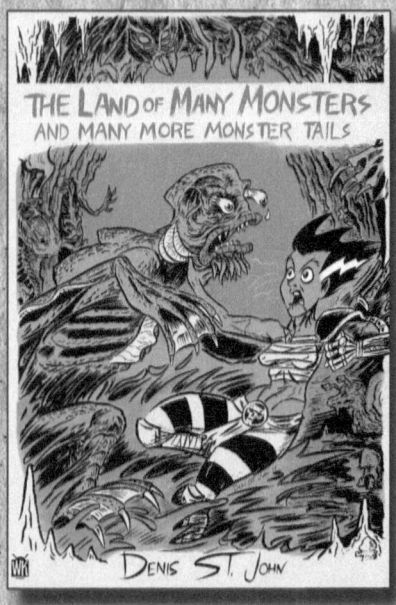
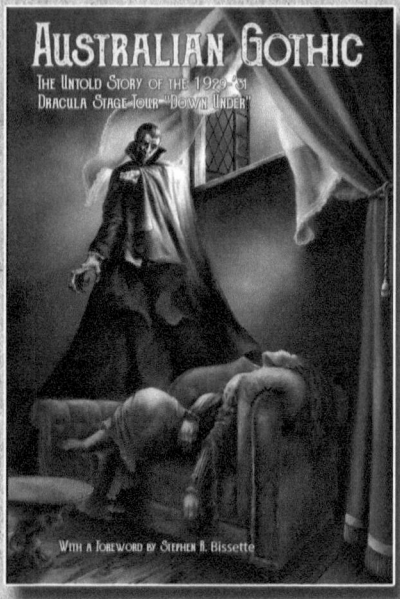
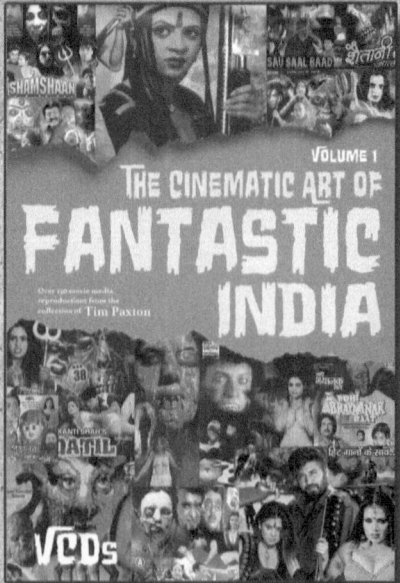
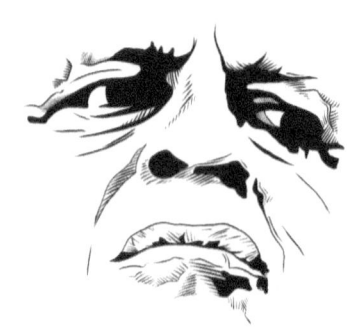

WENGSCHOPSTORE.COM

ANARCHY & MONSTERS

An Interview with Brett Piper
Parts 2 & 3 (of 6)

by Stephen R. Bissette

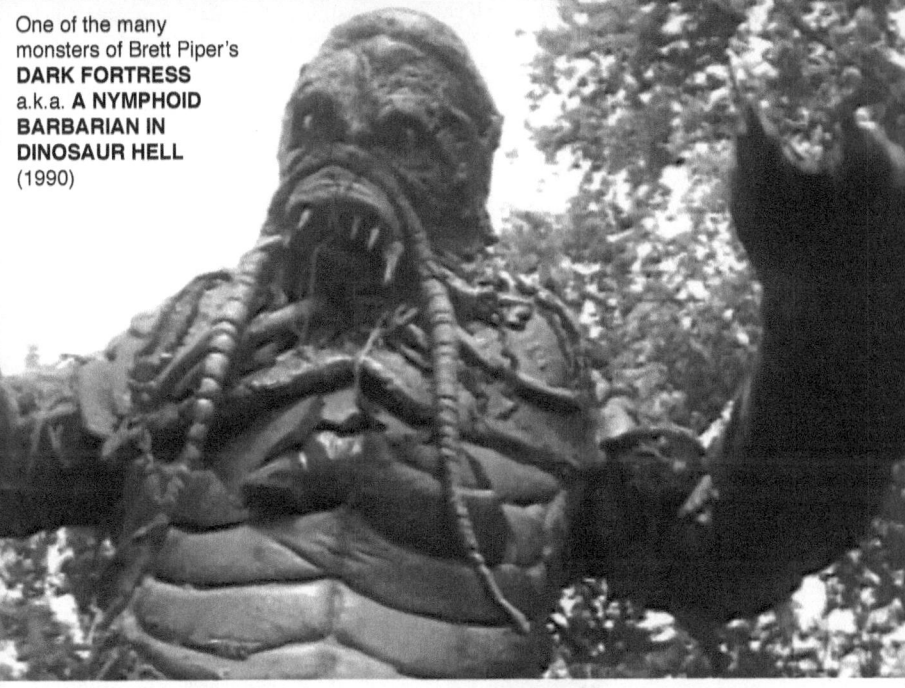

One of the many monsters of Brett Piper's **DARK FORTRESS** a.k.a. **A NYMPHOID BARBARIAN IN DINOSAUR HELL** (1990)

> "I'll tell you what the 'Brett Piper Universe' is about: anarchy and monsters. In all my movies the characters find themselves in situations, large or small, where they're on their own with no support from any kind of social structure... And there's monsters."
>
> — Brett Piper[1]

I'll not mince words: Brett Piper is the *only* American filmmaker who has continued to make the kinds of live-action-and-stop-motion-effects-creature-filled SF/fantasy/adventure films which Willis O'Brien and Ray Harryhausen used to make.

Brett has done so since 1982, non-stop. Brett does this without major studio money or support—or, actually, *any* kind of Hollywood studio money or support, ever, *period*. He's kept right on making his kind of SF/fantasy/monster movies without the benefit of name stars (well, there was *one*, who we'll

---

1 Email from Brett Piper to the author, September 3rd, 2016; the full context of this quote is contained in Part 2 of this interview (the section on **DARK FORTRESS**).

be talking about in this portion of our lengthy interview: ladies and gentlemen, Cameron Mitchell!), and without teams of animators, without assistants or gofers, without CGI enhancements, without squandering the gross national product of many small industrialized nations on single feature films.

Piper has rigorously maintained his private life as *private property*, and *Monster!* honors that. It's a matter of public record that Piper was born in 1953 in New Hampshire. In his own words, Brett "bought a Kodak Brownie 8mm movie camera when I was eleven; more cameras and more movies since then while supporting myself in construction, freelance art and design, newspaper composition, et bloody cetera."[2] Piper completed his first feature film, **MYSTERIOUS PLANET** ([1982] see "Anarchy & Monsters" Pt.1 in *M!* #32 [p.16]) at age 27, and he has worked steadily as an independent filmmaker ever since.

Piper completes entire features for less than most contemporary Hollywood features blow on one day of catering alone. Brett has mastered the staples of "old-school" special effects ingenuity, including (in almost every single film) stop-motion animation in the style of his heroes—Willis O'Brien, Ray Harryhausen, James "Jim" Danforth, Phil Tippett—but he also cites as influences "James Whale and the rest of the Universal gang... *[Roger]* Corman and Terence Fisher and (big-time) Hammer... John Huston

[2] Brett Piper, quoted in Kevin J. Lindenmuth's *The Independent Film Experience: Interviews with Directors and Producers* (2002, McFarland & Company, Inc.), p.147.

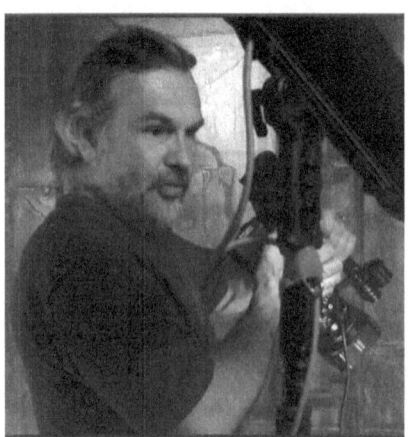

Hands-On Director: Brett Piper doing what an independent filmmaker does on the set of one of his inventive feature films—just about *everything*!

(the only director to whom I ever wrote a fan letter—and he wrote back!) and Orson Welles."[3]

Though he's a humble fellow, the fact remains that Brett is a one-man producer/writer/director/cinematographer/editor/special-effects expert. "I'm like one of those Japanese soldiers still hiding out on a tiny Pacific island twenty years after the war has ended," Piper says. "I'm doing special effects pretty much the same way they were being done in the twenties, before the invention of the optical printer (much less the computer). It's cool, I like it that way."[4] Even given this, feature films are a necessarily collaborative medium. Beyond working with the behind-and-before-the-cameras casts and crews, Piper has enjoyed a few creative collaborative partnerships along the way, some of which were indeed fruitful (if only briefly).

Brett Piper has done so steadily, quietly, and modestly, with scant recognition, for for nigh-on four decades now. He's continued making his kinds of movies without the accolades showered on his more prominent, better-bankrolled, and far less prolific and productive contemporaries. He is certainly invisible to the mainstream entertainment press, such as it is.

So? So, *what*? Piper can't do much of anything about it, save get to work on the feature film now being shot, now in post-production, now in the planning stages—in Brett Piper's world, it's the work at hand, not the lack of money or partners or fame, that counts.

In the grand scheme of things, neither fame, nor infamy, nor lack of fame or infamy has either bankrolled or crushed his dreams or projects. Given the systems and carnivore pits we laughingly call "distribution" and "distributors," Brett sees little choice when he's done with a movie: he entrusts each completed brainchild to whatever best-case-today agent, broker, dealer, or distributor might be interested or in reach, signs on those dotted lines, hopes for the best, then moves on to spawning the next beastly brood. Best to persevere and soldier-on with the work at hand, and get to work on the *next* feature film as soon as possible. The *business* of movies is a shark's game, and Piper knows it:

"*The worst part of making any movie is scraping up the money. It's marginally better to get some money maven to raise it for you, but then he's*

[3] *Ibid.*
[4] *Ibid.*, p.149.

going to want to call the shots himself and demand an inordinate kickback for doing so. I have nothing good to say on [the] subject... maybe three words: Be born rich.

The tendency of distributors to rip off the filmmaker is so entrenched nobody even notices it anymore. The deals are all outrageously slanted in favor of the distributor. One distributor admitted that under the terms of our agreement he was offering me there was no way I would ever see a dime, but he still couldn't understand why I refused to sign. I have had distributors offer me no salary and no percentage of the profits and still expect me to make films for them. The attitude of people in distribution is they are the pushers and we are the junkies, and sooner or later we'll have to come around."[5]

Despite often-insurmountable odds, Piper's films have landed distribution and are *seen*. He has abandoned a few unsold projects (i.e., a planned 1980s horror anthology feature, and **DINOSAUR KID**, which we discuss in this instalment), and totally disowned only *one* completed feature (i.e., **DINOSAUR BABES**, also discussed herein, in Part 3). In an era of ever-changing release formats and platforms, almost all of Piper's productions *have* seen distribution—including international distribution—and a couple have enjoyed remarkably long shelf-lives.

Brett doesn't seem to care, actually; "I just wanna make movies, you know?"[6] He is too concerned with the current and *next* production to fret over the fate of his past creations, most of which were sold outright to distributors or manhandled by business partners who were less than honorable. The eventual marketplace success or failure of his films neither fuels nor impedes Piper's current undertaking. You win a few, you lose a few; just get back to work! You name it, Piper has experienced it—shady business partners, shortsighted producers, broken promises, shaky deals, botched releases, shoddy mishandling of prints and video/DVD transfers—but he never gives up, and he still gives his all to every production. It's more a matter of absolute pragmatism than anything else, grounded in Piper's extensive knowledge of filmmaking and exploitation and genre film history. It is a track record that precious few other living (or deceased) writer/director/effects artist monster-movie-makers can or ever will hold a candle to.

---

5 *Ibid.*, pp.148-150.
6 *Ibid.*

It's about time Brett Piper's story is told. Hence, this multi-chapter *Monster!* interview with one of our all-time favorite filmmakers.

For Part 1, get your hands on a copy of *Monster!* #32 (March 2017, pp. 6-39). We're proud to be covering the entirety of Brett's body of work to date, in his own words: Parts 4 and 5 will see print in *Monster!* #34, Part 6 in *Monster!* #35—

—but here in Parts 2 & 3, we go back to the late 1980s and on into the 1990s towards the still-New Millennium with Brett Piper. From **MUTANT WAR** (1988) to **DRAINIAC!** (2000), we've got a *lot* to explore, and a LOT of monsters to savor! We'll be backtracking just a wee bit to touch base one last time with **BATTLE FOR THE LOST PLANET** ([1986] a.k.a. **GALAXY DESTROYER** overseas [see "A&M Pt.1", p.34]), and then...

MUTANT WAR (1987)

SRB: Did you broker/handle the BATTLE FOR THE LOST PLANET **distribution deal yourself with [New York City-based distributor] 21st Century—or were you working with a rep or an agent who took care of that?**

BRETT PIPER: I handled it myself. I used to look through *Variety*, especially the big AFM [American Film Market] issues and such, to find distributors who were handling cheap genre films, and saw a 21st Century ad for about a dozen of them, so I figured it was worth a shot. The usual phone calls and screeners followed, and he made an offer (again, a buy-out, all rights) which seemed acceptable.

SRB: There's a producer credited on BATTLE— **Charles Baldwin—who was also credited on** RAIDERS OF THE LIVING DEAD **[see "A&M Pt.1", p.29]. For** MUTANT WAR, **Charles Baldwin is co-credited, this time with Arthur Schweitzer. I don't see any evidence of you working with either of them again afterwards; who were these fellows, how did they work out for and with you, and how did you connect with them?**

BP: Baldwin had been the middle man between me and the money since **MYSTERIOUS PLANET**. I didn't know he was co-credited with Schweitzer on **MUTANT WAR**, but then I've never seen the finished movie. I certainly had nothing to do with either of them after **MUTANT**

WAR. I wish I'd had nothing to do with either of them *before* it.

SRB: Did the sale of BATTLE FOR THE LOST PLANET **to 21st Century Distribution bankroll** MUTANT WAR, **or had you already begun production on** MUTANT WAR **before** BATTLE **landed a distribution deal?**

BP: Schweitzer seemed reasonably pleased with **BATTLE**, and he and Baldwin began planning to make another film together; by which I mean they began planning for me to make another movie for them, only this time they would be the "producers" while I did all the work and actually got the movie made. Schweitzer was *supposed* to put up the money, although whether he ever came up with a nickel, I couldn't say. It was a total mess. Anyway, I pitched several ideas, and "Artie" (as Baldwin referred to his new best pal) shot them all down. I eventually realized that what "Artie" really wanted was **BATTLE** all over again, so I wrote a sequel which, unfortunately, he accepted.

SRB: Hence the casting of Matt Mitler as Harry Trent once again, making it a truly right-on-the-heels-of-BATTLE ***sequel. As best I can tell from what's out there, you had a smaller cast of characters for*** MUTANT WAR—***how well did you work with Mitler and your female leads (Kristine Waterman, Deborah Quayle) this time?***

BP: For the most part we worked together well. At one point Deborah and Kristine approached me, and Deborah *(not* Debbie—she was quite specific about that!) said, "I heard you had some trouble with your actors on the last movie. We just wanted to let you know that won't be happening with us." Which was rather sweet of them.

SRB: *Whatever the finances, you somehow landed Cameron Mitchell (as Reinhart Rex)—your highest-profile actor to date. What was that like, working with Mitchell?*

BP: It was very enjoyable. We had just the tiniest confrontation at the beginning of his shoot (he was only there for two days). He objected to some rather coarse dialogue his character was supposed to say. I explained my reasoning behind it—that the character, although now posing as some kind of "big man" in the post-apocalyptic world, was probably on the bottom rung of the social ladder before the change came, and in

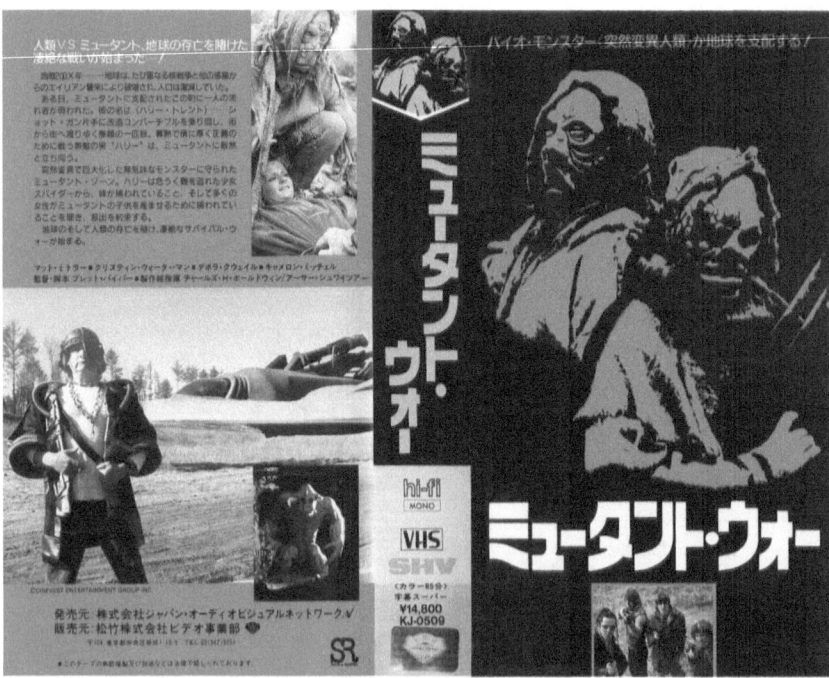

You Can't Get There From Here: Released almost everywhere else in the world except North America, this was the Japanese VHS packaging for Brett Piper's **MUTANT WAR /** ミュータント・ウォー(1987)

times of stress his real self showed through—and he nodded and accepted that, and said the lines. He also wanted his dialogue printed on cards so he wouldn't have to memorize it. I told him we'd do it the first day, but on the second it wouldn't be physically possible because of the location, so he'd have to know his lines. Which he did. I think he was testing me.

SRB: Sounds like you passed the test! Of course, he'd been in some pretty rough-and-ready movies in his career by then—

BP: We were shooting in an abandoned hydroelectric plant. It was a great location but not very accessible. He had to climb a rickety wooden ladder to get to a tiny room we were using as a holding cell. When we got there he looked around and said "This is the worst location I've ever been on in my life!" I said "Oh, I don't know. I've seen **MANEATER OF HYDRA**."[7] He shot me a look and snarled, "That damn picture made *money!*" Then he laughed like hell. Before every take, just as we were about to slate, he'd mutter, "Brett Piper is the best fucking director in the world!" I wish I'd saved those recordings. Some people might disagree.

Another time we were ready for a shot, and I looked around and couldn't find him. Someone told me he'd gone outside. I looked out the window and saw him, in his absurd Reinhart Rex costume, grabbing a couple of chili dogs from a lunch truck that had stopped at the factory next door. He'd gotten sick of waiting for me to break, so he handled the matter himself. The proprietors of the lunch wagon had recognized him, and he got his chili dogs free in return for an autograph.

A few years later, he was interviewed in *Fangoria*. They asked him about a bunch of his cheap genre pictures, including **MUTANT WAR**, and his response to nearly all of them was "Never heard of it." I wrote them a letter (which they printed) and said, **MUTANT WAR** might have been a lousy picture, but Mitchell had called it the worst set he'd ever been on in his life, and you'd think he'd remember *that!*

SRB: Despite that, years later, it sounds like Cameron Mitchell was a bright spot in this

---

[7] Brett was name-dropping one of Cameron Mitchell's 1960s Euro starring vehicles, the *other* Mel Welles' (who starred, natch, in Roger Corman's **LITTLE SHOP OF HORRORS** [1960]) carnivorous-vampire-plant opus **MANEATER OF HYDRA** (*La isla de la muerte*, a.k.a. **ISLAND OF THE DOOMED**, 1967), a Spanish-German coproduction directed by Welles under his occasional pseudonym of "Ernst von Theumer". And yes, that damned picture did indeed make money!

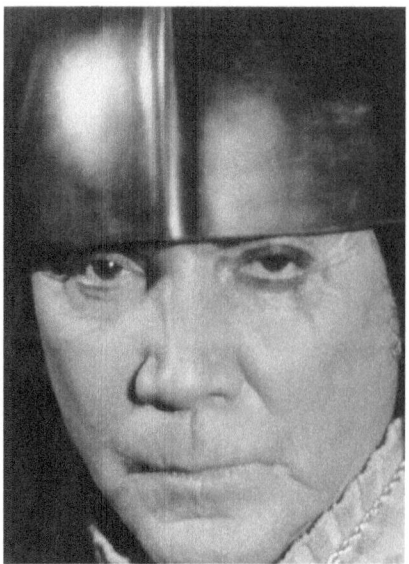

"This is the worst location I've ever been on in my life!" Brett Piper shot all of the Reinhart Rex (Cameron Mitchell) scenes for **MUTANT WAR** in just two days in a derelict hydroelectric plant in southern New Hampshire

grueling experience. Any other Cameron Mitchell memories you'd care to share?

BP: As I said, he was only there two days, so there isn't a lot to tell. He had HUGE hands. Make of that what you will. We had to double him in some shots after he left, so we'd put someone else in his costume, usually wearing an overcoat or something underneath to bulk them up, but in one shot we needed so show the character's hands doing something, and nobody's hands were big enough. Mitchell had hands like catcher's mitts!

After the first day of filming, we went to his hotel room to record some wild lines, and after the recording we sat around schmoozing. Mitchell was telling showbiz stories, and at one point he was trying to remember a name. He turned to me and said, "What was that guy's name, the artist who was friends with Barrymore?" and I said "John Decker." "Yeah, that's right, John Decker!" And he went on with his story. But I thought it was interesting that after knowing me only a few hours he just assumed that I'd know.

SRB: This had to be his only experience filming anything in New Hampshire; did he have any reaction to that?

BP: Mitchell never commented on his reaction to the Granite State. As far as I know, he only ever saw the airport, his hotel (which was adjacent to the airport), and the location. All these were in the most populous part of the state, so they would have been much like any unassuming airport, hotel, and abandoned hydroelectric plant you'd be likely to see.

SRB: How did you handle makeups and costumes this time around with the aliens, the mutants, etc.?

BP: Most of the costumes were made by a local woman I found (if I recall correctly) through some kind of crafts league. I was very pleased with her work, but I think one movie was enough for her. I designed and fabricated all the mutant makeups, but we hired a pair of makeup artists to apply them in some of the scenes. They did a good job, but we also had them do a couple of practical effects (laser hits and such) and they weren't quite as competent at that. Their ideas were pretty primitive, and that's coming from someone who's spent a lifetime working with outdated technology. But their methods were even cruder than mine, and less effective. Everyone has their own strengths and weaknesses.

SRB: There were some very cool monsters in MUTANT WAR. *How many stop-motion animation creatures and setups did you create for this production?*

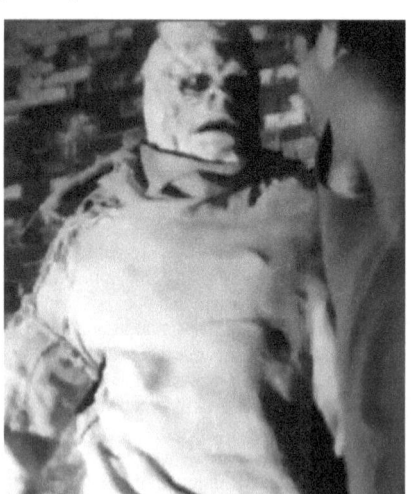

If You're Gonna Have a War, You Need Mutants! Bruce Osborne as one of Reinhart Rex's "formidable genetic creations," breeding stock for the **MUTANT WAR;** makeup by Brett Piper, Joe Rossi, and Ray Costigan

BP: Haven't seen the movie in decades, so my memory is a little fuzzy. But there was that bipedal monster at the beginning, a stupid-looking creature that Trent fights under the factory (whom we called "Goofy", for obvious reasons) and a return appearance by that Kirby-esque insect monster from **BATTLE**. There may have been others, I don't remember.

SRB: Where were your locations this time around? Did Baldwin and Schweitzer stay in New York and just leave you alone to just make the movie, once everyone was committed to doing the sequel?

BP: Again, all shot in southern New Hampshire, nothing more than twenty miles from my house. Schweitzer was from New York, Baldwin was local. Although Baldwin considered the two of them a team and the real movers behind the production, Schweitzer was more actively involved, all to the bad. He had nothing to do with the day-to-day work on the movie but made several "executive" decisions, such as insisting that the movie be shot in 35mm, which drove-up the expense and made everything much more difficult.

SRB: So, where was the money for all this coming from?

BP: I have no idea who ended up paying for this thing. For a while it was me. I kept waiting around for a contract or something to let me know I should start work, but nothing concrete appeared. It was all written in smoke. "Good faith" was Baldwin's by-word. We didn't need anything in writing, it was all "good faith", which turned out to mean whenever anything went wrong it was my fault, because I had nothing on paper to prove otherwise. Anyway, months passed and I kept asking Baldwin if we had a deal, and he'd say "Oh, sure, go ahead." I'd say "Do we have a contract?" and he'd say "No." I'd say "Do we have any money?" and he'd say "No". So I'd ask how I was supposed to pay for everything and he'd tell me to see his bookkeeper, a very nice and efficient lady, but when I'd talk to her she'd just shrug and say, "He hasn't said anything about it to me." Finally it's getting towards winter and I still have no definite go-ahead, so I start spending my own money. I put several thousand dollars into this thing just to get it moving, and finally we're shooting.

SRB: Did you end up getting—well, at least reimbursed? Making money?

BP: Gradually, in dribs and drabs, I got my money back, but I never made a nickel. I was supposed to be paid a fee of $20,000 for my work plus a percentage, but as far as I know Baldwin literally *gave* the movie to Arthur Schweitzer.

SRB: What was that all about?

BP: He had developed what I can only describe as an absurd schoolboy crush on his pal "Artie". Artie could do no wrong. Baldwin would point to effects I had done in the film and say, "Artie must have added that, you could never do anything that good". Artie ended up taking over the movie by calling the lab and having them send him all the original elements, which they did without getting a release from me, something they were not legally entitled to do. Then he bitched to Baldwin that I had screwed up by not delivering the movie by the agreed-upon date. When I pointed *[out]* that there *was no delivery date* (just as there'd never been a start date) Baldwin dismissed this objection with his usual comeback: "That doesn't matter, it's all *good faith!*" So after a year or so of grinding hard work, constant frustration and bungling interference from my "partners", I ended up with nothing. I consulted a lawyer, who told me that my "contract" was worthless, implying that it had been drawn up by an idiot. I'll let you guess who drew it up.

SRB: Given the business and production ordeal this represented, how did your participation end on MUTANT WAR, and what was it that you actually delivered to these bozos (35mm or 16mm, or video master)?

BP: They got the original 35mm negative from the lab without, as I said, my permission, so I no longer had any leverage at all. It was all shipped to New York to be conformed, and then a company called Rainbow Productions rushed through the post, the sound mix and whatever. I went to NYC and worked on it with them. They did it all in maybe a week. I was impressed that they could do it that fast, but it looked just like the rush-job it was, very poor. Schweitzer was trying to make some kind of convention, the AFM or something. Then afterwards he called me up and said it all had to be done-over. I told him as far as I was concerned he'd taken the movie out of my hands, and now it was up to him to finish it. He had a fit, called Baldwin and bitched, Baldwin called me and bitched, but it was clear by now that the whole thing was a disaster, and I just walked away from it. There was nothing more I could do.

SRB: Good God, no one could blame you there—what a completely toxic pair of

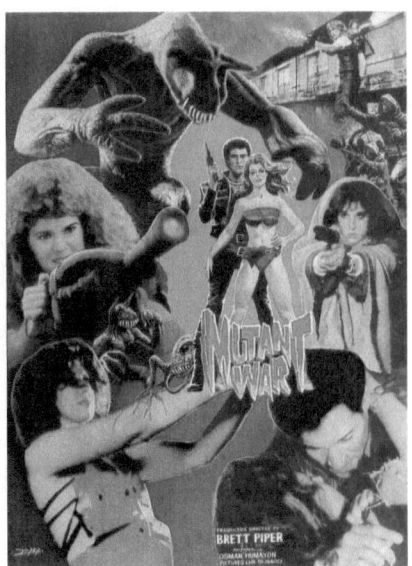

You *Still* Can't Get There From Here:
A lively Pakistani poster for Brett Piper's
MUTANT WAR

producers; this sounds insane! Did you have any sense of their doing anything with the film afterwards?

BP: The last I heard of it the title had been changed from **MUTANT WAR** to **MUTANT MEN WANT PRETTY WOMEN**. The Julia Roberts movie **PRETTY WOMAN** *[1990, D: Garry Marshall]* had just come out, and I guess Schweitzer thought he could fool people into believing she was in **MUTANT WAR** *[!?]*. That's the kind of "keen" thinking you have to deal with.

By the way, our assistant cameraman, Bob Becchio, had just finished working on a movie down in Massachusetts. When I asked him about it he shrugged and said "It was something called **MYSTIC PIZZA** *[1988, D: Donald Petrie]*. There's nobody in it." It was Julia Roberts' first big movie.

SRB: When I've been through similarly demoralizing creative ordeals/endurance tests, I have to do something for myself just to get my head back on straight. What did you do to pull yourself up and out after MUTANT WAR was behind you?

BP: There's not much you can do. Just chalk it up to experience and get on with your life.

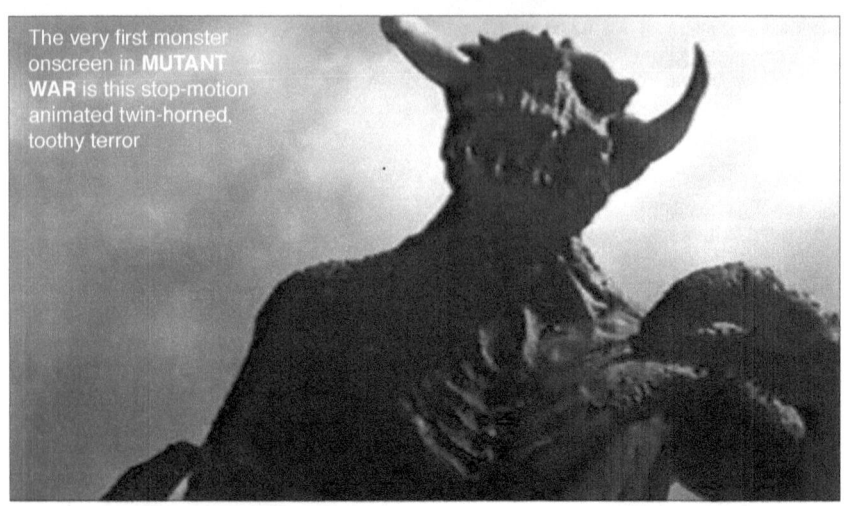

The very first monster onscreen in **MUTANT WAR** is this stop-motion animated twin-horned, toothy terror

DARK FORTRESS / A NYMPHOID BARBARIAN IN DINOSAUR HELL (1990)

SRB: At this point, your filmography is a bit of a quandary for me, Brett. It look like the very late 1980s and early 1990s, after MUTANT WAR, DARK FORTRESS *was your next feature film, but I recall you also had worked on personal projects (like* THE RETURN OF CAPTAIN SINBAD [c.1993-96]]*), and somewhere in all that you made the connection with Troma. Was* DARK FORTRESS *next for you?*

BP: **DARK FORTRESS** was definitely the next feature I did. Troma must have come later, because I first starting shooting things for them after they bought **FORTRESS**. **SINBAD** came at the tail-end of all this.

SRB: Did you bankroll DARK FORTRESS *yourself? Did you maintain complete control over this production?*

BP: **FORTRESS** was co-produced by Alex Pirnie, who raised the money. He'd been an actor in **MUTANT WAR**, and approached me afterward about our making a movie together. I had more or less complete control.

SRB: Alex also had a prominent role in DARK FORTRESS, *playing the lead villain, Clon—had you written the role with him in mind, then?*

BP: No, the screenplay for **DARK FORTRESS** was written before we'd even met. It may actually have been written before **MUTANT**

WAR—I think it was one of the stories I pitched to Schweitzer after **BATTLE**. But of course, if Pirnie was going to put money into a movie, he wanted to appear in it too, and he was a pretty good actor, so that was no problem.

SRB: According to various sources, Alex also appeared in a couple other roles in the film, as did your leads and some of the support players. I take it that was a budgetary decision—making the most of your cast—and what relations were "Reptilian Goon" players Ryan and Quinn Piper to you, and Melanie Pirnie to Alex?

BP: All kinds of people, including Pirnie, got into the lizard-man costumes at one time or another. My brother Quinn and Pirnie's daughter Melanie as well. Ryan, my nephew, played the little troll on the beach. He might have been nine or ten at the time. I thought I'd killed him at one point. After the lizards knock him into the water and I yelled "*Cut!*" he just lies there without moving. It was a brutally hot day and the water was freezing, so I was afraid he'd gone into shock or something. When I ran over to see if he was all right, he squinted up at me and said, "I didn't hear you say cut!"

SRB: Actually, Linda Corwin was pretty good in the lead role—she was convincingly feral throughout, aggressive, inhabiting the character. Was she comfortable dealing with the stunts and action sequences?

BP: She was fine with all that. In fact, I think she enjoyed it. The only thing she wouldn't do was the shot where Clon is feeling-up her boobs. She said—and I don't know if she was joking or not—"I wouldn't mind showing my boobs, if I had any!"

SRB: *That comes across in the film, for sure. She is a feisty heroine, and in many ways your most appealing protagonist to that point in your work; thanks in part to her character Lea,* DARK FORTRESS *manages to maintain an appealing combination of adolescent and adult fun, like a further-fantasized* ONE MILLION YEARS B.C. *Was that your intent, your narrative model? This was your first "caveman" movie, in a lot of ways.*

BP: I'd always wanted to make a true Harryhausen-style movie, an "epic" fantasy set in some kind of primitive world, but it seemed like quite a daunting task, considering how limited I was in money and resources. So I wrote a story that would have that kind of feel and setting—castles and monsters and medieval costumes and such—but with minimal characters and, I thought, manageable effects. When Pirnie came to me wanting to produce a movie, I figured it was time to give it a shot. I changed it from a period setting to some kind of alien world, but aside from that the script remained the same. I don't think the end result is a very good movie, but I do think I managed to rise to the challenge of creating another world on film fairly well. Considering.

SRB: *Actually, I'd like to push a bit more on talking about what was becoming a recognizable "Brett Piper Universe" at this point in your career. With* DARK FORTRESS, *we were now a number of films into a fantastic landscape that had certain consistent elements, whether terrestrial (*BATTLE FOR THE LOST PLANET*) or extraterrestrial (*MYSTERIOUS PLANET*): human characters at the fringe of savagery in an evolving or devolving tribal state, mutants, giant predatory creatures, etc. While there were certainly movies we'd grown up with that introduced those concepts (I'm thinking of* TEENAGE CAVEMAN, WORLD WITHOUT END, VALLEY OF THE DRAGONS, *etc.), and some pulp SF (Robert E. Howard's "Valley of the Worm" included), I get a real taste of Silver Age comics like* Mighty Samson, *or the later Jack Kirby* Kamandi, *and even more of a Richard Corben underground comix/*Heavy Metal *vibe (specifically* Rowlf, Den, *and his and Jan Strnad's* Mutant World *in the Warren magazine 1984/1994 in the late 1970s and early 1980s) from your films by the time we're into* DARK FORTRESS—*you even maintained Corben's mix of sexy, normal female and male survivors with militarized animalistic and/or deformed mutant tribes and bigger creatures higher up the food chain. Am I off-base, or were those comics you'd read and enjoyed?*

BP: I'm familiar with all the comics you mentioned, but the one I loved was *Kamandi*. It was published after I'd left home and was living on my own, so I still have all my old back issues. I remember a lot of flak to the effect that Kirby had merely stolen the premise of *Planet of the Apes*, but that's nonsense, like saying that **STAR WARS** was just a rip-off of

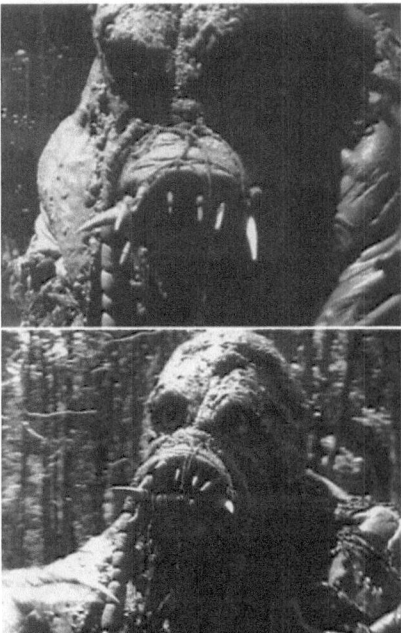

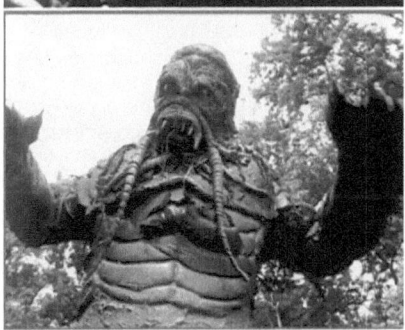

Three views of the man-in-suit swamp monster Brett Piper created for **DARK FORTRESS** a.k.a. **A NYMPHOID BARBARIAN IN DINOSAUR HELL**, anticipating the full-body-suit aquatic creatures he'd later construct for **THEY BITE** (1996) and **MUCKMAN** (2009)

Stephen R. Bissette   Brett Piper Interview Pts 2 & 3

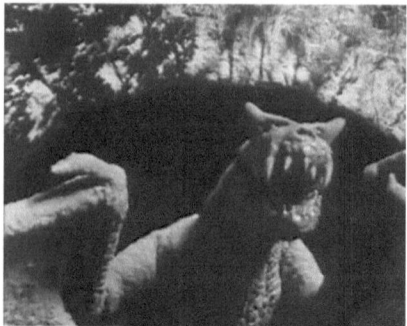

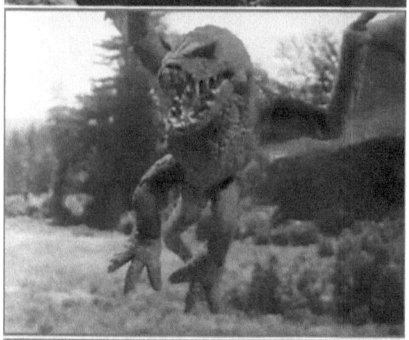

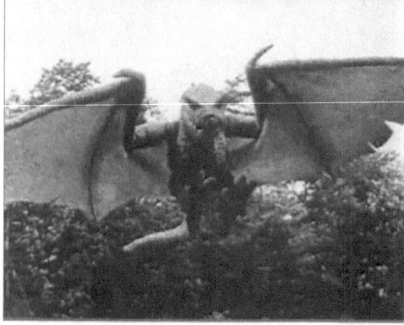

DARK FORTRESS' ptoothy pterosaur-like flying reptile in action: proof how far Piper's work had evolved in the just a few short years since his first flying stop-motion-animated monster in **MYSTERIOUS PLANET** (1982)

Flash Gordon because they were both about heroes in spaceships. That's like saying **HIGH NOON** *[1952, D: Fred Zinnemann]* is exactly the same as **BOWERY BUCKAROOS** *[1947, D: William Beaudine]* because they both have horses. So I suppose *Kamandi* must have been an influence to some extent, but then so were a lot of other things. That's just the way it goes. Everyone builds on what came before.

I'll tell you what the "Brett Piper Universe" is about: anarchy and monsters. In all my movies the characters find themselves in situations, large or small, where they're on their own with no support from any kind of social structure. Sometimes it's only one person *[DYING DAY]*, sometimes it's a whole planet *[BATTLE]*, but they're always on their own. And there's *monsters*.

By the way, I love **VALLEY OF THE DRAGONS**. I have no idea why. It just feels like a perfect Saturday Matinee movie to me.

SRB: I love VALLEY OF THE DRAGONS, too! In fact, growing-up with all those movies using ONE MILLION B.C. **[1940, Ds: Hal Roach Jr., Hal Roach]** *stock footage being on TV all the time, I've always loved VALLEY OF THE DRAGONS as being sort of the ultimate "K-Tel Greatest Hits" dinosaur stock footage movie. In hindsight, it really marked the end of an era, chronologically, while summing-it-up in so many ways. The creepy, fleetingly-seen "troglodyte" makeup was pretty great in that movie, too…*

BP: *"K-Tel Greatest Hits!"* I love that. I think another reason I like **VALLEY** is that I saw it before I'd ever seen **ONE MILLION B.C.**, which used to be pretty hard-to-find, so it was the first time I'd seen a lot of *[its]* great footage. Also, it just has everything—lizard monsters, Rodan, ape-men, Morlocks, cute cave-girls—I mean, that swimming scene with Danielle de Metz![8] I don't know why she's not more of a fan favorite. She was in **VALLEY**, **RETURN OF THE FLY**, **THE MAGIC SWORD**, and on TV in *Alfred Hitchcock*, *Thriller*, *Voyage to the Bottom of the Sea*.

By the way, do you have any idea where the opening stock footage of the Middle Eastern bazaar comes from? I happened to watch **VALLEY** and **CAPTAIN SINDBAD** *[Kapitän Sindbad, 1963, USA/West Germany, D: Byron Haskin]* back-to-back one night, and they open with the same footage, only in **SINDBAD** it's in color!

SRB: No, I don't know, but I'm going to go digging and try to find out, Brett.[9] Can I ask you about your own fantasy "world" in your

---

8   Correction: it's actually *Playboy* November 1958 Playmate of the Month Joan Staley whose swim sequence graces **VALLEY OF THE DRAGONS**; Danielle de Metz also plays a cavewoman in the film.

9   If anyone out there among the *Monster!* readership knows, let us know, please, and we'll pass your answer along to Brett.

films? There were certainly no stop-motion animation films predating yours that were set in any "universe" like yours! It's such a natural evolution for stop-motion animated feature films, but you were the one that took it forward and kept at it. Again, was that a conscious decision on your part—"I'm going to keep taking this further from the Harryhausen/ Schneer template," while extending their tradition (i.e., building stories around spectacular stop-motion animation set-pieces)?

BP: I think it was more an attempt to make Harryhausen-style movies within my budget restrictions. I couldn't afford to do things like **JASON** *[i.e., **JASON AND THE ARGONAUTS**, 1963, D: Don Chaffey]* or *Sinbad [a Harryhausen/Schneer series which began with **THE 7ᵀᴴ VOYAGE OF SINBAD**, 1958, D: Nathan Juran]*, recreating an entire bygone world, but I could create a post-disaster world and populate it with similar monsters. I'd still love to do a swashbuckling fantasy, especially aimed at a younger audience. I've written a few, but the money's not there to make them. The closest I've come is **DARK FORTRESS** and **RETURN OF CAPTAIN SINBAD**. Well, someday. It's good to still have goals later in life!

SRB: Was your intention, before Troma and Lloyd Kaufman were involved, that DARK FORTRESS be a medieval fantasy setting, or were you working the post-apocalyptic setting (the setting that Troma's added "prologue" insisted upon, once they had the film)?

BP: It was never post-apocalyptic. It was originally a period fantasy, and the setting was later changed to an Earth outpost on another planet. Various hints were dropped to that effect. The human characters were the descendants of the original colonists. When Troma made it a post-nuke story, I ended up getting a lot of flak for the inconsistencies this created. Then again, people constantly criticize movies without having the slightest idea how they ended up the way they ended up. They seem to think movies emerge full-blown from the mind of the creator, exactly the way he intended them. I don't think there's anything people criticize more and know less about than movies. Everyone thinks he's an expert, and most people don't know crap.

Dumbest criticism of **NYMPHOID / DARK FORTRESS**: one genius mentioned how stupid it was that Lea couldn't read, but she could speak English. Well, the world is full of people who can speak a language but not read it—like *everyone*

until the age of five or so! I don't mind intelligent criticism, but I resent being slammed by morons.

SRB: Was there anything you had scripted for DARK FORTRESS that you had to leave out— either not shoot, or cut out in your final edit— due to time or budget constraints?

BP: Not that I can recall. I don't think I've ever

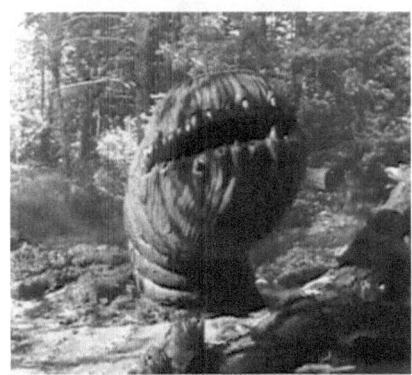

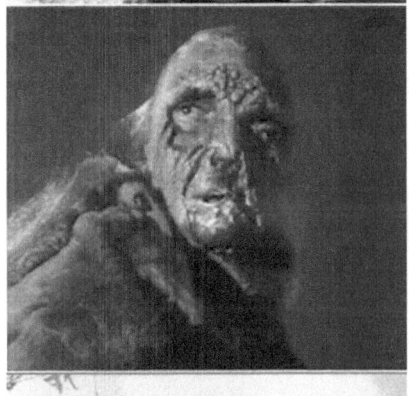

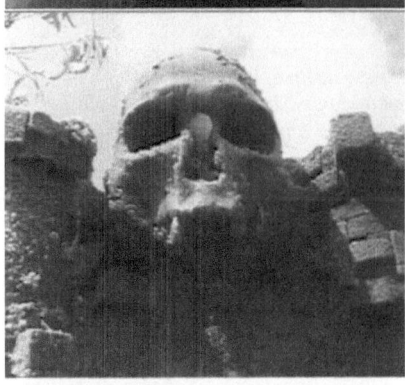

The alien monsters and environments of **DARK FORTRESS**—created via puppetry *[top]*, live-action makeup *[center]* and miniatures *[above]*—all the handiwork of Brett Piper.

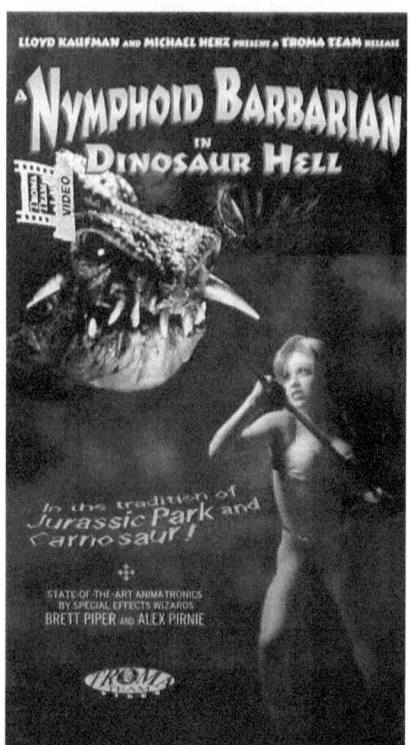

After playing the film theatrically and on cable, Troma waited until March 25th, 1997 to release **DARK FORTRESS / A NYMPHOID BARBARIAN IN DINOSAUR HELL** on VHS—with a bogus effects credit for Alex Pirnie

written a shot that I didn't manage to pull off, although frequently not as well as I would have liked.

SRB: Let's talk about the special effects and creatures, Brett. Were you working with larger animation models at this point, or did you just take—and have—more time to play with this one? The level of detail and illusion of life your monsters had/have in DARK FORTRESS was/is a real step-up from the earlier films, to my eye.

BP: I think I'd just improved my skills by then. The models were about the same size. In fact, one of them, the thing in the pit, was built over the armature of "Goofy" from **MUTANT WAR**.

SRB: DARK FORTRESS had a great lineup of monsters, on land, in water, in the air: outsized mutant insects, canines, bats, gators, and the simian/reptilian tribe subservient to Alex Pirnie's villain. It looks like you really cut loose; were there creatures you designed, built, and animated for DARK FORTRESS that you'd always wanted to work into a film?

BP: Not as I recall. The first two creatures I sketched and built were the monsters that battle on the top of the cliff; the canine creature and the rhinoceros beetle. The crocodilian swamp critter was a reworked puppet from a dragon movie I'd wanted to do. And as I mentioned, the creature in the pit was the reworked "Goofy" puppet from **MUTANT WAR**.

SRB: Were there creatures you worked-up for DARK FORTRESS purely because they would provide a challenge—push you in new ways you'd never played with before, or hadn't felt "up to" doing before?

BP: No, just monsters I thought would be cool.

SRB: Beyond the reptile-men makeups, how extensive were the live-action monster effects for DARK FORTRESS? It looks like you had a few more "props" (full-sized snouts, jaws, limbs, etc.) interacting with your actors than in previous films.

BP: The lizard creatures were strictly costumes, no real makeup involved. Clon's makeup was fairly elaborate, made more difficult by the fact that Alex Pirnie sweated like a herd of pigs, so the only thing that would hold his prosthetic scars on was surgical adhesive. There was extensive makeup for The Mysterious Stranger, full-sized heads for the giant worm and the crocodile creature. At the time, these were difficult to build because I was still feeling my way as to the best materials and processes to use. Today I would build them in half the time, and they would look five times as good.

SRB: So, you designed the "Reptilian Goons" as masks, gloves, and outfits, which made them much simpler to deal with than makeups. This must have sped things up, given how prominent a role those characters played in the film?

BP: Yes, that was the whole idea. Whenever we needed a lizard-man, someone could slip into one of those costumes in just a couple of minutes. I made the whole things myself, outfits included. In fact I made *all* the costumes for the movie, and I'm no seamstress! I was up all night before the first day of shooting finishing-up Clon's costume. I just had time to throw everything in the van and head off to the beach. I'd hired someone else, a friend of mine, to make them, but she simply didn't do the job. She never delivered a single costume until a week or so *after* we started shooting, when she just left a box of things on my doorstep which turned out to be entirely unusable.

SRB: So, what did you have in hand when DARK FORTRESS was completed—35mm or 16mm?—and how did the film end up with Troma and Lloyd Kaufman?

BP: **FORTRESS** was shot on 16mm negative, all silent with my Bolex, and post-dubbed. It was kind of funny—I got a bunch of the actors together after the shoot and we found a quiet spot in the country and basically reenacted the entire movie, just for sound. But for some reason they'd be as *quiet* as possible during the takes, even though the audio was what we were after! I still don't know what they were thinking. Anyway, I had the negative conformed and an answer print made, which was *horrible!* We screened it at the lab, and I couldn't believe it—the colors were way off, purple skies and blue grass and such, and I would have refused to accept it but Pirnie had planned a party that night to "premiere" the movie for his friends and he insisted on having the print. It was his money, so I finally gave in, but we couldn't afford to do it over, so that's the picture that has gone down to posterity. Someone once asked me if the weird color effects were a deliberate attempt to give the movie an alien quality. Afraid not.

SRB: Oh, man...

BP: Anyway, I started shopping it around. It was easier in those days; you just drew-up a list of companies that handled similar types of movies and sent them a screener. If they were interested,

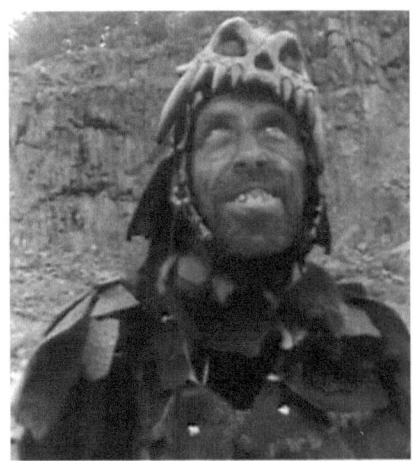

they got back to you. Ironically, one of the distributors was a guy who had earlier advised me to make a movie that was "all action, no dialogue", because that would be easier to sell overseas. When I sent him **FORTRESS**, he said, "I can't sell this—there's no dialogue!' There's a moral there, which is never listen to anybody. Eventually we got around to Troma. I had earlier pitched **BATTLE** to them, and they seemed interested, but they made it clear we would never make a nickel from them, so I passed. It turned out they *were* interested in **FORTRESS**, and made us an offer. It was a lousy offer, which is okay, that's where you start. We went back and forth—at one point they sent me an outraged letter calling the movie "unreleasable" for technical reasons, then came back a few months later with another, slightly-less-lousy offer. I would have held out longer, but while all this was going on Pirnie had decided he was now a producer and no longer needed his contracting company. As a result he was broke, and going to

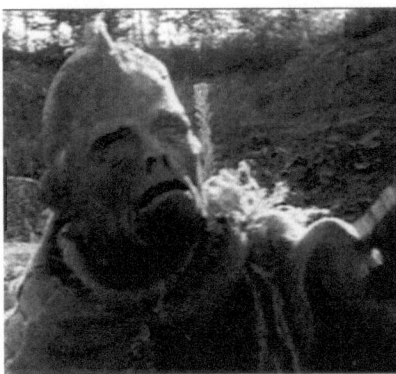
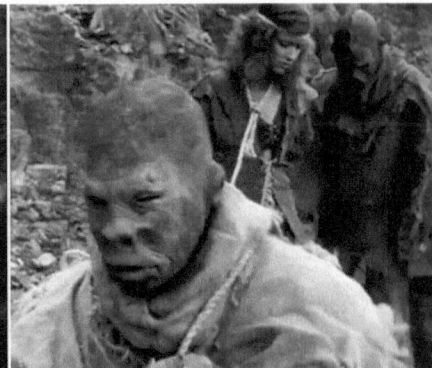

"To hell with you—you're *lizard meat!*" Alex Pirnie as Clon *[top]* and various Reptilian Goons with Lea (Linda Corwin) *[above, right]* in **DARK FORTRESS**

Stephen R. Bissette   *Brett Piper Interview Pts 2 & 3*   **139**

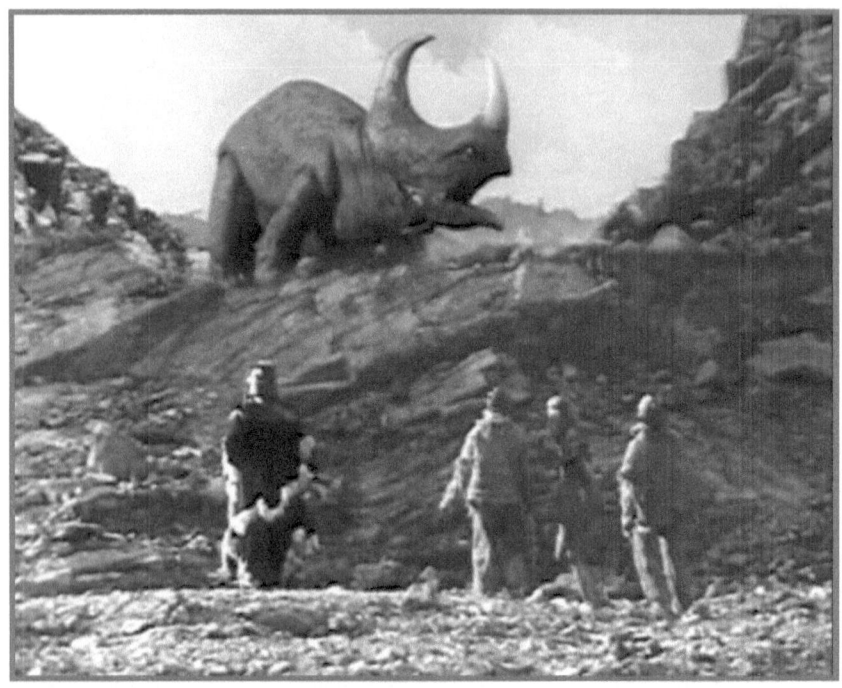

Dynastinaesaurus! The marvelous Rhinoceros beetle-like ceratopsian of **DARK FORTRESS** a.k.a. **A NYMPHOID BARBARIAN IN DINOSAUR HELL**, Brett Piper's inventive fusion of scarab and Cretaceous Ceratopia

lose his house, so (once again) I gave in to him and we accepted Troma's offer. It wasn't even enough to recoup our expenses. And *that's* how **NYMPHOID** was born!

SRB: So, then: the answer print was botched, color-wise; did that mean the negative was flawed? Was the negative intact, salvageable, or—?

BP: No, the negative was fine. New prints could certainly have been struck if anyone had cared to.

SRB: Would you have been delivering the negative to Troma as well as the answer print, or by 1990 was it video transfers only the studios worked with? For instance, what would have been shown to potential foreign distributors in May 1990 (the "official" release date noted online)?

BP: Troma got everything, negative included. They also got a ¾-inch video master made from the answer print which, as far as I can tell, is what they worked from in creating their new version. It certainly looked the same. I have no idea what Troma showed their sub-distributors.

SRB: Dumb question, but I have to ask: Did Troma confer with you about their plans— the new prologue, retitling it to NYMPHOID BARBARIAN—*or was it once again "a sale is a sale," and away she goes?*

BP: The first I heard that **THE DARK FORTRESS** had become **A NYMPHOID BARBARIAN IN DINOSAUR HELL** was when Al Pirnie told me. He expected me to be angry. I laughed my ass off. What did I care? It's not like they destroyed a masterpiece. It's different when, for example, Pop Cinema ruined **SHOCK-O-RAMA** *[2005]* in post. **SHOCK** was a pretty good movie that now looks like garbage. But **NYMPHOID**? Big deal!

SRB: NYMPHOID *has been a fixture of Troma's catalog since 1990, they've reissued it in almost every new format as they emerged. Was it a flat sale to Troma, no residuals, or have you seen revenue from the film since 1990?*

BP: Nope, not a dime. At one point Lloyd Kaufman even tried to convince me that **NYMPHOID** lost money for them, but I later spoke to an ex-employee of theirs who told me, not only had the movie been highly profitable for Troma, it had actually been their most successful movie in Japan.

***SRB: Oh, man. I** hate the fucking business— movies, publishing, comics, all of it. Love doing the work and the art; hate the business.*

BP: Couldn't have said it better myself. Movies have got to be the worst business in the world. I have a friend who made some movies financed by the mob in Vegas. He said, entirely serious, that he would rather make movies for Las Vegas mobsters than Hollywood producers, because the mobsters were more honorable men.

SRB: Buddy Giovinazzo once told me he was just happy Troma got his first feature COMBAT SHOCK **[1984]** *out there, in any form. Was there any satisfaction for you in your film getting out there, being seen, after what happened with the prior two features? Did* NYMPHOID *getting wider release lead to any further industry opportunities or contacts for you in the 1990s?*

BP: I suppose its exposure was somewhat gratifying. It did get a lot of play, because of the title, so kudos to Lloyd for that. It was mentioned on *Entertainment Tonight* and even in *The Wall Street Journal*. It's probably my best-known movie, although it didn't open any new doors for me.

SRB: Despite how Kaufman treated DARK FORTRESS, *you ended up working with Troma later in the 1990s. Was your doing special effects for one of the* **Class of Nuke 'Em High** *films your first post-*NYMPHOID *interaction with Troma? What was it like working in a creative capacity with Kaufman's team?*

BP: I want to make it perfectly clear that I bear no grudge against Troma over **FORTRESS / BARBARIAN**. They didn't do anything crooked or dishonest. They made us an offer we were perfectly free to refuse, but we accepted because Pirnie was desperate for cash. Anyway—Troma wanted "us" to do some effects for them because we (as in "I") could crank them out quick and cheap. Pirnie sort of brokered the deal, in return for which he was supposed to get a percentage. I'd cut him in because of his money troubles. I didn't find out until later that he'd convinced Troma he was responsible for the effects in **NYMPHOID** himself. He also later claimed to have co-created the **NUKE' EM HIGH 2** effects, which is why he shares credit for them on the film. In fact, he had almost *nothing* to do with them except for

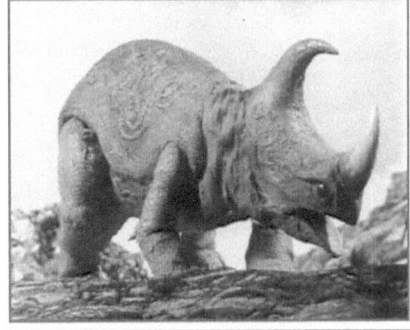

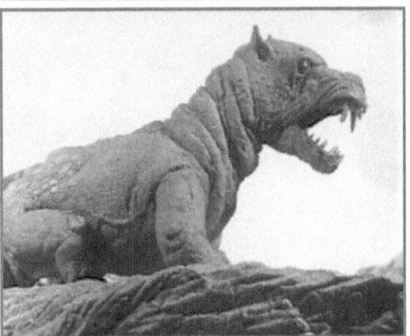

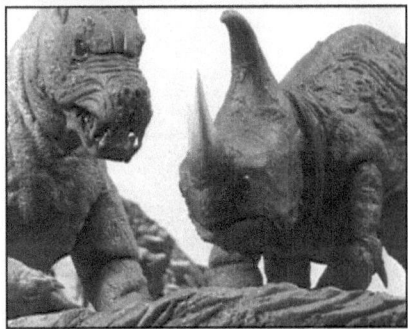

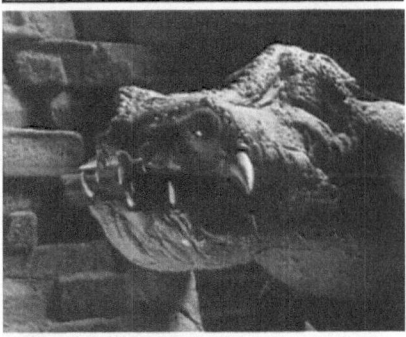

Monster Menagerie: Brett Piper's semi-saurians, pseudosynapsids, and threatening therapsids of **DARK FORTRESS** a.k.a. **A NYMPHOID BARBARIAN IN DINOSAUR HELL** are all imaginatively designed, sculpted, and animated

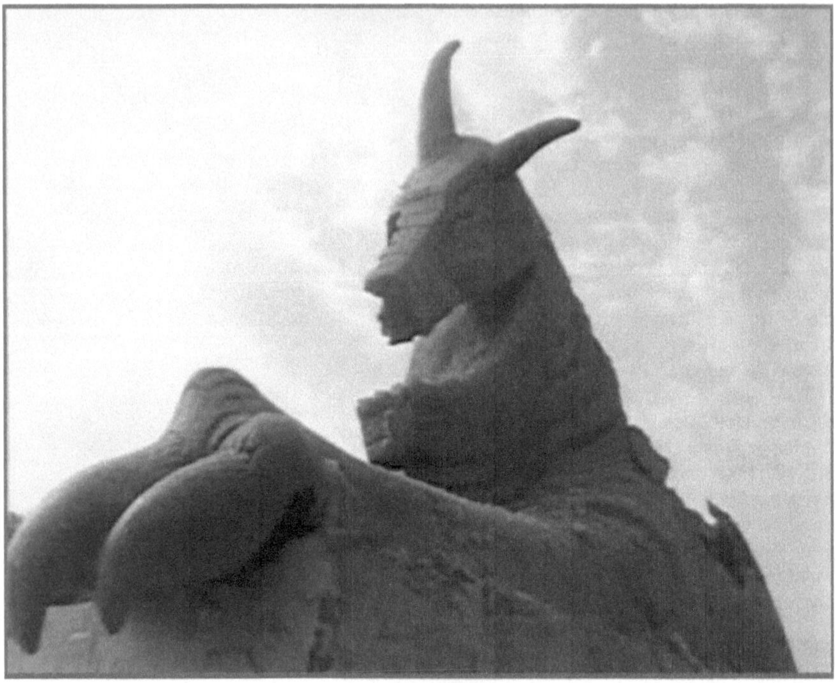

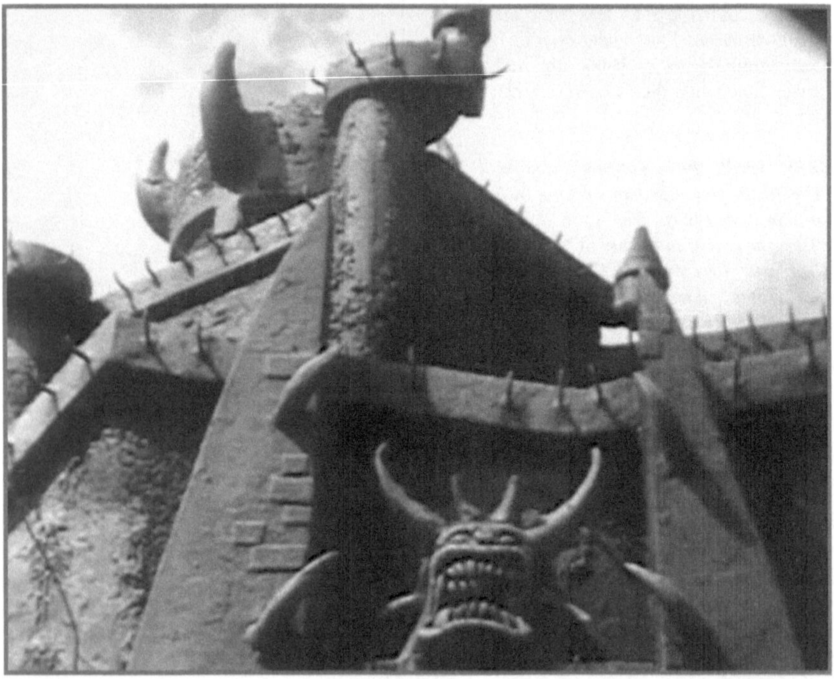

D.I.Y. D&D: Working with whatever materials were at hand, Brett Piper's **DARK FORTRESS** a.k.a. **A NYMPHOID BARBARIAN**'s lovingly sculpted miniatures use every illusion-of-depth-and-perspective trick in the old-school filmmaker's book to convey a sense of size, scale, and textural detail

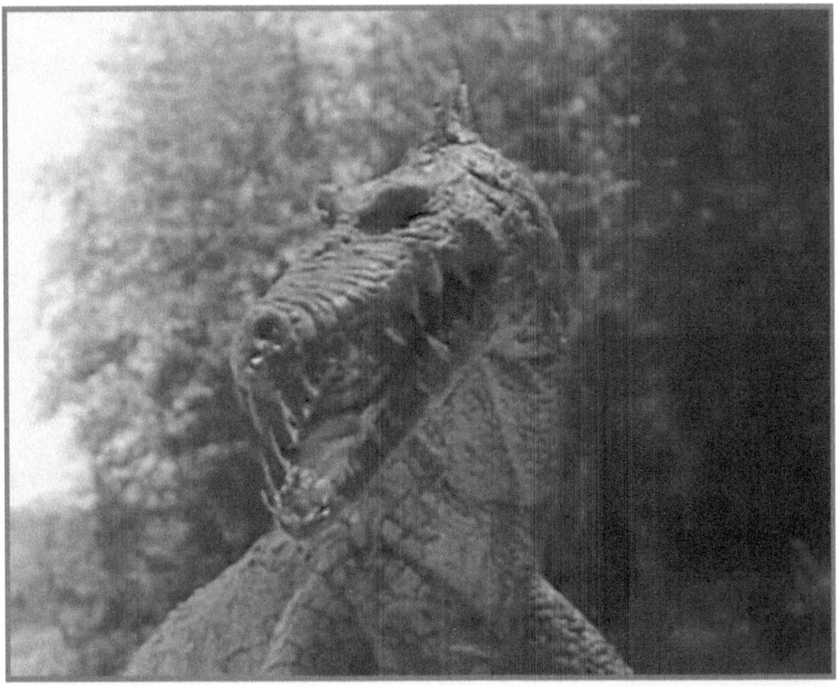

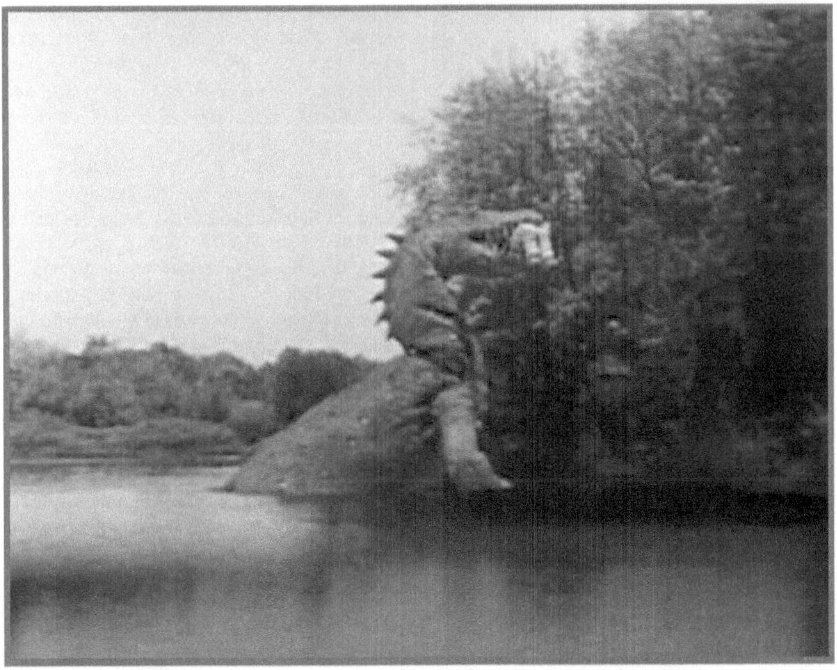

DARK FORTRESS a.k.a. **A NYMPHOID BARBARIAN IN DINOSAUR HELL**: "The crocodilian swamp critter was a reworked puppet from a dragon movie I'd wanted to do", Brett Piper explains

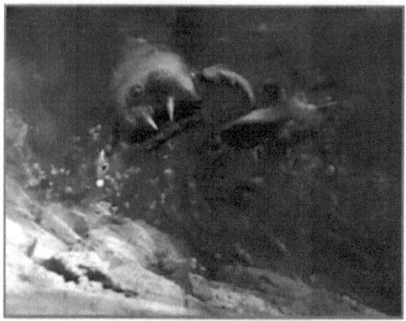
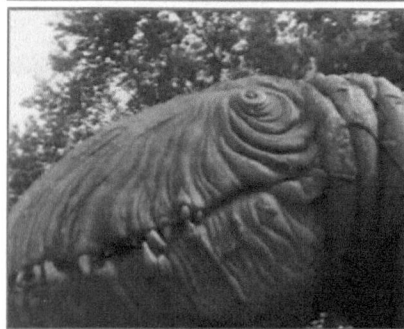
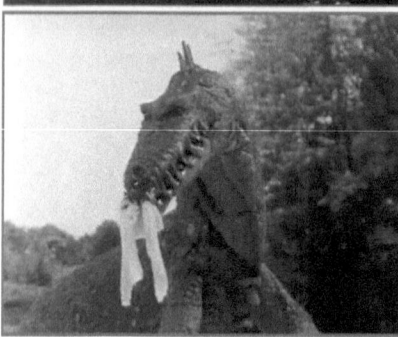

What Brett Piper conceived, designed, and executed to be alien invertebrates, outsized annelids and the carnivorous crocodilians of another world onscreen were retroactively explained-away as "post-apocalyptic" denizens of Tromaville when Troma changed **DARK FORTRESS** into a nonsensical futuristic fantasy instead

wearing the mutant squirrel suit I built. I did all the effects work myself, with very minimal input from Troma or the director, Eric Louzil. When I'd ask what they had in mind, they'd mostly respond "Whatever you think." At one point I bugged Louzil for some kind of storyboards until he finally sent me a sheet of yellow legal paper with a tiny square drawn in the middle and an X inside the square. Next to the X was the word "monster". That was all the creative input I got. So I struggled through and sent them footage

which they seemed happy with. There was even talk of my directing the next *Nuke 'Em High* movie, although I was already committed to **THEY BITE** *[1996].*

By the way, Pirnie was handling the money for this deal. Troma sent the check to him, but he stalled me for quite a while. Finally, we drove to the bank together so I could deposit my share. It should have been a few thousand dollars, but it was couple-hundred. "What happened to the rest of it?" I demanded. "I don't know," he said, and that was all I could get out of him. Troma didn't steal that money, I know that for sure, and it wasn't the last time Pirnie robbed me.

SRB: I had a friend I sometimes worked with who pulled such shit—nothing as bad as what you're describing, but, well, close. Awfully close. With friends like these—

BP: As I would often be reminded in this business, "No good deed goes unpunished."

SRB: Let's ride with this and detour at this point, for a while, and talk about the films by other filmmakers you did production and post-production work for, primarily contributing special effects or the like. Were there films made by others, prior to your finishing your own feature DARK FORTRESS, *that you'd had a hand in?*

BP: Nothing before **DARK FORTRESS**. Not much after, really, except for the few things I did for Troma, including a teaser trailer for **PSYCHO-BACKHOE** which I created over a weekend. I apparently have credit for effects in a lot of Polonia Brothers movies, but with a few exceptions it's mostly hand-me-down masks and props and such which I sent them rather than throwing them away. I have credits on movies I've never *heard* of!

SRB: Speaking of which: you received a "thanks" acknowledgment credit on Christopher Thies' shot-in-Massachusetts WINTERBEAST *(shot in 1986, 1989, released direct-to-video in 1992), and there was some fleeting stop-motion animation in the film; did you have anything directly to do with the film? As a consultant? Or was Thies just thanking you as an inspiration, given the proximity to your own New England filmmaking example?*

BP: I don't know why I would have been given a special thanks in **WINTERBEAST**. I had nothing to do with the making of the movie, although I knew the person who made it. I don't think Christopher Thies had much to do with the actual making of the film either. I met him just once. When **WINTERBEAST** was finished, he and Mark Frizzell, who I believe was the actual creator of the movie, came up to my apartment along with Mark's wife. They also brought a bottle of champagne, presumably in celebration. We watched the movie and afterwards Mark asked me what I thought of it. I said, "Do you want me to be nice or do you want me to be honest?" Mark and Chris both said "Oh, be honest!" I said, "Burn it and try something else." And Mark's wife, who up 'til then hadn't said a word, nearly shouted, "Listen to this man! *Listen to him!*"

DINOSAUR KID (*circa* 1992-93?) and THE RETURN OF CAPTAIN SINBAD (*circa* 1993-96?)

SRB: *Sometime after* DARK FORTRESS *was turned into* NYMPHOID BARBARIAN, *you worked on a couple of personal projects you allowed me to see (via loaned videocassettes) in the early-to-mid 1990s: some stop-motion and live-action* DINOSAUR KID *test footage, which was quite impressive, and* THE RETURN OF CAPTAIN SINBAD. *Which came first, by your recall?*

BP: I really can't remember. They must have been done very close together—they may even have overlapped. The two boys in the **DINOSAUR KID** test footage, my nephews Ian and Kyle, also did the voice of the boy in **RETURN OF CAPTAIN SINBAD**, and must have been nearly the same age at the time.

SRB: DINOSAUR KID *looked really* **neat!**

BP: It was an idea I shopped around when I heard **JURASSIC PARK** was being made. I've always wanted to do a dinosaur movie (still do), and it seemed like an ideal time to try to get one going.

SRB: *The novel was published in November 1990, and Universal bought the rights before Michael Crichton's novel saw print; I first saw it announced sometime in 1991, so you were shopping it around in what, 1992?*

BP: Maybe a little earlier, around the time the Spielberg movie was first announced. I figured if Spielberg was doing dinosaurs, it couldn't lose. But I learned an interesting lesson about the way the industry thinks. When I first approached studios about making it, **JP** was still in the works, so I was told, "No one wants to see a dinosaur movie, they're old-fashioned". When **JURASSIC** came out and became a mega-hit, I was told, "There's no point in making a dinosaur movie now, you can't compete with Spielberg". And afterwards, I was told, "It's too late now, why didn't you show us this earlier?" So what it came down to was, *whenever* I tried to pitch a dinosaur movie was the wrong time!

SRB: *I had a similar experience trying to shop my comicbook proposal* **S.R. Bissette's Tyrant®** *around to publishers in the early 1990s—you'd think selling a dinosaur comicbook or movie would be a no-brainer!*

BP: Especially when you consider how desperate distributors were to get their hands on dinosaur-themed movies after **JP** became such a huge success, and some of the really terrible films that resulted. One extreme example I remember is something called *Dennis the Menace, Dinosaur Hunter* which was a TV episode released on video—the cover featured a huge dinosaur looming over a house; an image which appeared nowhere in the movie.

SRB: *The models I recall in the* DINOSAUR KID *test footage you let me see were really excellent. What dinosaurs had you constructed for the film?*

BP: I'd built a *Megalosaurus, Saltasaurus, Stegosaurus, Centrosaurus* (in both stop-motion and puppet form) and an *Euoplocephalus*. I also made *Brachiosaurus* and *Pteranodon* armatures.

SRB: *Had you worked-up a full script for* DINOSAUR KID—*and if so, what was the story?*

BP: Yes, I did a full script and some large illustrations. It was a pretty generic story, in fact a little like my recent movie **TRICLOPS** *[see* Monster! *#30, pp.22]*, in that I had someone searching a lost valley for her missing brother. Hey, Howard Hawks liked to recycle his plots too, so what the hell! There's a kid along for the ride, and once in the valley they encounter not only dinosaurs but cavemen and a family of cowboys who, because of the nature of the valley, haven't aged since they stumbled into it a century ago. Since then a little girl has been born, who is about the same age as the titular Dinosaur Kid when the story takes place. Because she was born and grew up in the valley, she has a sort of psychic link to the dinosaurs. The story was basic, but I thought it would make a pretty good movie.

By the way, one of the people I talked to about **DINOSAUR KID** was Herbert Strock, director of **GOG** *[1954]* and **I WAS A TEENAGE FRANKENSTEIN** *[1957]*. We had a nice conversation, much of it about his career, but when we got around to discussing **DINOSAUR KID**, he told me flat-out, "It can't be made for the kind of money you're talking." Which was funny, because the figure I'd given him was *three times* what I actually needed.

SRB: You were SO on the money—the right idea at the right time, given the fact that Charles and Albert Band's PREHYSTERIA! **[1993] was awfully similar, and it made a fortune in video rentals, launching a series. At what point did you hear about Band working on what became** PREHYSTERIA! **for his then-new Full Moon Entertainment label?**

BP: I didn't know anything about **PREHYSTERIA!** until I saw the movie in a video store. It looked like fun, so I brought it home to watch with my nephews (the same ones you saw in the **DINOSAUR KID** test footage). They watched a little of it, started to get antsy, then about halfway through gave up and went outside to play. I never finished the movie either. A few days later, I was walking down the street with Ian, the older of the brothers, and out of nowhere he asks me, "What's the worst movie you've ever seen?" While I'm thinking about it, he shoots back "Mine's **PREHYSTERIA!**"

SRB: Adding salt to the wound, DINOSAUR KID **would have cost less to produce than** PREHYSTERIA!**—and would have been a far more interesting and entertaining film, I'd wager. What was your estimated budget, including everything? Would you have shot this in New Hampshire as well?**

BP: The budget was around $150,000—small change to Hollywood, but more than I've ever spent on a single movie to this day. We were looking at shooting parts of it in Puerto Rico. Not much jungle in New Hampshire.

SRB: Did you end up using the DINOSAUR KID **models in any future productions? Those really were lovely dinosaurs, what I saw in the test footage… sorry to keep saying it, but I so wish** we'd seen that film, and those creatures in motion!

BP: Most of them were used in (shudder) **DINOSAUR BABES** *[1996]*. The less said about which the better.

SRB: THE RETURN OF CAPTAIN SINBAD, **however, you did complete. This remains your only all-stop-motion-animated film, doesn't it? Were you emulating the classic "puppet films" (as Ray Harryhausen called them, in which he included his own fairytale short films) of the past with this venture?**

BP: Yes. My only all-puppet movie. I describe it as "Rankin and Bass meet Harryhausen". Also a slight nod to the many great East European animators (Jirí Trnka, Karel Zeman, etc.).

SRB: Did going stop-motion-miniatures only

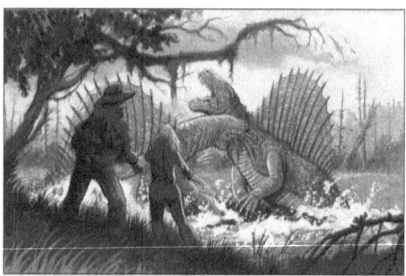

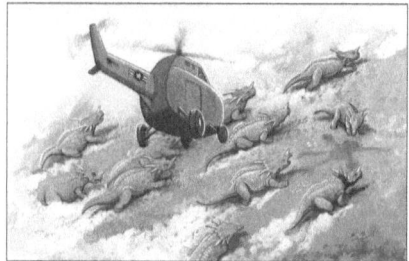

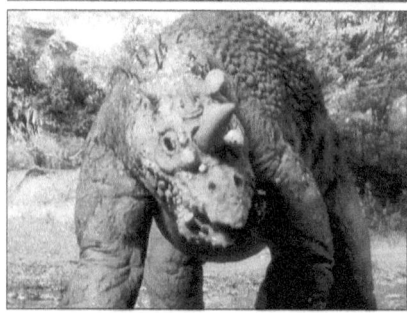

Brett Piper illustrations of sequences planned for **DINOSAUR KID** *[top, center]*; *[above]* one of the stop-motion creatures from Piper's **TRICLOPS** (2016)

simplify the production process (no need for locations, all that's necessary to shoot live-action footage, actors, etc.)?

BP: Yes, shooting all-stop-motion simplifies things a great deal in many ways. The hardest part of any movie, for me at least, is casting. Even when I worked in New Jersey and cast out of New York, it was horrendous. We'd put an ad in Craigslist or Backstage and get a thousand responses, but by the time we were through we were lucky if we found one or two we could use. In LA, I suppose it's much easier, but I've never worked out there. Maybe it's time.

SRB: CAPTAIN SINBAD is a charming adventure film. How many miniature environments did you create for the film, and how expansive was the largest of those?

BP: *Hah!* For a moment, I thought you said "expensive", in which case the answer would have been "not-very". None of the sets was big. They were all about the same size, about two feet by three or four. Various techniques were used to make them seem larger. I used a lot of false perspective, building sets that tapered into smaller backgrounds to give the illusion of depth. In some shots, for example the little boy climbing the stairs of Sinbad's castle, only the steps themselves were built to the scale of the model figure—the rest was a smaller miniature matted-in. And I had various-sized human figures too, tiny copies of Sinbad, and the villain maybe an inch high. The Grasp (the monster that Sinbad fights at the end of the movie) was only as tall as the main Sinbad figure himself (or should that be "*it*self"?).

SRB: Even the most stylized human characters are a real challenge for animators (in all media), and you'd never done anything like RETURN OF CAPTAIN SINBAD before. How did you approach that necessary component, and were you happy with the results?

BP: I think the figures weren't stylized enough, either in the design or the animation. I wouldn't have made them as non-realistic as Pal's Puppetoons, which could sometimes be a little too grotesque, but I think I could have given them a slightly more fantastic aspect.

SRB: It's also fascinating to see the monsters in SINBAD, and how differently they "play" from your creatures in the earlier live-action/animation feature films. Their design is more "plastic" ("cartoony," a non-cartoonist might

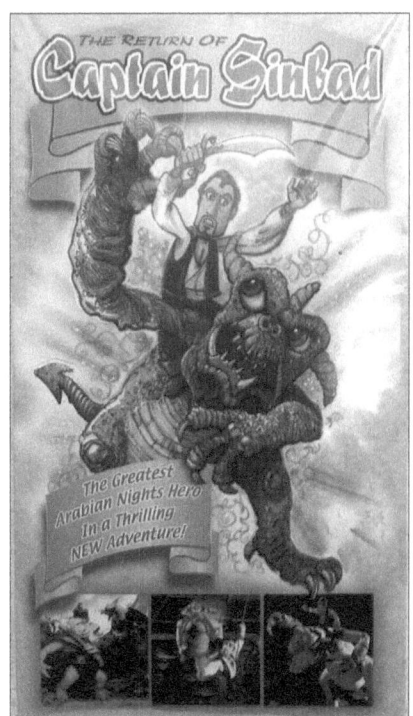

Brett Piper's **THE RETURN OF CAPTAIN SINBAD** actually had a legal US VHS release, using this box art (Sterling Entertainment Group, 2001)

say) and expressive, less-naturalistic, and their actions are also more flamboyant than in your other fantasy films. Was that a conscious shifting of gears for you, or did that playfulness with design and of motion just come naturally here, given the flavor of the project?

BP: I was after a more caricatured effect. In hindsight, I should have made the designs, the visuals more elaborate. They seem kind of bare-bones now. But it was an awful lot of work, and shortcuts have to be taken. The entire project, start to finish, only took nine months. There's only so much you can do in that amount of time.

SRB: You featured your nephew Kyle as your vocal "star", along with a couple adult performers—how did you go about "casting" your voice actors, at what stage did you do the recordings (before, and matched lip movement in the animation, or after, and had them "match" as best they could?), and were you satisfied with the results?

BP: The voices were all prerecorded, and I

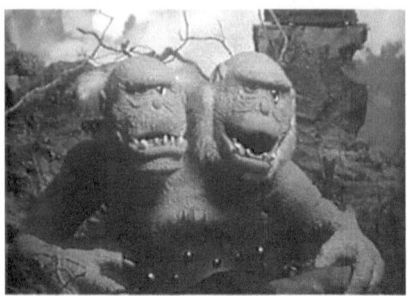

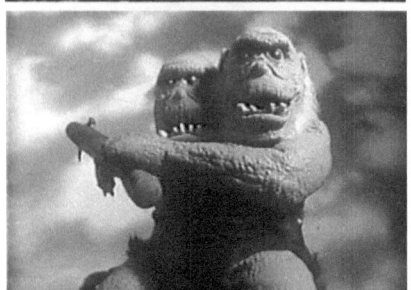

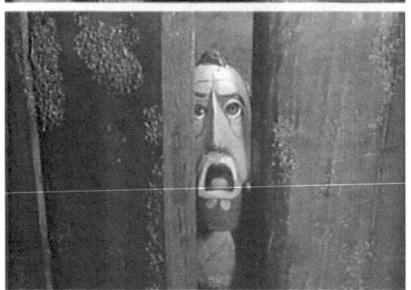

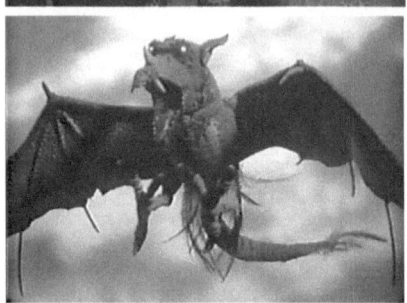

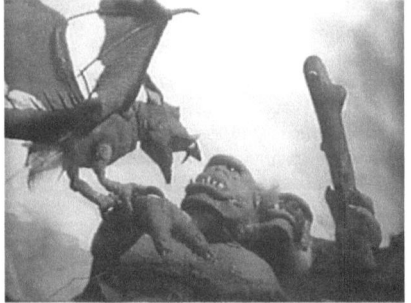

matched the animation to them later. Ian, Kyle and their cousin Matthew all recorded the boy's voice at the same time—the older two could read, Kyle was too young, so he just repeated what the older two were saying. In the end, everyone agreed that his voice was just *so damn cute* that I had to use it. He had trouble with one or two lines, but his brothers' voice and delivery were so similar that I substituted his readings and no one noticed. The other actors were people I knew. Al Pirnie did several of the minor voices, supposedly to pay off the money he still owed me over the **NUKE 'EM HIGH 2** fiasco. This would actually have been about ten times what I paid the other actors for doing far less work, but it allowed us both to put it behind us. The voice of Blowhole, the villain, was Steve Bulyga, a talented actor and comedian whom I'd worked with a couple of times, including **MUTANT WAR**.

SRB: If you'd had infinite resources, who would your ideal cast have been?

BP: My "dream" voice cast would have been José Ferrer as Sinbad, Keenan Wynn as Blowhole, and John Huston as Narrator. Not available!

SRB: How did you land Roddy McDowall to do the narration? Having grown up with some of his LP recordings of readings (including H.P. Lovecraft!), alongside his extensive movie career (child actor, actor, director), I was impressed by your working with him on this, and his contribution; kudos!

BP: Couldn't have been simpler. I looked up his address in *Who's Who* and wrote him a letter. A few weeks later I got a message from him on my answering machine. I called him back, we worked-out terms, and that was that. I never met him. He was on the West Coast, I was on the East, so I asked Deborah Quayle, who starred in **MUTANT WAR** and had moved to Los Angeles, to be my representative, so to speak, and meet him at a recording studio he'd recommended. She was delighted, told me later he was absolutely charming. I don't think it took him more than fifteen minutes to do the job. He gave me three different readings of each passage. It was perfect. What with Huston dead, McDowall was actually my first choice to do the narration—I mean literally, out of anyone living. So for once in my working life I got *exactly* what I wanted!

SRB: Congratulations on that score! The Wiegands, Ray and Dave, are credited as Executive Producers on SINBAD, and Mark Frizzell is created as Associate Producer. What

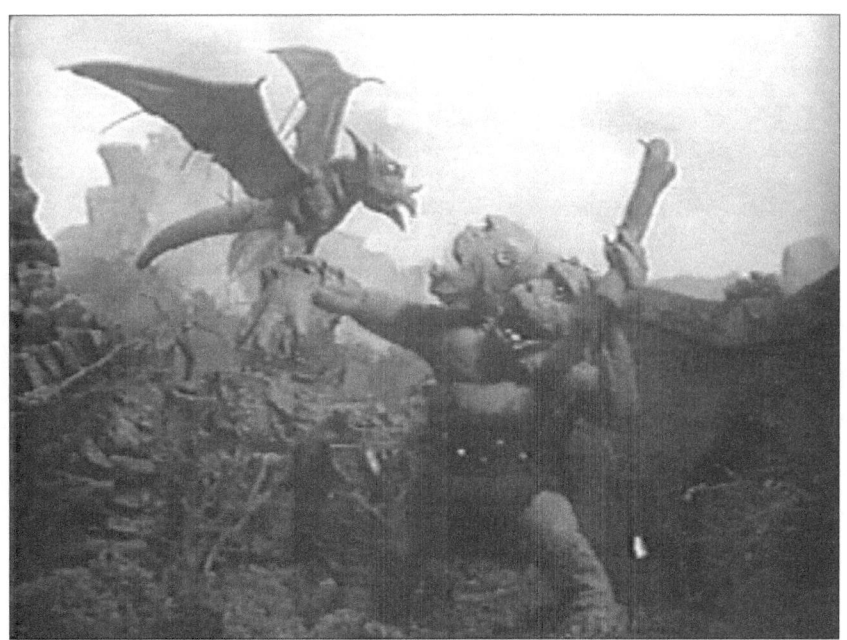

Facing Page & Above: A couple of marvelous monsters—and Sinbad! *[facing page, center image]*—from Brett Piper's **THE RETURN OF CAPTAIN SINBAD**. Its two-headed giant recalls the twin-domed creatures of the Fleischer Brothers' *Popeye the Sailor Meets Sindbad the Sailor* (1936), **THE THREE STOOGES MEET HERCULES** (1961), and **JACK THE GIANT KILLER** (1962).

was their involvement, and what did they do on the film?

BP: Mark, whom I've mentioned as director and animator of **WINTERBEAST**, introduced me to the Weigands. Ray was a successful chiropractor and Dave was his brother. Ray financed the movie, and Dave and Mark were supposed to market it when it was done. The original budget was $10,000. It ended up being $30,000. Roddy McDowall cost us another $10K and, unbeknownst to me, Frizzell, behind my back, was actually collecting a salary—he told Ray he was doing all the animation, and collected another $10K. In fact, he contributed *absolutely nothing*, and refused to help when I asked him to, so I did all the work on spec while he collected a paycheck. Ray finally found out, and the four of us had a luncheon meeting to discuss the situation, where Mark did the most blatant lying I've ever seen by someone who wasn't actually running for public office. He claimed that he was constantly offering to help but I'd refused to let him, shouting at him and threatening him when he offered. No mention was made of the money he'd received for doing absolutely nothing. Ray rather magnanimously suggested we put it all behind us, and as we were leaving the restaurant, Mark turned to me and said, "We're still friends, right?" I don't know how I kept my hands off him.

SRB: Good Lord—there's bottom-feeders at every level of this industry, aren't there?! When you initially tackled SINBAD, were you out to take a break from feature filmmaking after such an intense decade-plus (and such painful business dealings after the last couple features), or did you have a specific target audience and market in mind from the beginning?

BP: I thought if I made an animated childrens' film it had a good chance of making some money. I was wrong.

SRB: If only you'd collected the salary Frizzell was grifting—what did Dave and Mark do with the completed film?

BP: Nothing. As in *not a damn thing.* I ended up trying to sell the movie myself. I actually did make one sale, to the SyFy Channel back in the early days when they were hungry for product, but they never ran it—I suspect they bought it sight-unseen, and only later realized it wasn't a

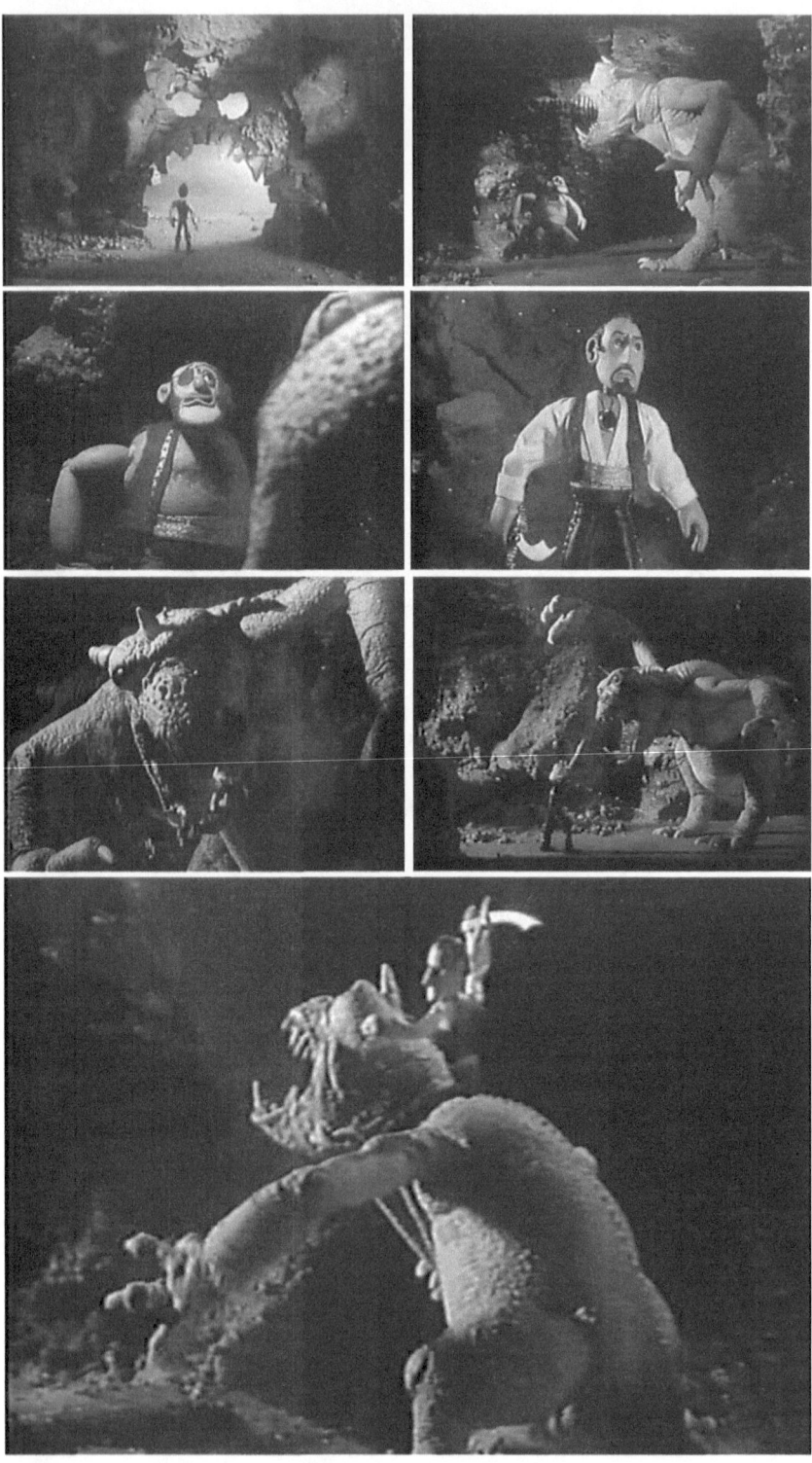

good fit for them. Aside from that, it went from distributor to distributor, most of whom went out of business, so the rights reverted to us. A couple of guys in Florida were marketing a bootleg version called **SINBAD AND THE BLACK DIAMOND**.

SRB: *I first saw SINBAD thanks to you— you allowed me to screen a copy back in the mid-1990s, when I first contacted you about a possible interview/article—and was later delighted to find it on VHS commercially, via Sterling Entertainment Group out of South Carolina. Alas, that VHS edition was from 2001—well over five years after you'd completed the film (more like eight, if the filmographies citing 1993 are correct)—a rather shoddy transfer (Sterling's VHS releases were all duped at LP or SLP speed), and late to the party with any VHS release . By that time, VHS was in the death throes of that format for rental or sale (DVD hit big in 1999). Did you see anything, anything at all, from the film? Did it sell overseas, or ever sell or play on television?*

BP: I never saw a dime from it. I sent the check from the SyFy sale to Ray Wiegand. It was made out to me so, I could have pocketed it myself, but I figure Ray was entitled to get some of his money back. He never even cashed it. At least SyFy ended up not paying for a movie they didn't run!

SRB: *I've seen more than one interview with you where you cite THE RETURN OF CAPTAIN SINBAD as still your favorite among your films. Does that stand, despite everything?*

BP: It was certainly one of my more fully-realized movies, in the sense that the finished product was closer to the concept I had in mind when I started it. It's probably still one of my best films, although I haven't seen it in decades. Maybe if I watched it again I wouldn't think so.

SRB: *Was that back in the days when SyFy was called the Sci-Fi Channel? They launched in September 1992; any recall of when this might have been, Brett?*

BP: It was still pretty new. They hadn't become the "all-*Sharknado*" network yet.

SRB: *Were there any other projects during this period—post-MUTANT WARS, pre-THEY BITE—you'd tried to get up and running? Were there any other production test reels to compare (in terms of manifested work: animation models, test footage, etc.) with DINOSAUR KID, projects you wanted to get off the ground but couldn't?*

BP: This would have been post-**NYMPHOID / DARK FORTRESS**. Pirnie and I were working on a project called **SHOCK-O-RAMA**, no relation to the movie of the same name I eventually made for EI/Pop Cinema, except that it was also an anthology picture. There would have been a mummy story, a kids-and-witchcraft episode, and a science fiction story about a robot monster in an abandoned subway tunnel. Only the mummy movie was ever shot.

SRB: *What became of that mummy episode you'd shot for the first SHOCK-O-RAMA? Was that ever shown or released in any form?*

BP: I have no idea what became of my elements. The negative was at a lab down near Boston, and wound up in the hands of a couple of "distributors" from Florida—I honestly don't remember how. But the movie itself, in workprint form (splices, dirt, grease pencil markings and all) later showed up on a three-part compilation video distributed by a Florida video company. I called them and made threatening noises and they agreed to pull it, but they refused to tell me where they'd gotten the print. They claimed they *didn't know*. "Are you telling me," I asked, "that the film just showed upon your doorstep one day, with no identification or any idea who left it there?" Yes, they said, that's exactly what happened. Well, *I'm* convinced. Sure.

SRB: *Both RETURN OF CAPTAIN SINDBAD and DINOSAUR KID were, together and apart, a concerted "stab" at reaching a viable family and childrens' video market. Given how that went—and especially how it* **didn't** *go—was that the impetus for jumping back into pure exploitation filmmaking again?*

BP: Well, you make what you can make. Opportunities arise and you take advantage of them (or *they* take advantage of *you*), and if the opportunities call for more exploitive material, that's what you end up doing.

More cavern monster action from Brett Piper's first all-puppet extravaganza, **THE RETURN OF CAPTAIN SINBAD**, including Captain Sinbad and the film's ruthless pirate villain. Brett completed his second all-puppet featurette, an excellent adaptation of H.G. Wells' *First Men in the Moon*, in 2017; we'll be covering that gem in the final installment of our interview

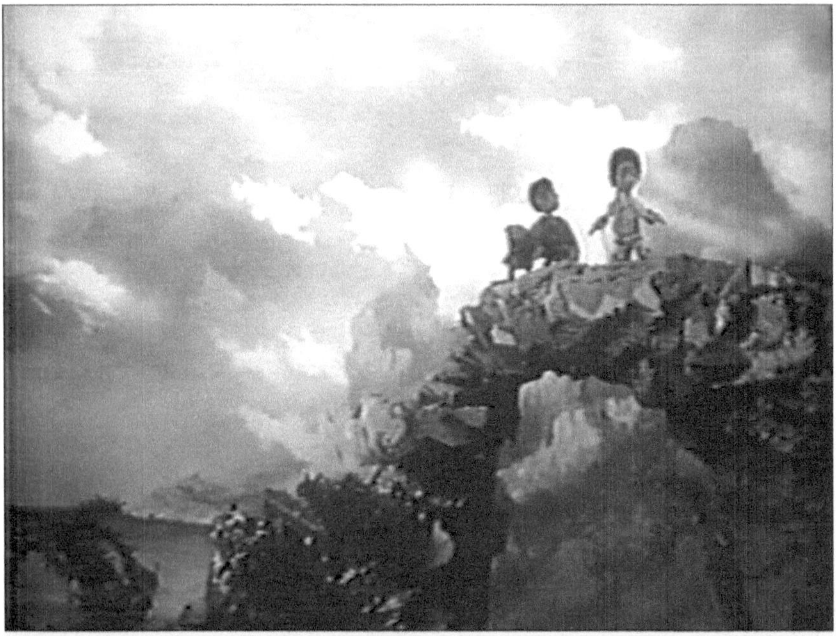

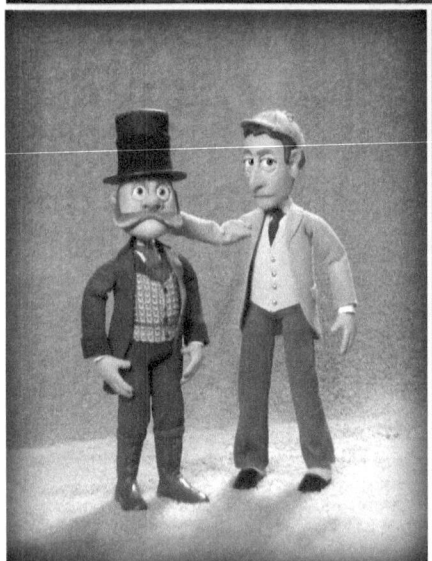
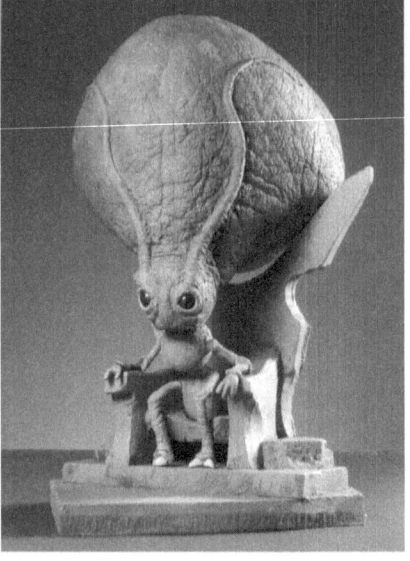
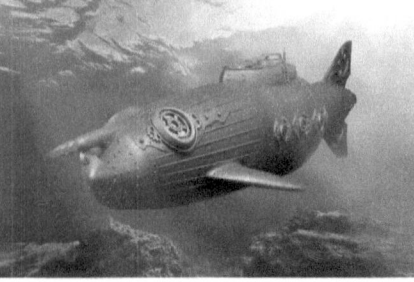

Painted Skies & Geological Formations: Haji and Prinsara amid one of the classical fantasy landscapes from Brett Piper's **THE RETURN OF CAPTAIN SINBAD** (1993/1996 *[top]*). Building upon the bedrock of **TROCS**, Brett has recently continued with new 'puppet' films, including adaptations of H.G. Wells *(First Men in the Moon, 2017 [above])* and Jules Verne (currently in production *[left]*). More in our next issue!

ANARCHY & MONSTERS
An Interview with Brett Piper
Part 3 (of 6)

By the early 1990s, Brett Piper had a number of feature films under his belt as writer-director, and he decided to accept a work-for-hire project (i.e., a production belonging to its producer, with Brett the "hired hand" engaged to make the movie *sans* ownership) that temporarily moved his base of operations from his home state of New Hampshire to sunny Florida. The project was entitled **THEY BITE**, and it was the first of Piper's features to satirize its own mode of production, lampooning the making of an independent adult film whose shoot is disrupted by the intrusion of alien oceanic invaders. It was rich comedic turf to which Piper would again return in his body of work, with far more creative freedom.

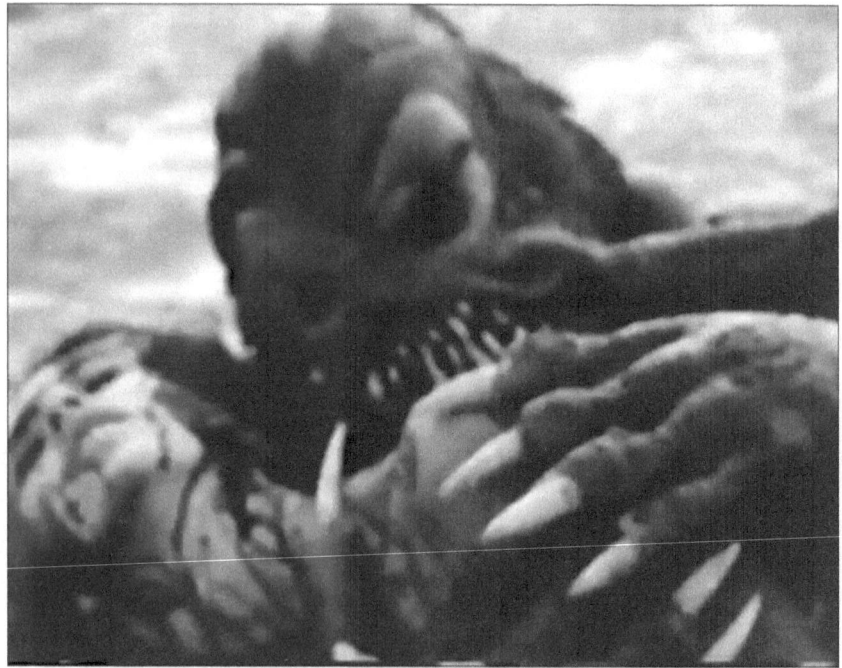

An alien "amphibinoid" claims the film's first victim (Blake Pickett) in Brett Piper's satiric **THEY BITE** (1995).

The production of **THEY BITE** was among the most heavily pre-promoted of all of Brett Piper's feature films—which remains the case, oddly enough, up to the present. "I got a fair amount of publicity on **THEY BITE**," Brett recalls, "before the film ever found a distributor. I'm not exactly a household name. Publicity is not my concern."[10] However, that promotion surfaced in a narrow venue of genre film publications (this was during the pre-internet, print-only era, after all). As Piper points out, that promotion also proved ill-timed—the film still lacked a US distributor when the articles/interviews saw print. Unfortunately, most of the subsequent coverage involved the "controversies" behind the film's production more than anything that might actually prompt a potential audience to seek out the movie.

That primary "controversy" was *supposed* to be the MPAA's threatening **THEY BITE** with an NC-17 rating for a dream sequence involving *Playboy*'s March 1988 Playmate of the Month Susie Owens[11] wielding a "toothy" vagina,

---

10 Brett Piper, *Kevin J. Lindenmuth's The Independent Film Experience*, Ibid., p.149.

11 The tradition of boosting low-budget genre feature film promotional and boxoffice potential by casting a magazine (specifically, *Playboy*) model goes way back. *Playboy*'s Miss May 1955 *and* Miss February 1956 Dianne Webber a.k.a. Marguarite Empey was queen of **THE MERMAIDS OF TIBURON** (1962), Miss August 1955 Pat Lawler was in **INVASION OF THE SAUCER MEN** (1957), **THE AMAZING COLOSSAL MAN** (1956) peeked in at Miss October 1955 Jean Moorehead while she was bathing in her bathtub, Miss January 1957 June Blair was among those on the **ISLAND OF LOST WOMEN** (1959), Miss February 1957 Sally Todd was in **THE UNEARTHLY** (1957) and **FRANKENSTEIN'S DAUGHTER** (1958), Miss May 1957 Dawn Richard was the gymnast attacked by lycanthrope Michael Landon in **I WAS A TEENAGE WEREWOLF** (1957), Miss November 1957 Marlene Callahan was in **THE MAGIC SWORD** (1962), Miss October 1958 Mara Corday co-starred in **TARANTULA** (1955), **THE GIANT CLAW**

revealed during lovemaking (a sequence that was, by all accounts, the brainchild of producer Links, and which Piper considered gratuitous). The lasting controversy ended up being Brett Piper's own candid assessment of his troubles with **THEY BITE** producer William J. Links in the cover article Bruce G. Hallenbeck wrote for *Femme Fatales* magazine,[12] the slick color "scream queen" companion zine to the highly-respected *Cinefantastique*.

Hallenbeck was (and remains) the most consistent and constant chronicler of Piper's career, and his even-handed and quite definitive coverage of **THEY BITE**'s production interviewed Piper, Links, and co-stars Blake Pickett, Christina

and **THE BLACK SCORPION** (both 1957), Miss November 1958 Joan Staley was in the VALLEY OF THE DRAGONS (1961), Miss June 1959 Marilyn Hanold was in **FRANKENSTEIN MEETS THE SPACE MONSTER** (1965), Miss July 1959 was Yvette Vickers of **ATTACK OF THE FIFTY FOOT WOMAN** (1958) and **ATTACK OF THE GIANT LEECHES** (1959), Miss September 1959 Marianne Gaba was in **MISSILE TO THE MOON** (1958) and **DR. GOLDFOOT AND THE BIKINI MACHINE** (1965), Miss June 1960 Dolores Wells was in **THE TIME TRAVELERS** (1964) and other AIP films, and Herschell Gordon Lewis and David Friedman's cast Miss June 1963 Connie Mason in **BLOOD FEAST** (1963) and **2000 MANIACS** (1964). There were many more popular men's magazine models who appeared in genre films from the 1950s to the 1990s. Susie Owens also appeared in the May 1993 issue of *Playboy* modeling as the comicbook heroine Flaxen; the character was originally "a logo/mascot for Golden Apple Comics in Los Angeles" (quoted from *http://www.herogohome. com/2011/08/06/out-of-the-vault-flaxen/* and also see *http://fraziersbrain.blogspot.com/2009/05/out-of-vault-flaxen-alter-ego.html*). Owens also appeared as the character in public venues and as a photo centerspread in the Dark Horse Comics and Golden Apple Comics *Flaxen* comicbook one-shot (1993, script by Mark Evanier, art by Richard Howell, Tim Burgard, and Jim Mooney), and a lackluster followup *Flaxen: Alter Ego* (1995, Caliber Comics, script by James Hudnall, art by Brian Michael Bendis and David Mack). The comic and character never caught on.

12 Bruce G. Hallenbeck, "Sex, Censorship, Salmon from Outer Space: Women With Bite: THEY BITE, 'the PLAYER of Horror Films,' was Hooked with an NC-17 Rating," *Femme Fatales* Summer 1993, Vol. 2, No. 1, pp.16-25, recommended. *Fangoria*'s short-lived companion magazine *Gorezone* #22 (Summer 1992) also published an article citing **THEY BITE**'s production, among other upcoming independent films, "How to Beat the High Cost of Dying," by Maitland McDonagh (pp.46-51; special thanks to William Wilson for the assist finding this article). McDonagh interviewed only producer Links, not Piper, and there's no discussion of any conflict or controversy in the *Gorezone* piece (which also covered the making of two other independent genre films, **THERE'S NOTHING OUT THERE** and **SMALL KILL**. McDonagh quite liked **THEY BITE**: "The result is a surprisingly successful mix of crude laughs and conventional scares whose biggest problem is likely to be distinguishing itself from the dozens of execrable horror/comedies cluttering up video stores' shelves"(p.51). To my knowledge, these were the only newsstand-distributed magazines to do give **THEY BITE** any coverage, with *Femme Fatales* having only limited newsstand distribution at that.

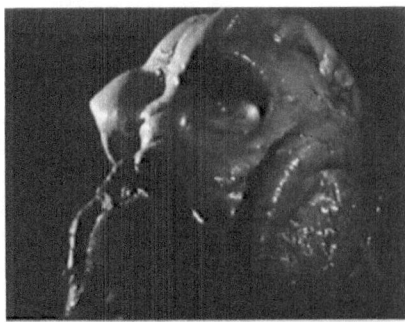
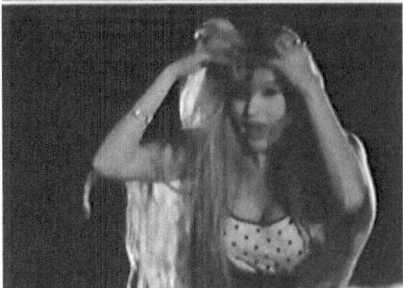
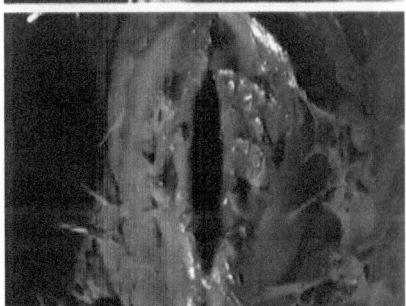
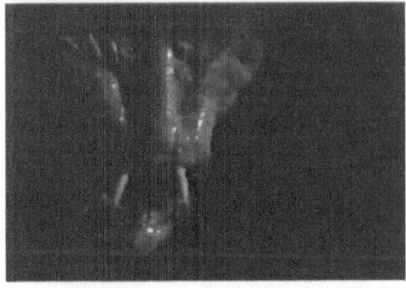

They Cut Bites: Images of the nighttime beach attack and *vagina dentata* from the censored-in-some-markets **THEY BITE** sequence featuring *Playboy*'s March 1988 Playmate Susie Owens. Sans an actual MPAA rating, MTI Home Video released two VHS editions of the film: an unlabeled one, which was uncut, and another (self-labeled "R" on the cassette label itself) which cut 30+ seconds from this sequence

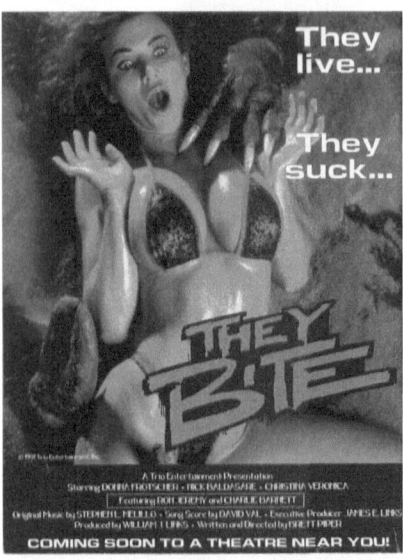

Ad slick for the planned domestic theatrical release of **THEY BITE** which never materialized

To date, Links still has only two films to his credit as producer: **DEADTIME STORIES** (1986, D: Jeffrey Delman) and **THEY BITE** (and, in his own words, he "was strictly an agent" for Piper's **DARK FORTRESS** a.k.a. **NYMPHOID BARBARIAN IN DINOSAUR HELL**: "I represented the sale to Troma films, and sold the film to Troma..."[16]). So, just *who was* "difficult to get along with"...?

The final paragraph of Hallenbeck's 1993 *Femme Fatales* article noted, *"THEY BITE's first theatrical premiere is scheduled for Korea. A regional theatrical engagement in the U.S. and a video release (both R-rated and unrated), are currently under negotiation."*[17] The Korean release may have manifested, but Links was unable to land any distribution for the film (as detailed in his subsequent interviews) until MTI Home Video's domestic home video release (box art copyright 1995, release date April 2nd, 1996). Footage of Susie Owens' *vagina dentata* sequence was included in all versions of the **THEY BITE** trailer included on VHS before the feature, and an image from the sequence appeared on the back of the slipsleeve cover art; the sex dream/nightmare sequence, however, did not appear in the R-rated version of the film.[18]

Veronica, and Susie Owens (who pretty much confirmed Piper's account, saying, "I know that Bill and Brett didn't get along. Bill has a tendency to be negative. Brett is more in my arena, while Bill is pissed-off at the world..."[13]). Each got equal "print" time, but the less-slick "scream queen" zines that followed simply interviewed Links, citing only Hallenbeck's interview with Piper as a point of departure, inflating his candor into a cudgel of sorts.[14] This led to fandom's unfair and disproportionate perception and caricature of Piper as, in the words of Links, someone "difficult to get along with"[15]—though a reading of the actual 1994 and 1995 interviews with Links makes it clear that the interviewers *themselves* were fanning the flames to incite Links. Needless to say, Piper's own record and subsequent filmography speaks volumes to the contrary, though he remains unafraid to discuss the ill behavior of producers and individual case histories, and always does so with discretion.

---

13 *Ibid.*, p.25.

14 See Hugh Gallagher, "THEY BITE: Interview with Producer William J. Links," *Draculina* #20 (Summer 1994), pp.25-31; and Ron Bonk, "Low-Budget Production Hell; Or, the Making of THEY BITE," *Alternative Cinema* #4 (Winter 1995), pp. 58-62. The contents page description of the latter sums up both interviews: "Producer William Links trashes everyone in explaining why his movie can't get a distributor" (p.3). There may have been other articles in other fanzines as well; these are the ones I currently have access to, with special thanks to G. Michael Dobbs for gifting them to me.

15 Gallagher interviewing Links, *Draculina* #20, p.31.

16 *Ibid.*, pg. 26.

17 Hallenbeck, *Ibid.*, pg. 25.

18 Some portion of the MTI videocassettes were labeled as being rated "R". However, there was no MPAA rating on-screen before the film or on the box art—it's just typeset on the cassette label itself—and there's no appearance anywhere in the packaging of the official copyrighted MPAA "R" symbol/rating. Self-imposed "R" or "Mature" labels occasionally appeared in direct-to-video releases, *sans* any actual submission of the film to the MPAA for a rating. MTI simultaneously released an unrated edition as well; it wasn't labeled as being unrated, the typeset "R" rating simply didn't appear on the original VHS cassette labels of the "unrated" versions (one such label is visible at brettpiper.com, see http://www.brettpiper.com/movies/theybite/cover+tape_theybite_USA_vhs_BIG.JPG). The unrated version inserts the *vagina dentata* sequence about one hour into the film: this three-minute-plus sequence begins in both the "R" and "unrated" versions with a shot of sunset at the beach as Kate (Susie Owens) argues with her long-haired beau (Vince Campiti [or Camiti?]) about her leaving a party to search for her sister Debbie (Pam Parker); she finds Debbie after dark, pinned down on the beach by a creature that punctures Debbie's abdomen with two barbed tentacles and "sucks" out her body's vitals, leaving a wet skeletal husk. Kate screams as she is attacked by a different creature with a vagina-like orifice in its chest; cut to her longhair boyfriend finding her laying barely conscious on the beach, dazed and incoherent but apparently unharmed. The "R" version ends there; the unrated version continues with the boyfriend inside a bedroom with Kate as he checks on her and finds her feverish. She awakens and aggressively flips him over onto the bed ("I'm hot, I'm *so* hot!") and removes her top, climbing onto and arousing him before removing her panties ("I've got something special to show you") to reveal a monstrous

The only dream sequence remaining in that version was Piper's brilliant black-and-white satiric trailer for the film supposedly being produced within the film, entitled "INVASION OF THE FISH FUCKERS".

With characteristic tenacity, Piper continued to make films, and the following interview instalment traces the even-more-troubled companion Florida feature which Piper ultimately disowned (though he is credited on the videocassette box art and film credits of **DINOSAUR BABES**, he has efficiently removed the credit from all online sources, including the IMDb), and his far happier independent production of **DRAINIAC!**. En route, Piper also made his initial connection and sale (as screenwriter) to Rutland, Vermont-based indy Edgewood Productions, which would soon play a major role in the next phase of Piper's body of work...

THEY BITE (1995)

SRB: THEY BITE is pure exploitation: an adult movie shoot is disrupted by ravenous amphibious humanoid monsters, which brings an ichthyologist into the orbit of the porn film's director, his cast, and his crew. THEY BITE satirizes the entire adult film industry. Given your own involvement with exploitation films—including occasional nudity and sexual situations, though always "soft" (as they say)—what's your own view on the porn film and video industry?

BP: My only objection to porn is aesthetic. Except for the brief "Boogie Nights" period in the '70s, there was never any attempt to make porno films entertaining as movies. **FLESH GORDON**, that was fun, but the porn elements were really extraneous. I've used nudity in several movies, but nudity is not pornography, even the supreme court accepts that. Nudity can be aesthetically pleasing, even in cheap genre movies, and I don't see why I'm not as entitled to utilize it as any painter or sculptor as long as the performers involved are comfortable with it.

SRB: Was there a mandate to riff off of then-still-fairly-recent successes like HUMANOIDS FROM THE DEEP, or was this a kind of movie—your CREATURE FROM THE BLACK LAGOON spin—you'd always wanted to play with?

BP: **THEY BITE** was strictly work for hire—too *much* work, as it turned out, for too little money, but them's the breaks. The producer's model was **HUMANOIDS FROM THE DEEP**, which I'd seen and thought was fairly well-made, but otherwise didn't care much for. "I want a movie with fish monsters and tits," I was told, "because fish monsters and tits never lose money." Where that nugget of wisdom came from, I couldn't say, but I sat down and wrote a script to those specs. After he read it he called me up and said (in some astonishment), "It's a *comedy!*" I said "You told me you wanted a movie with 'fish monsters and tits'—did you expect me to take it *seriously?*"

I had no particular desire to make a **CREATURE**

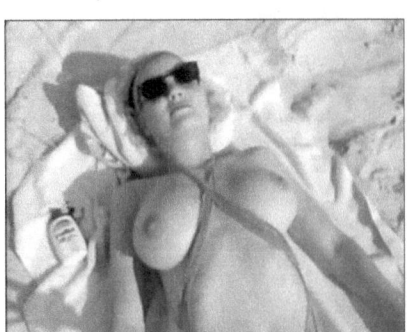

Tammy (Christina Veronica) bares skin to satisfy one of the demands of **THEY BITE** producer William J. Links: "I want a movie with fish monsters and tits, because fish monsters and tits never lose money!" Brett Piper made the nominal hero of **THEY BITE** (Nick Baldasare) a put-upon director of adult films, forever dealing with a boneheaded producer (George Mazzone) who pretty much embodies the kind of crap Piper had to deal with on the set

toothed maw in place of her vagina, which bloodily castrates him, spattering gore over his crotch, chest, and screaming face. Cut to: the same sequence seen earlier of the boyfriend finding Kate semi-conscious on the beach as before. Both versions cut to: exterior of the hotel at night, then to an interior corridor as pizzas are delivered to the adult film's cast and crew. Neither Kate nor her boyfriend are seen or referred to again in either version of the film: was it a nightmare, a vision, or a flash-forward? Who knows. The review posted on Amazon by "John's Horror Corner" on January 27th, 2013, refers to the *vagina dentata* scene quite specifically (@ https://www.amazon.com/they-bite-vhs-donna-frotscher/dp/630360806x?tag=indifash06-20): "the smuttiness somehow picks up yet more when random witness and beachgoer Katie (*Playboy* Playmate Susie Owens) is abducted by a sea monster's chest-vagina and becomes a monster herself with a toothy-mawed crotch hungry for...well, you know..."). At the time of this writing, the cut *vagina dentata* sequence is posted on YouTube—and with a transfer *much* sharper than the MTI US video release—at https://www.youtube.com/watch?v=sx9x-_bBowo. It has since been removed for (quote) "violating YouTube's Terms of Service".

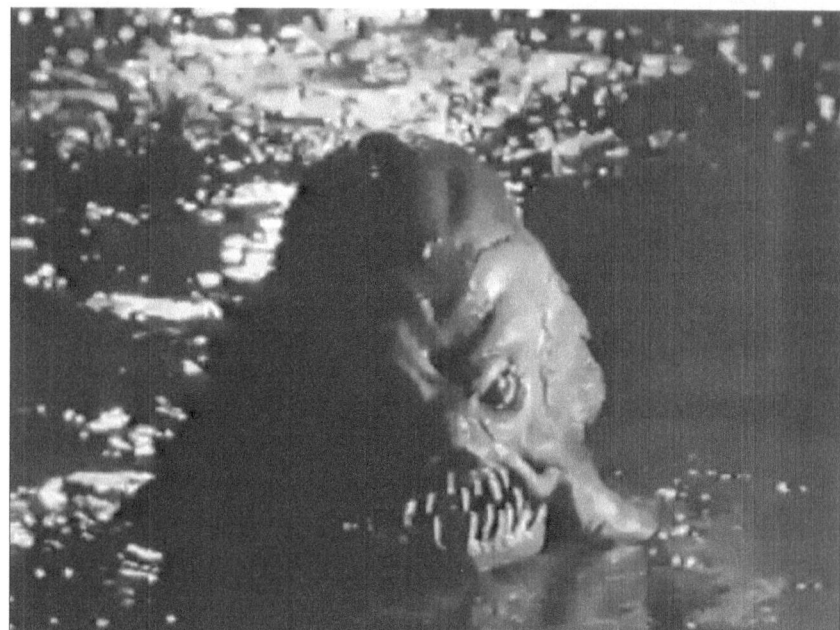

Surf's Up! One of the three amphibious humanoid monster designs Brett Piper created for **THEY BITE**, all constructed as live-action man-in-suit creatures

FROM THE BLACK LAGOON-type movie. I never cared for the *Creature* films, except the last one. I thought the Gill Man was a pretty boring concept for a movie monster.

SRB: You also made your "fishmen" beings from outer space, extraterrestrial monsters using the Earth as a feeding and spawning ground. You'd already done a lot with extraterrestrials in earlier films, but I wonder: did this story angle liberate your imagination in terms of creature design, or did it force you to stretch your budget even further?

BP: It didn't affect the budget much one way or another. I was trying to give the movie some kind of twist ending. When MTI eventually released the movie on video, they put the surprise ending on the front cover, which undercut the "surprise" element just a bit. They also misspelled everyone's name.

SRB: Ya, I remember that—it was right on the box art: "They Came From Beyond the Stars to Spawn in the Sea..." with the graphic of a starship in outer space above a close-up of one of the uglier fish/human hybrids on the front cover. Since it was work-for-hire, were you more intent on keeping to a specific budget and (especially) timeframe? How long did it take to make THEY BITE, from the "Yes, I'll do it" to delivery of final print?

BP: The budget was not my concern, or at least it was not supposed to be. Before we started shooting, I told the producer, "Either you're handling the money or I am. If you handle it, I don't want to hear anything about it. Keeping on-budget will be your problem." He, of course, was adamant that he would handle the money. Needless to say, we went way over-budget. This always happens when the money men insist on making all the decisions on what gets spent where. I've never seen it fail. Right at the beginning he called me into his motel room and handed me his checkbook. "Look at it," he said. "It's a checkbook," I said. "I've seen them before." He told me "we" were over-budget already. I reminded him that wasn't my responsibility. It all went downhill from there.

I should mention that by "over-budget" he meant he was spending more than he'd wanted to. There was never an actual budget in any real sense. That was the first problem.

SRB: So, the producer you're talking about who approached you would have been William J. Links. What was that dynamic, and what did you end up delivering to Links under the work-

for-hire terms (fully-edited completed feature, 16mm or 35mm, etc.)?

BP: What was the dynamic? That's pretty hard to answer. The short version is I struggled to get the movie made in spite of his constant boneheaded interference. To give you an idea of how bad that interference was, I had an acquaintance in the business who was absolutely convinced that Links was deliberately trying to sabotage the movie as part of some kind of tax scheme. He refused to believe that anyone could screw things up so egregiously through mere incompetence. Well, you had to be there.

I eventually delivered a fully-edited feature in 16mm with 35mm audio.

SRB: Who (if anyone) among the crew and cast helped you get through the process? I read that Steve Williams facilitated some aspect of production.

BP: I think Steve was credited as production manager or something. He was actually a big help in getting the movie done. Whenever we hit a snag, he was ready to pitch-in and try to find a solution. I remember when Links sprang an unexpected shoot on us one evening—he'd been out to a strip club and brought back three dancers to appear in the fake trailer for "INVASION OF THE FISH FUCKERS", which we were simply not prepared to shoot yet, but we improvised and shot anyway. We need a nurse's uniform, and Steve made a quick run over to a nearby hospital and talked them into lending us one.

SRB: You had some wild cards in the cast: XXX-star Ron Jeremy, Miami Vice's Charlie Burnett, Nick Baldasare as the film's porn director character, and so on. How did that cast come together for the film, and how well did they work together?

BP: By and large, the cast worked together well. The odd one out was Ron Jeremy. For some reason Links decided it would be shrewd to use Jeremy as his "spy", reporting back to him at night about how the shoot was going. There's nothing like throwing in a divisive element to make sure your shoot goes smoothly. Links would call me in to his room every night and inform me that his "sources" thought I was screwing-up, which usually meant I wasn't shooting enough close-ups of Ron Jeremy. That was Ron. One evening he showed us a tape of an Eddie Murphy concert where Murphy did a bit about Ron Jeremy. When the bit was over, Ron started to take the tape out

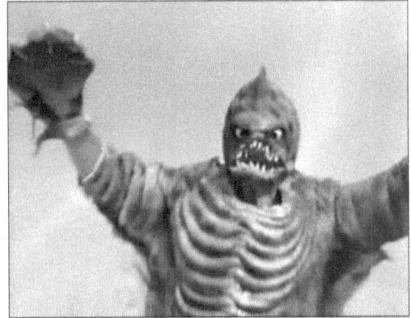

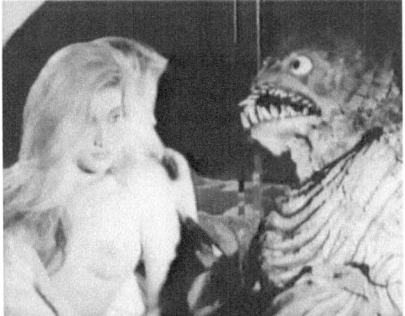

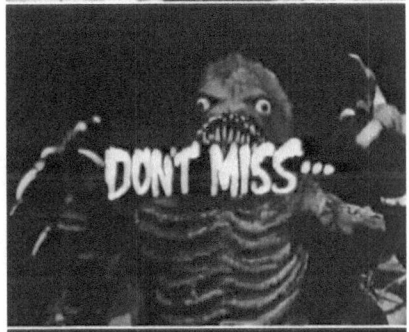

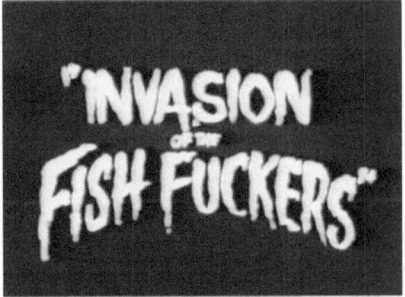

"Where Did They Come From?! What Were They After?!" Movie-within-a-movie trailer for "INVASION OF THE FISH FUCKERS", a filmmaker's nightmare featuring a faked fishman in the tradition of **THE BEACH GIRLS AND THE MONSTER** (1965)

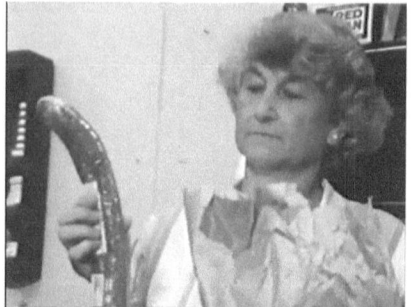
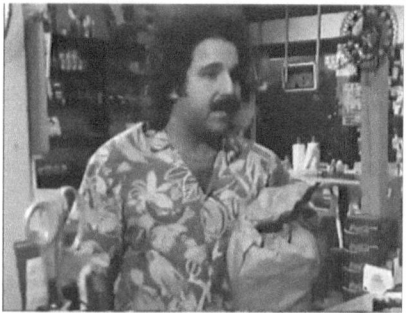
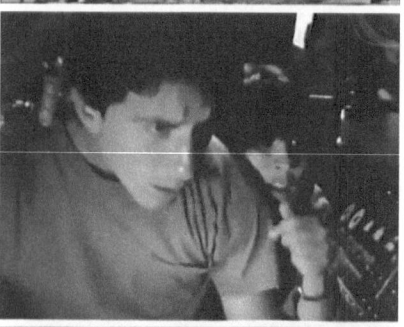
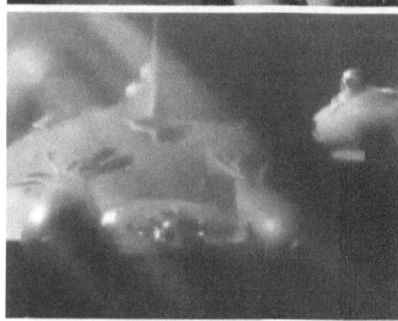

Top 2 Images: 1 sausage + 1 cashier (Margarette McLellan) + Ron Jeremy = a **THEY BITE** sight-gag! **Bottom 2 Images:** TB's hero Mel Duncan (Nick Baldasare) and ichthyologist Melody Duncan (Donna Frotscher) dive in a mini-submersible, only to find a submerged alien super-submarine *[bottom]*

of the VCR and we all said, no, let's watch the rest of it. Ron could not understand this. As far as he was concerned, once the routine was no longer about him, the show was over. He sat in a corner and sulked while we watched the rest of it.

Charlie Barnett was hired, I believe, through an entertainment broker in LA named Gerry Wolff *[sic?]*. He specialized in procuring "names" for cameos in small films. Other actors considered for the movie were Jan Murray, Jack Weston, and Frank Gorshin. Gorshin I believe actually agreed to do it, but backed-out at the last minute. Wolff also sent us some suggestions for some of the leads, up-and-coming people who were as yet not well-known. One of them seemed very promising, a very attractive young woman who we all thought might be good for the female lead. Everyone but Links, that is. "She's ugly," he'd snarl. "Links, she's not ugly, that ridiculous." "She's a dog". He finally admitted what he didn't like about her: "No tits." So she didn't make the cut. That was Sandra Bullock.

We hired local people through a casting agent in Tallahassee. When the time came for us to audition actors, she called me and said, "Whatever you do, don't bring your producer. He's so sleazy, if the actors meet him they won't want to do your movie." Fortunately, I had to be on my way by around five a.m., and Links liked to sleep late, so I managed to leave him behind. The woman we hired to play the lead, Donna Frotscher, was great—attractive, talented, easy to work with—and hardly any tits.

SRB: Brett, I also want to briefly come back to Alex Pirnie—his last listed film role was playing the Reverend Rex Stoner in this film. How did THEY BITE *bring your work with Alex to a close?*

BP: Pirnie and I were still on good terms at the time **THEY BITE** was made. I recommended him to Links as an assistant director/production manager based on our experience working together on **DARK FORTRESS**, where he'd been a real hands-on producer in the best sense, pitching-in and doing everything he could to get the movie made. The understanding was that if Links couldn't get a name to play one of the supporting roles, it would go to Pirnie. Rev. Stoner was the part that Frank Gorshin was supposed to play, so when he backed-out Pirnie got the part.

SRB: Wrapping-up on Alex and your work: You'd created the live-action monster suit,

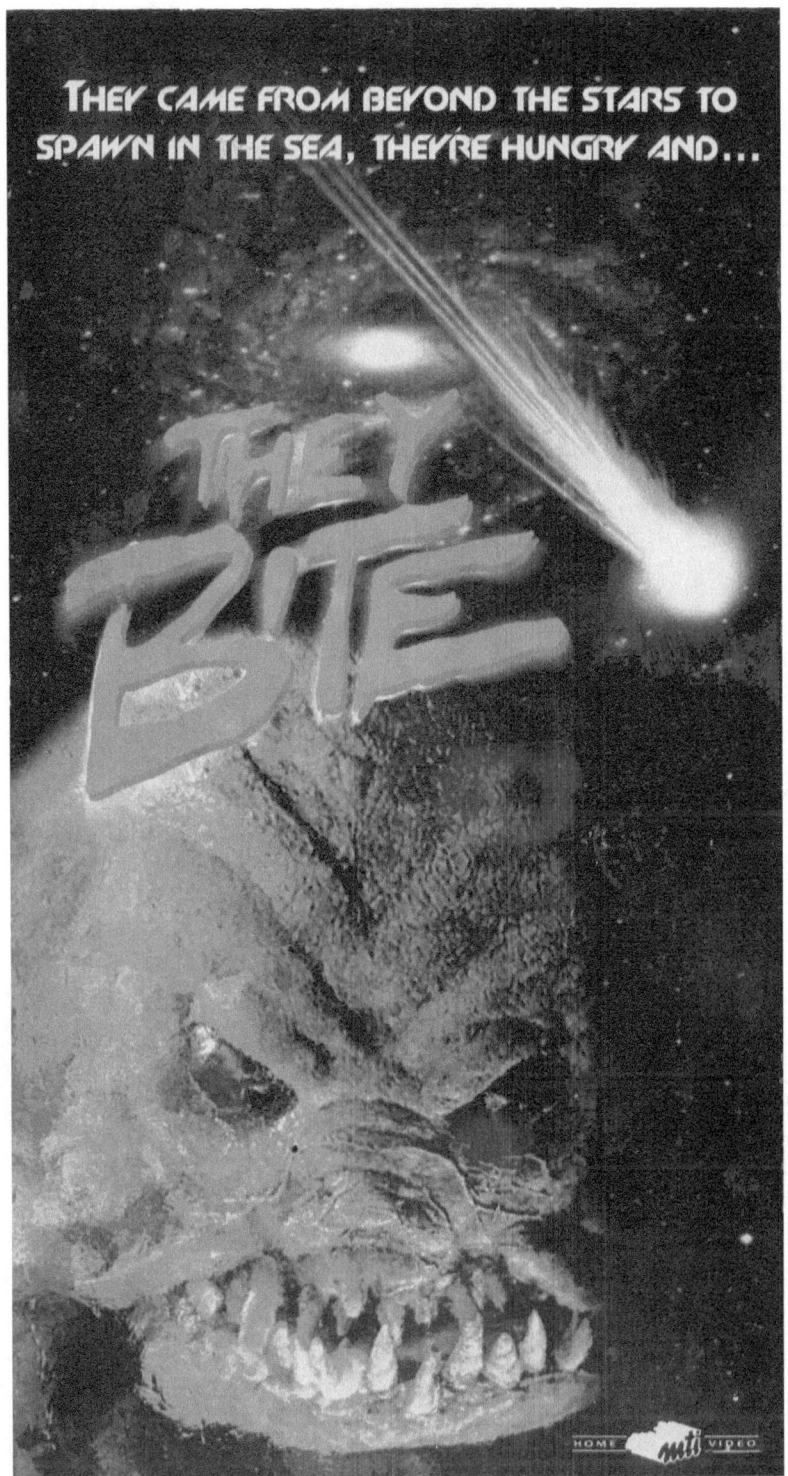

**FAST AND ENTERTAINING...
A FISH STORY WITH TEETH "FANGORIA"**

On a sunset Florida beach, a photographer captures on film more than he ever imagined, as a terrifying creature appears from the sea and devours his model.

So begins this odyssey into the unknown as a beautiful ichthyologist arrives to investigate reports of sea monsters terrorizing the beachfront and meets a young filmmaker who coincidentally is in town preparing a " monster " sexploitation film.

As the two compete to discover the truth behind the alien creatures they are drawn deeper and deeper into the ocean depths coming face to face with the alien vessel and it's terrifying secret.

A TRIO ENTERTAINMENT PRESENTATION
STARRING DONNA FROTSHER • NICK BALDASARE • CHRITINA VERONICA
FEATURING RON JEREMY • CHARLIE BARNET • SUZI OWENS
ORIGINAL MUSIC BY STEPHEN MELILLO • SONG SCORE BY DAVID VAL • EXECUTIVE PRODUCER JAMES LINKS
PRODUCED BY WILLIAM J. LINKS • WRITTEN AND DIRECTED BY BRET PIPER

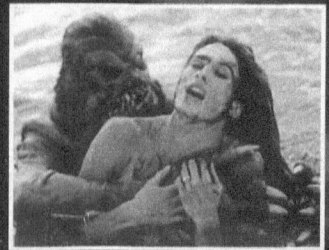
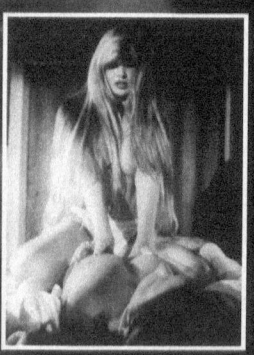
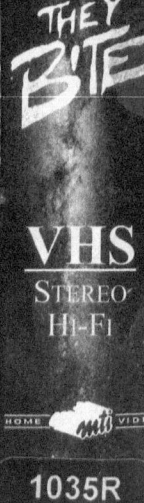

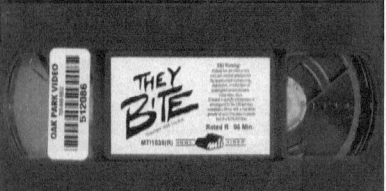

Previous Page & This Page: the MTI "Rated R" box-art (front cover + back cover) and cassette label *[left]* for their 1996 **THEY BITE** VHS release.

miniatures and effects sequences involving Tromie, a 30-foot-plus mutant squirrel, for CLASS OF NUKE 'EM HIGH PART 2: SUBHUMANOID MELTDOWN [1991, D: Eric Louzil], and you told me earlier how Alex was the performer in the Tromie suit. Did you have anything to do with the third Class of Nuke 'Em High film, THE GOOD, THE BAD AND THE SUBHUMANOID [1994, D: Eric Louzil]? Alex is listed in the cast as playing (ahem) "Mutant Squirrel's Internal Organs"—I know that entry was shot in Los Angeles, far from Troma's usual New York City and NJ locations—do you know what that involved, or did they just use your suit and footage shot for the second film?

BP: The third *Nuke 'Em High* movie was the one we'd discussed my directing, until it conflicted with **THEY BITE**. I'm not sure what Pirnie did on that. I wasn't personally involved with it at all. They simply recycled my work from the previous movie.

SRB: *How much time had you put into that Tromie monster suit and live-action effects sequence—was it something you had relative autonomy to shoot, or were you working closely with that film's director?—and did that in any way lay bedrock for the far more extensive man-in-suit work on* THEY BITE?

BP: I don't remember which came first, the Tromie or the fish-men. Tromie was actually a more difficult and elaborate suit than the amphibinoids. I had nothing at all to do with filming it. I just shipped it off and left it up to them.

SRB: *The "amphibinoids" effects work for* THEY BITE *primarily involved man-in-suit monster creation on a grander scale—and with the complications working in water with such effects. How many "suits" did you fabricate, and what were your preferred materials?*

BP: I made three suits. Originally they were all supposed to be identical, but I convinced the producer that three different monsters would be more interesting. I was primarily thinking that they'd be less boring to build—more work but less boring, which is the usual trade-off. Another effects artist was supposed to build them, some guy whose name I can't remember, but who had done some work for Troma. I did some sketches and sent them to him, and he got to work. After a while I started getting weird phone calls from him, panicked calls telling me he couldn't do the job, it was too much, he was quitting. I found out

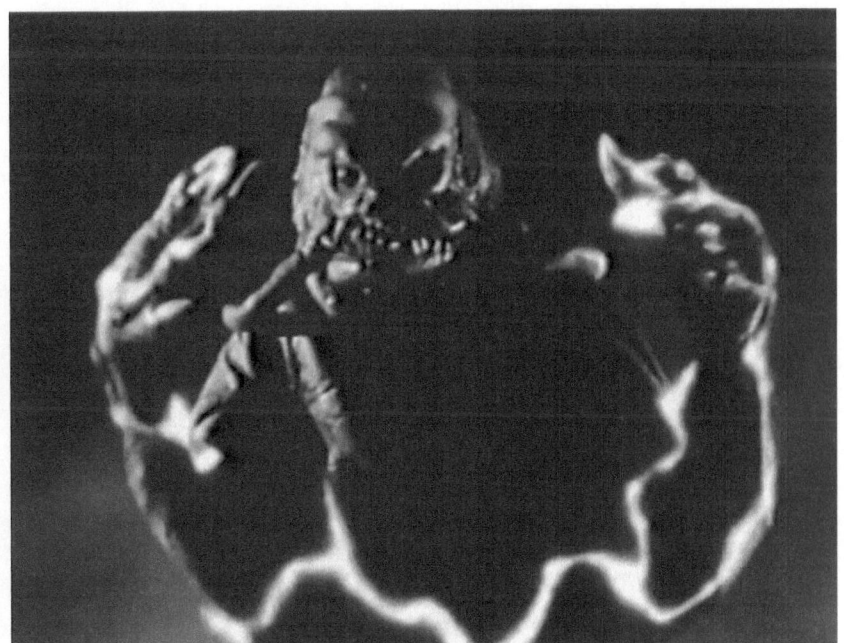

"You want to spend the rest of your life in a mental home?! This didn't happen!" In **THEY BITE**, partying teenagers attacked by a Piper "amphibinoid" are rescued by a blast of electrical energy, which fries the creature

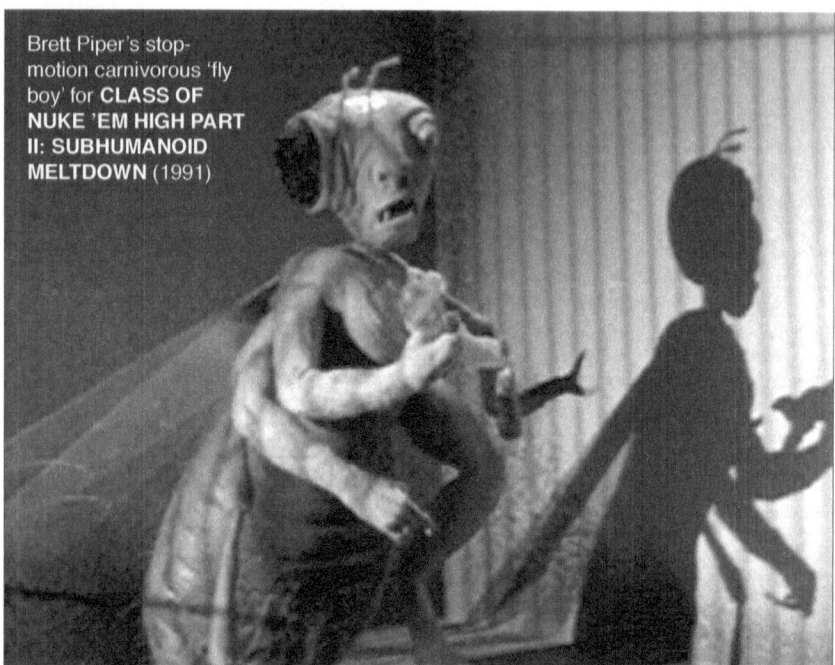

Brett Piper's stop-motion carnivorous 'fly boy' for **CLASS OF NUKE 'EM HIGH PART II: SUBHUMANOID MELTDOWN** (1991)

later that the chemicals in the foam he was using had anxiety-producing agents that were probably making him paranoid. He finally finished the suits and shipped them to me—collect. He wanted his money before we saw the suits, and with good reason. In addition to looking like crap, they were so shoddily made that they were falling apart as I took them out of the box.

I tried to repair one of them and make it usable, but it never really looked good enough, it was almost impossible to wear, and it kept falling apart. I finally had to build new suits from scratch, although the original suits are in the movie. The goofy-looking suits held together with duct tape and lighting clips were his. The tape and clips were only partly a joke—without them, the suits would fall apart.

The "real" monsters I made were all done Paul Blaisdell-style, built up in foam and latex over long underwear. They worked reasonably well and were fairly tough, standing up to the seawater okay, although they'd fill with sea organisms and really begin to stink, so every few days I had to fill a bathtub with hot water and Lysol and soak them in it. One day the hotel maid came in and saw one of the monsters propped up in a chair, drying. "You damn near scared the *hell* out of me!" she told me later.

SRB: There was almost no stop-motion or optical effects in THEY BITE, save for that finale. Did doing so many of the effects for the film via monster-in-suit keep post-production to a minimal scale? Were you able to wrap it up fairly quickly compared to your earlier features?

BP: There was supposed to be a small amount of stop motion in **THEY BITE**, some underwater shots of the monsters swimming. I built a small model fish-man, which actually looked pretty good, and shot some tests, but they didn't really fit with the rest of the film, so I scrapped them. Stop-motion isn't for every movie. Any advantages I might have gained by keeping the post on **THEY BITE** relatively simple were more than offset by Links' involvement. It seemed to drag on forever. I'd say finishing the movie took at least twice as long as it should have, which meant (since I was working for a flat fee) that I ended up getting paid half as much for my time.

SRB: Did this at all tempt you to stick with only live-action effects in future films? It's evident you didn't—stop-motion animation is clearly in your blood!—but I'm curious, given the monster-suit nature of THEY BITE (and your Tromie sequence for NUKE 'EM HIGH 2) if there was any temptation there...

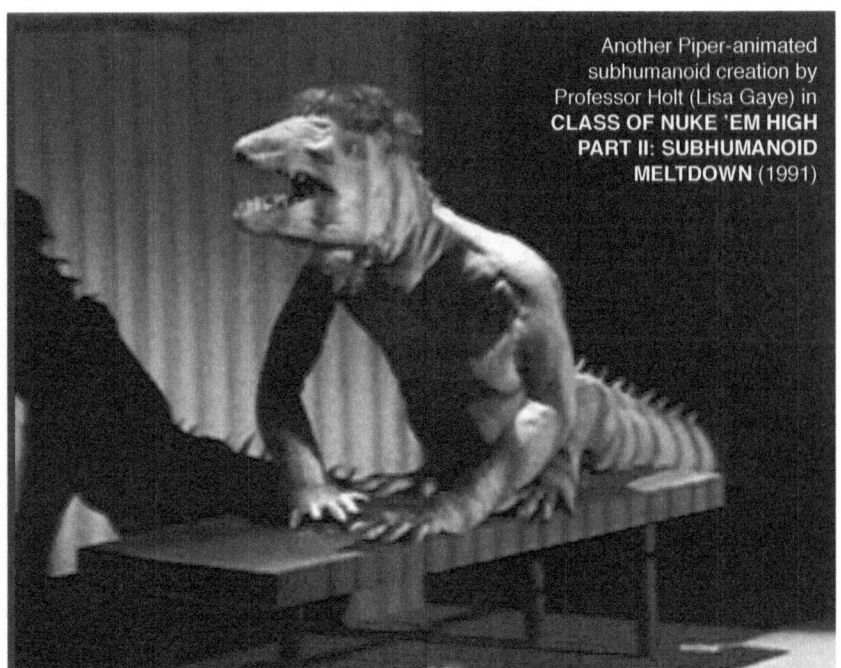

Another Piper-animated subhumanoid creation by Professor Holt (Lisa Gaye) in **CLASS OF NUKE 'EM HIGH PART II: SUBHUMANOID MELTDOWN** (1991)

BP: Well, remember I also did stop-motion for **NUKE 'EM HIGH 2**. I've never considered abandoning the technique, now less than ever. I'm one of the only ones still doing it (although other animators, in plugging their own projects, seem to ignore this), and it's kind of become my gimmick. I'm never going to make big-budget mainstream movies; the best I can hope for is a niche audience, which I'm fine with, actually, if I could ever make it pay. Stop-motion still has a big enough following and my budgets are low enough that it would seem like I could make a go of being the low-rent Harryhausen. You never know.

SRB: Oh, man, Brett, you've already earned that status, absolutely—hence this interview! One more question about CLASS OF NUKE 'EM HIGH 2: how extensive were the miniatures you constructed for the stop-motion animation in that film, what was it you delivered in terms of that stop-motion animation (16mm, 35mm?), and did you have anything to do with the miniatures that appear in the film with your Tromie monster suit?

BP: The miniatures in the stop-motion scenes were pretty bare-bones, cardboard walls and, I think, miniature bars to represent cells. This was primarily due to the lack of feedback I got from Troma—I didn't want to get too elaborate with the settings, because I had only a vague idea of what they wanted. I delivered 35mm elements to them, which meant that I couldn't shoot with my own equipment, so I rented space and cameras at Olive Jar Studios in Boston. You're probably familiar with them—they did a lot of stop-motions bumpers for MTV and the clay-animated lead-in for TNT's *Monstervision*. I got to use a rack-over Mitchell, just like Harryhausen! But I had nothing to do with the live-action miniatures.

SRB: Thanks for clearing that up. Though I know it was a work-for-hire, get-it-outta-here gig, THEY BITE was sold to MTI (which, at the time, was a pretty visible video label), it did get distribution into the video market in a more timely manner than your earlier features, and it did get a fair amount of pre-internet genre magazine coverage, and prompted your inclusion in at least one book (John McCarty's unfortunately-titled The Sleaze Merchants; *published April, 1995).*

BP: Someone involved with *The Sleaze Merchants*, I don't exactly remember who, later said to me, "The title doesn't really apply to you. You're cheap, but you're not sleazy."

SRB: I totally agree: the title wasn't appropriate to your body of work. But as a fan of your work craving information, I was thankful for the existence of that chapter. Did your work on THEY BITE have any benefits for getting a "next project" off the ground?

BP: I got no real benefit from **THEY BITE**. I've come to realize that in this business there's no value to "a little" success. Either you make **THE BLAIR WITCH PROJECT** and get all kinds of attention, or it's back to the same old grind, and I've never had my "**BLAIR WITCH**".

SRB: Did the production and filming of THEY BITE in Florida prompt you to consider doing any other filmmaking in that state? It had to be a pretty momentous change from making films in New Hampshire/New England...

BP: I did do one more movie in Florida (or part of one), which was **DINOSAUR BABES**. After those two experiences, I'm afraid the Sunshine State holds no particular allure for me.

DINOSAUR BABES (1996)

SRB: So, I hate to ask, but forgive me, I have to: Florida. Dinosaurs. DINOSAUR BABES...?

BP: **DINOSAUR BABES** was an idea I pitched to Lloyd Kaufman at Troma. Over the years I pitched a number of ideas to Lloyd, none of which worked out. The main reason seemed to be that Lloyd couldn't understand why anyone else should ever benefit from a deal. I remember discussing an earlier project with him, and after protracted negotiations over budget and other things, I brought up the question of what my remuneration was going to be, and his response was, "What do you mean? You get to make the movie." Anyway, I thought **DINOSAUR BABES** would be a good match, because I had the dinosaurs and he had the babes, but his response was basically, "Great, show it to me when it's done." Then Steve Williams found a couple of characters down in Florida who expressed an interest in "producing" it. I met with one of them and, unfortunately, they ended up agreeing to make the movie. You know, if I had my life to live over again (shudder), I'd say "No" a lot more.

SRB: Let's talk about his mentality a moment: I saw it all the time in my time in the video marketplace as a retailer, and I've certainly experienced and seen it first-hand in the publishing and comics fields, and dished-out to my students and alumni. Mercantile people, "money people," producers, distributors, guys like Lloyd Kaufman and Roger Corman: their business models are entirely dependent on creative folks like yourself, and yet they refuse to acknowledge any value to YOU, or your work. Have you lucked into any exceptions to the rule?*

BP: Uh—probably not. I mean, it varies, some "money people" value the creative end more than others, but by-and-large it's not considered primary. They don't feel (and I say this with some assurance based on conversations I've had with them) that they're dependent on us, they feel we're dependent on them. Their idea is that without money nothing gets done, so their part in the process is the more important, and everything revolves around them. And that any amount of money is worth more than any amount of work, by which I mean if I work my ass off for two years making a movie that a producer has sunk, say, $500 into, he still feels he gets to call the shots because *it's his money*.

Interesting quote: "Labor is prior to, and independent of, capital. Capital is only the fruit of labor and could never have existed had not labor first existed. Labor is the superior of capital, and deserves much the higher consideration." You know who said that? That damn commie radical Abraham Lincoln!

SRB: It drives me nuts, in negotiations, when I have to assert just that: how the creative work has monetary value, and nothing can follow without it. Of course, that is almost never the mercantile perspective; merchants—publishers, producers—see only their monetary investment as having value, hence greater clout. Given how you've proven, for decades now, how inexpensively you can initiate, create, produce, and deliver a feature film at such a modest budget, I just don't get how it is that nobody with sufficient bankroll to subsidize such a path ever steps forward. It's a long-time frustration—why can't, say, George Romero enjoy the kind of path a Woody Allen or Clint Eastwood does as a filmmaker? The remake rights alone to George's work would have amply rewarded such a "gamble," such risk-taking. Nina Paley wrote, directed, produced, animated and completed a pretty marvelous animated feature film—SITA SINGS THE BLUES [2008]—for peanuts; as far as I know, not one animation studio executive responded with "Quick! Get us a contract with Nina Paley!" You've made feature films that deliver solid entertainment, with stop-motion animation you create yourself; sans any of the

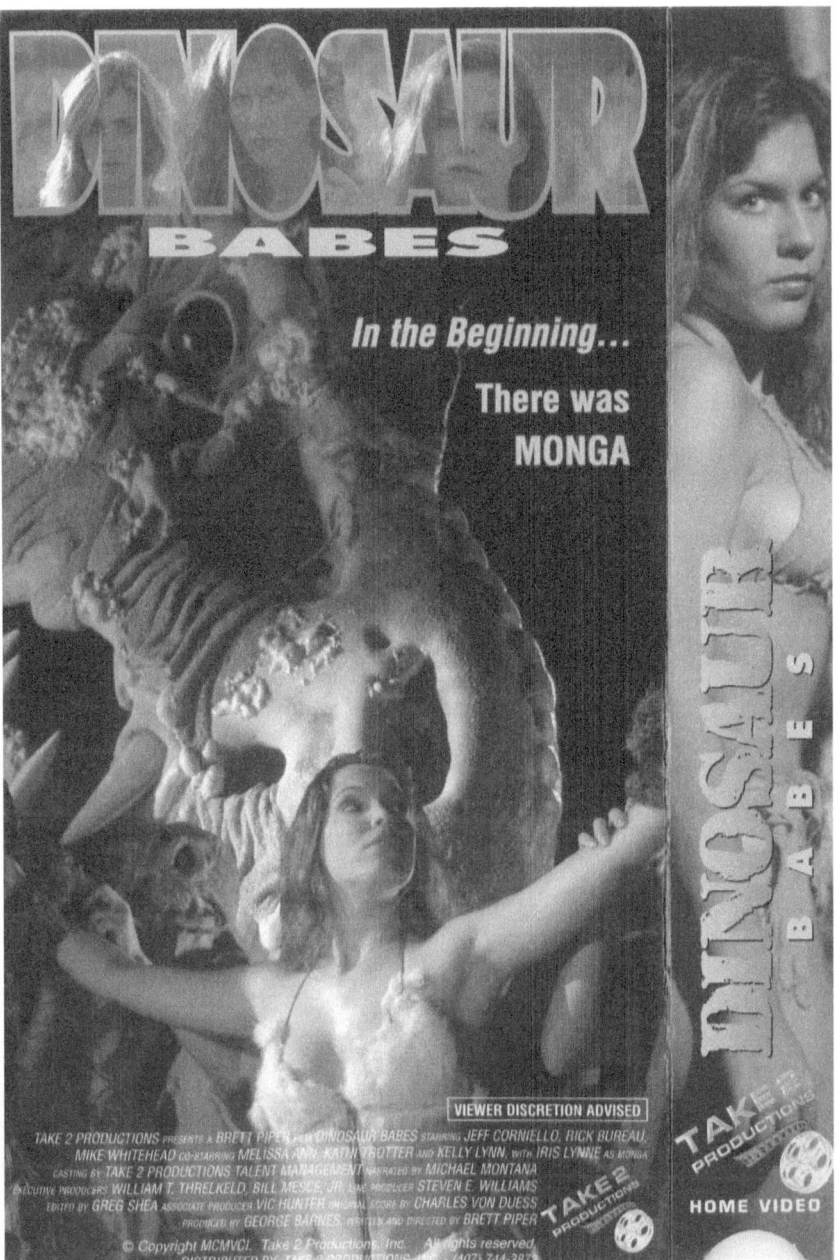

resources Harryhausen had, you continue to deliver. I don't get that Nina Paley's example, your example, doesn't attract money people who would just bankroll that kind of creativity, without micromanagement and meddling— just fund a string of films, knowing they're inexpensive to produce (by ANY industry yardstick) and some will work, some won't, but those that won't will get you to the next one. I know this is entirely rhetorical in nature, but are there any examples of a workable producer/creator or studio/creator relationship in existence that you'd embrace, in the best of all worlds?

BP: Sure. If I had an output deal where I

delivered "X" number of pictures and was paid X-plus dollars for each, that would be great, but it's not going to happen. Again, it's all about money. No one has ever gotten rich off any of my movies, so there's no reason for the money people to be interested. And the situation is only getting worse, because the industry is now dominated by a blockbuster mentality. It's no longer enough to make a decent profit, you've got to make a *fortune*, or nobody's interested. Back in the studio days, this wasn't true. Studios were factories turning out a product, and as long as each picture made a profit, all was good. Look at even a fairly recent example like AIP—when they hit their stride with the Poe movies, they were spending a few hundred thousand on each and making a million, million-and-a-half back, and that was good money. Not anymore. No one is interested in that kind of chump change today.

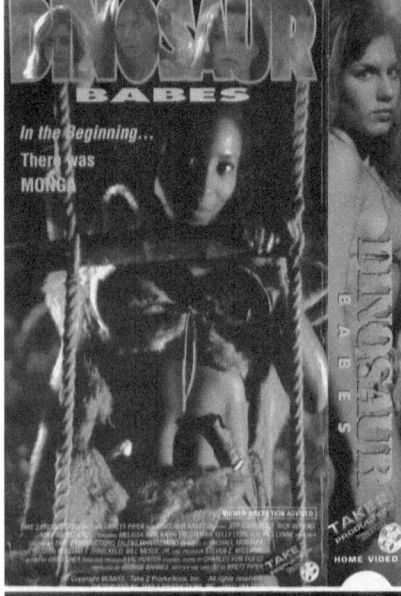

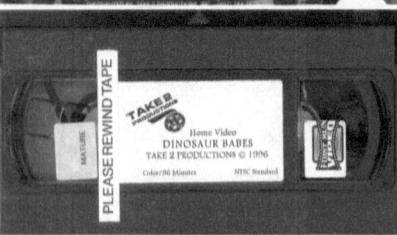

Previous Page & Above: Front and back cover art and videocassette for the fleeting (and disowned-by-the-filmmaker) Take 2 Productions VHS release of **DINOSAUR BABES** (1996)

SRB: If you're up for it, let's make our way through what it was SUPPOSED to be and SHOULD have been, then quickly deal with what it turned out to be.

BP: It was *supposed* to be a quick, fun little dinosaurs'n'cavegirls movie, a little like a poverty row version of **CAVEMAN** *[1981, D: Carl Gottlieb]*. What it turned out to be was an unmitigated disaster.

SRB: Did your involvement with this production begin while you were still in Florida, wrapping-up on or just after THEY BITE, or did you head back home to NH, then end up back in Florida working on what initially (I hope) promised to be your dinosaur/caveman movie?

BP: This was back in New Hampshire after I'd finished with **THEY BITE**.

SRB: So, You're back in New Hampshire. Was what footage you did shoot and complete shot in New Hampshire/New England, or was any of it filmed in Florida?

BP: All the live-action was shot in Florida. Only the effects were shot in New Hampshire.

SRB: How did it go from being an opportunity to make a "fun little dinosaurs'n'cavegirls movie" to whatever Take 2 Productions turned it into? Was there a point where you knew the film wasn't going to be what you intended, and what and when was that?

BP: Almost right away. I was given almost no time for preproduction, I was still building dinosaurs at night down in Florida after shooting all day. Once more, I really should have said, "Guys, this isn't working," and just walked away. I would have lost absolutely nothing.

SRB: Who were the producers at that point? William T. Threlkeld and Bill Mesce, Jr. were credited as executive producers on the VHS release that Take 2 Productions released, with George Barnes taking producer credit, Vic Hunter as Associate Producer—and Steven E. Williams was credited as Line Producer, meaning Steven actually did something tangible with you on the production?

BP: I'm not familiar with some of those names, which is typical. Cronies and people who did favors behind the scenes are always getting "producer" credit. George Barnes was the actual

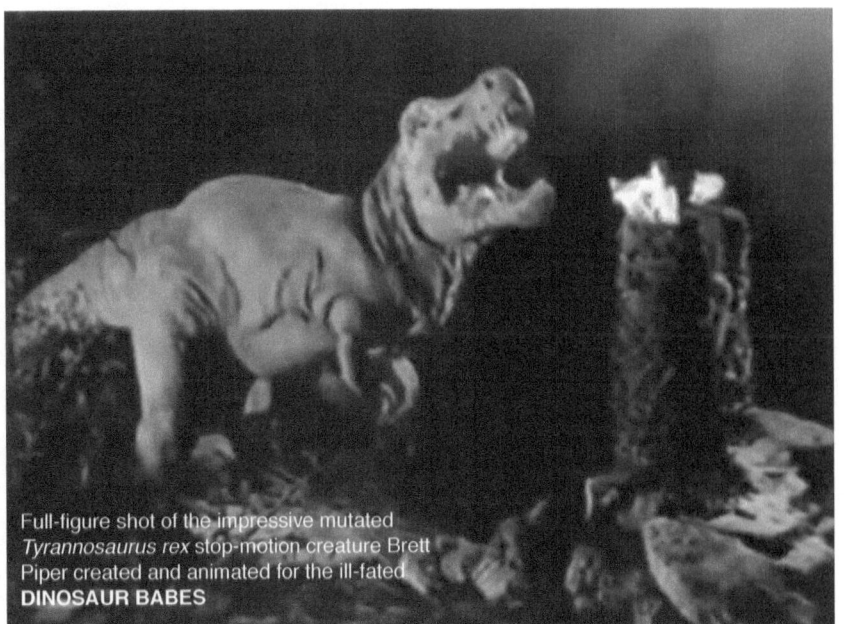

Full-figure shot of the impressive mutated *Tyrannosaurus rex* stop-motion creature Brett Piper created and animated for the ill-fated **DINOSAUR BABES**

producer, although unfortunately he was a hands on sort of guy who had no idea how a movie like this should have been made. He brought buddies onboard who were worse than useless, getting in the way and screwing things up. Steve Williams was actually the person who brought us together. Remembering how useful Steve had been on **THEY BITE**, I suggested he be hired as production manager. Unfortunately, this time around he was more hindrance than help. I have no idea what happened, but he seemed to have acquired an inflated idea of his authority. He considered himself one of the people who was running this show, which wasn't good. Barnes wanted to fire him, but I stuck up for him and kept him on. Well, in this instance (and in this instance only) Barnes was right, and I was wrong. It's funny (sorta), but at the beginning when things looked promising, Steve was very happy to take credit for bringing the project together, but at the end when it had all turned to crap he said, "Don't blame me, I didn't have nothin' to do with it."

SRB: Did the live-action filming in Florida include all the interaction with the full-scale dinosaur props—including nicely-staged action with the parasites, and puppetry involving that beautifully-detailed mutated Tyrannosaurus rex, the live-action Lambeosaurus, and extremities of the Centrosaurus—and the scenic miniatures (including the downed alien spaceship)?

BP: Yes, all that was done on location. Close-up and inserts were shot back in New Hampshire, including all the **KONG**-like scenes of the girls being sacrificed to the T-Rex miniature.

SRB: Your dinosaurs—the stop-motion models and the very detailed live-action puppetry—are really impressive, Brett, and quite paleontologically accurate per our understanding of these creatures circa the mid-1990s. You clearly put a lot of work into every one of them. Which ones had been created for *DINOSAUR KID*, and which did you create specifically for *DINOSAUR BABES*?

BP: The *Lambeosaurus* and the mutant *Tyrannosaurus* were built specifically for **DINOSAUR BABES**, the rest were made for **DINOSAUR KID**. There were actually dinosaurs shot—a *Stegosaurus* and a few others—that never made it into the feature. By that time I realized that the producers had taken the movie out of my hands, so I never bothered sending them the rest of the dinosaur footage. They wouldn't have known what to do with it anyway.

SRB: Your cast was led by your titular *DINOSAUR BABES*: Iris Lynn (a.k.a. Iris Lynne Sherman, who went on to do stunt work in TV and films like *JEEPERS CREEPERS* [2001, D: Victor Salva] and *OUT OF TIME* [2003, D: Carl Franklin]), Melissa Ann, Kathi

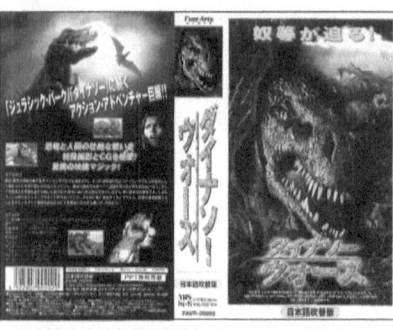

DINOSAUR BABES also secured Japanese VHS distribution in the late 1990s

Trotter, Kelly Lynn, supported by cavemen Jeff Corniello, Rick Bureau, and professional mixed martial artist Mike Whitehead (who also ended up serving time in prison for attempted sexual assault). How did you pull together this eclectic cast, and how were they to work with?

BP: It's funny—strippers and porn stars frequently use their middle names for stage names, and at one time the most popular middle name for girls was Lynn, so you find an entire cast made up of "Iris Lynns", "Kelly Lynns", "Shirley Lynns", "Melvin Lynns", *ad*-ridiculously-*infinitum*. I remember Iris Lynn, she was just a *tad* haughty (which actually fit the character) but good to work with, and I'm glad she went on to do other things. Kathi Trotter worked for the parks department, and supervised the auditions we held in a local park—she was the best-looking girl there, and got talked into starring in the movie, although she doesn't get star billing. She did a good job, but she wasn't really an actress, and this caused problems shooting the "sex" scenes, mild as they were. "Kelly Lynn" was Kelly Barnes, George's sister. Very nice, very attractive. By the way, the gangster "Machine Gun" Kelly's real name was George Kelly Barnes. I can't help wondering if that's coincidence.

As for the guys, I can't remember at this point which actor was which. I had no trouble with any of them. The big guy (Jeff?) was particularly funny. He did a slightly cruel but hilarious Lou Ferrigno impression.

SRB: Which members of the cast were involved in the New Hampshire shoot—the sacrificial sequences, any inserts requiring their participation—as well as the Florida shoot?

BP: None of the principles was involved in any New Hampshire shooting. I did hire a local model to put on some cavegirl outfits so I could shoot some blue screen to use with the miniatures, but I have no idea if any of that was used.

SRB: All in all, before you pulled out, how much time do you estimate you'd poured into the production?

BP: Very hard to say at this date. I was in Florida for maybe a month. I put in several more months doing post and animation back in NH. Maybe six months, but that's only a guess. I kept asking them when I'd be able to start editing, and they fed me some BS about technical issues. It eventually came back to me that they had started editing the movie without me. I called them on this, but they denied it, while at the same time boasting about it to people they knew I stayed in touch with. Like most dishonest people, they were also stupid. Eventually I just gave up and washed my hands of the project. I stopped calling them and I never heard from them again. Steve Williams sent them an email asking how the film was doing, and they threatened to sue him for harassment. Barnes later said in an interview that the main problem with the movie was that I was insane. That's typical of these types of people—like crooked politicians, they can't defend their own actions, so they slander you.

SRB: What did you end up delivering to the producer(s) that they were able to, then, completely make a mess of (and was it 16mm, 35mm, or video transfer only)?

BP: They had all the footage, except for the effects, right from the start.

SRB: The dinosaur animation footage you created and chose to withhold from this production: what did you do with it? Was it incorporated into a later film, or would that ever be possible?

BP: I tossed it.

SRB: Damn!—but, well, understood. Once, and only once, in my comics career I actually burned all the remaining original art in my possession associated with the project (all that remained and remains were pages that were later returned by the publisher); sometimes, you just want to torch the remnants and sow the fallow ground with salt. When did you discover they'd released what they made (or unmade) of your hard work on VHS to the video market, with your name and credit still on the film?

BP: I think it would be harder to destroy original

artwork than to destroy elements of a movie, because the original artwork *is* your creation—the books or magazines that appear on the stands are merely inferior copies. Whereas all the elements that go into a movie, the scripts and props and even footage, are not the movie, any more than nails and boards and paint are really a house. But getting back to the question, I'm not sure exactly when I realized that a bastardized version of **DINOSAUR BABES** had actually seen the light of day, although the review you wrote and sent to me may have been one of the first things I saw about it.

SRB: You've subsequently deleted DINOSAUR BABES from your filmography, including every online filmography I've ever found. I really appreciate your patience with these questions, Brett, thank you. This prompts the speculative question: what dinosaur film would you still enjoy making, if you had the opportunity, proper budget, time and the means, no limitations, no strings attached?

BP: I wrote a dinosaur movie several years ago very much in the *Star-Spangled War Stories* vein which I would still like to do. If and when I do it I'll throw out the last forty years of paleontological progress, and the dinosaurs will be very much Charles Knight/Marcel Delgado-style creations.

*SRB: Seriously, that would be **fantastic**! The DVD cover art for QUEEN CRAB! had the flavor of those **Star-Spangled War Stories** "War That Time Forgot" covers from the Silver Age—I would love to see you tackle that genre. Sci-Fi/SyFy has really debased it for some time with their clumsy "soldiers vs. giant whatsit" CGI features. I'd love to see what you'd do with it—and going old-school with the dinosaurs would be totally appropriate, and capture the flavor of those early 1960s comic book stories by Robert Kanigher and Ross Andru and Mike Esposito (Russ Heath, Gene Colan, and Joe Kubert also drew a few). Very cool.*

MOVING TARGETS (1998)

SRB: Let's shift gears: chronologically, your screenplay for the Rutland VT-based Edgewood action feature MOVING TARGETS [1998] follows sometime after the DINOSAUR BABES debacle, and your own next scripted-and-directed completed-and-released feature was DRAINIAC! [2000], a personal favorite of mine. What order did work proceed in after you washed your hands of DB, and were there any other projects you'd worked on hoping to find a home for during that four-year period?

BP: You know, again, it's ancient history. It all sort of blurs together in my mind. I'm sure there were other projects I tried to get going. One of them was called "CYBER-WOLF VS. THE LIVING DEAD". It was actually an idea Steve Williams had—or at least, he came up with the title—and the script I wrote was sort of like a Mexican monster mash movie, with the hero a werewolf who battled other monsters. But it never happened because Steve could never raise the money. I used to get that a lot. People who knew I could work cheap would approach me about shooting a movie for them if they could raise the money, but it never worked out. Well it did once, with Alex Pirnie and **DARK FORTRESS**, but he went broke right after that, so we never did another one.

I was asked to write **MOVING TARGETS** because they needed a script in one week, and they didn't know anyone else who could work that fast. I wrote it from an outline that made use of stock footage they had available. I turned over the script, got my money, and that was basically the only job I ever did for Edgewood where I didn't get screwed. I didn't think much of the finished movie, but that wasn't my problem. They cut out everything interesting, because

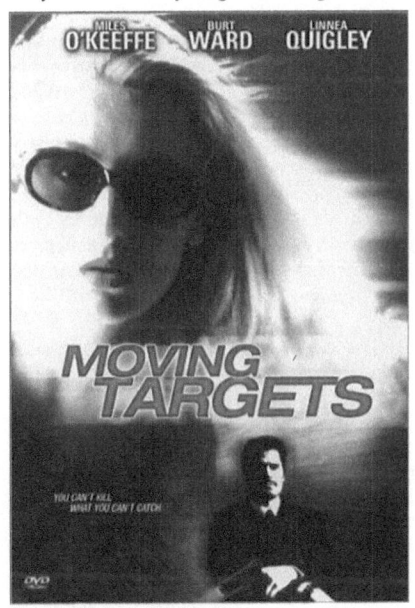

US DVD

it was "too expensive". What that really meant was it was too much like hard work. That's something I've noticed with various low-budget filmmakers—the minute a sequence becomes demanding, their first reaction is "Bag it, the audience will never know". Those are always the scenes that might have made the movie exciting or interesting. So sure, the audience never actually knows that there was *supposed* to be an effects scene or a chase sequence there, they just know they're watching a boring movie.

SRB: How did Edgewood hear of you, and how did they approach you to tackle that screenplay?

BP: We were introduced by Lloyd Kaufman. Edgewood had gone to Troma trying to set up some kind of co-production deal, and Lloyd told them about this other filmmaker (me) working on-the-cheap in New England, and suggested we get together. We'd known each other quite a while before **MOVING TARGETS** came along.

SRB: Building a movie around stock footage was a very Roger Corman-like concept: he'd done it with the early 1960s Russian SF films he had directors like Francis Ford Coppola, Peter Bogdanovich, and Curtis Harrington craft new footage around to create "new" films (yielding at least one good film, Harrington's QUEEN OF BLOOD [1966]). Arrow Video just released an insane DVD/Blu-ray set of three Corman productions carved-out of a Hungarian art heist movie, and Joe Dante, Jr. and Allan Arkush did the same with New World Pictures action footage to create their first feature for Roger in the 1970s, HOLLYWOOD BOULEVARD [1976]. Whatever they did with it, however much they cut back on what you'd scripted, I'm very curious: what was YOUR process? You or they screened the raw action footage available, and you worked from there, with a checklist of shots to be used, inserting as much stock footage as possible between cost-conscious interaction with your new characters and narrative?

BP: I was just given a checklist of items that needed to be worked into the plot.

What I find interesting about MOVING TARGETS in the context of your body of work is it's your first crime film: you'd had some "crime lord" elements in DYING DAY (the zombie master's rule, using the walking dead as his "hit men"), but other than that, this was a bolt out of the blue thematically. In MOVING TARGETS, an urban crime lord's attorney is murdered, his wife finds the computer disc containing the *dirty financials that the lawyer was killed over, and a detective and District Attorney have to keep her alive long enough to testify—though the detective's right-hand man is targeting her, too, since he's in over-his-head with gambling debts. You may have hammered it out in just a couple of weeks, but it's a solid little hardboiled crime drama, Brett. It would certainly have stood up as the setup for any network or cable crime show episode from the 1950s-early 1990s, and it's a decent concept for a feature film. Whatever the result from Edgewood, were you ever tempted to streamline operations and do another crime film of your own?*

BP: I hammered it out in *one* week! And it's not really my first crime movie, because it's not my movie at all. It's Edgewood's movie, I only wrote the script it was based on. I have no real desire to make a crime film. I like some of them (**THE ASPHALT JUNGLE** *[1950, D: John Huston]* comes immediately to mind; there must be others), but there'd be no scope for the miniatures and effects that are my real reason for making movies.

SRB: Were there any aspects of MOVING TARGETS *that you thought worked well, or at least made good use of the players? Was it your script that put so many female leads into roles this genre habitually made male characters (the detective, the District Attorney, etc.). They'd pulled together an interesting cast, to say the least: Miles O'Keeffe of TARZAN THE APE MAN [1981, D: John Derek] infamy as the crime lord; Linnea Quigley as the D.A.; the 1966* Batman *TV series' Robin, Burt Ward, as the corrupt Lieutenant; and a decent local actress Sue Ball as the detective (she was in Nora Jacobson's* MY MOTHER'S EARLY LOVERS *[1998], which is a fine regional independent feature).*

BP: Eh, I watched it only out of curiosity to see how my script translated to the screen. Not well. Burt Ward was fun.

SRB: We'll get into DRAINIAC! *first, but just for the sake of following through and establishing the connections: was it* MOVING TARGETS *that led to your subsequently working with Edgewood on your own pair of feature films a couple of years later,* PSYCLOPS (2002) *and* ARACHNIA (2003)? *[See* Monster! *#30 (pp.10-22) for coverage of both those films.]*

BP: As I said, we'd known each other for years. There'd always been talk of doing something together. It finally happened... unfortunately.

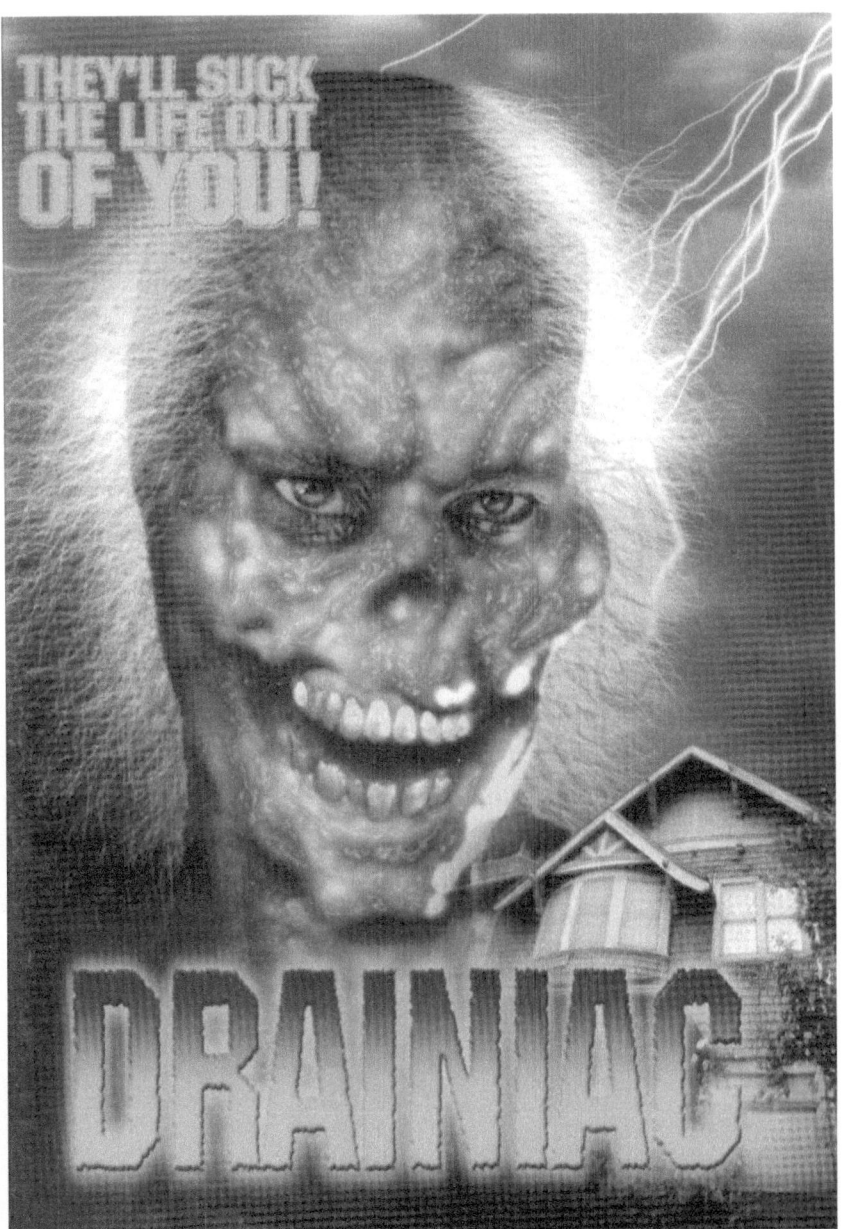

Uncredited Richard Corben-like DVD packaging artwork for the LMG label's release of Brett Piper's **DRAINIAC!** (2000)

DRAINIAC! (2000)

SRB: You were coming off a rough stretch at the close of the 1990s, and then you created one of your most inventive and audacious horror movies. What was the genesis of DRAINIAC!?

BP: My nephews taking a bath. They were very young and bathing together and, after the youngest, Kyle (who was maybe three or four at the time) was taken out and being dried off, his brother pulled the plug and the tub began to drain. Kyle saw the water swirling down the drain and began to panic, thinking his brother was going

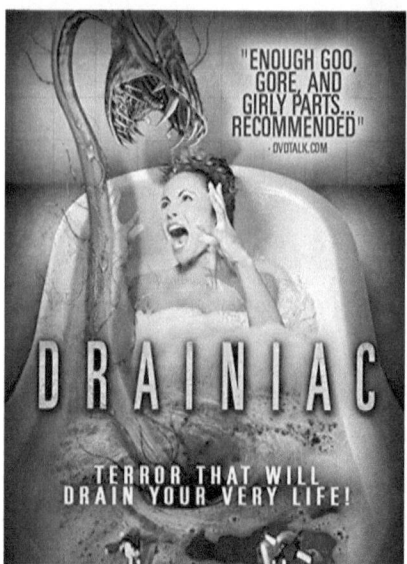

A very **THEY CAME FROM WITHIN** (1976)-like piece of **DRAINIAC!** promotional/packaging artwork

to be taken with it. "Ian, *get out!*" he started screaming, in absolute terror. *"Get out! Get out!"* And that's how **DRAINIAC!** was born!

It's funny—some reviewers slammed the tub scene as "gratuitous". It's actually the key scene of the movie. Of course, a lot of people don't know what gratuitous means anyway.

SRB: *Wait—the same nephew Kyle who was in the earlier films, who did the voice acting in* THE RETURN OF CAPTAIN SINBAD? *So, you'd been carrying this idea around in your head for some time?*

BP: Yes, I suppose so. But Kyle was very young when we did **SINBAD**, so there probably wasn't much time between them.

SRB: *Where was* DRAINIAC! *filmed, and how did you go about casting the film?*

BP: It was filmed in an abandoned house in Pelham, NH. The town administrator, Peter Flynn, was a big help in letting us film there. When I first mentioned I wanted to shoot a movie, his eyes lit up (*Ka-ching!*), but I had to let him know that there was no real money involved and, to his credit, he still helped us out. He went to bat for us at the town meeting where we needed to get permission. Somebody on the board suggested a fee of around $150 a day, which I couldn't possibly have afforded, and Mr. Flynn quietly said, "Well, I was thinking more like $50 a week." Which they accepted! But I had a very embarrassing moment with him. We were shooting one night, and he stopped by to say hello. I went to introduce him to the cast, but we'd been using the fog machine all night, and just as I was about to say his name, I had to stop and clear my throat, and he thought I'd forgotten it! He introduced himself, and I could see he was a little perturbed. It was the *fog*, honest!

The financing of **DRAINIAC!** was interesting. I happened to be chatting with a high school friend, Paul Costley—we were just sort of catching-up—and I mentioned that I'd been trying to figure out how little I could shoot a movie for, on film, and still have it look like something. I told him I'd come up with a figure of $10,000. He said, "All right, I'm in." "What do you mean, you're in?" "I'll give you the $10,000." And that was that! I hadn't even *asked* him, I was just making conversation. I wonder if he regrets it now. I still stay in touch occasionally. He's gotten some of his money back, but he's still in the hole for most of it.

The casting was the usual thing, which is to say looking under every rock until enough people turned up. I went to modeling agencies, casting agencies, online (still primitive back then), high school drama clubs. Two of the kids were real teens, which is something I normally try to avoid, but it worked out fine (although I had to postpone a couple of shoots due to soccer games). My friend Kati Preston, who runs a touring theater company called The Hampstead Players, suggested one of my leads for me. Georgia Hatzis, who played Julie, was suggested by a Boston actress who had auditioned for the part but was uncomfortable with the nudity. Georgia was from Easton, Pennsylvania and commuted on weekends, around a five-hour drive. Ironically (if that's the word), the film I just finished, **OUTPOST EARTH**, features another actress from Easton, PA—and she had to drive four hours in the *opposite* direction to get to our shoot.

SRB: *The special effects throughout are inventive and at times outrageous, and it was the first of your films where you really went all-out mounting a creepy, almost Lovecraftian atmosphere while really delivering "the grosseries," as my late pal Chas. Balun used to put it, without wallowing in the kind of onscreen gore you deplore. It's quite a tight-wire act!*

BP: Well, I prefer creepy to gory. This disappoints some people. One such person actually "accused" me of being gay because I didn't slash-up enough women in my movies. I can live without fans like that.

SRB: Were there any sequences you'd scripted or planned that didn't make the final cut?

BP: No, although few were as effective as I'd have liked them to be. I could do better now. I can do *everything* better now!

SRB: DRAINIAC! is, essentially, a film about a poltergeist infestation, via the vengeful water "demon", an elemental malignancy. When you were cooking-up the manifestations and materializations for the film, was the fact it was a water-being a liberating aspect, or was the liquidity of your creature and the effects work a bit of a logistical nightmare?

BP: Water effects are hard. Also, there was no water in the house we shot in. I had to bring in a sink and a tub and hook tubes and water jugs up to them to make them appear to work. For the bathtub scene we ran a hose from the fire station next door over to fill the tub. It was freezing in there too, so we only did the master shots in the house. I later brought the same tub home and duplicated a corner of the bathroom on my porch, and we shot the bulk of the scene there so Georgia could be warm. I had to carry the tub up some stairs by myself, but I'm a sturdy fellow.

By the way, the house was not in the isolated countryside, it was right smack in the center of town, between the fire station and a school, which meant that all the exterior dialogue had to be dubbed.

SRB: You use every trick in the book, and then some. What was your favorite set-piece or sequence in the film—the one that worked out and played on the screen just as you'd hoped it would?

BP: The bully being emasculated came off rather well (no pun intended. Or maybe.)

SRB: Point taken! I may have missed a disclaimer on the screen during the credits. Were any plumbers *injured in the making of this film?*

BP: No but the leading lady was almost killed.

SRB: OK, I'll bite: your leading lady—was that

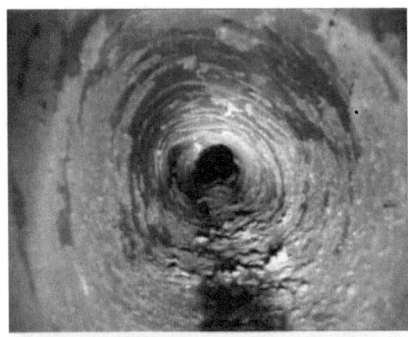
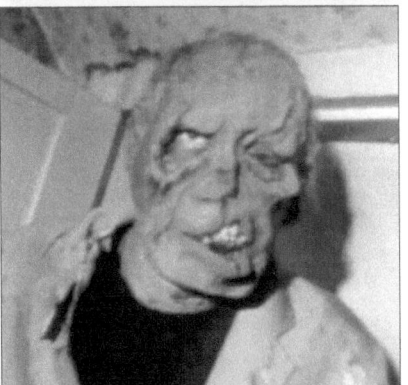
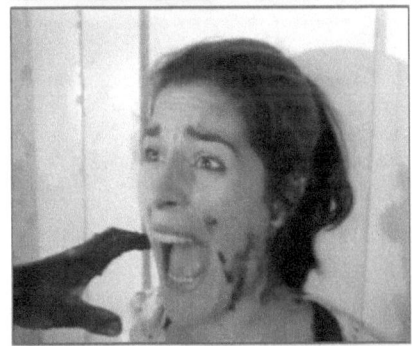
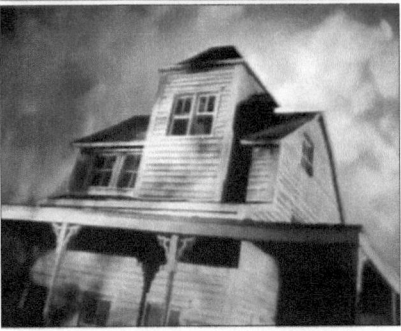

Evocative images from Brett Piper's **DRAINIAC!**, including a shot of screaming heroine Georgia Hatzis

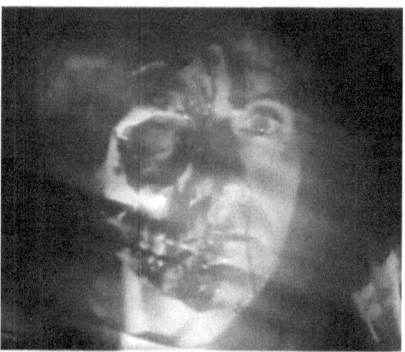
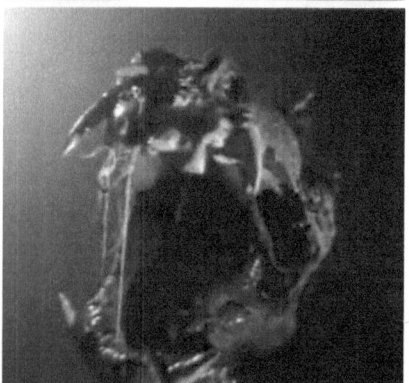
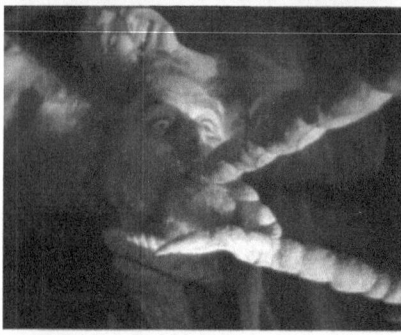
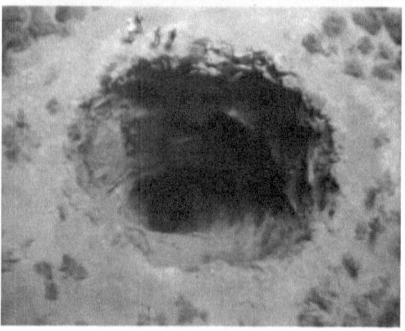

More visceral visages, septic screams, oral invasions and putrid plumbing from Brett Piper's **DRAINIAC!**

Georgia Hatzis?—was almost killed? What the hell happened?!

BP: We were doing the bathtub scene and one of the lights somehow tipped-over and fell toward the tub. I saw it falling and made a dive for it, and caught it as it bounced off Georgia's head. She didn't get hurt, and in hindsight the light was never going to fall into the tub—from that angle, the light-stand would have hit the rim and the light itself would have stopped a couple of feet from the water—but at the moment it was scary as hell. When the shock caught up with her, Georgia actually started crying for a moment. Not big embarrassing sobs, but a kind of quiet "What if?" reaction. It's *still* scary to think about it, all these years later.

SRB: God, that could have been disastrous—but you all survived, thankfully. A couple of your DRAINIAC! stars went on to some measure of fame—Georgia in television primarily, later landing a recurring role in the New Zealand TV series Short Poppies *[2014], and particularly Alexandra, subsequently acting in multiple feature and short film roles, television (*Flock *[2011-2012]), and working creatively behind the camera writing, producing, etc. (including directing a video game). But you directed them in their first-ever feature. How were they to work with?*

BP: I didn't know any of that, although I did get a Facebook message from Alexandra a couple of days ago. I'm glad they're doing well, they were very good to work with. It looks like some of them are doing better than I am! Well, good for them. I have no use for *schadenfreude*.

SRB: DRAINIAC! is a real estate nightmare movie—THE MONEY PIT à la THE AMITYVILLE HORROR (the movie that introduced leaky-liquids to the American ghost movie for mass audiences), with the creepy culprit in the plumbing—told from the point-of-view of the teenage daughter [Georgia Hatzis] stuck in the haunted house. This was your first narrative dominated by female characters; was that a stretch for you? Did you have input from family members, friends, or the actresses in the film [also including Alexandra Boylan and Samara Doucette], or did you just wing it?

BP: Nope, I just winged it. Although the character of the dad was based pretty much on my own father. That's why nobody finds him credible. I run into that a lot (the photographer in **SCREAMING DEAD** *[2003]* being another example)—whenever someone objects to the actions of one of my characters and says, "That could never happen in real life," it's almost always based on something from real life. This is what people really mean when they say "Truth is stranger than fiction." Fiction needs to be credible. Truth does not.

SRB: Rob Gordon went on to work in other films and some television, as did Todd Poudrier a.k.a. Todd Brendan (the melting hobo in DRAINIAC!), writer/actor Andrew Osborne (who'd done some work with Troma, in SGT. KABUKIMAN N.Y.P.D. [1990, Ds: Michael Herz, Lloyd Kaufman]), and one of your barflies in the cast was Mike Downey, who became a pretty prolific producer after his appearance in DRAINIAC! You also helmed Phil "Phip" Barbour as the enigmatic exorcist, Mr. Plummer; you worked with him again in PSYCLOPS, and Elizabeth Hurley also appeared in both DRAINIAC! and PSYCLOPS. How were they to work with?

BP: Wow—you know a hell of a lot more about these people than I do! Rob Gordon was the actor Kati Preston recommended to me, and he worked out very well, although being a little older than the other cast members and a little more experienced sometimes caused small conflicts. One of the other kids might suggest a bit of business, and Rob would come over to me and fume, "She's giving notes! She shouldn't be giving notes! Only the director gives notes!" Well, I like all the input I can get. I'm no dope; other people have good ideas too. Anyway, I was very happy with him in the film. Todd Poudrier and Andrew Osbourne I only worked with for an evening. Todd had read for either one of the kids' parts or the dad, I don't remember, but he was either too old or too young, so I made him a wino. Mike Downey was actually in the bar scene as Steve Bornstein's understudy, in a way. Steve was a good actor and fine as the dad, but he had a tendency not to keep in touch, so sometimes I never knew if he was going to available when I needed him. The bar scene was the first thing we shot, at a nearby Chinese restaurant, and Mike (also a good actor) understood that if Steve didn't show he would take over the Dad's role; if not he would be one of the barflies. By the way, the bald guy with the mustache was producer/money man Paul Costley.

Phip was a pleasure to work with, and brought a sort of old-school gravitas to a movie mostly filled with young people, giving it a nicer balance. Liz Hurley's part took maybe an hour to shoot against a black background. No sweat.

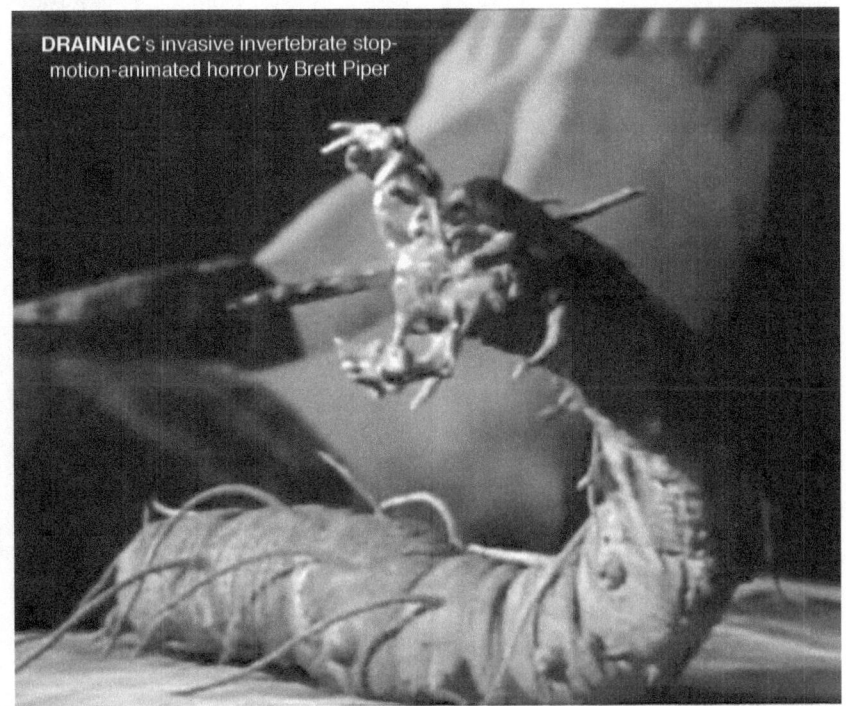

DRAINIAC's invasive invertebrate stop-motion-animated horror by Brett Piper

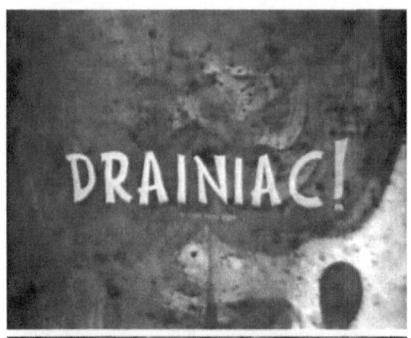
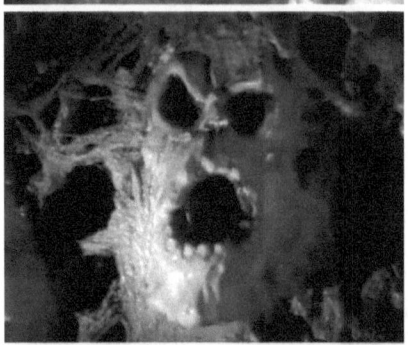
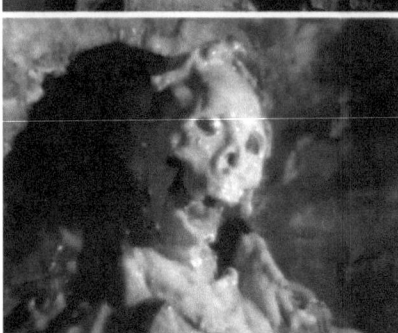
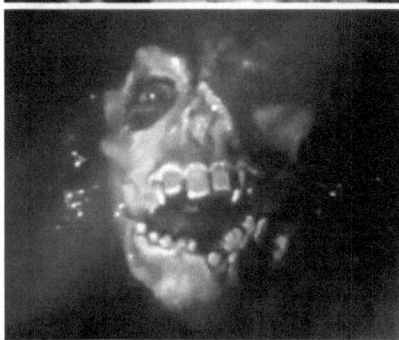

List all the melting movie men you can bring to mind: for Brett Piper, **DRAINIAC!** is more of an homage to his favorite 1990s Asian horror films than to **THE H-MAN**, **THE DEVIL'S RAIN**, **THE INCREDIBLE MELTING MAN** or **STREET TRASH**!

SRB: The stop-motion-animated creatures in DRAINIAC! were nasty, parasitic "things"— toothy annelids, penetrative tentacles, a ghost spider, bat-critters, and so on—but they weren't your usual gigantic creatures this time around: many were, I'd guess, not that much larger than the actual models you'd constructed. Was it easier working with small-scale critters this time out, or do the same sort of challenges in integrating live-action and stop-motion still apply, regardless of scale?

BP: Yes, they were all about the same size as they appear in the film. The difference in scale didn't really affect things much, but what did make things easier was not having them interrelate to the actors, something that was much more difficult with the resources I had to work with back then. All I could really do was in-camera effects, no rear projection, and certainly no traveling mattes, so showing actors and monsters in the same frame was always a headache. By the way, in the long shots the "demon spiders" were real spiders crawling around a miniature set.

SRB: Very cool. I'm curious about what might have fueled elements of DRAINIAC!. The packaging for and some reviews of the film mentioned THE EVIL DEAD, and I get that association, but other films also came to mind when I first saw DRAINIAC!. Sentient water-beings (therein spawned by H-bomb tests, not supernatural forces) were introduced in the Japanese gem THE H-MAN [美女と液体人間 / Bijo to ekatai-ningen, 1958, D: Ishirō Honda]; the opening with the homeless guys fighting over a bottle and one of them (Todd Poudrier) melting brings to mind the melting winos of STREET TRASH [1987, D: Jim Muro]; the wormlike parasites and the "tentacles-in-the-tub" sequence stick in the memory, as does the toilet-castration-by-water-demon, as echoes of David Cronenberg's SHIVERS a.k.a. THEY CAME FROM WITHIN [1975]. Were any favorite films of yours a direct influence here?

BP: It's funny—I showed the ending of **DRAINIAC!** to a friend of mine and her husband, who was from Hong Kong, and he remarked, "It looks like a Chinese ghost story." He's the only one who's ever made that comparison, and yet it was the biggest stylistic influence on the movie. The only two of the movies you mention that I've seen are **THE H-MAN** and **EVIL DEAD**, which were no influence at all (except that **EVIL DEAD** and **DRAINIAC!** are both cheap-ass movies—although **EVIL DEAD** cost *way* more than my film.)

SRB: Yes, I can totally see that, now that you point it out! Stupid me. I love A CHINESE GHOST STORY [倩女幽魂 / Sien nui yau wan, 1987, D: Ching Siu-tung]—I've shown it to my students a couple of times over the years (different groups of students), they always love it, too—as well as the more antic Hong Kong ghost films, like Sammo Hung's ENCOUNTERS OF THE SPOOKY KIND [鬼打鬼 / Gui da gui] trio. Any favorites of yours that inspired DRAINIAC! or your more recent films, any Asian ghost movies in particular?

BP: None in particular, just the overall feel of that genre, probably most typified by Tsui Hark's earlier films. They seemed to be an inspiration for Carpenter's **BIG TROUBLE IN LITTLE CHINA** (*[1986]* which I like a lot) as well, but Carpenter's film was even more inspired by American Westerns, which I gather it was supposed to be.

SRB: As a fellow New Englander who was trying to stay on top of the Chinese/Hong Kong/Chinese genre films of the 1990s back in the day, despite their being nowhere in theaters up here, were you keeping up with such films via catch-as-catch-can "gray market" videocassette dubs, the way I was at the time?

BP: I was originally introduced to Chinese ghost movies on Jonathan Ross' *Incredibly Strange Film Show [1988-89]*, and started hunting them down on VHS after that.

SRB: Understood. What happened with the completion of DRAINIAC!? First off, what did you complete (16mm or 35mm), originally?

BP: I only ever did one movie in 35mm, and that was **MUTANT WAR**. All the rest were 16mm. I'd had a "deal" with Edgewood *[Studios]* for them to do the post *[on **DRAINIAC!**]*—it was supposed to be a straight 50/50 participation, I'd shoot the movie, they'd provide post-production—but when the time came we had a "meeting" where they explained that I would also have to cover their "expenses", which came to almost three times what the movie had cost to make (and far more than I would have needed to simply do the post myself), so that killed that. Needless to say, this hadn't been mentioned before. They knew perfectly well I couldn't afford what they were asking. It was their way of reneging on the deal without, in their minds, appearing to do so.

SRB: For the record, given what's to come: that "deal" with Edgewood—that was originally about wrapping-up DRAINIAC!?

BP: Yes.

SRB: So, from there—

BP: While I was trying to figure out what to do next, I got a call from Mark Polonia. I had no idea who he was, but he'd read about my situation somewhere and volunteered to help me finish the movie. We talked a little and I ended up sending the work print and the video transfers to him in Pennsylvania. He match-cut the video and added basic audio effects, then I drove to PA for a long weekend and we completed the movie in a marathon three-day session.

SRB: DRAINIAC!'s postproduction was your first 'collaboration' with Mark Polonia, then?

BP: Yes. Afterwards we had an argument about payment—I offered him 25%, and he only wanted 10%. That turned out to be typical—the only times Mark and I have argued about money were when he asked for too little and I insisted he take more.

SRB: Thankfully, we'll be coming back to your working with Mark again! There's two versions of DRAINIAC! in existence, a 2000 edit and your preferred 2008 version; it actually had a rather unusual distribution history, originally hitting the video market right when VHS and DVD were vying for shelf space in video rental shops, which were still a pretty active market then. There were initially competing VHS releases in 2000—one with a zombie face looming over an ominous house with the tagline "They'll Suck the Life Out of You!" from Lincoln Media Group (who also issued it on DVD with the same packaging), and another (from the label Tapeworm) showing Georgia Hatzis in a bloody bathtub with a red, amorphous background revealing the skull-like demon's face—how did that happen?

BP: I have no idea who the hell Tapeworm are/is. The artwork you described is something I created when I was pitching the movie. No one else has ever used it, preferring variations that don't represent the actual movie in any way. **DRAINIAC!** was being handled by someone in LA calling himself American Film Partners. I believe he was actually a real estate broker who wanted to get into movies. Once I signed with him I got very little information about what was being done with the movie. This is quite common. Eventually I got no information at all, he simply stopped taking my calls or responding to my letters. When I'd had enough of this, I sent him a registered letter saying, in effect, "You're in breach of contract and I'm taking the movie back." The letter came back to me unopened, but refusing to acknowledge such a letter does not invalidate it, so I turned the movie over to EI/Pop Cinema. Unfortunately, this was right at the time that their own market was drying-up, so nothing much has happened with it.

SRB: Thankfully, DRAINIAC! enjoyed some legs via a later E.I./Shock-O-Rama 2008 reissue on DVD, with a far superior widescreen transfer and commentary track by yourself explaining, in part, the existence of new footage and this new edition. You cover some of this in that commentary, but for the benefit of this interview and chronology, could you summarize how all this went down? How did you hold onto or regain ownership necessary to the revamped 2008 DVD edition?

BP: Shock-O-Rama's version is in fake widescreen, cropped top and bottom, which actually degrades the image slightly, but [E.I. head honcho] Mike Raso felt that all movies have to be at least 16 x 9 now. There is no new footage in the movie, I merely enhanced some of the effects in post.

SRB: Given that revised and refined DRAINIAC! release—and I have to say, there's many of us who wish all your features enjoyed such a showcase on DVD, or even Blu-ray—I have to ask: if you were able to orchestrate similar restored and proper transfers of any of your earlier films, Brett, are there any you would favor for such treatment?

BP: Wow—I'd hate to see my movies rereleased in Blu-ray. That would be like telling a ninety-year-old actress "We're gonna shoot you in hi-def now—it'll be great, the audience will see every wrinkle!"

SRB: Well, yes, that pretty much sums that up!

———

©2017 Stephen R. Bissette all rights reserved; special thanks to Brett Piper, all images from Brett Piper's films © respective year of production, 2017 Brett Piper, unless otherwise indicated.

TO BE CONTINUED IN MONSTER! #34!

Coming Up: Monsters, Mummies, Mutants, Mucousy Malignancies and Misty Mundae as *Monster!* moves from the Green Mountain State to the Garden State—Edgewood to E.I. Independent Cinema—with Brett Piper's **PSYCLOPS** (see background image), **ARACHNIA, THE SCREAMING DEAD, BITE ME!, SHOCK-O-RAMA, BACTERIUM**, and much, much more!

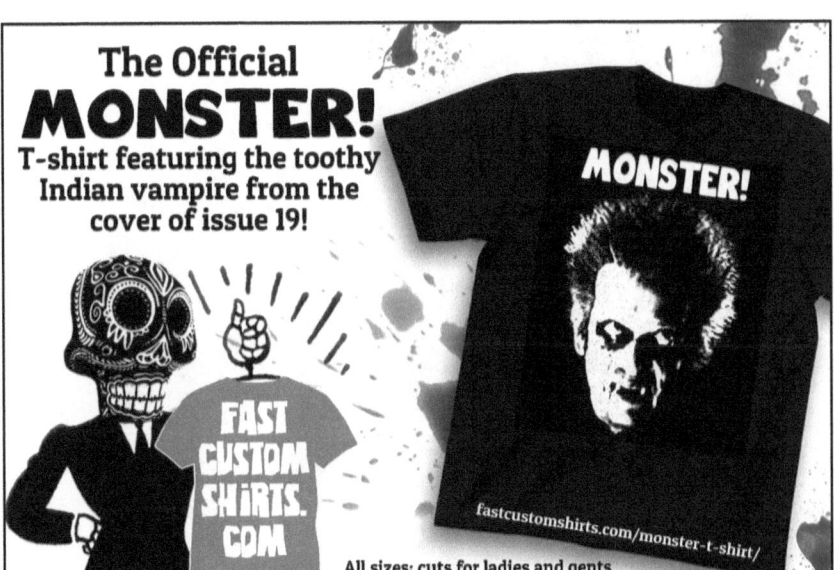

The Official MONSTER! T-shirt featuring the toothy Indian vampire from the cover of issue 19!

fastcustomshirts.com/monster-t-shirt/

All sizes; cuts for ladies and gents

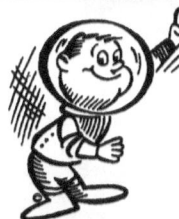

IF YOU THOUGHT WE ONLY PUBLISHED MOVIE MAGAZINES, THEN YOU NEED TO CHECK OUT THESE *ÜBER*-COOL BOOKS FROM WK BOOKS PUBLICATIONS:

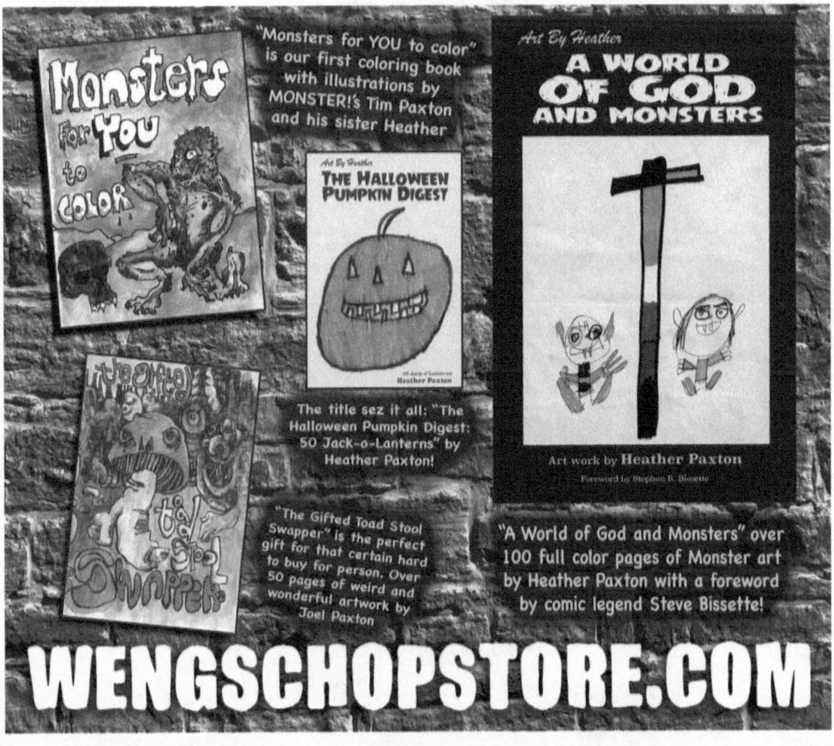

"Monsters for YOU to color" is our first coloring book with illustrations by MONSTER!'s Tim Paxton and his sister Heather

The title sez it all: "The Halloween Pumpkin Digest: 50 Jack-o-Lanterns" by Heather Paxton!

"The Gifted Toad Stool Swapper" is the perfect gift for that certain hard to buy for person. Over 50 pages of weird and wonderful artwork by Joel Paxton

"A World of God and Monsters" over 100 full color pages of Monster art by Heather Paxton with a foreword by comic legend Steve Bissette!

WENGSCHOPSTORE.COM

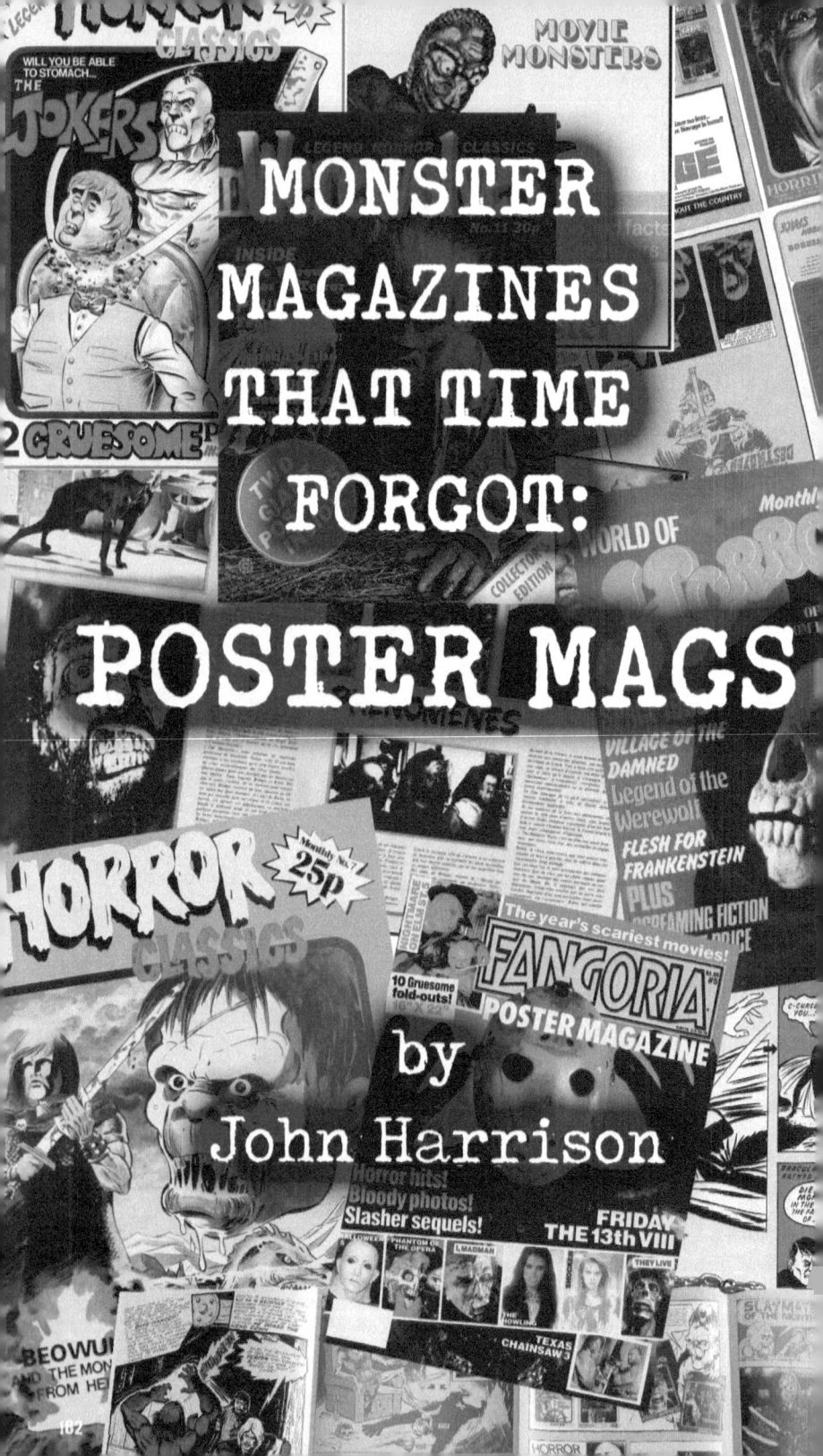

In this instalment of MMTTF, *I have decided to focus, not on an individual title, but rather on a specific* concept, *that of the fold-out poster magazines which became popular for brief periods, largely during the 1970s (they're having a bit of a "retro" resurgence now, in certain quarters of fandom). The idea behind the poster magazine was a simple and self-explanatory one: in terms of its page-size and cover designs, the package looks like a regular magazine when on the stands, but instead of it containing stapled pages, the whole thing was printed—in full-color—on a single large sheet of glossy paper, with one side generally containing a single giant image for use as a poster, while the reverse had several short articles or other items about whatever subject that particular poster mag was dedicated to, usually accompanied by smaller photos. The whole thing was then folded several times and simultaneously marketed as both a magazine and a poster, giving younger teenagers (the typical target audience) more bang for their pocket money. The dimensions of the poster when unfolded were about the same as a standard one-sheet movie poster (around 27 by 41 inches), although some were slightly larger (or considerably smaller) than that.*

The poster magazine as we came to know it seems to have had its beginnings in early-1970s England. Certainly, that is where the concept first took hold and became most popular. Kung-Fu Monthly *was a popular poster magazine that cashed-in on the martial arts craze from that period, with (*natch!*) most issues featuring Bruce Lee on the cover, as well as on the interior and fold-out poster.* KFM *was published by Felix Dennis, and proved to be a far 'safer' venture than his previous publication* Oz, *a controversial adult-oriented alternative/underground periodical that had gotten itself into some serious legal hassles in 1970 after it invited school kids to help edit and put together an issue. Like a number of other UK poster magazines,* KFM *also had editions published for sale in some overseas markets, including the US, where it bore a $1.00 cover price (the cover price in the UK being 25 pence; roughly the same at the exchange rate of that time).*

Science Fiction was another subject that proved popular for the poster magazine format in the UK. There was Sci-Fi Monthly *(which leaned heavily towards TV-related content like* Star Trek, Space: 1999 *and* Doctor Who*), a* Planet of the Apes *one-shot, and the short-lived* Sci-Fi Series *edited by Dez Skinn, which devoted issues to* The Six Million Dollar Man *as well as George Pal's ill-fated pulp adventure film* **DOC SAVAGE: MAN OF BRONZE** *(1975, USA). Later in the decade, there was a long-running series of* **STAR WARS** *(1977, USA) poster magazines (which got renamed after* **THE EMPIRE STRIKES BACK** *[1980, USA] and* **RETURN OF THE JEDI** *[1983, USA] were released), as well as* **CLOSE ENCOUNTERS OF THE THIRD KIND** *(1978, USA) and* Battlestar Galactica *titles.*

Other film genres also found themselves the focus of poster magazines too. There was Supercops *(which covered cinematic crime actioners like* **DIRTY HARRY** *and* **THE FRENCH CONNECTION** *[both 1971, USA], plus TV shows such as Telly Savalas'* Kojak*) and, of course, pop stars were also a popular subject (I had a couple of extra-large* KISS *poster mags, published in Australia by* TV Week, *whose posters adorned my bedroom walls for a couple of years). However, this being* Monster! *and all, it is the more horrific/monstrous subject matter which we are most interested in here and, while there was not a prodigious amount of monster movie-themed poster magazines published (certainly not in relation to the number of traditional-format monster magazines that were regularly appearing on the stands during the same period, anyway), there were a few noteworthy titles—not to mention a couple of oddities—that are deserving of coverage, which I will look at individually hereunder.*

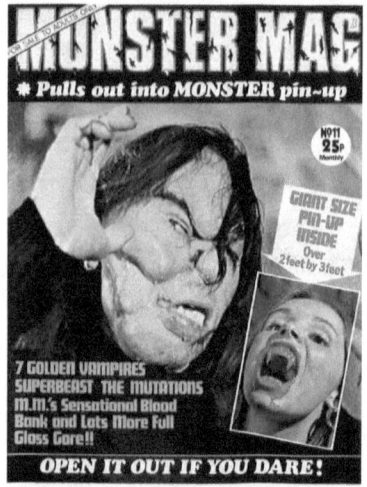
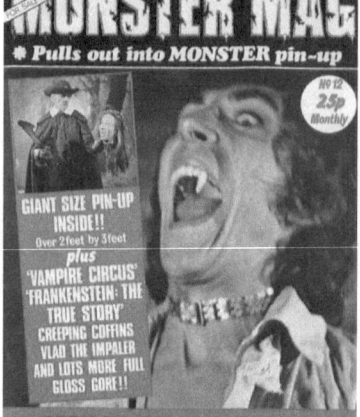
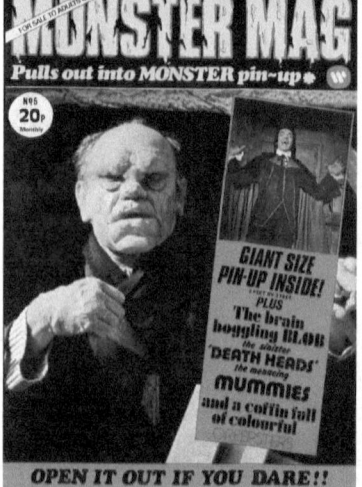

MONSTER MAG
(UK, 1973-1976; 17 issues)

The earliest and best of the genre poster magazines was the matter-of-factly-titled *Monster Mag*, which was published by Top Sellers in the United Kingdom (though issues were printed in several languages other than English for distribution on the Continent too). It was edited by the husband-and-wife team of Roger and Jan Cook, with Dez Skinn taking over for the final three issues. Running for a total of 17 issues between '73 and '76, the content of *MM* was very 'English'— and specifically, extremely Hammer Horror-heavy— one of the primary reasons why it is such a desirable title for collectors of material pertaining to the famous British fright factory. It also didn't shy-away from utilizing some of the more graphically visceral movie stills available, leading it to carry an "Adults Only" warning on the cover (something which, as Mr. Skinn tells us in the accompanying interview printed below, would of course have only served to give it an air of being [quote] "forbidden fruit" and thus increase its desirability with underage horror-loving youngsters).

"OPEN IT OUT IF YOU DARE!!" challenged the sensationalistic blurb on the first issue, whose cover was dominated by a close-up still of Christopher Lee as— *who else?!*—Dracula, his glaring bloodshot eyes indicating a recent slaking of his evil thirst. Lee was also the subject of the first issue's poster, which features a fabulous promotional shot of him as the Creature from Terence Fisher's **THE CURSE OF FRANKENSTEIN** (1957, UK).

While this landmark first issue of *Monster Mag* no doubt raised the eyebrows (and ire) of more than one concerned parent, it was the follow-up which really ran into trouble. When the English-language copies of *MM* #2 arrived in the UK from the printers in Italy, they were deemed to be offensive by the authorities, so all copies were seized and destroyed by officers from Her Majesty's Customs and Excise, leading it to become the most sought-after issue of the magazine (copies of the European version— commanding high prices—occasionally show-up today). Looking at it nowadays, it's difficult to perceive what exactly it was that UK Customs officials thought was so bad about the issue, to the point of not just banning it but actually going so far as destroying the entire print-run outright. There's nothing overly gory about the contents.

Open 'Em Out If You Dare!! **Left, Top to Bottom:** The covers to *Monster Mag*s #11 (March 1975), #12 (June 1975) and #5 (1974), with grotty grotesqueries from **THE MUTATIONS** and the movie version of **DOOMWATCH**, plus fangy Hammer Horrors (**TWINS OF EVIL** and **VAMPIRE CIRCUS**) as their prime selling points

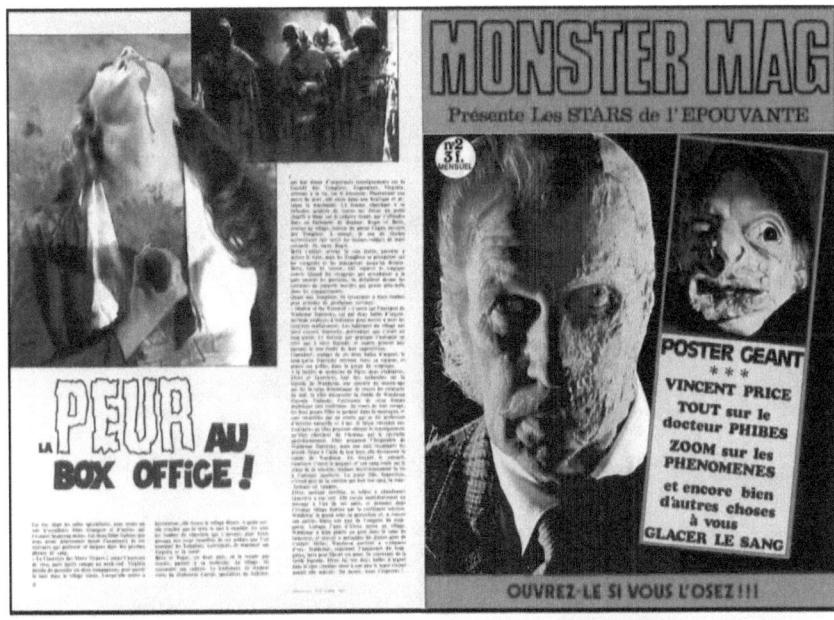

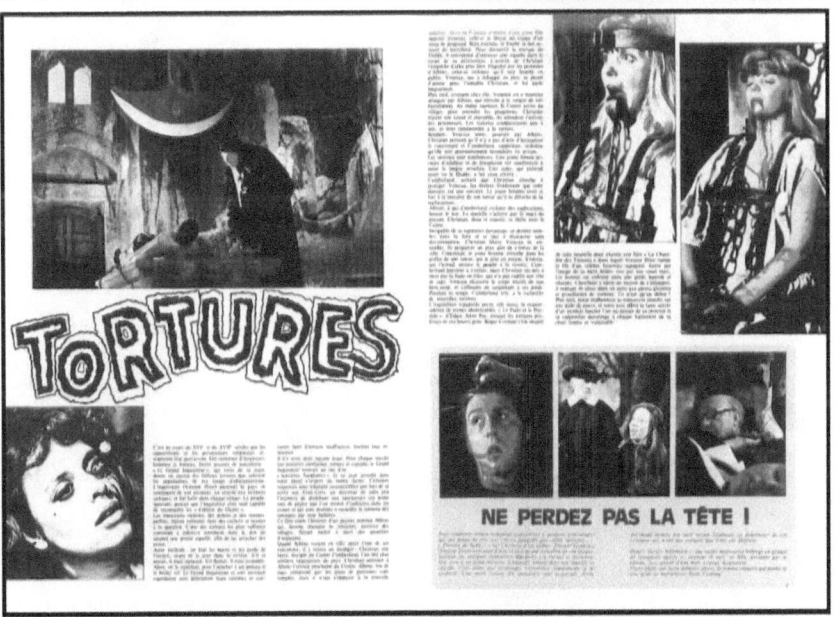

This Page & Next, Top: Triple diptychs of folded-out spreads from the French edition of the banned issue of *Monster Mag* (#2), which has recently been reprinted in all its gory glory in a belated English edition

Maybe someone was just in a bad or easily-outraged mood that day, and/or they took offense at that issue's "Focus on Freaks" angle, which seemed a tad more lurid and provocative than the usual cinematic vampires, werewolves and Frankenstein monsters. The poster for this issue does feature a rather ghoulish image of one of the unfortunate title characters from Jack Cardiff's effective oddity **THE MUTATIONS** (1974, UK), while one of the interior articles ran a photo of the human-headed dog from **THE MEPHISTO WALTZ** (1971, USA); either of which may have

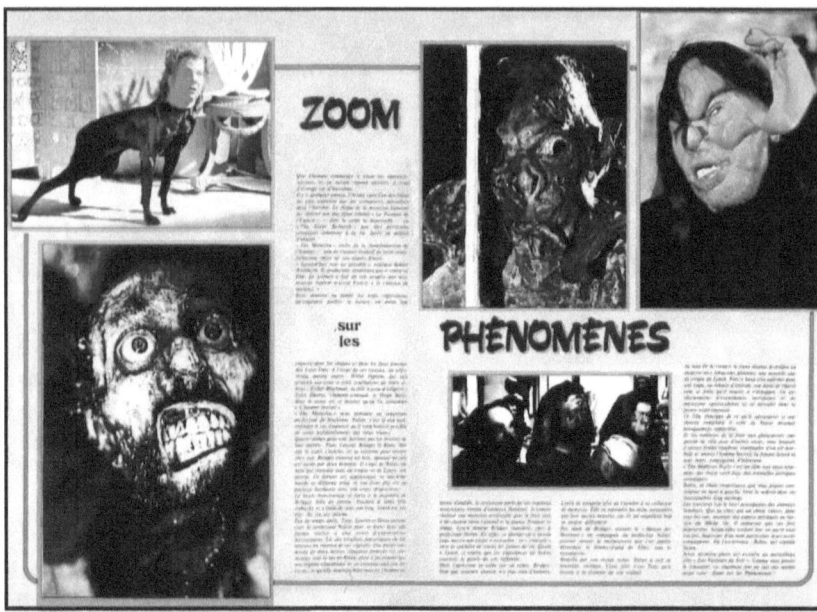

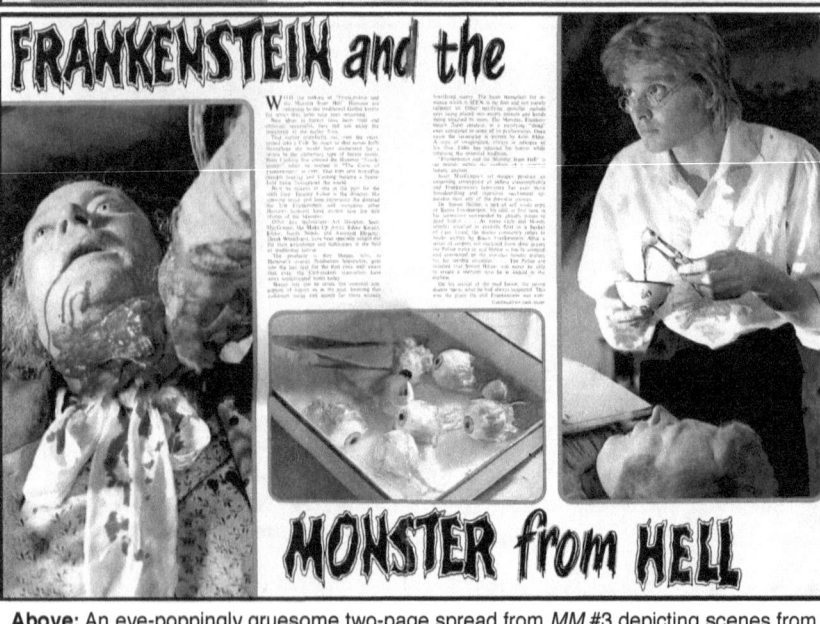

Above: An eye-poppingly gruesome two-page spread from *MM* #3 depicting scenes from Hammer Films' final *Frankenstein* franchise entry from '74 (that's Peter Cushing's co-star Shane Briant at right)

upset the delicate sensibilities of those arbitrary deciders of what constitutes good and bad taste. To play it safe and not risk a repeat incident, a local UK printer was soon found and utilized for future issues.

While the covers, articles and interior posters for *MM* were predominantly Hammercentric (with Christopher Lee, as always, a clear favorite), it still managed to cover a few non-Hammer oddities like **BEWARE! THE BLOB** and **BLACULA** (both 1972, USA), Larry Cohen's **IT'S ALIVE** (1974, USA), and even William Grefé's strange Florida-shot swamp-horror cheapie

DEATH CURSE OF TARTU (1966, USA [see *Monster!* #20, August 2015, p.74]). **THE EXORCIST** (1973, USA) also warranted some coverage, as did some British horror films that weren't produced by Hammer but were clearly inspired by them, such as Freddie Francis' underrated **THE CREEPING FLESH** (1973, UK).

When the Cooks left *Monster Mag* following the publication of its fourteenth issue, Dez Skinn—then only in his mid-twenties but already an experienced and recognizable name on the UK comics and film publishing scene—was brought in to take hold of the magazine's reins. Skinn would only publish three issues of *MM*, before ceasing the title to concentrate on *House of Hammer* instead. The first issue of *Monster Mag* published under Skinn (cover designated as Vol. 2 No. 1) differentiated itself by featuring **THE ROCKY HORROR PICTURE SHOW** (1975, USA/UK) on its cover, before the familiar visage of Chris Lee's Dracula returned on the following issue. The cover for the final issue of *MM* featured the lycanthrope from Freddie Francis' would-be Hammeresque Tyburn production **THE LEGEND OF THE WEREWOLF** (1975, UK), while the final poster was split-up into two images; the top half a still of Peter Cushing about to burn an alleged witch in **TWINS OF EVIL** (1971, UK), while the bottom half again featured Lee as Drac, this time meeting his demise on a busted wooden wagon-wheel spoke during the prologue of **DRACULA A.D. 1972** (1972, UK).

The original run of *Monster Mag* was dead, but like Dracula himself it could not stay buried forever... though its resurrection would not come for nearly *four decades*!

MONSTER MAG: TAKE TWO
(UK, 2014-present; 6 issues so far)

In 2014, Dez Skinn and original editor Roger Cook decided to resurrect *MM*, starting with an English-language reprint of the infamous confiscated-and-destroyed second issue, which Skinn painstakingly recreated by scanning in a rare French printing, digitally cleaning it up and translating and replacing all of the French text in English, using the same vintage fonts as the original, even retaining the original "1973" publication date and "15p" cover price for the sake of authenticity. Finally, collectors were able to fill that elusive gap in their collections, without having to take out a personal loan to do so!

This was only the beginning for the reborn *Monster Mag*. Skinn followed-up his reprint of *MM*

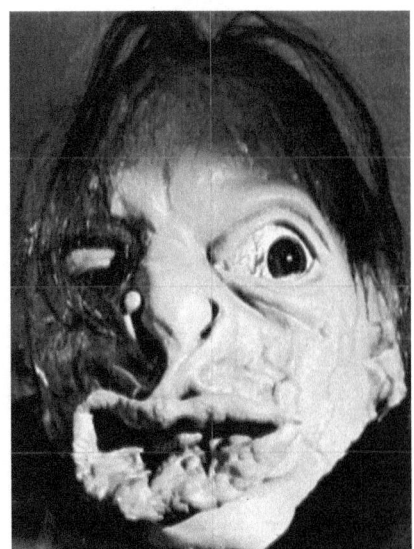

The complete poster from *MM*'s banned ish (#2), featuring a stomach-churning photo-portrait of the main monster from Jack Cardiff's **THE MUTATIONS** (1974)

#2 with the long-promised "Double X" special, originally slated for publication in November of 1976 but ultimately never delivered due to the magazine folding and Skinn moving on to *HoH*. Opening-out into a poster of a blood-soaked and barely-clothed Yutte Stensgaard (as the vampiric Mircalla/Carmilla in Jimmy Sangster's **LUST FOR A VAMPIRE** [1971, UK]), articles in the Double X issue (cover identified as Volume 2/Number 4) include pieces on Italy's Dario Argento, Spain's Paul Naschy and the beautifully-strange **HORROR EXPRESS** (*Pánico en el Transiberiano*, 1972, Spain/UK, D: Eugenio Martín), giving the issue a very European flavor.

Subsequent issues of the current run of *Monster Mag* have included reprints of the original first and third issues, plus a "Best of '76" special featuring Brian De Palma's **CARRIE**, Richard Donner's **THE OMEN**, Tobe Hooper's **DEATH TRAP** (a.k.a. **EATEN ALIVE**) and Dan Curtis' **BURNT OFFERINGS**; and, perhaps best of all, a *House of Hammer* special, which covers the origins and history of the classic British horror magazine (including the troubles it ran into with *Famous Monsters* publisher Jim Warren when it landed a US distribution deal). With text taking up only three pages instead of the usual seven, the *HoH* issue folds-out into not one, not two, but fully *three* large posters reproducing the covers of *HoH* numbers 7, 12 and 17.

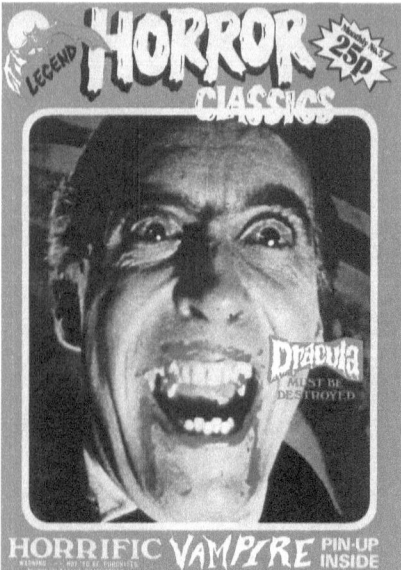

LEGEND HORROR CLASSICS
(UK, 1974-1975; 12 issues)

Briefly touched-upon in my article on *World of Horror* which appeared in *Monster!* #31 (November 2016 [pp.222-228]), *Legend Horror Classics* was put together by *WoH* editor Jim Shier after that magazine ceased publication following its ninth issue. *LHC* differed from *Monster Mag* in that it predominantly featured horror comic strips (most of them drawn by Kevin O'Neill) that folded-out and had a large monster portrait poster on the reverse. *LHC* enjoyed a decent run of precisely a dozen issues, with the last three being specials that focused on Vampires, Werewolves and the Frankenstein Monster respectively.

KING KONG POSTER MAGAZINE
(UK, 1976; one-shot)

When the much-hyped Dino De Laurentis-produced remake of **KING KONG** arrived in theatres in December of 1976—to good box-office but decidedly mixed reviews—it was accompanied by a flood of new merchandise that included board games, model kits, Topps' bubblegum cards, tin lunchboxes (with plastic thermoses), Halloween costumes, a 3D View-Master set (released in both standard and "talking" versions), a Colorforms play set, a set of promotional drinking glasses offered by Burger Chef, and much, *much* more. There were also several *Kong*-related paperbacks, books and magazines published (with the King making the covers of everything from *Famous Monsters of Filmland* and *Mad* to *Time* and *Circus*), along with this one-shot UK

Above & Below: The cover and 50% (i.e., one side) of the full spread of *Legend Horror Classics* #5 (its complete poster is on the next page at top left)

Printed in lurid full-color on quality 150g gloss paper, the new *MM* should be required reading for fans of 1970s horror, as well as those with a nostalgic pang for the monster magazines of yore. (See our accompanying interview with Dez Skinn for more on poster magazines in general and the history of *Monster Mag*, both then and now, in particular).

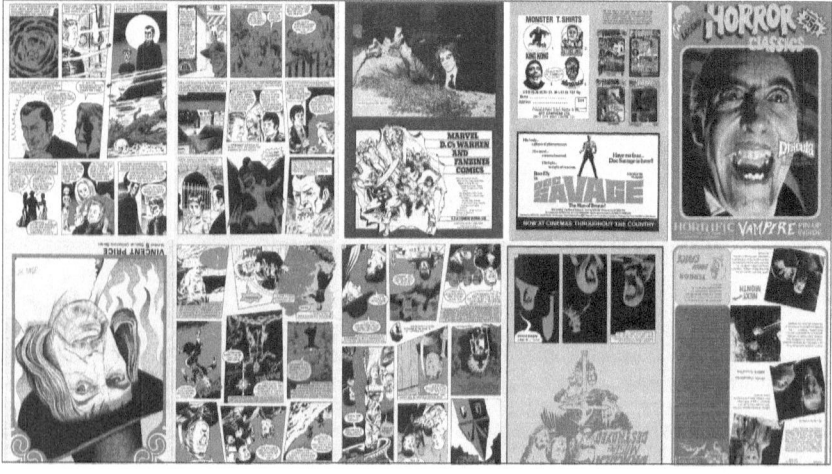

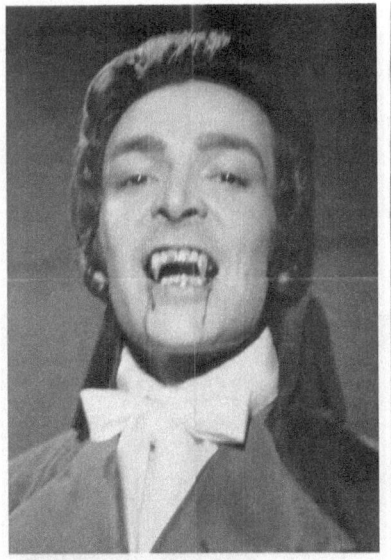
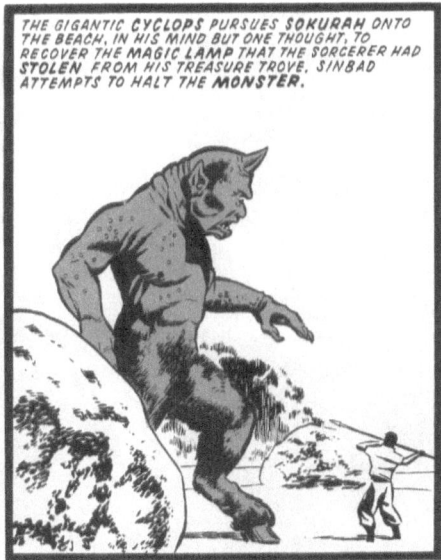
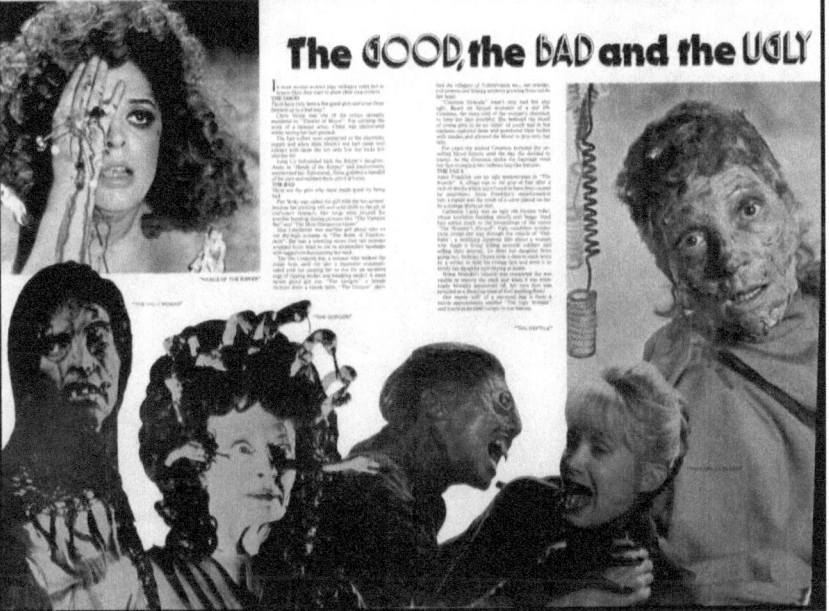

Top Left: The fangtastic poster of **TWINS OF EVIL**'s Count Karnstein (Damien Thomas) from *LHC* #5. **Top Right:** A panel of Kevin O'Neill "Cyclops" art from *LHC*. **Above:** Another garishly ghastly two-page spread from *Monster Mag* #5!

---

poster magazine, which was put out by the London-based Sportscene Publishers.

As suggested by its cover (which features both the '33 and '76 **KONG**s), the *KK* poster magazine delivers a nice balance of the old and the new. The bulk of the interior is taken up by two articles, both of them credited to one Vic Lime: a two-page spread looks back at the original **KK**, while the larger four-page piece is devoted to the remake and completely overdoes the hype surrounding its production and box-office potential (e.g., *"Every so often, the motion picture industry unleashes a movie of such staggering com-*

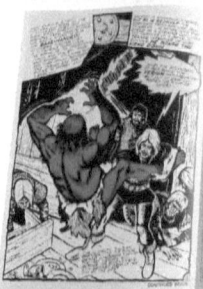 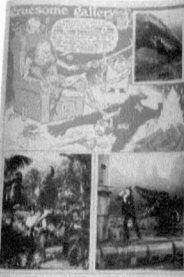 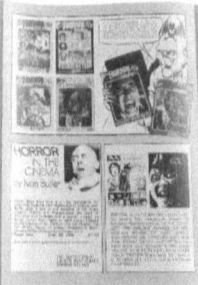 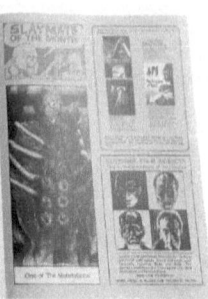

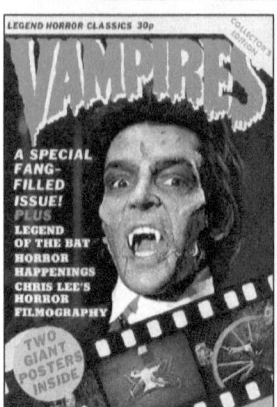 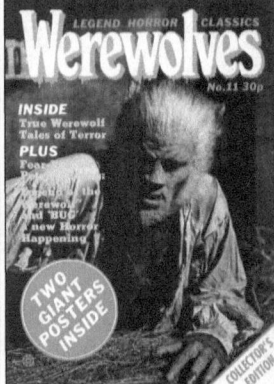 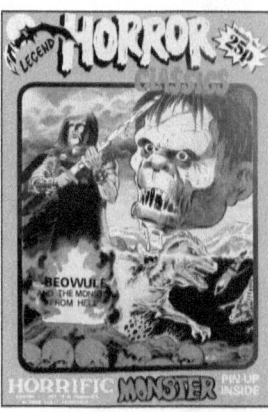

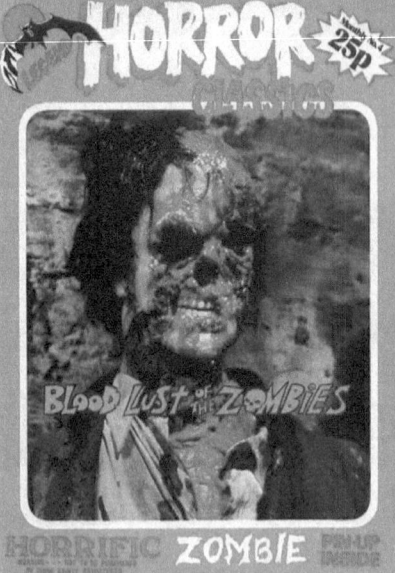 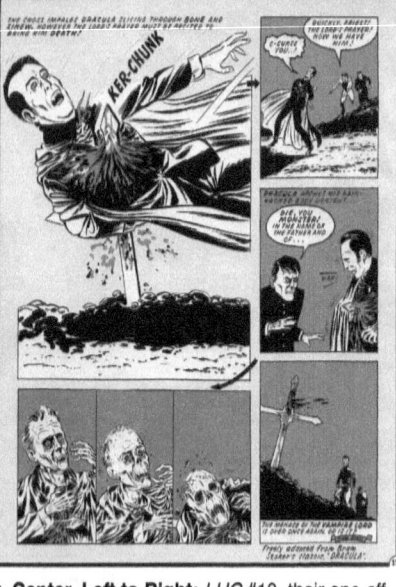

Top: Precisely 20% of *LHC* #7's total page-count. **Center, Left to Right:** *LHC* #10, their one-off "Vampires" special, once again featuring a still from **TWINS OF EVIL** (1971); the same mag's "Werewolves" special (#11, November '75), with David Rintoul as Étoile the lycanthrope from **LEGEND OF THE WEREWOLF** (1975) on the cover; and *LHC* #7 (1974), with cover illustration by their regular artist Kevin O'Neill. **Above Left:** The gnarly cover to *LHC* #4 (April 1975) features a shuddersome shock-shot from **DEATHLINE** a.k.a. **RAW MEAT** (1973). **Above Right:** A page of O'Neill artwork from his **TASTE THE BLOOD OF DRACULA** (1970) comics adaptation in *LHC* #5 mercial potentiality that it seems almost predestined to condemn all existing box-office records to a fate of instant oblivion").

Surprisingly enough, the *King Kong* poster magazine also contains a small text-only sidebar on **QUEEN KONG** (1976, UK), Farouk "Frank" Agrama's notorious spoof of the Kong legend starring Robin Askwith, Rula Lenska and Hammer Glamor gals Valerie Leon and Linda Hayden. Due to legal action from Dino De Laurentis, **QK** never saw release in either the UK or a number of other countries at the time, though an illustrated paperback tie-in for the film was nonetheless published by Everest Books in the UK (I talked about **QK** in my article on "The Great Giant Ape War of 1976/77", which appeared in *Monster!* #11, our classic *kaijū* special from November 2014).

The inclusion of **QUEEN KONG** gives a nice little oddball edge to the *King Kong* poster magazine, which opens up to reveal a colorful piece of art depicting the classic '33 Kong against a fiery red-and-yellow sunset, angrily pounding away on his chest as a squadron of pesky triplanes close in for the attack (this image is surprisingly evocative of a similar shot seen in Jordan Vogt-Robert's recent blockbuster **KONG: SKULL ISLAND** [2017, USA]... or rather, vice versa!).

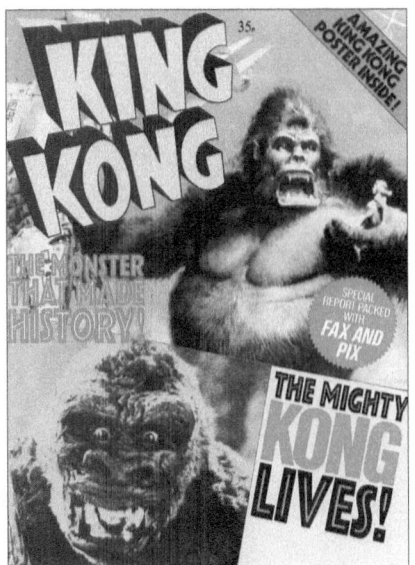

King Kong Poster Magazine (1977)

ISLAND OF DR. MOREAU
(UK, 1977; one-shot)

Though it boasted a decent budget for an American International Pictures (AIP) production and stars of the caliber of Burt Lancaster and Michael York, Don Taylor's 1977 adaptation of H.G. Wells' 1896 novel *The Island of Dr. Moreau* was met with something of a mixed reaction upon its release. It was in nowhere-near in the same league as Erle C. Kenton's classic 1932 pre-code version (titled **ISLAND OF LOST SOULS**) starring Charles Laughton and Béla Lugosi, nor was it as much pure pulpy fun as AIP's other two Wells' adaptations from the same period, Bert I. Gordon (a.k.a. "Mr. B.I.G.")'s **THE FOOD OF THE GODS** (1976, USA) and his follow-up **EMPIRE OF THE ANTS** (1977, USA). It was, however, *miles* better than John Frankenheimer's subsequent attempt at filming the story in 1996 with Val Kilmer and a bloated Marlon Brando (a messy, troubled production that was the subject of a 2014 documentary called **LOST SOUL**, which was much more fascinating viewing than the movie itself).

However, one thing which most people agree that Don Taylor's version got right was the Tom Burman-created makeup designs used to bring Dr. Moreau's experimental monsters (catchily dubbed "Humanimals") to life. So it certainly made sense for the *Island of Dr. Moreau* poster magazine to focus exclusively on the monsters, virtually ignoring the film's plot and its more fully-human characters altogether. Designed by one Bob Abrahams and published in the UK by the Interlink Publishing Company, the *IoDM* poster magazine folds-out into two half-size posters, placed in such a way that the posters could be separated and stuck on the wall individually. Their reverse sides are taken up by more photos of the Humanimals, accompanied by uncredited text that alternates between character profile and short fiction. There's also a short article on how to make a *papier-mâché* monster mask, which helps add something a little different to the content.

DAWN OF THE DEAD
(USA, 1978; one-shot)

Perhaps one of the most unexpected poster magazines from the late-70s was the one-shot published by MW Communications to tie-in with George A. Romero's now-classic zombie epic **DAWN OF THE DEAD** (1978, Italy/USA), which featured articles and a beautiful two-page

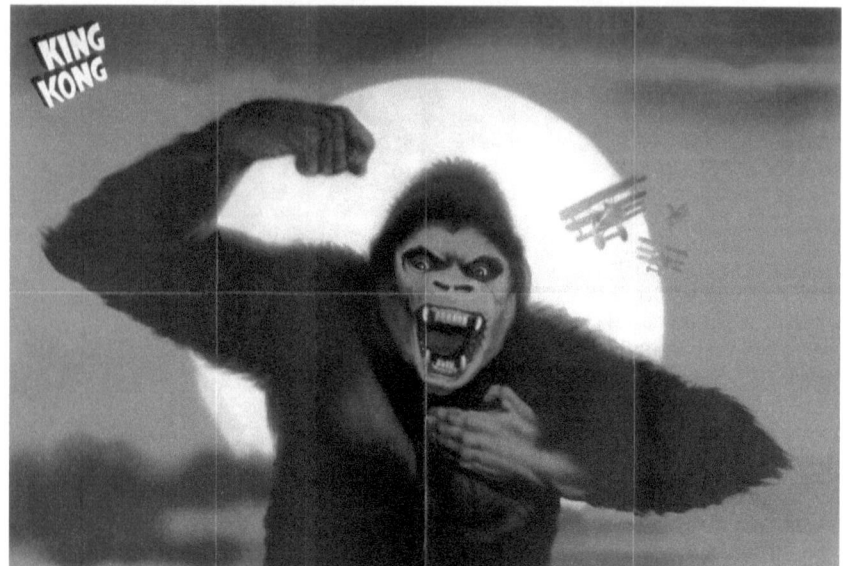

The spectacular fully-folded-out poster from 1977's *King Kong* poster mag; artist's name illegible

interior art spread by Jim Weholer, along with a main poster by Ron Mahoney. The back cover of this mag (whose cover identifies it as a "Poster Book") featured a full-page advertisement for a $6.00 **DOTD** T-shirt, cleverly designed so that a pair of denim overalls covers what promises to be a particularly gory section of the shirt's design (which featured the infamous 'bald zombie' with the red flannel shirt; a zombie that appears in the film for mere seconds but which became an integral focal point of the film's marketing/merchandising campaign).

It's certainly a great piece of original merchandise from this landmark and highly-influential film, which for such a violent movie that went out across America without a rating in order to avoid a certain "X" rating was, surprisingly, quite highly-merchandised on its first run. In addition to the poster magazine, there was also a tie-in novelization written by Romero and Susanna Sparrow (published in both hardcover illustrated trade paperback and mass-market paperback editions), a soundtrack LP featuring the classic Goblin score that was heard on the European cut, and even a **DOTD** board game!

ALIEN
(USA, 1979; 2 issues)

Ridley Scott's **ALIEN** (1979, USA/UK) was one of those films which united science-fiction and horror fans even at the same time as it divided them. Was it primarily a science-fiction space opera riding the success of George Lucas' **STAR WARS** (1977, USA), or was it more **THE EXORCIST** (1973, USA, D: William Friedkin) in space? I was one of those kids who was happy that the film seemed to perfectly blend both genres into one wholly satisfying and instantly-classic mix. I was only fifteen the year **ALIEN** came out and, being in Australia, I had to wait an agonizing *six months* for it to finally hit cinemas over here, after reading so much praise about it

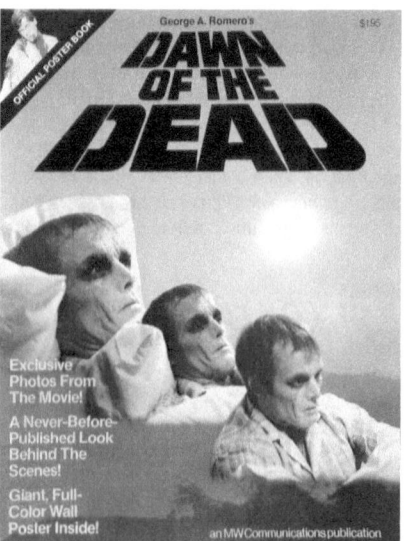

in magazines like *Famous Monsters of Filmland* and *Starlog*, buying the paperback novelization, 'making-of' book and comic book adaptation and trying my hardest not to look at or read any of it until I had actually seen the movie. Fortunately, when **ALIEN** did finally open in Australia later that year (just in time to catch the upcoming holiday season crowd), I skipped school that opening day and ended up seeing the movie *three* times in a row, and then *six* times more with various friends and family during its initial cinema run. **ALIEN** was definitely *my* **STAR WARS**, the movie I went crazy over in the same way that others went crazy for George Lucas' space opera.

Once I saw the movie and became completely seduced by virtually all aspects of it, I began to accumulate more **ALIEN** memorabilia: I bought the wonderful Jerry Goldsmith soundtrack LP, the Kenner board game, the trade paperback photonovel, the huge *Giger's Alien* book, and sent away to Captain Company in New York for a number of **ALIEN** T-shirt iron-on transfers too. Unfortunately, I never managed to find one of the notorious Kenner **ALIEN** dolls during the brief time that they were allowed on toy store shelves, but I did get the two great poster magazines that were published by Paradise Press in both UK and US cover-priced versions. Actually, I bought *two* copies of each issue, as one of the downsides of the poster magazine format was that once the poster was taped to the wall, you couldn't read the articles or look at the photos on the reverse anymore, so if you were a collector you would need to buy two copies of an issue.

Paradise Press were well experienced in the sci-fi poster magazine business, having published titles relate to *Star Trek*, **STAR WARS** and, later, David Lynch's **DUNE** (1984, USA). Like a lot of the early promotional materials for the film, the first issue of the *Alien* poster magazine shied-away from including any photos of the terrifying H.R. Giger-designed titular extraterrestrial itself, instead concentrating on other aspects of the film, such as the crew of the Nostromo (the grungy space towing vehicle aboard which the majority of the action takes place) and the derelict alien spaceship with its giant, long-deceased pilot (its ribcage ominously exploded outward in a grim forewarning of what was to come). The "Space Jockey", as the unfortunate extraterrestrial pilot became known, is also the subject of the first issue's poster. By the time the second and final issue of the *Alien* poster mag hit the stands, the film had been out for some time, so the design of the alien was no longer a closely-guarded secret, allowing the

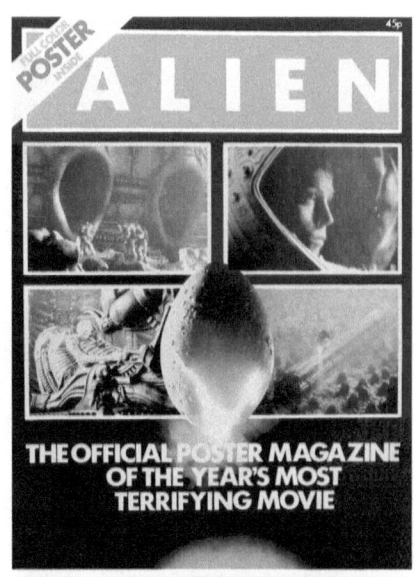

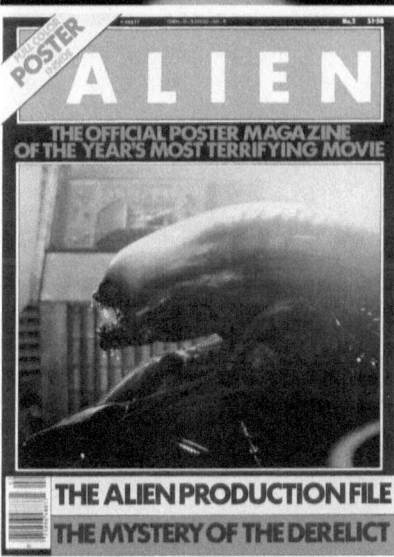

Issues #1 *[top]* and #2 *[above]* of the monster sci-fi movie hit's tie-in poster magazine

publishers to use a photo of the fearsome creature right on the cover, as well as in a couple of the interior articles, although the articles themselves concentrated more on the derelict spaceship and the interior of the Nostromo than the alien itself. The poster for this issue was split into two images, the top half featuring an exterior shot of the strange, horseshoe-shaped derelict spacecraft, while the bottom half contained an image of the Nostromo sitting on the foreboding, rocky terrain of the mysterious and inhospitable alien planet.

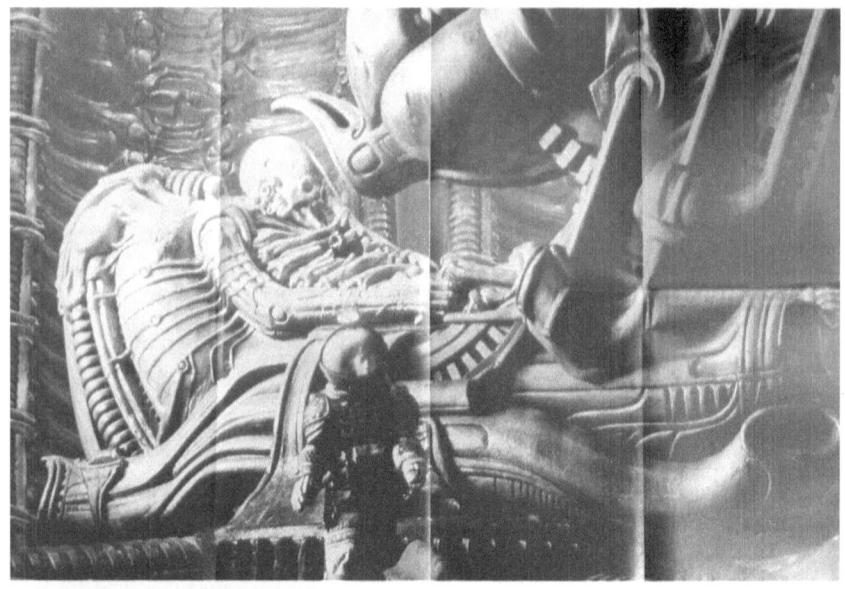

FANGORIA POSTER MAGAZINE
(USA, 1987-1990; 5 Issues)

By the mid-1980s, the kind of gory visuals that had landed *Monster Mag* in hot water were now commonplace within the pages of magazines like *Fangoria*, the US publication which had become as much of a bible to the 'Tom Savini/splatter movie' generation of that decade as *Famous Monsters* had been to the monster kids of twenty years earlier. *Fangoria's* older sister publication, the science fiction-oriented *Starlog*, had started publishing a poster magazine offshoot in 1983, and four years later the first *Fangoria Poster Magazine* hit the stands. Unlike the classic traditional poster magazines, however, *FPM* didn't fold out into a single poster. Rather, it was more like a standard magazine, containing no less than five double-sided 16" x 22" posters attached within the interior pages. Featuring more modern monsters such as Freddy Krueger, Jason Voorhees, Leatherface, Michael Myers and the occasional scream queen like Linnea Quigley or Elvira, *FPM* ran for just five issues, the final one hitting the stands in September of 1990. It was a fun title while it lasted, but it just wasn't the same experience as the classic fold-out poster magazines that had thrilled and warmed the blood of this horror fan more than a decade earlier.

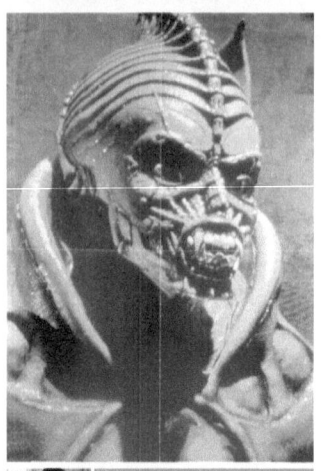

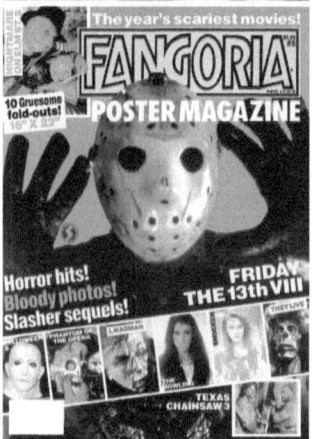

Top: The complete fold-out poster from *Alien* special #1, folds-'n'-all! **Left, Center:** *Fangoria's*, uh, sexy pinup of the slinky Syngenor from Bill Malone's **SCARED TO DEATH** (1981). **Left:** The cover to *Fango Poster Mag #5* (1988) flies in the face of *Monster!*'s strict "No Slashers Allowed!" policy; but whaddaya expect from that damned big lout Jason Voorhees?!

Interview: DEZ SKINN

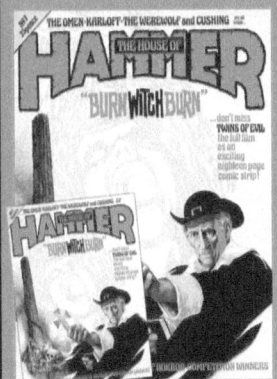
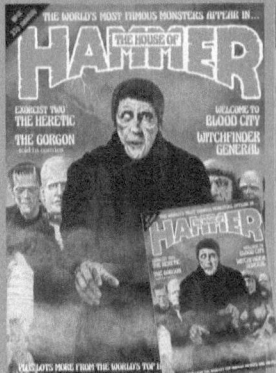
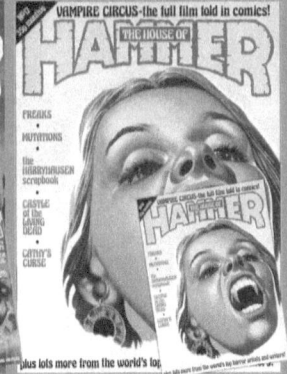

Unfolded HOUSE OF HAMMER posters ...each one FOUR times the magazine size!

House of Hammer posters (of the covers to #7, 12 and 17) are just some of Dez Skinn's current offerings

Often referred to as "the British Stan Lee", Dez Skinn has been one of the most important and prominent figures in the comics industry in that country for over four decades now. I first became aware of Skinn as the editor of House of Hammer *and* Starburst *magazines, both of which, as a fantasy film-loving teenager, I read religiously (though, of the two, I was much more partial to* HoH, *later retitled* Hammer's Halls of Horror *in hopes of broadening its appeal outside of the UK). Skinn also spent time during the '70s as the editor of the UK version of* Mad *magazine, put together hardcover annuals for genre television shows like* Planet of the Apes, Logan's Run *and* The Bionic Woman, *and edited a number of movie/TV poster magazines, most notably the* Sci-Fi Series, *which featured the likes of* The Six Million Dollar Man, **DOC SAVAGE: THE MAN OF BRONZE** *and* Doctor Who. *As related above, he also edited the final three issues of the classic poster magazine* Monster Mag, *and is the brains behind its current incarnation. Dez was nice enough to take time out from his busy schedule to answer a few questions regarding his work on poster magazines over the years...*

JOHN HARRISON: How did you come to get involved in publishing poster magazines, and what was the first title you put out?

DEZ SKINN: Having worked in comics for a few years, I was recruited as editor of the monthly UK edition of *Mad* magazine, along with fortnightlies *Tarzan, Korak* and *Laurel & Hardy* for Warner Bros in the mid-1970s. My brief was also to expand this teenage market division, so, working in Warner House in the heart of London's film world, I had easy access to major upcoming film material. I felt magazines and poster mags riding the back of each new film's massive publicity would be a good way to go.

So I produced one-shot titles on such films as **SINBAD AND THE EYE OF THE TIGER**, **DOC SAVAGE** and the like, but quickly learned that it was too hit-or-miss. The profits from each success were swallowed-up by later flops, and it was tough finding a new one worth publishing every month. My first poster mag had actually been a TV tie-in, *The Six Million Dollar Man*, with a little bit on *Doctor Who* to broaden the appeal.

John Harrison   Monster Poster Magazines   195

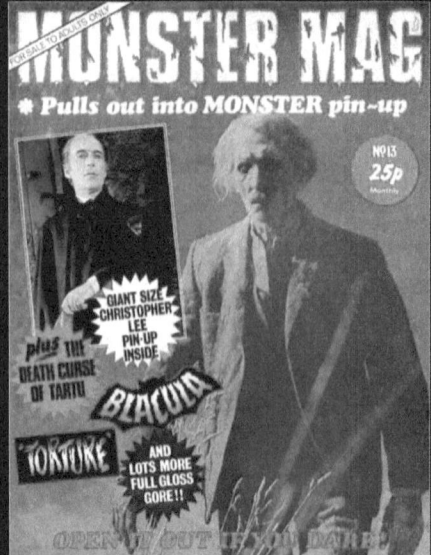 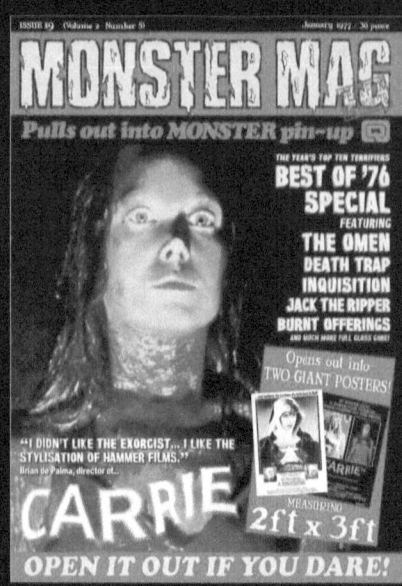

Monster Mags #13 and 19—celebrating the horror hits of the Scary 'Seventies!!

JH: *What were the biggest challenges in putting together a poster magazine?*

DS: The beauty of poster mags, as opposed to full-blown 48- or 68-page magazines, was that there was no real challenge, other than finding the best most commercial material to run. They were remarkably easy to fill, having only seven feature pages, plus cover and an eight-page poster.

JH: *How did the sale of poster magazines stack-up in comparison to the regular monster movie magazines?*

DS: There were no regular monster movie magazines over here at the time. There had been a few UK-produced attempts, but none had got past issue 10. Coincidentally, our distributor was responsible for importing the glut of mid-'70s US titles (*Movie Monsters, Monsters of the Movies, Quasimodo's Monster Magazine*, etc.) but only in small quantities, around 5,000 of each. *[Excuse me for butting-in and all, but as a horror-mad kid living in Swansea, Wales at that time, I eagerly snapped-up whatever issues of all three of those mags that I could find. Yes, I still have (most of) those very copies to this day! – SF.]*

JH: *Was it factored-in that a lot of people were likely buying two copies of each title, one to read/keep and one to tape to the wall?*

DS: No, I don't think our audience back then were quite so investment-minded. They just loved the gory photos and bedroom wall adornment!

JH: *What sort of shelf life did the one-shot poster magazines enjoy on the newsstands before any unsold copies would be returned?*

DS: It's a bit of a myth that a bimonthly or one-shot gets a longer shelf life than a more frequent title. Newsagents want to sell-out fast, so they invariably under-order. And the glut of titles constantly being produced meant that slow-sellers or perceived non-sellers would quickly be returned to wholesalers. The only exception to this would be the hardback Christmas annuals, usually stocked from September through to December, but they had far higher cover prices to justify their shelf space.

JH: *Much like those hardcover annuals, poster magazines seemed to be a uniquely British phenomenon, at least during the 1970s.*

DS: Indeed. Although Felix Dennis' poster mag *Kung Fu Monthly* was published in 14 countries and 11 languages at its peak.

JH: *Why did you relaunch* **Monster Mag** *when it ceased after its first 14 issues?*

DS: Rather than rack my brains with risky one-shots, I was looking for a continuing title, madly envious of *Kung Fu Monthly*'s success, and with all the horror material available, reviving *Monster Mag* seemed an obvious thing to do.

JH: How difficult was it to get the poster magazines printed for distribution in different countries?

DS: Being part of the international Warner Bros. publishing arm (under the Williams imprint), we printed in Italy, with all the text in black, so foreign editions could be "gang-printed" with only a black—language—plate change. This brought the unit cost down considerably, having a much larger international print run. Although we fell afoul of this when HM Customs and Excise refused to allow *Monster Mag* #2 into the UK. They considered its content unfit, and destroyed the entire print-run! An "Adults Only" flag was added to the cover from issue three, and a UK printer quickly sought.

JH: What inspired you to resurrect the poster magazine format in the 21st Century via the new Monster Mag title?

DS: It's absurd, really. It was somebody who recognised me in the local post office! He'd been a big fan of *Monster Mag* when growing-up, and was desperate to have the banned issue two. He was convinced there would be a market, were I to create an English-language edition. He told me how fans were eagerly snapping-up the German and French editions, whether they could speak the language or not, and even these often sold for more than £1,000. So I got my hands on a French edition, thanks to a kind fan, and 41 years after the original was pulped, translated it into English, published it and turned the world's most-scarce film magazine into a reality.

I also felt bad about dropping the title so suddenly back in 1975 when I launched *The House of Hammer* with the same editorial team, but with 48 pages instead of seven for their material. I'd actually promised in issue 17 that our next would be a "Double X Special". And it was, promised in 1976, delivered in 2014 as an all-new follow-up to the successful printing of issue 2.

JH: In many respects, the original Monster Mag was very much a 'video nasty' of its day. What do you remember most about the controversy surrounding it?

DS: *Monster Mag*'s original editor, Roger Noel Cook, wasn't really a film fan. But he absolutely adored being outrageous, doing everything totally over-the-top. So with *Monster Mag*, he didn't really care about what films he was covering, he just wanted the goriest, bloodiest pix he could possibly run. I think he realized that there was no such thing as negative publicity; anything in the news saying how shocking it was would inspire young teenagers to seek it out. I know from hearing from readers of the day that they'd been worried newsagents would refuse to sell to them. So it was a kind of 'forbidden fruit' they just *had* to taste!

JH: How has the new Monster Mag been received?

DS: I believe every magazine should have a unique selling point. It isn't enough to throw a few features and photos together when producing a magazine. They become interchangeable. So the relaunched *Monster Mag* is being produced as if it had never stopped. Its editorial slant, its USP, is that it still *is* 1977, so we only cover films that had been released by then, during horror's heyday. Before slashers dominated the genre.

This has struck a chord with those who grew up with the title in the 1970s. According to social media and our own letters page, its 100% nostalgic content and look take people back to those days, both those who were actually there in the 1970s and those who wish they had been!

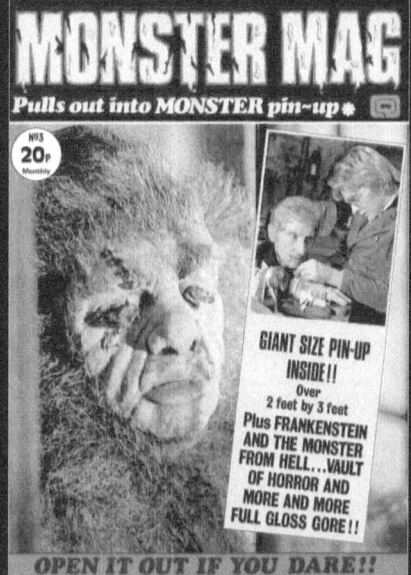

Monster Mag #3—stunningly-remastered quality edition of the 1973 classic!

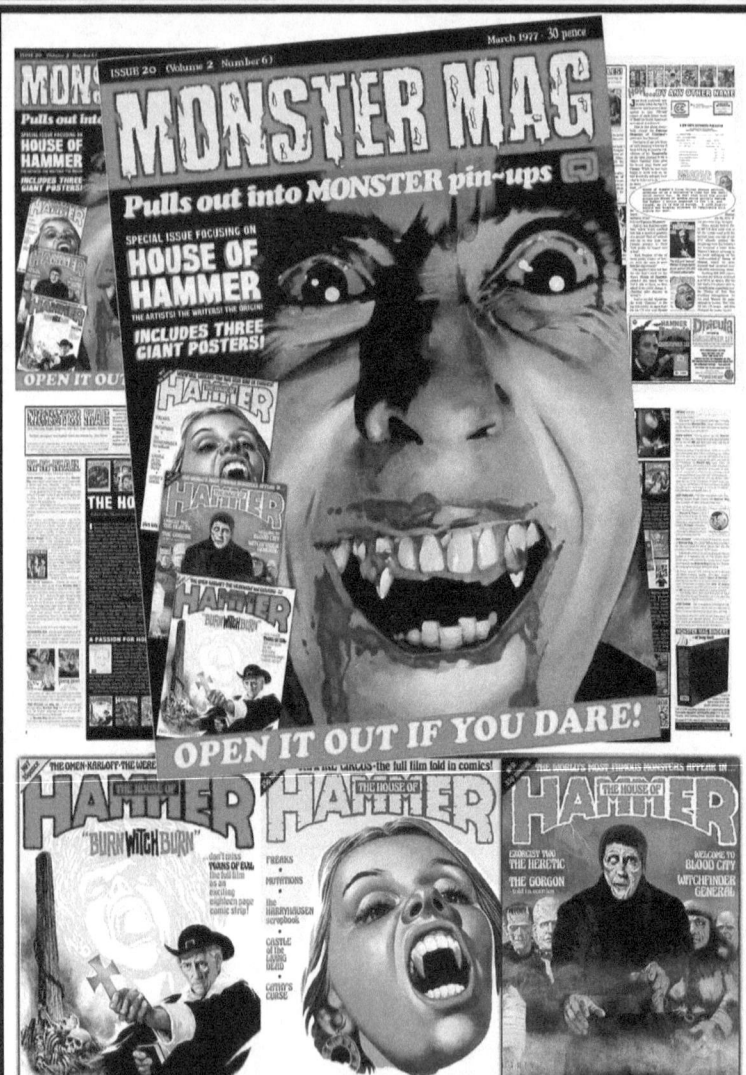

Hype for Dez Skinn's "The New" *Monster Mag* #20, the *HoH* poster special!—"*16 pages in total which folds out into two giant posters over 2 feet by 3 feet (335mm x 245mm) [...] People keep saying that most of those* House of Hammer *covers are worthy of being posters (even Hammer Films boss Michael Carreras said they were better than his film posters). So who are we to argue? This issue presents no less than three of ace artist Brian Lewis's cover paintings, all as giant posters. Plus the inside story on just how the magazine got started, why it changed its name so often and just what went wrong with the cover to issue #1. All this plus a look at the censored art from our adaptation of Vampire Circus.*" (see more @ https://www.facebook.com/MonstermagPostermag/)

Also, because of the scarcity and high price of the originals, our publishing programme is one of alternating between reprinting the originals and producing new 1970s-style issues.

JH: What are your long-range plans for the title?

DS: I look forward to the day when we will have all 17 original issues back in print, all in that glorious huge 3ft x 2ft poster size that was lost when the original downsized upon changing printers.

And I must admit, I'm seriously having fun producing it, especially the new ones. I'm putting far too much tender loving care into each and every page, sometimes spending hours just on creating title headings, but I don't view it as a "bottom line viability" project, it's something I just love doing. Some would consider it a limitation, having so few pages, but I consider it a challenge, seeing how much I can cram in. I also have a possibly unique way of working: I design each feature first, I get all the visuals placed so they're well-balanced and make an attractive layout. I then spend days adjusting color balance, so they're consistent across the spread. Only then do I start on the words, filling the gaps if you will. This is because I think design is all-important. Nobody is attracted to a magazine by its words. They're just reams of small squiggles. You need pull quotes, stand firsts and sub-heads which leap out at a potential buyer, that draw them into staying on the page. They're all-important selling points that most editors overlook in their desire to cram as many words in as possible. *[We stand guilty as charged!* ☺ *– Ye* M! *Eds.]*

JH: Everybody says that print is dying in the face of competition from digital reading and the internet. As somebody who has worked in print for almost 50 years, what do you think?

DS: I guess it's tough if you're focused on news coverage, as so many are. And they're always beaten to the punch by the internet, whether it's *Doctor Who Magazine* or *The Guardian* newspaper. But except for my 16-year stint producing the news trade magazine *Comics International*, my titles have never focused on the news. Even when I was producing the *Doctor Who Magazine*, or *House of Hammer* or *Starburst*, I took it for granted people would hear about new episodes or new films everywhere else. We focused on stuff that people *wouldn't* hear anywhere else. It stopped issues from looking dated on the news racks, because a cover's news scoop would quickly become outdated, then sales would plummet. It's short-termism. Insanity.

But *Monster Mag* lives happily in 1977, far from the rave for the latest news story. And it offers a three-foot by two-foot poster each issue, something the internet is incapable of providing!

[Author's Note: For more on Dez Skinn's remarkable career in publishing and details on how to order copies of the relaunched Monster Mag, *please visit* http://dezskinn.com/quality-shop-1*]*

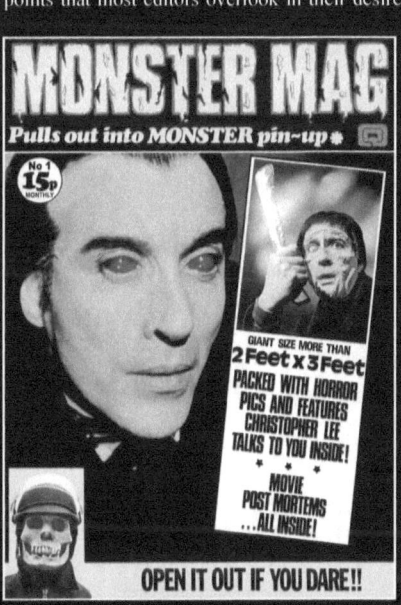

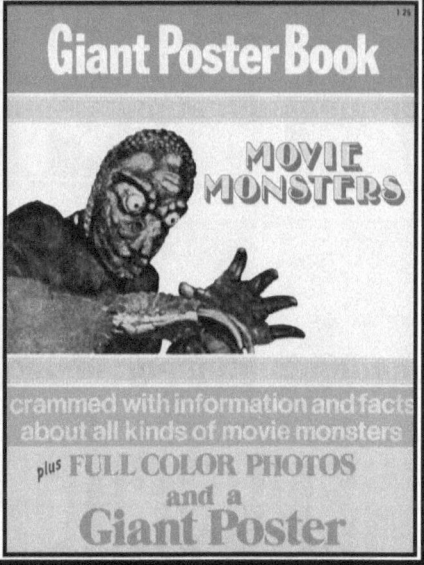

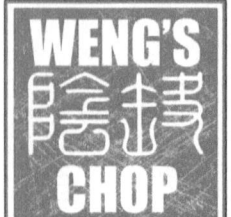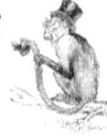

GRAB EVERY GLORIOUS DAMNED ISSUE!

Available at amazon or directly from the publishers at wengschopstore.com

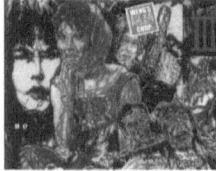
#0 - Wraparound CAT-III cover art by DB3

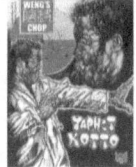
#1 - cover by DB3

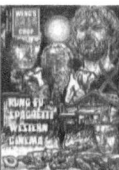
#2 (DB3 cover)

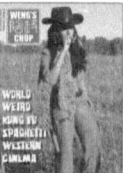
#2 (Bollywood Cowgirl cover)

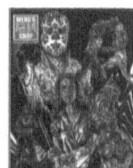
#3 (DB3 cover)

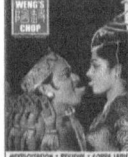
#3 (Nagin cover)

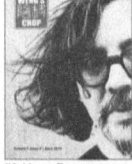
#3 (Jess Franco cover)

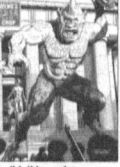
#4 (Harryhausen cover art by J.Yates)

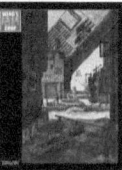
#4 (Tim Doyle cover)

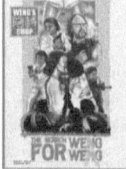
#4 (Weng Weng cover art by Matt O'Neill)

#4.5 Spooktacular (cover by H.Paxton)

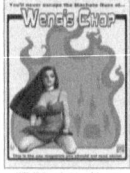
#5 (Machete Nuns cover art by Megh)

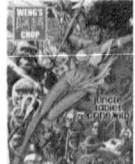
#5 (Jungle Girl cover art by Jolyon Yates)

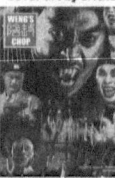
#5 (Jiangshi cover art by Bill Chancellor)

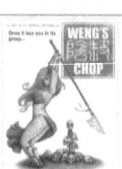
#6 (Jungle Queen cover by Megh)

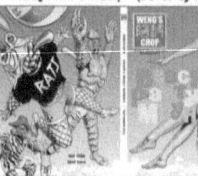
#6 (Beach Party Mayhem wraparound cover art by Jolyon Yates)

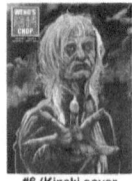
#6 (Kinski cover art by Kelly Forbes)

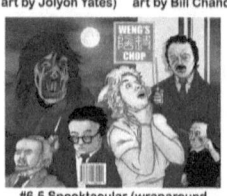
#6.5 Spooktacular (wraparound cover art by Joe Deagnon)

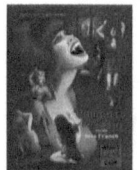
#7 - cover by Megh

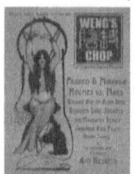
#8 - cover by Megh

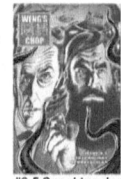
#8.5 Spooktacular (cover by J.Yates)

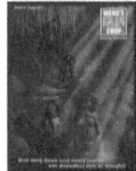
#9 - cover by Megh

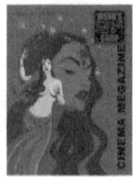
#10 - cover by Megh

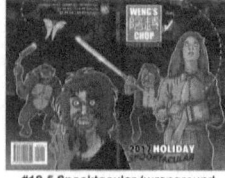
#10.5 Spooktacular (wraparound

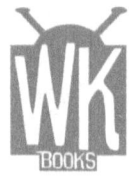

BOOKS YOU CAN HOLD

WENGSCHOPSTORE.COM

LAPACHHAPI: लपाछपी

A REAL GAME-CHANGER FOR INDIAN HORROR CINEMA!

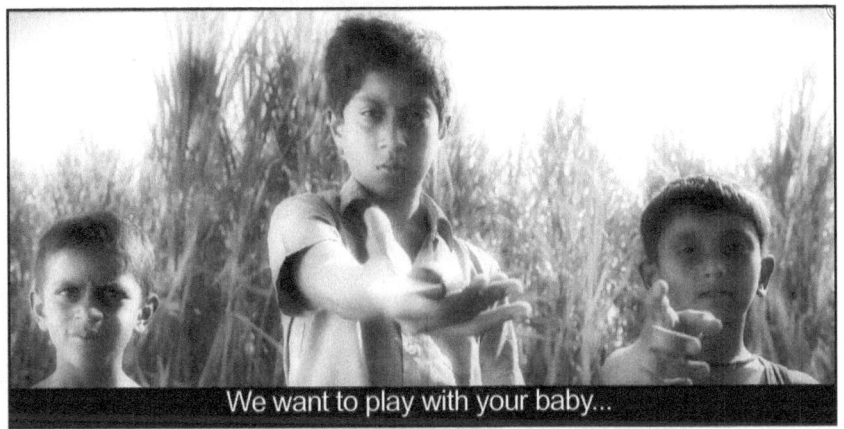

We want to play with your baby...

by Neil D'Silva

Horror is a decidedly *tricky* genre in India, especially in cinema. For several decades, Indian horror was monopolized by a few filmmakers whose brand of supernatural-monster horror became the very definition of the genre. The hangover from that is still so profound that new filmmakers with different concepts are finding it difficult to make their presence felt. It is good news for the genre, then, that Vishal Furia, a debuting director from Mumbai, has tasted success with his breaking-the-mold, game-changing Marathi horror flick, **LAPACHHAPI** (लपाछपी, 2016).

Lapachhapi is a Marathi word which means "Hide-and-Seek", the popular game played by children across the world. Most of the film—which features Pooja Sawant, Usha Naik and Vikram Gaikwad in the main roles—was shot (in broad daylight) at a village near Kolhapur, and almost all of its action plays out in a single house situated in the midst of a vast expanse of sugarcane fields.

The story tells of a young couple, Neha (Sawant) and Tushar (Gaikwad), who, due to circumstances, move to live in a small rural community. Their hosts at the village are their middle-aged driver Baburao, and his wife, Tulsa. Neha is carrying a baby and is in her eighth month of pregnancy. Given her condition, Tulsa goes all-out to make Neha feel at home. However, it takes only a couple of days for Neha to understand that *something* is amiss about the hosts and their hospitality. Behind the external veneer of their smiles and sweet talk, she can see something *ominous* looming. This shortly manifests itself in various bizarre paranormal forms. Most notably, Neha begins to have visions of children that no one else but she can see, and the expectant mother soon becomes embroiled in a tense game of hide-and-seek with them. Through this bizarre game, she has shocking revelations of what has been occurring in the house...

There are numerous things that quickly set this film apart from most contemporary Indian films. To begin with, the movie is in the regional language Marathi, which is spoken mostly in the state of Maharashtra, and which forms a niche within India itself. It is also interesting that the movie employs at least *two* dialects of Marathi:

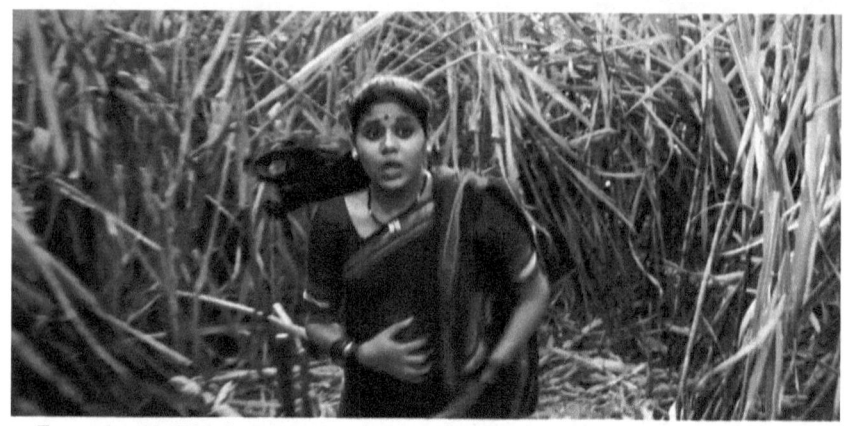

Terror Among The Sugarcane: A *very* pregnant woman flees from an unknown force through the tall grass in a scene from Vishal Furia's **LAPACHHAPI** (2016)

there is the more urban, sophisticated kind spoken by the protagonists, and then there is a much more raw and rustic dialect spoken by the rural hosts. This, along with the various other added local elements, provide insights into the indigenous culture, and the film scores extra points for its authentic details (examples being the woman preparing *chapatti*s on a *chulha*, the traditional dress of the locals, the set design of the house, the unending sugarcane fields crisscrossed with narrow paths, etc).

Unlike recent horror films in India, the movie plays out in a countryside setup and is, for the most part, shot on but a single location. There are no creepy monsters nor erotic scenes, and neither are there are any songs and comedic or fight sequences that have become the mainstay of Indian cinema. The very fact that it is a psychological thriller is a rarity in India, and it plays around with less than a dozen characters in total, including the three ghost children themselves.

Despite that, **LAPACHHAPI** has garnered recognition and awards in various international quarters, and has amassed quite a following locally as well (a full list of awards follows this article). It has transformed Furia into a blue-eyed boy for the horror-starved industry, with top-of-the-line producers now considering him for their future projects.

Interestingly, **LAPACHHAPI** also carries a social message—namely by being against female infanticide (which, sadly, is still practiced in some parts of India)—and this fact has been recognized in certain areas; for instance, at the 2016 Indiefest Awards, where the film won the Humanitarian Award, which makes it a rare (if not the *only*) film yet to win such recognition in India.

We got into a *tête-à-tête* with Furia to find out more about the insanity of it all. Insanity it surely seems to be, and passionate insanity even, because we learned that the movie was made against all odds (read: lack of funds) and, despite that, no creative compromises were made. Rarely is a filmmaker's movie debut so totally the director's personal vision, because there is always the outside interference by studios and producers to be contended with. As such, **LAPACHHAPI** is a total eye-opener for the industry itself. Perhaps the lesson to be learnt here is that, if a movie is made true to its original vision, it stands a better chance of achieving what it is striving for?

****

[We now follow-up with some excerpts from my interview with director Vishal Furia...]

Neil D'Silva: Good day, Vishal. It's a pleasure to have you in Monster! Tell us something about yourself to begin with, especially your connection with horror. When did you get interested in the genre, and, more importantly, what does horror mean to you?

Vishal Furia: To be honest, as a kid, I was quite intimidated by horror. The only exposure to horror back then was through bits and parts of the Ramsay films and the *Evil Dead*s on VHS, and I was extremely scared of those. But I could not stop watching them anyway, and wanted more and more of them.

Growing up, my house had no cable television, but my TV set used to capture a Star Movies signal late at nights. That was when I got to watch some good horror movies. Watching those movies, I developed my liking for horror. And then later on, when I watched Japanese and Spanish horror films, I began to hope that someday I would make a horror film too. A good horror film keeps the audience invested and makes them forget the world around them. The best part is that you cannot leave watching a horror film midway; you need a closure, or else the film haunts you for life. Maybe that's the hidden reason why my love for horror films developed.

ND: Is it true that LAPACHHAPI has become the first Marathi horror film ever to cross 50 days? This is an indication that the audiences have appreciated it. But how do you see the film? Did it do for you what you wanted it to do, both creatively and critically?

VF: I am not sure if it is the *first* Marathi horror film to do so, as in earlier days of cinema before laptops and mobile phones, it was quite easy for films to complete 50 days. But it is rare for a Marathi horror film to be in the theatres for more than 50 days in this time and age. To stretch it, it's rare that an Indian horror film completes 50 days these days.

Like any filmmaker, I started out with the hope that the audiences would like the film, especially young audiences and horror fans. That happened better than I expected. Among the many people who enjoyed the film were housewives and older audiences. That was an unexpected fan-base for the film, and they also recommended the film to others. This gave **LAPACHHAPI** a strong word-of-mouth, which made it sustain in theatres. People were looking for screens and making an effort to go watch the film.

Creatively, I could do complete justice to my film as my whole team believed in the film and stood by me while making it. Critically, we had decent success. It is not easy to please critics, but we fared quite well, I think.

ND: Since LAPACHHAPI is entirely your own concept, what were your experiences in finding a producer for it?

The way the producers look at horror in India is very disappointing. Either they want to make it a "horrex" (horror with sex), or they want to make comic horror, or they want to make cheap imitation horror (of some Blumhouse film, perhaps). In any of these scenarios, the horror goes out of the window and sex, comedy, or the songs come in and change the script into something else altogether. So, it became very difficult to find a producer who would believe in **LAPACHHAPI** and help me make it with complete honesty. That was a big reason why I chose to make the film in Marathi, as the Marathi audience is considered to be a mature audience that judges a film on its content and not on its commercial value. I found a great producer in Jitendra Patil, who also believed in the story and supported me to make the film with complete honesty and sincerity, without interfering at all.

ND: LAPACHHAPI is being hailed as a refreshingly different horror film, blending dark psychological and supernatural elements. A lot of that credit goes to the script. How did you develop it?

VF: I wanted to make a horror film which was purely Indian in its story and setup, as it is frustrating to see remakes and copies made in Bollywood every now and then. When I read the facts of female infanticide in India, I was horrified. I thought that if I have to make a horror film here,

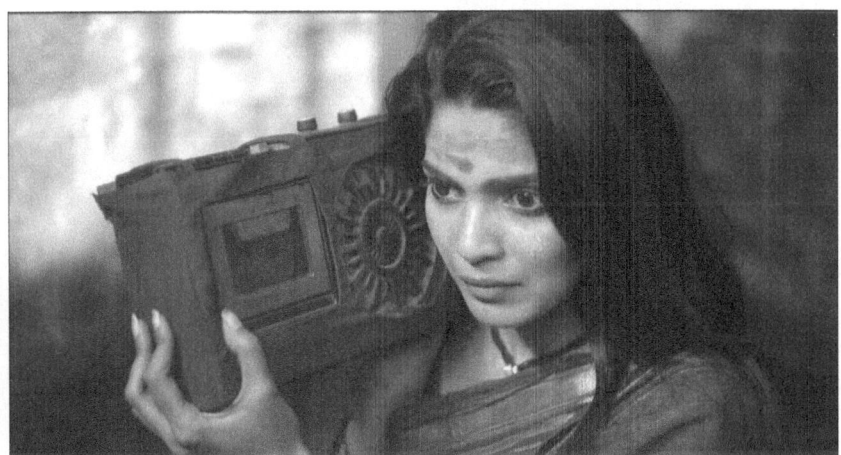
Pooja Sawant listens in shocked silence to the beat-up old cassette player layer which is one of the paranormal keys to unlocking the mystery surrounding the hauntings in **LAPACHHAPI**

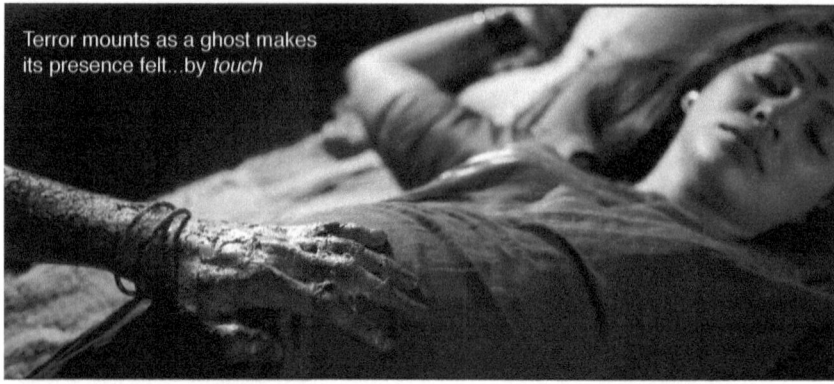
Terror mounts as a ghost makes its presence felt...by *touch*

then I should use these facts and stories that are pure horror by their very nature.

So, I came up with a story that was inspired by the psyche of people who indulge in such malpractices. Then Vishal Kapoor came on board to write the screenplay and dialogues of the film, and he elevated the story hugely. It was a difficult script to write, as we had to balance the horror and the social element of the script in such a way that the film stayed thrilling without losing the impact of the social message. I think we did quite well. The audiences could relate with the story and the message haunted them and stayed with them for some time after the film, as we are told by many people.

ND: Tell us something of your location shooting experience. Those endless sugarcane fields can get quite spooky at nights. How did your team keep their spirits high?

I was quite certain about the kind of location that I wanted, as the whole film is based in that one location. Finally, after looking at about a hundred houses, we found the final location. It was not even a house, but some creepy ruins of a house built 60 years ago and never used. So we actually constructed the house and the roads around it to make it shooting-friendly. It was scary to travel through the fields to the house back and forth. One makeup artist did see something in the night, screamed and fainted. She claimed to have seen a black figure in the fields. Also there were lots of snakes in the fields. Luckily, it all went well.

ND: From a technical point-of-view, LAPACHHAPI has broken some new ground. For one, most of the movie plays out in bright daylight, with the scares being right out in the open. The sounds, too, aren't the usual horror sounds, but music. How was all of this brought together?

VF: Yes, it was meant to be a day-horror. The idea being that the social theme on which it is based, female infanticide, is a horror that happens in broad daylight in front of our eyes, and we are still blind to it.

The sounds are mostly Indian, using regional instruments like the Tarpa. Music is an integral part of any film, especially horror. The music was composed by the music directors, Ranjan, Tony and Utkarsh. They came up with a score that it is unsettling and non-comforting. They did a great job with it.

ND: *LAPACHHAPI* is set in a rustic Maharashtrian village, and the story is quite rooted in traditional Indian customs. Despite that, the movie could break the barrier and get considerable appreciation out here in the West. How did you go about creating that universal appeal?

VF: I think India has a lot of horror stories that can be made into fantastic films which will appeal to a universal audience. **LAPACHHAPI** worked because the issues of violence against women are global and so audiences everywhere could relate to it. Also I have tried to make the film into an experience of living in that house lost in the sugarcane fields. Viewers loved that experience, and so could sympathize with the pregnant lady played by Pooja Sawant. Also, I believe that some people harbor evil thoughts in their minds which they are themselves not aware of. That stands true universally. Such an evil character was played faultlessly by Usha Naik, and it resonated with people all over the world.

There was also a lot of brainstorming over the adaptability of the film. We worked a lot over elements like language, the setup of the house, the costumes, the food they ate, etc. With costumes especially, I took calls such as to not have the driver Baburao wear a turban, as is usually worn by men in these parts. I felt the turban would have classed him differently, and that would have detracted from the universality of the film.

ND: How has Indian horror evolved over the decades? How does it compare with the '80s, when creature and monster horror films created a cult following of sorts?

Indian horror in the '80s was more about creature, monster, and the dead coming back. It was quite well-received at that time, as the audiences were not exposed to other kinds of horror. It was the setup and the thought that was more frightening than the horror itself. But as the audiences evolved, those films did not remain scary anymore. After that, some attempts were made to make good horror films, but then they all boiled-down to sex and comedy along with horror. I feel Indian horror has gone down over the decades. It needs a reboot.

ND: Do you think there is room for horror cinema in India? What kind of horror does the Indian horror buff want to watch?

VF: The Indian horror viewer is now exposed to good Hollywood horror. So they want to watch something that matches up to that. Sex is not a prerequisite for the audiences. They want more horror. There is ample space for horror as, currently, there is hardly anything that is purely horror in Indian films of the genre. All major Hollywood horror films have done great business in India, and none of them were erotic flicks. So it's time to give pure horror to the audiences, and I want to do that. I have started with **LAPACHHAPI**, and I hope more producers open up and put faith in filmmakers like me and take the genre forward.

LAPACHHAPI has won the following awards/accolades:

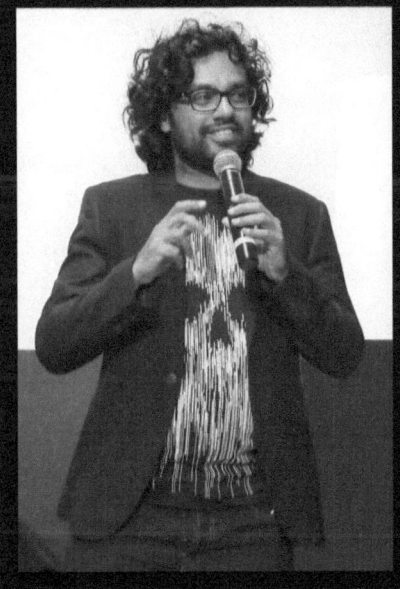

Director Vishal Furia discussing the film at a recent showing of **LAPACHHAPI**

2017 London Indian Film Festival (Official Selection)

2017 Edinburgh Festival of Indian Films and Documentaries (Official Selection)
Winner: **Best Lead Actor and Best Supporting Actor**

2016 Brooklyn Film Festival (Official Selection)
Winner: Spirit Award

2016 Madrid International Film Festival (Official Selection)
Winner: Best New Director
Nominations: Best Actress, Best Supporting Actress, Best Original Score, Best Editing

Spotlight Horror Awards: Gold Award Winner

Horror Hotel Film Festival, Ohio: Official Selection and fourth-place Winner

2016 Indiefest Film Awards
Award of Distinction: Best Humanitarian
Awards of Excellence: Leading Actress, Supporting Actress, Social Justice/Protest/Liberation
Awards of Merit (Special Mention): Cinematography

2016 Accolade Global Film Competition Awards
Awards of Excellence: Feature Film, Direction, Cinematography, Story / Writing, Original Score, Dramatic Impact

Special mention was made about **LAPACHHAPI** being given the Humanitarian Award by Indiefest Awards in 2016. Somehow, I don't think many horror films win this kind of an award!

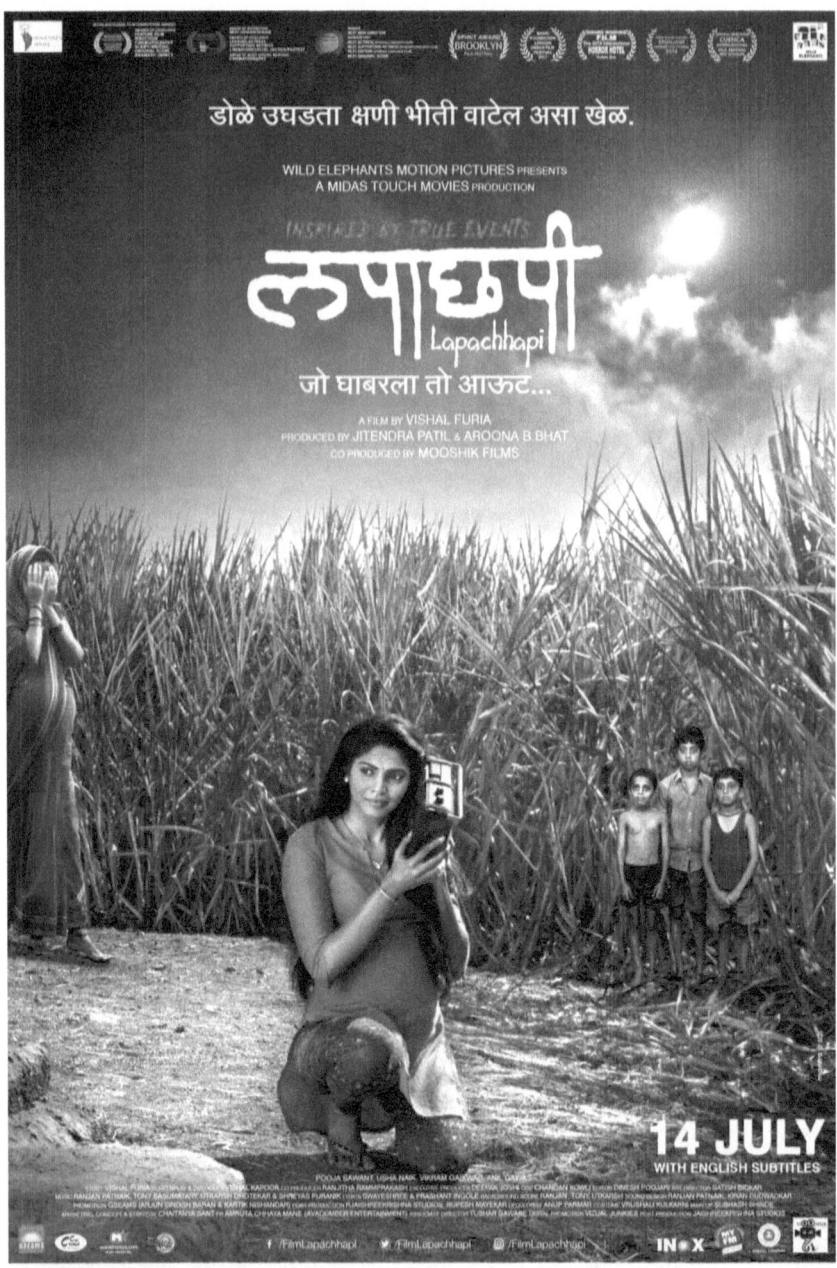

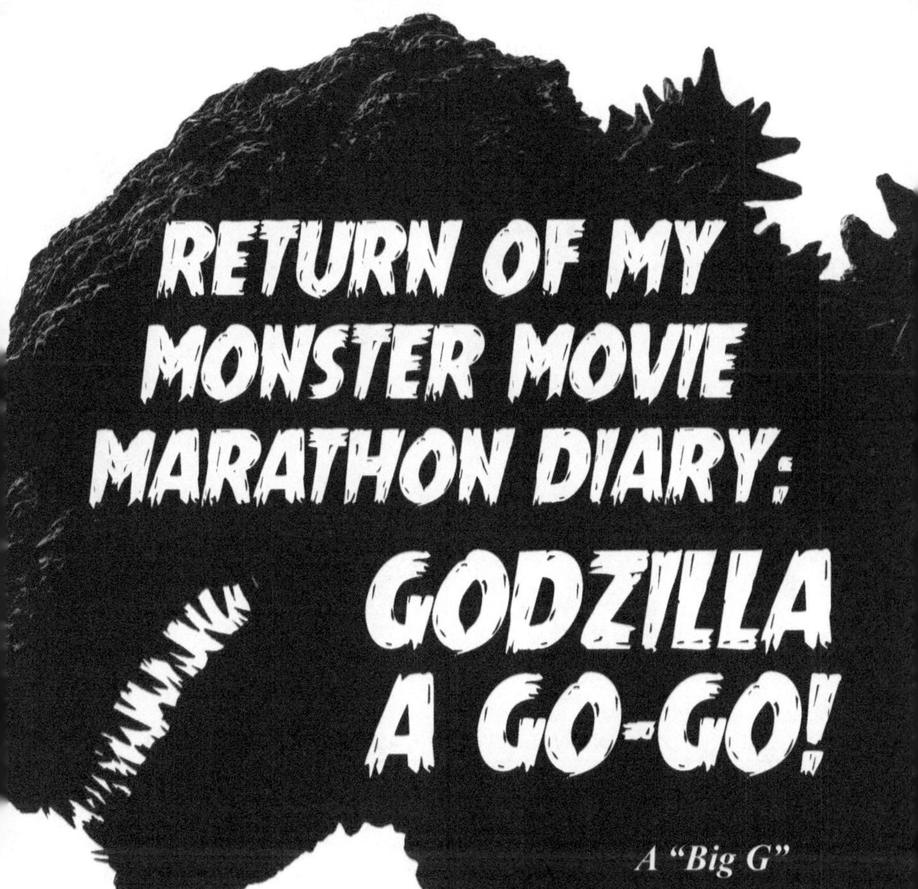

RETURN OF MY MONSTER MOVIE MARATHON DIARY: GODZILLA A GO-GO!

A "Big G" newbie's overview of Toho's Godzilla films, Chapter I: The Showa Era (1954-1975); or, how I spent my Christmas with Kaijū and loved every minute of it!

I honestly wanted to wrap-up "My Monster Movie Marathon Diary" back when Part 4 was published in issue #30 (June-July 2016) of this magazine, because I had gotten tired of the same-old/same-old SyFy fare that I was reviewing at the time. But you can't put a bad habit down. And as to my reason for reigniting this series of articles, you have Morbidly Beautiful to blame, as that website's excellent review of the WK Books goodies mentioned in my "MMMMD" series boosted my confidence to its limits.[1]

Since writing that aforementioned piece, I saw many more movies and TV shows, of all types...

by
Christos Mouroukis

---
[1] The article can be located online (@ http://morbidlybeautiful.com/wengs-chop/)

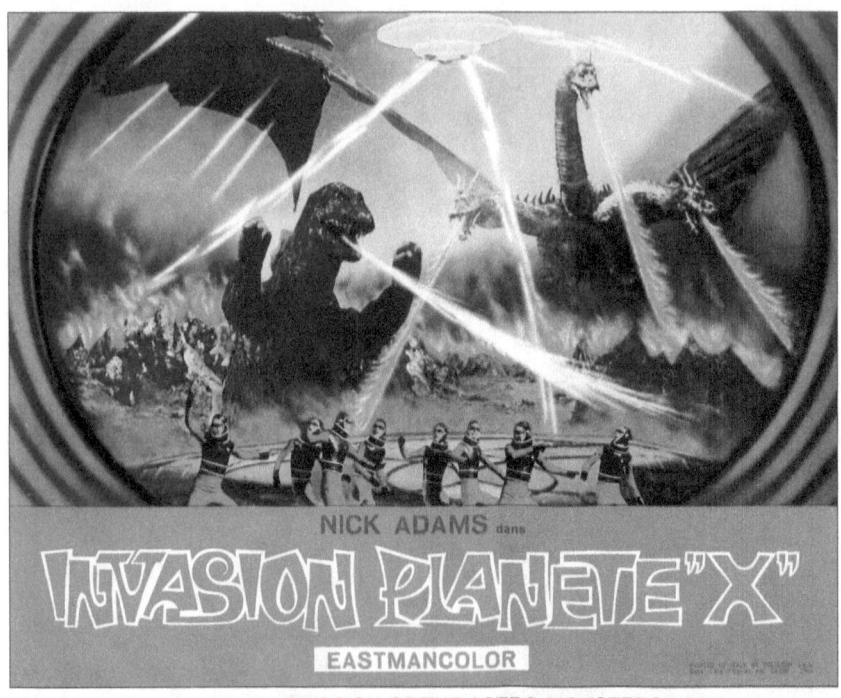

French poster for **INVASION OF THE ASTRO-MONSTERS** (1965)

In October 2016, I caught up with **CLASS OF NUKE'EM HIGH PART 3: THE GOOD, THE BAD AND THE SUBHUMANOID** (1994, USA, D: Eric Louzil), which was the *Nuke'Em* franchise's sole instalment that I hadn't previously seen; **THE SECRET LIFE OF PETS** (2016, USA/Japan, Ds: Chris Renaud, Yarrow Cheney), which wasn't as funny as I was expecting it to be; **CAPTAIN AMERICA: CIVIL WAR** (2016, USA, Ds: Anthony Russo, Joe Russo), which was as spectacular as these things can get; **X-MEN: APOCALYPSE** (2016, USA, D: Bryan Singer), which was as *boring* as these things can get; **DIRTY GRANDPA** (2016, USA, D: Dan Mazer), which was much sweeter than its reputation; **JOY** (2015, USA, D: David O. Russell), which is one of the most empowering films you're likely to come across these days; **DEADPOOL** (2016, USA, D: Tim Miller), which is one of *the* most entertaining superhero flicks I've ever seen, and certainly this year's best for the genre (even if— and probably *because*—Miller's film reads like a vastly-more-expensive *Toxic Avenger* movie!); the second season of *Gomorra: La Serie* (2014–), which was as good as the book it is based upon; and also the second season of *Scream: The TV Series* (2015–), in which the acting was as bad as the first time around (although the plot isn't as tiresome).

In November 2016, I caught-up with **MÖTLEY CRÜE: THE END** (2016, USA, D: Christian Lamb), a rockumentary on the final concert of the titular band, and for someone who grew up with their music, it is particularly moving (I must confess that I cried on more than one occasion whilst watching it!),[2] and the first season of *Luke Cage* (2016–), which is not so much about the titular character as it is about the Harlem community, and as such it is very welcome (I daresay that this slow-burn neo-*noir* is the closest thing you'll get to a 1970s Blaxploitation homage this year [i.e., 2016, as you'll recall]).[3]

In December 2016, I watched **SUICIDE SQUAD** (2016, USA, D: David Ayer), which has to be this year's *worst* superhero flick,[4]

---

2 I was introduced to Mötley Crüe when, as a kid, I went to the local record store (yes, I am old enough to have frequented such places and bought actual music that you could hold on your hands: be it CDs, cassettes, or vinyl!) *[Not to sound like a nostalgic old fogey or anything, but... those were the days!* ☺ – *SF.]* and asked the clerk if he knew of any bands that sounded like Guns N' Roses, whereupon he suggested The Crüe's *Too Fast for Love*: the album that changed my life!

3 Several references to Malcolm X in the opening credits and an awesome soundtrack helps, but I was rather left at a loss when I spotted a reference to **THE WARRIORS** (1979, USA, D: Walter Hill), of all things.

4 It suffers from a very weak screenplay (by David Ayer) that manages to turn a great idea into boring, by-the-numbers fare that cannot be salvaged by the endless

and **ALICE THROUGH THE LOOKING GLASS** (2016, USA/UK, D: James Bobin), which was surprisingly feminist.[5] But enough with that; I know that you are here for the monsters, so, without further ado, here's the Diary (Part 5) of the ones that have recently haunted my imagination…

I am a big fan of Japan's *Guinea Pig* (ギニーピッグ / *Ginī Piggu*) series, and Hong Kong's *Men Behind the Sun* (黑太阳731 / *Hēi tài yáng 731*) series, as well as other random Asian flicks, such as the sublimely splattery *chanbara* splice-job **SHOGUN ASSASSIN** (子連れ狼 / *Kozure Ōkami*, 1980, Japan/USA, Ds: Kenji Misumi, Robert Houston) and the sleazy *pinku eiga* entry **FEMALE MARKET: IMPRISONMENT** (凌辱めす市場 監禁 / *Ryōjoku mesu ichiba: Kankin*, 1986, Japan, D: Yasuaki Uegaki). Yet none of these films proved enough for me to start digging deeper into all the other exotic delights that the Orient has to offer. Sometimes I would think about starting to research HK "Category III" stuff, but then I didn't, and my friends and fellow film buffs keep on teasing me for being so Eurocentric and Americentric in my tastes. *[Whatever floats yer boat!* ☺ *– SF.]* Then, when Tim Paxton announced a while ago that one of our earlier issues would be focusing on *Kaijū* (怪獣) fare, I thought that enough was enough, and I had better overcome my anxieties of potential cultural misunderstandings, and tackle Toho's *Godzilla* (ゴジラ / *Gojira*) series, which, being monster-fests, I think are a great place for one to start. Better late than never! What's more, I had so much fun doing this that next issue I'll be back with more of the same. I opened my mind and I had a great time while doing so, and here's the report.

Other than writing about films, I also direct the occasional short. The very first one I ever directed (back in 1998) was *Godzilla*, in which my monster toys performed what was basically a **GODZILLA** (1998, USA/Japan, D: Roland Emmerich) rip-off scenario.[6] Amazingly, 19 years later it *still*

special effects (of the CGI variety) nor by the admittedly interesting character of Harley Quinn (played by Margot Robbie from **THE WOLF OF WALL STREET** [2013, USA, D: Martin Scorsese]). It is saddening, though, that Goths may find a lot to like here, and we are under serious threat of having people among us calling this a 'classic' 20 years from now. Isn't it funny when the rock tracks on the soundtrack are much better than the original multi-organ orchestral pieces?

5 This is the other film in which a dog has a flashback. Of course, the 'classic' originator was Wes Craven's **THE HILLS HAVE EYES PART II** (1984, USA/UK).

6 Luckily, not too many people have seen this, because, although I am not a stranger to humiliation, I don't think that I could bear explaining the stupidity of this particular subject.

hadn't occurred to me that I should at long last check out the Toho originals! Finally, in 2016, this sad state of affairs changed for the better.

The *Godzilla* series, like pretty well all other monster movies, was popular in Greece, if not as popular as westerns or martial arts flicks, or horror movies, for that matter. However, quite a few Godzilla-related tapes were released, including **THE VALLEY OF GWANGI** (1969, USA, D: Jim O'Connolly) which the obscure video distribution company Video Cronos misleadingly put out on tape as ΓΚΟΝΖΙΛΑ (or Γκονζίλα), which translates to "*Godzilla*", of all things (see scanned box art nearby). Oscar Video Production released **SON OF GODZILLA** bearing the box-cover title of **SON OF GOTZILA** [sic]. The ultra-obscure label Lucifer Video Enterprises[7] appears to have been quite monster-centric, and it released both **GHIDRAH, THE THREE-HEADED MONSTER** (三大怪獣 地球最大の決戦 / *Chikyū saidai no kessen*, 1964, Japan, D: Ishirō Honda) as well as the little-seen animated feature **THE SHIPWRECKED OF**

7 Accolades should be given to whoever was/were behind this label, as I can't imagine what it would be like in the ultra-conservative and widely Orthodox Christian 1980s Greece to register a company under the name of "Lucifer"!

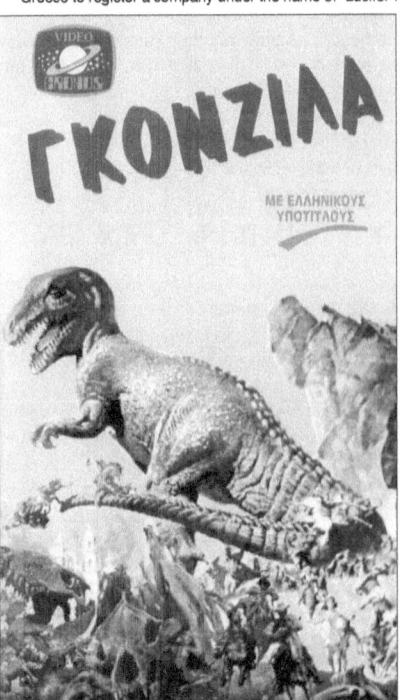

Greek VHS cover for **THE VALLEY OF GWANGI**, misleadingly retitled as "**GODZILLA**"!

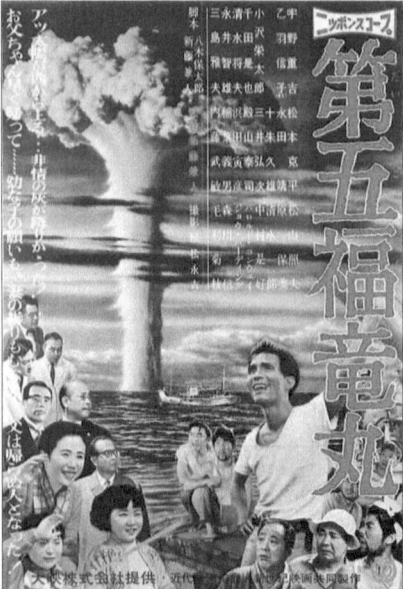

Japanese B2 poster for **LUCKY DRAGON NO. 5** (第五福竜丸 / *Daigo Fukuryū Maru*, 1959. D: Kaneto Shindo)

TERRA II (*Les naufragés de Terra II*, 1979, France, D: Alain-Christian Huber), which only barely has an IMDb entry (with less than 5 ratings as of this writing). Of course, countless other monster movies were released on tape in Greece, but these were the Godzilla-related ones that I managed to unearth in my collection.[8]

INTRODUCTION: "THE G-SPOT"

Gojira (ゴジラ) took its name from a hybridization of the Japanese words for the animals *gorira* (ゴリラ / "gorilla") and *kujira* (くじら / "whale"),[9] and it was introduced onscreen in Ishirō Honda's history-making franchise-launcher **GODZILLA** (ゴジラ / *Gojira*, 1954), a film which played a big part in founding the American "monster kid" craze (which is pretty much the reason why the present publication exists!), what with the multi-billion-dollar industry it created that aside from the films themselves featuring the monster (all of which will be reviewed in subsequent chapters of this column) also spawned toys, books, video games, graphic novels, and pretty much every other kind of merchandise that you can—or even can't—imagine. But in Japan, Gojira always had a much deeper reason for its existence rather than just being the simple spectacular giant monster that it was seen as in the West. Within just a decade prior to that aforementioned movie classic, Japan suffered both the atomic bombings of Hiroshima and Nagasaki (in 1945)[10] and the disastrous nuclear incident known as "Lucky Dragon 5" (in 1947),[11] and, although doom-and-gloom, paranoia-fueled Atom Age Cinema became widespread in America as well, in Japan it actually *meant* something much more serious and real. Godzilla, being a by-product of atomic anomalies and societal anxiety regarding the unknown dangers of nuclear radiation, has many peculiarities about it aside from its gigantic size, amphibious nature, fiery (radioactive) breath and booming roar/battle cry, and these qualities often vary from film to film (most will be subsequently discussed within the relevant reviews themselves when the time comes). What doesn't vary nor seems likely to change anytime soon is the fact that Godzilla, more than 60 years after its genesis, remains Japan's most widely-recognized pop-culture phenomenon, and the mighty monster's impact throughout the media around the world is unmatchable... pretty much like its devastating powers themselves.

Toho's *Gojira* franchise is the longest-running one in existence, and therefore it was inevitable that a lot of things about each era would vary, including the politics. The first 'era' is known as the Showa Era (1954-1975)—which is named after Emperor Showa (1901-1989)—and its first films are reviewed below (with more pending for next issue). The Showa classics are considered among fans to be the most 'suitable-for-kids/family-friendly' films of the series.

Tuesday, December 13th, 2016

GODZILLA
(ゴジラ / *Gojira*)

Japan, 1954. D: Ishirō Honda

Ad-lines: *"The legend begins...."* – *"It's Alive!"* – *"Civilization crumbles as its death rays blast a city of 6 million from the face of the Earth!"*

There's literally nothing to be said about this classic than what already has been, so the 1K-or-so words that follow put together the basics in introductory form, okay?

---

8   For more tapes from Greece, please refer to my "Greek VHS Mayhem" column over at *Weng's Chop*.
9   So you have to think twice before poking fun at Roger Corman's **SHARKTOPUS VS. WHALEWOLF** (2015, USA, D: Kevin O'Neill), which I previously reviewed in this column (see "MMMMD (Part 3)" [p.184] in *Monster!* #28/29, our Spring Special 2016 ish).
10 https://en.wikipedia.org/wiki/Atomic_bombings_of_Hiroshima_and_Nagasaki
11 https://en.wikipedia.org/wiki/Daigo_Fukury%C5%AB_Maru

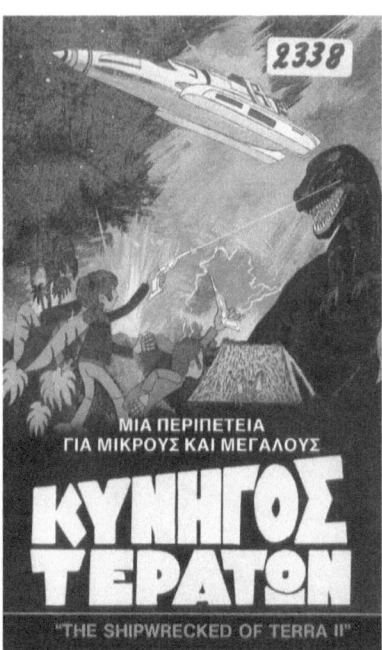
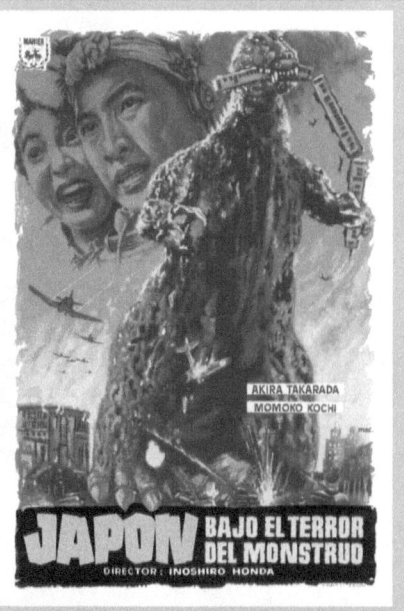
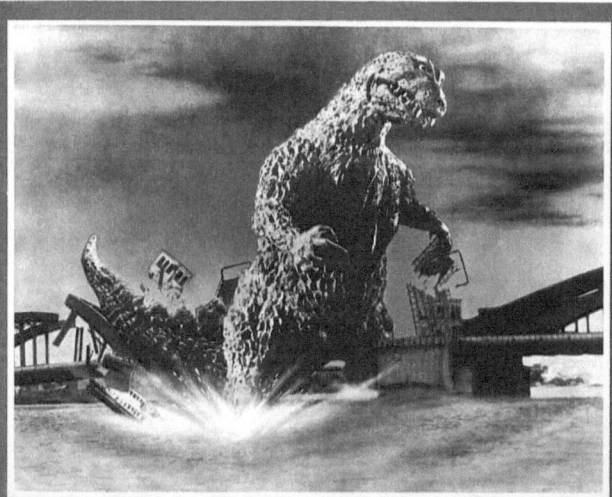
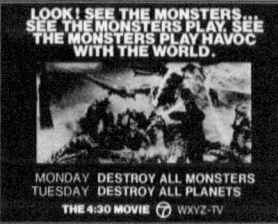

Clockwise, from Top Left: Greek VHS cover for **THE SHIPWRECKED OF TERRA II** (art unsigned); a Spanish handbill herald (with art by the great "Mac"/ Macario Gómez) and a spectacular Italian *fotobusta* for the history-making franchise-starter **GODZILLA** (1954); and, from back when local TV was actually fun, a WXYZ-TV ad from the Detroit Edition of *TV Guide* (for January 19th to 25th, 1974)

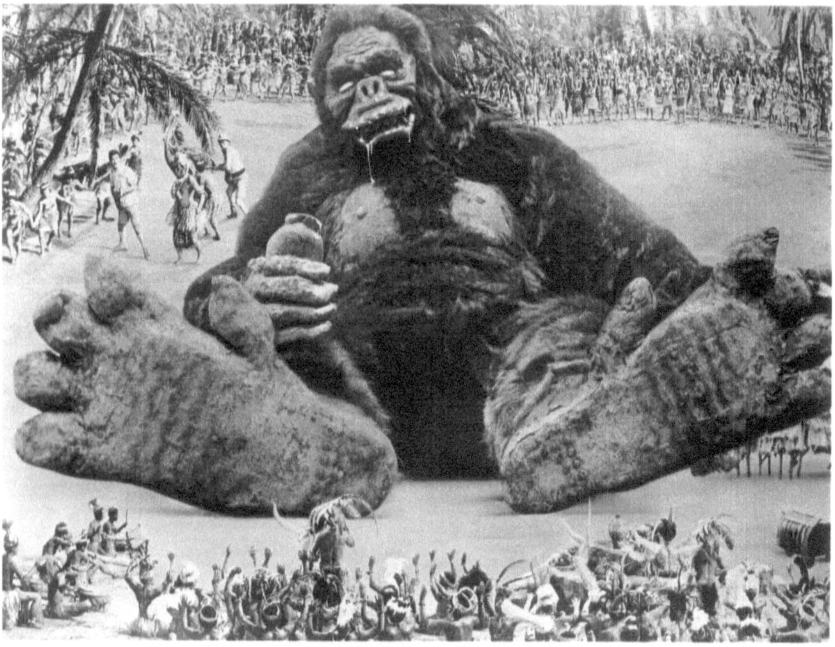

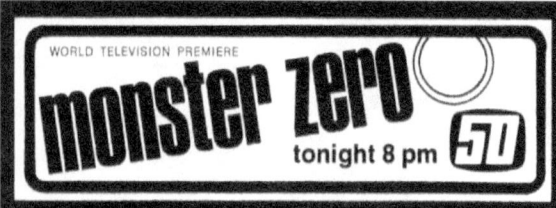

Above: An intoxicated Kong is worshipped by his mini-minions in a paste-up promo shot from 1962's **KKvG**. **Left:** A 1972 WKBD Detroit *TV Guide* ad-blurb: 'Zilla flicks were extremely popular TV fare in the '70s/'80s

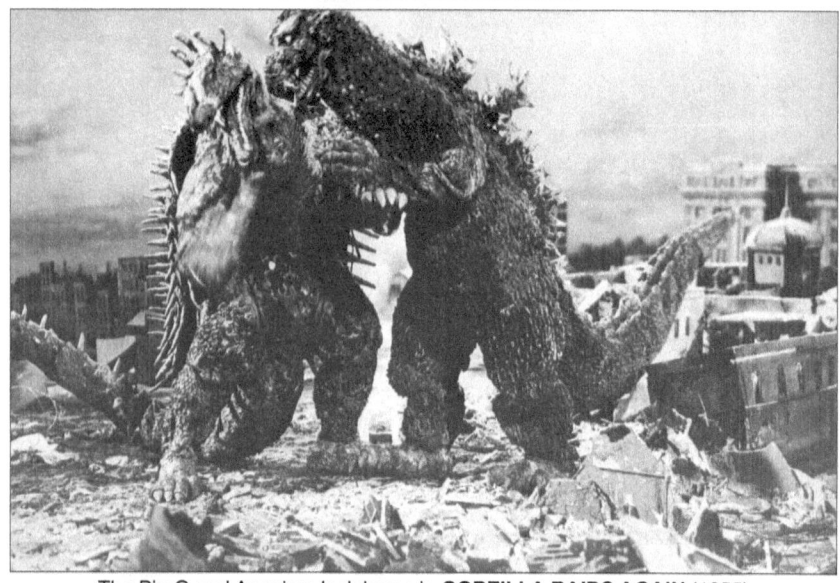

The Big G and Anguirus lock horns in **GODZILLA RAIDS AGAIN** (1955)

Godzilla A Go-Go

This classic kicks off on Odo Island, where the ships Eiko-maru and Bingo-maru are destroyed by a mysterious force. But behold, dear viewer, as some of the old folk of the isle suspect that these are the doings of the titular mythical creature. What's more, there are local legends about townsfolk sacrificing virgins to it, in what is the story's most *"What the fuck?!"* moment. Fear not, ignoring the locals' mumbo-jumbo, Godzilla shows up again to destroy several homes and even kills a few people, but one weird character seems more concerned about his dead cows than the loss of human life! Once Odo is vacated by the poor locals in a mass-evacuation, the government sends in palaeontologist Kyohei Yamane-hakase (the great Takashi Shimura, from Kurosawa's **RASHŌMON** [1950, Japan]) to investigate, and he discovers gigantic footprints, informing the protagonists that they are dealing with some species of dinosaur. The evidence make it quite clear that this is an exceedingly LARGE beast indeed (at one point it is guesstimated to be around 50 meters tall), and that its amphibian nature and characteristics—such as the fire that it can throw out with its breath like a dragon—scream that its creation was the result of a hydrogen bomb blast. The story then should be very familiar with monster movie fans, as a few conservative voices (i.e., the army) are trying to find a way to kill the beast, whilst more progressive voices (i.e., the scientists) want to study it. It is the Army that has its way with the proceedings, though, and an electrified 30-meter-tall fence is constructed, but it proves no match for our favorite monster, which comes stomping into Tokyo and pretty much flattens everything in sight, in what has to be the 1950s' most-spectacular sequence of monster destruction.

All of the above make for a great film, but it would be even greater had it ended at this point. What happens instead is the film runs for an anticlimactic approximate half-hour of 'overtime', with a long 'conclusion' featuring people discussing pseudo-science in a not-very-scientific manner. Another problem that I had with the film was its depiction of women, mainly that of the female lead Emiko Yamane (Momoko Kōchi, who reprised her role in a few sequels; more on them later), who seems to be there only to look worried, and is seemingly incapable of doing much else; but I guess that was the deal in real life in the mid-1950s too, and people didn't really know any better. But, me being a newbie watching this for the first time (yes, I am ashamed it took so long!), I must admit that I was here for Godzilla and the special effects, and—well—the monster was amazing (and it absolutely lived up to its

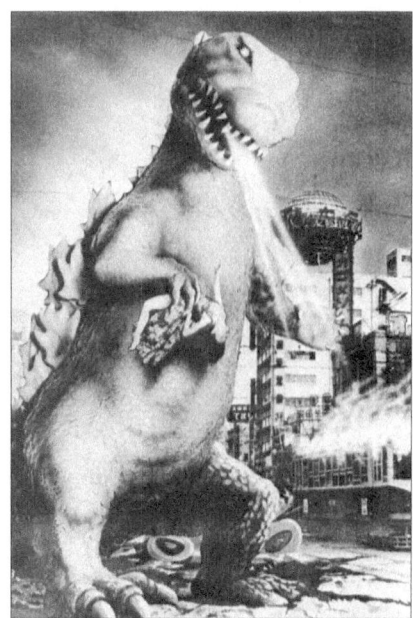

A heavily-retouched still used to promote **GODZILLA** (1954)

reputation)[12] and the SFX were seamless (which is a stunning fact, considering that this was made more than six decades ago, and it still holds up better than *all* of the modern crap that I usually review). What's more, the cinematography by Masao Tamai (of **FLOATING CLOUDS** [浮雲 / *Ukigumo*, 1955, Japan, D: Mikio Naruse]) puts most Hollywood product of the era to shame, and the memorable soundtrack by Akira Ifukube (of **THE BURMESE HARP** [ビルマの竪琴 / *Biruma no tategoto*, 1956, Japan, D: Kon Ichikawa]) is now stuck in my head and doesn't look like it's going away anytime soon.

I watched the original full-screen Japanese version (with English subtitles) at 1.37:1 (black-and-white), but I am aware that most monster kids in the West watched the Americanized version (released in a heavily-reedited cut by Embassy Pictures under the title **GODZILLA, KING OF THE MONSTERS!**, featuring additional scenes starring Raymond "Ironside" Burr), which in turn was also released in Japan in a messed-up widescreen format. On a similar note, in 1977,

---

12 Kazuyoshi Abe was originally hired, but due to the too-humanoid physiology of his designs, the collaboration did not proceed further. The more dinosaurian designs of Eiji Tsuburaya (special effects director), Teizō Toshimitsu (monster builder) and Akira Watanabe (art director) were used, and the team went for the suitmation process instead of stop-motion animation. Haruo Nakajima and Katsumi Tezuka were the duo that wore the Godzilla suit.

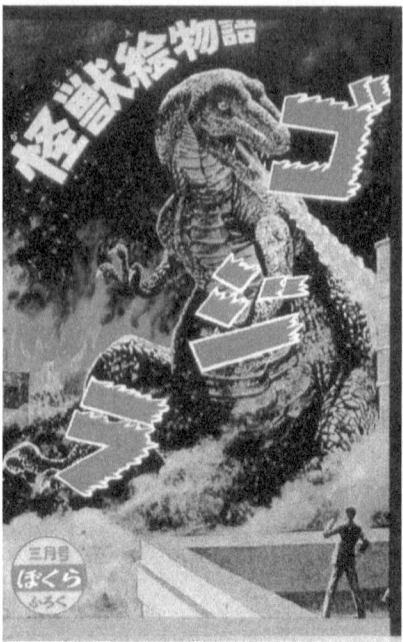

1955 Godzilla *manga* cover

Italian fantasy film legend Luigi Cozzi released a 'colorized' version. I haven't seen either of those two versions, so can't comment on them.

The most commonly-acknowledged inspiration for this legendary film is **KING KONG** (1933, USA, Ds: Merian C. Cooper, Ernest B. Schoedsack), but in reality producer Tomoyuki Tanaka conceived the idea after watching the highly-successful dinosaur-from-the-deep spectacular **THE BEAST FROM 20,000 FATHOMS** (1953, USA, D: Eugène Lourié), and Tanaka actually penned an outline (which he tentatively called *The Giant Monster From 20,000 Leagues Under The Sea*) whilst on a flight back from unsuccessful negotiations about a project he was hoping to make (called *In the Shadow of Glory*). Shigeru Kayama was quickly hired and penned the 50-page treatment, which was turned into a screenplay by Takeo Murata and Ishirō Honda. Shot in 51 days, utilizing mostly the backlot of production/distribution studio Toho and made on an approximate $175,000 budget (amounting to the most expensive Japanese movie ever made at the time), it grossed $2.25-million in its native Japan only. It didn't sit too favourably with the critics, but it won the Japan Movie Association Awards' prize for Special Effects and was nominated in the Best Picture category, as well.

As mentioned in the introduction above, Godzilla is now a cultural icon/phenomenon (the many Toho sequels will be examined throughout subsequent chapters of this column) and, in 2004, on the film's 50th Anniversary, Godzilla received a star along Hollywood's Walk of Fame. The movie and monster's influence in popular culture is unsurpassed, and even George Lucas has gone on record to say that the miniature work here (most-prevalent in the Tokyo destruction sequence) influenced his work on **STAR WARS** (1977, USA/UK).

Monday, December 19th, 2016

GODZILLA RAIDS AGAIN

(ゴジラの逆襲 / *Gojira no gyakushū*; a.k.a. **GIGANTIS, THE FIRE-MONSTER**)

Japan, 1955. D: Motoyoshi Oda

Ad-line: *"Roasting Anything in Its Path!"*

During a routine day at work, airplane pilots Shoichi Tsukioka (Hiroshi Koizumi from **MOTHRA** [1961, Japan, D: Ishirō Honda]) and Kōji Kobayashi (Minoru Chiaki from **RASHŌMON** [1950, Japan, D: Akira Kurosawa]) wind up landing on the island of Iwato, where they soon come across the titular monster, fighting another giant monster—namely Anguirus, which looks like a turtle with thorns on its back, and which, as we learn later, is an ancient enemy of Godzilla.

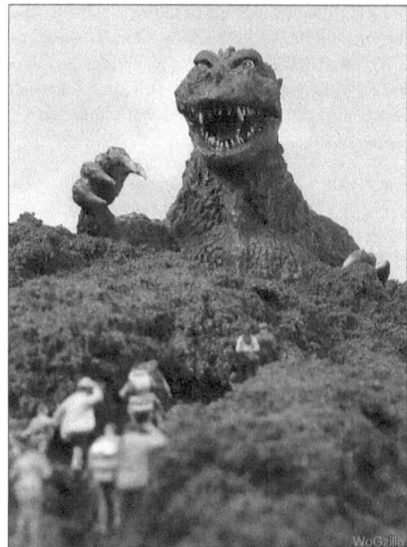

Godzilla dwarfs the very mountains themselves in this model kit from the early 2000s

The authorities in Osaka are informed, and at a meeting—complete with a screening of clips from the first movie—archaeologist Kyohei Yamane-hakase (the returning Takashi Shimura) comes up with the theory that has this particular 'new' Godzilla shares the same background with the first (it was sprung from the same batch). Both this Godzilla and Anguirus (a.k.a. Angilas [アンギラス / *Angirasu*]) were brought to life by the same hydrogen bomb detonation referred to in the first film. The problem is that it is impossible to kill this second Godzilla.

Our title monster soon attacks Osaka, but a well-organized action plan (involving an electrical blackout and jet fighters), forces the beast to temporarily leave the area. An unfortunate side effect of the blackout is that a group of criminals take advantage of it and succeed in escaping from custody. What's more, their violent escape generates a huge fire in the city, which manages to attract the attention of Godzilla, and the monster now returns to counterattack Osaka even more fiercely than before. Anguirus then shortly rejoins the fray and attacks Godzilla once more... Which monster will win and what will be left of Japan in the aftermath of their epic battle?

This was the first film in the Toho franchise to have Godzilla battling another monster, and the concept went over so well with audiences that it was repeated many, many times over in the subsequent slew of sequels. I watched the original Japanese version with English subtitles (at 1.37:1, black-and-white), but most Western Hemisphere monster kids first saw this in its English-dubbed version, entitled **GIGANTIS, THE FIRE MONSTER**,[13] which Warner Brothers released on American shores in 1959 on a double-bill with either the 'extraterrestrial JD' guilty pleasure **TEENAGERS FROM OUTER SPACE** (1959, USA, D: Tom Graeff) or the G-less *daikaiju* movie **RODAN** (1956, Japan, D: Ishirō Honda), depending on what area you happened to live in.

GODZILLA RAIDS AGAIN's screenplay by Takeo Murata (**GODZILLA** [1954]) and Shigeaki Hidaka (based upon a story by Shigeru Kayama) is occasionally problematic; for example, such awkward moments as when one of the pilots flirts his girlfriend over his radio while on duty. However, the direction by Motoyoshi Oda (**THE INVISIBLE AVENGER** [透明人間 / *Tōmei ningen*, 1954, Japan]) is top-notch, and so are the special effects by Eiji Tsuburaya (returning from the original). Godzilla looks spectacular, as (usually)

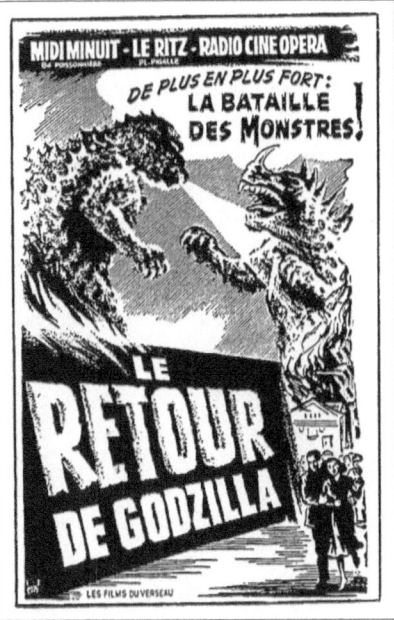

French newspaper ad for **GODZILLA RAIDS AGAIN** (1955)

always, and the new version of the monster was a welcome addition that resulted in an unforgettable battle royal onscreen. Produced by Tomoyuki Tanaka, it comes highly recommended indeed.

Tuesday, December 20th, 2016

KING KONG VS. GODZILLA
(キングコング対ゴジラ / *Kingu Kongu tai Gojira*)

Japan, 1962. D: Ishirō Honda

Ad-lines: *"The motion picture screen beckons you to adventure that thrills the emotions with shock and terror!"* – *"Now an all-mighty all-new motion picture brings them together for the first time in the colossal class of all time!"* – *"The most colossal conflict the screen has ever known!"*

Pacific Pharmaceuticals C.E.O. Tako (Ichirō Arishima from **INCIDENT AT BLOOD ISLAND** [待ち伏せ / *Machibuse*, 1970, Japan, D: Hiroshi Inagaki]) is disappointed with the television shows that carry his company's advertisements—incidentally, these opening minutes work as an excellent commentary on the media of the

---
13 Originally the plan was to make a new film (entitled "THE VOLCANO MONSTERS") that would utilize the great special effects of the Japanese original, but the project never materialized.

day—and since he has a strong influence on their content, he is looking for the next best thing in order to boost their ratings so more people will see his commercials. He finds just that when he is informed that a gigantic monster lives on the nearby Faro Island. This monster is none other than King Kong (Shoichi Hirose wore the ape-suit), but it is not the *only* monster on the island, as we also get to see what I think is the greatest attraction in the present show: namely a gigantic monster octopus, which is so visceral that it looks very ahead of its time and wouldn't seem at all out of place in a 1970s David Cronenberg film. In the meantime, an American submarine destroys an iceberg (seriously, this scene is better than all the ice-related SFX seen in **SUPERMAN** [1978, USA/UK/Panama/Switzerland, D: Richard Donner] combined!) in which the original Godzilla (here with Haruo Nakajima in the suit) was asleep, essentially unleashing the monster. Thus, for the third film into the series, we have *three* monsters to contend with! That said, the octopus isn't in it for too long, as Kong is quick to defeat it (these are not spoilers, as this happens very early on and primarily works as a means to establish how powerful Kong is, mainly because he was new to the *G* franchise). The authorities send Kong off to sleep and then try to drag the beast away to Japan (via air-lifting him using helium-filled balloons—no, I'm not making this up!), but Godzilla is also on its way to Japan for a little bit more destruction and mayhem. Inevitably the two title monsters have their first brief battle there. Tokyo doesn't just sit idly by waiting for its newest demolition this time out, and an electric fence is constructed, which works against Godzilla, but it seems to not only be harmless against Kong but also gives him extra power (of the electrical kind, I suppose). What's more, Kong, as he always does, captures a girl with whom he becomes enamored (namely Mie Hama, from the present film's loose semi-sequel [*sans* Godzilla] **KING KONG ESCAPES** [キングコングの逆襲 / *Kingu Kongu no Gyakushū*, 1967, Japan/USA, D: Ishirō Honda]). The authorities send Kong to sleep once again before luring he and Godzilla into a final battle. Which monster will win and what will be left of the South Pacific in its wake?!

In 1960, animator Willis O'Brien (**KING KONG**) proposed a treatment to RKO for a film that would be called "KING KONG MEETS FRANKENSTEIN", in which the titular monstrous duo would solve their differences in San Francisco (just what Frankenstein or his monster would be doing in Frisco is anyone's guess!), but later on he changed the title to "KING KONG VS. THE GINKO" instead. The story was turned into a screenplay by George Worthing Yates (of **IT CAME FROM BENEATH THE SEA** [1955, USA, D: Robert Gordon] fame) under the title *King Kong vs. Prometheus*. No American studio was interested, however, for the simple reason that there was no way for the ambitious script to be produced on a low budget, and the concept was eventually taken to Toho, who changed Kong's opponent to become Godzilla, their reigning King of the Monsters. RKO was paid an estimated $200,000—a princely sum for the time—for the licensing of their King Kong character and registered trademark...and the rest is history!

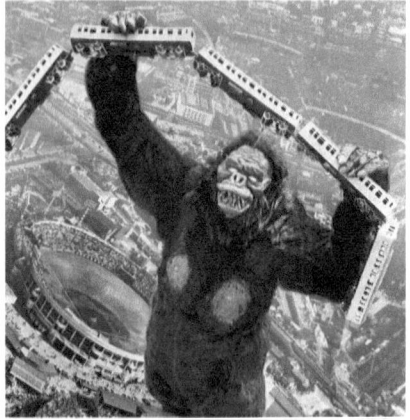

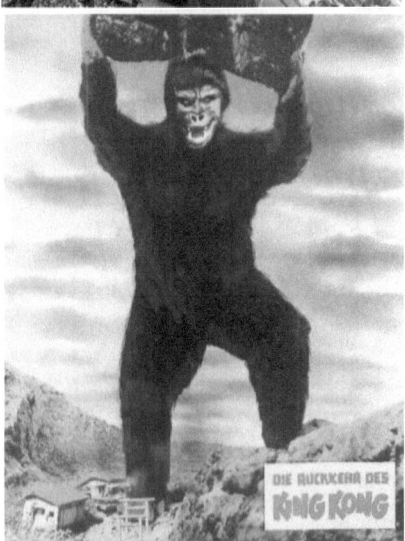

Above: Two odd promo items for KKvG. The bottom image is a heavily-retouched German lobby card in which ol' Kong looks *nothing* like the suit that appears in the film

I watched the original Japanese version with English subtitles (at 2.35:1 and in color; this was the first-ever *Godzilla* production to employ that aspect ratio), but a very different US release version also exists. Although the present film has been heavily criticized in regards to how extremely 'family-friendly' it became (for example, the humanized mannerisms of the two monsters do indeed border on the idiotic at times), one thing that is rarely noticed by critics is how politically incorrect it often is. Take, for example, the scene in which the explorers hand out cigarettes to natives and a kid asks if he can have one too, so they promptly hand him a cig, saying that he shouldn't tell his mom about it (and then his mom takes one too!). The combination of these two widely different aspects make this a surreal viewing experience indeed. Some matte painting work may be unfortunate, and some of the special effects don't look very convincing, but the scene in which Kong forcibly stops a train and grabs the heroine from inside it is still breath-taking to behold more than a half-century on. Made on an estimated budget of $200,000 and grossing a then-astonishing $1.25 million, this is the most widely-released Godzilla film of all. A sequel was announced ("CONTINUATION: KING KONG VS. GODZILLA"), but it unfortunately never got made; instead, Toho went on to make sequels all the more frequently.

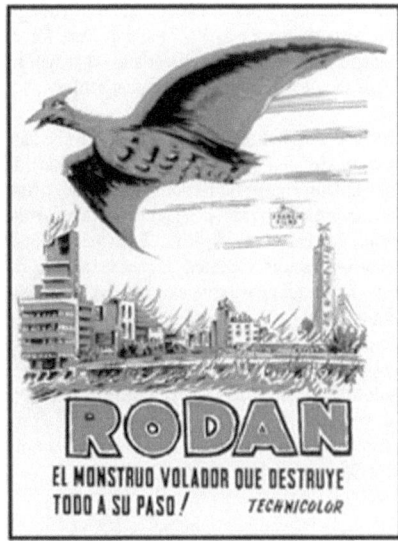

Argentine poster for **RODAN, THE FLYING MONSTER** (1956)

Saturday, December 24th, 2016

RODAN, THE FLYING MONSTER

(伊福部昭 - 空の大怪獣 ラドン / *Sora no daikaijū Radon*)

Japan, 1956. D: Ishirō Honda

Ad-lines: *"Most horrifying hell creature that ever menaced all mankind!" – "Thundering out of unknown skies – The super-sonic hell-creature no weapon could destroy!"*

Miners Goro (Rinsaku Ogata, later seen in **INVASION OF THE ASTRO-MONSTERS** [1965, Japan/USA, D: Ishirō Honda]) and Yoshizo (Jirō Suzukawa, from **SEVEN SAMURAI** [1954, Japan, D: Akira Kurosawa]) disappear mysteriously whilst at work, and it's not long before the latter is found dead by unknown causes. Fast-forward to a few days later, and more miners, along with a couple of police officers too, are slaughtered by some sort of subterranean monster. But it's not long before the eponymous winged wonder actually shows itself (it is of an ancient species of dragonfly called Meganulon), and unfortunately it doesn't look too impressive, even though it appears menacing, as firepower has no effect against it. What's more, there are at least *two* flying monsters (Rodans) herein that fly over Japan

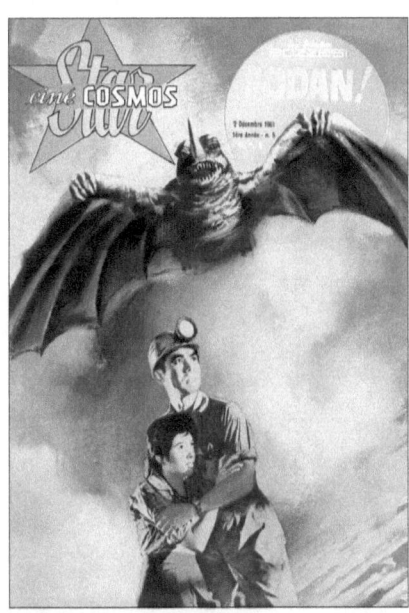

Star-Cine Cosmos' Italian *foto-romanza* (December 2nd, 1961) of **RODAN** (1956)

terrorizing its citizens, and if that's not enough, they also spawn eggs! Will the Japanese forces manage to overcome the threat and what will be left of the nearby city when the dust settles…?

This was the first of Toho's *kaijū eiga* to be shot in color (by cinematographer Isamu Ashida), in 1.37:1. Unfortunately, I couldn't score an original Japanese version, so I had to work with the awful English-dubbed print, in which subpar American actors imitated Japanese actions in ways that might easily be characterized as racist (but then I'd imagine that Japanese actors played racist depictions of Americans in films of the day too, so I guess it all evens out). Be it the copy's fault, or the film's actual qualities, this is one of the very few films that sent me to sleep. Considered a classic by many, it is nevertheless my least-favourite Ishirō Honda film.

Monday, December 26th, 2016

MOTHRA
(モスラ / *Mosura*)

Japan, 1961. D: Ishirō Honda

Ad-lines: *"Incredible! Inconceivable! World Wrecked As Monster Hunts Human Mates!"* – *"What Bizarre Spell Do The Tiniest Women In All The World Hold Over The Mightiest Monster In All Creation?"* – *"Fabulous! Fantastic! Two Doll-Sized Beauties Worshipped By a Winged Behemoth!"* – *"Earth Quakes As Monster Seeks Tiny Mates!"* – *"Love-Crazed Monster Crushes World!"*
An expedition to the presumably-uninhabited Infant Island results in the discovery of a few natives and leaves a handful of explorers sick by what appears to be radiation illness. These events attract the involvement of the press, and a lot of 'comedy' ensues (actually, most of the film under review is played as a comedy; one of the main performers here is Frankie Sakai, a famous comedian). The authorities arrange a new expedition and, much to everyone's amazement, two pint-sized young ladies (the identical twins Emi Itō and Yumi Itō) are discovered, who, instead of speaking, make keyboard-like musical sounds. Of course, these twin tiny wonders are captured, and off they are sent to Tokyo to be put on display as sideshow freaks, but they haven't had the last word yet (or their first, for that matter!), and they go on to spiritually/telepathically communicate with the title monster's egg, which soon births a gigantic flying insect of the order Lepidotopera that is quick to launch a devastating aerial assault on Japan.

The screenplay by Shin'ichi Sekizawa (**KING KONG VS. GODZILLA** [1962]) was adapted from the novel *The Luminous Fairies and Mothra* by Shin'ichirō Nakamura, Takehiko Fukunaga and Yoshie Hotta; the story is now considered a classic and somehow unique, because the monster is not totally menacing, but actually has some sort of benevolent motivation behind what it does. The direction by Ishirō Honda is, as always, top-notch, but at over 100 minutes long, this might benefit from 30 minutes-or-so of judicious cuts (the lengthy monster-free introduction is particularly boring). I watched the original Japanese version (with English subtitles), but many Western monster kids first discovered this in its English dub, which ran considerably shorter. A 62-minute version was belatedly released in Japan in 1974.

Tuesday, December 27th, 2016

MOTHRA VS. GODZILLA
(モスラ対ゴジラ / *Mosura tai Gojira*; a.k.a. **GODZILLA VS. THE THING**)

Japan, 1964. D: Ishirō Honda

Ad-lines: *"Nothing Like This Ever on the Screen!"* – *"See The Armies Of The World Destroyed! See The Birth Of The World's Most Terrifying Monster! See The War Of The Giants!"*

The most-recent disaster to strike a Japanese village is a typhoon, and journalists Ichiro Sakai (Akira Takarada, from **GODZILLA** [1954])

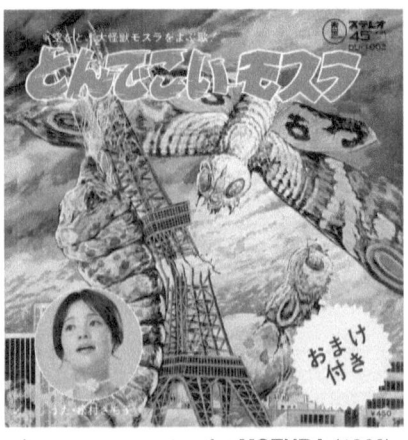

Japanese *sonorama* for **MOTHRA** (1962)

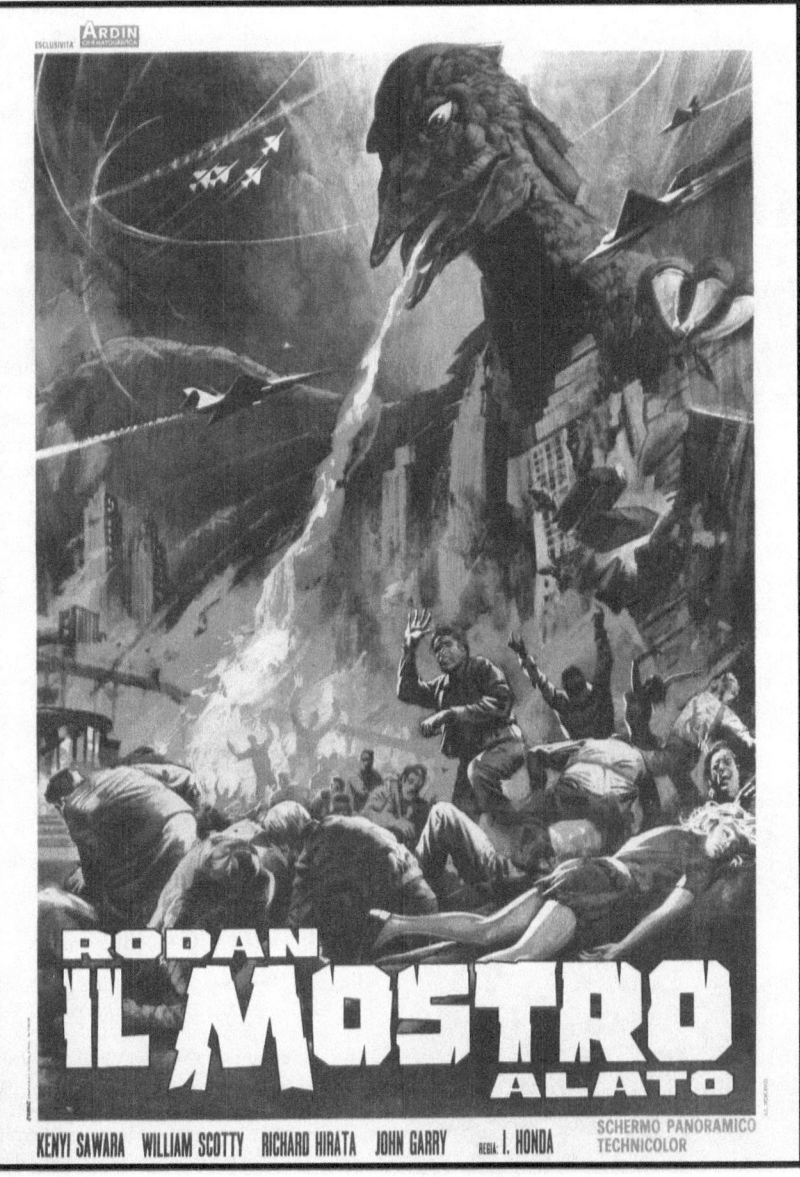

'68 Italian reissue *due-fogli manifesto* for 1956's **RODAN**; amazing art by Mario Piovano/Studio Paradiso

and Junko Nakanishi (Yuriko Hoshi, from **KILL!** [斬る / *Kiru*, 1968, Japan, D: Kihachi Okamoto]) cover the disaster in the aftermath. A giant egg is soon discovered, and powerful businessman Kumayama (Yoshifumi Tajima, from Kurosawa's **THE HIDDEN FORTRESS** [隠し砦の三悪人 / *Kakushi toride no san akunin*, 1958, Japan]) is quick to get a-hold of it, and his intentions are not good either, as he wants to turn things into a sideshow. The first thing he does is arrange a meeting with his boss, Jiro Torahata (Kenji Sahara, from **RODAN, THE FLYING MONSTER** [1956]), and it is together that they will come across the tiny Shobijin twins from the reviewed-above **MOTHRA** (1961), and the pint-sized ladies inform the men that the egg belongs to that creature. The plan doesn't go too well, however, as the two men attempt to kidnap the ladies and turn them into a sideshow as well, but the tiny duo luckily

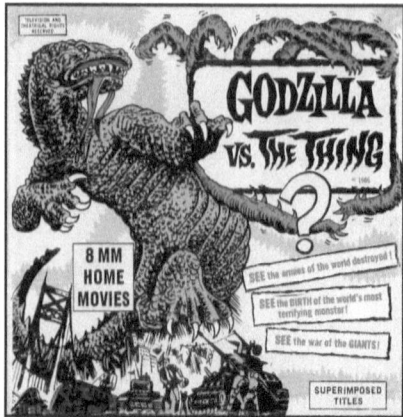

US 8mm movie box for **MOTHRA VS. GODZILLA** (1962)

escape. They link-up with two journalists and Professor Miura (**MOTHRA**'s Hiroshi Koizumi) to share the information with their more positive ears. Godzilla soon wakes up and, in the film's greatest moments, attacks Nagoya; a sequence which is extremely powerful, especially when we see the struggle of the humans, which is highly reminiscent of situations during wartime. Now Mothra must be brought aboard

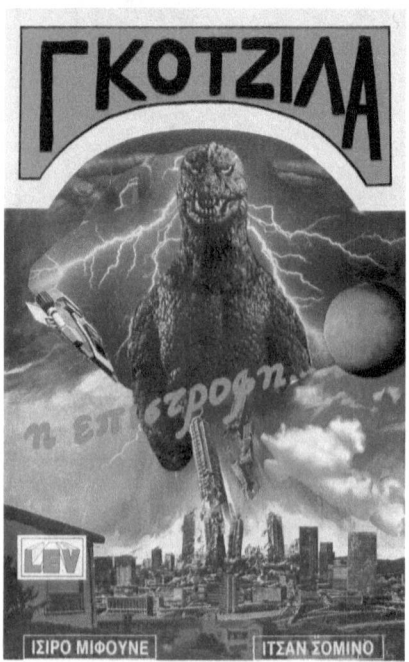

Greek VHS cover for **GHIDRAH THE THREE-HEADED MONSTER** (1965)

in order to defeat Godzilla. Which monster will win and what will be left of Japan when they get through…?

Judging from what my eyes can tell, the Toho team perfected their craft with this entry, as the rear-screen projections are pretty seamless, creating spectacular—and above all, *believable*—visuals. I had the pleasure of watching the original Japanese version (with English subtitles) at a gorgeous widescreen 2.55:1 aspect ratio which left me speechless (the cinematography by Hajime Koizumi [**MOTHRA**] is flawless), but Western world monster kids back in the day got to watch its Americanized version, christened **GODZILLA VS. THE THING**[14] by stateside distributors American International Pictures (which featured additional footage that was actually shot by Toho for this particular release) who paired it up on a double-bill with the Eastern European SF classic **VOYAGE TO THE END OF THE UNIVERSE** [*Ikarie XB 1*, 1963, Czechoslovakia, D: Jindrich Polák]).

Wednesday, December 28th, 2016

GHIDRAH THE THREE-HEADED MONSTER

(三大怪獣 地球最大の決戦 / *San daikaijū: Chikyū saidai no kessen*)

Japan, 1964. D: Ishirō Honda

Ad-line: *"The Three-Headed Monster battles Godzilla, Mothra and Rodan for the world!"*

Although detective Shindo (Yōsuke Natsuki from **YOJIMBO** [用心棒 / *Yōjinbō*, 1961, Japan, D: Akira Kurosawa]) does his best to maintain the safety of the Princess of Sergina (Akiko Wakabayashi, later seen in the James Bonder **YOU ONLY LIVE TWICE** [1967, UK, D: Lewis Gilbert]) on her way to Japan, the latter's plane is bombed, but much to the former's surprise she turns up alive and well. Only problem is, she claims to be a prophet from another planet. What's more, her predictions begin to come true, and these include the resurrection of Godzilla and Rodan…

---

14 This could be a nod to **THE THING FROM ANOTHER WORLD** (1951, USA, Ds: Christian Nyby, Howard Hawks).

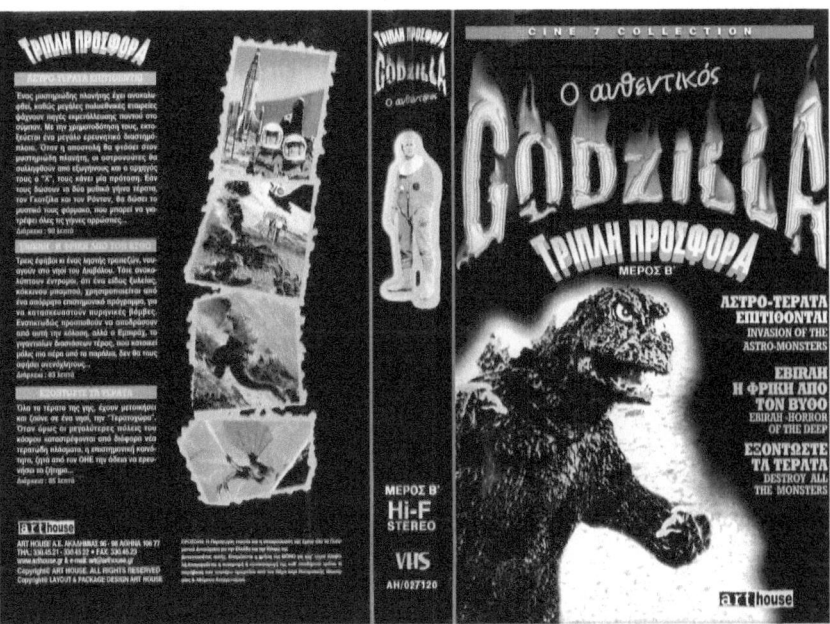

Greek Godzilla VHS three-pack

Enter the Princess' uncle (Shin Ōtomo, also from **YOJIMBO**) who, as we learn, was behind the bombing and who now sends hitman Malmess (Hisaya Itō, later seen in **THE WAR OF THE GARGANTUAS** [フランケンシュタインの怪獣 サンダ対ガイラ / *Furankenshutain no Kaijū: Sanda tai Gaira*, 1966, Japan, D: Ishirō Honda]) to The Land of the Rising Sun, for a second attempt. This too is prevented, though, because the Shobijin twins (played by button-cute actresses Emi Itō and Yumi Itō once again) warn the Princess on time. A further attempt is prevented because Rodan and Godzilla and their destructive business put everything else on hold.

Princess Selina comes up with one more prediction, and this is about the titular monster, King Ghid(o)rah, who is quick to make an appearance and begin trashing the joint. Will the Japanese authorities manage to arrange the creatures' forces to turn this monster mash-up to their favour, or will Tokyo and its environs be totally trashed yet again?

In Japanese mythology, "Eight-Forked Serpent" (a.k.a. *Yamata no Orochi*) is a dragon with eight heads, and it was the one in this particular legend that the titular creature herein was based upon. Throw in Godzilla and Rodan, and—*VOILA!*—you got the ultimate in monster mash-ups! Written by Shin'ichi Sekizawa, executive-produced by Tomoyuki Tanaka, and directed by Ishirō Honda, you could read success all over this one's forehead, yet the results are far from that. The credits reveal snippets from the action that would come later on, yet things don't look as spectacular as they were supposed to. What's more, the rampant sexism all over, makes this more dated and laughable than exciting. For example, a female scientist is observing the sky when a meteor falls, so she then duly informs the male scientists. A bit later, the Princess, during one of her public speeches, is asked by a man in the audience what sex she is.

The bottom line is that this is more historically important than it is actually enjoyable (it's overall pretty boring, as well), as this is the first time the tiny twins are referred to as "fairies" (although this is not expanded upon further), it's also the only time we see future series regular Ghidrah acting independently (more on that in the reviews below), as well as the first time that Godzilla turned into a heroic character (a role that he will pretty much maintain in every subsequent sequel).

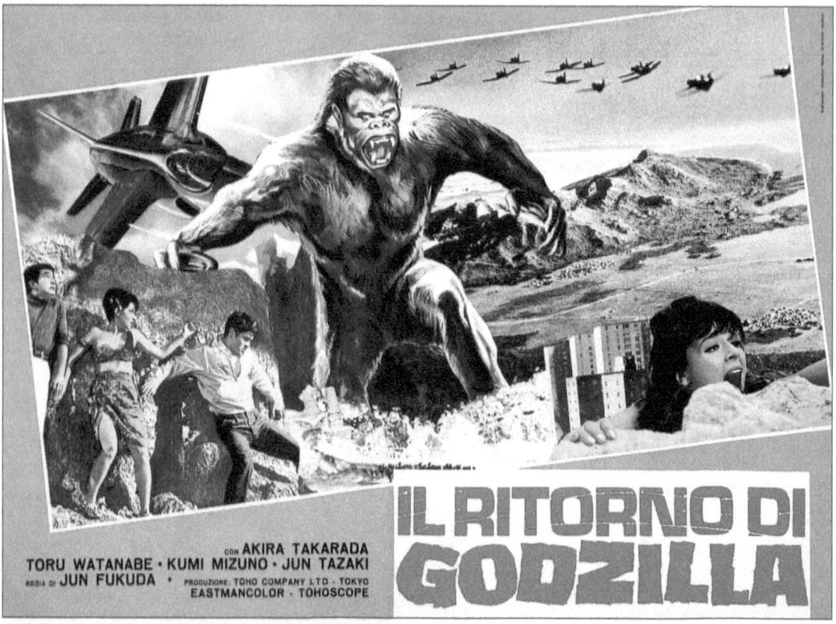

Thursday, December 29th, 2016

INVASION OF THE ASTRO-MONSTERS
(怪獣大戦争 / *Kaijū daisensō*; a.k.a. **MONSTER ZERO**)

Japan/USA, 1965. D: Ishirō Honda

Astronauts Fuji (Akira Takarada from **GODZILLA** [1954]) and Glenn Amer (Nick Adams from Nick Ray's **REBEL WITHOUT A CAUSE** [1955, USA]) land on Planet X, where they come across the Ghidrah (キングギドラ / *Kingu Gidora* a.k.a. King Ghidorah), the triple-noggined dragon from the previous film. The natives (i.e., aliens) explain how the three-headed monster is attacking them non-stop, and they ask if they could have the assistance of Godzilla and Rodan in order to defeat the threat; in exchange they would give humans the cure for cancer. The people of Planet X don't do much waiting and shortly appear on Earth in their spaceships uninvited to take Godzilla and Rodan back to their homeworld, where the monstrous duo successfully battles Ghidrah away. You would now expect the aliens to deliver the cure for cancer to us, but they're not the most benevolent of people, as it turns out. You see, they present humankind with a tape which should supposedly contain the instructions to make the cure, but instead it contains an ultimatum which essentially demands

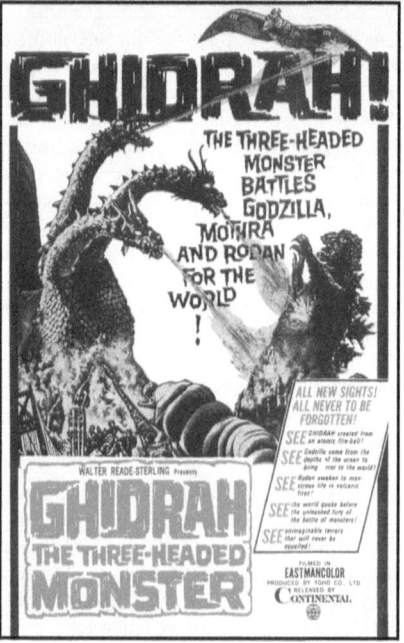

Top: In a bid to fool audiences into believing they'll be seeing more than just Godzilla fight a giant shrimp, we have this misleading mid-'70s (i.e., "Dinokong"-era) Italian *fotobusta* for **EBIRAH, HORROR OF THE DEEP**. **Above:** US poster art is generally much more straightforward

that we Earthlings surrender to Planet X, otherwise the trio of mighty monsters now controlled by them will be sent to our globe to run amok. Is there any hope for the humanity? *[Is there ever any hope for humanity?! Least of all these days. ☺ – SF.]*

I had the pleasure of watching the original Japanese color version with English subtitles at 2.35:1, but most western monster kids originally saw the American version (which had several alterations in the editing, plot and dubbing, etc.) which co-producing studio United Productions of America (UPA) released under the title **MONSTER ZERO** (on a double bill with the same director's **THE WAR OF THE GARGANTUAS** [1966]) some five years after it was made (in 1970), probably to cash-in on star Adams' then-recent passing. It was produced by Tomoyuki Tanaka, written by Shin'ichi Sekizawa, and directed by Ishirō Honda.

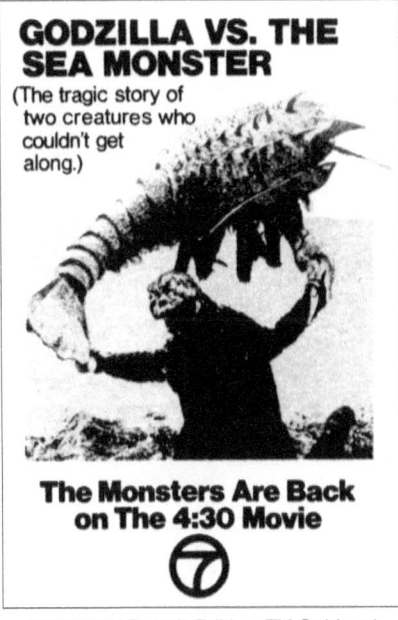

WXYZ-TV Detroit Edition *TV Guide* ad (February 26th to March 3rd, 1972)

Friday, December 30th, 2016

EBIRAH, HORROR OF THE DEEP

(ゴジラ・エビラ・モスラ　南海の大決闘 / *Gojira, Ebira, Mosura Nankai no Daikettō*; a.k.a. **GODZILLA VS. THE SEA MONSTER**)

Japan, 1966. D: Jun Fukuda

Ad-line: *"This is one lobster you don't want to order!"*

Just so you know, I originally began this review with a lengthy, random, distasteful and entirely self-indulgent pair of paragraphs (totalling almost exactly HALF the total word-count of my review) about a topic which had absolutely nothing whatsoever to do with Godzilla movies, although I did try to tie it in with them in some facile, flimsy way. However, upon rereading said paras prior to submitting my final draft of this article, I judiciously elected to omit it entirely and stick to the subject instead. Besides, I realize that *Monster!* has certain standards of decorum to uphold, so I decided that the contents of my combo ramble/rant really didn't belong here. *[Good on ya, Christos! Way to use editorial discretion there, bud! If only that Mongo McGillicutty would take some pointers from you! – eds.]*

In this one, the terrorist team Red Bamboo are controlling the titular monster, while also exploiting the natives of Infant Island by forcing them to labor for them, but the poor people hope to have their revenge on their cruel oppressors by waking-up Mothra (the twin fairies are this time played by Pair Bambi). Meanwhile, the dormant Godzilla gets awoken from his slumber once more thanks to receiving a heavy jolt of electricity, and off he goes to fight the baddie monster, as well as another one named Daikondura too. Which monster will prevail and what will be left of the miniature sets once they get through stomping the living shit out of them…?

This film begun life in development under the title "OPERATION ROBINSON CRUSOE", and it was originally conceived as a King Kong concept, but when that didn't come to fruition, Toho kept the screenplay by Shin'ichi Sekizawa and simply replaced the monstrous gorilla with Godzilla. It is a very peculiar entry, as it appears that director Jun Fukuda went for full-on/all-out comedy, and he mostly succeeds at it, as most of the protagonists are little more than caricatures rather than actual characters. Also, the extensive shootouts seem out-of-place, and they simply aren't good enough to compete with those seen in other actioners from the era; for example, those from Italy. We do get the occasional wonder, including the underwater scenes (that look better than the rest of the film), and the scene in which two humans get 'forked' by Ebirah is a quite

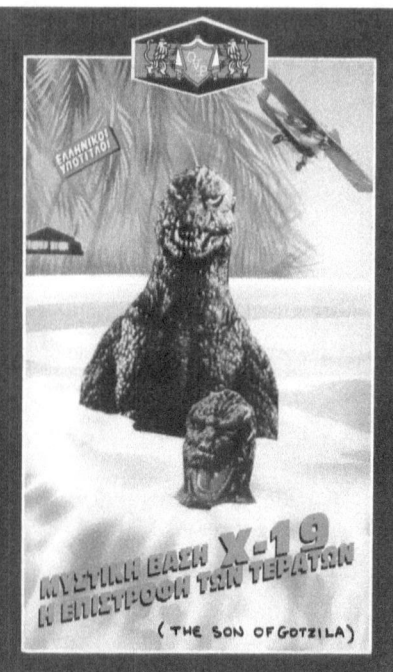

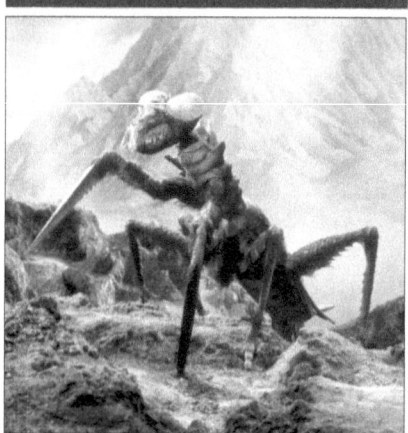

Top: '80s Greek VHS cover for **SON OF GODZILLA** (1967). **Above:** One of the film's way-cool giant mantis marionettes/rod puppets

boob tube, as this is 'family-friendly', TV-grade entertainment all the way. I may have been a bit harsher on this one than I perhaps might have been for the simple reason that my copy is not in very good condition, so this may have negatively colored my opinions of it.

SON OF GODZILLA
(ゴジラの息子 / *Kaijū-tō no Kessen Gojira no Musuko*)

Japan, 1967. D: Jun Fukuda

Ad-lines: *"Japan's Greatest Foe Delivers an Heir!"* – *"Ever see a monster hatch from a monster egg? You will!"*

On an out-of-the-way tropical island in the South Pacific, some scientists are working on a weather-control system—this would be awesome, but to an extent it is not so very different from the negative effects of climatic change and pollution—which (guess what?!) goes horribly wrong when a radioactive balloon malfunctions and this results in the super-enlargement of three incidental local praying mantises to gargantuan dimensions. The first thing these monstrous mantids (known as Kamacuras [カマキラス / *Kamakirasu*] a.k.a. "Gimantis" in the Anglo-dubbed print) do is bother an equally gigantic egg—containing the baby Godzilla, Minya a.k.a. Minilla (ミニラ / *Minira*)—which they further harass once it hatches. Papa Godzilla shows up, kills all but one of the mantises and takes the Godzilla pup under his protection; which essentially means teaching him tricks, such as how to emit the famous flaming breath (Minya manages to muster-up some smoke-rings instead). But these are not all the monsters the picture has to offer, and we are soon introduced to the main villain: a gigantic spider (クモンガ / *Kumonga*; known as "Spiga" in the stateside dubbed version). Which monster/s will win and what will be left of the island of the experiments?

Okay, you can't take kids' stuff like this seriously. This went straight to television in the US, and it clearly resembles Saturday morning programming (the scenes in which Baby Godzilla acts like a puppy dog, complete with supposedly cute tricks, etc., are quite pathetic to witness). Director Jun Fukuda's full-on comedy approach doesn't work for me, and the budget that it was given is considerably lower at this stage in the series, and these lowered production values mainly reveal themselves in the gruesome moment. The rest of the film is mostly kids' stuff, though. **EBIRAH, HORROR OF THE DEEP** is notable for being the first *Godzilla* film not to receive a theatrical release in the USA, as it went straight to television (licensed by Walter Reade Organization), but a little-known fact is that, prior to these broadcastings, one outfit called Continental Pictures did exhibit the film in a few theatres. It's hardly surprising that it subsequently got unceremoniously consigned to the two main monsters (i.e., Godzillas Sr. and Jr.), which look amateurish. The film is not without its merits, though, as the insectoid/arachnid baddie monsters do look quite impressive, as does the extended climactic sequence amidst fake snow. The film was written by Kazue Shiba and Shin'ichi Sekizawa, and it was produced by Tomoyuki Tanaka.

Sunday, January 1st, 2017

DESTROY ALL MONSTERS
(怪獣総進撃 / *Kaijū Sōshingeki*)

Japan, 1968. D: Ishirō Honda

Ad-lines: *"Monsters of Mass-Destruction." – "The Battle Cry that could Save the World!"*

Set in the then-futuristic year of 1999 (not very 'futuristic' now, I know!), this film would have us believe that world peace has finally arrived, because the United Nations Science Committee have gathered together all the monsters from the previous films and corralled/confined them safely on one small island. However, an alien race called Kilaaks or Kilaakians (キラアク星人) have infiltrated the island's team of scientists and, in order to terrorize our planet's leaders into submitting, they proceed to unleash the captive monsters on the world. For this, we see them destroying famous cities (for example, Godzilla takes New York, and Rodan takes Moscow!). Of course, the international powers collaborate successfully to ensure that the monsters are once again under the aegis of the humans, but the aliens haven't had the last word—or laugh—yet, and they unleash their own attack-beast, namely Ghidrah (a.k.a. King Ghidorah). Can the rest of the friendly monster mob win the ultimate battle against the evil three-headed one, or are we potentially doomed to total destruction yet again…?

This begun life as "ALL MONSTERS ATTACK DIRECTIVE", but during the developmental stages that early draft's monster line-up was changed (e.g., some monsters were replaced by the ones we got in the final film). Toho had big plans for this one, as it was intended to be the final *Godzilla* outing (yet its success led to still more sequels [reviewed below]), and it was the studio's twentieth *kaijū eiga* (Toho made numerous other monster movies besides the ones

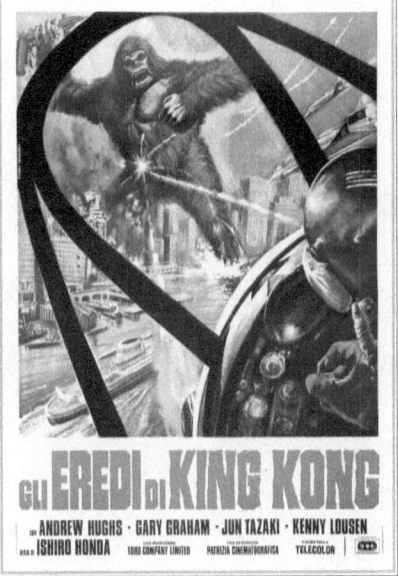

Italian *due-fogli manifesto* for **DESTROY ALL MONSTERS** (1968). The reason why the title and artwork (by Studio Paradiso) so misleadingly promise Kong being the film's star—he isn't even *in* it!—is that this poster was for its 1977 rerelease in Italy, at the height of the media 'mania' surrounding Dino De Laurentiis' then-recent *KK* remake

reviewed here. I'm primarily covering those within Godzilla's story arc and canon). It also marks the return of Ishirō Honda to the director's chair, and with that the return to greatness, really, as, aside from being a highly entertaining film (I mean, with so many monsters, and a screenplay by Honda and Takeshi Kimura that is set all over the world, not too much could go wrong!) it is also a very well-crafted one. It's also incredibly spectacular, and is hands-down my all-time favourite Godzilla movie. Even the title designs at the beginning are special this time around, and for the gorehounds among us there is a surgery scene (which may not be as gruesome as it could be, but it is still quite strong, considering that this is family fare) and…earring-pulling (*OUCH*)! **DAM** was produced by John Sirabella and Tomoyuki Tanaka, and it was released in the USA by Samuel Z. Arkoff's and James H. Nicholson's American International Pictures (AIP) in a version that was dubbed into English and had a few changes made in the editing (I watched the original Japanese version instead, with English subtitles and in a gorgeous 2.55:1 widescreen print). This is one that you should *not* miss!

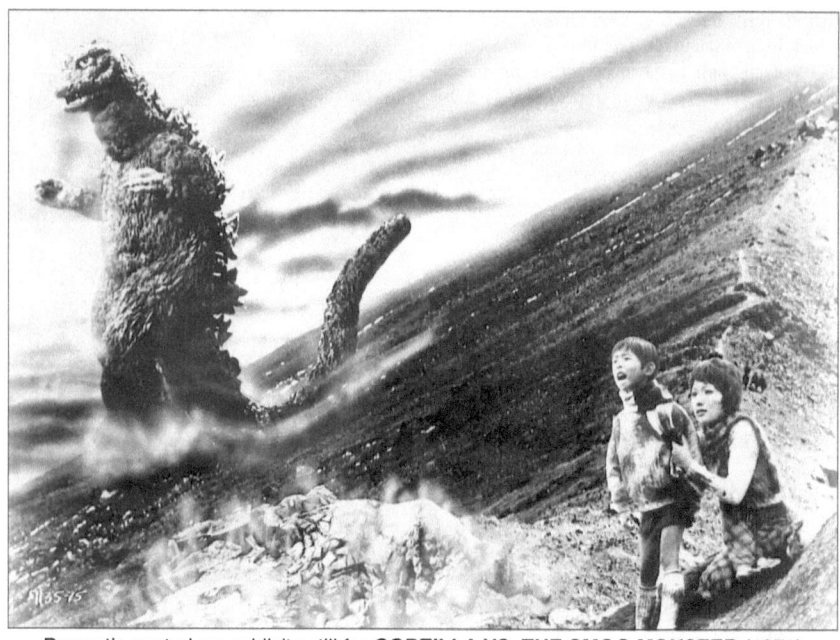

Dramatic pasted-up publicity still for **GODZILLA VS. THE SMOG MONSTER** (1971)

Tuesday, January 3rd, 2017

GODZILLA'S REVENGE

(ゴジラ・ミニラ・ガバラ オール 怪獣大進撃 / *Gojira-Minira-Gabara: Ōru Kaijū Daishingeki*; a.k.a. **ALL MONSTERS ATTACK**)

Japan, 1969. D: Ishirō Honda

Ad-line: *"See: Prehistoric Monsters Crawl Out of the Hidden Depths of the Earth and Take Revenge against the Living!"*

Set in the radiation-polluted Kawasaki area of Japan, this one concerns a young boy named Ichirō Miki (Tomonori Yazaki, from **DUEL IN THE STORM** [嵐の果し状 / *Arashi no hatashiji*, 1968, Japan, D: Akinori Matsuo]) who is mercilessly bullied by his schoolmate Gabara (Yū Sekita from **SON OF GODZILLA** [1967]). Ichioro's best friend is inventor Shinpei Inami (Hideyo Amamoto, from **YOJIMBO** [1961]), who has just created a transportation machine/computer that transports the harried Ichirō to the place of his dreams: namely Monster Island, where he is quick to befriend Godzilla's son, Minya/Minilla. Problem is, the friendly mini-monster and the human kid shortly come under attack by the dinosaurian Gabara (ガバラ), the clacking-pincered crab-monster Ebirah (エビラ / *Ebira*), and a trio of Kamacuras (カマキラス / *Kamakirasu*) mantises. We are soon introduced to the main attraction—Godzilla, natch!—who in turn fights further monsters and also some airplanes. But maybe the kid *wasn't* actually transported anywhere at all in the first place, and it was all only a dream? Whether this is the case or not, Ichirō has more problems back home in Kawasaki, and these include a duo of adult villains, Senbayashi (Sachio Sakai, from **YOJIMBO**) and Okuda (Kazuo Suzuki, also from **SON OF GODZILLA**). The kid hero will have to employ all the defensive/offensive tactics he learned from his monster friends in order to defeat the more mundane threats that he ultimately faces.

Although most of these early entries in the series are 'family-friendly' to da max, this one gets particularly ridiculous, as it seems to have been targeted to toddlers, and not very *clever* ones at that (it was released at Christmastime). There is some consolation in the fact that it runs for a mere 69 minutes (at least the Japanese version with English subtitles that I watched did), even though it still feels like three hours! Audiences realized this, and it was the least successful Godzilla film up to that point in Japan. In the USA, monster kids were introduced to it under the title **GODZILLA'S REVENGE** (whose Americanized version was a bit different in spots), which played on some double-bills with either the superior sci-fi potboiler **NIGHT OF THE BIG HEAT** (1967, UK, D: Terence Fisher) or Ishirō Honda's **THE WAR OF THE GARGANTUAS** (1966). **GR** is not entirely without its merits, as Genta Kano's "Monster March" theme tune is particularly brilliant, and you can actually even have some fun with the film in a campy *Batman* TV show (1966-1968, USA) kinda way. Overall, this feels much akin to what a *Godzilla* film would look like if it was directed by Ted V. Mikels…which may or may not be a bad thing, depending entirely on your viewpoint.

Saturday, January 7th, 2017

GODZILLA VS. THE SMOG MONSTER
(ゴジラ 対 ヘドラ / *Gojira tai Hedora*; a.k.a. **GODZILLA VS. HEDORAH**)

Japan, 1971. D: Yoshimitsu Banno

Ad-lines: *"Creature of Slime and Sludge Spawned by Pollution's Poison Threatens to Destroy the Earth!"* – *"Out of Pollution's Depths It Slithers! Breathing Poison…Leaving a wake of deadly slime… Destroying all in its path!"* – *"Our environment is doomed!"*

Due to all the rampant pollution in the sea, a hideous amphibious muck-monster named Hedorah (ヘドラ) is born from out of the filth. It resembles a gigantic lump of shit and, what's more, it also even hurls giant turd-balls at its adversaries! This excremental monstrosity, of course, proves no match for our hero monster Godzilla, and it quickly, uh, runs away, scared for its life. But the monstrous villain proceeds to incorporate even more pollution into its system, then transforms into a titanic flying turd to launch further attacks on humanity. In typical Western movie fashion (some shots reveal such an influence), because Tokyo just ain't big enough for the both of them, there will be a showdown between the two titular monsters in the final reel. Which one will emerge victorious…?

This one is unique in that it introduced an all-new monster as its menace (the previous entries always reused monsters from older films), and although the budget and shooting schedule were notoriously small (this was shot in a mere 35 days on an estimated budget of $250,000), the shortcomings don't actually show, since said monster actually looks great (all scatological jokes aside, Hedorah is my favorite baddie monster in the series). What also look great are the opening titles (Toho seems to have gone beyond the call of duty with their designs here), although the overall 'hippie' sensibilities prove to be lacking when a scene down at the beach introduces us to some flower kids dancing awkwardly to a rock band. Also, although this is PG-rated fare, the imagery is occasionally rather gruesome (often due to the treatment of its ecologically-conscious subject matter). Overall, if you can imagine 1970s Troma producing a clone of **THE BLOB** (1958, USA, Ds: Irvin S. Yeaworth, Jr., Russell S. Doughten, Jr.), you'll have a pretty good idea of what this feels like. I watched the original Japanese version (with English subtitles) at 2.35:1 (in color), but monster kids in the U.S. of A. were introduced to it via the Americanized version released by Samuel Z. Arkoff (entitled **GODZILLA VS. THE SMOG MONSTER**), which wasn't too different from the original. Sadly, executive producer Tomoyuki Tanaka was so dissatisfied with the direction of Yoshimitsu Banno (who also penned the screenplay with Takeshi Kimura) that the latter's plans for a sequel to be set in Africa were consequently cancelled.

Tuesday, January 10th, 2017

GODZILLA VS. GIGAN
(地球攻撃命令　ゴジラ対ガイガン / *Chikyū Kōgeki Meirei: Gojira tai Gaigan*; **GODZILLA ON MONSTER ISLAND**)

Japan, 1972. D: Jun Fukuda

Ad-lines: *"Space Monsters War with Godzilla for the Earth!"* – *"Alien Monsters Threaten to Destroy Mankind!"*

Hostile space aliens are—predictably enough—planning the overthrow and domination of Earth once again, this time by taking on the forms of our dead, also conspiring to bring King Ghidorah (キングギドラ / *Kingu Gidora*) and Gigan (ガイガン / *Gaigan*) to their aid in the process. Godzilla is quick to realize this, so he sends his friend Anguirus (アンギラス / *Angirasu*) from **GODZILLA RAIDS AGAIN** [1955]) to check on what's up. In case you are wondering how, let me tell you that this time out the two

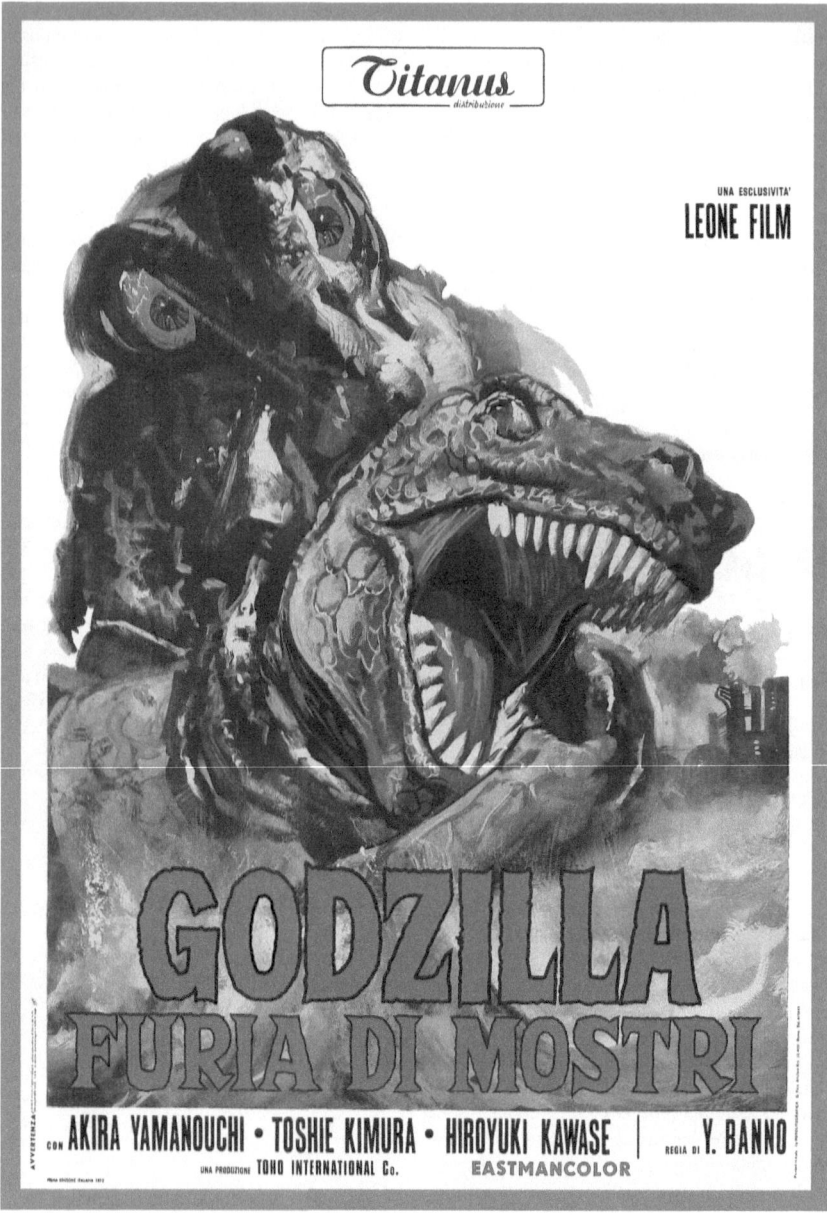

Italian *due-fogli manifesto* for **GODZILLA VS. THE SMOG MONSTER** (1971)

monsters communicate with each other in their own strange language, which is translated into Japanese in comic book-style word balloons. The problem is that the Japanese forces mistake Anguirus' good intentions for bad ones and send the well-intentioned monster on his way. Godzilla will have none of that, and he allies with his spiny buddy Anguirus for a big battle against the baddies King Ghidorah and Gigan. Which monster duo will win and what will be left of the miniature sets once they get through…?

This magazine covers plenty of monster movies in which suspense is built up—until you see the disappointing creature(s) in the end and they blow it. But the film under review is the exact opposite, as in the second half you actually get *too much* monster action (probably more than you would have asked for, anyway); although, unfortunately, the monster designs are nothing to write home about. However, the lengthy destruction sequence during the spectacular conclusion is amazing, to say the least (possibly the finest half-hour the franchise had to offer in the early 1970s), and it works well for the big payoff. If you can imagine a movie with poor-looking monsters that nonetheless wreak some spectacular havoc, you'll have a good idea of what this looks like. The first half is curious, though, as it resembles a spy film (complete with a confusing 'devil-may-care' plot that goes nowhere), which is none-too-surprising considering the successes of the James Bond movies at the time. Another peculiarity is that Godzilla actually *bleeds* herein (yes, there is brief gore to be seen), which makes sense since this was made in 1972 (but not too much if you consider its mild PG rating).

I had the opportunity of watching an excellent 2.35:1 widescreen color print of the original Japanese version (with English subtitles), but stateside monster kids caught up with this in an Americanized version entitled **GODZILLA ON MONSTER ISLAND**, which was mildly different.

Wednesday, January 11th, 2017

GODZILLA VS. MEGALON

(ゴジラ対メガロ / *Gojira tai Megaro*)

Japan, 1972. D: Jun Fukuda

Ad-lines: *"Underground horrors attack!"*

"I fell into a burning ring of fire / I went down, down, down / And the flames went higher / And it burns, burns, burns / The ring of fire / The ring of fire..." |– from "Ring of Fire" (1963), by Johnny Cash. (The lyrics to this song are appropriate to this review, which you may understand only if you have seen the ending, and which I shall not reveal, as we *do not* do such unethical things as that in this mag.)

Due to further nuclear action on the part of irresponsible governments, the creatures of the Monster Island are once again awakened, including Rodan (ラドン / *Radon*), Anguirus (アンギラス / *Angirasu*), and Godzilla, but only the latter remains for the rest of the film. Meanwhile, the cult of Seatopia, which has suffered aplenty due to humans' polluting ways, seeks revenge against

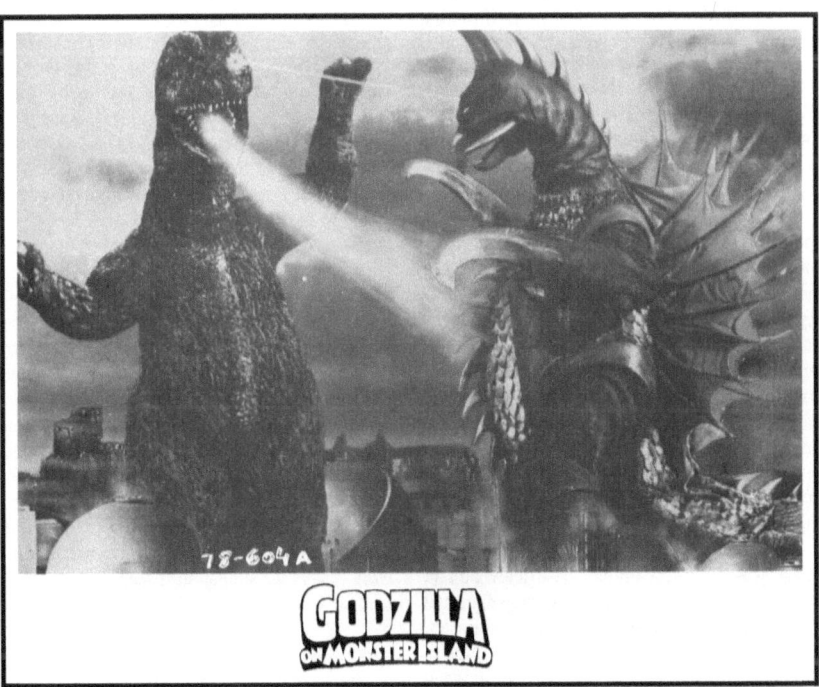

US lobby still for **GODZILLA VS. GIGAN** (1972) under its alternate stateside release title

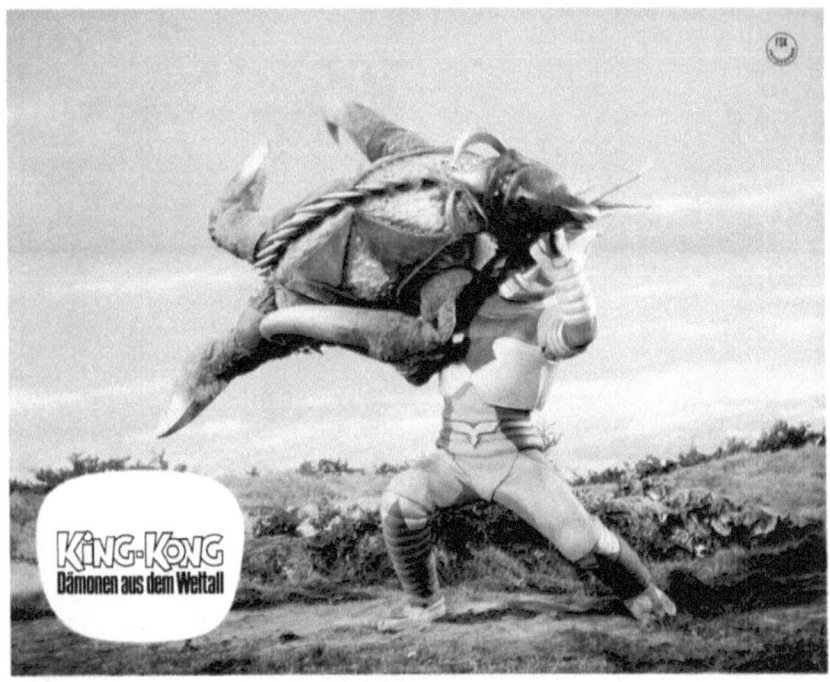

Oh, those German film promoters and their deceptive lobby cards! This time it's one for **GODZILLA VS. MEGALON** (1972), for which Kong only appears in the title yet again. *Why?* Simple: because this card showing Jet Jaguar giving Gigan the ol' heave-ho is for a mid-'70s release intended to cash-in on "Dinokongmania", that's why

us, and for this they invoke their monstrous deity Megalon (メガロ / *Megaro*), who is positively *gleeful* about wreaking major havoc on Earth. Luckily, our planet has the answer in the form of Professor Goro Ibuki (Katsuhiko Sasaki), his nephew Rokuro (Hiroyuki Kawase) and his buddy Hiroshi Jinkawa (Yutaka Hayashi), who control an awesome-looking humanoid robot called Jet Jaguar (ジェットジャガー / *Jettojagā*) that can fly and perform all sorts of other amazing feats. But the good robot is no match for the marauding monster, so Godzilla is required to lend it an assist. The people of Seatopia will have none of that, though, and they employ the services of the Nebula aliens, who in turn bring on the wrath of Gigan (ガイガン / *Gaigan*, last seen in **GODZILLA VS. GIGAN** [1972]). Which monstrous duo will win and what will be left of Japan…?

There was a contest on Japanese television in which the best drawing out of those submitted by kids would be turned into a film character, and Toho's reps went for Jet Jaguar (originally christened "Red Arone" by the kid that designed it, and pretty much resembling Ultraman [ウル

トラマン / *Urutoraman*] or one of his family). However, the initial film that was to be called "JET JAGUAR VS. MEGALON" did not sit well in the development stages, so Godzilla was brought aboard. As everyone who has seen the film knows, however, there isn't much Godzilla action to be seen in it, and this is indeed still primarily a Jet Jaguar flick…and, frankly, not a very *good* one at that.

At least Jet Jaguar looks amazing, as do his monster opponents too. Gigan's blade-like claws are fascinating, and Megalon's driller hands never fail to impress, but all the monster action is saved for the very end, and the rest of the torturous length consists of a dull spy-like plot—that goes nowhere—featuring some of the least-exciting car chase scenes that 1970s cinema ever produced (remember, this was the era of the Italian cop thrillers and actioners, whose dynamic stuntwork makes the subpar stuff seen herein pale by comparison).

I had the opportunity to view a gorgeous widescreen (2.35:1) color print of the original Japanese version (with English subtitles) that was so clean and clear that the wirework was visible on more than one occasion. The print that I saw makes the film look better than it deserves, because the cinematography by Yuzuru Aizawa (from Kurosawa's **THE BAD SLEEP WELL** [悪い奴ほどよく眠る / *Warui yatsu hodo yoku nemuru*, 1960, Japan]) resembles a 1960s film, making this—presumably intentionally?—appear at least a decade older than it actually is. **GODZILLA VS. MEGALON** was obviously made with children in mind as its audience, and the soundtrack by Riichirō Manabe (**GODZILLA VS. HEDORAH** [1971]) is incredibly cartoonish; so much so that sometimes it at times becomes inappropriately silly. And what's more, any attempt at drama fails miserably. On a positive note, though, Godzilla does bleed again, and so does one of the human actors, which may not be too surprising considering this was made in 1972, but it is surprising enough for a PG-rated film (although the Americanized version opted for brief cuts in order to achieve that rating).

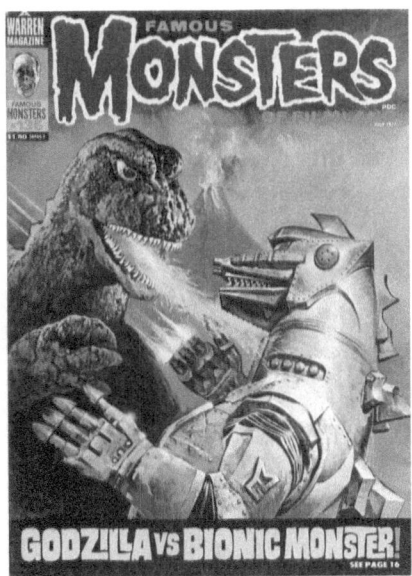

Basil Gogos' spectacular cover art for *Famous Monsters of Filmland* #135

Thursday, January 12th, 2017

GODZILLA VS. MECHAGODZILLA

(ゴジラ 対 メカゴジラ / *Gojira tai Mekagojira*)

Japan, 1974. D: Jun Fukuda

Ad-lines: *"Mechanical Titan of Terror!"* – *"Put the Monster to the Metal!"*

Masahiko Shimizu (Kazuya Aoyama) discovers an alien metal—the sound of it made me think of heavy metal bands who play music that is not of this world—which he demonstrates to Professor Hideto Miyajima (Akihiko Hirata from **GODZILLA** [1954]). It is then that the film goes ape-shit bananas with archaeological expeditions and another spy movie-like subplot that leads straight to nowhere.

However, things do get better when a monster that looks like Godzilla arises to create mass-destruction in Japan; which is peculiar, to say the least, as we have come to understand that The Big G is a goodie monster (at least in the then-most-recent of his films), and his former comrade-at-arms the monster Anguirus a.k.a. Angilas (アンギラス / *Angirasu*) is equally as surprised as we are by the unexpected development. Fear not, though, G-fans, as the real deal shortly shows up, and the previously-seen 'baddie' version turns out to be an alien-controlled impostor which, beneath its deceptive covering of *faux* lizard-skin is in reality a machine: complete with rocket-launching fingers, laser beam-shooting eyes, and other extravagant technological gizmos that blow our minds! What's more, the human-sized aliens that control the rampaging robot monster

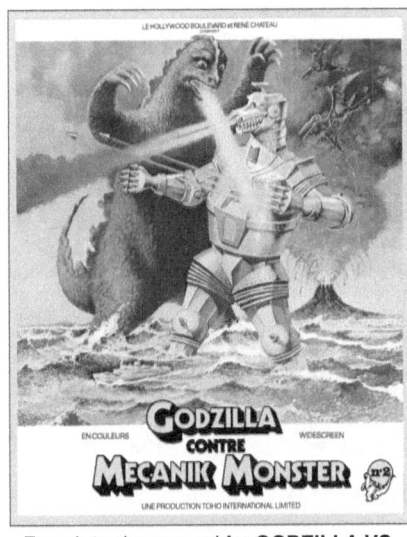

French tradepaper ad for **GODZILLA VS. MECHAGODZILLA** (1974)

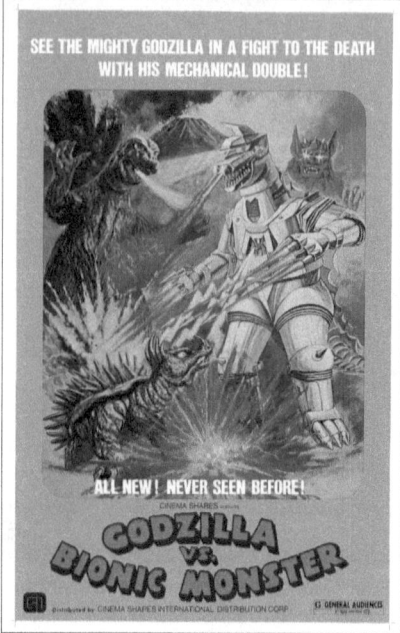

US one-sheet poster for **GODZILLA VS. MECHAGODZILLA** (1974)

have the ability to transform into apemen—shades of anthropoid supervillain Dr. Gori (ゴリ博士 / *Gori Hakase*) in the TV show *Spectreman* (スペクトルマン / *Supekutoruman*, 1971-72, Japan)—usually when they are just about to croak. Plus, they also bleed *green* blood! Luckily for him (and us!), Godzilla has the formidable leonine godmonster King Caesar (キングシーサー / *Kingu Shīsā*) in his corner to help him deal with this new threat, which is essentially yet another of the many would-be alien invasions he thwarted over the course of his lengthy career.

Sure, the monster designs here are impressive enough, but too much time is wasted on humans talking at each other whilst traveling aboard an ocean-going vessel, and this is seldom a sign of good drama (just look at all the other 'shipboard' movies that were total duds, including Amando de Ossorio's third *Blind Dead* entry **THE GHOST GALLEON** [*El buque maldito*, a.k.a. **HORROR OF THE ZOMBIES**, 1974, Spain], starring Jack Taylor, and James Cameron's major sinker **TITANIC** [1997, USA], starring Leonardo DiCaprio).

Although it was released in Japan with loads of fanfare from Toho—largely because it was their franchise's 20th Anniversary—the Americanized version (which had a quite a few alterations made to it) that originally went out under the title **GODZILLA VS. THE BIONIC MONSTER** and then as **GODZILLA VS. THE COSMIC MONSTER**—after the producers of *The Six Million Dollar Man* (1974-78, USA) took exception to the earlier title's unauthorized usage of the copyrighted then-topical buzzword "bionic"—failed to generate too much attention among the kids it was targeted at.

Saturday, January 14th, 2017

TERROR OF MECHAGODZILLA
(メカゴジラの逆襲 / *Mekagojira no Gyakushū*)

Japan, 1975. D: Ishirō Honda

Ad-lines: *"Metal meets Monster." – "From a black hole in space... They came to conquer Earth!"*

This is a direct follow-up to the preceding film, in which Interpol employs the services of the Akatsuki submarine in order to search for the remains of the titular robot monster Mechagodzilla (メカゴジラ / *Mekagojira*) that will hopefully lead them to its alien inventors. Instead, they come across an equally-evil *daikaiju* beastie known as Titanosaurus (チタノザウルス / *Chitanozaurusu*). The problem with **TOM** is that a *lot* of the action plays-out inside the submersible, and since this is no **DAS BOOT** (1981, West Germany, D: Wolfgang Petersen), the results are often monotonous, to say the least.

Although believed to be dead, Titanosaurus' creator and all-round madman Dr. Shinzō Mafune (Akihiko Hirata from the original **GODZILLA** [1954]) is planning to bring about the end of the world, and in order to do so he conspires with alien leader Mugal (Gorō Mutsumi from **GODZILLA VS. MECHAGODZILLA** [1974]), who in-turn controls the titular robot monster. The malevolent monstrous duo is unleashed on Tokyo, and wholesale havoc is wreaked by them. Will our friendly neighbourhood Godzilla be able to stop them...?

Yukiko Takayama (of **THE TALE OF GENJI: A THOUSAND-YEAR ENIGMA** [源氏物語 千年の謎 / *Genji Monogatari: Sennen no Nazo*, 2011, Japan, D: Yasuo Tsuruhashi]) was the winner of a competition organized by Toho, and his screenplay was turned into this film by returning original director Ishirō Honda. Truth be told, it is in actuality a very *boring* story, especially in the many scenes showing humans endlessly interacting with one another, all of which is somehow redeemed by the spectacular ending with its great destruction footage. It is also occasionally silly (wait until you see the robot surgery scene, and the one with the alien leader whipping his minions in an awkward B&D+S/M moment!), but the occasional snatch-glimpses of greatness—largely thanks to the stunning cinematography by Sokei Tomioka (from **GODZILLA VS. MECHAGODZIL-LA**)—really save the day; the last shot in particular (depicting Godzilla in the ocean waters) is a real work of art, and it makes a fittingly poignent end for the Showa era.

I had the pleasure of watching the original Japanese version (with English subtitles) at 2.35:1. It proved a box-office flop in Japan, and it was released theatrically only briefly in the USA under the title **THE TERROR OF GODZILLA**. Fear not though, as Toho would be back with a vengeance in less than ten years... but *that* is a story I shall be saving until next issue. Be there or be stomped!

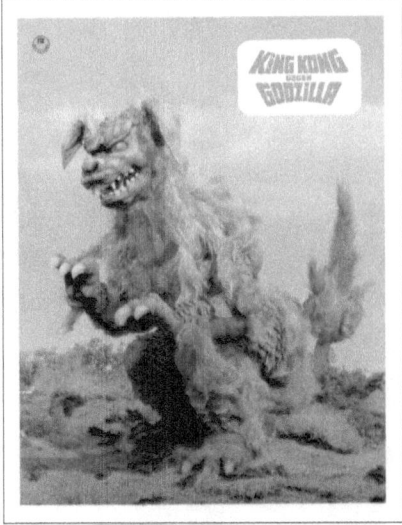

Below: Japanese lobby card for **GODZILLA VS. GIGAN** (1972)

Another misleading German lobby card, this one for **GODZILLA VS. MECHAGODZILLA** (1974). At least Godzilla is in the title, and King Caesar *kinda* looks like King Kong... well, he's a *mammal* with *hair* at least, anyway!

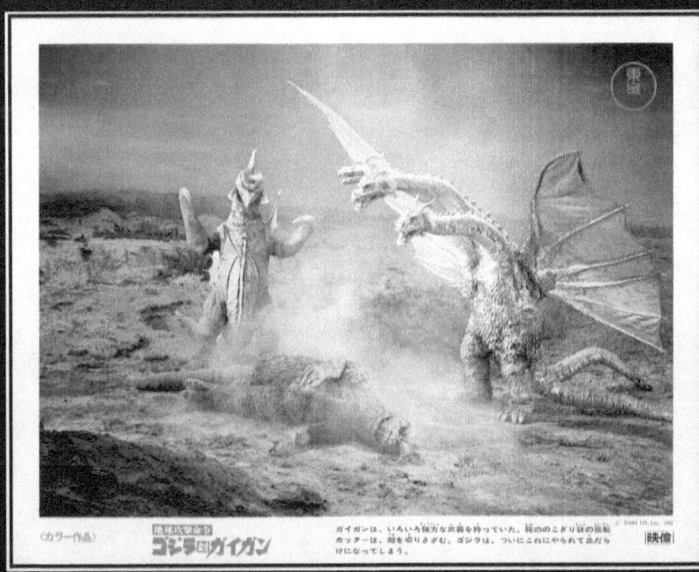

Y'all be sure to come back for Monster! *#34, in which "Son of My Monster Movie Marathon Diary" (essentially, Part 6 of your all-time favorite column) will present you with a newbie (i.e., Yours Truly)'s film-by-film overview of the* Godzilla *series' Heisei Era (1984-1995) and Millennium Era films (1999-2004), along with other assorted goodies besides!*

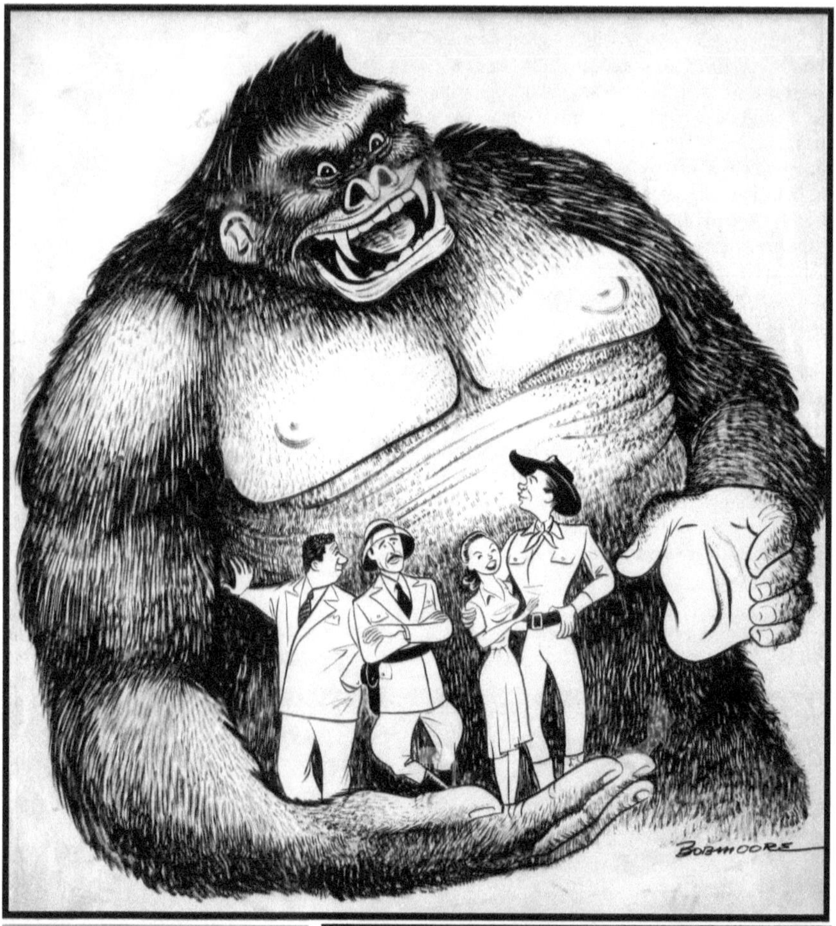

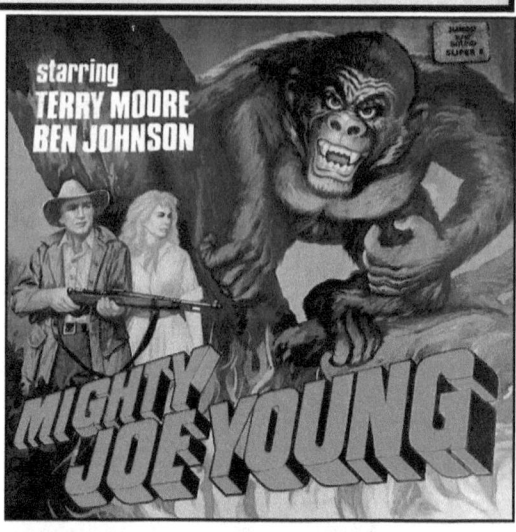
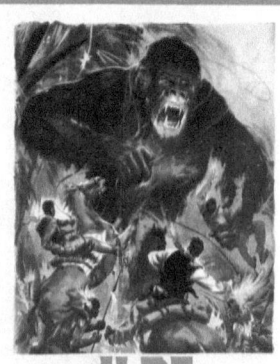

Top: Bob Moore caricature promo art for **MIGHTY JOE YOUNG** '49. **Above:** 400ft sound Super 8 film box. **Left:** MJY's Italian *locandina*; art unsigned

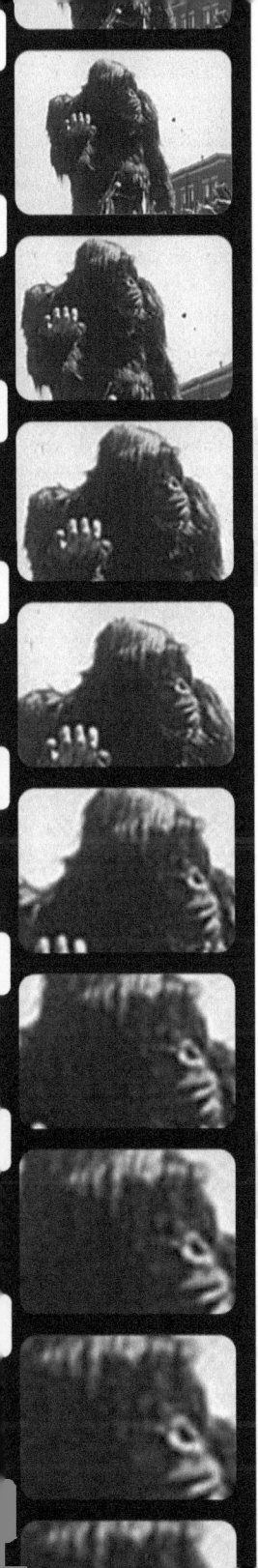

MONSTER! ROADSHOW:
Recently Discovered 8mm Footage Makes a Monkey Out of *M!*

by Stephen R. Bissette & Mark Nelson

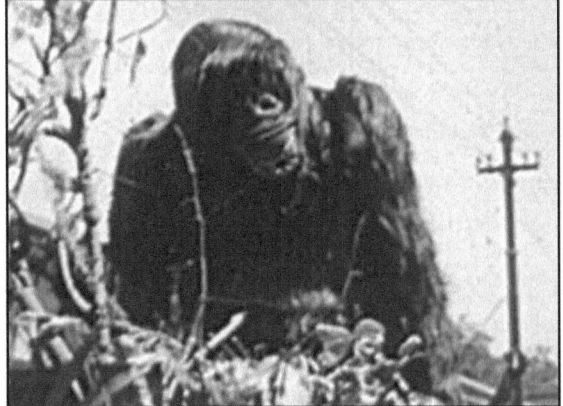

Did Mighty Joe Young visit Massachusetts in 1949? *Read on!*

In June 2017, Mark Nelson's day-job dropped some never-before-publicly-seen home movie footage into his lap that showed a gigantic animated monster gorilla. He was gobsmacked. Using the internet to 'tap' yours truly on the shoulder to say, "Hey, look at *this!*" Mark wrote:

> "Transferred some 8mm from 1949 the other day for a client, and came across a short clip of a giant Kong-looking 'robot' in a city street. Have you heard of anything like this?"

Have a look at the frame grabs yourself, shown here for the first time anywhere. With the kind permission of the living owner of the 8mm footage, we present these images and the following.

The proprietor of the 8mm footage, who shall remain nameless, told Mark that the footage "was shot by her father, who died long ago. He was stationed all over the world in the military, but she did say he was in MA for a while."

We scrambled to try and find out where and when the monster ape movie footage may have been filmed. "Pretty sure the reel was labeled as Fitchburg, MA, 1949," Mark noted, "but I could be wrong. I'll upload the video in a few so you can see it in motion… the film box said Fitchburg, MA on it, but that might have been referencing other material earlier on the reel. The majority of the reels were shot in Europe, but this all seemed to be domestic footage surrounding the damn dirty ape".

Monster! Roadshow Mystery

My first-best guess was that this would have been an elaborate promotional stunt to ballyhoo the local release of RKO's **MIGHTY JOE YOUNG** (1949)—the year would be correct, and it's also possible the robotic giant ape wasn't constructed for the promotion, but an acquisition, repurposed for promotional purposes. I know of at least a couple of giant-size 'animatronic' gorillas that existed in the 1930s and 1940s, having seen photos and diagrams of them in vintage back issues of *Popular Mechanics* and similar digest-format science-and-invention "do it yourself" magazines. I've a few photos in my collection of the giant ape mechanical animatronic built for the May 1933 Chicago World's Fair, and there's a photo of that mechanized simian on page 77 of *Modern Mechanix and Inventions*' June 1933 issue (see pp.239, 241-242+247 of this ish of *M!*).

"That's what I figured, that this was **MJY** promo," Mark replied, "and the person who filmed it just casually assumed it was *[King]* Kong."

Upon double-checking what was actually written on the film reel box, Mark noted, "The film box was marked 'King Kong,' but I think that was more a point of reference, for the shooter (might not have retained the *[MIGHTY JOE YOUNG]* film title, but knew what to call a giant ape) than an accurate account of what the Mech-Ape was promoting.... There's also the possibility that the '1949' I noted was the expiration date on the Kodak box, as I haven't had a chance to get back to the camera shop to verify that date was written on it by the shooter."

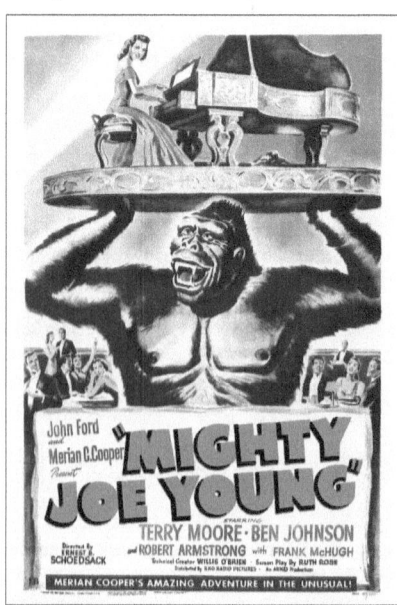

US one-sheet poster; art unsigned

Then again, if 1949 *isn't* the year of the filming, well, all bets are off!

It *is* possible that the giant ape was on display to promote one of RKO's many theatrical rereleases of **KING KONG**. RKO reissued **KING KONG** theatrically *four* times in the 1940s and '50s: 1942, 1946, 1952 and 1956, and one time earlier, in 1938, which is when the cuts to appease the by-then-heavily-enforced Motion Picture Code were made.

While I can say with some conviction that Mark and I are pretty sure **MIGHTY JOE YOUNG** would have been the tie-in *[You'd win that bet!* ☺ *– Mongo McGillicutty]*, it's entirely possible the big gorilla was just a touring big gorilla—or perhaps touring to promote a circus coming to town.

****

Taking a different approach to hopefully identifying the where-and-when of the 8mm footage, Mark scrutinized the footage for clues having nothing to do with the Mech-Ape or what film it might have been promoting. "I did grab another still of a fleeting glimpse of downtown signage, in case anyone could use that to pinpoint the location…"

Take a look at the frame grabs yourself, and let us know if anything rings a bell for you, *Monster!* reader. There is a downtown Dreamland Theatre (spelled with an 're', not 'er') visible in the 8mm footage, the only easily visible landmark that might provide a clue as to where this mechanical monster ape was making such a splash. While the Dreamland Theatre marquee is readily visible in the footage, no other downtown business signage can be discerned—the names are only partially visible, at best—and it's almost impossible to narrow down precisely where in North America this footage was originally filmed.

An online search turned up a few possibilities, but none of them in Fitchburg, MA. Curiously enough, the *Jungle Jim* monster entry **KILLER APE** (1953) was visible on the marquee in a photo accompanying an online listing for the long-defunct Dreamland Theater (note 'er'!) in Lorain, Ohio, closer to Tim Paxton's stomping grounds. "This was a neighborhood theater on Broadway," *cinematreasures.org* writes. "It opened in 1917. It suffered damage from a fire August 18, 1947 and reopened April 7, 1948. It closed in the mid-1980's and now serves as a church."[1] Digging deeper on the Cinema Treasures website, I found evidence of two Dreamland Theaters in Massa-

---

1 http://cinematreasures.org/theaters/10895

chusetts: one now closed (Lynn MA), one still open (Nantucket), but no theater by that name in Fitchburg. The Lynn closed in 1929. There used to be a Boston theater named Dreamland, but that venue changed from Dreamland to another name in 1928.[2] Mark did some searching to determine if it might have been the Nantucket location, but no dice:

"I'm doing a Google Street View for the Nantucket theater, but the area (possibly radically changed since 1949) lacks the tall brick downtown buildings on the side opposite the marquee."

Another online source on movie theaters, *cinematour.com*, listed a Detroit, Michigan Dreamland Theater ("7510-16 Oakland St [CLOSED]") and a Monongahela, Pennsylvania Dreamland Theater (also "CLOSED").

Consulting the listings for "Theatre Circuits in the United States and Canada" in my hard copy of the *1949-50 International Motion Picture Almanac*, we find that year that Dreamland Theatres/Theaters (or just 'Dreamland' or 'The Dreamland') were in Tulsa, Oklahoma (part of Milton Starr's Bijou Amusements Co. chain out of Nashville, TN), Herington, Kansas (part of H.E. Jameyson and Robert M. Shelton's Commonwealth Theatres chain based in Kansas City, MO), Macon, Mississippi (of the Connett Theatres chain out of Newton, Mississippi), Denton, Texas (amid the massive Interstate Circuit, Inc. chain out of Dallas, Texas), and that Lorain, Ohio Dreamland owned of operated by the Dreamland Theatrical Co. (Mrs. Nazera Zegiob, General Manager). There was also the Livermore Falls, Maine 'Dreamland' (part of the Maine & New Hampshire Theatres

---

2 http://cinematreasures.org/theaters/united-states/massachusetts?q=dreamland&status=all

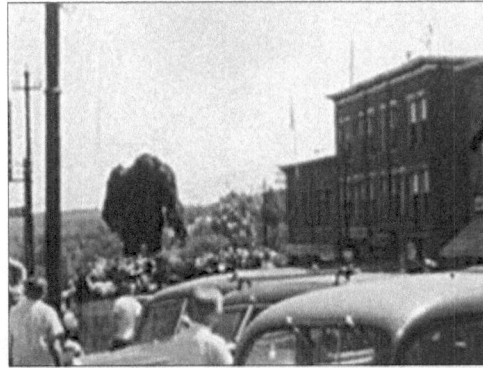

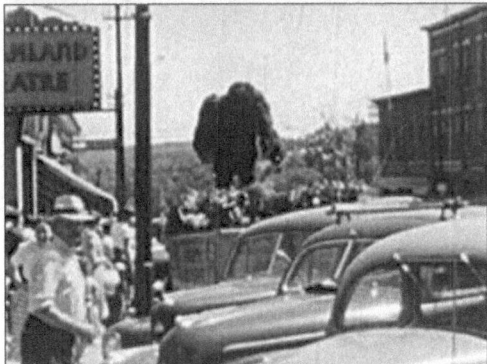

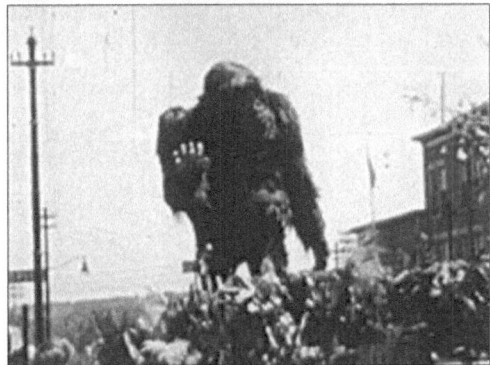

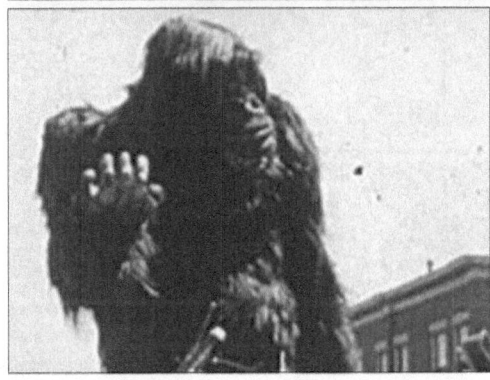

Grainy frame-grabs taken from 8mm showing the 'mystery monkey', which, according to some sources, was a refurbished version of a model originally manufactured by the Messmore & Damon firm of NYC (see following sidebar)

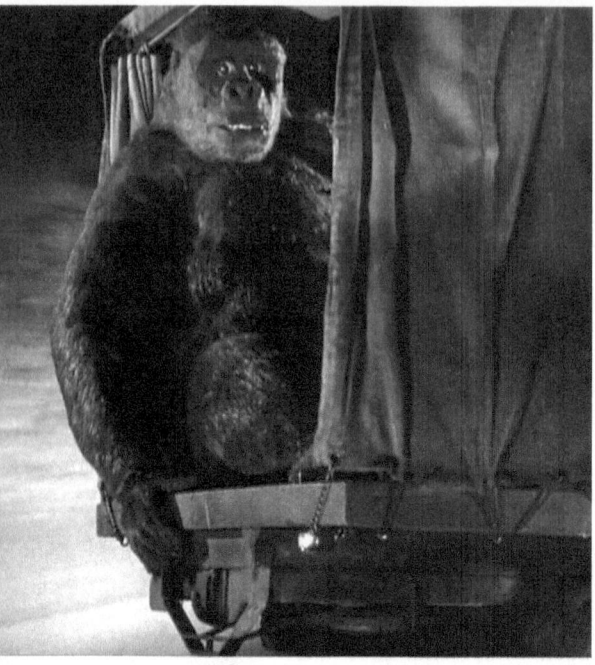

The Truck Stops Here! The 'real' Mighty Joe took rides on no less than two trucks in the actual film itself. But did a mechanical *doppelgänger* of him do likewise to promote his movie, that is the question? **Below:** A die-cut promotional mobile (note that wee hole punched into the very top of it for the string to be threaded through so it could be hung up) and an advance teaser newspaper ad for the film advertising cardboard cut-out Joe masks that were given away *gratis* at some venues

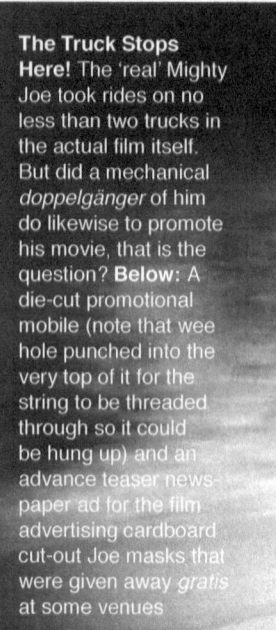

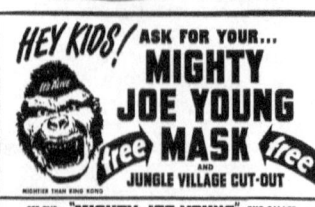

Co. out of Boston, MA, "affiliated with Paramount"); this was one of the theaters specifically cited in the May 3rd, 1948 Supreme Court decision in *United States of America v. Paramount Pictures, et. al.* case and the consent decree.[3] According to *cinematreasures.org*, "The Dreamland Theatre opened about 1908 with live shows and films, then films only. It lasted into the 1960's."[4]

In Canada, there was also the Dreamland in Edmonton, Alberta (part of the Famous Players Canadian Corp., Ltd. chain out of Toronto, Ontario; another Paramount affiliate).[5] According to the *1949-50 International Motion Picture Almanac*, there was not even *one* Dreamland in Massachusetts or New Hampshire.

Then again, the listings only offer the moniker "Dreamland", with no indication whether each was a theat*er* or a

---

[3] *1949-50 International Motion Picture Almanac*, edited by Terry Ramsaye (1949, Quigley Publications): Tulsa, Oklahoma's Dreamland, p.447; Herington, Kansas, and Macon, Mississippi, p.452; Lorain, OH, p.454 (and again on p.491, listed as part of the "Zegiob, Mrs. N, Theatres" chain; Denton, TX, p.464; Livermore, Falls, ME, p.470; Theaters with names that were *close*: the Dream in Fowler, Indiana (p. 442), Dream in Coeur D'Alene, Idaho (p. 482), and Dream in Jeffersonville, Indiana (p. 485). The Livermore Falls, ME Dreamland was cited in the "Paramount and RKO Consent Decrees" on p. 675. The Livermore Falls, Maine 'Dreamland' was also of special interest to me since it was owned by the Maine & New Hampshire Theatres Co. out of Boston, MA, "affiliated with Paramount", who also owned seven theaters in NH and the Flynn and Majestic in Burlington, VT and Capitol in Montpelier, VT—theaters I grew up seeing movies at for most of my childhood and young adult life.

[4] http://cinematreasures.org/theaters/51051

[5] *Ibid.*, Edmonton, Alberta, p. 456

theat*re*. It's possible, too, that "Dreamland Theatre" *wasn't* a MOVIE theater, but rather a live theatre—in which case, we'd be barking up the wrong trees entirely.

A momentary detour: It's astonishing in hindsight how many small town theaters used to operate in North America. Maine had more theaters than almost any other New England state, except for Connecticut, and even the smallest towns seemed to support more than one theater (there were *seven* theaters in little ol' Fall River, Massachusetts). There were other amusements to be found in the search—three theaters named "Cozy," seventeen (17!) named "Manos" (after the owner of the chain; and I bet **MANOS, HANDS OF FATE** never kissed a single one of those screens!), and only one "Kickapoo". My personal favorite theater names from the 1949 listings included a Wisconsin town with two theaters, the "Gay" and "Co-Ed", which is handy; Willamina, Oregon had the "Gay-Way", there were two "Gopher" theaters in Hibbing, Minnesota, and, in Fargo, the Fargo (I hope they lasted long enough to play **FARGO** at the Fargo in Fargo!). I noticed a Wisconsin theater named "Badger"—but have yet to discover a "Woodchuck" in Vermont!—while Beaverton Oregon boasted the "Beaver" theater. *[Circa the early/mid-'70s, there was also an adults-only—if non-XXX—theater called Le Beaver (later just plain Beaver) on Park Ave. in Montreal, Québec! – SF.]* I'm easily amused. Speaking of which, it's kind of amazing how many theaters in 1949 were called "Amusu" (as in '*amuse-you*'; get it?), one was actually called A-Mus-U (in Kosciusko, Mississippi), and another named the Bad Axe *rules*. Morrisville, Vermont (which had the Bijou during my lifetime) had a theater called Tegu (named, not after the lizard, but after chain owner Andrew Tegu of St. Johnsbury, VT), and there was another theater called "Needles" and one named the "Hoo-Hoo" (Gurdon, Arkansas)!—OK, back on task:

Mark took another approach to possibly solving this mystery. "I'm trying to work on the names of the businesses seen on that street," he wrote.

"One I want to say is Myrt's, but 'Kong' obscures one or two letters. Next door is a restaurant/market with Coke signs on either side of the name, but the image isn't sharp enough to make it out. I also see a Krueger Ale sign, though that may not be much of a clue to location. Looking at the blur of the sign/banner on the back of the truck bed that houses 'Kong', I think I see an 'M,' and possibly **MIGHTY JOE YOUNG** on the side. Of course, this might be my mind trying to fool my eyes in making a declaration that I want to believe".

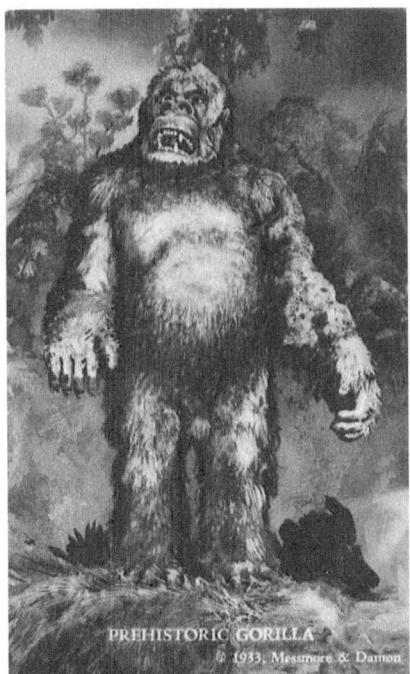

The same make of giant ape as was later used atop the **MJY** publicity truck(s?); souvenir postcard from the '33 Chicago

RKO-Radio's **MIGHTY JOE YOUNG** opened July 23rd, 1949[6]—so unless evidence turns up to the contrary, we're going to stick with our 'best guess' that this supersized animatronic gorilla model was touring the countryside to promote **MIGHTY JOE YOUNG**'s release on a regional basis. *[It is indeed a VERY GOOD guess!* ☺☺ *– Mongo.]* In the end, Mark was resigned to the fact we'll likely never know. "There just didn't seem to be enough concrete evidence (visually) of location to be able to nail where that was", he wrote me in December 2017. "Though the more I look at that truck hauling the MegaMonkey, the more it looks like the **MIGHTY JOE YOUNG** logo from an angle on the banner".

So, the **MIGHTY JOE YOUNG** Mystery Case remains, for now, a *Monster!* mystery…

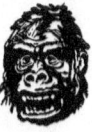

©2018 Stephen R. Bissette and Mark Nelson, all rights reserved; images from the film footage appear with the permission of the original 8mm film owner.

6 *Ibid.*, p. 535

SIDEBAR:

*[/Editors' Note: As an addendum/appendix to Messrs. Bissette & Nelson's preceding item on the theme, we now present further food for thought—which hopefully ain't just 'bananas', Mongo! ☺ —on the subject of **MJY**'s publicity campaign...]*

GOIN' APE OVER *MIGHTY JOE YOUNG*;
or, even a Giant Gorilla Can't Make a Monkey Out of *Monster*!

by Mongo "Missing Link" McGillicutty

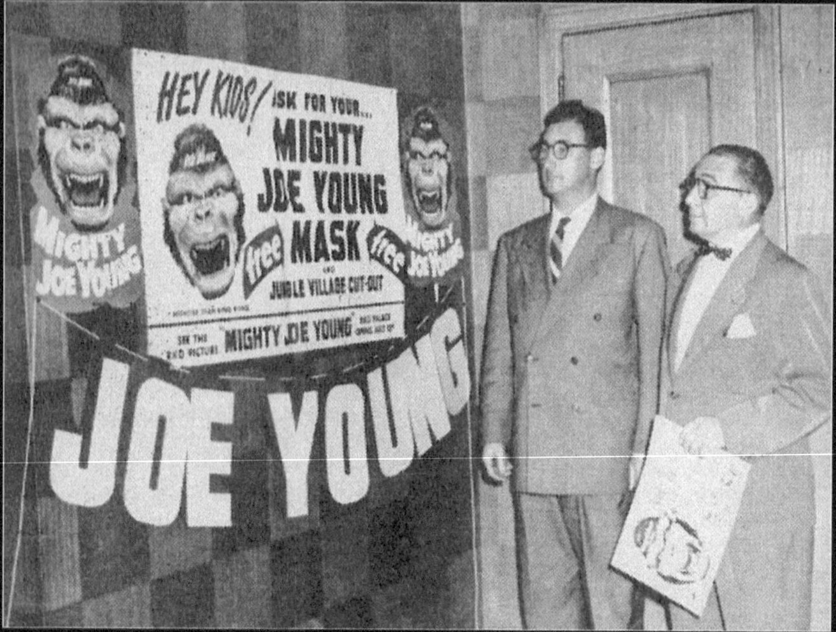

Messmore & Damon, Inc. press item titles (from *Popular Science Monthly* for November 1931 and June 1933 respectively): *"Hidden Motors Give Life to Prehistoric Monsters"* — *"Mechanical Monster 'EATS' Girl on Movie Stage"*

Lyrics from the song-sheet for M&D's 1936 promo jingle "The World a Million Years Ago" (words and music by Kenyon Scott): *"The world a million years ago had dinosaurs that we all know existed from our records of today / The Stegosaurus and his sons the Brontosaurus (forty tons) with Tyrannosaurus... / In eras mesozoic followed by the zenozoic [sic], then dimetrodons and pterodactyls grew..."*

Undated catalogue listing for one of the company's best-known products, which was manufactured by them from 1933—tellingly enough, the year of the original **KING KONG**'s release—up until at least the early 1970s, reportedly: *"Giant*

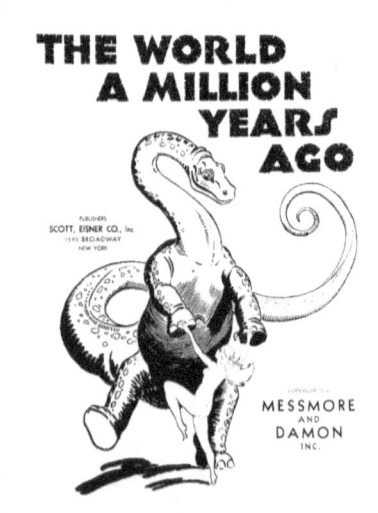

240   *Goin' Ape Over Mighty Joe Young*   Mongo McGillicutty

size mechanical Gorilla swings arms, sways and turns head-
-------$1800.00" (we're not sure when that price dates from,
but it's a hefty sum for any era!)

A souvenir postcard (see illo on p.239) of the original M&D motorized gorilla was sold at the '33 Chicago World's Fair, where the actual figure (and others made by the same company, including various dinosaurs) was featured in its own diorama as part of a then-state-of-the-art exhibition entitled "The World a Million Years Ago". Printed on the card's reverse is the following caption pertaining to the artist's rendering reproduced on its obverse:

"*[The] World a Million Years Ago, Feature Attraction at 'A Century of Progress,' Chicago, 1933. PREHISTORIC GORILLA—PLEISTOCENE PERIOD. This monstrous gorilla is Messmore & Damon's conception of Gorilla Life in the Pleistocene Period, just prior to the arrival of the Java Ape Man.*"

****

History tells us that the looming 10-foot-tall figure—estimates as to its exact height tend to vary somewhat from source to source, though it seems to have been within the 8'-10' ballpark—was manufactured by Messmore & Damon, Inc. of New York City. Demonstrating its quite fluid motorized movements, vintage newsreel footage of the very same ape—nominally implied to be "King Kong" by narrator Joseph Cotten's throwaway line of voiceover (evidently simply because the producers didn't want to spring to rent a clip from the actual movie, so went for a cheaper 'substitute' instead)—appeared in the episode of David L. Wolper's series *Hollywood and the Stars* (1963-64, USA) entitled "Monsters We've Known and Loved"; ironically enough, who should show up in the very next clip after this one than Mr. Joseph Young of Africa himself in an authentic snippet of footage from his own film. *[Those wanting an albeit-only-fleeting if priceless look-see at Messmore & Damon's "Prehistoric Gorilla" in operation might want to check out the upload of said show on YouTube. Simply key-in "Monsters We've Known and Loved" for a link to it.]*

Relatedly, at his post there dated December 24th, 2011 (see first link listed below), Classic Horror Film Board member MovieMatt posted the photograph reproduced hereabouts depicting a group of kids and a dog posing with Messmore & Damon's Giant Gorilla, as well as those photos showing the XL 'dummy' ape (see p.242) used to promote **MJY** the movie atop a van or truck in 1949. At the same post, MovieMatt posited—albeit rather laconically, requiring us to 'read between the lines' a tad—the possibility that a motorized gorilla of the same (or similar) M&D model may have been used as an 'MJY' substitute for promotional purposes…including in the sorts of on-the-street promos described in the Bissette/Nelson piece? While we have no way of knowing at this point how many such ape-topped vans and/or trucks may have been used—presumably just one?—judging by all appearances, it seems a distinct possibility that such a Messmore & Damon-manufactured gorilla was indeed 'cast' as Mighty Joe for the purpose. MovieMatt's post also provides

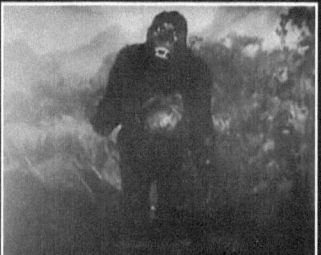
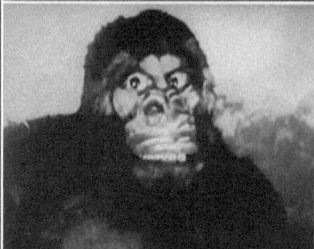
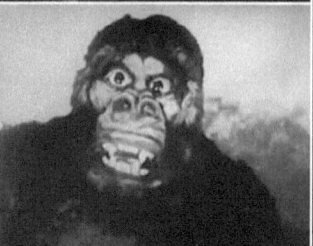
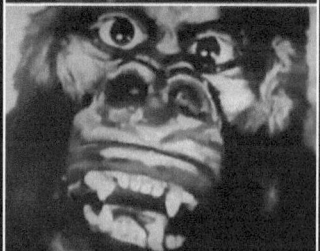
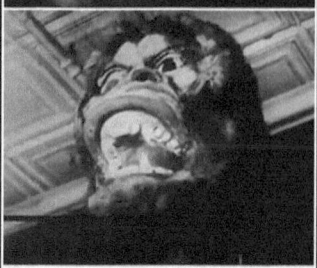

Above: M&D's mechanical gorilla in action, as seen in "Monsters We've Known and Loved". **Preceding Page, Bottom:** Sheet music for the M&D show's '36 jingle

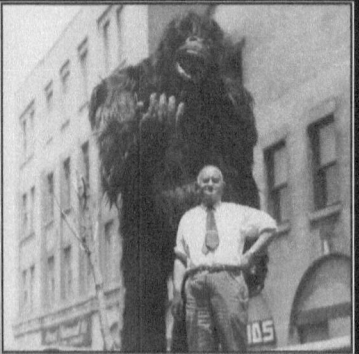

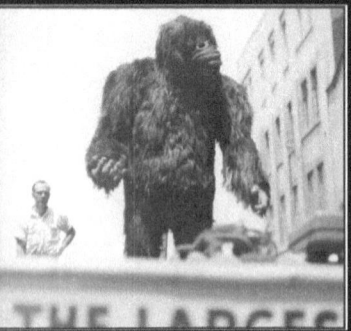

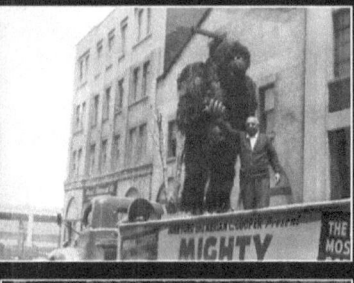

a couple of links (see third and fourth links attached below) to other posts elsewhere (i.e., at the Lagoon History Project [LHP] website, dedicated to historical research concerning Farmington, Utah's Lagoon Amusement Park) that delve further into the 'mighty mystery', which might well run as deep as the deep web itself! Apparently, more than one person 'in-the-know' out there is of the opinion that the **MJY** publicity-drive ape originated at M&D. So we'll leave it at that for now, until such time as any further substantive evidence arises.

****

[And now for some further dope on Messmore & Damon themselves, a subject which might well bear digging deeper into in a future issue of Monster!]**

As per their plug on the back of the same postcard previously quoted-from above, the firm (quote) "...reconstructed life size animated, colossal, prehistoric animals with life-like motions and natural sounds". M&D was founded in 1916 by George H. Messmore and Joseph Damon, and, in regards to their mechanical replicas of animals, the same postcard ad-blurb just quoted also further proclaimed they were the "First to show them inside and outside for exhibition purposes." According to other sources, M&D's products also included mechanized versions of more mundane modern animals, including both an equine (1939's "Horsepower" installation [*"Mechanical Horse Gallops Realistically"*]) and a ruminant (*"Robot Cow Moos and Gives Milk"* [!!]). According to an online article posted on October 28th, 2013 by one Alison Oswald at the site Lemelson Center for the Study of Invention and Innovation (see second link given below), Messrs. Messmore and Damon

[...] *designed and constructed parade floats, dioramas for museums, exhibits for expositions, displays for department stores, scenery, exhibits for corporate clients, and for film, theater, and television. Most of their parade and department store work featured animated mechanical devices.* [They...] *brought to life huge dinosaurs, tigers, mastodons, dragons, other monsters, and even cows. One of their creations was a life-sized (48 feet long, nine feet high, 4,000 pounds) mechanized reproduction of a dinosaur, Amphibious Dinosaur Brontosaurus (aka "Dolores" or "Dino"). It could laugh, breathe, roll its eyes, shake its head, and move its jaws. It was a must see. Created for the Century of Progress International Exhibition (1933-1934), "The World a Million Years Ago," Dino was made of layers*

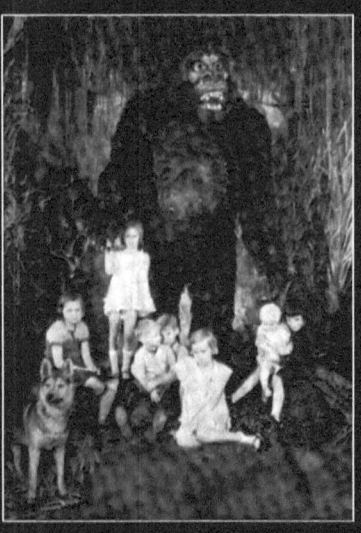

Left, Top 3 Pics: Shots of MJY's truck-top mechanized 'stand-in' during the film's promo push of 1949. (Note the partially-visible movie title on the side of the vehicle in the third pic.) **Left, Bottom:** Photo from Messmore & Damon's sales catalogue, depicting the $1,800 ape mentioned on pages 240-241

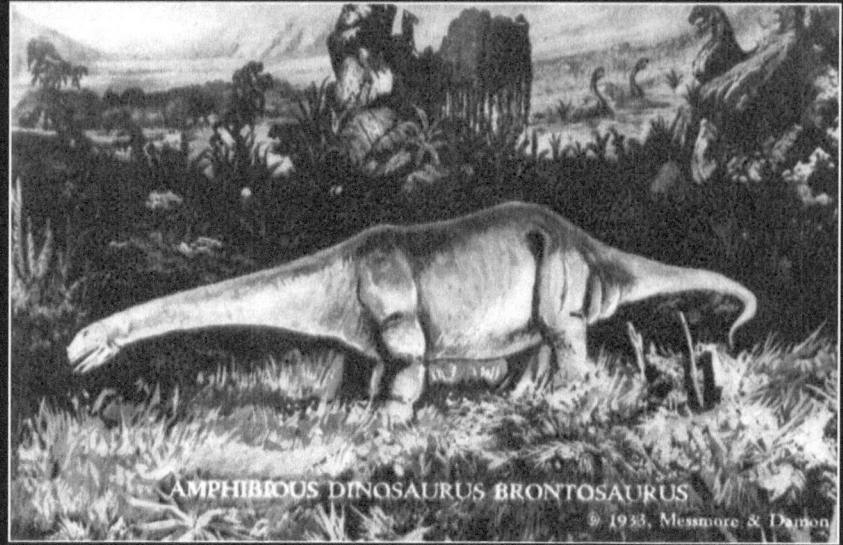

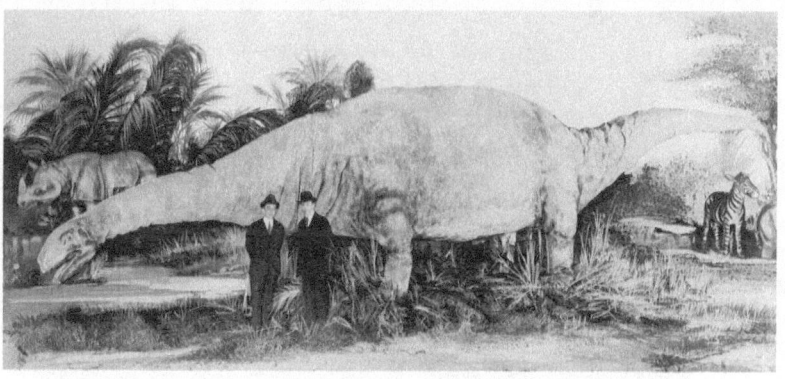

"AMPHIBIOUS DINOSAUR BRONTOSAURUS"
47' IN LENGTH – 9¾' IN HEIGHT – MOVES MECHANICALLY. REQUIRES TEN
MOTORS TO WORK EYES, HEAD, NECK, HIPS, STOMACH, SIDES AND TAIL.
THE ORIGINAL SKELETON IS AT THE AMERICAN MUSEUM OF NATURAL
HISTORY – NEW YORK CITY.   MESSMORE & DAMON - INC.
                                  404-8 W. 27th ST. N.Y.CITY

This Page: A pair of souvenir postcards—the top one an artist's rendering, the other a photograph—depicting one of Messmore & Damon, Ltd.'s dino dioramas at the 1933 World's Fair in Chicago. That's Messrs. M&D themselves standing next to "Dolores" the Brontosaurus in the image directly above. On the left-hand side of page 244 *[from top to bottom]* are depicted cutaway diagrams of the creature's (to quote Zacherle!) 'internal workings'. **Right:** A trade ad for the company from the 1960s. **Following Page, Top & Center Left:** Postcard of the Dimetrodon from "The World a Million Years Ago", and an M&D employee works on the then-unfinished dino's figure

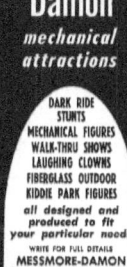

Mongo McGillicutty   *Goin' Ape Over Mighty Joe Young*

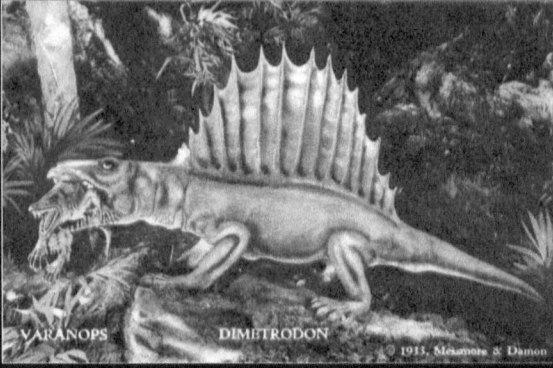
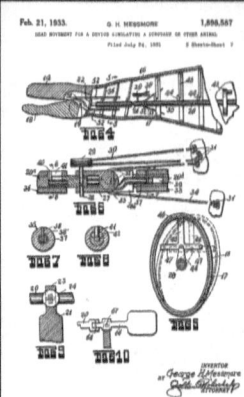
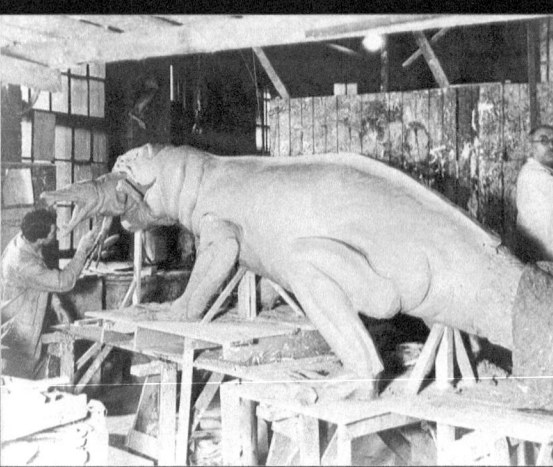
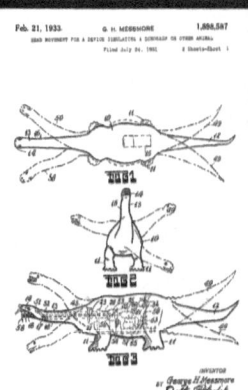
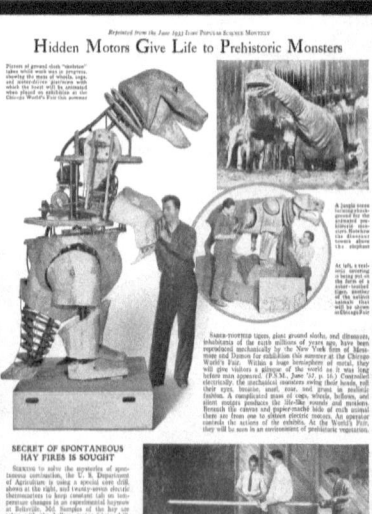
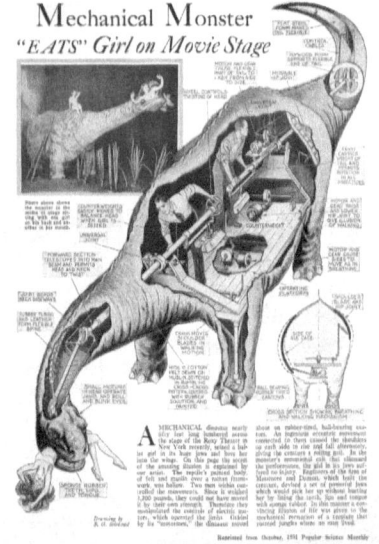

Goin' Ape Over Mighty Joe Young — Mongo McGillicutty

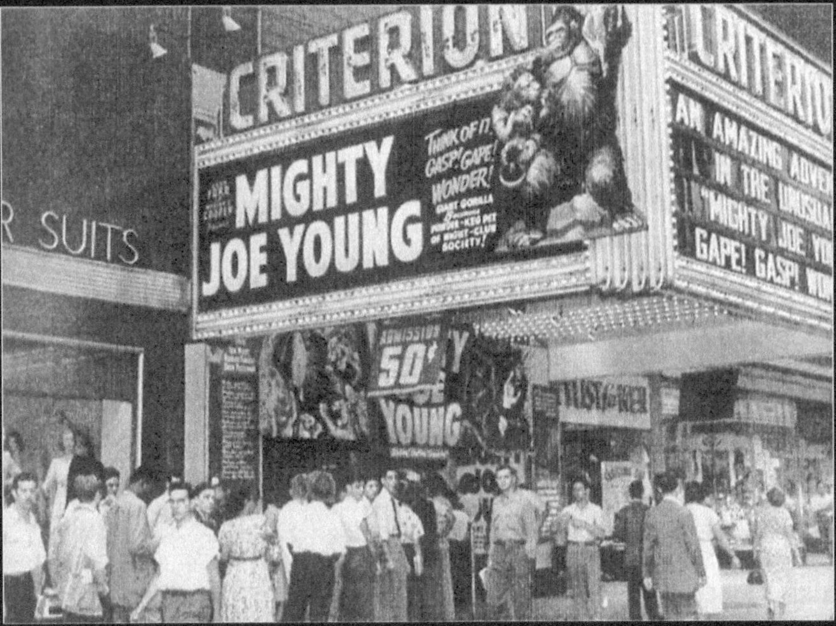

of chicken wire, canvas, rattan, papier-mâché, and paint. A human ran a complicated series of motors, chains, ball bearings, gears, cranks, counterweights, and universal joints that worked in concert to create a spectacular experience. The dinosaur was capable of moving its head in all directions and it had a moveable jaw. George Messmore's 1933 patent (US Patent 1,898,587) stated "the jaw was intended to hold a dancer so that the dancer may be lifted up by the animal for entertaining purposes."

****

In another bit of **MJY**-related hoopla/hyperbole, to promote the film's initial '49 release in New York City, a stunt-person was hired to dress up in a low-rent 'gorilla' suit—complete with sneakers!—and hand-over-hand it across a highwire that was stretched tautly between two local tall buildings especially for the occasion. About this event, of which only sparse documentation seemingly remains extant today, Craig Scott Lamb, co-moderator of the fine, long-running Facebook group Ape Suit Cinema (see fifth link listed below), turned-up a couple of extra tidbits of information—and still more pics, which we reproduce here—at an unnamed French website explaining how it was the manager of a Broadway cinema called the Criterion who staged said choice publicity stunt, much to the surprise and appreciation of a throng of gawping onlookers on the sidewalk far below; unfortunately, neither the names of the monkey-suited daredevil who per-

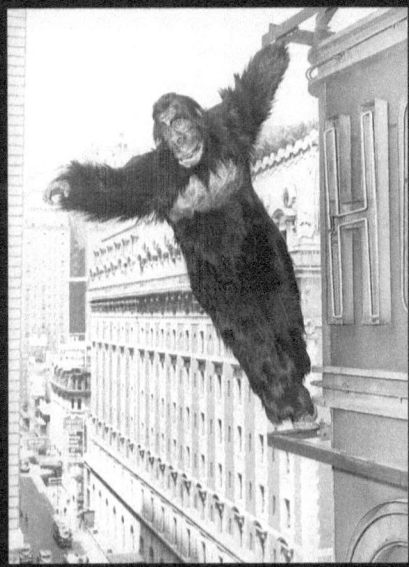

Top: The Broadway theater whose imaginative proprietor—in an act worthy of the movie's impresario Max O'Hara (Robert Armstrong)—staged a spectacular publicity stunt to promote **MIGHTY JOE YOUNG**'s 1949 debut in The Big Apple. **Above:** The stunt's gorilla-suited performer clings precariously to the side of a skyscraper either before or after performing the daring feat. Obviously the running shoes were intended to provide better traction!

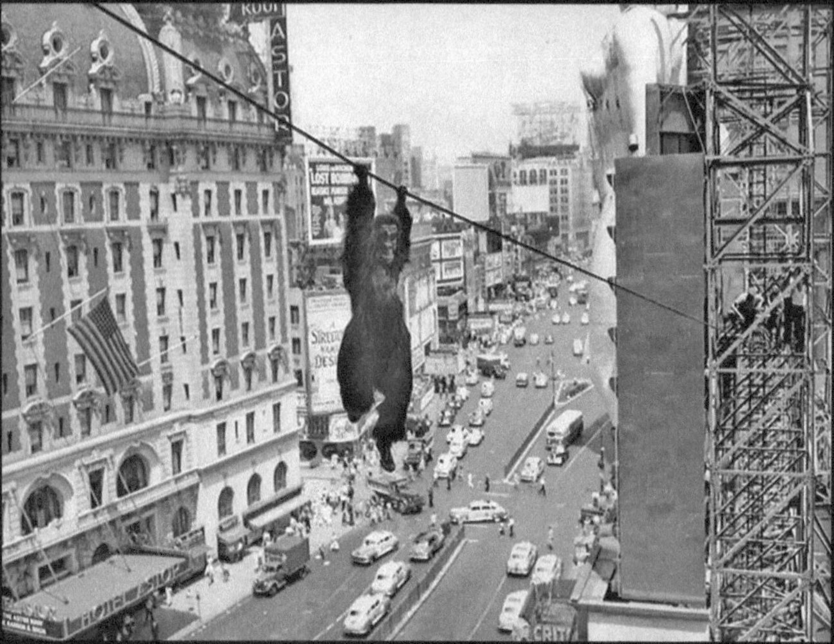

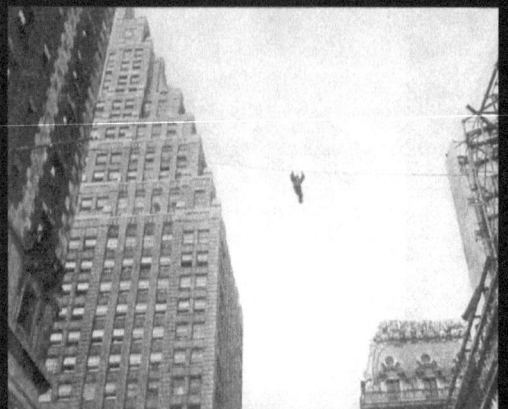

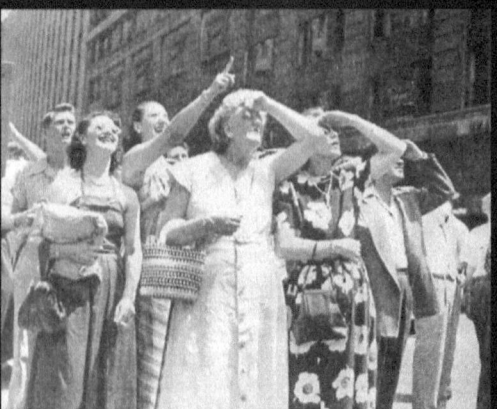

formed the dangerous acrobatic stunt nor the manager of the movie-house were given.

In summation, even back at a time when moviegoers went bananas for ballyhoo in the real, physical world and buzz was generated more by simple word of mouth as opposed to largely 'ethereally' in the online environment, all the advance hyperbole surrounding **MJY** in '49 didn't result in (as per a gag line heard in the movie) "big money for the big monkey", due to the fact that the film was not a massive earner upon its initial release; hence, no "SON OF MIGHTY JOE" was hurried into theaters to capitalize on the new ape on the block's (non-existent) craze, as had happened with 1933's quickie insta-sequel **SON OF KONG** in the immediate aftermath of **KING KONG**'s smash box-office success internationally well over a decade before. While paying punters

Top to Bottom: You'd need nerves of steel and the strength of a gorilla to perform a stunt like this! We can only wonder if a safety net was provided, and whether the performer had decent insurance coverage...*if any!*

of the day didn't exactly throw their dough Joe's way first-run, chiefly due to its numerous TV airings and home video releases, his movie nevertheless did develop into a sizeable fan favorite that proved belatedly profitable in subsequent decades—hence its hit 1998 Disney remake starring Charlize Theron, Bill Paxton and an often-CG Kong (albeit also featuring superlative/state-of-the-art practical gorilla suit work by Rick Baker too). It was the popularity of **MJY** '98 that, for better or worse, helped pave the way for Peter Jackson's entertaining if way-too-overdone **KONG** reboot in 2005.

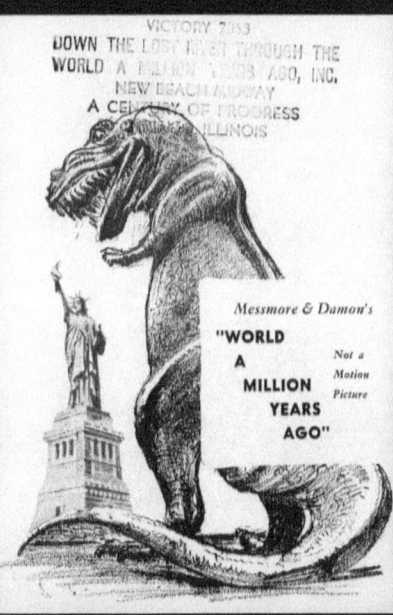

Kaijū **Kong!** Spectacular ballyhoo at the **SON OF KONG** premiere in Taishokan, Asakusa, Japan in 1933. We haven't got a clue what the origins of this giant ape are, but it sure does stand out in a crowd!

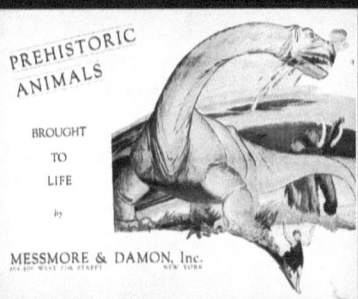

Above & Right: A pair of vintage M&D ad-flyers. **Below:** The dust-encrusted head of M&D's World's Fair '33 gorilla now resides in the collection of pioneering monster kid Don Glut (see seventh link below). *[Image courtesy of his website Don Glut's Dinosaurs]*

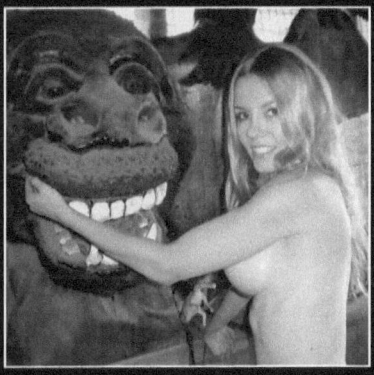

LINKS OF INTEREST:

https://www.tapatalk.com/groups/monsterkidclassichorrorforum/look-what-i-found-t41336.html
http://invention.si.edu/extraordinary-attractions-be-amazed-must-see
http://lagoonhistory.com/project/missing-link-located-in-hairy-heredity/
http://lagoonhistory.com/project/gorilla/
https://www.facebook.com/groups/317964048317049/?ref=br_rs
https://www.aber.ac.uk/en/news/archive/2017/11/title-207857-en.html
http://www.donglutsdinosaurs.com/messmore-damon-giant-gorilla

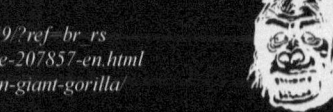

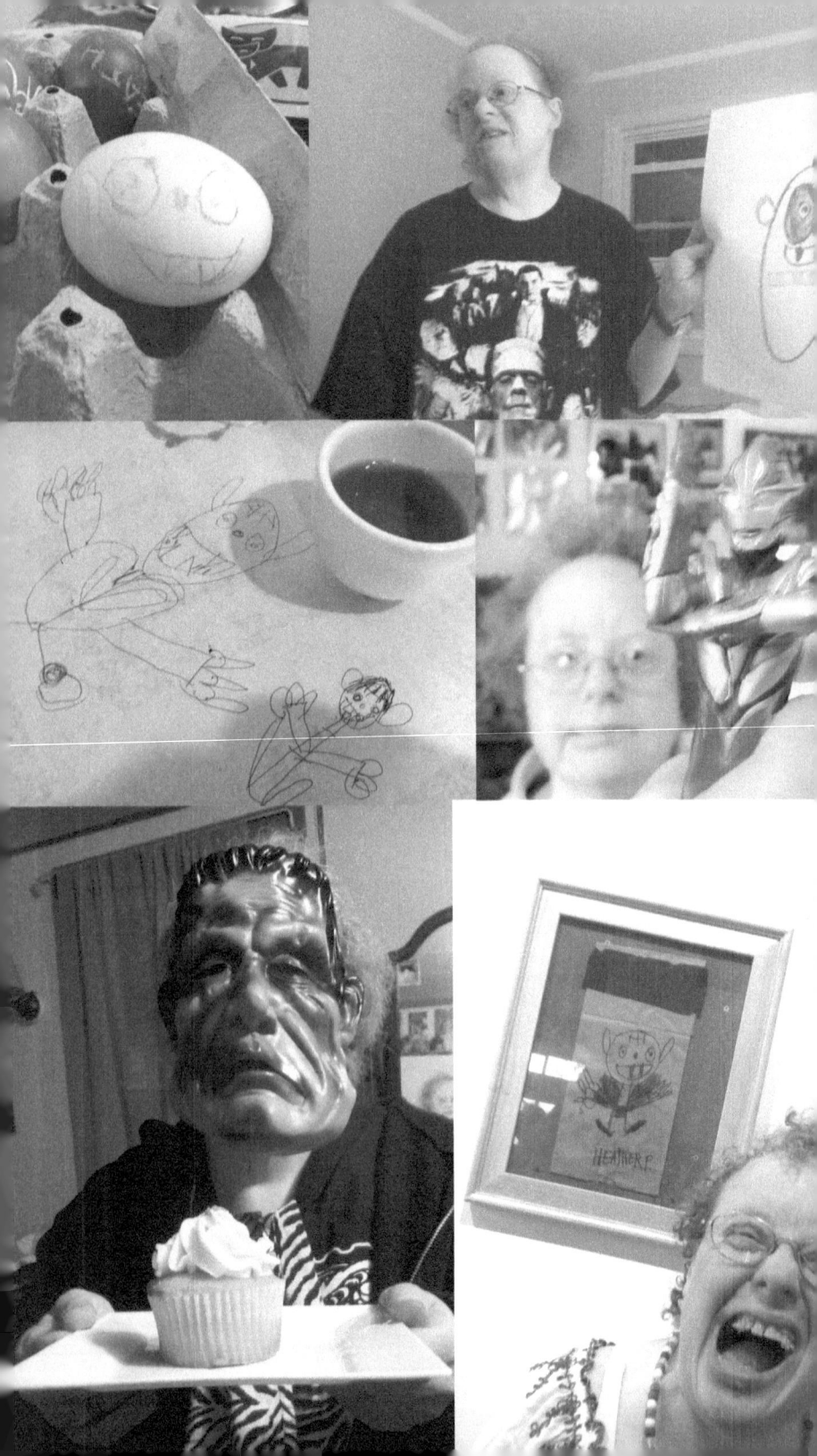

REVIEWS:

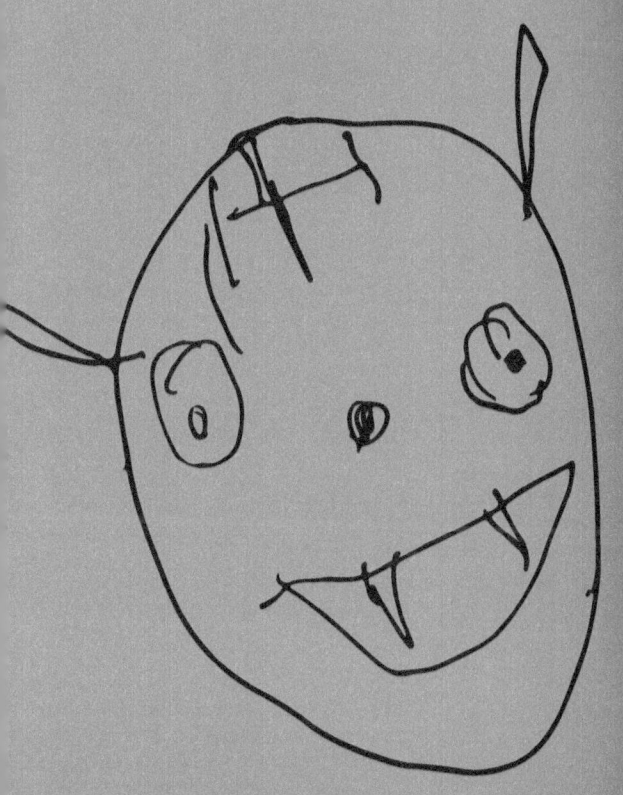

Art by Heather™

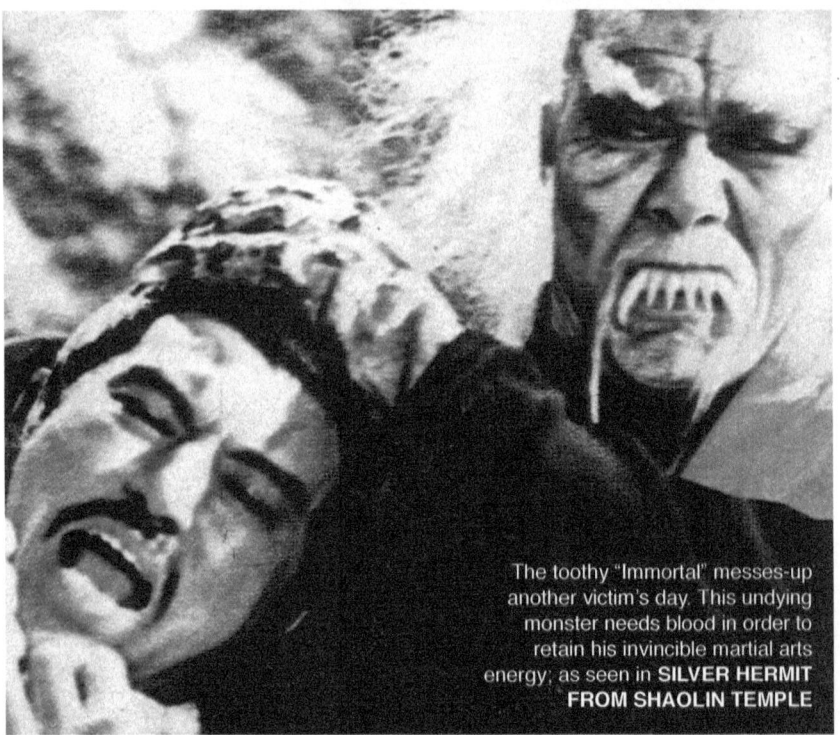

The toothy "Immortal" messes-up another victim's day. This undying monster needs blood in order to retain his invincible martial arts energy; as seen in SILVER HERMIT FROM SHAOLIN TEMPLE

SILVER HERMIT FROM SHAOLIN TEMPLE

(碧血洗銀槍 / *Bi xue si yin qiang*, a.k.a. **THE SILVER SPEAR**)

Reviewed by Steve Fenton

Taiwan, 1979. D: Peng "Roc" Tien

Anglo trailer narration: *"He was framed, trapped by deceit, and his hopes in the future destroyed! His task: to find the guilty party and bring him to justice!"*

(You'd never guess there was actually a monster in this judging by the above hype, which might fit any number of movies with a vengeance theme, whether they be of the MA variety or otherwise. Neither do either of the film's two user reviews at the IMDb mention anything whatsoever about it. But there *is* one to be found in it, so stick with it!)

Just for the record, this is a heavily-revamped (pun most definitely intended, considering the theme!) rewrite/revision of a review I did which first ran in the debut issue (1993) of Colin Geddes' long-gone-but-not-forgotten Far Eastern cinema fanzine, *Asian Eye* (subtitled "The Occidental Tourist's Guide to Oriental Pop Cinema"), for which I contributed slews of reviews over the course of its sadly only brief run; it folded—both figuratively and literally—after issue #2 in 1995, more's the pity.

This period *wuxia* (武俠) chop-socky adventure comes complete with monstrous supernatural ingredients, which adds some extra zing to an otherwise standard yin-versus-yang plotline. Just so long as you don't go in expecting too much, the easily-amused might find some entertainment value in the film, which would likely be pretty much a total dud (or at least far lesser) without its more fantastical content.

As just about everyone and their dog knows by now, for the two or three people out there who might not be aware of the fact, the Hong Kong kung fu renaissance of the early/mid-'70s sparked by the phenomenal smash popularity of Bruce Lee, resulted in tons (and *tons*!) of one-shot cash-ins, as well as plenty of loosely-related martial arts movies released in "series" form (often even when they weren't actually parts of the same series whose names they dropped at all, but merely in-name-only capitalizations). These latter type included—to list only a few of the virtually countless generic subgenres of 'fu flicks—umpteen *One-Armed Boxer/Swordsman, 18 Bronzemen* and *Flying Guillotine* titles (both of the "legit" and illegitimate types). As well as in HK (and elsewhere, for that matter; everybody *was* kung fu-fighting, after all!), Taiwanese producers also hopped on the bandwagon, churning out a whole horde of "imitation" *wuxia* movies of their own, as in the case of the one currently under discussion. Incidentally, in my original version of this review, such was the comparative dearth of readily available data on the subject back in the pre-internet days that I mistakenly guessed both that **SHFST** was not only of HK origin rather than from Taiwan, but produced in 1975 as opposed to some four years later. My, how times have changed since then! Now all it takes is a quick look-see on the IMDb and a minute or so's cross-referencing at the HKMDB to find all the factual details needed. Talk about progress! Also, since my original evaluation of **SHFST**, when I don't think I was paying as close attention as I should have been, and overlooked some details, I have somewhat modified my less-than-favorable opinion of it. Upon looking at it with all-new eyes, I spotted many more positive attributes that I either totally missed or simply ignored the first time round. So consider this my reappraisal, albeit mixed in with much of my old one.

Back in the '80s and '90s, if you were to visit your average well-stocked video rental outlet, chances were good that you might find a specific subsection of the "Action" section proper clearly marked "Martial Arts" (or words to that effect). Back in the day, this would probably have been a confusing jumble of Lee / Chan / Norris / Van Damme / Chiba / Segal / Kosugi titles, "NINJA" this-or-that obscurities, or outright Jackie Chan rip-offs and lame Bruce Lee clones (e.g., Bruce Le and Li, *ad nauseam*. Although, to be fair, nowadays even many so-called substandard Lee imitators have since developed quite faithful fan-bases of their own, it should be said). Hoping to blur the lines between more "official" franchises and unofficial ones, a sizeable quantity of titles utilized "SHAOLIN" something-or-other—not that said operative word could be copyrighted anyway, mind you—as a selling tactic, resulting in a plethora of releases with such titles as **THE SHAOLIN INVINCIBLES** and **MERCENARY MONKS FROM SHAOLIN TEMPLE**, *ad infinitum*. Indeed, so many films bear the Shaolin seal of approval that even today it's incredibly difficult to know in advance of watching just what the "fu" you're getting into! Although I'm occasionally partial to a good no-frills chop socky kick-flick, I must confess that, as far as this voluminous full-contact genre goes, I generally gravitate towards the more outré examples, given the choice; most especially the kind that involve mystical abilities and outrageously over-the-top action, including fighters with superhuman techniques (e.g., high-jumping aerial trampoline/wirework maneuvers and such) and/or off-the-wall/out-to-lunch paranormal elements (e.g., demoniacal villains with pulsing, serpentine extendo-tongues three times better-hung than Gene "I-can-lick-my-own-asshole-better-than-one-of-my-groupies" Simmons'). Now, all that said, if a 'fu-fest goes all-out and can actually boast of a bona fide *monster*, all the better…

Thankfully, **SILVER HERMIT** fits all these criteria/categories (well, except for elongate oral organs [although it does have real long teeth in it!]); and rest assured that if it *didn't* fit that final one mentioned, it wouldn't even be in this mag to begin with! Back in around 1992 or so, when I first exposed myself to this particular title under review, of all the lurid boxes lumped-together in the martial arts rack where I discovered it, it was **SHFST**'s cover which boasted the only illustration in the lot that really attracted my ev-

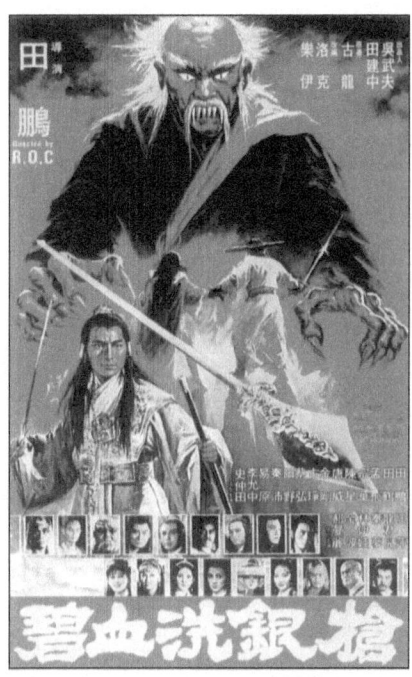

Chinese poster for **SILVER HERMIT FROM SHAOLIN TEMPLE** (artist unknown)

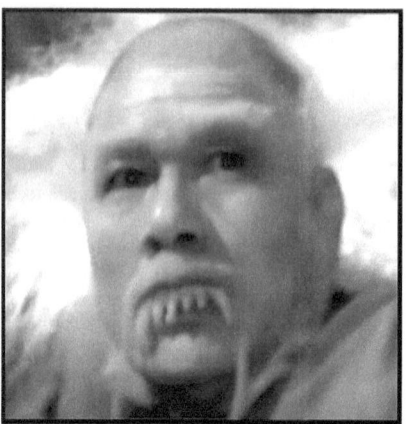

Everyone knows you should *never* mess with the guy in a KF movie with long white hair...or fangs!

er-vigilant Asian eye (*wink*). Said art depicted a grey-haired, jagged-fanged devilman—albeit, surprisingly enough, *not* the titular "Silver Hermit", as you might be led to expect—in the process of choking some luckless Chinese dude. Of all the other more mundane MA VHS tapes on display, *this* was the one that looked like the most-likely candidate for snagging my frugally-rationed rental bucks. We live and learn, as they say! (Having said that, it did have its moments, even if, to misquote Aristotle here, "The whole *isn't* greater than the sum of its parts".)

The lilting, jangly mandolin-heavy instrumental opening theme sounds better-suited to a traditional Neapolitan *sceneggiata* melodrama—or perhaps a Greek wedding?—and, although one Stanley Chow is credited hereon for the musical score, it sounds to me like this particular track might well have been lifted from a different movie (a practice which was far from unknown to occur in Asian movies, be they the MA kind or otherwise).

At a renowned martial arts academy known as the Green Jade Villa, nestled deep in the Shaolin Valley ("What a beautiful place!"), an MA tournament is held by its queenly proprietress Madame Green Jade (Meng Chin?) in order to determine who will wed her (quote) "haughty, strange, beautiful" maiden daughter, the Princess (Doris Chen?), who has recently come of age, so—ready to get "plucked from the cherry tree" (so to speak [*wink*])—she is now eligible to tie the knot with the lucky winner. Brought in to judge the contest—who better but!—is a quintet of monks from the nearby Shaolin Temple. Unfortunately, when a flagon of poisoned wine puts three out of the four proposed contestants in the tourney out of the running— just for the record, those named Green Lotus Blossom and Red Leaf both die, while Shining Spear is saved from the poison by an antidote just in the nick of time— suspicion perhaps understandably falls on the sole unpoisoned contestant, our valiant hero Mai Yu-lung, alias "Silver Hermit" (director/star Roc Tien, who also choreographed all the fighting; he has a bit of a "David Chiang" quality about him at times). Thus he is forced to become a fugitive from ruthless Shaolin justice while endeavoring to clear his sullied name. Because we know right from the get-go that the prime suspect's merely the innocent patsy in an organized frame-up involving all sorts of complicated chicanery/skullduggery, the fact that he's ultimately going to beat the rap is a foregone conclusion.

Scripted by Lo Keh from a novel by Ku Lung, **SHFST** was released in the USA by Joseph Lai's IFD Films & Arts Ltd. in 1982, in an English version prepared for Lai by Vaughan Savidge; which was the version reviewed here, as issued in a domestic VHS edition during the mid/late '80s by the notorious cheapie American video, Saturn Productions. Technically, at least, the film—a passable emulation of the lucrative Shaw Bros.' polished style from rival indie HK producers—is quite well-mounted. It possesses nice cinematography (which looks good even when reduced to fullscreen, as in Saturn's old domestic VHS version), along with elegant medieval costumery, as well as an eye-pleasingly picturesque winter snowscape locale in the early portion that somehow contrasts neatly with the numerous sword/spear clashes (whose colliding weapons' deafeningly over-amplified metallic clangs threaten to burst our eardrums!). For instance, the first confrontation seen in the movie between two of the contestants—namely Green Lotus and Red Leaf—just for a sportsmanly pre-contest "warm-up" takes place in an idyllic, snow-carpeted woodland glade amidst white-frosted trees festooned with blossom-buds. As the pair go at it with their shiny jabber-stabbers, the fluid, alternately dollied/crane-mounted camera swoops and glides all around them, observing them through snowy tree-branches as they battle with balletic grace, their full-length winter-cloaks swirling about their bodies while never once becoming snagged on their weapons. The organic fluidity of the cinematography here (and elsewhere) greatly augments and complements that of the agile participants, making for a most pleasing visual composition indeed. Without doubt, it's the film's elegant and at times eloquent cinematography (by Yung-cheng Ho) that amounts to its strongest suit.

That said, however, much of the slowly-paced narrative consists of a succession of talking heads uttering confoundedly inane and/or just plain surreal dubbed dialogue (certainly nothing unusual for the genre, as any fan well knows!). For instance, one woman exhorts passionately, "Hold me...hold me...choke me till I *die*!" In response, her male companion (evidently a user/endorser of Palmolive?) exclaims, "Good! Then I'll kill you with my lovely hands!" As if that unexpected outburst wasn't sufficient indicator what a weirdo he is, he subsequently matter-of-factly announces, "I had decided to kill this bitch when I first laid eyes on her". (Gee, how's *that* for the flipside of love at first sight?!) These odd lines are spoken by English dubbers with such nonchalance you'd think they were discussing nothing more serious than favorite recipes for Szechuan-style *ma po* bean curd or something!

Despite the convincing density of its period detail and heavily over-amped clangor of sword on sword and foot on face, the refractive nature of the drama makes it hard to become too deeply involved in the proceedings. This convoluted (read: disoriented) scenario is only mildly enlivened when a vampire named "Immortal" (let's hope not!) shows up and puts the toothy nibble on a few necks. This suitably long-in-the-tooth (i.e., senior citizen) blood-biter is about as far removed as you can get from *gyonshi/jiangshi* ("hopping vampire") traditions, but its only real connection to the more Eastern European species is its serrated upper row of choppers, canines all (it also has a bit of a hunched back and razor-sharp talons), as well as its need to suck blood, of course. It seems highly likely that this more western world-style vampire was intended to cash in on the Shaws'/Hammer's then-still-fairly-recent "crossover" fright/'fu co-production, **THE LEGEND OF THE 7 GOLDEN VAMPIRES** (七金屍 / *Qi jin shi*, 1974, Hong Kong/UK, Ds: Roy Ward Baker, Chang Cheh [see review on p.229]).

A few of **SHFST**'s action sequences are handled quite capably, but the plot of the Anglicized print simply does not jell into a satisfyingly coherent whole, though possibly even in its original Mandarin it might not have made a whole lot of sense either. Much of the blame must rest with the cumbersomely-translated script, which is delivered in English by some of the most lethargic- and disinterested-sounding voiceover actors ever heard. Some of the unconvincing sound effects add to the air of artificiality (for instance, so-called "horses' hoof-beats" sound especially risible, particularly while going at a full gallop!). I seem to remember reading somewhere or other that **SHFST** (whose Anglo export print clocks-in at around 84 minutes) ran far longer—possibly as much as 20 minutes more?—in its original Taiwanese version. This seems highly likely, judging by the fractured/fragmented narrative of the dubbed version. Characters' names (e.g. "Master Jet", "Doctor Jade", "Flying Hawk", etc.) are dropped seemingly at random, adding to the cluttered clusterfuck that is the dub-job. There are all sorts of things that don't make sense and really aren't worth the effort of clarifying anyway. And speaking of clarity—or rather, the lack thereof—an apparently pretty awesome, rapid-fire nighttime battle goes down between the baddies and some silver ring-slinging Shaolin monks, only the image on Saturn's old video print is so dark, we can barely make out a thing. Since so much of the latter half of the action takes place after dark—when Immortal's up and about, working the "graveyard shift"—a lot of stuff gets lost in darkness, making an already confusing movie considerably more disorienting still. And not only that, viewers must perform backflips (albeit of the more mental kind) with all the agility of a Shaolin-trained kung fu master in order to unravel the convolutions of the plot's multi-layered subterfuge, so best not to even bother *trying* to figure out if it all makes sense or not. Talk about a muddle!

Appearances by the aforementioned Immortal, potentially the film's saving grace, come few and far between, it should be said; in fact, albeit kept in the shadows, he doesn't even first show himself until the 39th minute, close to the midway point of this shortened (?) print. I'm actually tempted to think that perhaps some of his scenes got left on the cutting room floor when **SHFST** was reedited/dubbed for the English-speaking market by its distributor Joseph

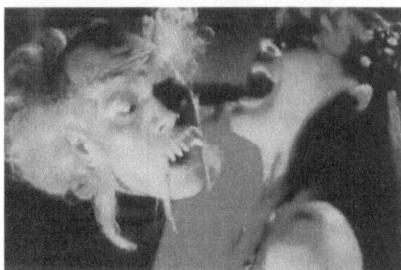

Unhappy Hooker: Immortal visits a prostitute for a night-bite

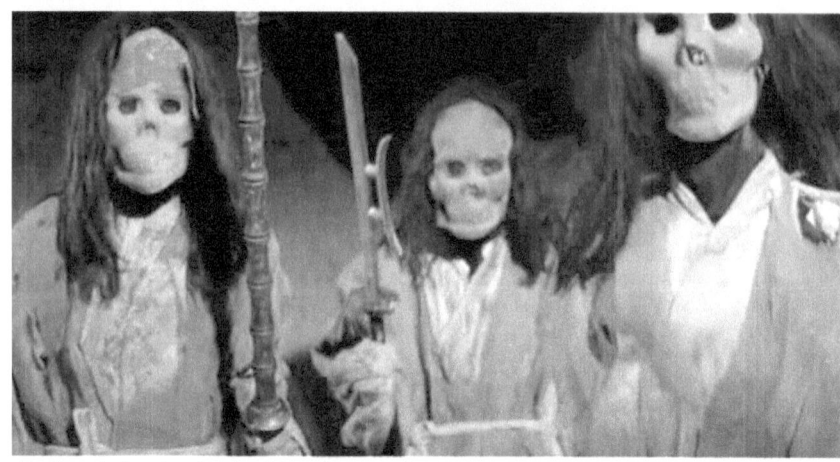

Skullheaded undead of the Shaw Brothers/Hammer Films co-production **THE LEGEND OF THE 7 GOLDEN VAMPIRES** hop along to the kill!

Lai. Whenever Immortal—who, despite his ironic name had been killed two decades earlier—reappears (he and his minions march under thirteen black flags), bloodshed and devastation are sure to follow ("He is not a human. He's a *beast*! ...He needs blood in order to retain his martial energy"). Instinctively sensing his evil presence, dogs bark their heads off when he's on a nocturnal prowl. His initial victim is a vain courtesan who boasts out loud to herself "There isn't a man in this world I can't seduce!" before promptly getting neck-bit; yes indeed, we know it was by a bona fide vampire, as the encounter leaves two whopping great bloody contusions on her corpse's alabaster throat. ("That little whore *[...]* was killed by a vampire, and all her blood was sucked out!" exclaims a local man the following day. "What's that? A *vampire*?!" asks his buddy incredulously. "*Yeah!*" replies the other). For the record, this vampire (originating from ancient Persia, of all places) has returned to China after many years absence to seek revenge on the household of the Green Jade villa ("Immortal has returned!" announces an underling ominously). A skilled martial artist himself (*natch!*), in one scene the bloodsucking demon makes short work of those aforementioned Shaolin monks, sending them packing with their strings of prayer beads between their legs. During the final third, Immortal dominates much of the action, and his various violent encounters with different enemies are handled with some impressive aplomb...if only we could see what was going on more clearly!

Adding another spooky *frisson*, a mysteriously wraith-like, veiled female flower-seller materializes from out of nowhere ("Jasmine! Anyone wanna buy some jasmine? ...One flower costs one life"), but she is not what she seems to be; in actuality a villainous she-warrior who switches faces as effortlessly as Fantômas, simply by putting on and peeling off her rubber face-masks as required. There's also a quartet of mysterious characters dressed in full-length navy blue robes emblazoned with "Yin/Yang" symbols, topped with oversized felt hats. Oh yeah, and let's not forget him known as Iron Axe ("...because I am renowned for my axe skill" [*what else?!*]), the sickly, sinister warrior with an echoey, rumbling voice and a hand-shaped birthmark (?) on his chest, who, to alleviate an unspecified illness, must constantly suck back raw hens' eggs straight from the shell, seasoned with plenty of salt. "You're *not* the vampire", deduces Hermit our hero, rightly sensing another red herring.

The finale picks-up here and there, but that's really neither here nor there. Too well-produced to classify as a full-fledged gobbler, at least in its sub-par Saturn incarnation **SHFST** is neither audacious nor uniformly inept enough to really entertain on a truly "goodbad" level either (unlike aforementioned notorious **THE SHAOLIN INVINCIBLES** [雍正命喪少林門 / *Yong zheng ming zhang Shao Lin men*, 1977, D: Hou Cheng], another Taiwanese chop-socky cheapie which at least features high-jumping 'fu fighters in ratty-ass ape suits doing the maddest mad monkey-style kung fu ever!).

When all is said and done, **SILVER HERMIT FROM SHAOLIN TEMPLE** is rather too on the bland side for my liking (I repeat: at least going by its Saturn video version), neither pro-

THE LEGEND OF THE 7 GOLDEN VAMPIRES
(七金屍 / *Qi jin shi*, a.k.a. **THE 7 BROTHERS MEET DRACULA**)

Reviewed by Andy Ross

UK/Hong-Kong, 1974. Ds: Roy Ward Baker, Chang Cheh

Trailer hype for the film (under its US alternate release title **THE 7 BROTHERS MEET DRACULA**): *"Black Belt Against Black Magic... in the Greatest Battle of All Time as The 7 Brothers and Their One Sister Meet Dracula... while vampires drink the blood of the virgins and turn them into zombies! You haven't seen kung fu until you've seen the seven brothers and their one sister in action against Dracula! ...Die, Dracula, die! See the ten-thousand-year-old monster disintegrate before your eyes as the seven brothers and their one sister meet Dracula!"*

As a lifelong fan of Hammer horrors, I've always found myself swimming against the tide when it comes to the subject of **THE LEGEND OF THE 7 GOLDEN VAMPIRES**. Emerging from the studio's latter-day renaissance, unlike **CAPTAIN KRONOS – VAMPIRE HUNTER** (1974, UK, D: Brian Clemens) and **VAMPIRE CIRCUS** (1972, UK, D: Robert Young) this "East-meets-West" kung fu shocker continues to be a subject of sharp division. Speaking as someone who was equally fascinated by the martial arts mastery of the legendary Bruce Lee,

voking a strong adverse reaction, nor a particularly strong positive one either. Except for some decent battle scenes—the ones we can actually *see*!—it's largely just ho-hum, and mainly only questionably of note for its over-usage of the term "bitch", which is flung around as freely as at a convention of male divorcees who got royally shafted by their exes in the divorce settlements; running said epithet a close second on the audio track is the word "bastard".

In closing, when renting martial arts movies, remember what Confucius say: "You can't judge a 'fu flick by looking at the cover". From what's on display here, I'd be interested in checking-out a properly widescreen, English-subbed print with the brightness/contrast settings at a far more legible level and a not-so-fuzzy picture (pretty tall order, I know!). There really is some nicely-done action occurring onscreen, if only we could see it clearer! Viewing the film in its original version with more optimal quality may not make the garbled plot much (if any) easier to comprehend, but at the very least some of those too-dark action scenes should hopefully register more easily on the eye; especially ol' Immortal's crazy climactic rampage, during which he growls and roars like a lion and really smashes shit up before having his final confrontation with the hero.

NOTE: Under its other perhaps better-known Anglo a.k.a., **THE SILVER SPEAR**, this film should not be confused with **THE DEADLY SILVER SPEAR** a.k.a. **SHAOLIN'S SILVER SPEAR** (血連環 / *Xue lian huan*, 1977, Taiwan, D: Sung Ting-mei), a comparatively "straight" MA actioner starring Jimmy Wang Yu.

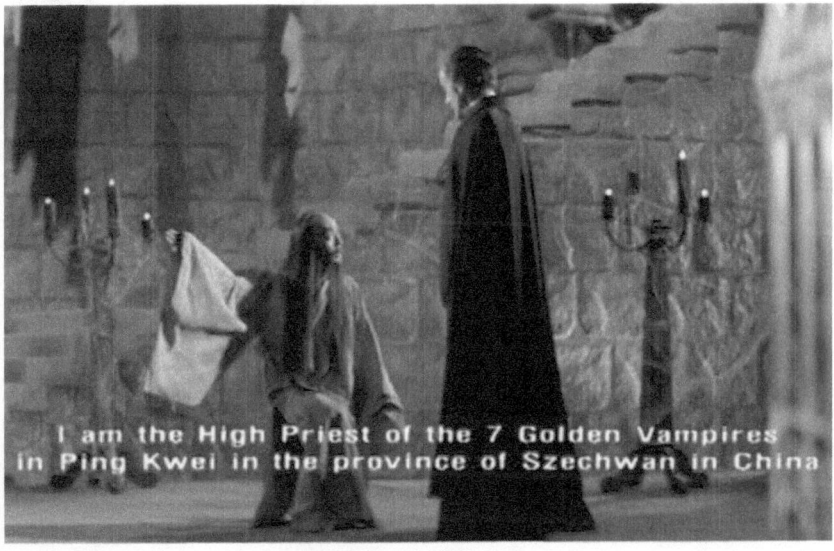

I am the High Priest of the 7 Golden Vampires in Ping Kwei in the province of Szechwan in China

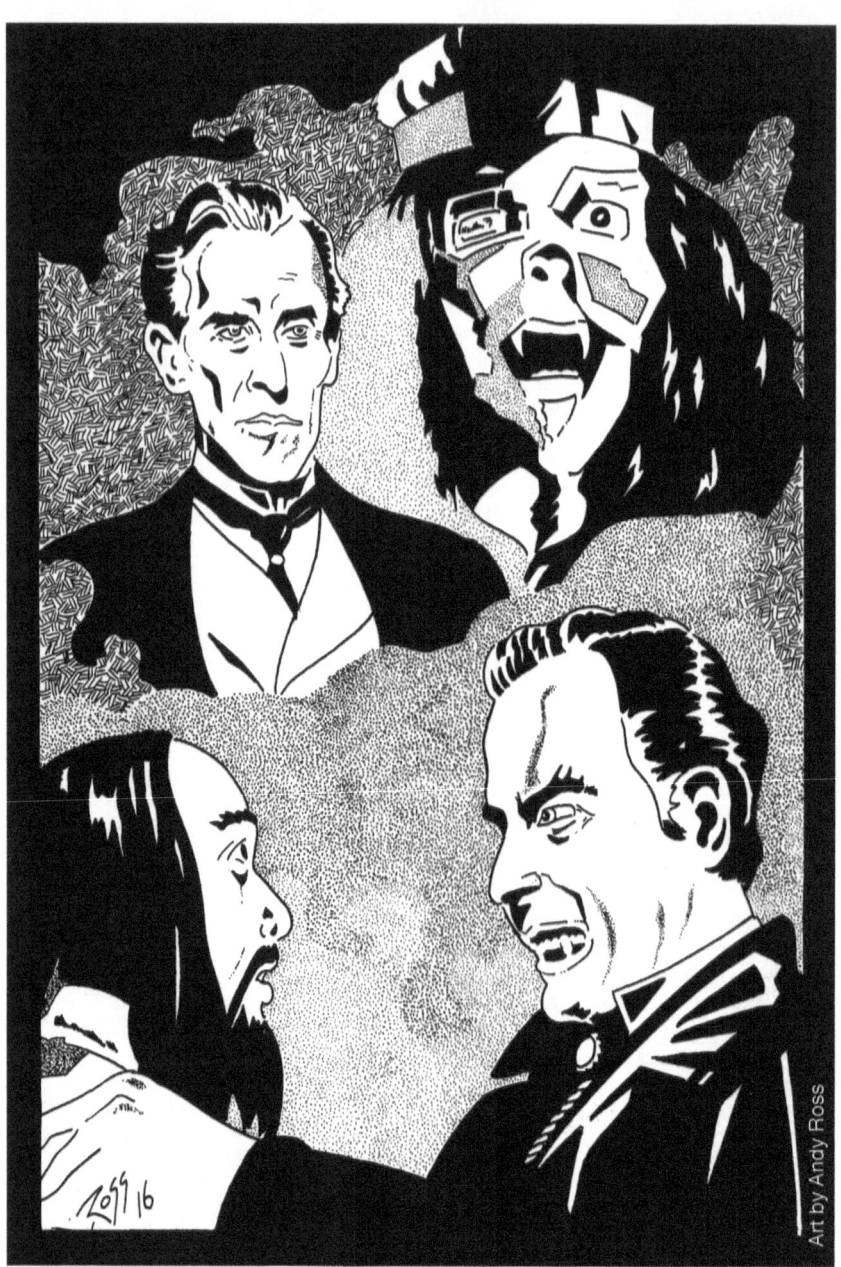

the film's blend of oriental adventure and vampire horror was a match made in heaven. Co-produced by the Shaw Brothers, filmed extensively on location and starring Hammer stalwart Peter Cushing (reprising his oft-repeated Professor Van Helsing role), chronologically speaking, **THE LEGEND OF THE 7 GOLDEN VAMPIRES** represented the seventh instalment of the cycle launched by Hammer's **DRACULA** (a.k.a. **HORROR OF DRACULA**, 1958, UK, D: Terence Fisher). Unjustly derided by Hammer historians, the film was to prove a bold move by the studio that, by 1974, was no longer *the* horror movie powerhouse anymore. Conceived at a time when British horror product had—quite literally—saturated the market, whilst the end result might not have achieved the desired effect, it was no less bold in its attempt to try something different.

Transylvania, 1804. Upon reaching the end of his far-ranging pilgrimage from the Orient to Eastern Europe, Kah (Chan Shen), High Priest of the Order of the Seven Golden Vampires, seeks the aid of Count Dracula in a bid to reestablish his grip on a diminishing empire. A prisoner within the walls of his own castle, the Vampire Lord is all too eager to lend a hand to the exotic traveler. Taking possession of Kah's physical form and now free of his earthly bonds, the Count duly sets out to exact his revenge on humanity. Moving forward a century to 1904, and in front of a disbelieving audience at Chunking University, Professor Lawrence Van Helsing (Peter Cushing) delivers a lecture on the vampires of Chinese legend. Relating the story of a rural village purportedly plagued by the cult of the Seven Golden Vampires, and of a farmer who stood valiantly against them, Van Helsing's lecture strikes a raw chord in a student by the name of Hsi Ching (David Chiang [**THE RETURN OF THE ONE-ARMED SWORDSMAN** (1969, Hong Kong, D: Chang Cheh]). Claiming to know the exact whereabouts of the village whilst insisting that the story is true and that the farmer referred to was his grandfather, Ching offers proof when he presents Van Helsing with a medallion that had once hung around the waist of a Golden Vampire. After it was stolen by Ching's late grandfather (likewise played by co-star Chiang), the vampiric victim of the theft then killed the thief in revenge before expiring itself. (One down, six more to go!)

Agreeing to accompany the young man back to his village and aid in the elimination of the remaining half-dozen ringleaders of the vampire threat, Van Helsing—funded by the wealthy widow, Vanessa Buren (Julie Ege, from **MUTATIONS** [a.k.a. **THE FREAKMAKER**, 1974, UK, D: Jack Cardiff]) on the strict stipulation that she can tag along for the adventure of it, which she does—is summarily joined on the expedition by his dashing son, Leyland (Robin Stewart, from **THE HAUNTED HOUSE OF HORROR** [1969, UK, D: Tony Tenser]). Ably supported by Ching's uniquely-talented siblings (five brothers and one sister, Mai Kwei, played by the wonderful Shih Szu) the group embark on a journey that is fraught with danger every step of the way.

I'm of a mind that the aspects of **THE LEGEND OF THE 7 GOLDEN VAMPIRES** that served

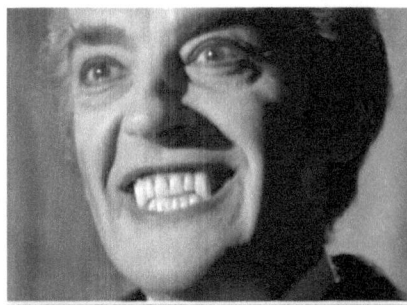

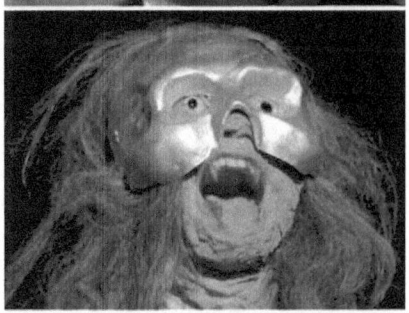

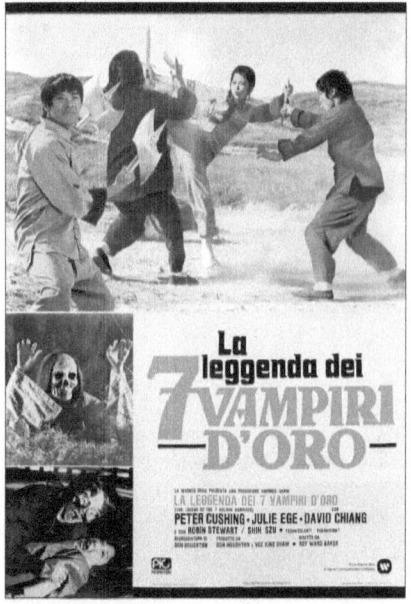

Top to Bottom: John Forbes-Robertson as the pasty, blue-faced Count Dracula bares his fangs; as does one of the masked, crumbly-skinned 7 Golden Vampires (and no, the other 6 don't look any better!); plus an Italian *soggettone* for **THE LEGEND OF THE 7 GOLDEN VAMPIRES**, which prioritizes its Asiatic aspects of martial arts and the macabre over the names of the Euro-brand actors who are headlining the picture

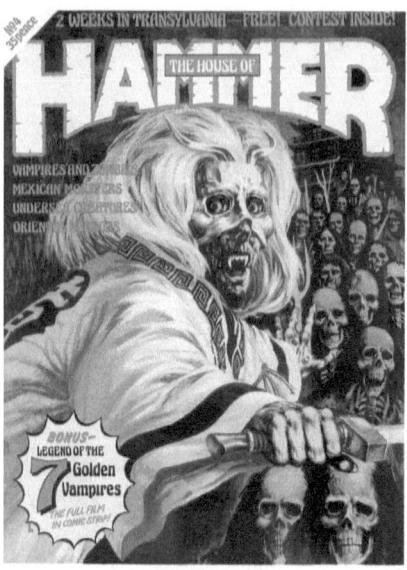

The House of Hammer magazine #4 (1977); art by Brian Lewis

to distance the "Hammer faithful" were the ones I personally enjoyed the most. First and foremost, is the oft-maligned prologue (and fleeting climactic) appearance of the Count himself. Having read the script and turned the role down, Christopher Lee summarily made way for the grand theatrics of John-Forbes Robertson. Taking its cue from the visually dynamic creations of Asian cinema, the Dracula we see here is a wildly exaggerated one. With his generous eyebrows, heavy makeup and booming vocal performance (overdubbed by David De Keyser), this particular version of Dracula belonged very much within the realms of Far Eastern superstition. Instantly recognizable as a demon to East Asian viewers, that Forbes-Robertson's appearance continues to offend Western audiences remains something of

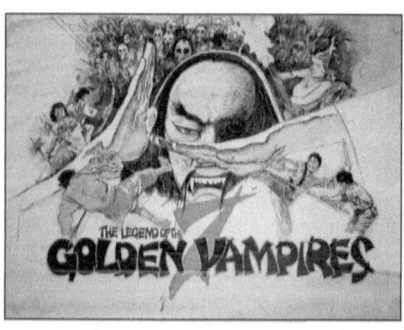

An early conceptual sketch by artist Vic Fair for the film's British quad poster

a moot point. As a joint British/Chinese venture (with cast and crew drawn respectively from their creative stables), in order for the film to appeal to its intended audience, it likewise had to appeal to two vastly-polarized cultures. Those more in touch with the (by no means subtle) nuances of Asian cinema can readily brush aside the cynicism in respect to Forbes-Robertson's performance as the nefarious Count. Indeed, if we view **THE LEGEND OF THE 7 GOLDEN VAMPIRES** as a Far-Eastern horror film with Western influences, then this particular incarnation of Dracula acquits itself rather well. Another aspect of the film's production that invited scathing criticism was its "below-par" fight sequences. By now more accustomed to the rapid fire mastery of Bruce Lee (whose last film **ENTER THE DRAGON** (1973, Hong-Kong/USA, D: Robert Clouse]) was released posthumously a year earlier), British audiences were to find Hammer's kung fu antics rather tame by comparison. That said, the larger-scale combat scenes in **THE LEGEND OF THE 7 GOLDEN VAMPIRES** (considering the amount of stunt actors involved) are remarkably well-choreographed and, of the film's three major set-pieces, both the early ambush scene and the siege on Pingwei village continue to crackle with a vibrant energy.

Lastly perhaps, is the film's depiction of its myriad vampire antagonists. Split between the Golden Vampires themselves and a vast army of decrepit, skull-faced living dead minions, again the influence is unashamedly Asian. Sporting gold face coverings, their hair wild and their skin in a state of advanced decomposition, the ghoulish inhabitants of **THE LEGEND OF THE 7 GOLDEN VAMPIRES** are among the most striking of Hammer's monstrous creations. Filmed in slow-motion and set against a wonderfully creepy score by James Bernard (whose last name is conspicuously misspelled in the opening credits as "Benard" *[sic!]*), the sight of the ramshackle undead army advancing on Pingwei (some of them [sort of] skipping—if not actually *hopping*—as per the conventions of Chinese ghost stories) is as creepy as it is memorable.

Setting aside the facets of the film that have inherently divided its audience, one is rarely made aware of the film's rather rich and sprawling milieu. One of a handful of Hammer films that were to abandon the homey familiarity of their usual haunts in Iver Heath, **THE LEGEND OF THE 7 GOLDEN VAMPIRES** (alongside the straight actioner **SHATTER** [奪命刺客, a.k.a. **CALL HIM MR. SHATTER**, 1974, Ds: Michael Carreras, Monte Hellman; guest-starring Cushing)

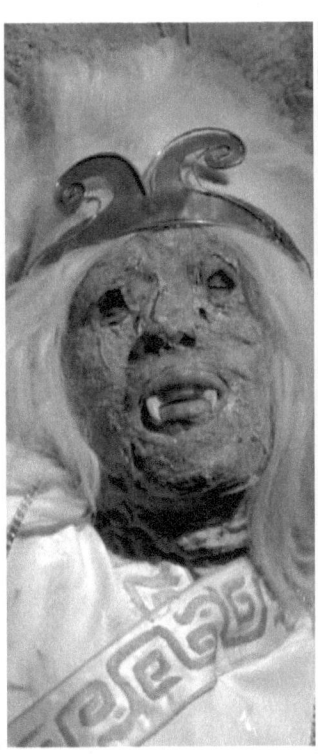
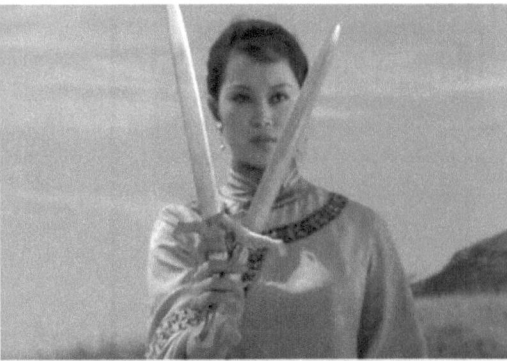
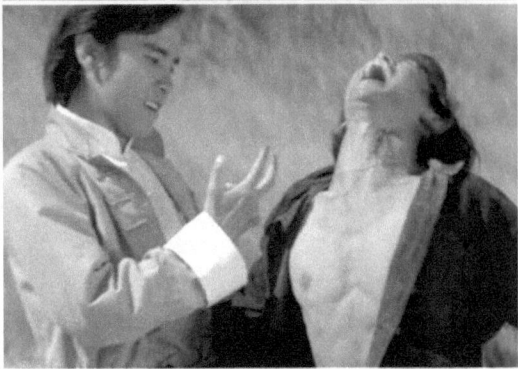

Above Left: The crumbling, mummy-like look of a recently-deceased Golden Vampire. **Top Right:** Shih Szu has a pretty deadly set of fangs herself... **Above Right:** ...and so does David Chiang, for that matter!

was filmed extensively on location in Hong Kong and China. Adding a sense of otherworldly reality to the proceedings and placing its European protagonists firmly in uncharted territory, the redundancy of the foreigners' presence is never more apparent than when they are forced to sit it out on the sidelines twiddling their thumbs while allowing their Chinese counterparts to take center-stage during the MA combat scenes (although the Van Helsings, both father and son, do pitch in their fair share during the later set-tos between the living and the not-quite-dead).

Another energetic outing for the Hammer veteran, in his last appearance as Professor Van Helsing Peter Cushing remains as "hands-on" as ever. Not one to shy away from the more physical demands of the role, whilst Cushing was to spend the majority of the film under the protective wing of the brothers, when their number dwindles, it's Van Helsing who finds himself in the thick of the vampire-slaying action. Providing excellent support for Cushing in what (due to the language barrier, proved to be an arduous shoot) are Robin Stewart (from the 70's TV sit-com *Bless This House*) as Leyland, martial-arts star David Chiang as the brother's spokes-person Hsi-Ching and Shih-Szu as the instantly endearing Mai Kwei. Somewhat redundant to the proceedings however, (but whose wealthy widow Vanessa Buren funds Van Helsing's expedition) is Julie Ege, a blonde Norwegian actress who was first

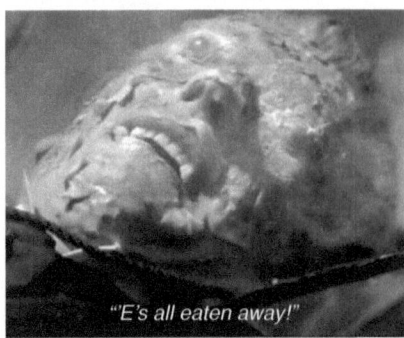

"E's all eaten away!"

As per his usual cinematic contract, Drac gets vanquished and quickly dissolves into the typical fried-egg-eyed, blistering, rotten mess. Oh well, it's a (un)living!

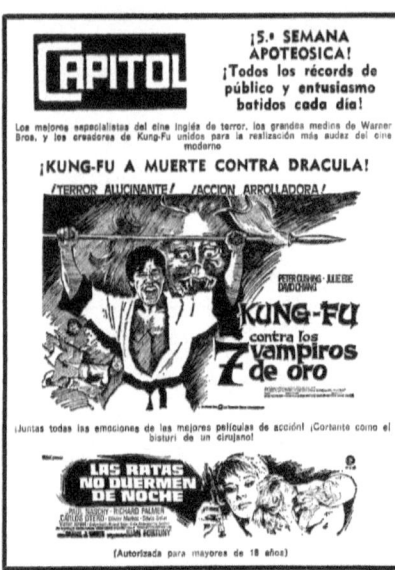

Spanish newspaper ad for **THE LEGEND OF THE 7 GOLDEN VAMPIRES**

"revealed" to Hammer fans in **THE CREATURES THE WORLD FORGOT** (1971, UK, D: Don Chaffey).

THE LEGEND OF THE 7 GOLDEN VAMPIRES is somewhat of a stable-mate to **CAPTAIN KRONOS – VAMPIRE HUNTER**, in that it sought to combine elements of both action and horror. *[It also included a smaller element of the Far East—this time Japan—in the form of title character Horst Janson's trusty samurai katana – SF.]* Whilst it might not be the best of Hammer's *Dracula* series, it is by no means the worst, either. Visually rich, wonderfully-scored and with never a dull moment, **THE LEGEND OF THE 7 GOLDEN VAMPIRES** remains one of Hammer's most energetic and thoroughly enjoyable offerings.

BAD MOON

Reviewed by Dennis Capicik

USA, 1996. D: Eric Red

Cursed with lycanthropy, Uncle Ted (Michael Paré) stares-down Thor, his nephew's highly-intuitive and protective German Shepherd, and remarks rhetorically, "He knows an old dog when he sees one."

Based on Wayne Smith's novel *Thor* (Random House, 1994)—which the titular family dog narrates in the first person!—Smith's novel is one of many books as told through the eyes of an animal or multiple animal characters. Jack London's *The Call of the Wild* (Macmillan, 1903) about a Klondike sled-dog named Buck whose feral instincts come to the fore when he returns to the wilderness, is perhaps one of the more famous examples to take this approach. This was soon followed by *White Fang* (Macmillan, 1906), London's follow-up of sorts, which, in an interesting flipside, charts the *domestication* of a feral dog as opposed to its return to the wild. As with many film adaptations of London's work, Buck and White Fang never narrate the actual films themselves, but are most always presented as integral, central characters, which is what director Eric Red has also done with the Rin-Tin-Tin-like canine hero of **BAD MOON**, his reworking of Smith's novel.

While on an expedition deep in the Amazonian rain forest, Ted and his girlfriend Marjorie (Johanna Marjorie Lebovitz) are viciously attacked by a werewolf, and of course, Ted survives the attack—if far from unscathed, as we shall see—to return stateside. Yes, you guessed it: after being bitten by the werewolf which, in a wolverine-like fury, viciously slaughtered his GF, just as expected, Ted has come down with a bad case of lycanthropy. Three months later, after having exhausted every possibility for a cure, his strange and incurable affliction having left doctors completely baffled, he decides to look up his sister Janet (Mariel Hemingway) and her son, his nephew Brett (Mason Gamble), who are currently living in a rural area outside of Seattle. However, unbeknownst to him, Janet's and Brett's (quote) "overprotective" dog, a large German Shepard named Thor—his doggie senses tingling—immediately deduces that something is *very* amiss with Ted...

Simplistically plotted and to-the-point, **BAD MOON** has a lean, less-than-80-minute running time, cutting its exposition down to the absolute bare minimum needed to tell its story. As described by director Eric Red in his audio commentary (which is included on Scream Factory's slick-looking Blu-ray), the jungle-set intro definitely (quote) "opens with a bang". Caught off-guard while making love in their spacious tent (cue plenty of nudity even in the R-rated cut), a classic-styled—and absolutely *kickass*-looking—bipedal werewolf literally pulls Marjorie away right in mid-*coitus* and proceeds to tear her apart in most gruesome fashion indeed, while Ted, although injured, grabs a handy shotgun and blows their vicious wolfen attacker's head clean off—actually, the close-to-point-blank shot pretty much *atomizes* it!—as a (quote by Red) "hurricane of blood and flesh" fill the screen. This prologue, whose sheer ferociousness and savagery definitely takes the viewer by surprise, then fades/segues into majestic aerial views of densely-forested mountains in the Pacific Northwest region. It's an absolute corker of an opening, and even the obviously studio-bound if colorful sets standing-in for the Amazon jungle give it the look and feel of a quaint '60s jungle adventure gone insane.

As the camera flies over the vast landscapes, it narrows-in on an out-of-the-way, bucolic house (and yes, this *is* British Columbia, Canada standing-in for the outskirts of Seattle), where Brett and Thor cheerily play together out in the front yard; it's that picture-perfect image of an all-American family homestead. In an interesting and worthy change from Smith's novel, Brett no longer has both his parents and two siblings, which only reinforces Thor's guardian/protector status—depicting him almost like a surrogate father figure of sorts—and this dynamic also allows Hemingway's character to be a much-stronger heroine. She, like Thor, will also stop at nothing to protect her family. As evidenced in the very next scene, a fast-talking conman (Hrothgar Mathews in an entertainingly skeezy turn) pretending to sell a product called the Magna Reading Project provokes Thor, who instinctively attacks, which was this flopsy's ploy all along, so he could cash-out on a fraudulent settlement, unaware that Janet is a member of the bar ("Don't mess with a lawyer on her *own* turf!" she warns him). Sure, this scene may be a little heavy-handed, but it's an admirable set-up for the upcoming confrontation with Uncle Ted, and one which also highlights the potential dangers of the 'modern' single-mother family.

Upon first meeting Ted (who only makes his presence known to her months after his return from the Amazon Basin), Janet and Brett are naturally excited to see him, but are concerned for his well-being living alone out in the woods in his Airstream trailer. "Don't you use that razor I bought you for Christmas?" asks Janet jokingly as she brushes the scruff on his face, which he quickly—and frustratedly—answers with, "Yeah, maybe to slit my own throat". While Janet knows something may be afoot, she acquaints his odd behavior to him being her (quote) "flaky brother". However, in a much more interesting elaboration, both Thor and Brett discover a whole lot more about Ted, a subplot which further emphasizes the innately inquisitive natures of both children and animals. While snooping about in the Airstream, Brett discovers a copy of *The Lore of the Werewolf* (possibly shades of Sabine Baring-Gould's 1865 book on mythological werewolf lore, *The Book of Werewolves*?), plus also some vials of blood and various other odd-

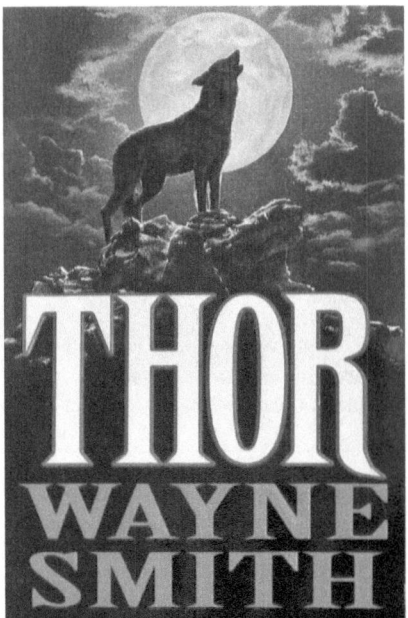

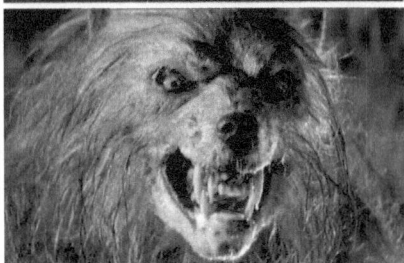

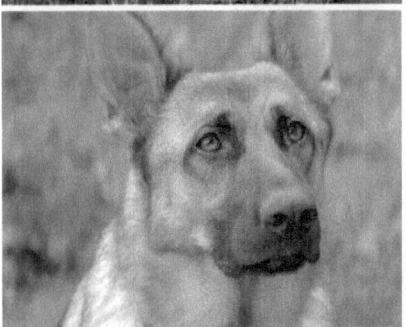

Top: Random House's mass-market '94 edition of the novel on which **BAD MOON** is based. **Center:** Some decent practical effects raise the quality-bar on this fine mid-1990s werewolf outing. **Above:** Hero of the film is a German Shepherd named Thor, who must deal with a rather unpleasant human pseudo-cousin—his owner's Uncle Ted—who is running amok. As Ted remarks, "He knows an 'old dog' when he sees one"

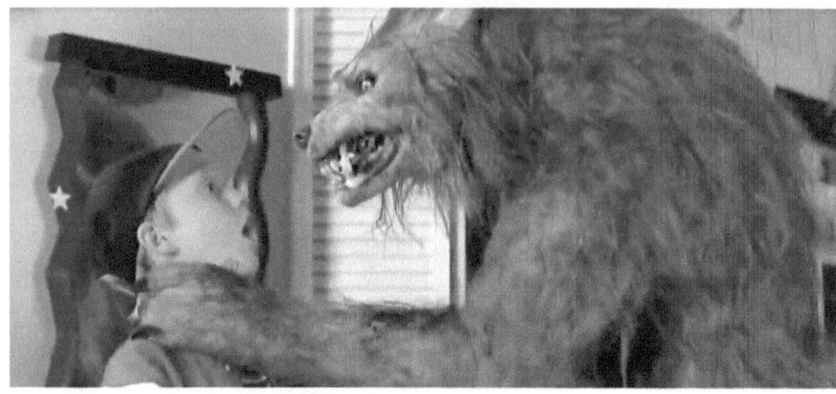

Lupine Lunacy: Uncle Ted gets out-of-hand when he confronts his nephew in full werewolf form and the shit really hits the fan!

ities. Meanwhile, Thor scours the area and finds some shredded human remains hanging from a tall tree high up the trunk. And then, when Ted and Thor first truly meet, the dog slowly—almost respectfully—walks towards the man, who calmly says knowingly, "We're two of a kind, pal". Later in the film, when Thor realizes the danger Ted poses to *his* 'pack', he continues to diligently stand guard outside the man's trailer, watching, waiting and even going so far as to 'mark' his territory when he pisses on a wheel of Ted's trailer,

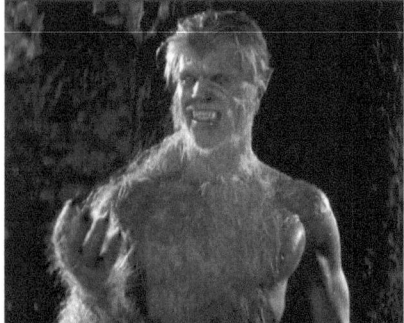

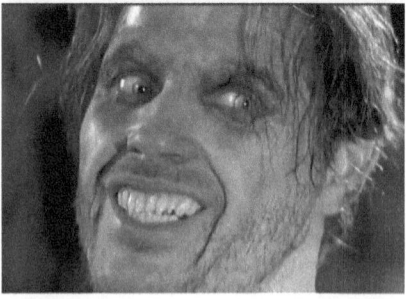

Michael Paré easily gives the strongest performance in the film, convincingly conveying all the necessary pathos and frustration (*à la* Lon, Jr.) as he deals with his affliction

which is now parked closer to home—too close for comfort?—in his sis' backyard. This pissing scene can be taken as a comedic moment, as it does provoke a chuckle, but it resonates far more effectively if taken seriously, interpreted at a deeper level. As, like the rival alpha males vying for leadership they are, Ted and Thor continue to size-up and psych-out each other, the human says cockily to the canine, implying that a violent confrontation between them is inevitable in the very near future, "In good time, old boy. In good time…"

At the same time, the film also pokes fun at—or *does* it?—some of the more commonplace aspects of werewolf lore. In a prime example of this, young Brett is seen watching Stuart Walker's **WEREWOLF OF LONDON** (1935, USA) on television, prompting knowing laughter from his uncle at the film's preposterous genre rules, which that most werewolf movies abide by—such as silver bullets and full moons—rules which Brett idealistically and adamantly defends ("*That's* the way it works"). Begging to differ, Ted, who most definitely *knows* better from firsthand experience, confidently suggests that, "*Any* moon will do the trick", not just a full one. In an amusing and possibly deliberate quirky touch on the filmmaker's part, most of these 'supposed' werewolf legends originated in George Waggner's and Lon "Larry Talbot" Chaney, Jr.'s **THE WOLF MAN** (1941, USA), and in particular Curt Siodmak's screenplay, so it's a nice touch that Walker's film—which *doesn't* follow these so-called 'rules'—is the one shown playing on TV. In yet another funny moment, when Thor is mistakenly blamed for killing the conman from the opening scene and forcibly taken off to the pound by the ASPCA, Ted—the beast within him starting to show itself even while he's still in human form now—calmly strolls over to Thor's kennel and vindictively pisses all over *his* house.

Michael Paré easily gives the strongest performance in the film, convincingly conveying all the necessary pathos and frustration (*à la* Lon, Jr.) as he deals with his affliction, and even when he becomes increasingly angered and a possible threat to both Janet and Brett, this sudden change in his temperament is also effectively portrayed. Even if it does—at times—come across as rather cartoonish, at the same time, it could also be argued that he too is fighting to hold onto what *he* believes is rightfully his, creating an interesting dichotomy between wild beast and tamed beast, one which harkens back to London's *The Call of the Wild*. At the same time, Ted expresses his vulnerability around humans and, however subtly, seeks help for his affliction and believes in the (quote) "restorative power of love" and that "family is everything", which he believes is his last possible chance to cure himself. Earlier in the film, his late-night runs in the woods are used as an excuse to handcuff himself to the boles of big trees in order to prevent him from roving free while in his transformed state and killing any more innocent people, which the police have predictably attributed to some kind of wild animal… you got that right, occifers!

Less interesting, but no less important, Mariel Hemingway and Mason Gamble are also well-cast. They provide the film with the necessary potential victims worth caring about, and play well alongside Paré; even if, in the end, they are overshadowed by his powerhouse performance. Portrayed by one Primo, our doggedly loyal (pun intended!) hero Thor—a truly magnificent and charismatic specimen of his breed indeed—has an imposing and prodigious presence on camera, and even though he went through a reported six months of training beforehand to prepare him for the demanding role, a few scenes nonetheless remain in the film where his trainer couldn't coax the necessary menacing growling or snarling out of him as he faces-off with Uncle Ted (that happily wagging tale in some scenes is a dead giveaway that he isn't anywhere near as angry as he's supposed to be playing!). As for his ferocious "dialogue", Thor's growls and snarls were later dubbed-in and, although it's a minor gripe, it's worth mentioning just the same in comparison to other 'stunt dogs' in, let's say, Samuel Fuller's **WHITE DOG** (1982, USA) or Lewis Teague's **CUJO** (1983, USA), wherein both title animals come across with such naturalness and conviction it's easy to forget that they *are* actors who just happen to be canines.

Lensed with assurance by Jan Kiesser (who also lent his talents to Tom Holland's '80s favorite, **FRIGHT NIGHT** [1985, USA]) in sprawling Panavision 35mm anamorphic, the film seems at odds—in a positive way—with its modest $7 million budget. For one particular scene, in which a forestry worker is gorily mauled to death, Red and Kiesser effectively replicate the fog-enshrouded forests of Waggner's much-celebrated atmospheric visuals in **THE WOLF MAN**, and even though much of the present film takes place at night, everything looks crisp, clear and impressively lit. Thankfully, Red and Kiesser also never shy away from showing their werewolf: a magnificent combination of mechanical animatronics and a man-in-a monster-suit (stunt coordinator was Ken Kirzinger) created by veteran SPFX artist Steve Johnson, which at times has a rather feline quality to it, facially speaking. It's a stellar piece of work, which not only looks great on camera, but is actually quite terrifying to behold. Unfortunately, a climactic transformation late in the film (which, by the way, begins just fine), quickly degenerates into some truly *awful* CGI morphing effects, which have, mercifully, been eliminated from Red's director's cut featured on Scream Factory's lush Blu-ray. Trust me, it *really* is that much better without it!

Although the new millennium saw the release of both John Fawcett's **GINGER SNAPS** (2000, Canada) and Neil Marshall's **DOG SOLDIERS** (2002, UK), two hugely-impressive indie werewolf films, the largely forgotten **BAD MOON**

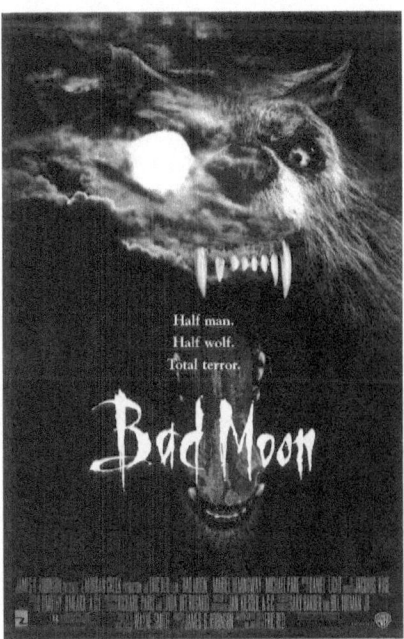

US poster

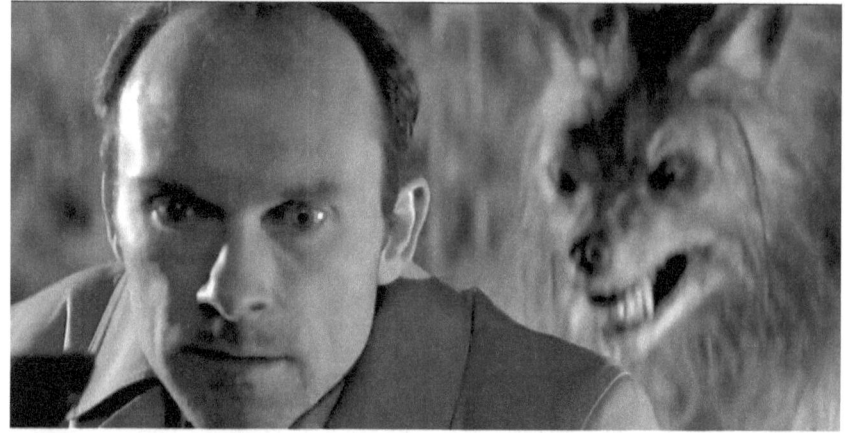

Wolf At The Door: All-too-convincingly playing a would-be scam artist, Hrothgar Mathews subsequently receives his exceedingly nasty comeuppance for being such a total douchebag

may (debatably) not be in the same league as those particular films or other earlier contemporary werewolf films such as Joe Dante's **THE HOWLING** (1981, USA) or John Landis' **AN AMERICAN WEREWOLF IN LONDON** (1981, USA) either, but it's most definitely worthy of attention as a novel take on one of the screen's classic monsters.

BONE TOMAHAWK

Reviewed by Andy Ross

USA, 2015. D: S. Craig Zahler

When I was a youngster, the Western genre was never one of my favorites. Whether that's down to my late father's obsession with all things Wild West (and the seemingly endless loop of John Wayne and Audie Murphy features) or, as a British kid, their lack of cultural significance for me, is sincerely hard to say. Perhaps the honest truth (as a lover of all things fantastic) is that the Western genre (with its vast, open plains and bleak, desert settings) simply failed to ignite my juvenile imagination. *Shock! Horror!* Whilst many reading this might be shaking their heads in disbelief (and perhaps even questioning my sanity), the Western staples of cowboys versus Indians and posses tracking down outlaw gangs were resoundingly lost on me. Naturally aware that Westerns (whilst far from actual factual lessons in American history) were morality plays wherein the forces of good sought to vanquish the forces of evil, those seemingly endless gunfights served no other purpose than to numb my younger self to the core.

Whizzing forward some three decades, the emergence of by-far-more-gritty and historically accurate fare (e.g., **DANCES WITH WOLVES** [1990, USA, D: Kevin Costner], **TOMBSTONE** [2003, USA, D: George P. Cosmatos]) was to witness a rather radical overhaul of my previous reservations. With the first of these productions being a grounded and honest depiction of The Plains Wars and the second a gutsy reenactment of the events prior to and including The Gunfight at the O.K. Corral, the harsh realities of life in the era were rather refreshingly being made apparent. Far from the clean-shaven heroics that had (in my mind) dominated the genre, the events and characters of the contemporary Western seemed far more sincere than those proffered by their predecessors. Forged on acts of individual courage, of dreams and aspirations made manifest and of unfathomable bloodshed, the sprawling frontier of the American West was by no means a territory that was "won" with ease; an observation that these modern-day offerings seemed determined to prove.

As two very distinct film types, the onscreen marriage of the Western and the Horror had been sporadic to say the least. Set within a specific time period and having their own very unique tales to tell, the addition of supernatural elements into the Wild West mix might well have seemed superfluous. Whether an independent low-budget feature or larger-scale, multi-million-dollar production, at the very heart of the filmmaking process lies the necessity to take an occasional risk. Whilst it's true that not every gamble pays off, in the case of **BONE TOMAHAWK**, the audacious union of such disparate genres (unusually enough) was to pay dividends. A stripped-back survival horror set in the closing years of the 19th Century, whilst **BONE TOMAHAWK** ticks all the boxes in respect to setting, characterization, narrative and pace, it is also a presentation in three progressively-more-menacing parts. Making its bloody intentions plain within the opening few minutes, **BONE TOMAHAWK** begins with a cold-hearted display of human cruelty and then proceeds to build further upon the concept. Eking-out a living through ambush, robbery and murder, two fugitives (Sid Haig from Rob Zombie's **THE DEVIL'S REJECTS** [2005, USA] and David Arquette from the *Scream* franchise; an offbeat pair-up if ever there was one!) unwittingly find themselves on an ancient tribal burial ground. Having been spooked by an eerie series of howls, when Buddy (Haig) is introduced to the business end of an arrow, his panicked partner Purvis (Arquette) hot-foots it to the safety of the nearest sleepy outpost. Further compounding his situation, when "Buddy" (as Purvis now chooses to introduce himself) is spotted stashing his ill-gotten gains for later collection, the town's Sheriff Franklin Hunt (Kurt Russell) confronts the stranger at the local saloon. A firm-but-fair lawman, Hunt is immediately suspicious of Buddy's erratic demeanor. After shooting the ne'er-do-well in the leg as he attempts to flee upon being accosted, Hunt dispatches gentleman gunslinger John Brooder (Matthew Fox) to secure the medical expertise of doctor's assistant Samantha O'Dwyer (Lili Simmons). While currently tending to the broken leg of her rancher husband Arthur (Patrick Wilson), Samantha agrees to remove the bullet and to monitor the patient in the hours thereafter.

As the sun rises on a new day, Sheriff Hunt is summoned to a nearby farm where a young stable-lad has been brutally murdered during the night before. Upon returning to the jailhouse to report his findings to his subordinate First Deputy Nick (Evan Jonigkeit), Hunt discovers that the jail's occupants (Buddy, Samantha and Nick) have all up and vanished amid obvious signs of a violent struggle. Studying a rudimentary bone arrowhead found at the scene, the town's Native representative identifies the assailants as hailing from a legendary tribe known as the Troglodytes. A hybrid cave-dwelling species that is greatly feared due to their ravenous fondness for eating human flesh, whilst their Native informant feels obliged to reveal the rumored location of the troglodyte camp, he doesn't have the stomach to embark on a suicide mission. Insisting (against Hunt's wishes and in spite of his leg injury) that he join the rescue effort, Arthur is determined to rescue his kidnapped wife, come what may. With the aged Second Deputy Chicory (Richard Jenkins) and the impulsive John Brooder completing the quartet, the men ride out in pursuit…

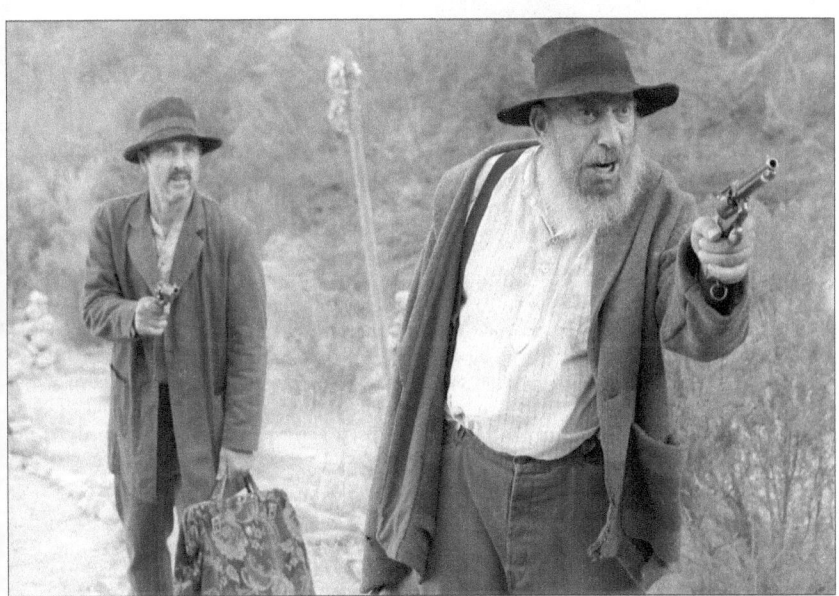

Two fugitives confront what they think are normal humans they can shoot and be done with it, but that's not the case with the monstrous beings in **BONE TOMAHAWK**

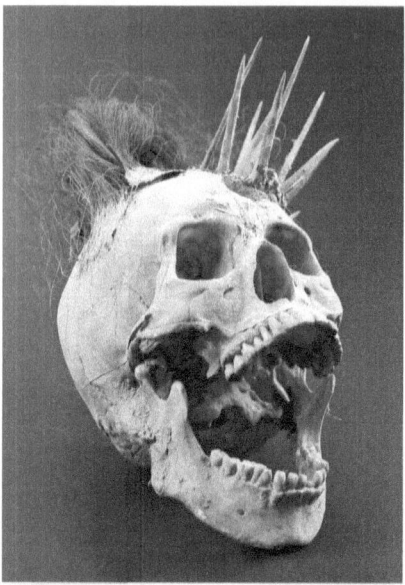

Having previously watched Quentin Tarantino's **THE HATEFUL 8** (2015, USA) and remembering how sold I was on the performance of Kurt Russell in it, I entered **BONE TOMAHAWK** with no clear-cut advance idea of what I was about to watch. Naturally, I was expecting a rugged western along similar lines to Tarantino's eighth cinematic feature, but it should go without saying that I, being a diehard horror fan, found myself rather pleasantly surprised.

As an observer accompanying the four unorthodox heroes on their quest, and inasmuch becoming increasingly attached to their polarized personalities and in-fighting, I entered into the film's final act anticipating nothing more than the obligatory conflict and resolution. Imagine my surprise then when **BONE TOMAHAWK** chose instead to present me with a darkly sinister and incredibly brutal denouement. Whilst the driving force behind Zahler's film was the courage and determination of the four pivotal players, its dynamism comes from the group's eventual confrontation with the primitive and bestial Troglodyte clan. Possessing certain thematic similarities to both Neil Marshall's **DOG SOLDIERS** (2002, UK) and the same director's **THE DESCENT** (2005, UK/USA), **BONE TOMAHAWK** proffers a monstrous archetype that (besides having evolved into a whole new species) is physically, savagely superior. Utilizing all-over whitish body paint in order to blend seamlessly into the dusty desert backdrop, the Troglodytes are cold and calculating killers. They communicate via wolf-like howls through a cartilaginous extension in their voice-boxes, and have similarly developed an appetite for human flesh. As one of the most primitive representations of the monstrous archetype, these hulking creatures are neither wholly man nor beast, but instead are a curious hybrid of both. Although they craft brutal weapons from the bones of their prey—hence the film's evocative title—there is nevertheless a savage beauty (of sorts) attached to these creatures. Relatively unaffected by the intrusion of civilization and yet dependent upon its generous larder for their sustenance, these are creatures (were it not for Purvis' and Buddy's intrusion) that would have remained on the fringes of society. In an act of revenge when outsiders infringe on their territory, the Troglodytes deem to deal with the problem via the only means they know how and, in all honesty, it's *not* a pretty sight!

With its sole oversight involving a gaffe in continuity (it'll hit you as it did me, which, to

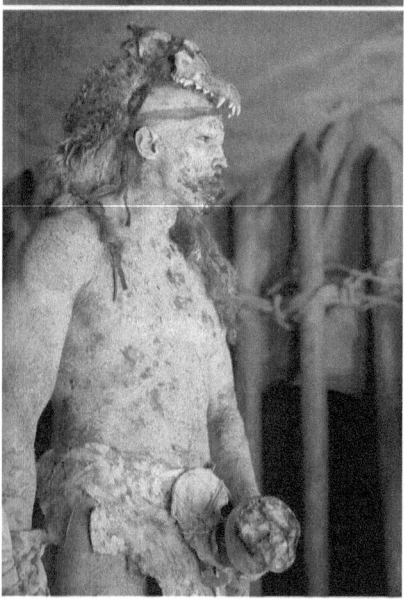

There is no backstory given for the mutated ogres that hunt and devour humans in **BONE TOMAHAWK**. However, that isn't to say they were entirely fabricated by S. Craig Zahler for the film. 'Cannibalistic' monsters are not uncommon in Amerindian folklore and mythology. It seems that just about every tribe has their own variety of giant man-eating ogres that terrorized the lands. For example, the "Basket Ogres" of various Northwest Coast tribes were a race of beings who caught and ate humans on a regular basis be honest, was well after the event), **BONE TOMAHAWK** (besides its rare status as a horror-themed Western) is an education in what can be achieved whilst thinking outside of the box. Suffice to say, the ensemble cast of Russell, Wilson, Fox, and Jenkins are quite excellent in this one. Portraying well-rounded and individually-driven characters, whilst all have their own very human traits, the means by which the four outgrow their personal differences and forge a solid group dynamism is rather stylishly delivered. Given the subject matter covered in great depth by *Monster!* (as per its title) when I suggested the film for consideration, the first question that was asked of me was "Is it a *monster* movie?" Had that question been asked of me midway through watching the film, I'd have resoundingly responded in the negative. It's only when the true savagery at its core reveals itself that it does indeed fit the "monstrous" criteria. Featuring monsters of both the human and the inhuman variety (the former in the form of great cameos by Haig and Arquette, playing lowlife predatory cut-throats), a storyline that serves to keep the viewer hooked and—yes—some decidedly bleak and foreboding desert settings, **BONE TOMAHAWK** is of an ilk that seeks to combine one cinematic genre with another and succeeds in doing so quite magnificently.

TICKS

Reviewed by Dennis Capicik

USA, 1993. D: Tony Randel

Trailer narration: *"It started out small, a part of Mother Nature's wonder... But then, they grew... and* GREW*! Unimaginable! Unthinkable! Unbelievable! ...Where civilization ends, the* nightmare *begins!* **TICKS**... *It's not* nice *to mess with Mother Nature!"*

Whether it be subtle or extreme, most individuals have some sort of phobia in regards to insects and/or arachnids, big or small, and this ill feeling of ours towards so many kinds of arthropodic creepy-crawly has, perhaps subconsciously, always caused 'big bug' movies to draw an audience, whether out of repulsion or for pure entertainment.

With the proliferation and testing of thermonuclear weapons throughout the '50s, monster movies began to shift their focus from Gothic horrors onto science fiction, and in particular, the aftereffects of this then-new technology, which is still misunderstood and mistrusted to this day. Irradiated insects were perfect fodder for the next crop of monsters; ones that lived among us in our backyards, and even right in our homes. Produced by Warner Brothers, giant, rampaging ants were the focus of Gordon Douglas' **THEM!** (1954, USA), one of the first—and

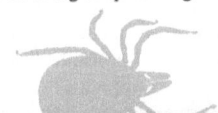

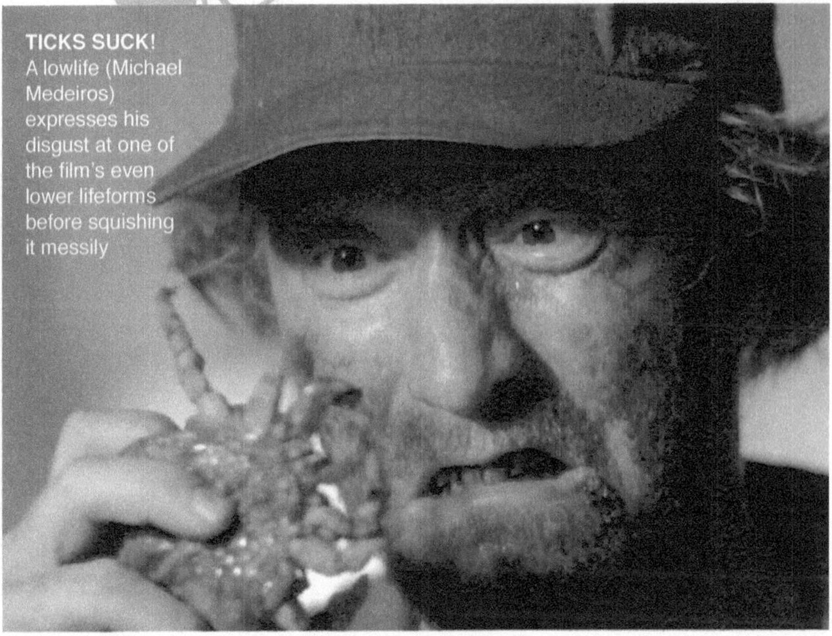

TICKS SUCK!
A lowlife (Michael Medeiros) expresses his disgust at one of the film's even lower lifeforms before squishing it messily

still best—examples of 'killer bug' movies. Others, such as Jack Arnold's **TARANTULA!** (1955, USA), Nathan Juran's **THE DEADLY MANTIS** (1957, USA), Edward Ludwig's **THE BLACK SCORPION** (1957, USA) and Bert I. Gordon's **BEGINNING OF THE END** (1957, USA) soon followed, plus numerous more besides. When the unpredictable and ghastly effects of radiation poisoning began to lose its attraction among enterprising producers and directors, toxic waste became the next big ecological blight on the block to blame (e.g., Bert I. Gordon's **EMPIRE OF THE ANTS** [1977, USA]), and in one particular instance, a freak earthquake unleashed a new strain of mutant, flesh-eating, incendiary cockroaches in William Castle's and Jeannot Szwarc's **BUG** (1975, USA). In the '80s, biological experimentation was the cause for still more mutant roaches in Terence H. Winkless' **THE NEST** (1988, USA), while in Frank Marshall's big-budget—and financially highly-successful—**ARACHNOPHOBIA** (1990, USA), as per its title the film overtly plays-up to people's paranoias about feisty arachnids (as the ads said: *"Eight legs, two fangs and an attitude"*), but in Tony Randel's **TICKS** (1993, USA), herbal steroids used to enhance local rural marijuana crops accidentally create a horde of nasty, mutated, bloodsucking ticks—which are easily one of the more *revolting* bugs among the countless species to be found in the insect world.

As part of the Wilderness Project, a group of 'troubled' (i.e., mostly real annoying!) L.A. youths are taken out into the forests north of the city by their adult custodian Charles (Peter Scolari, from the short-lived TV sitcom *Bosom Buddies* [1980-82, USA], in which he co-starred alongside Tom Hanks) and his girlfriend Holly (Rosalind Allen), a romantically-involved couple of enthusiastic social workers. Led by Tyler Burns (Seth Green), who is trying to get over his lingering fear of getting lost in the woods as a kid (a subplot which doesn't really go anywhere), this group of 'kids' consist of every imaginable teenage cliché possible. There's trash-talkin' Darryl (Alfonso Riberio), who's a wannabe badass 'gangsta' from the hood—which is actually quite difficult to swallow after seeing Mr. Riberio for all those years as pampered rich boy Carlton Banks on *The Fresh Prince of Bel Air* (1990-96, USA)!—who goes by the unlikely street name of "Panic" and also brings his dog Brutus along for the ride; then we've got good girl Melissa (Virginya Keehne); spoiled rich-girl Dee Dee (Ami Dolenz) and her obnoxious buff jock boyfriend Rome (Roy Oriel); as well as Kelly (Dina Dayrit), a quiet, meek girl who is (quote) "a victim of her own troubled mind". Upon their arrival at the Camp Madeleine Campgrounds, they're greeted with open hostility by the locals ("What brings you to our neck of the woods?"), especially by Jerry (Michael Medeiros) and him-known-only-as Sir (Barry Lynch). It seems when the local logging

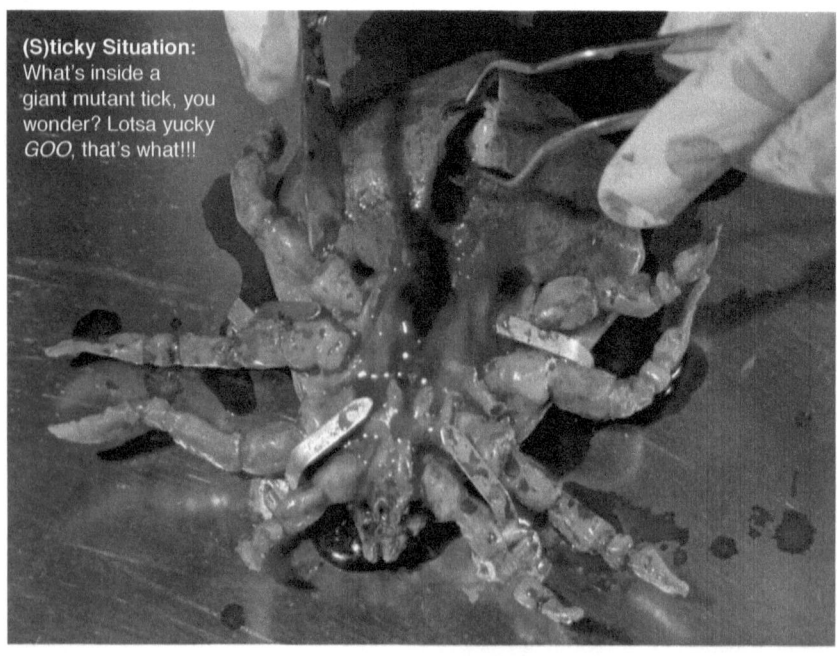

(S)ticky Situation: What's inside a giant mutant tick, you wonder? Lotsa yucky *GOO*, that's what!!!

plant closed down and laid-off all its employees, the townsfolk instead resorted to (quote) "illicit means of gettin' by" and started numerous grow-ops. However, in order to increase the growers' profits, Jarvis (the always-great Clint Howard), their 'chemist' of sorts, experimented with some backyard horticulture and began using steroids to enlarge the pot plants' buds, only to unwittingly have much of this home-brewed concoction seep into the ground. This seepage infects and mutates all the ticks, which soon overrun the plantation and its environs, Camp Madelaine included.

Originally conceived by visual effects guru Doug Beswick, though far-from-original, the somewhat messily-scripted scenario still manages to push all the right buttons, with plenty of enthusiastic and over-the-top F/X work courtesy of K.N.B. EFX Group. Oversized, blood-squirting ticks that burrow painfully under their victims' skin provide plenty of fun for undiscriminating horror fans, and it's all further bolstered by a fast-paced finale involving most of the principal cast battling for their lives against an ever-increasing swarm of voracious, hard-bodied ticks. Tough to kill due to their exoskeletons, the best defense against these vicious little buggers seems to be fire, which causes them to explode in spectacularly splattery fashion, like blood-filled oversized popcorn kernels. Brimming with 'old-school' practical F/X, the token 'perils of steroids' angle is also half-heartedly—if rather ridiculously—explored, but it at least allows for a bravura showstopper towards the end of the film wherein a titanic tick gorily erupts from the carcass of a recently-deceased not-so-happy-camper who had indulged in too much recreational steroid abuse.

In spite of all the gooey fun to be had, much of **TICKS** is actually pretty slow on the uptake, populated by a variety of woefully-underwritten characters taking up—some might say wasting—much of the film's relatively brief running time, a brevity which may be conveniently blamed on the project being (quote) "under-scheduled", according to director Randel's commentary. Transposing the much-used standard 'slasher film' formula (including the summer camp setting), **TICKS** actually has quite a lot in common with Danny Steinman's mean-spirited **FRIDAY THE 13TH: A NEW BEGINNING** (1985, USA), albeit minus that film's nasty edge…and with oodles upon oodles of skittering, splattering monster ticks, of course! As with most unidimensional, one-note movies such as this, most of these characters are merely brought together to become bug fodder, and in one of the more potentially interesting

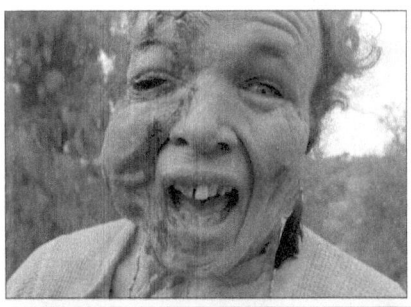

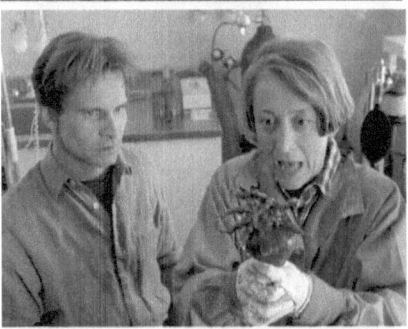

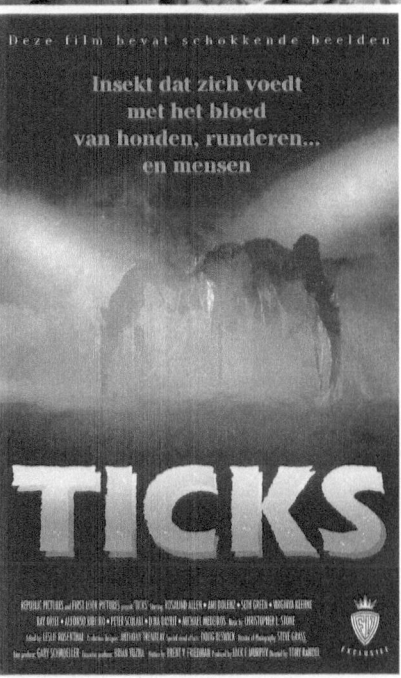

Top: Clint Howard laughs maniacally as he proclaims "*I'm INFESTED!*" with the title buggers in **TICKS** (1993). **Center:** *Ticked-Off!* Peter Scolari and Judy Jean Berns get up-close-and-personal with one of the oversized bloodsucking critters in the lab. **Above:** Dutch VHS cover

CURSE OF THE BLUE LIGHTS

Reviewed by Steve Fenton

USA, 1988. D: John Henry Johnson

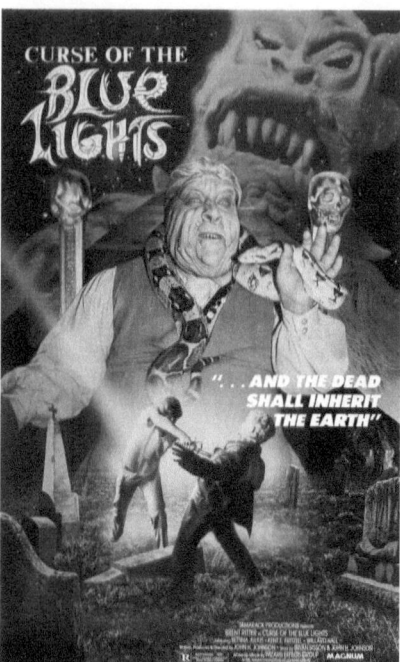

US poster

Choicest excerpt of dialogue: *"These ghouls or goblins with green faces. They looked* bizarre. *They had these* huge *hands, all gnarled-up, like tree bark or something. And they had these incredible* warts *all over their deformed faces!"*

Despite its paltry 3.8 rating there when I first looked up this film at the site a couple of years ago—said rating has since jumped a fraction of a decimal point to a whopping 3.9 on the Sphincter Scale in the interim!—the actual individual user reviews themselves for this title up at the IMDb are generally quite favorable towards it (e.g., "Fabulously insane monster mash", "Lightweight but pleasing cheesy schlock"). One reviewer even went so far as to call it "The best I've ever seen". So, this combined with what little—if *anything*!—I remembered reading about this film back around at the time of its initial release, had my expectations primed for something not just a little bit different, but hopefully something extra-special too. Hope springs eternal in the human breast (or is it *beast*?), as they say! So here goes nothin'…

In hopes of avoiding any potential spoilers, I made a point of avoiding reading too much either online or elsewhere about this shot-in-Colorado creepy-cheapie prior to finally—at long last!—sitting down to watch it (I've been planning on doing a write-up about it in *Monster!* for ages, and Sunday, October 8th, 2017 [Thanksgiving long weekend up here in Canada/Kekistan] proved to be the lucky day).

At the small town of Dudley, somewhere deep in America's "Bread Basket" (you know, where all the so-called "deplorables" supposedly live, in so-called "Fly-Over Country"), while tilling his field on his tractor, an old dirt farmer has a fateful fatal encounter with a living scarecrow (played behind a sackcloth hood by Willard Hall) that is actually *something else* altogether in disguise. No sooner has the stiff-legged, zombie-like creature—in actuality an undead ghoul named Forn—raised a shovel to behead the fallen farmer (albeit firmly off-screen), than the action abruptly cuts to stilted scenes of 'character development' involving our protagonists, over-the-hill subplots involving Tyler and his (quote) "trial by fire" to face his demons within the woods, this barely-developed character arc allows him to 'evolve' in record time to become the rather nominal hero. To this end, hillbilly horticulturists Jerry and Sir, baddies through and through, are also introduced to further ratchet-up the suspense and propel the story forward, and, much like Karl Hardman's divisive Harry Cooper character in George A. Romero's seminal **NIGHT OF THE LIVING DEAD** (1968, USA), they also provide the necessary tension and in-fighting during the film's climactic bug siege.

Budgeted at just over $1 million, **TICKS** had its biggest exposure via home video when theatrical engagements for low-budget stuff like this began to dry up, but despite the film's modestly-budgeted approach and rather hare-brained plot developments, Tony Randel's **TICKS** still clicks as a wholly appropriate 'creature feature', with plenty of 'old-school' visual viscera on view.

If you're in the mood for a tick-flick, this one is about the only game in town, but it shouldn't get under your skin too much.

'teens' all. Their plan is to—what else?!—party-down at a local spot called The Blue Lights (as per the title; no, it *isn't* some trendy nightclub!), which earned its name on account of mysterious lights spotted in the night sky high above it, that *may* be caused by UFOs, or might possibly even be of outright supernatural rather than merely inexplicably paranormal origin. Another local legend—or is it perhaps a *true* story?—tells of The Muldoon Man ("…some kind of missing link or somethin'…"), an ancient, petrified statue-like figure of a misshapen humanoid monstrosity that had originally been discovered in the vicinity by an archaeologist name of Muldoon—its namesake—then became lost under macabre and tragic circumstances many decades previous.

Sure enough, while trekking through the bush to the chosen party site and having only just borne witness to eerie azure illuminations (i.e., two neon-blue dots moving against a plain black background) overhead in the heavens, our 'teenage' heroes/heroines happen across what may well be nothing less than The Muldoon Man him—er, *it*—self, buried in the earth with just one gnarly-knuckled, monstrous hand showing aboveground (no, we're not made privy to its facial features as-yet). No sooner have the delayed partiers brought local cop Officer Fox (Marty Bechina) to the scene of their startling discovery to show him what they stumbled upon than they realize their find—as per the hoary cliché—has up and vanished in their brief absence, prompting a reprimand by the policeman for their act of apparent mischief, who then goes on his way with a stern-but-friendly caution for them not to be causing any more trouble. Their partying plans now having been put aside, the group of inquisitive youngsters instead determine to get to the bottom of the mystery they themselves have partially helped set into motion…

All evidence points to the excavated statue having been dragged-off in the direction of the in-aptly-named Sunny Hills Cemetery, where, along with his equally homely 'colleague' Bor (Kent E. Fritzell), the aforementioned Forn—his former scarecrow disguise now abandoned—works as a hench-thing in service of the obese, bluish/greenish-faced boss ghoul, known as Loath (the top-billed Brent Ritter, wearing effective demonic prosthetic makeup, including contact lenses and pointy teeth, latter of which sometimes cause him to slur his words in an unintelligible manner). Here the fiendish ghoul-boys (a.k.a. "Workers of the Darkness") brew-up a horrid humanary stew (or rather, *soup*) using a maggot-ridden male cadaver, which they melt down into a bubbling

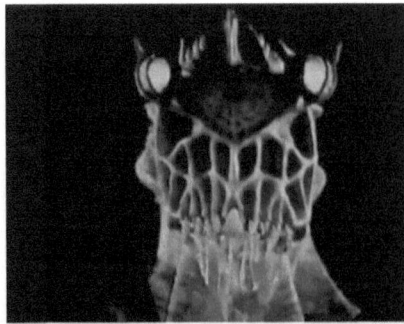
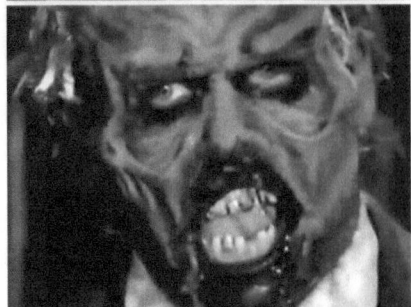
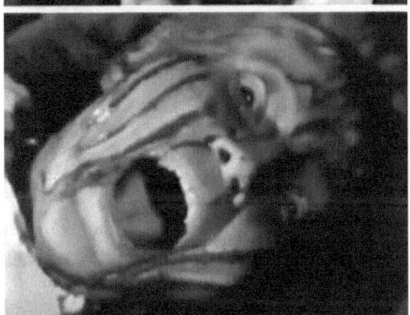
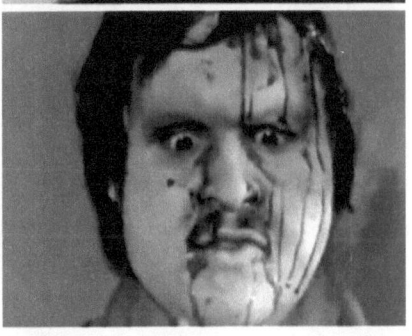

4 shots from **COTBL. Top to Bottom:** The obligatory false-scare scene with a 'kid' in a monster mask; a zombie mugs for the camera; the crazy witch woman, about to overact her last; and some big galoot begins to bleed from the brain

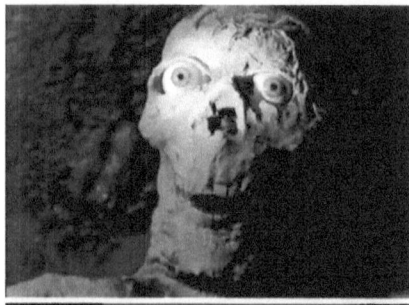

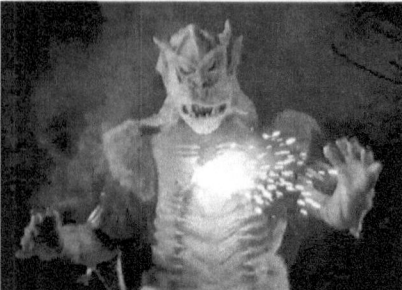

Top: This googly-eyed corpse from **COTBL** sure looks happy to be dead! **Above & Bottom:** The Muldoon Man, er, in da house!

puddle of gruesome glop prior to 'transfusing' it into The Muldoon Man's inert corpse, which underwent a process of petrification rather than simply succumbing to putrefaction and decomposing. Having overheard Loath's plans for he and his frightful flunkies in the near future, after the trespassing 'kids'—twentysomethings all!—unwittingly give their presence away, the ghoul master orders Bor and Forn to capture the trespassing humans forthwith, or else pay the penalty for failure. As it turns out, without a certain ornate metal disc (of talismanic powers) that is vital to Loath's scheme to resurrect the long-dormant Muldoon Man, this resurrection cannot be carried out as foretold, and that talisman is now in the possession of one of the youths, having been removed from the chest of The Muldoon Man at its burial place prior to its disappearance.

Looking for answers as to why dark forces had claimed the lives of more than one of their number during the previous night, the survivors visit a local witch woman (Bettina Julius, hamming it up horrendously with maximum histrionics) to get the lowdown on both the strange disc and The Muldoon Man. "It waits for a chance to enter our realm and reign forever over mankind," she informs our heroes regarding the latter before offering to lend them an assist in preventing this very thing from happening; a silly-looking 'macramé balaclava' (for wont of a better term!), an ancient book and an interdimensional portal in the form of a mirror—and of course loads of mock-'occult' mumbo-jumbo—are only parts of the witch's supernatural solution. Just when you think the actress playing her couldn't possibly get any hammier if she tried, she becomes possessed by a dark power, Deadite-style, and goes way off the deep end into an all-out gibbering frenzy. It's only right before her character kicks the bucket that she actually manages a semblance of more understated, naturalistic acting (even if it mostly just seems that way due to simple contrast, but better late than never).

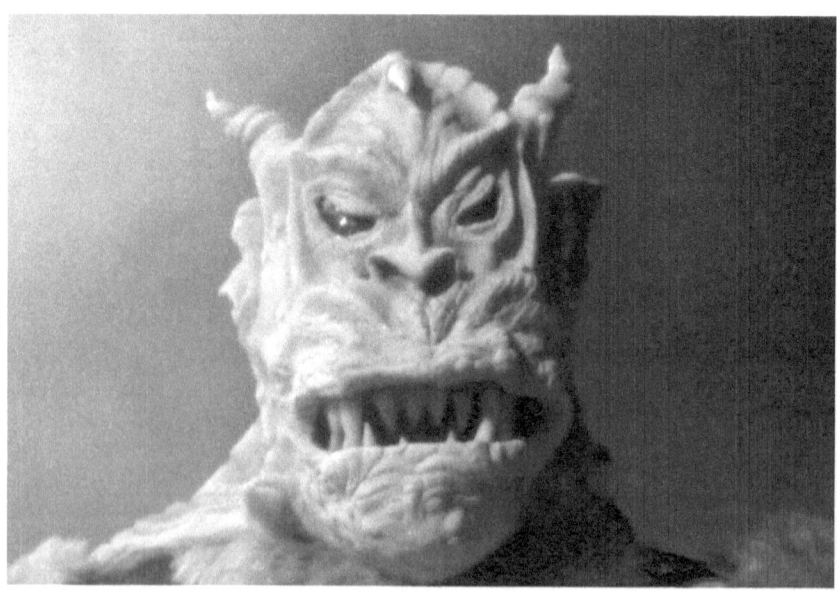

As the loathsome Loath of the (quote) "ancient ghoul clan", as befitting his star billing—despite doing double-duty as key grip on the production too—Ritter gives what is by far **COTBL**'s most competent, commanding performance, and his rotund frame and prim-'n'-proper 'upper crust English' delivery kept on reminding me of Aussie "Hitchcock lookalike/soundalike" Frank Thring (from Philippe Mora's **HOWLING III: THE MARSUPIALS** [1987, Australia], in which he steals scenes from the titular—*um*—werewolves). Unfortunately, while it's Loath who gets to mouth most of the best lines, we can't say for sure, as, evidently caused by the fake fanged dental appliance crammed into his gob, his pronunciation was thrown-off considerably, causing many of his words to come out garbled/slurred and decidedly hard to understand (although I distinctly heard him lispily namedrop HPL's "lost Yog Sothoth" at one point; this while sat upon a diabolic throne amidst gloomy mood lighting fondling [and waggling his tongue at] a modest-sized if living, breathing constrictor snake, yet).

As for the film's behind-the-camera credits, when we notice it at all, the thin synthesized score by Randall Crissman seldom suits the action that's occurring as it plays, not even the end-credits crawl. Writer/producer/director J.H. Johnson also functioned jointly as both the film's DP and its editor too. The by-turns amateurish and passably slick SFX makeup and prosthetics were the work of the Wizard Effects Group (partly consisting of assistant director Bryan Sisson, who also co-wrote the original story and functioned as an assistant editor). Many of the cast and crew also doubled—maybe even *tripled*?—as members of the walking dead.

One guy sinks into a grave as if into quicksand, swallowed-up without a trace into the earth, which closes-up over him like a sphincter afterwards. Having been held captive in the ghouls' domain, he subsequently reappears unharmed and *apparently* (note italics) normal…for a little while, anyway. Having at last regained possession of the magical talisman, Loath invokes its resurrecting power to empty-out the graveyard surrounding his mansion ("…I beseech you, mighty empirical disc, bring forth your messengers of doom!"), whereupon, sooner than you can say "**PLAGUE OF THE ZOMBIES**" three times fast, the two surviving heroes are forced to contend with a horde (okay, maybe *20*, tops) of shambling undead corpses in order to rescue their girlfriends from the grisly ghoul-fiends' clammy clutches. Just as the boorish Bor—whose three-digit manual extremities (I hesitate to say 'hands') rather resemble anthropomorphized pig's trotters—is preparing to melt-down the gals to help 'rehydrate' and reanimate The Muldoon Man (who seems to have a bottomless appetite for liquefied human bodies), their boyfriends burst into the dungeon to thwart the monsters' plans, precipitating the climactic concatenation.

Does The Muldoon Man get to walk the earth anew? Yes, he does, I will tell you that much. Quite a *lot*, actually (if by no means very fast). Because if he *didn't*, would you ever be pissed-off at me for not warning you beforehand! In closing, **CURSE OF THE BLUE LIGHTS** is a fun, unpretentious bit of nonsense that, in these days when so much obscure (and in some cases debatably undeserving) schlock is getting released in deluxe Blu-ray editions with all the fixings, seems overdue for the same treatment. I don't doubt it'll be all the more enjoyable if given a pristine release in an optimal format.

DRY BONES

Reviewed by Sebastien Godin

USA, 2013. Ds: Gregory Lamberson, Michael O'Hear

Gregory Lamberson has long stood as one of the most unsung names in the indie genre world. His 1988 directorial debut **SLIME CITY** has a decent cult following, and **JOHNNY GRUESOME** (2018, USA), his upcoming film adaptation of his beloved novel (I had the immense pleasure of working on the film version as its behind-the-scenes documenter), has been getting quite a lot of buzz lately in the low-budget horror world. But among his most-undervalued if nevertheless worthwhile works is the 2013 micro-budget creature feature **DRY BONES**, a film that tackles the subject of one of the most-beloved (and feared!) of childhood terrors: the dreaded monster under the bed!

Young Andy (Mark Goodfellow) lives in abject fear of the decrepit beast living under his bed. Nobody seems to believe him until his abusive father (a comically over-the-top turn by **BASKET CASE**'s Kevin Van Hentenryck) is mysteriously killed when threatening his son. Flash-forward to years later, and Andy has become a down-on-his luck middle-aged man who now prefers to instead be called Drew (played by co-director Michael O'Hear of **SNOW SHARK** [2011, USA, D: Sam Qualiana]). Drew returns to his childhood home in the hopes of repainting and selling it with the aid

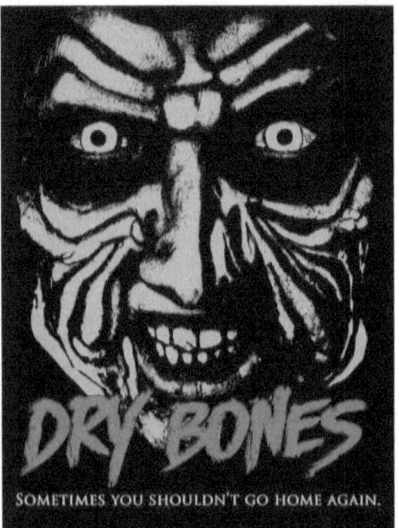

of his alcoholic friend Tom (Paul McGinnis, from **FRANKENSTEIN'S PATCHWORK MONSTER** [2015, USA, D: Emil Novak]. As time progresses, we become aware of just how luckless Drew really is when corpses—with their life essences sucked right out of them—begin popping-up, bringing him to the unwanted attention of emotionally-distraught police officer Carl (John Renna, from **PORKCHOP 3D** [2012, USA, D: Eamon Hardiman]). Just when things couldn't get any worse, the monster under his bed reveals itself to be real…and it's a *succubus*! The diseased, phallic-winged demon (Debbie Rochon, who has appeared in more B-horror movies than you can count; including **TEENAPE VS. THE MONSTER NAZI APOCALYPSE** [2012, USA, D: Chris Seaver] and **SHE WOLF RISING** [2016, USA, D: Marc Leland]) has some dark, twisted plans in mind for Drew. Can he escape this twisted childhood nightmare-turned-reality…?

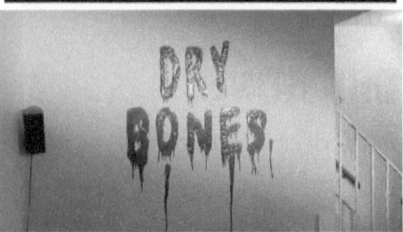

DRY BONES is one of the more lower-budgeted efforts that Lamberson has given us, and it's very clear right from the get-go that this is a micro-budget production in every sense of the word. However, what it may lack in terms of technical slickness, it more than makes up for with its sharp, witty script and excellent cast of characters. O'Hear plays his character very stiffly, but in a manner that absolutely works in his favor. McGinnis and Renna make colorful supporting figures, and the appearances of other Lamberson regulars like Bob Bozek and Alex McBryde round-out a pretty likable cast. The show is obviously stolen by Rochon, who plays her monstrous antagonist with sadistic glee, unhindered by the mounds of makeup she's covered in.

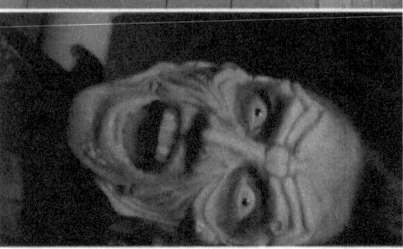

The gore effects are limited (as is the bloodshed in general) but the dried-up victims of the creature are delightful, while the beast itself is the product of some fairly impressive makeup effects. The musical score is also a treat, principally supported by an excellent rendition of "Dem Bones" by Sealcats. The song plays an important role in the film, so it only makes sense that it would be given a very special treatment. Even if you don't enjoy the movie itself, then there's no doubt in my mind that you won't be able to get this tune out of your head for a long, long while after the end credits have rolled.

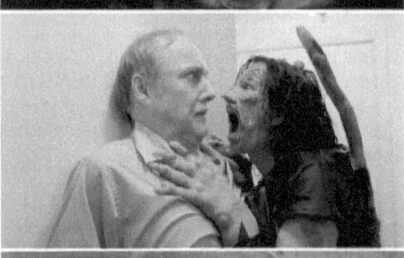

Left, Top to Bottom: The poster and a selection of frame-grabs from **DRY BONES'** trailer (viewable on YouTube, natch), featuring Debbie Rochon as the diabolical demoness and a cute-'n'-cuddly "Nerf" cadaver that looks every bit as cheerful as the one on page 272 does!

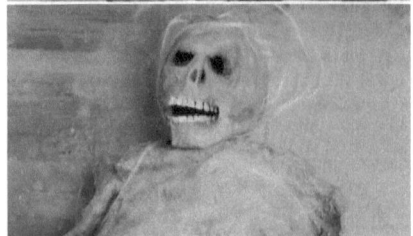

Creature Feature Reviews

Ultimately, **DRY BONES** is neither among the best micro-budget horror films out there, nor is it even one of Lamberson's best works either. However, it *is* an excellent example of just how important a solid script and likable characters can be to a genre piece. So often we forget that horror is capable of conveying more pathos, fun, emotion and sadness than any other genre. Within its brisk 87-minute runtime, the film manages to deliver all these various emotional beats without once losing its momentum or suffering from the dreaded tonal whiplash that can so easily plague even the strongest of screenplays.

For all of its faults, **DRY BONES** never falters in delivering a fun story via people we can connect with and enjoy spending time around. It manages to be a mature exploration of childhood fear and trauma without losing its sense of energy or fun, balancing good old-fashioned spooky joy with real-world struggle and a dash of modern day shocks. In a world where indie horror is growing more and more pandering towards its target audiences, it's very nice to see that people like Greg Lamberson still recognize all of the potential the genre has to offer. And on those merits alone, I'd say that **DRY BONES** is well worth picking up.

YOUNG-GOO AND DINOSAUR ZUZU

(영구와 공룡쭈쭈 / *Young-guwa gongryong Zzu-Zzu*)

Reviewed by Sebastien Godin

South Korea, 1993. D: Hyung-rae Shim

This is going to be a bit of an odd one for me, as I've never had to review an unsubtitled foreign film before. The film is reportedly very hard to come by, and the copy that I watched looked to be cobbled-together from various source prints. This resulted in some occasionally difficult-to-see moments and a very shoddy attempt at a 5.1 mix. But that didn't hinder my enjoyment, as I had a pretty decent time with this bizarre South Korean comedy from the director of the notorious **REPTILIAN** (the North American release title of 용가리 / *Yonggary*, 1999, SK). The titular beast(s) here bears a striking resemblance to the original Yongary, as seen in **YONGARY, MONSTER FROM THE DEEP** (대괴수 용가리 / *Taekoesu Yonggary*, 1967, SK, D: Ki-duk Kim), with its traditional dinosaurian figure, horned snout and ability to spew flames from a conveniently placed (and not very well-hidden!) nozzle in his

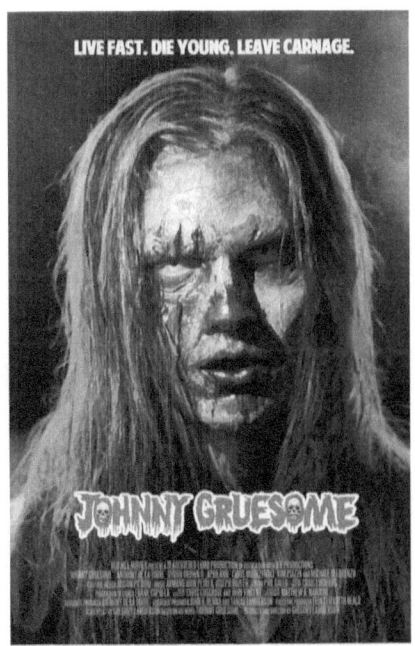

Director Gregory Lamberson's newest entry into micro-horror filmmaking

mouth. The result is an admittedly unimpressive but immensely charming beast that has a lot of heart, and is very enjoyable to watch during both its cutesy comic relief scenes as well as the shockingly violent rampage sequences (one particularly unexpected moment of gore involves Zuzu's rampaging mother melting a whole room full of terrified humans with her fiery breath), and one can see the beginnings of writer/director/producer/star Hyung-rae Shim's obsession with largescale monster violence (later more fully-realized in his aforementioned **REPTILIAN** and the infamous South Korean blockbuster **D-WAR** [디워, 2007, SK]).

This reaches something of a strange middle ground between Hyung-rae's comedies (which is where he earned his fame and eventual superstardom in South Korea) and his later big-budget *kaijū*-style disaster thrillers. The plot is pretty straightforward, even with no subtitles and atrocious audio. Hyung-rae himself either plays an "actual" child or else a very childish adult (hard to tell) who finds himself befriending a baby dinosaur named Zuzu. Eventually, after a good few sequences of shenanigans, both of them are kidnapped by some criminals. Too bad for the villains, Zuzu's mother shows up to find her offspring, leaving a fiery trail of destruction in her wake.

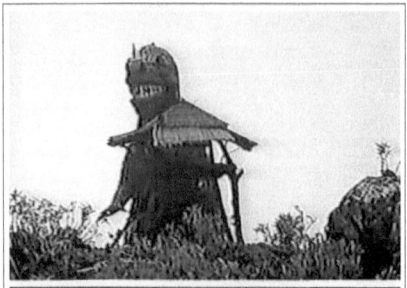

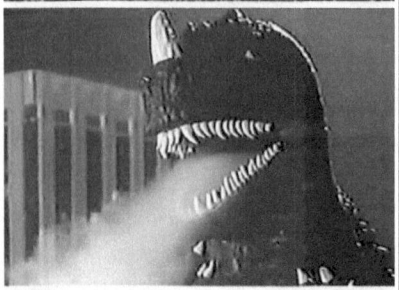

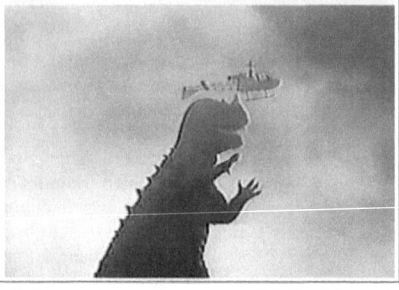

Following in the footsteps of **GORGO** and **GAPPA, THE TRIPHIBIAN MONSTER**, the mother/son tag-team of **DINOSAUR ZUZU** make short work of any human interference in their tightknit family unit!

Sound familiar? Well it should. Nearly identical scripts were the basis for the beloved British giant monster adventure **GORGO** (1961, D: Eugène Lourié) and the obscure but fairly-well-beloved *kaijū* comedy **GAPPA, THE TRIPHIBIAN MONSTER** (大巨獣ガッパ / Daikyojū Gappa, 1967, Japan, D: Haruyasu Noguchi; better-known in North America under the hilariously inaccurate title **MONSTER FROM A PREHISTORIC PLANET**), both of which feature angry monster parents wrecking cities in hopes of finding their children. Now, simply throw in some bizarre slapstick and a strangely mean-spirited climax (albeit, with a fake-out that helps soften the blow for younger viewers) and that's pretty much what you get here. It's silly, weird, sort-of-fun and sort-of-annoying, but always fascinating to watch.

As far as I know, there has never been an overseas release of **DINOSAUR ZUZU**, even in bootleg form. The poorly-transferred version I watched can be found through digging around online, and that may be the best we're ever gonna have. I won't go so far as to say it's a film that's deserving of a pristine Blu-ray release, but it is one that should be seen, if only for the completist *kaijū* aficionados who are craving something a little on the wilder side.

THE FLESH EATERS

Reviewed by Les Moore

USA, 1962. D: Jack Curtis

US trailer narration: *"It takes just* ten *seconds for* **THE FLESH EATERS** *to strip the last bit of flesh from any living thing! ...They stood alone, surrounded by the most abominable threat ever faced by human beings! ...One-by-one, half-mad with terror, they turned upon each other. What was the dread secret of this horror that was born out of science and madness? Was there no way to escape...***THE FLESH EATERS***?!"*

Castaway floatplane flyer Grant Murdoch, our been-around-some hero, comes to a frightening realization: *"...We've stumbled onto a* living horror*!"* He subsequently comes to another one a short time later: *"There's something* weird *out in that water! Something that eats the skin right off ya!"*

I was originally due to have this review run in *Monster!* #32 (March 2017) as a companion-piece to Matt Bradshaw's fun-'n'-funky **FLESH EATERS**-themed comic strip-format review, but since I'd already gotten something in that ish beforehand, when the mag's page-count escalated to well above that of our usual-sized issues' (i.e., up, up and away into the stratosphere!), this Yours Truly's present **TFE** write-up got justifiably bumped ahead to this ish instead.

This movie had long been touted as one of the true pioneering efforts of splatter cinema, ranking right up there with "founding father" Herschell Gordon Lewis' **BLOOD FEAST** (1963, USA). While **TFE** is certainly not as consistently gory as **BF** is—the fact that it was shot in flat B&W contributes greatly to that (although, in my opinion, blood can actually look all-the-more-disturbing in monochrome)—it probably did stress the violence permissibility envelope of many early-'60s US moviegoers. As such, for all its tawdriness and seediness, it nevertheless remains an important landmark in the "evolution" of modern gore-for-gore's-sake movies (be it for better or worse; now that there's really no longer any envelope left to stress, the only place for goregrinders to go is well beyond the pale into increasingly sickening excesses that nobody needs to see... even if so many *want* to).

An approaching hurricane combined with his crate's technical problems cause seasoned-if-down-on-his-luck marine pilot Grant Murdoch (Byron Sanders) to engineer a forced seaplane landing nearby to a desolate Atlantic isle. Also aboard the light aircraft is a temperamental, self-pitying alcoholic/neurotic movie star—your stereotypical prima donna/drama queen—named Laura Winters (Rita Morley), who is traveling 'incognito' to her next movie shoot down Province Town way in the company of her loyal secretary/confidante, a much classier lassie with an even assier chassis name of Jan Letterman (Barbara Wilkin).

Almost immediately upon the protagonists' arrival 'safely' back down on *terra firma*, veteran Hollywood heavy, the top-billed Martin Kosleck (1904-1994), who was often cast as Nazis during the war years and beyond, shows up as soft-spoken (but creepy) marine biologist Prof. Peter Bartell, this after unexpectedly trudging ashore from out of the drink dressed in full SCUBA gear; a get-up which, at first sight of him advancing towards them through swirling, windblown whorls of beach-fog, causes the two surprised female castaways to react as though they've seen the very Creature from the Black Lagoon himself ("I'm very sorry if I frightened you. This equipment must make me look like one of those creatures from a horror film", Kosleck drolly deadpans in that familiar carefully-modulated Teutonic speech pattern of his). Within minutes of their encountering Prof. Bartell, the exploring Ms. Winters discovers a human skeleton while "beachcombing" and lets out a horrified shriek which alerts the others, who promptly come a-running. Being the supposed 'expert' in such matters, Bartell—whom, you'll recall, is a marine biologist (or so he says, anyway)—calmly and casually explains that the fleshless (as in completely picked-clean to the point of bleaching it!)—if still virtually fully intact—skeleton is attributable to (quote) "sharks". (Yeah, *right*, doc! Pull the other one, it's got barracudas on! Not that, to give him credit, our canny flyboy hero, who's been around a bit, actually falls for this shaky shark's tale

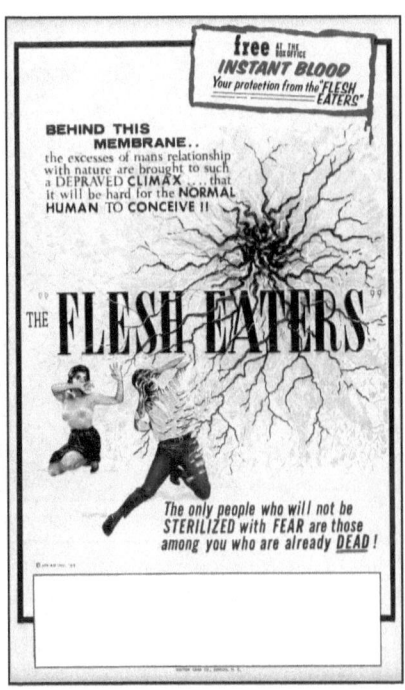

Striking US poster art which is reminiscent of SF paperback covers of its day

for even a second, mind you.) Later, ominously enough, mountains of de-fleshed fish carcasses begin mysteriously appearing washed-up on the beach (shades of the irradiated ones in **BEHEMOTH THE SEA MONSTER** [a.k.a. **THE GIANT BEHEMOTH**, 1959, UK, Ds: Eugène

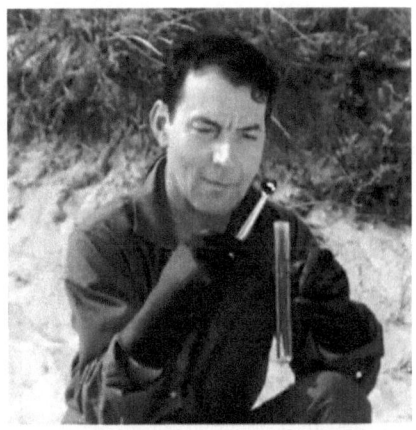

Martin Kosleck picks up a luminescent Flesh Eater specimen—represented by simple squiggly scratches on the film emulsion—with tweezers prior to popping it into a test-tube

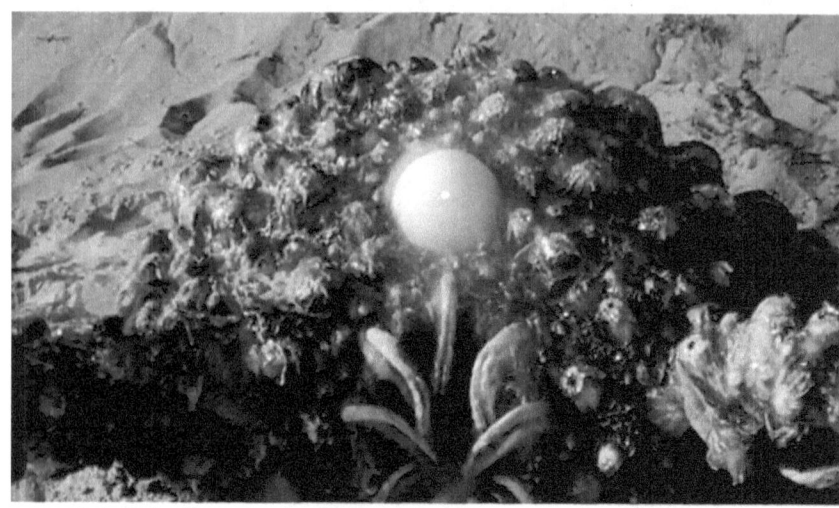

A giant-sized communal organism stalks human prey in **THE FLESH EATERS**

Lourié, Douglas Hickox; see *Monster!* #12, p.79]). Our heroes soon discover that the hungry culprits are millions upon millions of carnivorous aquatic microbes (often economically-if-effectively rendered onscreen as flickering scratches etched right into the film emulsion itself). These tiny creatures—self-described as a "microscopic parasite" by Kosleck's character (who knows *way* more than he's letting on, as well we know!)—infest the waters surrounding the island in abundant quantities rather like plankton, possessing appetites more insatiable than malnourished miniature piranhas. And are constantly multiplying...

It comes as no real surprise to either Murdoch or the audience that Dr. Bartell (who in one scene is contemptuously described by the ever-acting-up castaway actress as both "an egghead with a microscope" and a "little tin god!") is responsible for the new microbial lifeform's creation; part of still-ongoing experimentation he began while working for Nazi biochemists ("...a very low order of science", he confesses) in Norway following WW2. While searching for a means of curing viral infections, the scientists unwittingly and accidentally created... well, *y'know*. During some rather sleazy flashback scenes that prefigure such Nazi atrocity exploitationers as **ILSA, SHE-WOLF OF THE S.S.**, scientists oversee the feeding of "naked" (i.e., tactfully revealing no naughty bits) female prisoners to their indoor swimming pool-full of the so-called flesh eaters. These scenes and others were chopped from both old TV prints and Monterey Home Video's erstwhile available (*circa* the '80s) Beta/VHS cassette copies of **TFE**. Upon witnessing their no-budget seediness and too-suggestively implied nudity, I can well see why.

To get her back in like kind for her earlier cold-bloodedly cutting put-down of his manhood, while suddenly revealing a wide swathe of his all-too-familiar mean streak in the process, Kosleck sneeringly accuses her of being "all body and no brain!" But then, considering that the catty high-tone bitch *had* just attempted to both figuratively and literally emasculate him using only her cruel mouth, she pretty much got what she deserved, and we actually find ourselves siding with the villain in this particular instance. Not that we're even fully supposed to realize he *is* one quite yet, mind you, although his rather gleefully sadistic verbal comeback definitely does hint that his true colors might be a whole lot darker than some of his mildly suspicious companions-of-circumstance are starting to strongly suspect. Also, while usual character actor Kosleck's name wasn't exactly a household one, chances are he would have been well-known enough at that time even to the 'new generation' of monster kids that had grown up since his heydays (*circa* the 'Forties). After making one of his earliest appearances of all in the mildly SF-themed early talkie **ALRAUNE** (1929, Germany, D: Richard Oswald), Kosleck went on to appear in such Hollywood horror movies as **THE MUMMY'S CURSE** (1944, D: Leslie Goodwins)—playing the figuratively and literally backstabbing Egyptian henchman, Ragheb—as well as appearing in **THE FROZEN GHOST** (1945, D: Harold Young), **HOUSE OF HORRORS** and **SHE-WOLF OF LONDON** (both 1946, D: Jean Yarbrough; all four of those just-cited titles originated at Hollywood's hottest horror house, Universal), later appearing in a bunch of US sci-fi TV shows too.

Meanwhile, back at the island, an obnoxious (and frankly unbelievable) character named Omar (Ray Tudor)—a hep-talking, philosophizing (and also rather ridiculous) beatnik—washes ashore on his makeshift wooden raft. But it only amounts to a short stopover for him. (***ATTENTION: SPOILER ALERT! #1***) Omar's overacting and ludicrous dialogue are thankfully conclusively silenced when Bartell 'hospitably' offers his latest 'guest' a cocktail spiked with several of the flesh-eating organisms. Squealing in agony ("There's something inside me! It's eating its way out!"), Omar promptly expires due to a bloodily perforated stomach—*YOWCH!*—in what are perhaps the film's most sadistically mean-spirited and unpleasant moments, while Kosleck stands coldly and idly by recording his victim's agonized reactions as he dies with cold analytical detachment.

(***ATTENTION: SPOILER ALERT! #2***) For the memorably weird climax, Bartell electrifies the ocean around the shoreline. Conse-

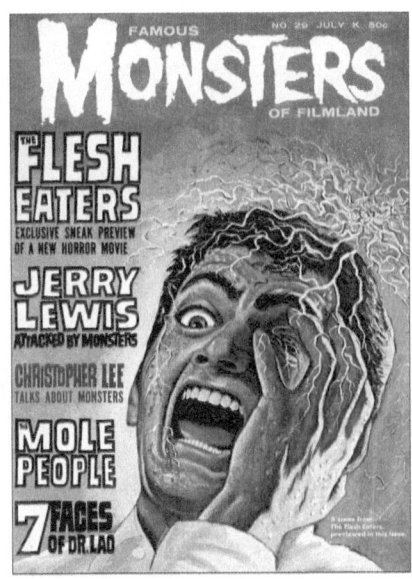

Basil Gogos did this luridly eye-grabbing **FLESH EATERS**-themed cover art for *FM* #29 (July 1964)

quently, all the unicellular flesh eaters coalesce into a single gigantic entity with the potential to obliterate (i.e., devour) all Humankind. This humongous, acephalous, tentacled mega-protozoan thingy towers over the island c/o optically-enhanced miniature effects that are waaaayyy better than you have any right to

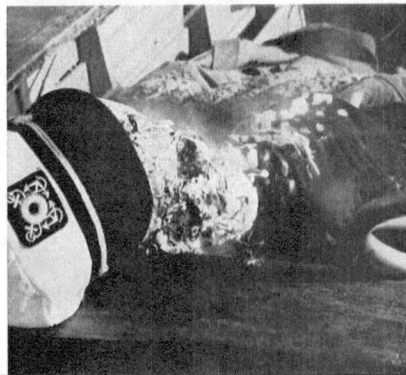

This opening spread (pp.4+5) of a special promo for the film in *Shriek!* magazine #1 (1965) depicts a gruesome image that was often cut from TV prints

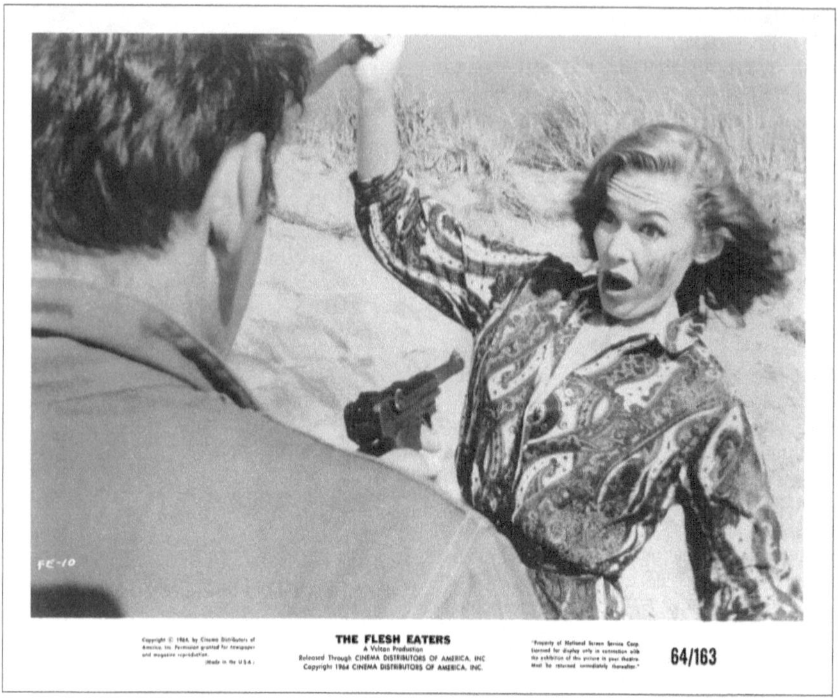

Laura Winters (Rita Morley) is about to get curtly chopped-down by Dr. Bartell (Martin Kosleck)'s quick-draw Luger in this unexpected moment from the film; US lobby still

expect from a low-low budgeter such as this. I won't give away the simplistic ending, but I will tell you that **TFE** was capably—and often quite stylishly—edited by none other than soft/hard porn artisan Radley Metzger (the future "Henry Paris") in his formative pre-skin salad days. Kosleck meanwhile went on to play one Basil Malko, a similarly anti-American mad

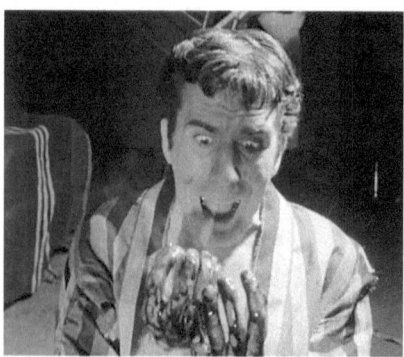

After feeling a churning in his guts then sudden excruciating pains inside him, Omar the garrulous beatnik's horror truly begins when his stomach wall splits open…and that's only the start *of it!*

scientist who messed around with pond-slime-green, algae-like flesh-absorbing bacterial life-forms in the cheap-ass Yankee 007 rip-off, **AGENT FOR H.A.R.M.** (1966), directed by no less than Gerd Oswald, of *The Outer Limits* (1963-65) fame and acclaim. In that decidedly discount wannabe cash-in, very little of much interest happens, and it is mostly only of any interest whatsoever on account of its quite stellar 'psychotronic' cast (which also includes future Eurotrash cinema sex kitten Barbara Bouchet).

Although obviously produced on a budget about as slight—if not all-out scrawny—as its "slimline" star's build was, rather than even attempting to blow us away with impressive production values right from the get-go, right at the outset, in a directorial decision presumably primarily intended to ensure that sufficient funds were saved to sock into its oftentimes quite remarkably well-done FX work, **TFE** instead merely switches scenes from NYC to its primary island location without further ado or delay. Why? Because, as any low-budget filmmaker worth their salt well knows (a cosmic given which holds every bit as true today as ever), shooting in rural locales without having to resort to either building or renting special sets for the occasion saves on bucks big-time. That said, while cost-effective, shooting in such a seemingly out-of-the-way place as serves as the main location here must have added to the rigors of the shoot in far from inconsiderable ways, simply due to the inhospitable terrain and clime (the weather does indeed appear exceedingly unpleasant for much of the runtime, as though the makers purposely opted to shoot on the shittiest days they could get, and this aesthetic decision does add a great deal to the dreary bleakness of the milieu; indeed, few other monster movies of its day attain such high levels of grimness, griminess and grittiness). While **THE FLESH EATERS** may arguably fall just a few nibbles shy of attaining the all-out "lost classic" status which some well-meaning enthusiasts sought to bestow on it once upon a time, it can easily rank up there with such visceral "so-'bad'-they're-great" schlockers as **THE BRAIN THAT WOULDN'T DIE** (1962) and **THE HORROR OF PARTY BEACH** (1964, both USA), and in terms of its script, direction and performances, it generally surpasses both of them, aesthetically speaking.

NOTES: If you were to go solely by what the IMDb says—when it comes to that site, as with doctors, it's sometimes best to get a second opinion—you'd assume this movie originated in 1964; however, the print clearly bears the official copyright year, in Roman numerals, of MCMLXII (=1962). The otherwise quite nice widescreen copy which I freely confess I downloaded courtesy of Vuze via an online torrent site (So shoot me! Just don't be committing any indignities on my corpse afterwards, OK? Else I'll come back and haunt you) was missing both the "Nazi atrocity" flashback scenes and the momentary startling/striking red-tinted climactic sequence which had been intact on Sinister Cinema's erstwhile (circa '90s) videocassette transfer print, which was how I first saw **TFE** back in about 1992 or thereabouts. Not to be confused with the film's secondary female lead Barbara *Wilkin*, tertiary cast member Barbara *Wilson* had previously appeared in several other creatures features: namely Herbert L. Strock's **BLOOD OF DRACULA** and László "Leslie" Kardos' **THE MAN WHO TURNED TO STONE** (both 1957, USA), as well as Virgil W. Vogel's **INVASION OF THE ANIMAL PEOPLE** (*Rymdinvasion i Lappland*, 1959, USA/Sweden).

FRANKENSTEIN 2000: AFTER DEATH

(*Frankenstein 2000 – Ritorno dalla morte*; a.k.a. **RETURN FROM DEATH [FRANKENSTEIN 2000]**)

Reviewed by Eric Messina

Italy, 1991. D: "David Hills"/Joe D'Amato (r.n. Aristide Massaccesi)

"D'Amato"/Massaccesi, quoted from Martin Coxhead's combo article/interview "Man of a Thousand Pseudonyms" (which ran in *Gorezone* magazine [#18, 1991]): *"I'm trying to be an Italian Roger Corman."*

Screenwriter Antonio Tentori, interviewed circa 2013, long after the director's death: *"He ['D'Amato'/Massaccesi] did erotic films, and then hardcore porn, but his true passion was always horror. [...]* **FRANKENSTEIN 2000** *is an evident sign of Aristide's [...] passion for fantasy, horror and thrillers. [...] He gave me this script to revise, because he wanted to do* Frankenstein, *he wanted to do a modern* Frankenstein. *He wanted to make a film that referred to Mary Shelley's book and to the first* Frankenstein *films by*

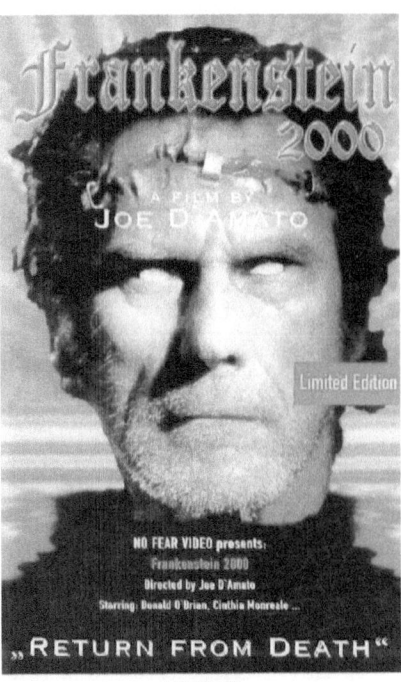

US DVD

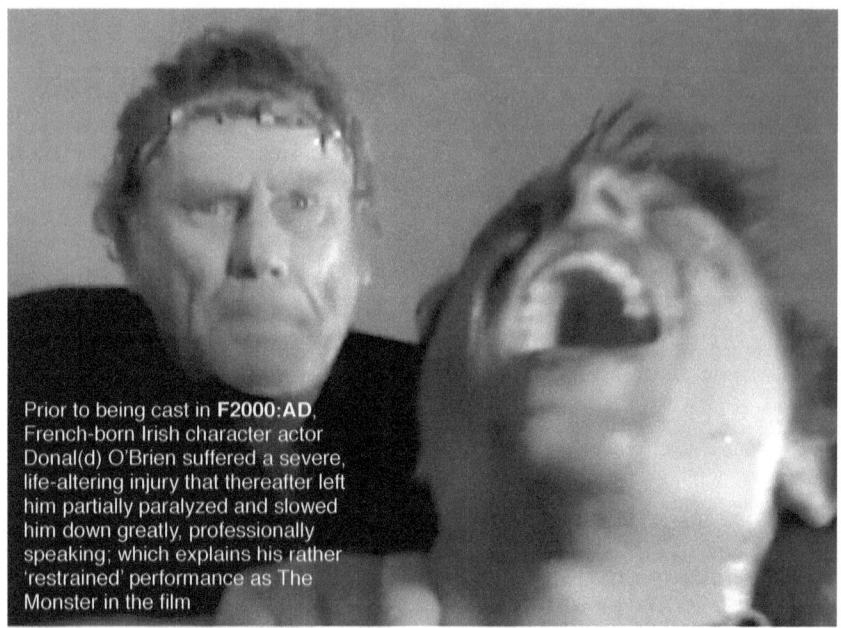

Prior to being cast in **F2000:AD**, French-born Irish character actor Donal(d) O'Brien suffered a severe, life-altering injury that thereafter left him partially paralyzed and slowed him down greatly, professionally speaking; which explains his rather 'restrained' performance as The Monster in the film

James Whale, about the famous monster. [...] It is a splatter film, remaining in line with Aristide's style, but less than **BEYOND THE DARKNESS**, **ANTHROPOPHAGUS**, **ABSURD** and some of his previous horror films. But it still has some very violent scenes. There's a rather evident reference to James Whale's **FRANKENSTEIN** and Mary Shelley's book when the monster comes back to life in the morgue. [...] Another thing to note is the presence of Donald O'Brien, who is the main actor, the monster. [...] By chance, Donald O'Brien fell in his home. Thus, one side of his body became semi-paralyzed, and his hand was slightly cramped. When he was chosen to play Frankenstein [i.e., The Monster], he played the role [...] in such a convincing manner that he seemed like a monster. But it was all due to that domestic accident, which caused him to acquire this sort of limp."

Unidentified actor playing a cop, regarding O'Brien as The Monster: *"It was* huge *and* horrible*!"*

After a lengthy career of dishing-out the sleaze with Laura Gemser (a.k.a. "Moira Chen") as the *über*-slutty journalist protagonist of the most unappealing, uninhibited and offensively repulsive hardcore porn that manages to offend even the most jaded raincoat-crowd viewer, Aristide Massaccesi ([1936-1999] better-known to teeming legions as "Joe D'Amato") attempted a new career direction. Practically all of the *Emanuelle*—*sans* one "m" to differentiate them from the "official" *Emmanuelle*—films share common elements, interjecting snuff, bestiality and cannibalism (etc.), all in the interests of some viewers' sexual arousal—not me though, I'm *normal*!

Among D'Amato's sizeable body of work, such fare was his mold-ridden bread-and-butter throughout much of the '70s and '80s (often while partnered with George Eastman [r.n. Luigi "Luca" Montefiori] and Gemser [r.n. Laurette Marcia Gemser], the former of whom sometimes penned scripts for the director). Soon after this phase of his career, D'Amato mellowed-out somewhat and founded the notorious cheapjack exploitation outfit Filmirage, with which most fans of extra-shitty Eurotrash movies are familiar; its most universally-famous example being the notorious **TROLL 2** (1991, Italy, D: "Drake Floyd"/Claudio Fragasso). D'Amato never made a film that wasn't trying to rip something off or capitalize on some cinematic subgenre or other, but his work is always (well, *usually*) over-the-top and enjoyable on a fucked-up "What-am-I-witnessing?!" level of depraved extremity. Filmirage farmed-out directorial duties to up-and-coming young filmmakers and, at their best, bankrolled such higher-end cult hits as Michele Soavi's first directorial feature, the stylish *giallo* **STAGEFRIGHT: AQUARIUS** (*Deliria*, a.k.a. **BLOODY BIRD**, 1987, Italy). At the other end of the scale, they also produced their own threadbare in-house exploitation product, including such monster/horror cheapies as: "Claude Milliken"/Claudio Lattanzi's **ZOMBIE 5: KILLING BIRDS** (a.k.a. *Killing Birds: Raptors*, 1987), "Humphrey Humbert"/Umberto Lenzi's **GHOSTHOUSE** (*La casa 3*) and "Martin Newlin"/Fabrizio Laurenti's **GHOSTHOUSE II** (*La casa 4*, a.k.a. **WITCHERY**, both 1988), as well as "Humbert"/Lenzi's **HITCHER IN THE DARK** (*Paura nel buio*, 1989), George Eastman's **METAMORPHOSIS** (*DNA formula letale*, 1990) and "Raffaele 'Raf' Donato" (actually the pseudonymous Massaccesi)'s **DEEP BLOOD** (a.k.a. *Sangue negli abissi*, a.k.a. **SHARKS**, 1990), among others.

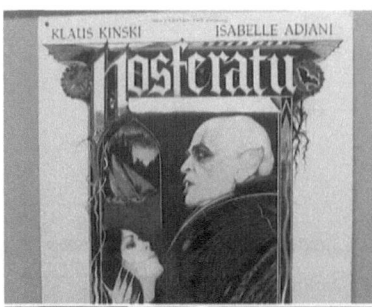

This present film, however, is way *tame* in comparison to much of his canon, but don't be disappointed, because it works well enough for the easily-entertained and, yes, it *is* trying to rip-off several films at once, such as **DEMENTED** (1980, USA, D: Arthur Jeffreys): namely the scary dollar-store masks; and **PATRICK** (Australia, 1978, D: Richard Franklin): the part about telekinetic energy emanating from someone in a coma. (The former of those two just-cited titles, a rape/revenge movie starring usual porno cocksman Harry Reems, includes a scene that is similar to one in **F2000:AD** depicting dudes in scary Halloween masks assaulting a female victim. The scene where this occurs shows one dude in a Don Post Freddy Krueger mask, during which the editor keeps clumsily cross-cutting back and forth with great obviousness to a poster for **NIGHTMARE ON ELM STREET 4: THE DREAM MASTER** [1988, USA, D: Renny Harlin]). Possibly they're hoping to trick you into thinking that the *actual* Freddy's in this dingy lowbrow production rather than merely a woefully tawdry imitation?! Actually, in the back room of a video store, there are tons of "celebrity cameos" made in the form of various memorabilia seen; they're not actually, physically there, of course. Some of the celebs that appear without their knowledge are Marilyn Monroe and Jason Voorhees (starring in **FRIDAY THE 13TH: THE FINAL CHAPTER**, 1984, USA, D: Joseph Zito), as well as Klaus Kinski in the artwork for Herzog's **NOSFERATU THE VAMPYRE** (*Nosferatu: Phantom der Nacht*, 1979, Germany). The attacker in the vampire mask actually says, "Let me suck your neck like Dracula!" I mean, how *unoriginal* can you get?! Purely in the interests of some more facile namedropping, they also zoom-in on a poster of Christopher Lee, and another for Kubrick's **A**

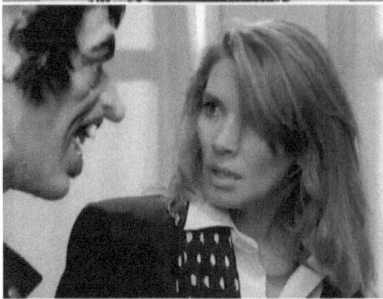

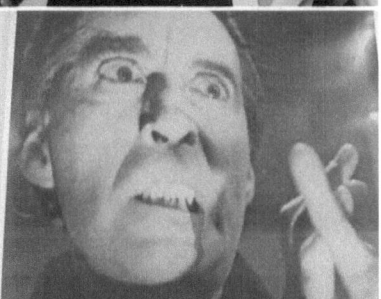

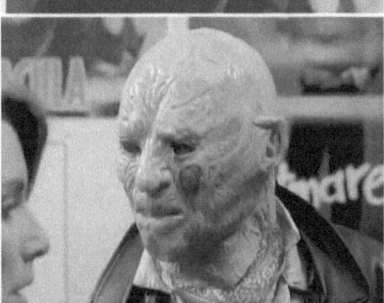

> Evidently in hopes of generating some 'cult cred' with fans, **F2000:AD** brazenly name-drops other vastly superior movies, intermixing scenes of low-rent actors performing in cheap knockoff monster masks with emphatically in-your-face close-ups of international horror movie icons as seen on posters for their films, like they think they're fooling *anybody*. Rather than come across as in any way 'hip' or 'stylish', this tawdry technique only smacks of absolute desperation!

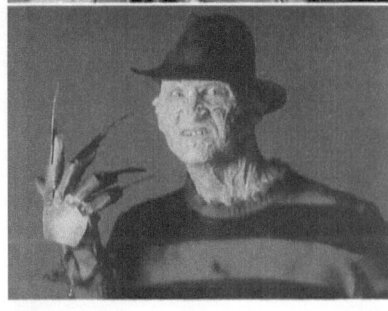

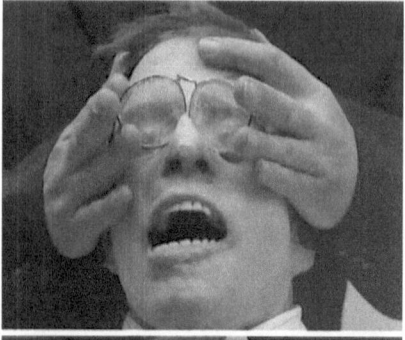
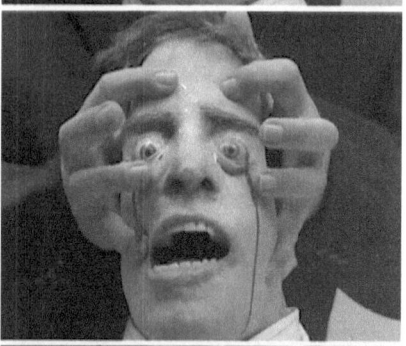
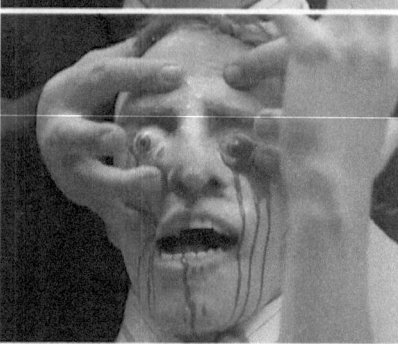
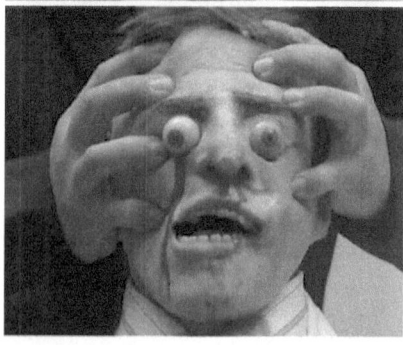

There's no caption we could come up with that could possibly do proper justice to what's happening in these pictures, so we ain't even gonna bother trying to think of one. By all means make up your own!

CLOCKWORK ORANGE (1972, UK). You just know this is a cheap-ass movie with little of its own to offer when they have to lean on other films as a crutch like this!

They try *so-o-o* fucking hard to bash Irish-born prolific spaghetti western player Donald (r.n. Donal) O'Brien—another not-infrequent D'Amato employee—into that pivotal role made internationally famous by Boris Karloff, but it's all circumstantial, and nothing here is related to Shelley's source material other than nominally. Playing an ex-pugilist who winds up being reanimated from the grave, the former "Dr. Butcher" actor mostly just appears exhausted and half-asleep as he lumbers around in the oversized bolt-necked-style blazer and clunky shoes combo, while they shine some eerie green lights on him in faint hopes of evoking the look of Karloff's signature monster. Coincidentally, both films I reviewed for this issue just happen to feature O'Brien. Of course, like everything else D'Amato directed, they're trying to capitalize on a more-famous product: in this case the originating Universal Frankie Monster, but being as this *was* the early '90s—some 60 years after James Whale made Karloff a big-time star—it's almost laughable in its belatedness. I mean, at the time people were way too busy doing the "Bartman" or watching *Arsenio Hall* to notice a bad Italian *Frankenstein* rip-off!

There's no mad scientist or Igor, so obviously the tacked-on copyrighted Mary Shelley character was just an afterthought. O'Brien plays Rick (or what I mistook as "Slow" Rick). There's some corrupt police officers in this German town, where the streets display lots of German beer ads. You see, Rick is there to protect a Mrs. Georgia Danson (Cinzia Monreale), who repeatedly experiences paranoid hallucinations about her moptopped son and at one point even sees his severed head flying through the air! Her son looks suspiciously like that "Bob" kid played by Giovanni Frezza from the Fulci movies (on some of whose scripts the present film's co-scripter Antonio Tentori worked), with a voice that sounds like it was dubbed by a middle-aged woman (!?). I was nervous that I'd have to suffer through more ear torture again, but thankfully the kid here doesn't say much. *Signora* Monreale is practically unrecognizable in her Danson role herein, the actress' most-popular previous role being as Emily, the blind, bleached-blonde clairvoyant from Fulci's **THE BEYOND** *(...E tu vivrai nel terrore! L'aldilà*, 1981, Italy). The woman who dubbed her voice on this one has an extremely thick Noo Yawk *[sic]* accent, which gives it some unintentional hilarity. They also give her the unexplained ability to use her mind to levitate objects, which reminds me of the female character from the

Brit parodic fantasy TV series *Garth Marenghi's Darkplace* (2004).

Two extremely crooked cops are in cahoots with the monster-masked punks from the rape scene. They both have slovenly hair, and one even has a ponytail: that would *never* fly in the real police force! Every male in this film seems to want to sexually assault Mrs. Danson. (What's the point?! I don't get it!) She suddenly slips into an inexplicable coma, and "Slow" Rick is the only one who can read her telepathic thoughts. At one point, he does a Herman Munster impression and really hams it up. There's a head-crunching scene where the victim's animatronic-eyeball-bulging face oddly resembles the puppet effects from the Lou Reed video for "No Money Down" (1986)! Towards the ending of **F2000:AD**, the film plunges into even more surreal territory. During a Nazi-themed party, people disco-dance around Swastika flags, and there are pictures of Hitler everywhere. What the hell's going on?! I was flabbergasted. Is it meant as a *joke*...? I'm not so sure, but I found it all very distracting, and it's never really explained. They just proclaim it a costume party, one girl wears a giant wind-up clock outfit, and I guess the Nazism is included just for the head-scratching shock value of it; although, that said, perhaps communist hammer-'n'-sickle flags might be a lot more shocking; the commies, of course, being by far the most monstrously murderous political regime the world has ever known. Frankie, who now has oozing stiches dripping off his forehead-wound, makes it to the party, though, where he proceeds to throttle the guests. Monreale's character is now languishing under heavy sedation elsewhere, but uses those mysterious, miraculous mind powers of hers to off those on her shit-list with the aid of her unquestioningly obedient "Caligarian" slave.

When all is said and done, this is a pretty horrible film, but if you're a fan of ridiculous, schlocky Eurotrash cinema, then you will probably dig it, as with most other '90s Filmirage garbage (it sounds lots nicer if you pronounce it "*garr-baaage*", with a strong French inflection).

FRANKENSTEIN '80
(Mosaico)

Reviewed by Les Moore

Italy, 1972. D: Mario Mancini

Starting the 'trend' of tacking random future years onto movie titles following the prime selling point's name—in this case a highly familiar if much more than four-letter F-word—the better part of two decades prior to the present title under review, we got **FRANKENSTEIN 1970** (1958, USA, D: Howard W. Koch). In the additional two decades since the present film **F '80** was made,

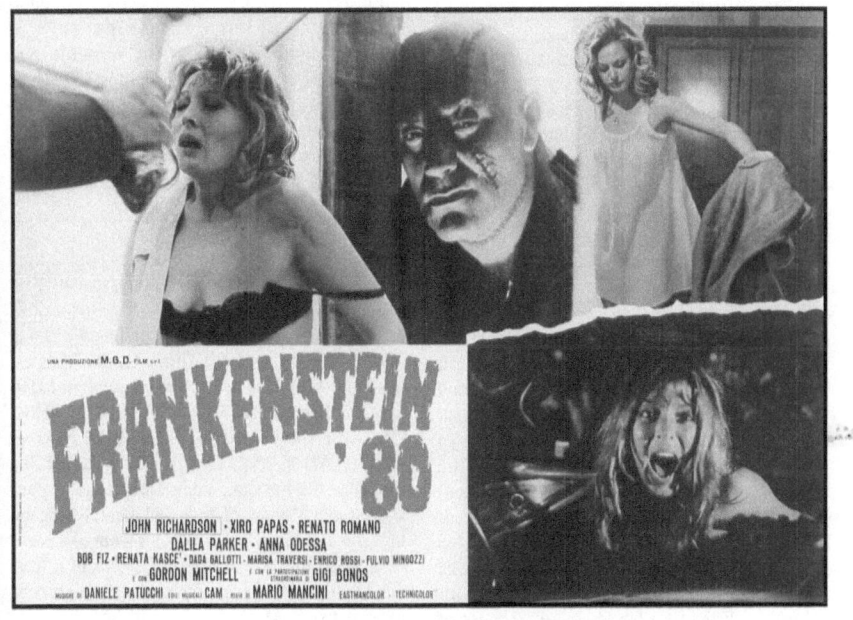

Italian *fotobusta* for Mario Mancini's **FRANKENSTEIN '80**

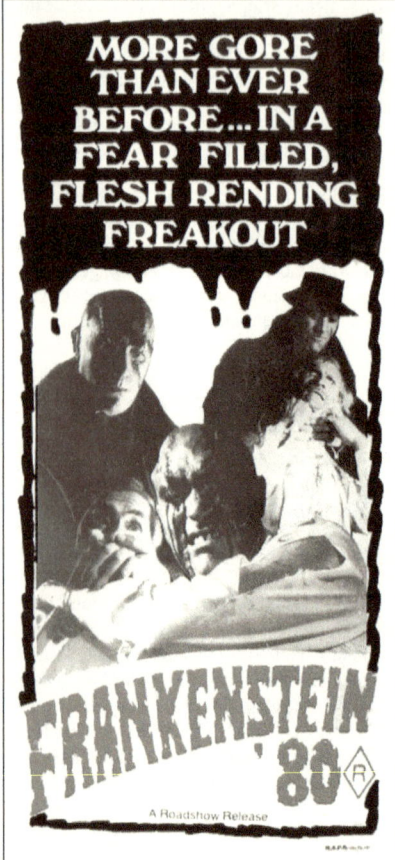

Australian daybill poster

there were **FRANKENSTEIN 90** (1984, France, D: Alain Jessua; released in Germany in '85 as **FRANKENSTEIN 2000** [confused yet?!]), **FRANKENSTEIN 95** (*Frankenstein: Une histoire d'amour*, 1974, France, D: Bob Thénault) and **FRANKENSTEIN 2000: AFTER DEATH** (*Frankenstein 2000: Ritorno dalla morte*, 1991, D: "David Hills"/Joe D'Amato [see p.281 this very ish]). As was such a commonplace practice in the German movie marketplace—rather like how so many otherwise-unrelated spaghetti westerns (and even some made-in-Hollywood ones, for that matter) were released as nominal/faux "Django" titles there—so too were scads of foreign-made monster movies nominally—and oftentimes inexplicably—retitled "Frankenstein"-this-or-that in Germany; as in the case of **THE PROJECTED MAN** (1967, UK, Ds: Ian Curteis, John Croydon [see *Monster!* special double issue #28/29, p.12]), whose German title became "**FRANKENSTEIN 70**" (shades of that late-breaking Karloff entry cited off the top of this paragraph). But don't even get me started on all the Godzilla/Gamera and other Japanese *daikaiju-eiga* imports that got inappropriately tagged as "Frankenstein" flicks in Germany, else we'll be here all day!

And so, after that shakily-connected segue, on to **FRANKENSTEIN '80**, which is neither a sequel nor a prequel, or in any other way related—other than by its *Frankenstein* reference—to any of the films mentioned above; much the same way that none of those others are in any way related to one another either. So why am I even mentioning all this at all? Just for the sake of some mildly interesting trivia and to make like a know-it-all, that's why. This here fine publication you be holdin' *is* a fanzine, after all: it's what we do! ☺

Usual cinematographer Mario Mancini—an ex-assistant to respected DPs Ubaldo Terzano and Enzo "*Trinity*" Barboni—is typically associated with lower-end commercial Italo fare, a category into which his tawdry spaghetti western three-pack of **DJANGO... ADIOS** (*Seminò morte... lo chiamavano il castigo di Dio!*), **HERE IS DURANGO, PAY UP OR DIE** (*Arriva Durango, pago o muori*) and **WANTED: SABATA** (*Wanted Sabata*, all 1971) well fits, as they all originated from the same sweaty armpit/underbelly of the Roman film industry as much of the rest of his far-from-high-profile work did. Yes indeed, through no fault of his own, with those titles just cited Mancini earned the dubious distinction of lensing no less than *three* (3) of the all-time worst Spaghetti Westerns ever made; all of which make the poorest of "Miles Deem"/Demofilo Fidani's cost-conscious-if-generally-enthusiastically-staged oaters look like the heights of High Art by comparison. (Which is *still* quite the accomplishment, come to think of it...)

As for his work which more pertains to the kind of stuff this here mag (as per its title) usually covers—i.e., anything with monsters in—Mancini's earlier works as a cameraman included canning (under DP Giuseppe La Torre) Guido Malatesta's irresistibly kitschy prehistoric peplum **FIRE MONSTERS AGAINST THE SON OF HERCULES** a.k.a. **COLOSSUS OF THE STONE AGE** (1962), starring American bodybuilder Reg Lewis as the beefcake and sultrilicious English superstarlet Margaret Lee—clad in a fetching animal-fur, um, 'cocktail dress' (for wont of a better term!)—as the cheesecake. Not only did it have that latter prime selling point going for it, but the fab-fun **FIRE MONSTERS** also boasted some pretty awesome full-size animatronic dinosaurs by Carlo Rambaldi too (none other than Bruno Mattei served as sound editor on the production, which provides another neat link to Italian cinema's penny-pinching poverty row production houses [bless 'em!]). Further on into the '60s, by which time Mancini had risen to the rank of Director of Photography, he served in that capacity on **KING OF KONG ISLAND** (*Eva, la Venere selvaggia*, 1968, Italy, D: "Robert Morris"/Roberto Mauri), the infamous and immortal jungle girl/killa gorilla laff-riot starring Brad Harris, Esmeralda Barros and a bunch of guys in the rattiest/tattiest ape-suits you ever saw (assuming you never saw **THE MIGHTY GORGA** [D: David L. Hewitt, 1969, USA], that is!).

Although a period piece rather than set in contemporary times like F '80 is, **FRANKENSTEIN'S CASTLE OF FREAKS** (*Terror! Il castello delle donne maledette*, 1974, Italy, D: "Dick Randall"/Robert H. Oliver), another lowly horror/sexploitationer on which Mancini functioned as DP, dabbled in some similar themes of marauding man-made monsters molesting underclad starlets at every opportunity. The present film is even more cut-price than that earlier one, so in hopes of upping its virtually nonexistent production values, it lays on lots more skin and gore than its marginally more 'respectable' predecessor did, and for that we can all be thankful...for the simple reason that, without these purely gratuitous additions, odds are it would be as-good-as-unwatchable!

Later still, Mancini moved up in the filmmaking pecking order to become a 'full-fledged' director of sorts; at least for this single film, anyway. His contributions to international popular culture included one of Italian exploitation cinema's more outrageous horror sleazy-cheapies (I suppose it might be classified as a "sexy shocker"): namely *MOSAICO* / "Mosaic", better-known to Eurotrash cinema freaks the world over as **FRANKENSTEIN '80** (1976), for which Mancini also co-wrote the script, his sole credit in that capacity too. Starring both the much-monstered John Richardson and Gordon Mitchell, this was a sloppily-stitched-together celluloid creation— the cinematic equivalent of a tawdry *sesso e orrore fumetti* ("sex and horror comic")—every bit as dire as any entry in the lowly western 'trilogy' which Mancini had committed to emulsion some years before it...but don't let that stop ya, as it's arguably about ten times as entertaining!

For this unrepentantly sleazed-out, skeezy exercise in cheap, sensationalistic entertainment, Mitchell guest-stars as none other than obsessive-

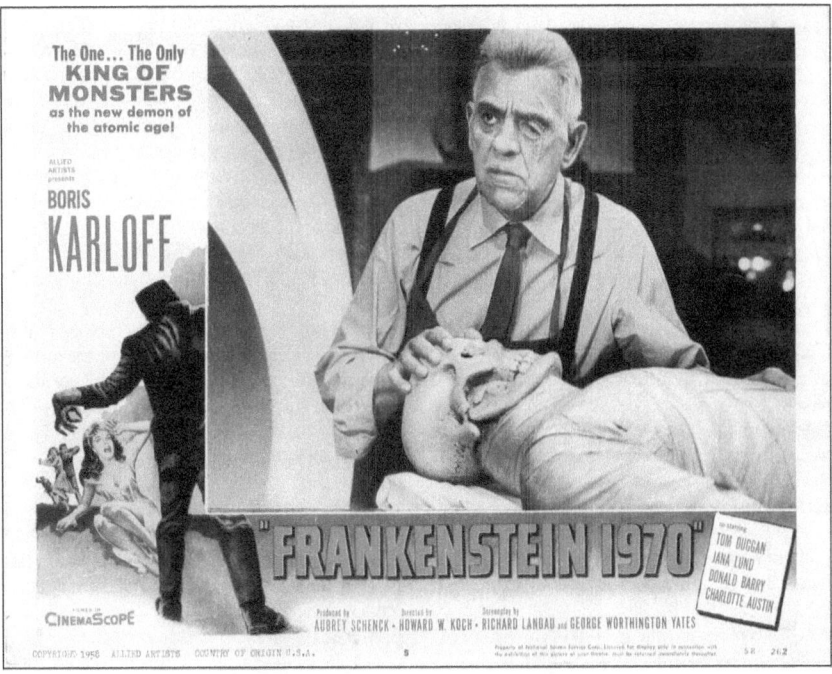

In Howard W. Koch's **FRANKENSTEIN 1970** (1958), Karloff as Baron Victor von Frankenstein thought he had the market in facial scars cornered—until **FRANKENSTEIN '80** rolled around, that is!

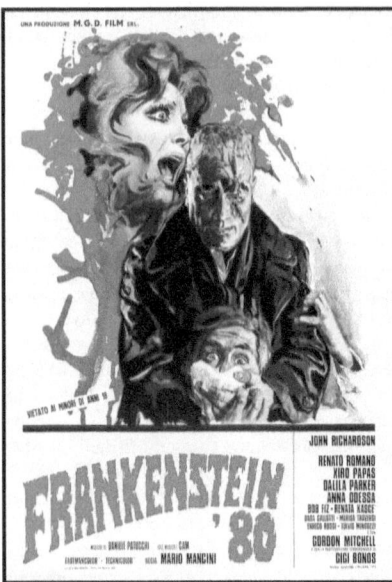

Italian *due-fogli manifesto*; art unsigned

ly-dedicated pathological anatomist and surgeon Dr. Otto Frankenstein (creator of titular patchwork creation, just in case you hadn't guessed already). Sporting greying blond hair and silvery sideburns and by now very much in the twilight years of his once-prosperous Italo movie career, Mitchell—whose ambulance-chasing character leaves a lingering after-scent of formaldehyde in his wake wherever he goes—is shown gleefully mucking about amidst all the awful offal, removing livers, eyeballs and what-not (e.g., "I begin the testicle transplant..."), before—***ATTENTION: SPOILER ALERT!***—winding-up unceremoniously offed with a big-bladed banana knife by his own creation, the murderous Mosaic ("The *real* monster is that Dr. Frankenstein!").

During one scene in **F '80**—set at a seedy grindhouse movie theatre-*cum*-striptease venue—the title patchwork monster-man gorily throttles a naked stripper in her dressing room; this while (background announcer's quote) "that great western hit 'TUCSON SAM', starring Wild Bill Brown" plays in the background. Appropriately enough, heard from off-camera but never actually seen, said fictitious film-within-a-film includes imitation 'spaghetti western' music, whinnying horses and gunshot sound effects.

As is so typical of these low-end Continental exploitation quickies, actors who might ordinarily fill only the slightest, most peripheral of parts in more 'upscale' productions get their names boosted up the cast-list a few notches higher than usual and are given bigger roles to play than they usually got. In a prime example of this, cast herein in a far-more-prominent light than was the norm for usual glorified extra/bit-parter Xiro Papas (1933-1980), an Italian-born-and-based actor of evident Greek descent whose first name was typically Italianized to "Ciro" (roughly pronounced "Chee-roh") on domestic releases, at such times as he was even credited at all, which was by no means always. Largish—albeit neither overly big nor tall, if photogenically 'ugly' (if far from all-out hideous), even when wearing only minimal special makeup—a typical role for Papas was the looming, bald-headed hunchbacked bloodsucker (billed on Anglo prints as "The Vampire Monster"!) in "Paolo Solvay"/Luigi Batzella's enduringly endearing tit 'n' fang-fest **THE DEVIL'S WEDDING NIGHT** (*Il plenilunio delle vergini*, 1973, Italy), starring Mark Damon and "Sara Bay"/Rosalba Neri. That said, come to think of it, his final known film role—that of Lupo in same-director Batzella's batshit nasty Nazisploitationer **THE BEAST IN HEAT** (*La bestia in calore*, 1977, Italy)—probably edges this earlier one out in terms of notoriety among most fans of such lowest-common-denominator stuff as this.

Thanks to Prof. Schwarz's newly-developed so-called "anti-lymphocytic serum"—a clear sky-blue fluid resembling mouthwash in a glass bottle neatly-labeled with strips of Dymo tape (anyone old enough to remember what that is will remember it well!)—a humanoid monster comes into being... His role as said monster in **F '80** probably amounts to Papas' meatiest part ever, both figuratively *and* literally. Playing Dr. Frankenstein's crazy-quilt patchwork creation assembled from sundry corpses—hence his name, "Mosaic"—pathos-ridden human monster ("...ugly sonofabitch...") Papas lumbers about a generic indeterminate locale (Italy? Germany? I assume the latter, but who can say for sure!) bloodily dispatching incidental victims, usually in the form of topless prostitutes. His mental and physical states deteriorate still further when his unnaturally-created body begins to reject its transplanted brain, with expectedly garish/grisly results.

It's hilarious to witness the desperate lengths to which this post-synched flick's Anglo voice-dubbers went while attempting to match-up the English dialogue with the movements of all the Italian-speaking actors' mouths! Strangely enough, even though stars Richardson and Mitchell (both of whom were dubbed by others' voices after-the-fact hereon) deliver their lines in apparent English throughout, the lip-synch is sometimes so off that they also appear to have originally been speaking in a foreign tongue (although, now that I mention it, it sometimes appears as though the former was also delivering his lines in Italian for some scenes [?]). For lengthy stretches showing Mitchell's mad medico character hard at work in his lab/operating theatre, rather than have him actually speak, his expository monologues are spoken from behind a surgical mask whilst he tapes his procedures orally on a nearby audiocassette recorder. As was clearly the express intention of this tactic, the dubbing team get a breather during these scenes as, because we can't see his lips moving anyway, all they have to do is let 'his' English words play back over shots of his masked face to sustain the 'illusion' (!) that he's actually the one mouthing them.

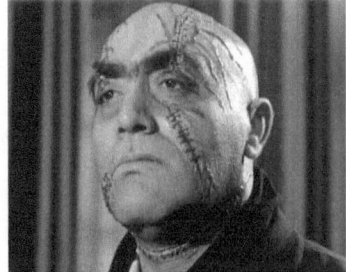

Elsewhere in the cast, then very much approaching the tail-end of his movie career, seasoned comic performer/character actor Luigi "Gigi" Bonos ([1910-2000] the youngest of a trio of brothers, actors all, who outlived both his only-slightly-older brothers by many decades) tries his darnedest to maintain an air of human dignity while putting in a low-profile 'cameo'. Without ever uttering a single word of dialogue and truly looking the part in his filthy tramp's rags—essentially replaying one of his stock comic music hall characters from way back in his better days—Bonos appears as a bumbling old rummy who gets his head incidentally crushed under an engine block in a junkyard by Papas' marauding man-made monster. Elsewhere, during another outrageous sequence that resembles a horror *fumetto* come to life, a female butcher gets bloodily bludgeoned to death by same with a huge soup-bone in a meat-locker, for no other reason than simply being in the wrong place at the wrong time.

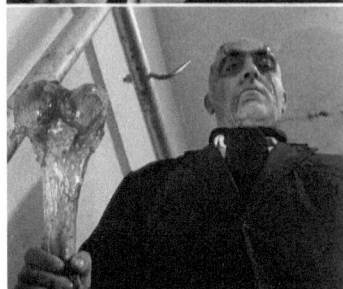

As cheapozoid Italo splatter-schlockers go, there are many substantially better ones than **F '80** to be had, without doubt; by the same token, though, there are many that are a whole helluva lot *worse*, if in a far-less-glorious (and gorious *[sic!]*) way. For this enjoyably ludicrous exercise in no-mind, no-budget nonsense—which includes plentiful gratuitous blood-'n'-guts and T&A (complete with some obligatory unkemptly bushy '70s-style mega-muffs!)—Richardson received top billing as crime reporter Karl Schellen (a tabloid hack who is at one point very-sarcastically-indeed referred to by some smartass as "Hemingway"). Along the way getting to go on a hot date with Sonia (local sexpot Dalila Di Lazzaro, whose last name was hereon given as "Parker"), the daffy doc-

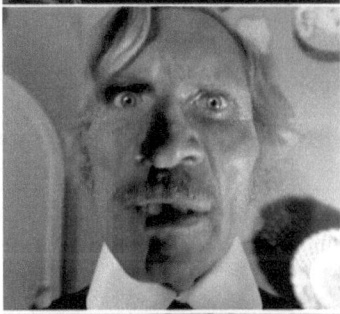

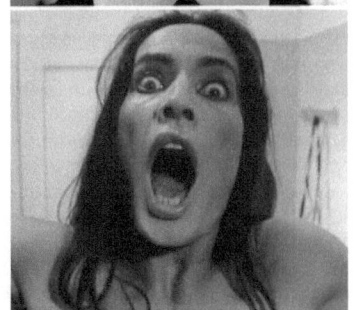

Right, Top to Bottom: Boasting a sloppily-stitched-together mug only a mother (or a *Monster!* reader) could love, the monstrous Mosaic (Xiro Papas) runs around terrorizing incidental ingénues at every opportunity—including bludgeoning one to death with a HUGE soup-bone in a butcher's meat locker—much to the chagrin of his creator, Dr. Frankenstein (Gordon Mitchell)

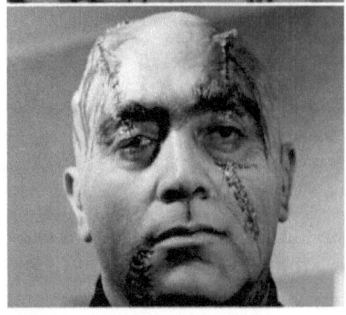

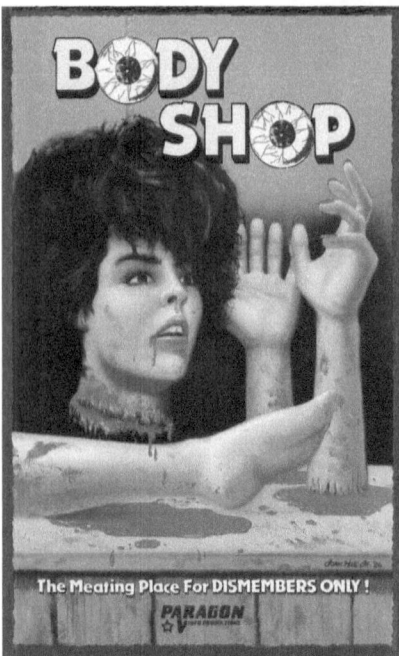

Goriously [sic!] tacky VHS box art from Paragon Video, one of the 1980s' premier sources for, um, unusual cinema

tor's hottie niece ("We'll eat out..."), Richardson ultimately comes to grips with Frankenstein's pathetic piecemeal 'progeny' while manfully maintaining a straight face throughout. Just a couple years further on, Richardson, a future main-squeeze of Brit scream queen Martine Beswick who got his prestigious start in Italo-horror/monster flicks way back in Mario Bava's superlative B&W masterpiece **BLACK SUNDAY** (*La maschera del demonio*, 1960) but who was generally not the most emotive of thespians, had to try even harder not to laugh as the 'name-brand' star of "Al Bradley"/Alfonso Brescia's chintzy poverty-row **STAR WARS** wannabe **COSMOS: WAR OF THE PLANETS** (*Anno zero: Guerra nello spazio*, a.k.a. **BATTLE OF THE STARS**, 1977); although, credit where it's due, he did manage to close his over-two-decade-long stint in Italian movies by appearing in a couple more certified horror classics (i.e., Riccardo Freda's above-par *giallo* **MURDER SYNDROME** [*Murder Obsession*, 1981] and Michele Soavi's flashy occult thriller **THE CHURCH** [*La Chiesa*, 1989]), so at least he went out on a high note with what was definitely much more of a bang than a whimper. However, as for the actor's obvious lack of commitment to his indifferent, take-the-money-and-run performance in **F '80**, it evidently stemmed from the fact that he knew he was appearing in a total turkey, so why bother even trying at all.

Daniele Patucchi's interesting experimental 'avant-garde jazz' (for wont of a better term) tuneage includes passages of amelodic/off-key, minimalistic plonked piano notes reminiscent of a funeral dirge, appropriately enough. At other times too, his compositions seem to be striving to endow a fittingly discordant mood to the decidedly out-of-whack proceedings. Mostly though, music takes a back-row seat to all the penny dreadful *grand-guignol* going on. Future real-life successful Italian TV exec Renato Romano (another spaghetti western alumnus, as were Richardson and Mitchell both to even greater degrees) appears in a straight-faced comic relief part as crabby police chief Inspector Schneider, who is all-the-more bad-tempered than usual due to trying to quit smoking and having not gotten his nicotine fix in days while presiding over his incompetent subordinates' botch-job of an investigation. Just to be extra prickish and take it out on everyone else, he vindictively imposes a strict no-smoking ban on all his underlings at the precinct until such time as they solve the case of the monstrous mutilation murders that have been plaguing the city.

This low-end Italo-splatter cheapie recently became made available on Blu-ray (of all things!) via '84 Entertainment; of which release Dennis "Un-popped Cinema" Capicik gives us the lowdown in our back pages' "Vid Info" section (p.339).

THE BODY SHOP

Reviewed by Steve Fenton

1972, USA. D: J.G. Patterson, Jr.

Better-known to teeming dozens as **DOCTOR GORE**, this justifiably notorious shot-in-Charlotte, NC cheapo-creepo might superficially not seem like it fits this zine's (relatively) stringent criteria for what constitutes a creature feature at first glance, it mainly being more of a sexploitation-tinged splatter chop-'em-up and all. However, as its highly-Frankensteinian plot does concern a wacked-out medical maniac who constructs an all-new composite human being—which he then brings to unnatural life—out of parts (including BIG tits!) of various dead bodies, it totally fits our requirements for inclusion, not *despite* but *because* of the fact that Doc's man-made "monster" just happens to be a bodaciously-stacked *über*-boober babe (Virginia

"Jenny" Driggers), which makes it fit *my* personal requirements all the more! This is one of those seriously *warped* examples of fringe-flick fuckery that makes you seriously question the sanity of its creators (or rather, its main creator Mr. Patterson, alias reputedly once-regionally-popular Carolinan stage performer "Don Brandon", a.k.a. "America's No.1 Magician"), who deserves the lion's share of the blame—and especially most of the accolades!—for the mind-bogglingly mesmerizing, truly one-of-a-kind monstrosity that he, in his sublime madness, has wrought; by that I mean both the movie itself and the alluringly attractive "she-monster" who features prominently in it). After the tragic premature passing of his never-seen but presumably luscious (quote) "former pin-up model" wife Anitra, grieving and lonesome surgeon Dr. Brandon determines to create a replacement in her image, in the process improving on all her, eh, imperfections ("We'll be together again, except this time you'll be *perfect*!" – "I want a mate, but this time a perfect one; perfect in *every* way. She must be beautiful, she must have *everything*…").

The, er, anti-photogenic "Brandon"/Patterson possesses a decidedly oddball brand of charisma, largely on account of his strangely appealing voice…and not because he's such a great thespian either! Far from it, in fact. Yet his amateurishly awkward line-readings, uttering dialogue custom-written by he himself but sometimes obviously ad-libbing on the spot, make for inexplicably compelling listening, aided-and-abetted greatly in the visual aspect of his performance by his eccentrically unpredictable facial expressions (googly roly-poly eyeballs and authentic warts included!), odd mannerisms and stilted movements. Here known nondescriptly as "Greg", Doc's stereotypical, generic hunchbacked lowercase "igor" (if I may be so bold as to reference the kiddie-oriented CGI cartoon **IGOR** [2008, USA, D: Tony Leondis] in this comparatively highly dubious a context) is played by chubby, carrot-topped, bearded actor Roy Mehaffey, whose wild mane of frizzy-frazzled ginger hair is almost of Afro proportions, like it's constantly standing on end due to static electricity. He constantly "smokes" an unlit cigar-stub, and his unconvincing "hump" largely looks like he's going about with a volleyball (or sometimes a couch cushion) stuffed up his jumper! Major props to Mr. Mehaffey (wherever he may be today) for playing this character with the proper combination of tongue-in-cheek humor and, er, deadpan seriousness. Exemplifying this nutty flick's D.I.Y. ethic perfectly is the bizarre sequence wherein the dotty doctor and his severely stooped-over, mutely mewling assistant methodically—and interminably!—encase the (unseen) fresh corpse of a female experimental subject in a body-length "cocoon" of crinkly tinfoil fastened to the operating table with good ol' all-purpose duct-tape (!!) then attach itty-bitty alligator clip electrodes all over it—including to the raised "tit"-shaped areas of the form-fitting foil directly over where the nipples would be… if there was actually a real woman inside it rather than (for the most part, anyway) merely an immobile dummy, that is. The following attempted revivification scene brims with whizzbang Kenneth Strickfaden-style electrical effects as Doc cranks-up his lo-tech gadgetry in hopes of raising the dead. With its low-key, high-contrast lighting, exaggerated shadows, rapid-fire editing and sundry extreme close-ups of an assortment of dials, gauges, electrometers and other zapping/sparking "sciencey" gizmos, this lively sequence and a similar later one amount to the film's most ambitious, energetic and enthusiastically-staged sections.

After all the would-be revivifiers' dedicated efforts to infuse life into the corpse, however, it winds up getting too-well-done by an electrical

This regional newspaper ad is as crudely put together as the movie itself; the same surely can't be said for its "monster", played by superstacked starlet Jenny Driggers overload, so off into the nearby acid vat it goes for instant disposal. No sooner has the bloodied if shapely bod of another newly-deceased young woman (Linda Faile, convincingly playing dead, all wide-eyed and gagged) been delivered directly to the lab inside a trunk sealed with still more duct-tape (!!) than the staunchly-devoted pair harvest it of any useable parts. Much like Paul Naschy was inclined to do (and who can blame him!) in his own self-penned and sometimes self-directed productions, after first hypnotizing them to do his bidding, Patterson gets to make out with a non-stop succession of comely ingénues, smooching up a storm with them while they try real hard to pretend they find his aggressive amorous advances the greatest turn-on ever. After meeting, making-out with then drowning a bikini bimbette (Jan Benfield) down at the beach before dragging her off to his mad lab, she has her legs hacksawed off at the thigh-top by him for the simple reason that Doc—you gotta start somewhere, right?—wants to use her torso ("perfect" except for the fact that it's now totally limbless, albeit with the dead head still attached!) as the foundation for his piecemeal creation ("We must add to our collection!"). Next, with his sly, swivelly eyes on harvesting her shapely hands, after using more instant mesmerism to finagle her away from her date at a local bar, Dr. Brandon takes home an easy pick-up (attractive actress Jeannine Aber, whose sole known other film appearance came the following year in the obscure thriller **THE NIGHT OF THE CAT** [1973, D: Jim Cinque], which, perhaps not just coincidentally, also featured the present film's Ms. Driggers in a supporting part). Next up: the arms! These are forcibly removed from a beautiful busty blonde secretary (the obviously-pseudonymous "Candy Furr" [howzat for a perfect porn alias!], in her single known screen role) during a scene that makes us feel all the more queasily guilty for the simple fact that her big bare breasts are juxtaposed with the sawn-off stump of her armless shoulder; simply because we know her "missing" arm is only stuck down through a hole in the table, with a hunk of raw steak hiding the spot where it goes through, allows us to better appreciate the one-time-only actress' bountiful bazooms for the blatant titillation tactic they are (I'll try to refrain from making a grossly distasteful "He should've just taken her knockers instead!" joke here). After that, another victim has her eyeballs yanked out with a vicious-looking pair of pliers-like forceps!

When the bodacious body beautiful formed of mixed-and-matched bits-'n'-pieces finally breathes her first, she is 'reborn' from death a total *tabula rasa* ("No prejudices. No inhibita-

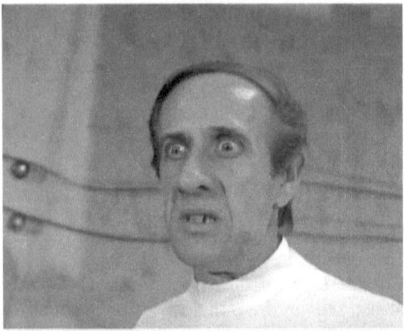
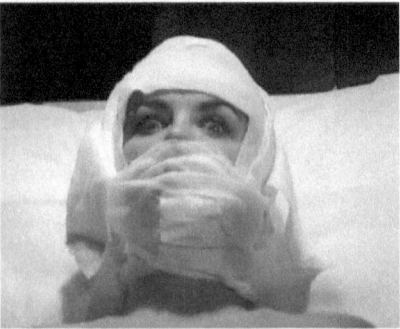
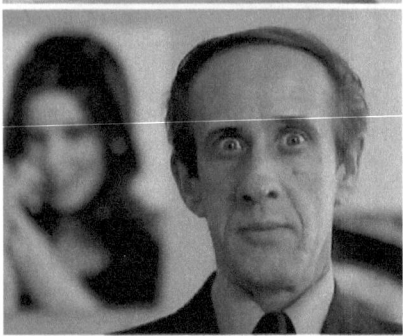
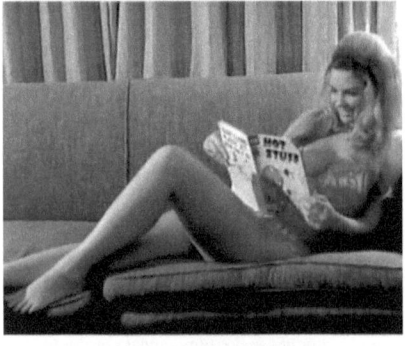

Watch out, girls! The irresistible "Dr. Gore" has his googly-woogly bedroom eyes on you! **Above, Bottom:** Ms. Driggers digests some appropriate reading matter as Doc's recently-created monstress tions [sic!]"), thus making her eminently moldable and manipulable to the highly libidinous doc's will. When he catches Greg apparently in the midst of making time with Anitra—actually, the total reverse is true, despite all appearances—he first hurls a beaker filled with a highly-caustic chemical in his hunched henchman's face then lodges a massive meat-axe smack in his hump before then unceremoniously shoving him into the acid bath. Naïvely childlike in mind yet sexually inquisitive and fully mature (and *then* some!) of body, with fickle and promiscuous mating habits, Anitra subsequently puts the moves on a chunky trucker who stops by the house on an errand—literally to "haul some ashes", no less!—then skips out to parts unknown solo to have her own ashes hauled by whatever next man happens along. Believe it or not, at precisely the 77-minute mark, a medium shot of the entire clapperboard is seen stuck in the dead-center of the screen, even while a scene is unfolding behind it! Talk about *surreal*. Clearly this was a holdover artifact from the unfinished print that was considered lost and remained unreleased for over a decade. While it's easy enough to figure out how the gore FX techniques—augmented by figurative smoke and literal mirrors—were accomplished, there's no denying that they were done with some panache, heavily reliant on Patterson's patented sleight-of-hand tricks as a practicing prestidigitator. And, while the way-too-bright-red blood is obviously only of the stage variety, the various fetishistically dwelled-upon scenes of beautiful women having parts of them matter-of-factly severed, leaving mere bloody stumps, are undeniably quite unsettling to behold. All-in-all, **THE BODY SHOP / DOCTOR GORE** makes for an utterly fascinating viewing experience! I'd say "Let me count the ways," but I wouldn't know where to start, that's how many there are, so I'll leave it at that.

A smoothly-sung, fittingly morbid if maudlin C&W ballad entitled "A Heart Dies Every Minute" is performed live at a bar for real by local act Bill Hicks and the Rainbows. Correct me if I'm wrong, but I'm tempted to believe that the portly, redheaded Mr. Hicks is none other than the more normal clean-cut alter-ego of Mehaffey's disheveled/deformed Greg character. Odds are he's not (?), but it's tempting to conjecture on such a possibility. If anyone out there has the skinny about this, by all means let me know!

NOTES: As a note of related trivia, those who gravitate towards ultra-dark/demonic deathcore-*cum*-black metal sounds (*not* my favorite kind of HM by a long shot, I must confess, but I will partake of the odd tune now and again)

might wanna give the Italian band Dr. Gore's stuff a spin (their repertoire includes such, ehh, 'upbeat' [i.e., high-speed] ditties as "Freshly Decomposted" *[sic?]*, "Postmortem Blood Ejaculation", "Viscera", "Back from the Grave

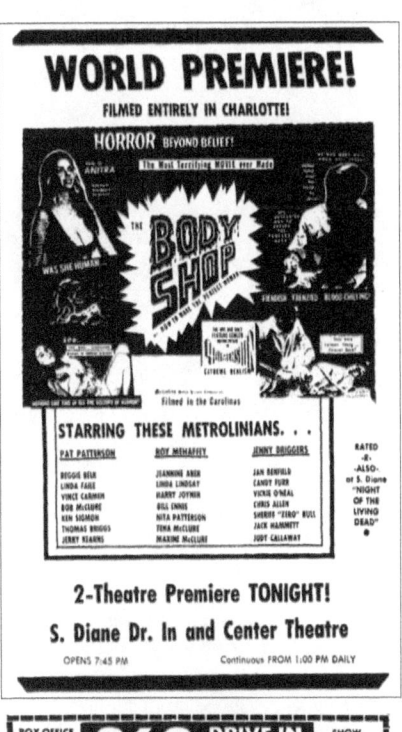

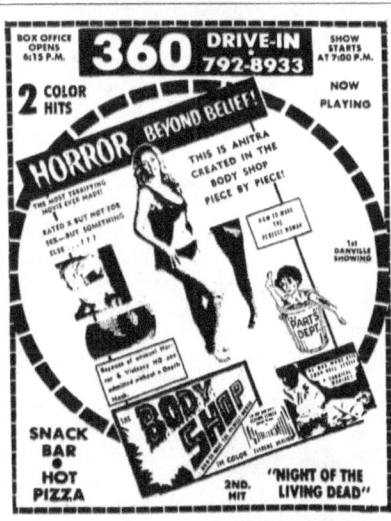

Regional US newspaper ads for **THE BODY SHOP** a.k.a. **DOCTOR GORE**. **Top:** For the world premiere in Gastonia, North Carolina (April 6th, 1972). **Above:** From Danville, Virginia (December 1st, 1973)

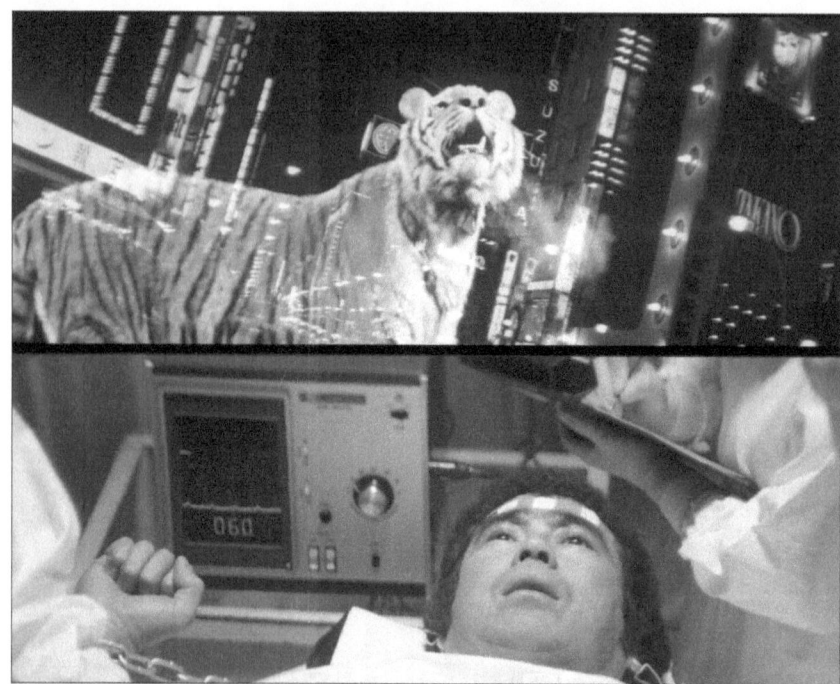

Above: Made at a time when the Japanese movie industry was severely strapped for cash, what **WG:EL** lacks in production values it at least attempts to make up for in the sheer lunacy of its plot! Whaddaya mean "How come Sonny Chiba doesn't get to wear no werewolf makeup?" Cuz he's such a fearsome, badass mutha, he don't *need* any, dat's why!

WOLF GUY: ENRAGED LYCANTHROPE

(ウルフガイ 燃えよ狼男 / *Urufu gai: Moero ōkami-otoko*)

Reviewed by *Jeff Goodhartz*

Japan, 1975. D: Kazuhiko Yamaguchi

Translated text-blurbs from the film's Japanese trailer: *"Lunar Cycle, Day 3 – New Moon, An Awful Night... Trouble Comes Bursting In Again! [...] I Am The Wolf Man – Proud and Gentle-Hearted. [...] In Pursuit of Something Bizarre... Her Claws Will Rip and Shred! The Horror of the Tiger's Claws [...] A Curse! Hatred! A Grudge Incarnate! [...] The Plot Gets More and More Complicated. [...] The Wolf Guy's Blood Boils! [...] Lunar Cycle, Day 15 – Full Moon, Time To Counter-Attack! Muscles of Steel! The Invincible Wolf! Extreme Violence and Heroism! Shin'ichi Chiba's Latest Work. Relentless Wolf Action! A Hard-Hitting Action Epic [...]"*

to Kill Again", "Obsession of Mutilated Bodies", "Grotesque Corpse Sculpture", and let's not forget the catchy "Hacksaw Disfigurement", which may or may not reference **DG** the movie in its, uhhh, lyrics, which are more utterly unintelligible than most of this genre due to their being roared / howled / growled / snorted / bellowed / squealed [etc.] in some sort of guttural inhuman language... but then again, maybe it's just *italiano* [?]). And then, on a completely unrelated note (other than by name only), there's the hour-long doc *Dr. Gore* (2009, France, D: Pauline Pallier), concerning, not the present film's Pat Patterson, but rather French horror/splatter filmmaker Antoine Pellissier; still another project that entirely feasibly derived its title from the Patterson flick, which gained quite a lot of notoriety during its '80s home video heydays under its **DG** retitle.

Creature Feature Reviews

WG:EL dares to answer the question; when is a werewolf movie *not* a werewolf movie…?

This film existed for many years as little more than an urban legend here in the West. It first came to my attention just over a decade ago via the book *Outlaw Masters of Japanese Cinema*, by Chris D. Though the blurb was only a sentence or two long, it was descriptive enough that it sent my imagination soaring. Could it be? The great Shin'ichi "Sonny" Chiba as a crime-fighting werewolf?! Sure the book suggested that this wasn't quite the case, but I still couldn't get that notion out of my head. Fast forward a few years to 2010 when as if a collective prayer was answered, the almost mythical movie showed up in the form of a torrent via an uncut (!) TV airing in Japan. Even better, it was fan-subbed in English by some very kind and considerate souls. Since I couldn't do torrents at that time (and *still* can't, come to think of it), I had to wait a bit longer for it to show up as a gray market DVD-R. Sure the print was a pan-and-scan job of lesser quality, but I didn't care at the time, considering the scarcity of it. Now, roughly seven years later, Arrow Video comes along with a newly-discovered print and gives the film the full Blu-ray treatment for us Chiba and vintage Japanese exploitations fans to properly gawk at!

Based on a manga written by Kazumasa Hirai, the film centers on one Akira Inugami (Chiba) who, as we see in flashbacks to his childhood, is the sole surviving member of a clan of supernatural werewolves who were hunted-down and slaughtered for no apparent reason other than fear of the unknown (isn't that *always* the case?!). Now all-grown-up and an ace crime-fighting reporter, Akira stumbles upon a scene where men are being murdered by some unseen force; the latest victim running through the streets, terrified for his life and seeing the ethereal image of a tiger in the sky before being literally ripped to shreds in the goriest manner possible. Akira decides to dig around, and quickly discovers that the victims were all members of a rock band that had gang-raped a poor girl named Miki (Etsuko Nami). Seems Miki made the mistake of falling in love with a well-to-do young man whose powerful father frowned upon their romance; so much so, in fact, that it was he himself who ordered the raping. As if that weren't bad enough, the gang also infected Miki with syphilis in the process (truly a heartfelt story of forbidden love, no?!). Driven mad by the experience, Miki spends her time as an addict while performing as a singer in a strip-club. At nights, her desperation and rage manifest in the form of an invisible spirit-tiger that systematically hunts down and slaughters the lowlife gang members responsible for her

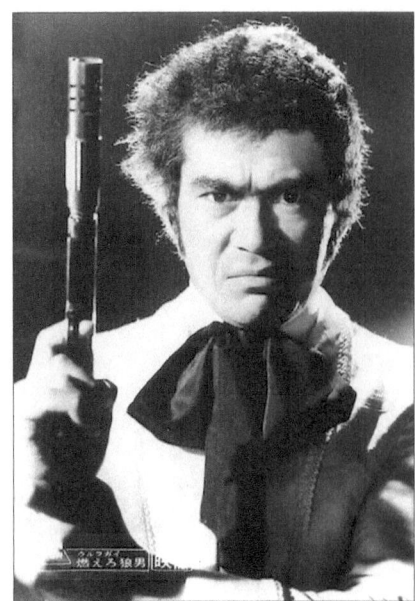

This is about as fuzzy as Chiba ever gets in his werewolf form; Japanese lobby still for **WG:EL**

violation. Worse still, both Miki and Akira (who takes great pity on her and wishes to help) soon find their paths dogged by sinister shadowy underworld types who wish to use each of their supernatural abilities to assassinate high-ranking politicians and the like.

Let's just get this part out of the way: there are *no* actual, literal, genuine werewolves visible anywhere in **WG:EL**. None as in *none*, nada, nuthin'! With a film title that twice mentions our hairy two-footed fiend, one tends to have certain expectations. For me, initially, it was the vision of Chiba in a kind of "karate Paul Naschy" mode, or at least something along the lines of Henry Hull in **WEREWOLF OF LONDON** (1935, USA, D: Stuart Walker). Well, that *didn't* happen, and the reasoning behind it would at first seem perplexing. That is, until one discovers that this is actually a loose sequel to the once-nearly-as-rare-and-now-even-*rarer* **CREST OF THE WOLF** (*Ōkami no monshō*, a.k.a. **HORROR OF THE WOLF**, 1973, Japan). That film featured a teenage version of the Akira Inugami character (as played by Tarō Shigaki), who, if memory serves (I no longer have a print of it, nor did I make the connection between the two films until recently, as my old VHS dupe was *sans* subtitles), spends much of the film getting harassed by local school bullies until finally transforming into a vengeful werewolf, sporting one of the goofier masks seen in the genre. Though containing dollops of

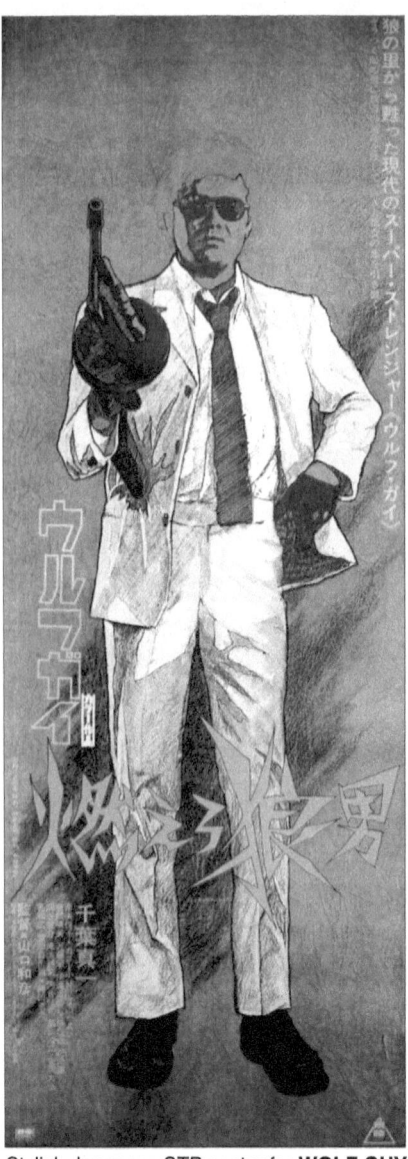

Stylish Japanese STB poster for **WOLF GUY**

ない / *Zubekō banchō: zange no neuchi mo nai*, 1971] and **KARATE BEAR FIGHTER** [けんか空手 極真無頼拳 / *Kenka karate kyokushin burai ken*, 1975], to name but a few) seems unaffected by this and goes full-steam-ahead with his usual brand of crazed, overwrought concepts and visuals. Sure he may sometimes lack fundamental storytelling technique (try watching the middle section of the otherwise-hugely-enjoyable **SISTER STREET FIGHTER** without wondering where the missing reel is hiding!), but it's usually of little consequence. His films exist as "B"-grade instant gratification, and on that level, **WOLF GUY** delivers. After one gets over the initial disappointment over the lack of said Lycanthropes, they will find many a nasty pleasure here; even more in fact than in most Japanese productions from this period (and that's saying a *lot*). Fans of karate-style action will enjoy watching an even-more-amped-than-usual Chiba taking out various flunkies with unbridled ferocity. It also has a wonderfully funky, psychedelic music score (God, how I love those guitar licks!) that fuels the action in a most agreeable fashion. The real benefactors however are the gorehounds and sleaze mavens who will find this a particularly nasty '70s-style assault on their sensibilities (or more accurately, lack thereof). The very idea, for instance, of having the downtrodden Miki character (surely one of the sadder, most pathetic and put-upon female characters in exploitation cinema) ultimately go from victim to enemy is a pretty diabolical conceit that will likely cause some amount of queasiness in all but the most hardened genre fans. Speaking of queasy, I'll admit I started to squirm in my chair just a bit during the sequence where the captured Chiba has his blood literally ripped from his body in order to infuse a genetically created man-wolf (one that *does* very vaguely resemble the Henry Hull variation, with large eyebrows and bushy widow's peak. Unfortunately, this is where I come to the first of two moderate complaints with the film. Firstly, this artificially-enhanced wolf guy *should* have been a major plot contrivance. Instead, it exists almost as an afterthought; being introduced past the midpoint and then done away with quickly thereafter. Indeed, what sets up to be a major wolfen smackdown amounts to little more than the would-be combatants leaping about for a few moments until the fake wolf guy erupts in spattering blood and dies. I get the idea that Akira's supernatural blood would not mix with that of a mortal, but couldn't these two have at least landed a few punches and kicks first?! Secondly, the other disappointment comes at the climax when Akira is ultimately and sadly pitted against an enraged Miki (who is jealous of Akira's affection toward another female). After a fair amount of buildup, the anticipated spirit tiger vs.

gore (no **TEEN WOLF** this!), the almost "cute" mask likely led the filmmakers to drop the idea of any kind of physical transformation for the follow-up. Director Kazuhiko Yamaguchi (who helmed **SISTER STREET FIGHTER** [女必殺拳 / *Onna Hissatsu Ken*, 1974], **WANDERING GINZA BUTTERFLY** [銀蝶渡り鳥 / Ginchō Wataridori, 1972] and its same-year sequel **SHE-CAT GAMBLER** [銀蝶流れ者 牝猫博奕 / *Ginchō Nagaremono: Mesuneko Bakuchi*], **DELINQUENT GIRL BOSS: WORTHLESS TO CONFESS** [ずべ公番長 ざんげの値打も

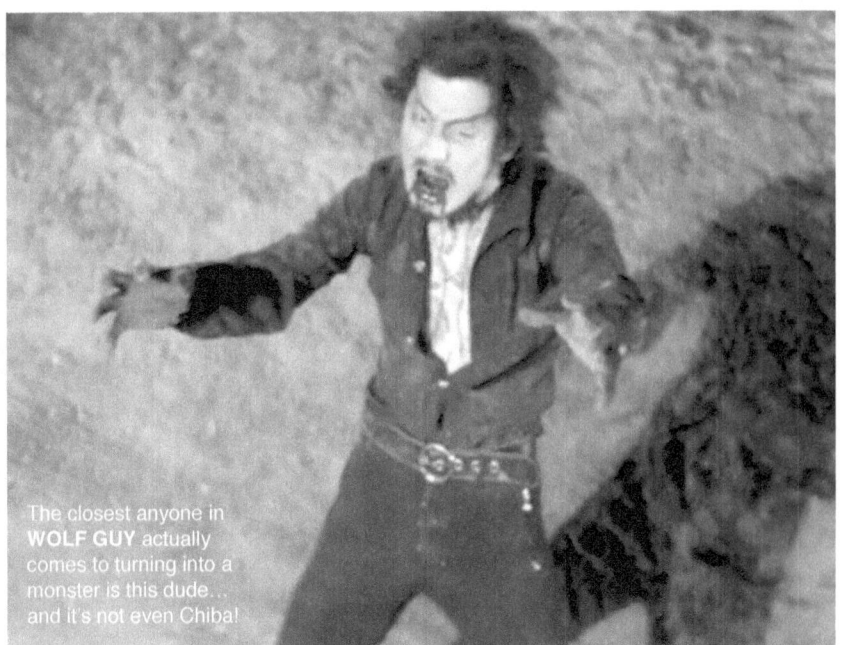

The closest anyone in **WOLF GUY** actually comes to turning into a monster is this dude... and it's not even Chiba!

supernatural wolf never really happens. Indeed, the final 30 minutes in general felt rather rushed. The results left me—as an action fan first, mind you—feeling a little frustrated over what *might* have been. Regardless, this is still an upper-level Sonny Chiba vehicle. Maybe not on the level of either **THE STREET FIGHTER** (激突！殺人拳 / *Gekitotsu! Satsujin Ken*, 1974, D: Shigehiro Ozawa) or **THE EXECUTIONER** (直撃！地獄拳 / *Chokugeki! Jigokuken*, 1974, D: Teruo Ishii), but certainly good enough. Bottom line: despite some drawbacks, the world is still a much better place with outrageously oddball movies like this one inhabiting it.

Arrow continues their high-quality standard with this two-disc (one Blu-ray and one DVD) release. It's a beautiful widescreen transfer that instantly renders the—nonetheless much-appreciated at the time—DVD-R bootlegs obsolescent and expendable. The bulk of the extras are three separate interviews (conducted in Japanese with English subtitles). First up is "Kazuhiko Yamaguchi: Movies With Girls". In it, the director offers a flip attitude regarding his experience with **WOLF GUY**, stating "I didn't really want to make it", admitting he was unfamiliar with the comic and expressed a disinterest in classic werewolf films. Hey, sounds like the *perfect* guy for the gig, right?! He found Chiba to be "very intense with his character" and seemed impressed with the way he built-up his performance. Next up is "Toru Yoshida: B-Movie Master". This in-

terview with the film's producer is more detailed and enlightening. Among what's discussed is the fact that he also didn't wish to do the film, at least initially (sensing a pattern here!), but, unlike Yamaguchi, he didn't care for Chiba; stating he was not a good actor (!) and that he preferred a more realistic style of action to Chiba's karate choreography. Also unlike the previous interviewee, Yoshida did like the idea of shooting a werewolf movie, but laments not having the budget to do it properly, and therefore not taking it as seriously as he might have. The line that truly floored me here was Yoshida's statement, "If I had put more effort into this one, I think it might have become as groundbreaking as Masked [Kamen] Rider" (!). As a *huge* fan of '70s-style Japanese TV superhero shows in general and *Kamen Rider* (仮面ライダー / *Kamen Raidā*) in particular, this made me weep. He also shared some sad stories involving writer and friend Fumio Konami. The third and final interview is "Sonny Chiba: A Life in Action Vol. 1." Sadly, the great man doesn't even mention the subject matter in his segment, but nevertheless gives a pretty cool interview anyway. Chiba heartily discusses the art of action choreography and comparing how it's done currently in the US versus Japan (he is *not* very complimentary to his homeland here). He also credits director Kinji Fukasaku for first noting and then helping to draw-out the action star in him. I was, however, left wondering where and when Vol. 2 will make a digital appearance. Rounding-out the extras is a terrific trailer that leaves little to

THE SECRET OF THE MUMMY
(*O Segredo da Múmia*)

Reviewed by Martín Núñez

Brazil, 1982. D: Ivan Cardoso

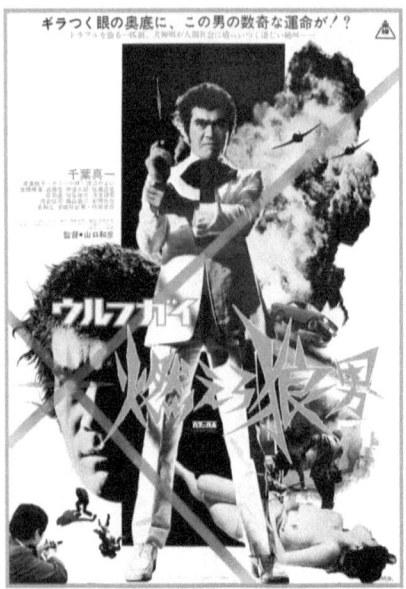

Weird horror-themed cinema was alive and kicking in Brazil during the early 'Eighties. It's strange to think about a country as big as Brazil and realize what little one knows about its cinema. It is a country that has given us some extraordinary singers, musicians and writers (etc.) over the years, although we still have much to learn yet about the nation's quite substantial and prolific movie industry.

Most horror enthusiasts are at least in some way familiar with the works of Brazilian cinematic master José Mojica Marins—a.k.a. "Zé do Caixão", his evil alter-ego *[informally known to many Anglos as "Coffin Joe" – ed.]*—and some of the more-curious, cinematically adventurous ones would likely know about the flourishing sexploitation phenomenon that hit Brazilian cinemas in the late 'Seventies and early 'Eighties, largely consisting of sleazy, bizarre, cheap and ugly so-called "erotic" films that were better-known in the imagination (how *could* it?!) and a booklet with some very fine liner notes penned by one Patrick Macias, author of the thoroughly entertaining and easily-digestible book *Tokyoscope: The Japanese Cult Film Companion* (VIZ Media LLC, 2001).

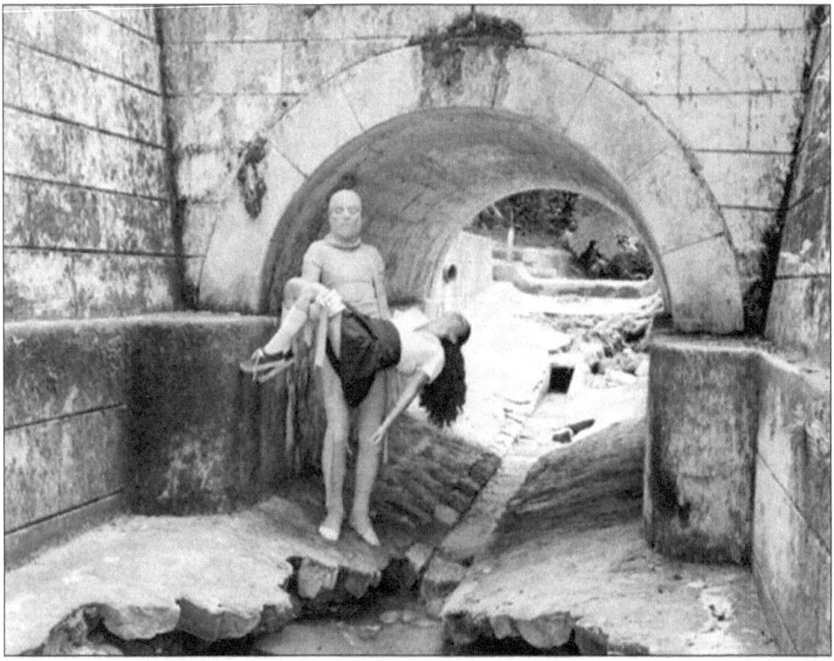

As with all traditional movie monsters, the embalmed undead thing from **THE SECRET OF THE MUMMY** strikes the classic pose with an unconscious damsel

Creature Feature Reviews

the vernacular as *Pornochanchadas* (which not only feel like but actually can be translated as "pigstyporn" [¡!]). These bad-taste, lowest-common-denominator sleazefests were shot in the slums following the outbreak of the global AIDS epidemic; and yeah, they are indeed every bit as *filthy* as they sound!

In this same period, Brazilian filmmaker Ivan Cardoso started his career, mostly due to his devotion for horror movies, especially those made by the aforementioned Mojica Marins, the mentor of many a Brazilian filmmaker who realized that there was no better way to learn about making movies than going out and doing just that. We should remember that Mojica Marins started shooting his horror efforts without having ever even watched the classics beforehand, so consequently his movies turned-out to be weirdly unique ones that are not for the weak-nerved/hearted, and Cardoso seems to have emulated his master (if in a more "highbrow" sense), at least in the case of this particular movie. Also, he was an energetic creative force who not only wrote but also produced and directed his personal cinematic visions.

Cardoso began his filmmaking career with *Nosferato no Brasil* ("Nosferatu in Brazil", 1970), which was shot on Super 8. *Nosferato* has more simple enthusiasm than anything else going for it, but it works nonetheless, and already shows some of the experimental *vive* which Cardoso added to almost all of his early work; a kind of no budget/experimental cinema that, despite all its faults, has an overall charm that works just fine...at least with *me*.

A few years later, Cardoso made the first-ever documentary on Zé do Caixão: a 26-minute short entitled *O Universo de Mojica Marins* ("The Universe of Mojica Marins", 1978), a film that mixes-up footage from Marins' movies along with backstage sequences with various voiceover discussing Zé do Caixão's work, plus includes personal testimonials from The Man himself. I can well recall the emotion I felt when I grabbed a fourth-generation VHS dupe of this documentary back in the '90s because with all its flaws it is a perfect document to understand Mojica Marins' phenomenon and cinema, both elements that walk together in Brazilian pop culture. We have to remember that Zé do Caixão figure was so huge that besides his movies he made Comic magazines and records. It has been said that Brazilian parents still scare their children with Zé do Caixão's character. Anyway, this documentary is a good example to start handling Cardoso's work as a mix of cerebral editing combined with horror fanaticism.

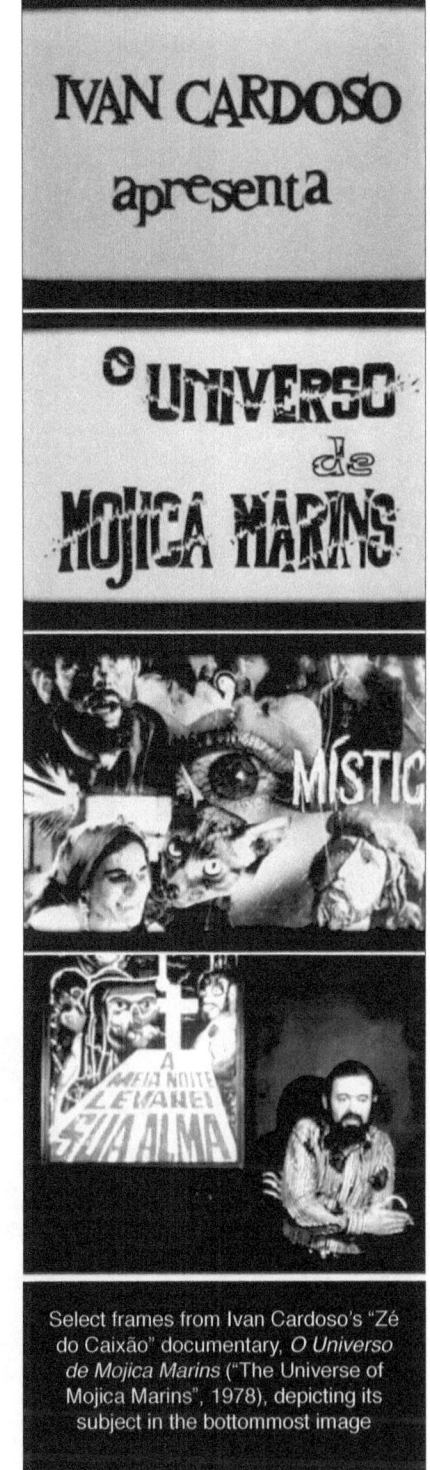

Select frames from Ivan Cardoso's "Zé do Caixão" documentary, *O Universo de Mojica Marins* ("The Universe of Mojica Marins", 1978), depicting its subject in the bottommost image

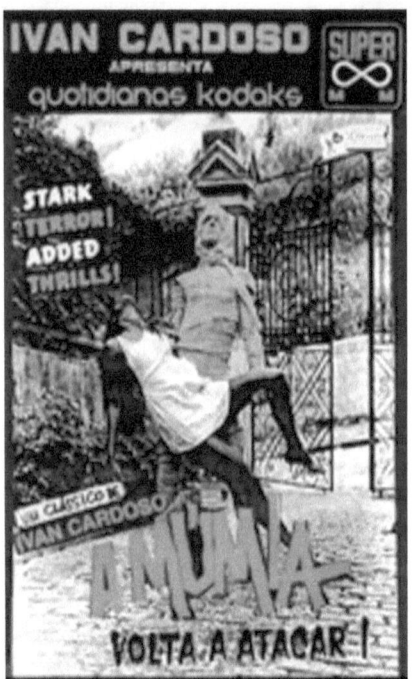

Brazilian 8mm film cover for an earlier Cardoso mummy outing, the 25-minute short *A Múmia Volta Atacar* (1972)

But it wasn't until 1981 that Cardoso started shooting his first full-length feature, and it's a movie that has to be seen to believe. Is it weird? *YES!* Is it experimental? *YES!!* Is it funny? *HELL YES!!!*

Released one year later, **THE SECRET OF THE MUMMY**, produced by Embrafilme / Mapa Filmes / Super 8 Produções Cinematográficas, is a movie that is assuredly not to everyone's taste, mostly because it has a heavily comedic tone that was highly unusual in Brazilian popular cinema back in the day. And that's not all, as the movie dares to push the outer limits of genre cinema, not only in its plot, but also in its aesthetics.

Obviously inspired by classic horror movies, these movies' elements function here mainly as *homage*. Strictly speaking, though, this isn't a "classic"-styled horror movie, despite its featuring the likes of a mummy and a mad doctor (as well as some insane T&A/sex-filled exploitation sequences!).

Like most South American movies of those years, **SECRET** has virtually *zero* in the way of production values, and this can be confirmed by the seemingly arbitrary use of both color and black-and-white film stock, to evidently no real narrative purpose; simply because, out of necessity, the director shot it on whatever kind of film he happened to have handy at the time. I can imagine Cardoso scanning over the shooting schedule then checking what stock he had available to use. Due to these decisions, we see B&W takes combined with color ones but, as sometimes tends to happen, the randomly mismatched film stock integrates quite flawlessly due to the overall experimental/artsy final result.

But, you ask, what is the plot all about...?

Professor Expedito Vitus (a famished South American Boris Karloff lookalike) is obsessively

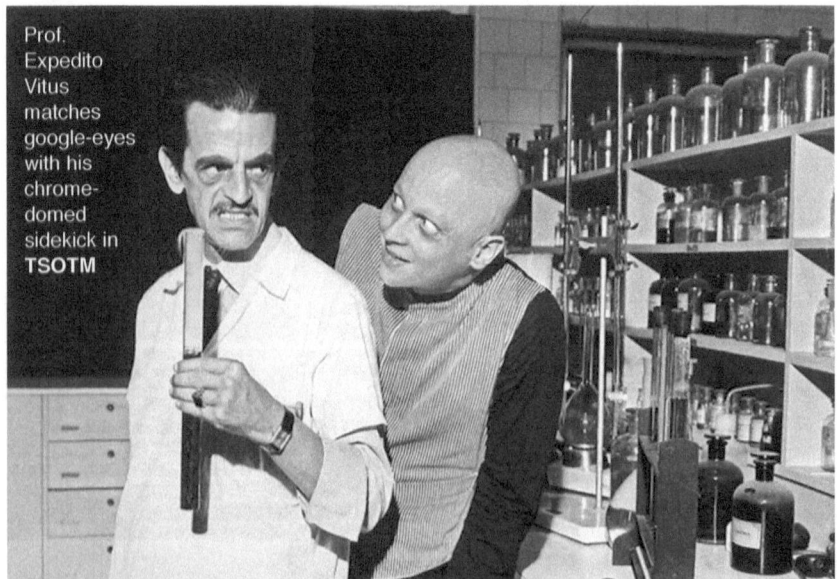

Prof. Expedito Vitus matches google-eyes with his chrome-domed sidekick in **TSOTM**

searching for the *Mumia de Runamb* ("mummy of Runamb"), so in 1954 he travels to El Cairo after finding a map that used to be the property of another scientist (this one played by no less than José Mojica Marins/"Zé do Caixão" himself!). However, said map was divided-up into eight separate sections, so the movie opens with the mysterious murders of each individual part's owners. These killings are not violently presented, and are pretty well-shot and edited, providing a highly entertaining introduction to the story. In this way, after getting the eight pieces of the map together, Cardoso shows professor Vitus on a sandy Brazilian location, edited-together with some 8mm stock footage depicting Egypt's pyramids and sphinxes. Clearly the film stocks here do not match, but they possess this lovely low-budget charm that succeeds in elevating sheer creativity and willpower over basic economical restrictions.

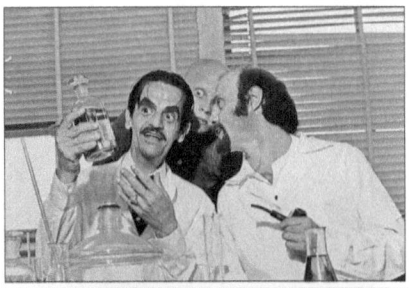

Vitus' discovery generates instant media coverage, so, after we see several newspapers discussing the professor's success, Cardoso installs a recurrent device that runs throughout the whole movie to that places the story into context: fake, well-shot newsreels, like those projected in cinemas prior to the main feature not so very many decades ago. In this first newsreel we see a triumphant professor Vitus returning to Brazil, but this sequence also works to present Vitus' personality and his various enigmatic studies.

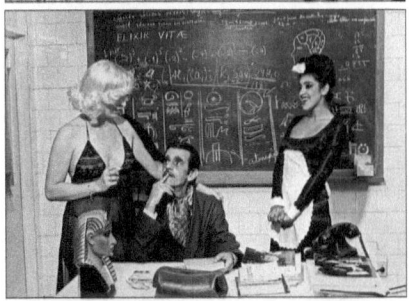

After this, Cardoso introduces us to the prof's everyday life; various happenings occurring at his laboratory, his weird studies, hieroglyph-filled blackboards and his female partner Gilda (played by a blonde bombshell with virtually no acting skills whatsoever). Due to the movie's satirical feel, these overacted issues utilizing several actors ends up being a good vehicle to propel the narrative, as half of **SECRET** is absurd comedy, after all.

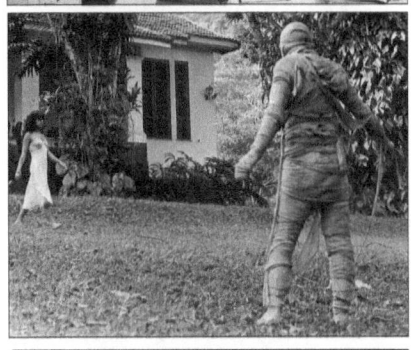

The gorgeous Gilda is the first (along with we lucky spectators!) to learn of Vitus real intentions: that is, to prove to the scientific community how wrong they were about his Elixir of Life, a drug he claims is capable of bringing the dead back from the grave. This elixir was previously tested on Igor (!), his henchman (who also happens to be an operatic tenor!), who was injected with this fluid and thereafter attained eternal life, in the process turning his character into the kind of typical mad doctor sidekick we all adore in these kinds of movies. Obedient and loyal, this baldheaded assistant will kill without hesitation when his master commands him to.

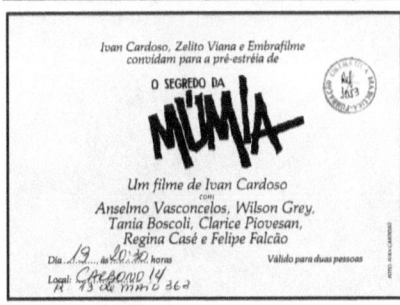

Top to Bottom: Three more scenes from **THE SECRET OF THE MUMMY** (1982), plus a view of the reverse side to one of the stills *[above]*

But things are not easy for the good ol' professor, as an inopportune character will show up during this stage in the form of a journalist named Everton (yes, Brazilian movie characters' names are *weird*!), who is investigating the murders of the former map owners and follows the clues that lead him to Professor Vitus. In order to get into the house, Everton must flirt with the professor's

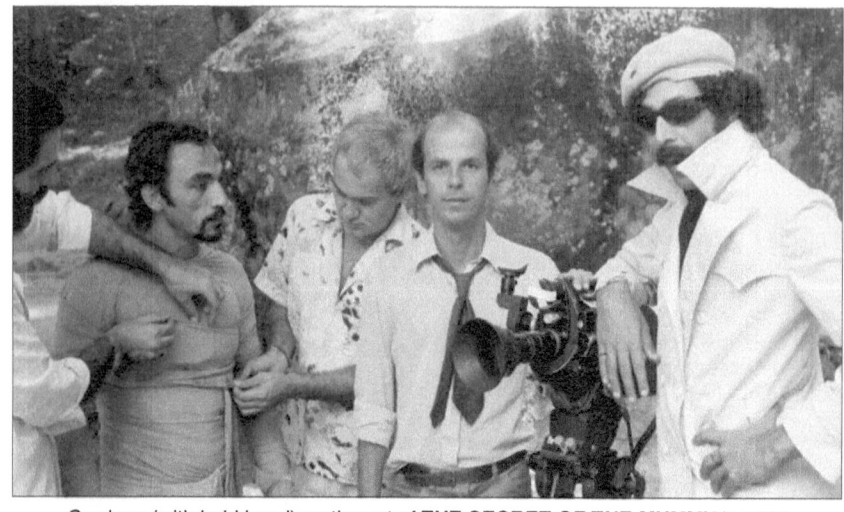

Cardoso (with bald head) on the set of **THE SECRET OF THE MUMMY** in 1982

hot brunette assistant Regina (Regina Casé, a successful Brazilian actress), who also happens to be Igor's lover—their sex scene is so weird and awkward that it results in one of the movie's highlights.

At this time, the story of Runamb the Mummy is exposed. Millennia ago when he was alive, this hedonistic Pharaoh had enjoyed the carnal pleasures during orgies, while seeking to win the affections of Nadja, his former lover. Runamb, a big consumer of white-trade slaves, looked for Nadja in every woman he bought, but since none of these satisfied him, he proceeded to kill each of them. This obsession to find his Nadja remains with him even in his mummified version. Upon being captured, tried and judged, Runamb was then sentenced to death and to be mummified as his final punishment. This sequence is one of the most interesting in the movie, mostly due to its editing.

After another fake newsreel covering the "Miss Brazil" pageant, via a single shot utilizing silhouettes, Cardoso pays tribute to the famous "*It's alive! It's alive!! It's alive!!!*" scene from James Whale's **FRANKENSTEIN** (1931, USA). That film's title character is elsewhere also present here in the book studied by Vitus to create his life-restoring elixir, as it was written by one "Arthur Frankenstein".

And now things get more interesting… Runamb's recently-bought-to-life mummy starts a killing spree, which, while not violent, leads to the *weirdest* element of the film: after murdering some male victims, the mummy kidnaps women in order to take them to Vitus' dungeon, where several girls are used as guinea pigs for his experiments. You have to watch the "chicken-girl" to see just how *weird* this movie is! The female cast perform their sexy sequences as readily as they do the ones involving cannibalism.

Absurdism, love affairs, satiric overtones, overacted comedy, hot ladies, sleazed-out lesbianism, mad doctors, horror movie homages and

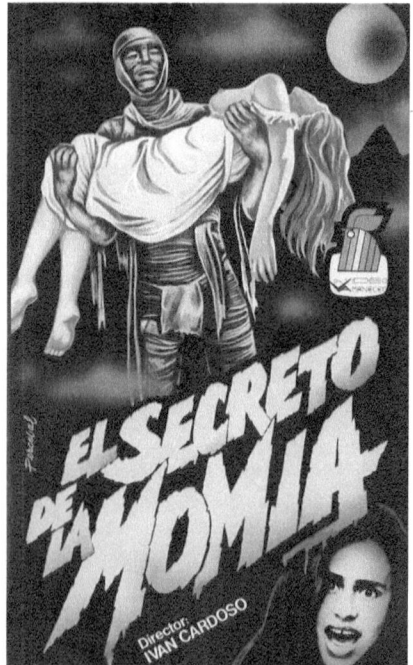

Hispanic VHS cover; art by Perceval

intellectualism all converge to total a movie like no other. Believe me, this is *not* the classic horror-themed black comedy, nor the senseless amateur horror homage, let alone along the lines of the kinds of horror comedies being made in the United States during that era. This is a movie that only Cardoso would have made in the context of Brazilian popular cinema and, believe it or not, **SECRET** actually works *great*! Despite its lack of either any budget or gory SFX (barring a single simple, gory decapitation) and its many technical difficulties, the final product stands tall mostly due Cardoso's unique approach to horror comedy and its crazy plot.

Cardoso had an irregular and uneven career as filmmaker later on, but he was able to deliver some other horror-related gems that you might be reading about within these pages in the near future. *[Feel free to write about more of Cardoso's works whenever you like, Martin! ☺ – SF.]*

If you like weird world cinema, by all means give **THE SECRET OF THE MUMMY** a try. Chances are you won't be disappointed.

THE INTRUDER WITHIN

Reviewed by Eric Messina

USA, 1981. D: Peter Carter

ABC-TV teaser trailer narration: *"Someone's finally gone too deep! Something's finally been awakened!"*

I remember seeing the box for this on video store shelves in the '80s, along with **DEMENTED** (1980, USA), **ALIEN PREY** (a.k.a. **PREY**, 1977, UK, D: Norman J. Warren) and **DR. BUTCHER M.D.** (1980, Italy), but never had the opportunity to rent it. All I can remember was that it had a giant orange Gigeresque monster on the cover. I soon forgot about it until the deadline for the next issue of *Monster!* crept-up on the agenda, so decided to dial it up on YouTube to see whether it was a total shit-fest or a lost classic....actually, it's a bit of both, if a lot more of the former than the latter. Yes indeed, it's another **ALIEN** (1979, USA/UK) rip-off, albeit catering to more conservative network TV tastes, but what it lacks in gore it certainly makes up for with unintentional laughs.

It begins in the most random and irrational way possible, with an obscure reference to Martin Luther King's famous "I have a dream" speech. So already we've been set up for a rough ride! How dare a dopey TV movie-of-the-week allude to

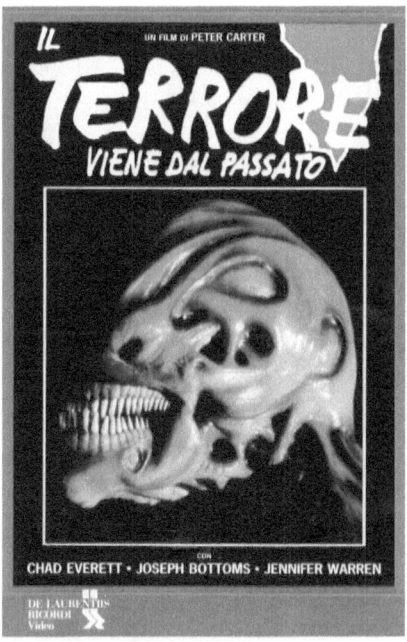

De Laurentiis Ricordi Video's Italian VHS cover for **THE INTRUDER WITHIN**

that prophetic civil rights leader in such a throwaway manner! Sure, it doesn't stand a chance, but I like this movie's moxie anyway! A squirmy Horshackesque goofball (played by Matt Craven) awakens from a nightmare, but unfortunately he is also actually living one on an evil corporation's offshore oil-rig called Zortron (love that name)! Chaos ensues faster than you can don a Caterpillar P-5000 robo-exoskeleton and yell *"Get away from her, you BITCH!"* Jennifer Warren, one of the tough females on the crew, is no Sigourney Weaver—to be fair, though, she's not trying to be, and the male characters primarily dominate the heroic duties. A few years later, Warren appeared in the toxic waste zombie potboiler **MUTANT** (a.k.a. **NIGHT SHADOWS**, 1984, USA), co-starring Wings Hauser and helmed by former Al Adamson stuntman John "Bud" Cardos (with an uncredited assist from Mark Rosman).

For **THE INTRUDER WITHIN**, in the interests of ratcheting-up the "human drama", the Zortron deep-sea drilling rig's self-proclaimed tool-pusher and head roughneck Jake (Chad Everett, who has a Tom Skerritt-style mustache going on) and a brash young uni-browed dude (played by Joseph Bottoms) clash over who's *really* in charge, causing friction and in-fighting among the employees at the isolated work station. There's all kinds of bickering and gender politics going on in this awful work environment. Oil rigs must

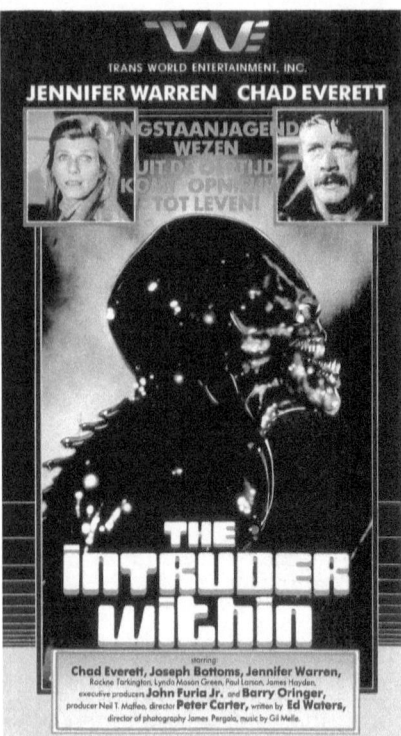

THE INTRUDER WITHIN's Dutch VHS cover

have had lax policies on sexual harassment, because that's exactly what happens later on. *[Since so few females actually worked on oil-rigs—especially of the offshore kind—in the early '80s (even less than do today), chances are drilling companies didn't have any policy about it at all! ☺ – SF.]* It gets worse as a Xenomorph slithers up from a piece of hardware called a "shaker" and chomps on a crew member's arm, for which it gets blasted with flares; as a result, the grayish-red toothy critter gets vaporized—well, *that* was easy! More lunchroom zaniness ensues, and the roughnecks' late co-worker's fatality is chalked-up as having been caused by a lamprey-like creature that injected venom not unlike that of a Portuguese man-o'-war into its victim. They don't really go into detail, but it seems like this creature is much more of an aquatic terrestrial threat than an intergalactic one. There's never any evidence of a spaceship (most likely due to basic budgetary restraints), and this monstrous being simply gets dumped aboard the rig from the oil pump and proceeds to infect various members of the crew.

The acting is mostly decent enough, but the level never rises above the quality of, say, a particularly freaky episode of *CHiPs* (1977-83, USA).

Scotty, the geologist with the uni-brow—who, to make matters worse, also sports a Marjoe Gortner-style 'white guy' 'fro on top of it (literally!)—seems to be hiding something. That Styrofoam plateful of spiny sea urchins he was bogarting in secret sure looks suspicious! Yep, that's confirmation enough for me to know that this dude shouldn't be trusted! One of the spiked echinoderms pokes one old geezer's finger, and he starts reacting badly, like he might have been infected with something or other. He begins to attack people on the rig, and it seems that he's now become extra-sensitive to light, which could be 'subtle' foreshadowing pointing to the potential means of battling the oncoming creeper invasion later on. Scotty keeps fucking around with the sea snails while the crew snap at each other snarkily during lunch as the stress levels continue to rise among them. One dude named Chili (Canadian actor Michael Hogan) even turns into Crazy Ralph from **FRIDAY THE 13**ᵀᴴ (1980, USA, D: Sean S. Cunningham) and warns everyone that "They're all *doomed*!"

If you love the snail-paced relationship dynamics of a certain copyrighted Yaphet Kotto (*et al*) space flick but wished that pesky drooling bug would quit interrupting the action, then you'll dig this one. The way these alien shlubs pop up and zoom about looks and sounds like one of my favorite arcade games of the '90s, *Xenophobe*. That Bally Midway game was another item in the nostalgia craze of the Ridley Scott franchise. That trend—which continues to this day in one form or other—also includes **GALAXY OF TERROR** (1981, USA, D: B.D. Clark) and **FORBIDDEN WORLD** (1982, USA, D: Allan Holzman). Best you watch those two first before you bother with this blander neutered, watered-down televersion. Don't get the wrong idea, though: I had a blast during this film, and there's lots of unintentional chuckles (and even outright guffaws) to be had.

Scotty, the sleazy science guy (allegedly a geologist, but with a keen interest in zoology, especially when it comes to unknown lifeforms) has the same mentality as Ian Holm's automaton 'company man' character in **ALIEN**, and prioritizes the strange new species over ours. Since this is network TV, they can't show how horny these beings are—*WHEW!* Thank the censors for that! Hence, it's only *implied* that they want to mate with the three poor females on board, violating the shit outta the sexual harassment policy. Thus, it borrows ever-so-slightly from **HUMANOIDS FROM THE DEEP** (1980, USA), the Roger Corman flick about amorous bikini-chasing monsters. If I had to choose in a hypothetical scenario between seeing a better Ridley Scott/Dan O'Bannon rip-off like the aforementioned '81 flick

GALAXY OF TERROR on a big screen or this on the box at home, I would've already been warming-up the car to head out to the theater! You can't really compare this present movie to that all-star exploitation classic, because it spawned an entire rape-tentacle anime subgenre, while the present one maybe at best succeeded in lulling some insomniacs into a deep slumber before they had to get up early for work the next morning.

THE INTRUDER WITHIN's derivative creature was played by Joe Finnegan, who was a stunt man in everything from **APOCALYPSE NOW** (1979, USA/Philippines) to **ZAPPED!** (1982, USA). When the toothy monster is finally revealed, it looks like a combination of "The Chatterer" from **HELLRAISER** (1987, USA) and an **ALIEN**esque crustacean with 'roid rage! The grand finale has it climbing to the top of the rig, and good thing there's a bunch of crude oil about, because once a flare-gun ignites it, the monster goes up like a Christmas tree!

The effects are pretty dark and tough to see at times, but James Cummins, who wrote and directed the choice 'poodle-monster' film **THE BONEYARD** (USA, 1991), worked on them. Peter Carter, director of this TV movie, also made the effectively creepy **DELIVERANCE**-inspired backwoods thriller **RITUALS** (1977, Canada), starring Hal Holbrook. While **THE INTRUDER WITHIN** is very obscure and copies are now scarce, it's not *really* worth checking-out. However, if you absolutely *must* see everything either directly or indirectly spawned by H.R. Giger/**ALIEN**, then by all means check it out if you ever happen to spot it on YouTube (as of this writing there were at least two full-length rips/uploads in English at the site).

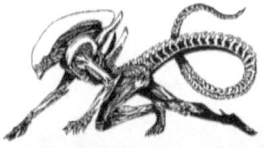

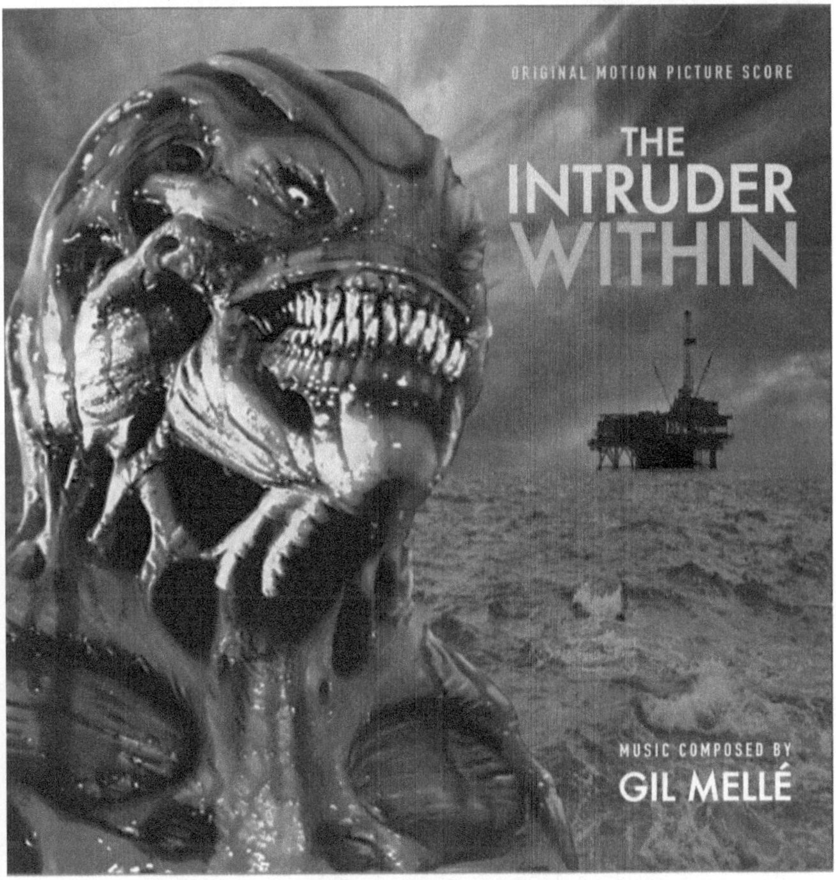

If only the film itself were even half as exciting as the cover of its soundtrack is!

"The house?" Alice had enquired, with a sudden crooked look on a face that Nature, it seemed, had definitely intended to be frequently startled; *"The house?"* |– from "The Looking-Glass" (1923), by Walter de la Mare

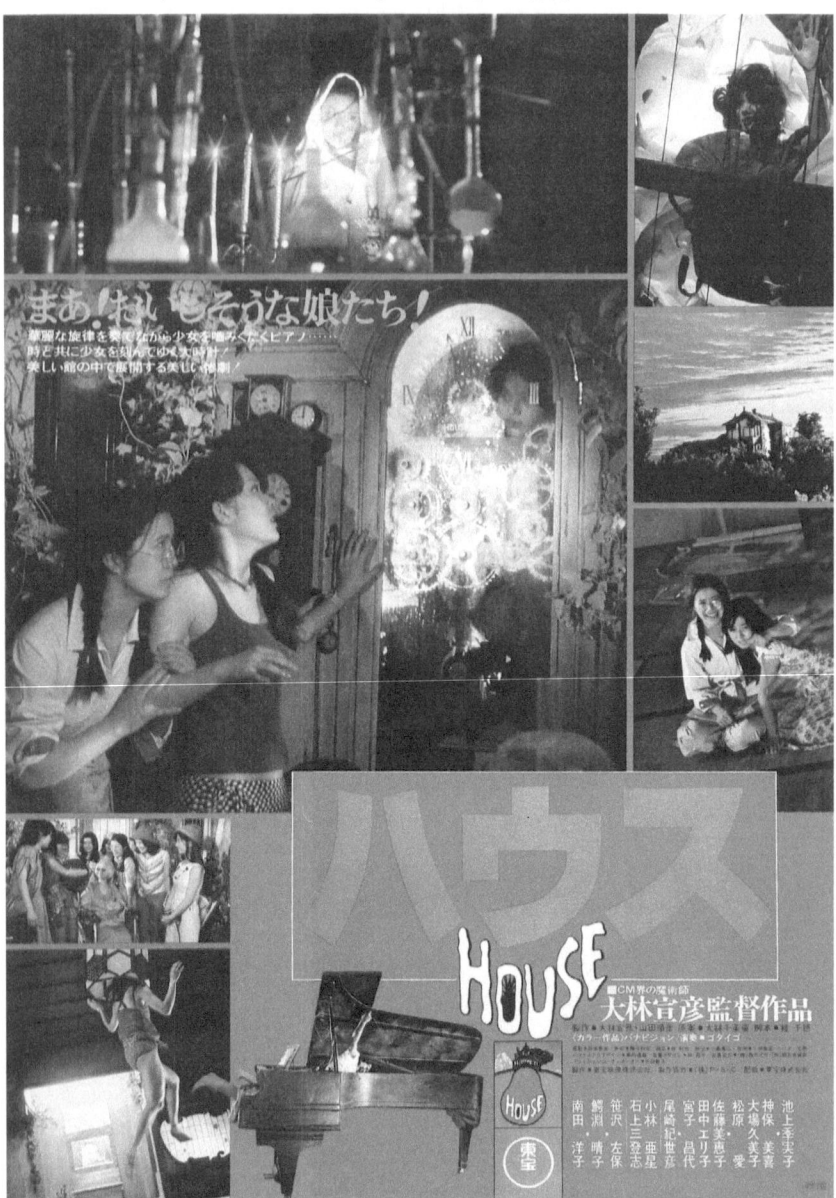

"Even when the body decays, you may always live on in the heart of another together with the love of that person. Therefore, the story of love must always be retold. So that the one you love can live on forever. Live forever, the feelings of the beloved, which never fades, only one promise... That is Love." |– Consecutive lines of translated Japanese dialogue from the English subtitles to Criterion's domestic disc edition of **HOUSE** (1977)

KEYS TO THE HOUSE
Turning Experimentation Into Expression!

by Michael Hauss

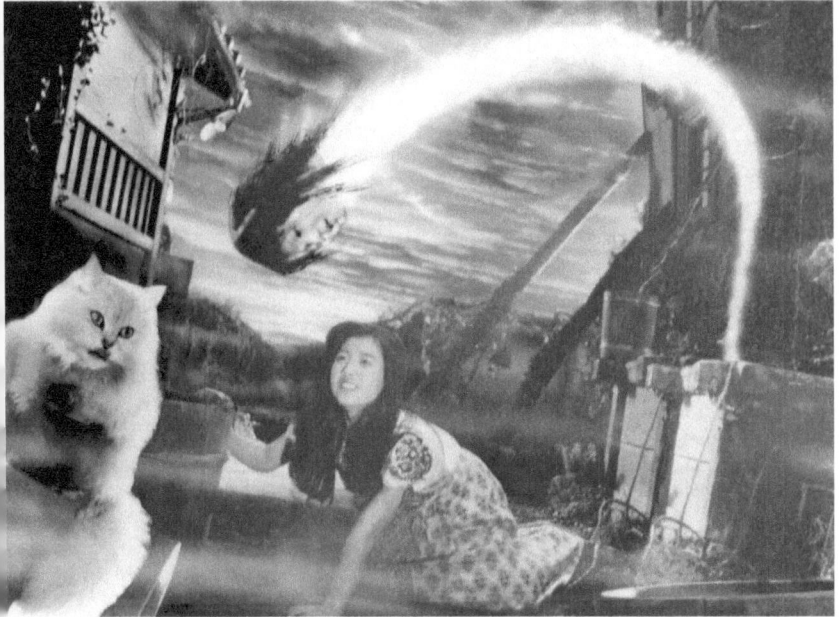

A cut-'n'-paste promotional montage for **HOUSE**. Believe it or not, the film itself gets *way* crazier than this!

My first by-chance viewing of Nobuhiko Ōbayashi's astonishing film **HOUSE** (ハウス / *Hausu*, 1977, Japan) was a copy of it in Japanese, without English subtitles, courtesy of *Monster!* magazine guru Tim Paxton. That first viewing left me dazed and confused, feeling that some of the insanity that unfolded on the screen *might* be explained…if only I could understand what was being said onscreen. So, I rushed to buy The Criterion Collection release of the film, with English subs. Boy, was I *wrong* about understanding this film, even *with* the aid of subtitles! It seemingly *doesn't want* to be understood on 'normal' terms, that's how confoundedly cryptic and couched in enigma its scenario is, and stubbornly goes out of its way to remain. The narrative is sewn-together with ideas which, while seemingly unconnected, ultimately coalesce into one to form a profoundly moving whole that requires the viewer to put the pieces together themselves, its events often being open to our personal interpretation. There is no mistaking, even though lightheartedness and absurdity abounds, that the film's narrative is more than merely a bunch of cut-ups, quick edits or random unassociated snippets of ideas; it's much deeper than that, but, then again, at the same time, it *isn't*. A visual feast, **HOUSE** is a gleeful celebration of the very art of filmmaking itself, basing its foundations firmly upon Japan's tried-and-true wealth of *Bakeneko* (化け猫 / "changing cat") or *Kaibyō* (怪猫 / "ghost-cat") legends and *Yūrei* (幽霊 / "ghost") stories out of local folklore, literature and cinema. However, none of the just-cited *bakeneko*, *kaibyō* or *yūrei* tales (be they oral, in print or on celluloid) ever dived deep into the bottomless well of utter insanity quite like **HOUSE** does while expanding—even stretching right to the point of snapping—their basic fantasy framework into far-flung worlds well beyond our ken. It exists in a universe of all-out, no-holds-barred fantasy that none of its genre progenitors/predecessors had ever ventured into before it, nor would have ever *dared* to, being so tradition-bound as such

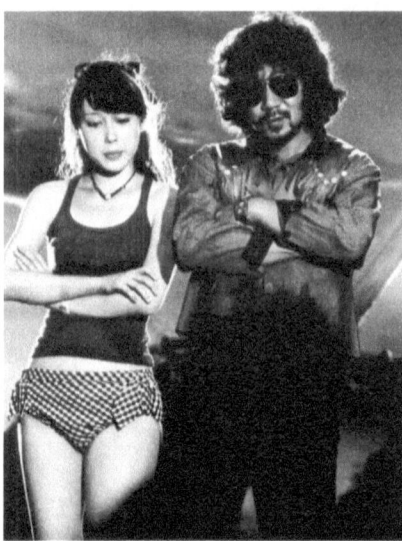

Actress Miki "Kung Fu" Jinbo and **HOUSE** director Nobuhiko Ōbayashi on the set of the film in 1977

fare generally is. **HOUSE**, on the other hand, breaks from such kabuki theatre-based traditions with an almost anarchic, cathartic glee, yet still succeeds in retaining some of its quintessential 'Japaneseness' in the process.

****

Seven schoolgirls, whose seasonal break from classes has been altered by a pair of unrelated incidents, set out on a journey that lands them smack-dab in the realms of the unreal! Oshare (Kimiko Ikegami, who plays three roles herein), was due to spend the summer holiday with her father (Saho Sasazawa), a wealthy, successful composer. Having recently returned from scoring a film in Italy, Dad tells Oshare, "Leone said it's even better than Morricone's"; 'Leone' obviously referring to the great Italian director Sergio Leone and 'Morricone' being his frequent collaborator, the world-renowned composer Ennio Morricone, of course. In addition, Oshare's father—a widower—has a secret he wishes to confess to his doting daughter. That secret is revealed to be the 'new' woman he plans on marrying, and the one who is set to accompany the girls on their upcoming vacation. The self-centered and possessively territorial Oshare spitefully rejects her father's lover Ryōko Ema (Haruko Wanibuchi), taking the white scarf that woman affectionately places around her neck—a symbolic flag of surrender?—and throwing it contemptuously into the air. Heartbroken that her father has found himself another woman, whom he assures his daughter will become a replacement/surrogate for her deceased birth mother, Oshare decides to write her auntie (Yōko Minamida), her late mom's sister, to ask if she can go visit her for a spell. "I'm sorry that I write this letter, even though we hardly know each other", she writes. "Please do not think badly of me. I'm close to tears at the moment. I want to go back

A specially-posed group shot of all the girlfriends in **HOUSE**. *[From left to right]* Melody (Eriko Tanaka), Prof (Ai Matubara), Gorgeous a.k.a. Angel (Kimiko Ikegami), Kung Fu (Miki Jinbo), Fantasy (Kumiko Ohba), Mac (Mieko Sato) and Sweet (Masayo Miyako)

to mother's home districts, and let you comfort me in Mummy's place. Please let us come". The very next day, her aunt's response arrives in the mailbox via the beautiful long-haired white cat that had visited Oshare the night before (which she'd dubbed Snowflake, whose actual name is Blanche and who fills a key role in the action throughout). In her letter, Auntie hospitably welcomes the girls to her home: "Come to me… *come to me…*"

The seven girlfriends are not referred to by their birth names, but are instead given names that best fit their stereotypical attributes in the eyes of their chums. So, we have arguably the 'prettiest' of the bunch, the vain Oshare, alias "Gorgeous", as well as tough tomboy "Kung Fu" ([*Kunfū*] Miki Jinbo), who performs energetically enthusiastic martial arts on a dime, "Prof" ([*Gari*] Ai Matubara), who is the 'smart' one (as her studious spectacles superficially indicate), "Fanta" (short for "Fantasy" [Kumiko Ohba]), whose mind at times dwells in the land of make-believe, "Sweet" ([*Suîto*] Masayo Miyako), who is an obsessive homemaker/housekeeper, "Mac" ([short for 'stomach'!] Mieko Sato), a chubby greedy-guts who enjoys eating, and "Melody" ([*Merodî*] Eriko Tanaka), who is musically-inclined. In a surreal journey by first a train and then a bus, the vacationing septet finally arrive in the rural village, where the titular house, Oshare's aunt's ancestral home, is situated. The girls are welcomed-in by "Auntie", as they all come to informally call her; a sickly white-haired woman who is bound to a wheelchair and, unbeknownst to them, is actually a *yūrei* spirit-being in mortal human guise. Shades of the fairy tale witch in the candy cottage from "Hansel and Gretel", she presents an enticingly—if deceptively—wholesome, saccharine front to her prospective victims, who initially don't suspect that anything sinister lies in wait for them behind her beguilingly smiling façade of maternal hospitality, although, in a bit of foreboding foreshadowing that doesn't bode well for their future, they do note how creepy her house is upon their arrival (it certainly doesn't look like the kind of place to have a framed plaque reading "Home, Sweet Home" on the wall, that's for sure!).

****

The Japanese have many stories—usually scary ones!—concerning a kind of *Yōkai* (妖怪 / "supernatural creature") known as the *Bakeneko*. This is a cat that, due to having lived a long natural life, has transitioned from being an ordinary feline to one possessing supernatural powers which, while they can be used for good, are oftentimes used in the furtherance of Evil (typically

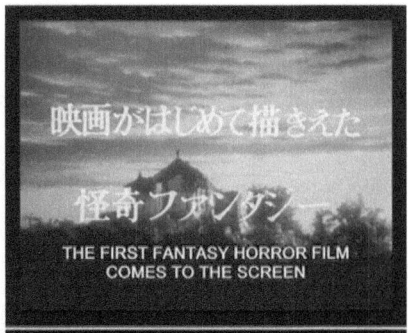

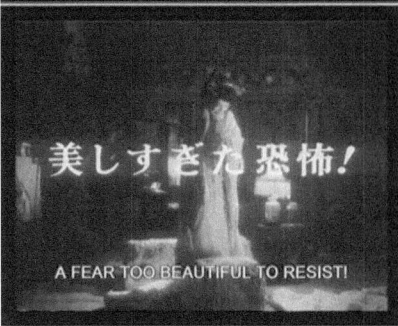

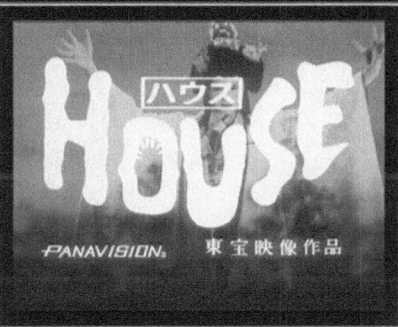

Screen grabs from **HOUSE**'s trailer

to exact vengeance on immoral humans who have wronged them in some way. Since 'vengeance' typically means 'justice' in such scenarios, any evildoings done in its furtherance might almost be regarded as acts of goodness in the long run, at least when applied to the moral resolution of a fable). Through ancient transcribed texts, verbally passed-down folk tales and *ukiyo-e* (浮世絵) art prints, stories of these creatures proliferated over the centuries, eventually becoming the subjects of Japanese motion pictures as early as 1914 (when several short [?] films were made on the theme), and the subject matter has carried on over more recent decades with the likes of the J-horror hit **JU-ON: THE GRUDGE** (呪怨じゅおん / *Ju-on*, 2002) and its equally *yūrei*-fraught sequel **JU-ON: THE GRUDGE 2** (呪怨2じゅおん2 / *Ju-on 2*, 2003, both D: Takashi Shimizu),

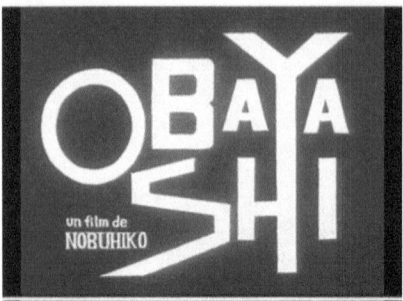
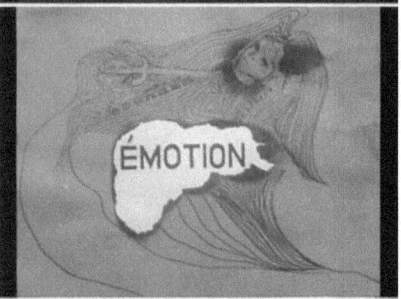
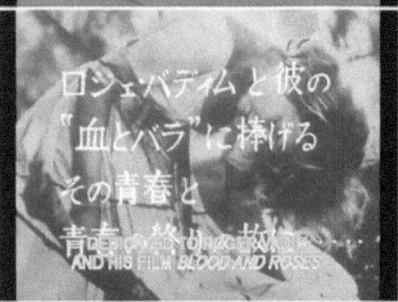
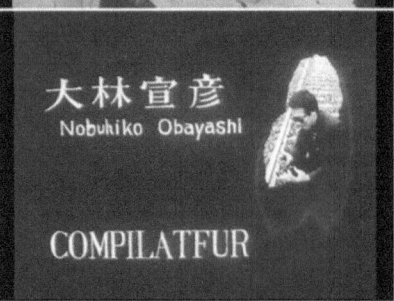

A quartet of frames from the title sequence to Nobuhiko Ōbayashi's 1966 short subject *Emotion* (伝説伝説の午後=いつか見たドラキュラ だドラキュラ / *Émotion: densetsu no gogo = itsukamita Dracula*), one of which—the third from the top—acknowledges French filmmaker Roger Vadim and his vampire film **BLOOD AND ROSES** (*Et mourir de plaisir*, 1960, France/Italy)

both being more recent successful variations of the form that incorporate key elements of the legends about ghostly felines into their scripts, as did **HOUSE** more than two decades before (both a ghost-kitty and a ghost-*kiddy* are to be found in the *Ju-on* mythos). Other noteworthy examples of local Bakeneko cinema are: **GHOST CAT OF ARIMA PALACE** (怪猫有馬御殿 / *Kaibyō Arima goten*, 1953, D: Ryohei Arai), starring typecast "*bakeneko* actress" Takako Irie (1911-1995), who appeared in similar roles in several such films; **THE GHOST CAT OF OTAMA POND** (怪猫 お玉が池 / *Kaibyō Otama-ga-ike*, 1960, D: Yoshihiro Ishikawa); **THE GHOST-CAT CURSED POND** (*Kaibyō nori no numa*, a.k.a. **BAKENEKO: A VENGEFUL SPIRIT**, 1968, D: Yoshihiro Ishikawa); and **THE HAUNTED CASTLE** (秘録怪猫伝 / *Hiroku kaibyō-den*, 1969, D: Tokuzo Tanaka). The *yūrei* in their various forms were also the subject of a good many Japanese films, including, most famously, Masaki Kobayashi's sumptuous cinematic canvas **KWAIDAN** (怪談 / *Kaidan*, 1965) and Kaneto Shindō's two moody B&W *kaidan eiga* **ONIBABA** (鬼婆, 1964) and **KURONEKO** (藪の中の黒猫 / *Yabu no Naka no Kuroneko*, 1968), that latter film also being a key entry in the afore-noted *bakeneko* / *kaibyō* subgenre. *[See Steve Fenton's "Terror of the Were-Kitties" article (pp.41-67) in Monster! #10 (October 2014). If all goes well, he is planning on belatedly having another instalment of that very occasional feature ready in time for M! #34 (or 35!). Incidentally, there is also a vengeful Japanese female feline spirit—in this case of a tiger—to be found in this issue's loopy lycanthropy actioner **WOLF GUY** (1975), starring Shin'ichi "Sonny" Chiba, which is reviewed by Jeff Goodhartz on p.294. – Eds.]*

****

Nobuhiko Ōbayashi (大林 宣彦, born in Hiroshima Prefecture in 1938), the director of 1977's **HOUSE**, the present film under discussion, was approached by Toho Pictures to write a film treatment along the lines of the blockbuster Steven Spielberg film **JAWS** (1975, USA), of all things. The fact that Toho would approach such a filmmaker as Ōbayashi to write such a clone is, quite frankly, bewildering to me. Up to that point, he was primarily known for his experimental short subjects of the 1960s, which include the filmmaker's important formative symbolist/surrealist effort *Emotion* (伝説伝説の午後=いつか見たドラキュラ たドラキュラ / *Émotion: densetsu no gogo = itsukamita Dracula*, 1966), a film of thinly-veiled horror tropes, symbolically-stylized violence and black humor that displays Ōbayashi's at-times-kinetic, organic sense of motion and fondness for the spontaneous. Dedicated to director Roger Vadim's elegantly arty vampire film **BLOOD AND ROSES** (*Et mourir de plaisir*, 1960, France/Italy), *Emotion*—alluding to (quote) "that Dracula we once knew"—possesses a haunting, dream-like structure whose non-linear narrative is virtually impossible to synopsize coherently; much the same can likewise be said about Ōbayashi's later film **HOUSE**. Beautifully-shot and edited in a freeform, sometimes staccato and at times seemingly-at-random 'word-association' style, *Emotion*'s score largely consists of light, xylophone-heavy jazz and its audio track intermittently alternates back-and-forth between narration in English and subtitled Japanese (although sometimes there aren't any Anglo translations for the native language at all). Interestingly enough, due to the fact that it's dedicated to a classic French vampire movie with lesbian overtones and concerns two girls "from the sea", Emi and Sari, who meet and become friends in a fairy tale world whose denizens also include a traditionally-attired if oriental male bloodsucker (who, amusingly enough, sucks his victim's blood from their jugular through a drinking-straw!), the short often prefigures the future poetic *gothique* works of Francophone fantasist Jean Rollin. As the philosophical black-caped, umbrella-toting vampire in *Emotion* pontificates in English at one point: "Love is a gentle wildflower, a flower that won't wilt in the heat of the summer sun. A fevered passion hidden in one's breast, never to be frosted-over by doubt", echoing some of the same sentiments later re-expressed in **HOUSE** (as in the dialogue quote from it at the beginning of this article). The '66 short closes with another English line, "Farewell, Dracula. Farewell, you"; ending on an odd note made odder by the atypical cadence of that final word.

Ōbayashi's use of both the camera and editing suite as experimental tools is prominently evident in *Emotion*, and it is also of utmost importance in the director's later film **HOUSE**, as it is in most of his other experimental films and television commercials too. Prior to making his commercial feature debut in '77 with **HOUSE**—he had previously made the 71-minute experimental drama **CONFESSION** (コンフェッション＝ハルカナルアコガレギロチンコイノタビ / *Haruka naru Akogare Girochin Koi no Tabi*, 1968)—Ōbayashi was also known for directing a number of high-profile television commercials featuring famous Hollywood actors (including the likes of Kirk Douglas and Charles Bronson). The proposed **JAWS** clone offered him was quickly aborted by Ōbayashi (although it's indeed interesting to conjecture about what an inventive cinematic stylist like he might have conjured-up for such a project!), as the director instead began gathering ideas for his first full-length mainstream feature, approaching his then 10-year-old daughter Chiguma in regards to what

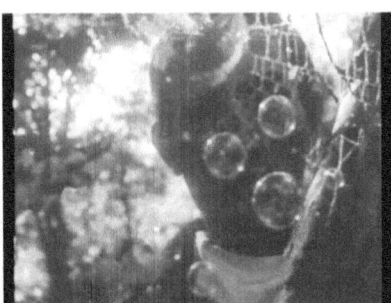
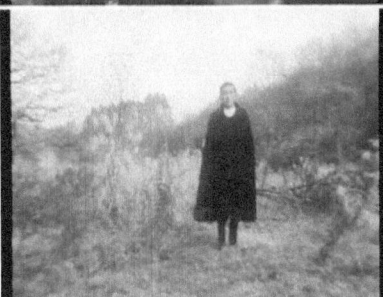
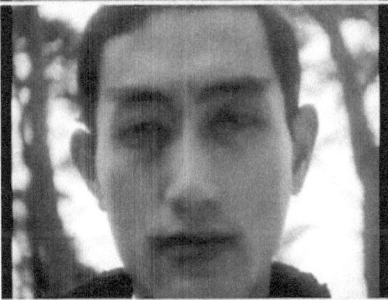
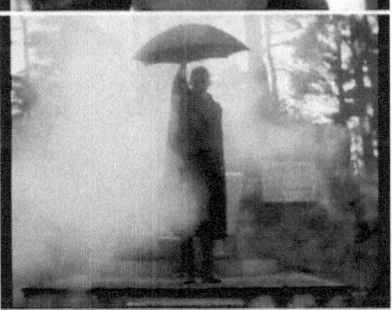
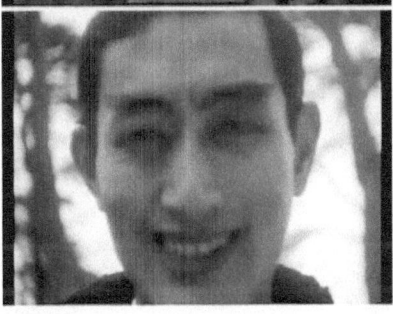

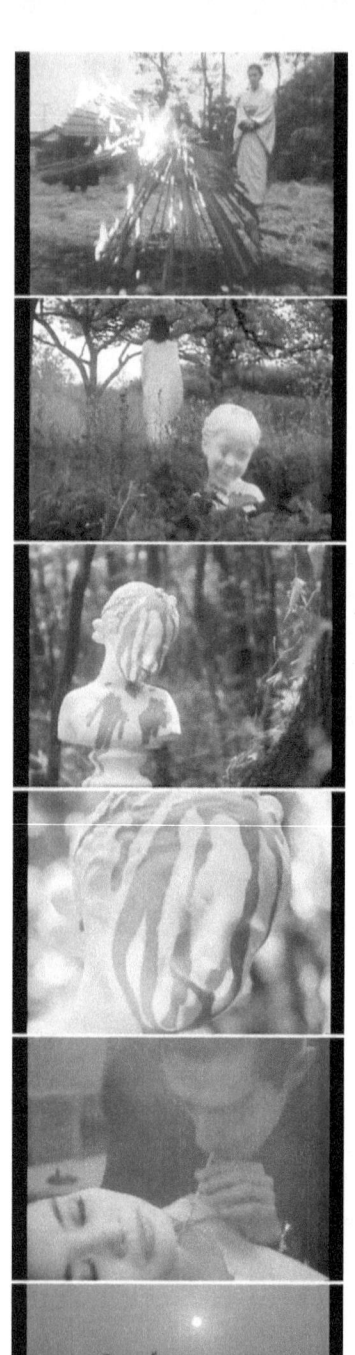

kind of film he should make. After proclaiming to him that Japanese films were "boring", she began recalling instances from her young life that had heavily impacted her in a horrific and/or fantastic way, and these anecdotal recollections eventually gave birth to scenes that were included in the movie: including the fantasy involving the mirror, the beach ball-sized watermelon bought by Mac being hung down into the well on a length of rope for chilling, the massed 'mattress attack' on Sweet, and other ideas.

Chiho Katsura was brought in to write the script, taking ideas from both the father and daughter and weaving them around a standard ghost-cat 怪談 / *kaidan* (loosely-translated, meaning "weird tale") and infusing it with bits-and-pieces of a short story he had read by the author Walter de la Mare (1873-1956), entitled "The Riddle" (first published in *The Riddle and Other Stories* [London: Selwyn & Blount, 1923], it was reprinted in the author's anthology *Collected Stories for Children* [London: Faber & Faber Ltd., 1947]). De la Mare, an English poet, novelist and short story-writer, is best-known for his ghost stories, including his most famous one, the unsettlingly Lovecraftian "All Hallows" (1926), about an isolated rural church haunted by entities from somewhere 'other' than *here*, possibly up to and including living gargoyles ("...there are devilish agencies at work here..."). In "The Riddle", seven grandchildren (four boys and three girls, of assorted ages) go to live with their grandmother ("...it was not a pretty house...") and, although strictly forbidden to enter the spare bedroom of her home—which contains an old ornately-carved, red silk-lined oak chest—they are, naturally enough, spurred-on by simple instinctual childish curiosity rather than dissuaded by the warning from entering the room; each child does so, either singly or in pairs, only to perish inside the box, vanishing from this world entirely ("Someday maybe they will come back to you, my dears", explains Granny to the gradually-depleting survivors. "Or maybe you will go to them...").

In **HOUSE**, the home of Oshare's aunt, which has belonged to her family generationally for many decades, metaphorically 'ate-up' the seven young female visitors ("The girls were... *eaten*!"), much as the wooden chest had done to the same number of children in the "The Riddle". Neither the house nor the chest themselves *per se* are ultimately the culprits in either the film or the book, but, metaphorically speaking, the deaths they bring about represent the death of innocence itself, and the end of childhood prior to being 'reborn' into adulthood. The girls in **HOUSE**—all 'teens' of similar ages—are travelling far away from their families on a collective journey towards womanhood, each equipped with something supposedly

This Page & Preceding Page: A series of non-consecutive images from Ōbayashi's *Emotion* (1966), a playful experimental exercise that revels in cinema purely for cinema's sake, and which, amongst other things, has tongue-in-cheek (and drinking straw-in-neck!) fun with certain long-standing traditions concerning vampire folklore inherently desirable about them, such as a stereo-typical personality trait, physical characteristic or behavioral quirk, *et cetera*. However, their trip from adolescence to becoming full-fledged women is cut short by an intrusion of the past: which *no one* can escape, come what may. One-by-one, each of the girls, who, while performing the one main characteristic or act of vanity which most defines them—as in the case of the conceited Oshare (a.k.a. "Gorgeous"), who endlessly applies makeup while staring at herself in the mirror—are also destroyed by those same clichéd characteristics. (Interestingly enough, while the slight similarity may be only coincidental rather than intentional, this particular 'comeuppance by poetic justice' aspect of **HOUSE** is rather reminiscent of The Seven Deadly Sins [a.k.a. capital vices] being utilized as a central plot device by Jean Brismée's atmospherically eerie Belgian/Italian horror shocker **THE DEVIL'S NIGHTMARE** [*La plus longue nuit du diable*, 1971; see *Weng's Chop* #8.5, p.65], in which Euro scream queen Erika Blanc played a seductive succubus from hell who tempts various victims into committing said sinful acts [i.e., pride, greed, lust, envy, gluttony, wrath and sloth], thus resulting in their deaths and eternal damnation.)

A few other points of reference that **HOUSE**'s screenwriter Katsura may have used from the works of de la Mare are from two other short works by the author that were likewise included in the above-cited '23 collection *The Riddle and Other Stories*, those being the possible vampiristic relative in the story "Seaton's Aunt", and the use of a mirror—in which is seen the 'reflection' of a fanged female vampire in **HOUSE**—as a potential reality-defying portal in "The Looking-Glass" (the heroine of which is named Alice, clearly after the leading lady of "Lewis Carroll"/Charles Lutwidge Dodgson's *Alice Through the Looking-Glass* a.k.a. *Through the Looking-Glass and What Alice Found There* [1871]); the same volume also includes such other prime de la Mare ghost/horror stories as "The Creatures", "The Tree", "Out of the Deep" and others.

****

Once completed, **HOUSE**'s script was quickly greenlighted for production, yet no director at the fabled Toho Pictures would touch the film, many feeling that it might well end their careers should they accept such a difficult assignment. Hence, the script was placed on the shelf by the formerly flourishing if then-cash-strapped production house, and if not for Ōbayashi's herculean efforts to keep the project alive, his film would never have seen the light of a projector at all. Initially, Ōbayashi was flatly refused the opportunity to direct the film for Toho, as, being an 'outsider',

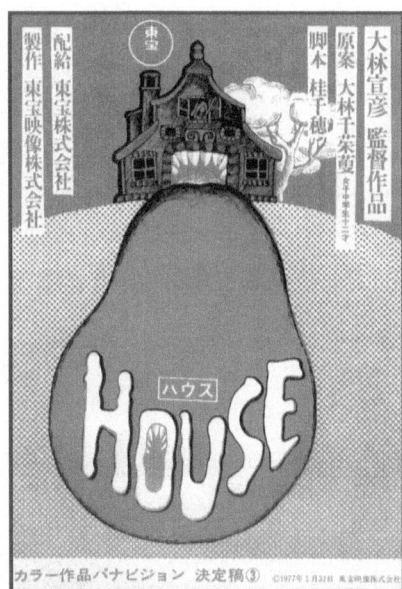

Anglo DVD cover design for **HOUSE**

he did not belong to the studio's cliquish fraternity. Therefore, what the canny future director of **HOUSE** did was begin to generate a buzz in the various media in hopes of getting a groundswell of public interest going that might precipitate him getting the movie made. He asked his old friend Asei Kobayashi (who also appears in the film as the roly-poly, sinisterly jovial 'comic relief' character called "The Watermelon Man"), to compose a score for the as-yet-unmade film. After at first flatly refusing to get involved in the project, Kobayashi finally relented, albeit with one slight condition: he asked Ōbayashi if he could bring in a band called Godiego to write the music, using his own themes. These musical artists' resulting compositions—which range from beautiful classical-inspired pieces to overblown Japanese funk ("J-funk"?) to light and airy post-psychedelic prog-pop—is at times the virtual aural *antithesis* to the action seen occurring onscreen, yet this high contrast in the audiovisual components helps make the experience all the more emotionally troublesome—albeit in a stimulating way—in one's eyes/ears and mind as a result.

The soundtrack received its release a year before the film was distributed in theaters, and it became a hit. That was not the only thing that helped to get the film made, however. There was also a radio drama produced, and a manga published; all this and more adding to the relentless campaign to at last get **HOUSE** 'built'... which eventually did happen, obviously (otherwise

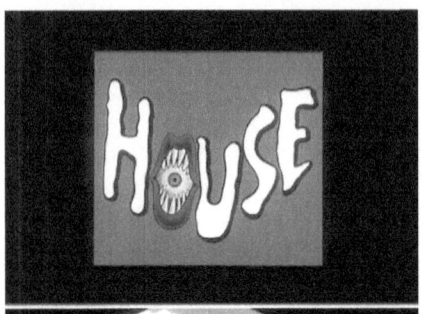
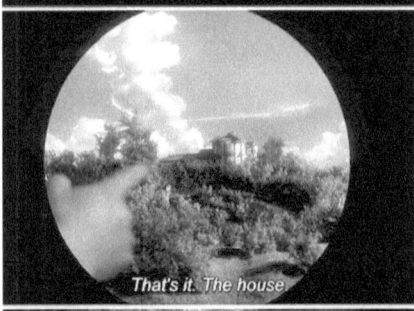

That's it. The house.

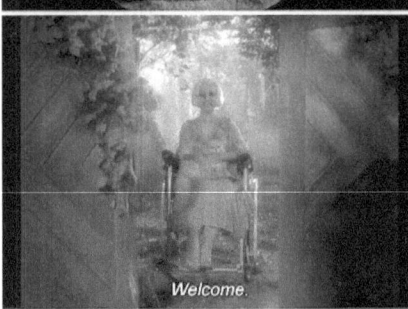

Welcome.

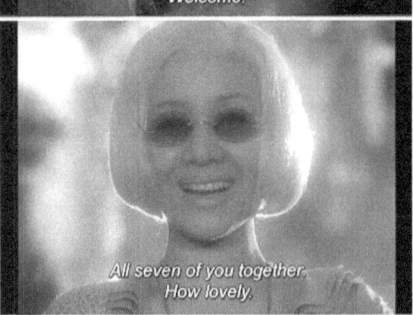

All seven of you together. How lovely.

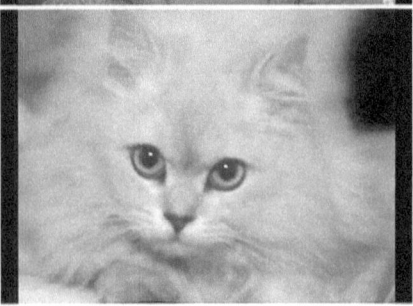

this article wouldn't exist!). Toho Pictures simply couldn't turn a blind eye anymore, and their execs finally gave Ōbayashi permission to make his long-forestalled film. The film technicians at Toho, at first hesitant to work with this 'trespasser' on their turf, eventually joined forces to help him create his visionary and unforgettable piece of purest Cinema. Upon being completed and released, **HOUSE** went on to become a huge hit in Japan, although, for the most part, the critics were not kind in their appraisal of the film. Even some industry insiders and certain of Ōbayashi's co-workers on the film were not enamored with its well-deserved success, some even believing that the film might actually spell the end of Japan's then-ailing cinema industry once and for all. In the late '60s, after a decade of steady decline, as more televisions sets were brought into Japanese homes, the once-prosperous major film studios felt the huge drop-off in theatrical attendance/box-office returns, and some studios were forced to either switch gears by, for instance, becoming involved in the production of television programming, or else close their doors altogether; as the Daiei Motion Picture Company (大映映画株式會社 / *Daiei Eiga Kabushiki Gaisha*)—home of the *Daimajin* (大魔神), *Zatōichi* (座頭市) and *Gamera* (ガメラ) franchises—were obliged to do in 1971, after filing for bankruptcy following several decades of solvency (the company was formed in 1942 as Dai Nippon Film Co., Ltd). Thus, many studios had to downsize and, in order to compete, started including ever-increasing amounts of nudity, sex and violence in their films; things which TV audiences could not see at home, so proved popular/profitable in cinemas. This would in-part account for the marked increase in production of ピンク映画 / *pinku eiga* ("pink films" a.k.a. "eroductions") in the so-called "Pinky Violence" genre, and filmic violence in general escalated as never before. As the "Sexy/Shocking 'Seventies" rolled onwards, cinema came to include more-and-more gratuitous skin, sin and horrific bloodshed, which was born out of necessity: it was either survive or die, both in the films themselves and basic reality too.

Casting the present film was something which Toho Pictures wanted no part of and, as a consequence, this chore was thrust firmly into the busy hands of Ōbayashi himself. He cast actresses whom he knew, from them working in his commercials and on other independent projects. All

---

These 2 Pages: In addition to cats—specifically, *one* cat *[left]*—**HOUSE**'s whole host of textural motifs includes *[opposite]* a plethora of circular/spherical/globular objects, such as fishbowls, watermelons, severed human noggins and…eyeballs!

Creature Feature Reviews

the young women chosen were, for the most part, novices, with the only professional amongst the principal seven players being youthful leading lady Kimiko Ikegami. The American-born (in NYC in 1959), Japanese Ikegami was still actively acting as of this writing, and besides her dual role as both Oshare and her mother in **HOUSE**, she is best-known for her performances in **THE MAN WHO STOLE THE SUN** (太陽を盗んだ男 / *Taiyō wo nusunda otoko*, 1979, Japan, D: Kazuhiko Hasegawa), which stars the legendary Bunta Sugawara, and **THE GEISHA** (陽暉楼 / *Yōkirō*, 1983, Japan), directed by the great Hideo Gosha, which tells the story of a beautiful geisha named Momowaka, her life, loves and personal tragedies, whose title role was played with amazing depth and aplomb by Ikegami herself.

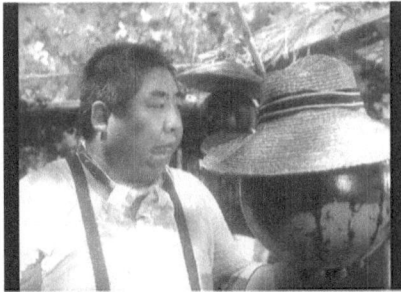

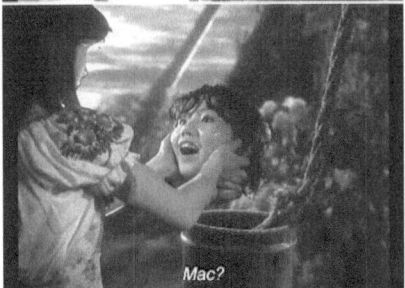

Unfortunately, the movie careers of the six remaining lead actresses in **HOUSE**'s cast were never fully realized, with most appearing in but a mere handful more films apiece. Kumiko Ohba, who played Fanta(sy), accrued some 22 acting credits, the crime-drama **VILLAGE OF DOOM** (丑三つの村 / *Ushimitsu no mura*, 1983, Japan, D: Noboru Tanaka), being her best-known role, with **HOUSE** marking her motion picture debut. The charismatic Miki Jinbo, who appears in the film as the high-kicking Kung Fu, appeared in only eleven films in total, with **HOUSE** numbering her third onscreen appearance. Ai Matsubara, has only four IMDb credits, with **HOUSE** being her first, but she is probably best-known to western audiences for playing Rako in the wildly-popular made-for-TV movie and spinoff miniseries *Shogun* (1980, D: Jerry London), co-starring Richard Chamberlain and Toshirō Mifune. The rest of the girls' credits are as follows: Meiko Sato (as Mac), five credits, this production being her second; Eriko Tanaka (as Melody), **HOUSE** being her sole credit; and Masayo Miyako (as Sweet) in the first of her three onscreen roles. "Saho" Sasazawa ([1930-2002] proper name Masaru Sasazawa), who played Oshare's father, was not a professional actor. He is best-known as a novelist, with many of his novels having been adapted into motion pictures and television shows, his most popular being the *Kogarashi Monjiro* (木枯し紋次郎) series of novels, which saw adaptations to Japanese television on a number of occasions. In 1961, the period novelist won the Detective Story Writers Club Prize for *Hitokui* ("Cannibalism"). His other works include *Manekarezaru Kyaku* ("Uninvited Guest") and *Roppongi Shinjuu* ("Love Suicide in Roppongi").

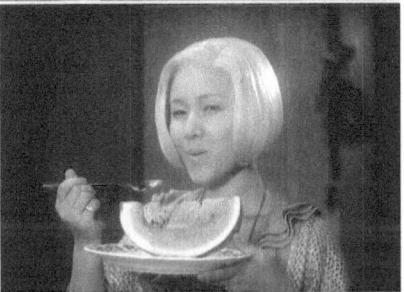

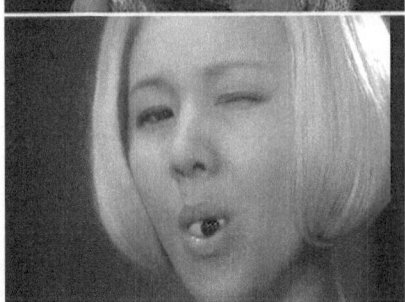

In the interview included on The Criterion Collection's Blu-ray/DVD release of his film,

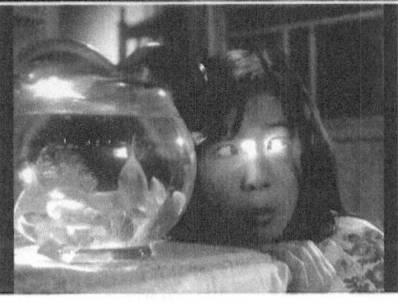

Ōbayashi says something that to me holds the key to better unlocking **HOUSE**'s secrets: he states that he wanted to turn his "experimentation into expression", this by at times juxtaposing reality and fantasy in his narrative constructions; taking the viewer on a journey through the world of the fantastic, wherein things do not need to be explained in a linear, logical manner and leaving it up to the viewer themselves to fathom any 'deeper meanings' to be had, and to construct a narrative within their own minds to compensate for the lack of basic logic and predictable plot movements ("Things are going just as Fantasy imagined", says one character of another in passing, tellingly enough). The film never gives viewers a chance to wrap their intellects around the step-by-step—if *not* in neatly-arranged order!—narrative, instead taking one off-guard and making one say to oneself, *this* is not correct, *this* does not fit, and how the heck did the plot get *here*?! The music is another of the film's primary disturbances as, like I mentioned above, it often simply *doesn't fit* the subject matter (at least by usual standards of criteria). This mismatch incites a certain disdain within one's mind, at least initially. Until, that is, you realize it wasn't composed solely to play on our emotions, but to exist as-is alongside them, to take all the biases we have regarding a certain logical combination of music and drama and make these surreal juxtapositions collide/coincide. This amounts to an uneasy merging, for sure, but it does make one constantly acutely aware of the action/narrative unfolding onscreen *and* the soundtrack separately, each/both at the same time (if not always in the same 'space' as one another).

Nobuhiko Ōbayashi continues making films to this day, including such brilliant efforts as the sci-fi romance **THE LITTLE GIRL WHO CONQUERED TIME** (時をかける少女 / *Toki o kakeru shōjo*, 1983), the horror movie **THE DISCARNATES** (異人たちとの夏 / *Ijin-tachi to no natsu*, 1988), and the criminal

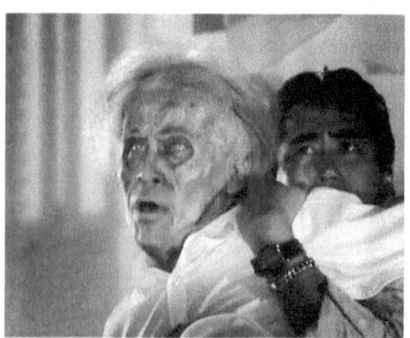

A scene from Ōbayashi's 1988 film
THE DISCARNATES

biopic **SADA** (SADA〜戯作・阿部定の生涯 / *Sada: Gesaku Abe Sada no shōgai*, 1998), to name but a few. He further worked with Chiho Katsura, the scripter of **HOUSE**, on a few other films, including **THE DESERTED CITY** (廃市 / *Haishi*, 1984), the anime **KENYA BOY** (少年ケニヤ / *Shounen Keniya*, 1984, Japan), **CHIZUKO'S YOUNGER SISTER** (ふたり / *Futari*, 1991, Japan), plus **GOODBYE FOR TOMORROW** (あした デラックス版 / *Ashita*, 1995) and **HANAGATAMI** (花筐, 2017). Chiho Katsura, among his many outstanding writing credits, also did work for the notorious movie studio Nikkatsu Corporation, scripting such risqué films in the company's prolific "Roman Porno" *pinku eiga* line as **RAPING!** (暴る！/ *Yaru!*, 1978, D: Yasuharu Hasebe), **ZOOM IN: RAPE APARTMENTS** (ズームイン 暴行団地 / *Zūmu in: Bōkō danchi*, 1980, D: Nasosuke Kurosawa) and the extra-infamous **ZOOM UP: THE BEAVER BOOK GIRL** (ズーム・アップ ビニール本の女 / *Zūmu appu: Biniru-bon no onna*, 1981, D: Takashi Kanno), among others.

****

The aforesaid Ghost-Cat films of yesteryear form the main nucleus of the present *faux* fantasy/horror film, but other uniquely Japanese fantastical inspiration sources are also woven into the film's complexly dense (some might say impenetrable!) fabric. The titular residence may at first *seem* to be the antagonist—the main 'monster', if you will—but it is its individual everyday household items—which, in ancient paganistic Shinto beliefs, are each said to be inhabited by individual spirit-entities—that are the objects (here used as plot devices) which consume the young girls, including the piano that consumes—fingers first, fittingly enough!—the musician Melody ("...it felt as if the piano *bit* me!" she exclaims beforehand); the flopping futons that attack Sweet ("The mats and sheets leaping on her like beasts!") in a feather-festooned sequence; the looking-glass which breaches realms to capture a soul; even the refrigerator—a major source of sustenance and consumption in the modern world—proves to be a gateway to another plane of existence, and it is at one point referred to as being "sick" by Auntie, who uses it as a portal to elsewhere at will. However, all the evil haunting her home—whose poltergeist-like activity includes all those ordinarily immobile objects assuming a life of their own—is telekinetically manifested by the matronly aunt herself, who, unbeknownst to the girls, has died, but, her body lives on. In a bit of a twisted nod to the infamous Countess Elizabeth Báthory legend (see Andy Ross' two-part article about same in *Monster!* #'s 28/29 [p.136] and 30 [p.115]), she consumes the more youthful females, thus gradually reverting from an elderly woman bound to a wheelchair who becomes increasingly restored to youthfulness and vitality herself as each of the girls' lives is taken and their life essence is consumed around her, infusing the vampire's own body with their stolen vitality and vivacity. Other Japanese folklore is introduced in the guise of assorted possessed household items, of the 'species' of *yōkai* known as 付喪神 / *Tsukumogami* ("tool kami"); basically, normally-inanimate implements/utensils that have been invested with unnatural life and movement by their inhabiting spirits. These include the *tsukumogami yōkai* called a 暮露暮露団 / *Boroboroton* ("tattered futon"), the haunted mattress (or napping mat); 妖怪ウンガイキョウ / *Ungaikyo* ("clouded-out mirror"), the possessed looking-glass; and the *Zorigami*, a possessed clock which absorbs one of the ill-fated girls into its inner workings without missing a tick. All of these 'possessed' possessions fall under the above-noted *Yōkai* category classified as *Tsukumogami* ("tool kami"). One memorably out-to-lunch sequence involves a decapitated airborne noggin known as a *Nukekubi* ("prowling head"), a subspecies of the type of stretchy-necked, head-extending *yōkai* known as *Rokurokubi* (ろくろ首, 轆轤首), *kaidan* standbys both. Yet another supernatural entity is of course the anti-Auntie herself, who, as mentioned above, is revealed to be a ghostly 幽霊 / *Yūrei*. In the aunt's case, in life she had such a yearning hunger to be reunited with her beloved, long-lamented fiancé even after death that this obsession would not let her rest peacefully in her grave. Ergo, even after shuffling off this mortal coil, she is still consumed by the same hunger for his love, and her restless 霊魂 / *reikon* ("soul" or "spirit") reenters into the physical world once more, bound on fulfilling her life's—and death's—desire, no matter what the cost to others.

HOUSE has the trappings and/or staples of many horror film clichés, including at the outset when Fanta takes a picture of the beautiful Oshare, in a hooded robe, and tells her that she resembles a witch from a horror movie. The unfolding action is spoken-of by the girls as if it has seemingly come from a horror flick… and a very old, *odd* horror flick at that. Even an out-of-place *homage* to **JAWS** is inserted—albeit a ludicrous moment indeed—so **HOUSE** does thus retaining something of that original idea from Toho that Ōbayashi should direct a clone of Spielberg's killer shark hit after all, here dis-

Face To Face: In an enchanted mirror, Gorgeous and Auntie seemingly blur into one… or is it merely an optical illusion caused by the reality-defying looking-glass, perhaps?

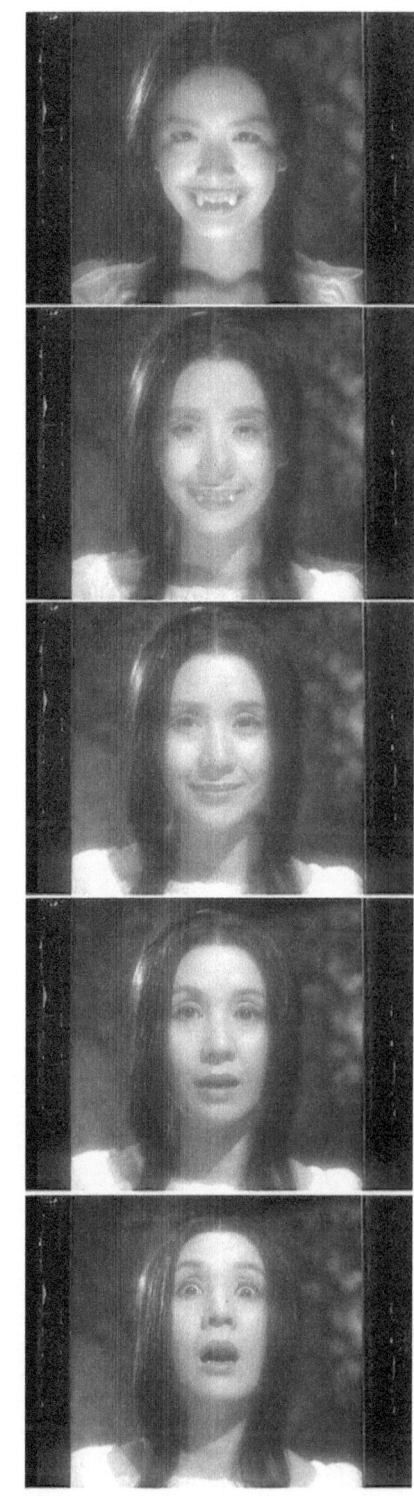

Monster Movie Reviews

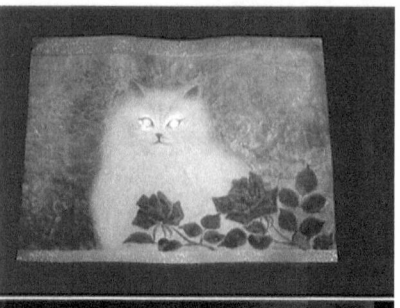
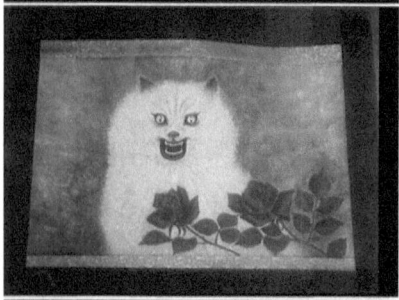
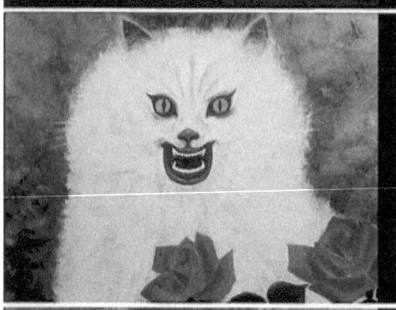
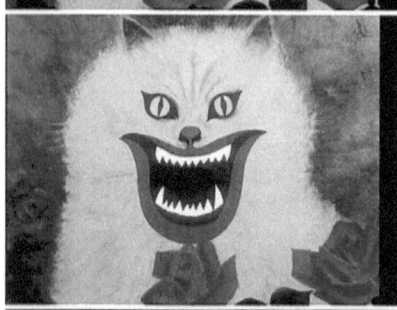
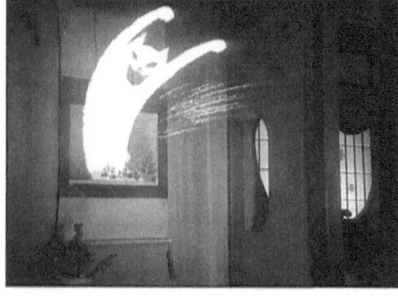

torted beyond all recognition by the filmmaker. Oh, and speaking of nudge-nudge/wink-wink in-jokes here, let's not forget an adult male passenger on the bullet train to Auntie's house, who is seen reading a copy of the great book *A Pictorial History of Horror Movies*, by Denis Gifford (London: Hamlyn, 1973). At the start of this same sequence—at roughly the 16:00-minute mark—director Ōbayashi, sporting a slouch hat and sunshades, puts in a sly background cameo out on the railway platform, overshadowed by the gaggle of excited heroines in the foreground, who jostle him aside in their girlish eagerness to board the train and get underway, leaving their director behind stranded at the station when the conveyance's sliding doors slam shut in his face!

While presenting its young female protagonists as being thoroughly modernized, the film nevertheless then proceeds to confine them to the past. A few points are raised to further emphasize this point, including a female gym teacher who is to be married during the break from school, yet the marriage is of the old-fashioned prearranged kind. In a similar throwback to traditional beliefs, the Mr. Tōgō character (played by Kiyohiko Ozaki) is looked upon as the savior of the girl's situation, as he gallantly rides to their rescue, after he was to accompany them to Auntie's house, but missed the bus because of an accident involving a bucket getting securely stuck to his backside (!). Mr. Tōgō has many trials and tribulations in store while getting to the house, but after finally arriving and inquiring at a fruit stand where the girls had stopped-off before arriving at Auntie's, he gets magically turned into a bunch of (fittingly phallic) bananas…so much for the manly hero of the 'helpless' girls!

The backstory of the aunt spans the Second World War, the dropping of the atomic bomb upon Japan, and a promise of love that is never-dying. We learn she was engaged to be married to a man who was due to take over the family medical practice following the war. He promised Auntie that he would come back. However, while the other soldiers began gradually returning from military service, Auntie's fiancé was not among them. She promised to wait for him forever if necessary, and still does even on into the present-day. After arriving at her house, Fanta attempts to take a picture of the girls and Auntie together but, with a flash of green from Blanche the cat's eyes, the camera is lifted clear out of Fanta's hands and breaks after crashing to the ground; this possibly being a vampire-like reaction by Auntie to the silver nitrate that was in the film (or possibly because she knew that her undead image wouldn't register in the emulsion of the exposed photograph, so she wished to prevent it from being taken?). Auntie's home—her boudoir especially—is bedecked with numerous pictures of the white ghost-cat. As played by Yōko Minamida (1933-2009), Auntie Karei Hausu comes across as a playful creature, who, much like a feline, toys with her 'food' to torture it before killing and devouring it. The radiant Minamida was only 44 years old at the time this film was made, but she really does convincingly sell the part of the elderly—or at least aging—woman, which was a pivotal role in the film. Her professional steady resolve and character development help to offset the acting deficiencies of the younger actresses, who were not really merely acting but rather reacting to the music that Ōbayashi played for them during the shooting of the movie; this to give the girls the 'motivation' to honestly and cheerfully move about during their many scenes, while rhythmically and emotionally responding to the score. As for Ms. Minamida, the veteran actress took a risky chance by accepting the part, as she realized that she would likely thereafter become typecast as a matronly performer for the remainder of her career. Yōko Minamida's movie credits include many classics of Japanese cinema, to list but a few here: including **THE CRUCIFIED LOVERS** (近松物語 / *Chikamatsu monogatari*, 1954, D: Kenji Mizoguchi), Seijun Suzuki's brilliant **VOICE WITHOUT A SHADOW** (影なき声 / *Kagenki koe*, 1958), **A SUN-TRIBE MYTH FROM THE BAKUMATSU ERA** (幕末太陽傳 / *Bakumatsu taiyōden*, 1957, D: Yūzō Kawashima), **YOKIHI** (楊貴妃, 1955, D: Kenji Mizoguchi) and **PIGS AND BATTLESHIPS** (豚と軍艦 / *Buta to gunkan*, 1961, D: Shōhei Imamura). Haruko Wanibuchi, who plays Ryōko herein, isn't really expected to do much of anything other than look elegant and beautiful, which she does (elegantly and beautifully!). She continued to work sporadically in film, and two roles from more recent years displays her versatility as an actress, including appearing as Cat Woman in the film **ANGEL** (2005, Japan) and also appearing in the amazing cheesy futuristic samurai film **ZIPANG** (黄金孔雀城 / *Jipangu*, 1990, Japan, D: Kaizō Hayashi), in which she plays the Queen. It was in 2005 when the aged actress first began exhibiting signs of dementia, and she retired from showbiz the following year, some three years before her death in 2009.

Director Nobuhiko Ōbayashi, wanted to make a fantasy film (if not an 'ordinary' one) as opposed

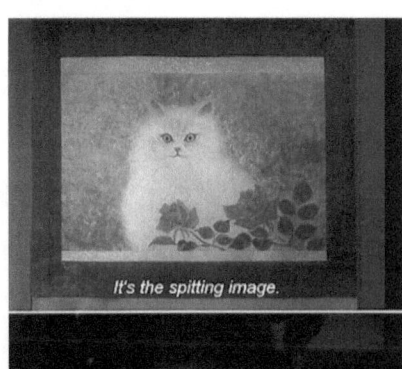
It's the spitting image.

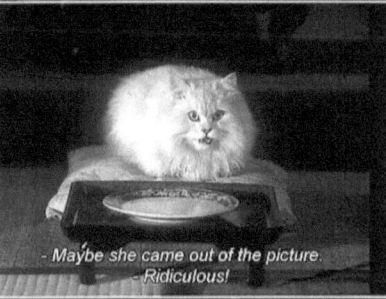
- Maybe she came out of the picture.
- Ridiculous!

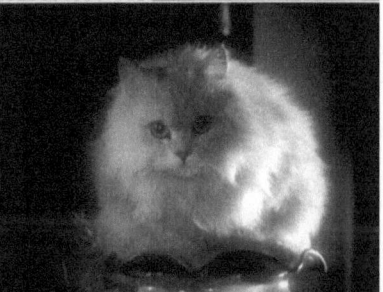

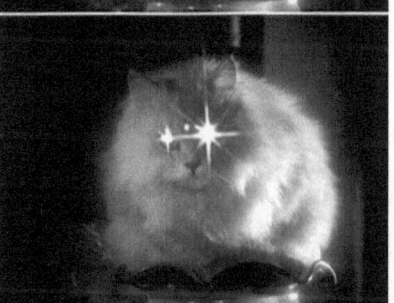

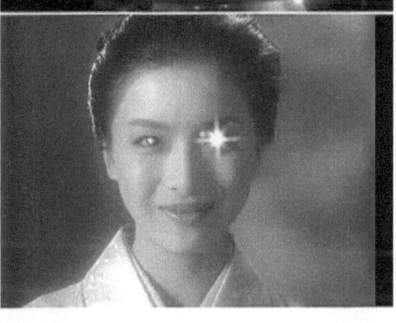

As her magically transforming painted portrait ably conveys, Blanche the pure-white kitty-cat of the **HOUSE** is by no means what she outwardly appears to be, and her fluffy, cuddly-cute exterior actually masks a voracious vampiristic ghost!

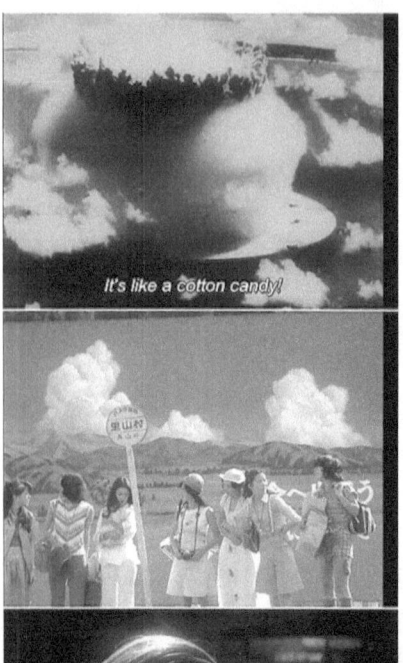
It's like a cotton candy!

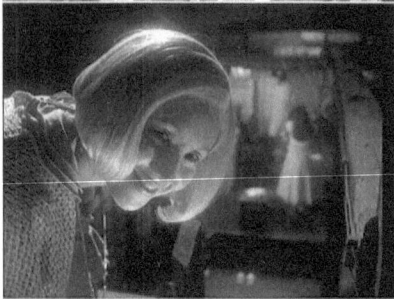

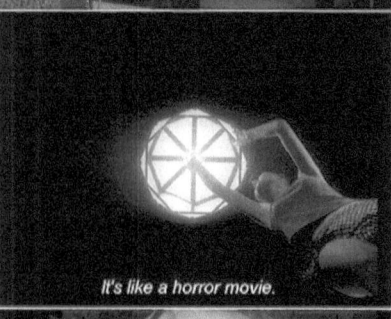

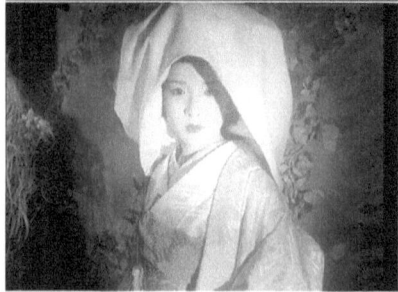
It's like a horror movie.

to an outright horror film with touches of horror. He opted to make **HOUSE** in a fantasy vein, with a ghost as the basis of the plot ("Ghosts *don't* exist", says one of the girls, tantamount to whistling in the dark), yet he chose to exaggerate the fantastical milieu way beyond anything previously presented on film, twisting the concepts of quasi-reality/fantasy by escaping from the standard established ghost story narratives. Having been born in Hiroshima, in 1938, World War Two and the A-Bomb were very real and horrifying happenings in his early life, and aspects of which Ōbayashi wished to include in his film's narrative. The young actresses—all of whom were born post-War—didn't know of anything but peacetime. The actors from older generations, including Ms. Minamida as Oshare's aging aunt, knew only-too-well about the devastation which war wrought. Ōbayashi also stated in the Criterion interview how he wanted to include the atomic bomb as a major theme in the film, this manifesting itself after Oshare's parents had gotten married, intermingled with a brief bit of stock footage showing the terrible nuclear device in mid-devastation mode (during which its puffy rising mushroom cloud is ironically equated with "cotton candy").

The title house is so inexorably tied to the past that to not connect it to the war and the carnage that happened during it would be a serious oversight. As the young girls' lives are each greedily consumed by the life/love-hungry aunt, their young lives are abruptly cut short in midstream by the her callous bitterness and the evil spirit within her manifesting itself, creating a scenario not unlike that of a war being waged inside her home in microcosm. When dispatched, the lady of the house's victims are done-in in a grotesquerie of extremely violent ways—although these scenes are softened somewhat by being tinged with absurdist, cartoonish comedy (indeed, various kinds of cel animation techniques are incorporated into the action throughout)—with the carnage and deconstruction of the girls being presented as horrifyingly gruesome, just as the effects of the war were both mentally and physically on its millions of victims. The atomic bombs may have been dropped on Hiroshima and Nagasaki more than 30 years before this film was made, but the long-term effects on the people of Japan are still dissipating all these years later, even more slowly than radioactive fallout. The war not only destroyed both her lover's present

---

By turns darkly disturbing and wittily whimsical (etc., etc., etc.), **HOUSE** weaves a rich cinematic tapestry around itself and its audience that is as organic as life—and death—itself.

and the aunt's future, so too, in turn, does she destroy the futures of the girls as a direct consequence.

Surprisingly enough considering what a highly visual experience it is, there were no storyboards created for the filming of **HOUSE**. The effect that Ōbayashi most strived for during the shoot was spontaneity. As he states in the interview, "At the time Japanese cinema was all about realism". He didn't want realism, he wanted the fantasy element, the innovation, to show through, not based on reality, but rather on the *fantastic*. Each day of filming was a day of technical experiments. Turning those experiments into expression was the filmmaker's ultimate goal with this heavily-personalized production.

The ending of the film is left open for interpretation (as is much of the rest of it, for that matter). Oshare's father's bride-to-be, Ryōko Ema, courageously elects to go—in her first official challenge of (step)motherhood—to retrieve Oshare from Auntie's house and bring her back into the fold/under the wing of the newly-blossoming family unit whose matriarchal figurehead she shall be. Oshare's real mother had died when she was but six, and for ten years after her death Oshare's father had given their daughter his full love and attention, spoiling her shamefully. Now this new woman was going to take her father away from Oshare (or so she thought), and was vying to replace her biological mother with a surrogate (i.e., herself). The father even says at one point, "It's been eight years since your mother died. We should start to slowly bring happiness back into our lives", possibly implying that their existence together had been unhappy (at least following the late wife/mother's death) and that a cathartic external force was needed in order for the pair to at last achieve some degree of contentment in their lives. The Ryōko character is glamorously/romantically introduced, each and every time, with the wind gently blowing her hair and scarf and with a look of superficial ambiguity on her lovely visage. When the external force that was Ryōko entered the troubled family home, the ball started to roll faster and faster downhill, possibly towards calamity. With the surrender to Ryōko by Oshare rebuffed, the 'war' had commenced anew and, like World War II, its effects rippled through the generations of Oshare's family. Upon finally arriving at *the* house, Ryōko asks where Oshare's friends are. To which Oshare replies, "They'll soon wake up, hungry. One always wakes up if one has hunger". Just as Auntie did in her long-lingering yearning for her dead fiancé, so too will the possessive and demanding Oshare's appetite for the solitary love of her father continue to live on…

"An old cat can open doors, but only a ghost-cat can close them! If one is hungry enough, one always wakes up!"

****

HOUSE can truly be regarded as a masterpiece of the fantasy genre. The fact that the film straddles the tenuous fine line between coherence and incoherence so shakily at times forces the viewer to assimilate some of the alien or un-connectable plot devices in unique ways. If the mind is not open to the experience, then the film's tenuous world of fantasy can never really be reached, let alone dwelled within.

If you read between the lines/frames some, it *might* all be interpreted as a metaphor/allegory for how the domestic milieu—while it is traditionally meant to provide shelter for and nurture family members—can also be a source of their destruction from right within the very foundation of the family unit: the home itself becoming a virtual battleground. In **HOUSE**, the title dwelling as a combatant/destroyer of lives is not merely presented figuratively, but quite literally, with the ruling matriarch of the place (and, much more indirectly, the patriarch of another home) being the main instigator/perpetrator of all the horrors that transpire beneath its roof and between its walls.

Ever-insatiable, as the film ends, a cartoon caricature of the house even swallows-up the end credits themselves, which scroll right into its open, fang-filled, tongue-lolling maw (i.e., front door)…indicating that—*yes!*—it is still hungry for more, even after all those it has already consumed beforehand.

*[*Author's Note*: Much of the information gathered for this article was sourced from the lengthy interviews with Nobuhiko Ōbayashi, his daughter Chigumi and* **HOUSE***'s screenwriter Chiho Katsura on Criterion's Blu-ray release. Said release represents the first time that the film has ever been released on home video in the United States.]*

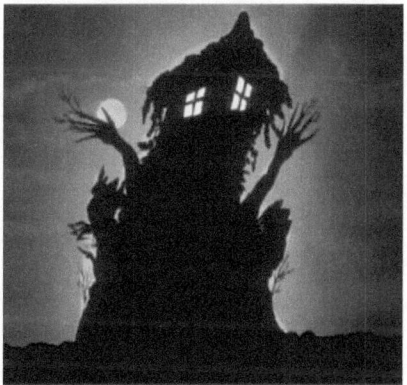

MUSINGS ON THE MUMMY (2017)

by Troy Howarth

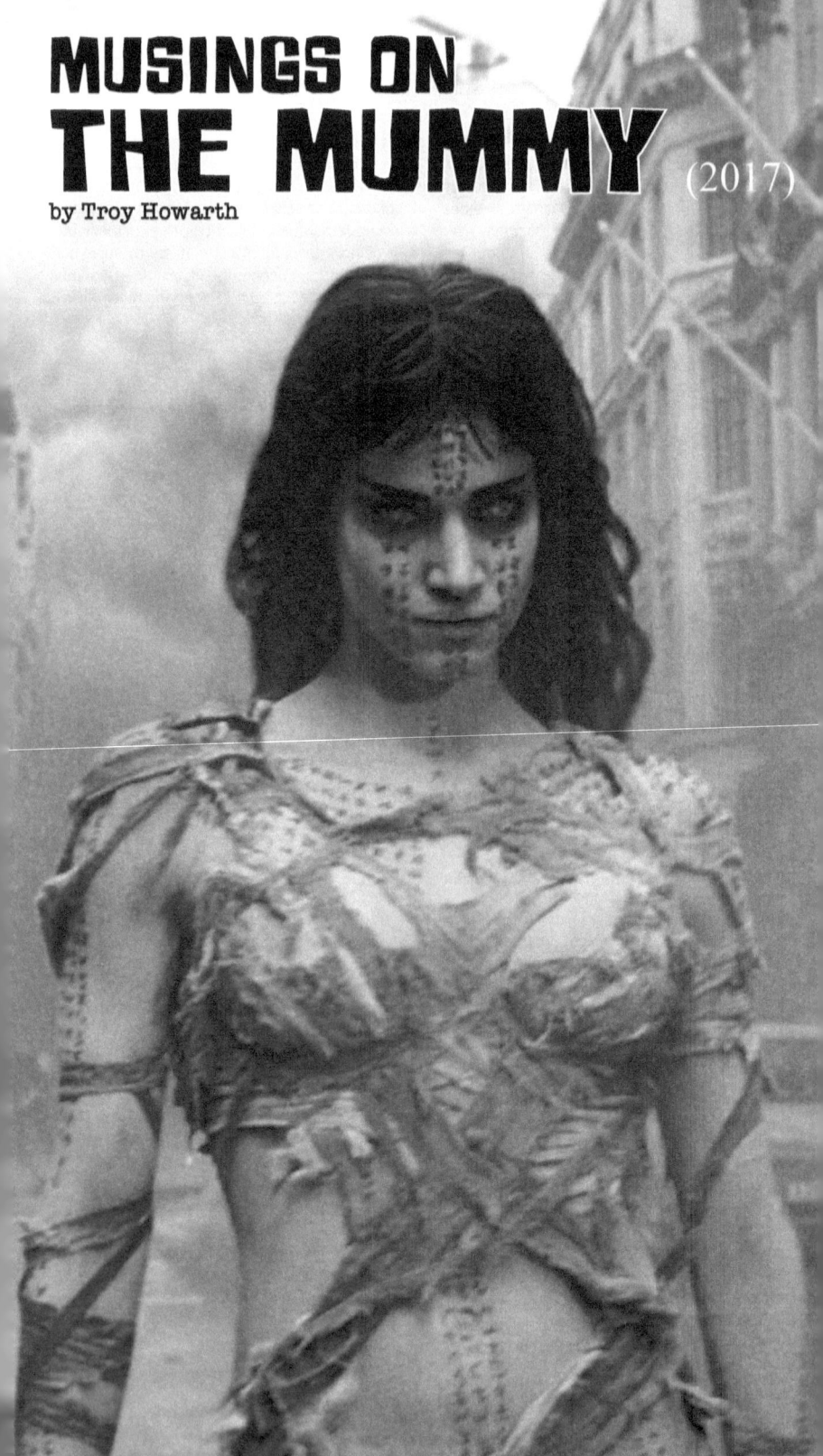

By way of full disclosure, I must confess: I am not *anti-remake*. *I* do not *seize-up into a quivering rage* when I hear that a film—even a beloved favorite—is being given the "all-new" treatment. My attitude has always been, quite simply: if the new version is good, we will have two good films to appreciate instead of just one; and if it sucks, well, the original is unaffected—indeed, it will shine that much brighter by comparison. There is also a practical side to welcoming remakes, reboots, "reimaginings", or whatever the hell you want to call them: very often the studios will reissue the original films in new special editions in order to capitalize on the momentum surrounding the latest production. And on that level, I can say something positive about Alex Kurtzman's new take on **THE MUMMY**: it surely is no coincidence that it—as part of a proposed new series of films under the Dark Universe banner (more on that in a jiffy)—has been accompanied by the arrival of the entire 6-film series of Universal-produced mummy films of the 1930s, '40s and '50s (up until and including the titular monster's inevitable run-in with Abbott & Costello [see pp.26-29]) on Blu-ray. So that's nice, at least. Now, as to the new film itself...

First things first, let's get this "Dark Universe" subject out of the way... When I first saw the trailer for the present film earlier this year (i.e., 2017), preceding a screening of **ALIEN: COVENANT** (a flawed film, but infinitely more satisfying than the one under discussion), a bad feeling crept over me: not only was this film pointing to the absolute certainty that the type of horror-fantasy cinema that I know and love is *dead*, but it also seemed to indicate that Universal, in their infinite wisdom, has elected to reboot their famous horror franchises in the spirit of a superhero franchise! The film itself definitely confirms this, without any shadow of a doubt. Usually, when embarking on a potential franchise, the idea is to burst out of the gate at full speed—but if **THE MUMMY** is any indication, the future of Dark Universe is not only bleak...it's also highly questionable. There's clearly a thought here that the so-called "new and improved" approach to classic horror characters is to revise them into some sort of superhero mold, with plenty of action and a notable lack of character. Now, lest we get too teary-eyed and sentimental, it can be said that characterization is a trifle lax in even many of the horror films we know and love—but at

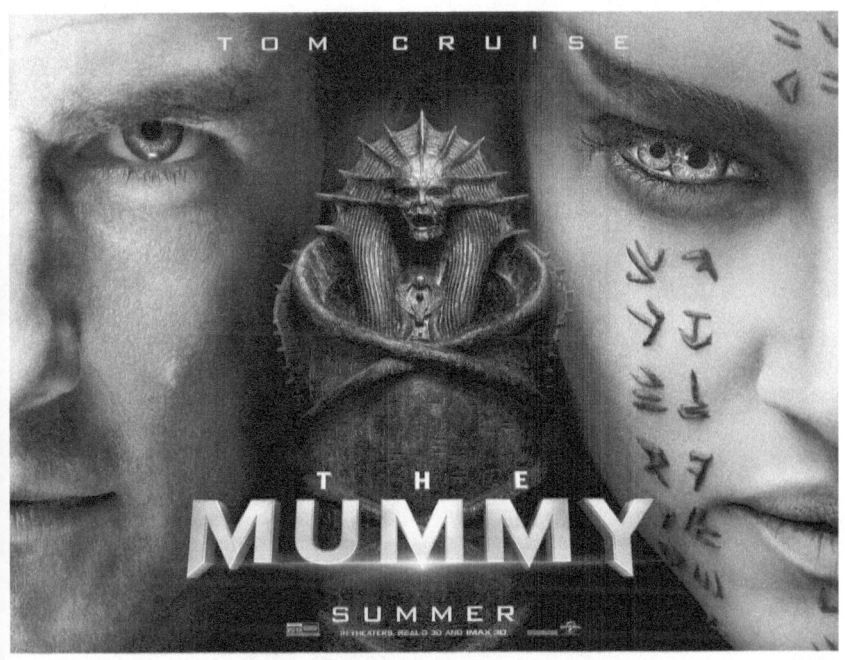

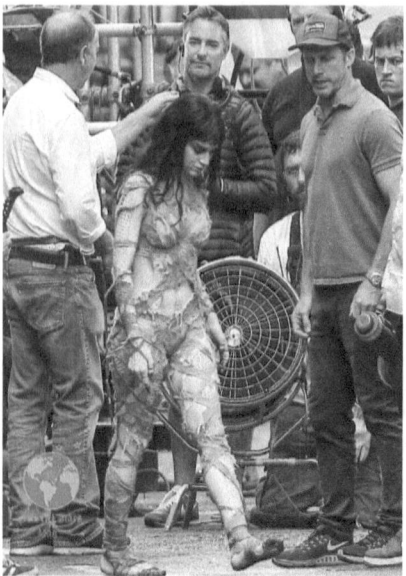

She went for a little walk…in her skivvies! Sofia Boutella struts her stuff on the **M** '17 set

least those films were relatively honest in their intentions and focused on delivering the goods where it counted. Watching **THE MUMMY**, it's as if the people involved haven't seen a horror film in *years*; they kind of *vaguely* remember what all those old musty mummy movies were like, however, and they hope to avoid the pitfalls of making their film too old-fashioned and "dull" by amping-up the action and increasing the scope and the spectacle in overcompensation. Fair enough, I guess. It's not as if the 1932 Karl Freund film would play very well for a contemporary youth-based audience anyway, truth be told. But the strange sorcery which has transpired in the process has made the present "mummy" film into a sort of weird hybrid of action and thrills where the horrific and the atmospheric have no opportunity to develop.

Another point worth considering is the casting of a major superstar in the form of Tom Cruise. Now, I freely admit, I find Cruise a rather grating person in interviews, and I am not a fan of his image in general—but as an actor, I tend to give him credit: he tends to gravitate towards good material, and he's always shown a desire to work with talented directors. Don't believe me? Look at his résumé: he's been directed by Martin Scorsese, by Francis Ford Coppola, by Stanley Kubrick, by Ridley Scott, by Brian De Palma, by Michael Mann… but, you get the picture. When he's cast in the right role and is being guided by a director who knows how to draw out his talent, he can be quite good. I still remember the furor surrounding his casting as Lestat in **INTERVIEW WITH THE VAMPIRE** (1994, USA), with author Anne Rice being particularly incensed, but even she changed her tune when she saw what a very fine job he had done in the role. In short, the guy's got talent and, unlike a lot of major box office stars, he seems to actually *care* about the quality of the films he appears in. Which makes his involvement in **THE MUMMY** that much more perplexing. For one thing, his presence is a distraction. You get the feeling that he simply *does not* belong here as soon as he shows up, and that feeling never really dissipates. Cruise's smarmy, athletic screen presence is well-suited to the macho, sleight-of-hand universe of the **MISSION: IMPOSSIBLE** franchise, but here he is unable to summon the sense of mystery and romanticism which is apparently meant to be a part of his character. He's okay while playing-up the mercenary aspect of his character, but when it comes to investing the role with anything of real weight and substance, he fails miserably. For another, it may seem a churlish point to make, but given that Cruise is a superstar of the first rank, you're dealing with a man who makes more money per film than most of us will ever see in our entire lifetime. As such, good on him for being choosy and trying to do films that actually have a bit of substance—but here you can't help but feel like punching him for taking the money and laughing all the way to the bank! His name will surely help to bring in audience members, at least at first, but as the dismal reviews and lukewarm word-of-mouth begin to circulate, well…good thing he has **AMERICAN MADE**, a much-more-interesting-looking "based on a true story" affair coming out later this year. He will need a hit after this—and that film will perhaps help to smooth-over any audience backlash which may greet his participation in such an utterly vapid and brain-dead exercise in pure unbridled cynicism and greed.

I guess it's clear by now that I was not taken with this film, but my distaste for it goes well beyond a nostalgic connection to the various mummy films produced by Universal, Hammer Films, and beyond. No, it cuts much deeper than that. I knew full-well going into it that **THE MUMMY** would not be a reprise of the Karl Freund classic. I knew also that it would not owe much, if anything, to the very-nearly-as-good version produced by Hammer in 1959. The presence of a shapely, sexy mummy may be reminiscent of Hammer's 1971 **BLOOD FROM THE MUMMY'S TOMB** (based on Bram Stoker's *The Jewel of Seven Stars* [1903]), but the resemblance is only superficial at best. No, this is very much its own unique take on the material. And, as such, I was ready to run with it and at least find it to be an enjoyable popcorn movie of sorts. My optimism was crushed early on due to the barrage of over-the-top but curiously lifeless action scenes, and absolutely *nothing* occurs in it to make up for this sort of assembly-line mentality approach. The story—such as it is—involves a soldier-of-fortune named Nick Morton (Cruise, of course) who inadvertently unleashes the forces of darkness when he stumbles onto the excavated tomb of the Egyptian princess Ahmanet (Sofia Boutella). Ahmanet marks Nick as "the chosen one" and sets about trying to involve him in a ritual which will give her full sway over humanity, while allowing Nick to be reborn as a god among men. Meanwhile, Dr. Henry Jekyll (Russell Crowe) and his minions are anxious to stop Ahmanet, even if it means killing a lot of innocent people in the process.

It took no less than *six* credited writers (David Koepp, Christopher McQuarrie, Dylan Kussman, Jon Spaihts, Alex Kurtzman and Jenny Lumet, just to let the record show) to concoct this complicated witch's brew. But in truth, it might just as well have been jotted-down on the back of a cocktail napkin during happy hour at the local Buffalo Wild Wings restaurant. The sad thing is, all of these people have backgrounds in writing much better films than this. Yes, everybody has a bad day. But this seems a classic case of having too many cooks in the kitchen, and no doubt everybody had their own "unique" idea of how to revise the mummy films of yesteryear, and everybody's ideas more-or-less cancelled themselves out as the film was dragged through the soulless machinery of the filmmaking-by-committee attitude which informs so many Hollywood blockbusters.

Suffice it to say, the story is ridiculous, the characterizations are nonexistent, and the film seems to have an awfully hard time making up its mind about exactly what it's supposed to be. Is it tongue-in-cheek or serious? Scary or goofy? Horror or action? It's a little bit of all of the above, truth be told, and it's not very effective at any of them. The action scenes are all very loud and very bombastic, but they grow wearisome through repetition. The touches of horror are reliant on hoary clichés—as in *Eeeeee-oooo! Like, that beetle* totally *just crawled into that guy's ear!*—and play out very much like some grandma's idea of what constitutes a horror movie. And without characters to become really involved with, it all amounts to a lot of sound and fury signifying nothing.

Horror buffs may amuse themselves spotting "in-joke" references to other films—James Whale's **THE BRIDE OF FRANKENSTEIN** (1935) and Tobe Hooper's **LIFEFORCE** (1985) included—but surely people are over this non-stop game of "spot the reference" by now?! Therein lies the problem with films being made by film buffs, and that is arguably a big part of the reason why so many of the great horror films of the past were made by people who didn't care a damn about referring to this film or that film. The worst and most utterly pointless of these long-winded points of reference occurs via Nick's ongoing dialogue with his dead friend, who appears periodically to remind Nick that he's up the creek without a paddle. If you guessed that this sounds a lot like John Landis' **AN AMERICAN WEREWOLF IN LONDON** (1981), congratulations: you've undoubtedly seen a lot more horror films than the people involved in this mess ever have.

With the somnambulating Cruise merely going through the motions on autopilot, the more demanding roles are assigned to Sofia Boutella (**KINGSMAN: THE SECRET SERVICE**

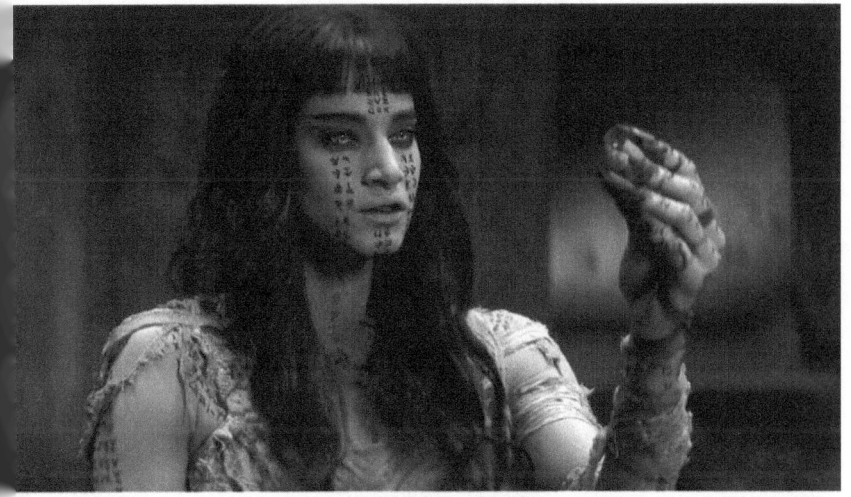

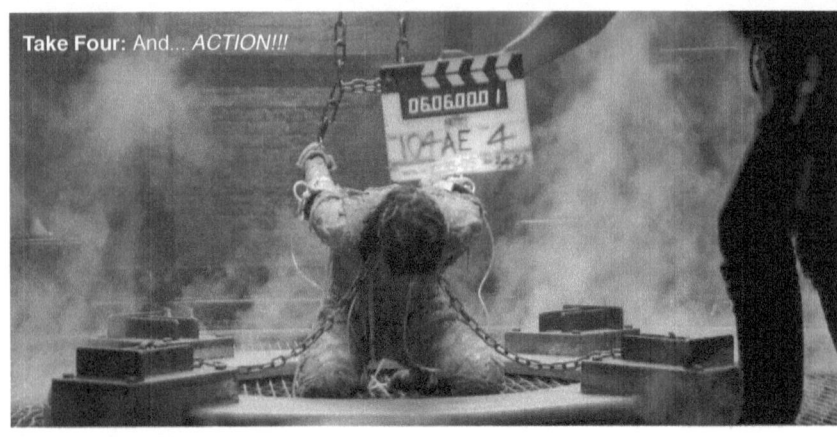

Take Four: And... *ACTION!!!*

[2014]) and Russell Crowe (**GLADIATOR** [2000]). Boutella has real charisma and screen presence, but she's stuck playing what is essentially an unplayable character. Ahmanet is established as evil incarnate, and that's mostly just the level at which she's required to play. But when some attempt is made, late in the game, at making her appear more pitiable and tragic, it comes as far too little, far too late. For reasons which are never made clear, Ahmanet is given two sets of irises and pupils in each eye, and her face is covered with Egyptian hieroglyphics—but all that succeeds in doing is make her look like some sort of very early-era punk rocker chick. Boutella does her damnedest to convey an air of mystery and danger, but the special effects are called upon to do the heavy lifting, and she gets lost in the process. As for Crowe, there's no denying his skill as an actor, but he was either too disinterested or too hamstrung by the lousy material to make much of an impression here. The inclusion of Jekyll/Hyde indicates the sort of approach that Dark Universe will evidently be taking in future, and one can only hope that if this film continues to perform poorly, they will rethink the idea of using him or other characters as a sort of "link" between one entry and the next. Crowe gets to quote Dr. Pretorious (Ernest Thesiger) from the aforementioned **BRIDE OF FRANKENSTEIN** when he toasts to "a new world of Gods and monsters," but he never conveys the sort of strength and intensity which marks out his best performances. Like Cruise, he simply appears to be onboard with money in mind, and when he transforms into Mr. Hyde (after suffering a bit of trouble with his body disobeying him, which elicits unintended chuckles by way of memories of Peter Sellers' eponymous character in Kubrick's **DR. STRANGELOVE, OR: HOW I LEARNED TO STOP WORRYING AND LOVE THE BOMB** [1964]), it's a very sorry sight to see indeed.

Ultimately, one is left wondering how a film that cost so much money (in the range of $125-million, without factoring in advertising costs) could not only look so *drab* and unremarkable, but also how it could ever have been approved to go into production in the first place with such a shambolic screenplay to work from. Perhaps whatever good intentions were behind it got lost in the process, but the end result is bound to disappoint genre fans—and it's unlikely to do much for viewers looking for action and adventure, either. If the so-called "Dark Universe" is able to weather the storm of this their first ill-fated outing, then hopefully the creative heads behind the upcoming **BRIDE OF FRANKENSTEIN** and **THE INVISIBLE MAN** will think long and hard about what made the originals of these films so special to begin with—and then plan, and write, accordingly. Ultimately, this film will likely be remembered as something of a low-point for its star, and fans needn't comfort themselves with the thought that it might encourage younger people to seek out the old films which inspired it; not only are many of them seemingly allergic to "old" movies to begin with, but it's hard to imagine this film inspiring anybody to seek out other films which might be anything like it, either!

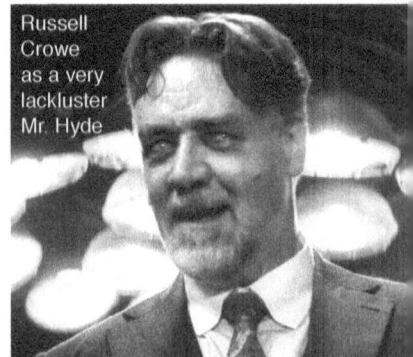

Russell Crowe as a very lackluster Mr. Hyde

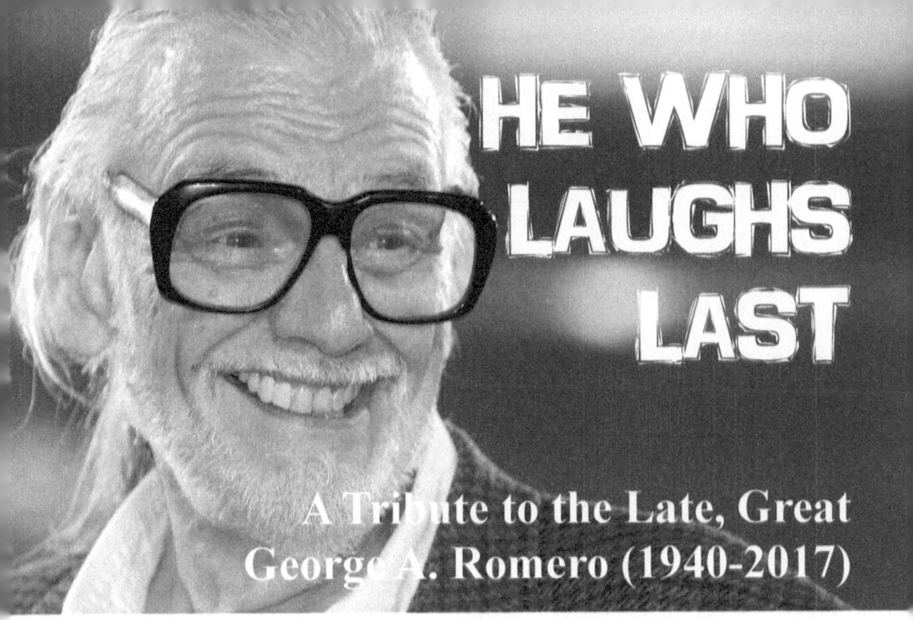

HE WHO LAUGHS LAST

A Tribute to the Late, Great George A. Romero (1940-2017)

by Troy Howarth

When I think of George A. Romero, I *don't* think of zombies. I *don't* think of gore. I think of the man's *laugh*. I never had the privilege of meeting the man, I'm sorry to say—he was one of many people I hold in high esteem, whom I always held out hope of someday meeting... but it was just not to be. However, down through the years, I have listened to *every* audio commentary he ever recorded, and I have watched *every* interview with him or pertaining to his work that I've ever stumbled across. And you can be sure that at some point in those commentaries or interviews or retrospectives, he would let loose with *that laugh*! It came from the lower depths, alright, and it denoted a man of great warmth, humor and humanity. He was the kind of guy you could imagine sitting with over a beer and having a laugh over movies and the insane world of politics. Above and beyond everything else, he came across like a *good guy*—and in the world of movies, that's by no means always something that's synonymous with talent.

Truth be told, he wasn't on my mind on Sunday, July 16th, 2017. I was going about my usual business on a typically slow and boring Sunday, when all of a sudden I saw the sad news pop up in my Facebook feed. I didn't believe it at first; I've seen too many celebrity death hoaxes to accept it based on but a single report. But the report did come from a reputable source—*The LA Times*—and the truth began to set in: *Son-of-a-bitch!* George Romero really *is* dead! It's weird when people we admire die—we seldom get to interact with these people. They aren't even aware of our existence. And yet, for us, they are an integral part of our lives; they help to shape who we are. George Romero was one such person. Back in the early 2000s when I lived in Pittsburgh, I was told that Romero was prone to eating at the Sushi 2 restaurant in Shadyside. I hate sushi, and I was too afraid to go there in the hopes of possibly seeing the man. The timing would have had to be just right, for sure, but stranger things have happened. But *then* what? Do you interrupt the man eating his meal just to go up and blather at him like an idiot? Many would, but my basic shyness and good manners (believe it or not!) would have held me back, even if I had spotted him. Besides, I told myself, he'd surely do a convention at some point, and I'd get to see him that way. Romero did do plenty of convention appearances, but they were often far away from me in Johnstown, Pennsylvania. I missed my chance back in the day when he surely was doing

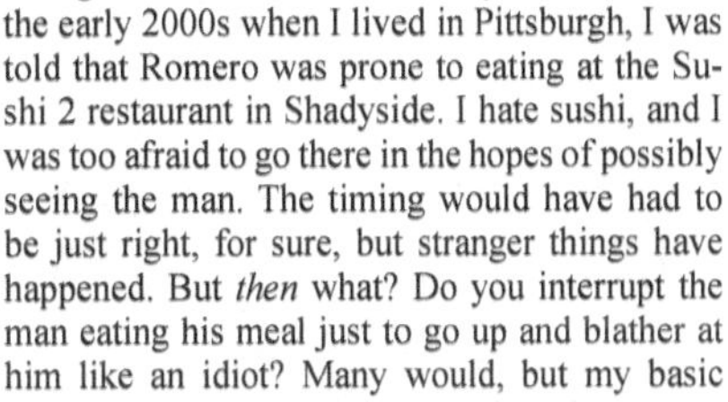

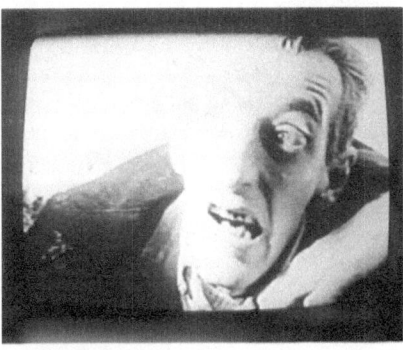

NIGHT OF THE LIVING DEAD '68 TV screen shot by Colin Geddes, circa 1990

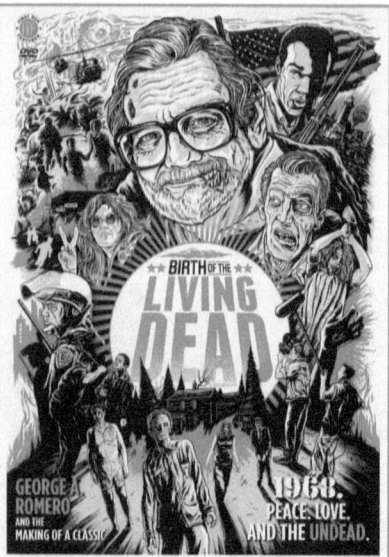

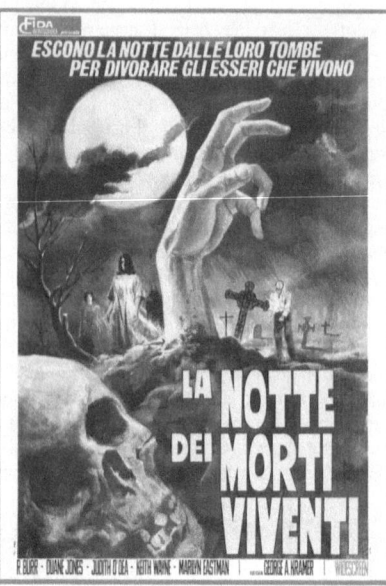

Top: US poster for the **BIRTH OF THE LIVING DEAD** documentary. **Above:** Italian *quattro-fogli manifesto* for **NOTLD**, the film that launched a thousand Italo imitations!

appearances in Pittsburgh; now, as I write these words, he's joined the roster of names along with the likes of Lucio Fulci (1927-1996), Jess Franco (1930-2013), Sir Christopher Lee (1922-2015), and many others who have moved on to The Great Beyond—people I so desperately wanted to meet, yet, sadly, never had the chance to...or, worse still, those whom I'd had a chance to see at some point, but passed-on for one reason or another.

The fact of the matter is, while Romero is gone in body, he will *never* really die in spirit. His work lives on. People will continue to dissect his films and argue over their merits. Some stubbornly persist in decrying him as a one-trick pony without any discernible style. It's true he wasn't a grand stylist in the tradition of Mario Bava or Dario Argento, but he came from a background in editing, and that's the way to an understanding of his style as a filmmaker. Romero's best films are brilliantly *edited*—often by the man himself—and they build tension through montage, as opposed to elaborately-choreographed camera movements. Romero also came from a more guerilla style of filmmaking, which he learned doing commercial work and industrial shorts in Pittsburgh. He didn't necessarily have access to the most hi-tech equipment, but it never really mattered: his sense of urgency and his flair for drama and black comedy—as well as shocking, visceral violence too, of course—comes through loud and clear in his best films. Even many of his weaker films have certain moments that make them special.

Sadly, in his later years, Romero found himself in a difficult position within the film industry. He was never an 'insider'. He rejected Hollywood—and Hollywood rejected him in return. Filmmakers took inspiration from him and built massive successes atop ground that he had ploughed years before. Many viewers of AMC's megahit series *The Walking Dead* (2010–) love to opine about how the show is so special because of its non-undead characters, *not* because of the zombies. Well, guess what? The same is true of Romero's films. Yes, his zombie films do feature memorable viscerally gruesome highlights, but they *aren't* focused purely on the ghouls: they instead focus on the dynamics of whatever living human characters are gathered-together in the scenario, desperately trying to salvage what little is left of humanity before it's too late. So, sorry to shatter the illusion, folks: but there's nothing more "depthy" and meaningful in *The Walking Dead* than we haven't already seen in the groundbreaking work of George Romero; he simply did it a lot more economically, and with a lot less melodramatic posturing (and padding!).

Sure, Romero's perspective may have been fatalistic, but the fact that he basically loved humanity—foibles and all—shines through plain as day. Even his zombies themselves began to take on more character over time: after the personality-free ghouls of **NIGHT OF THE LIVING**

DEAD (1968), they began to take on a quirkier vibe in **DAWN OF THE DEAD** (1978)... and then, in **DAY OF THE DEAD** (1985), we were introduced to him affectionately known as "Bub", a semi-domesticated zombie who made it abundantly clear that these creatures still have some vestige of humanity left in them, despite since having become ravening cannibalistic monsters that are technically dead, yet still very much alive. Yes indeed, the monster isn't "them", it's *us*—and our inability to get along with and collaborate, cohabitate and work together in harmony for the common good is the very thing that shall be our undoing. Having established himself so firmly in horror with **NOTLD**, Romero found it difficult breaking free from the genre it. He tried to early on with the romantic dramedy **THERE'S ALWAYS VANILLA** (1971), but nobody cared, and the film flopped; to be honest, it really isn't all that good anyway, though Romero diehards/completists like myself still want a copy in their collection regardless *[I have it! ☺– SF]*. Romero accepted his 'typecast' fate with his usual good humor, but he found himself painted into a corner: after a certain point, nobody cared about him if he was trying to do anything *but* a zombie movie. It would have been easy for him to become bitter, but if he was, he didn't show it.

He set about trying think of new ways to reinvent the genre, and managed to come up with some inspired ideas in the likes of **LAND OF THE DEAD** (2005) and **DIARY OF THE DEAD** (2007), although **SURVIVAL OF THE DEAD** (2009) proved to be a little too much running back to the same well too quickly, and the end

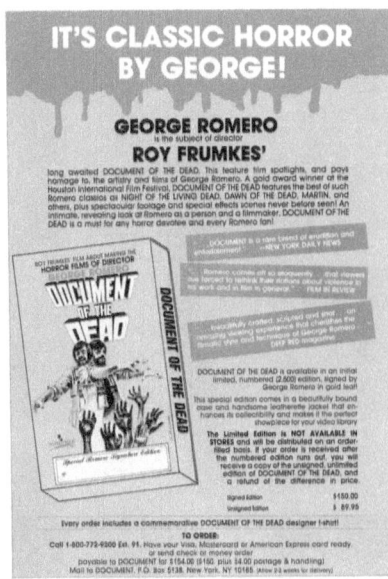

DOCUMENT OF THE DEAD home videotape mag ad

result was a bit on the stale side. Sadly, it would prove to be his final work as a director. He still had ideas, and wanted to realize them, but even when you're working on a small scale, you need sympathetic financiers and supporters, and for Romero, that simply wasn't forthcoming. In Hollywood, you're only as big as your last hit, and—let's be honest—Romero hadn't made much of

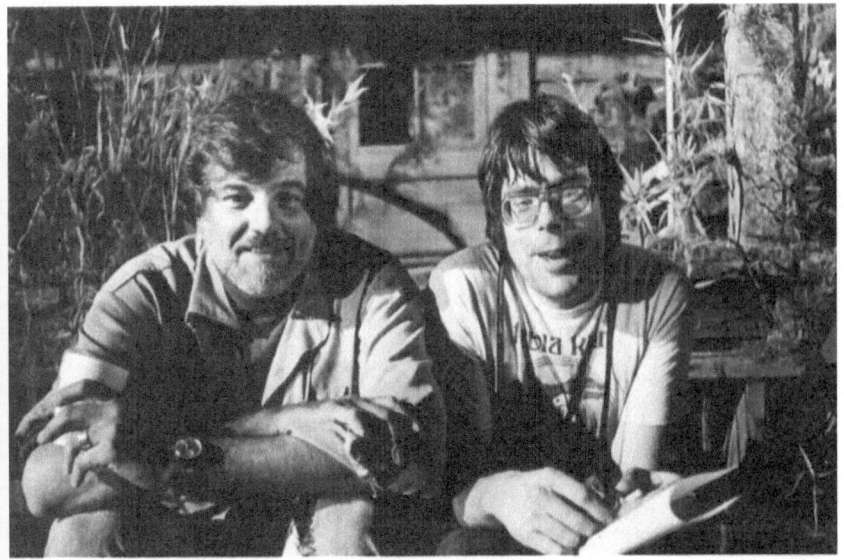

With Stephen King on the set of **CREEPSHOW**

Ho-o-old It! A behind-the-scenes shot from **MARTIN** (1977), with actors Lincoln Maazel and John Amplas, cameraman Michael Gornick, and next to Gornick, we have a distracted Romero

a dent at the box office in a long, long time. I remember going to see **LAND OF THE DEAD** with a group of friends on its opening day; this was my "**STAR WARS**", my opportunity to get my geek on! Hardly anybody showed, however, and it was regarded as a commercial disappointment, though it sold well enough overseas to prompt a couple more *Dead* films before the whole thing pretty much just ran dry altogether. *The Walking Dead* took over as the next big zombie epidemic and, depending on your point of view, it either added something new to the formula…or simply plodded along back over the same old ground that Romero had explored so well in his earlier films. That it was so successful and acclaimed might have stung a bit; that he himself couldn't even raise financing anymore must have really rubbed salt in the wound. Yet through it all, in public at least, he maintained his good humor. He was opposed to the fast-moving 'running' zombies seen in some of the more-amped-up modern horror films (including the 2004 remake of **DAWN OF THE DEAD**) and he let it be known that he wasn't necessarily the world's biggest fan of *The Walking Dead*; some cynics saw that as simple sour grapes from a bitter old man, but come on: he was entirely entitled to his opinion, no matter what you may think of the whole *WD* phenomenon.

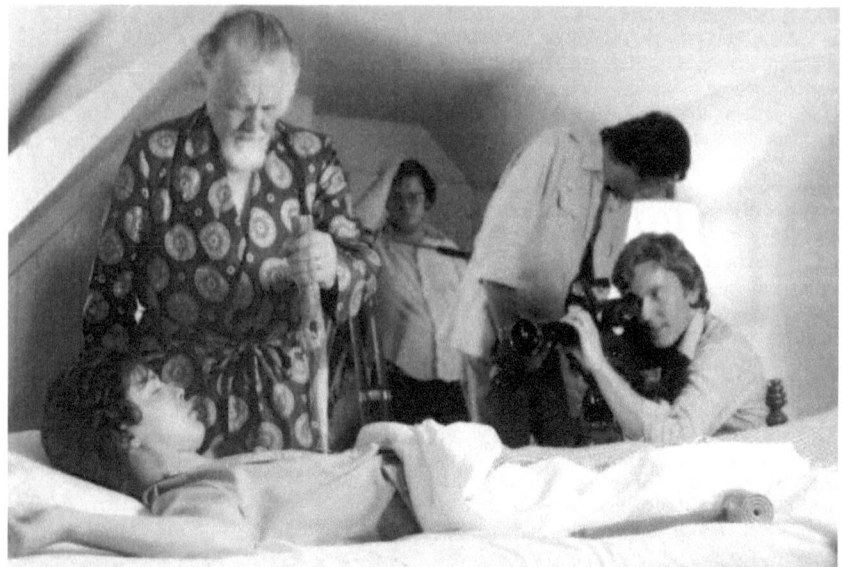

DAY made the cover of Chas. Balun's seminal *DR* magazine in '88

For a time in the 1990s, Romero appeared to have dropped off the map altogether. I still remember seeing an interview with him where he talked about being put under contract at Universal. He said he made more money than he had ever seen in his life, but every project he had in the works became stuck in development hell, and he didn't succeed in getting anything off the ground. He was attached to **THE MUMMY** (1999, D: Stephen Sommers). He was attached to **RESIDENT EVIL** (2002, D: Paul W.S. Anderson). They were made, but not with him at the helm. Who knows how his own versions of those particular films would have turned out, or whether they would have connected with audiences and spawned lucrative franchises? Success in Hollywood is measured by thee almighty dollar, and Romero's ideas just didn't fit in with the whole 'blockbuster' mentality. He finally managed to get a small, low-key, Canadian-made horror movie called **BRUISER** (2000) off the ground. Some fans felt it marked a sad comedown for Romero, while others—myself included—saw it as a fascinating continuation of his themes and obsessions, that was only mildly compromised by an unsatisfying finale. The film didn't make money, but it at least announced that he was still out there, and that he was still ready-and-willing to make movies. When he finally did get a film off the ground through Universal, it was something of a deal with the devil: he wouldn't be free to make it quite as 'splashy' as its predecessors, at least not for theatrical showings, but **LAND OF THE DEAD** afforded him a larger budget and slicker hardware to play with. Romero had problems navigating the waters of studio-sanctioned moviemaking, with its emphasis on rigorous planning and scheduling, but he nonetheless managed to deliver a film of real wit and intelligence. Crucially, the whole home video environment had changed, as well, making it possible for him to justify playing along with the MPAA for theatrical screenings, while knowing that his vision would ultimately be preserved on DVD in a gorier 'unrated' cut. That **LOTD** ultimately failed to connect with audiences on a large scale is a shame but, really, I don't know that it would have changed his career much even if it had been a hit: Romero was always an outsider, so the odds of him continuing to work within the confines of a major studio, after all the aggravation he had endured, don't seem very likely. It's just a shame that the kind of big ideas he often had called for resources that were often well outside his reach; I still regret his not getting to tackle Stephen King's *The Stand*, for example, and I will always wonder what the 'bigger' version of **DAY OF THE DEAD** would have been like, though I flat-out adore the end result, anyway.

Sooner than regret and bemoan what he was unable to do, however, it's important for us to celebrate and remember all that he *did* accomplish. Virtually singlehandedly, he helped to create and define the modern horror film. His combination of social commentary and go-for-broke shock effects won him millions of fans, and his influence can still be strongly felt in the genre to this day. Everybody remembers the zombie films, but let's not forget his other unique gems: his downbeat 'vampire' serial killer thriller **MARTIN** (1977) was his personal favorite of his own canon, and it happens to be mine as well; his offbeat satirical drama **KNIGHTRIDERS** (1981) is a potent and heartfelt exploration of consumerism and the death of a certain type of idealistic utopia; **CREEPSHOW** (1982) is still the most successful translation yet of the EC comics aesthetic and sensibility to celluloid; while **MONKEY SHINES** (1988) is a sharp psychological thriller which takes on heartbreaking proportions if you're an animal lover like me. The work speaks for itself. For me, the hits far outnumber the misses, but even if he had made only one good film, **NIGHT OF THE LIVING DEAD** would be enough to ensure his place in the history books.

Now that we have braced ourselves for a world without Romero in it, let's be glad that he was here, and that, during that time, the technology existed which allowed him to preserve his macabre, often bitingly funny visions on celluloid. And be glad, too, that *that* laugh and those sage observations of his about the difficulties involved in getting it all done on time and on budget are preserved for posterity on DVD and Blu-ray, thus enabling us to sit down and bullshit with George for many years to come.

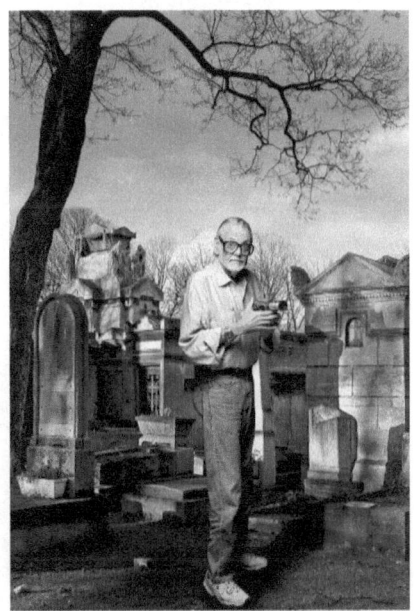

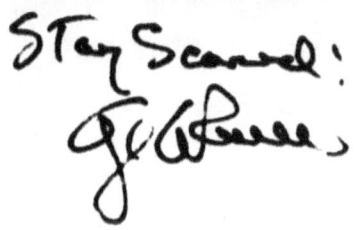

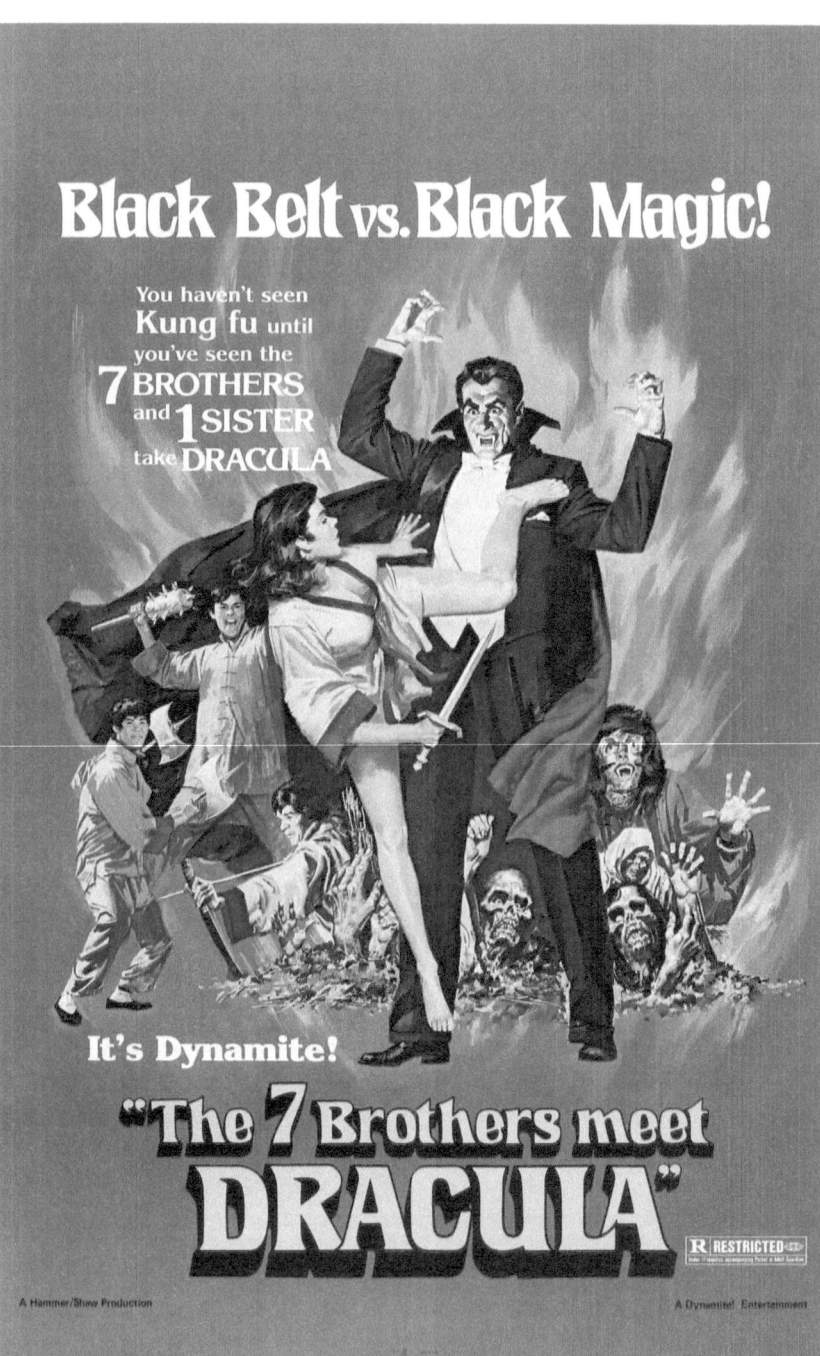

Alternate-titled US one-sheet poster for **THE LEGEND OF THE 7 GOLDEN VAMPIRES**; art unsigned

MONSTER! #33 MOVIE CHECKLIST
MONSTER! Public Service posting: Title availability of films reviewed or mentioned in this issue of MONSTER!
Information dug up and presented by Steve Fenton and Tim Paxton.

Doctor Who and other Brit TV Sci-Fi / Horror Series *[pp.70-95]* – Originally produced by Independent Television (ITV) / Associated British Corporation (ABC), the vintage juvie-oriented B&W SF teleseries *Pathfinders in Space* (1960-61) *[p.72]*, starring Gerald Flood, Peter Williams and George "**WOMAN EATER**" Coulouris, was issued on British Region 2 DVD by the UK's Network label via Studio Canal in 2011, this as a Trilogy set that includes the full serials *Pathfinders in Space*, *Pathfinders to Mars* and *Pathfinders to Venus* (whose combined running time is a whopping 525 minutes and whose individual episode titles include the likes of "The Valley of Monsters", "The Venus People" and "The Creature"). *PiS* has also been made available on domestic DVD-R by Sinister Cinema. As for the ABC/ITV sci-fi series *Out of This World* (1962, UK) *[p.72]* only a single episode (i.e., "Little Lost Robot") out of a total of 14 made is known to have survive. It was issued on Region 2 DVD in 2014 by BFI. Considerably more remains of the similar-format later BBC series *Out of the Unknown* (1965) *[p.72]*, but it is also incomplete (any remnants—in this case enough to fill a 7-disc box set—are likewise available on R2 disc from BFI). As the "Trivia" section for *OotU* at the IMDb tells us: "*The series suffered from the BBC's lack of a proper archiving policy until 1978. It was BBC policy before 1978 to wipe master tapes and reuse them for other programmes, hence saving money and storage space. The total number of editions known to exist on film or videotape stands at twenty (and a half) out of 49. Additionally, visual excerpts from eight episodes are held, plus various off-air audio sequences from 16 installments.*" As with all the British Broadcasting Corporation (BBC)'s series' vast array of its other serials, each of the following *Doctor Who* adventures can be acquired on DVD via BBC Video (often in conjunction with Warner [Bros.] Home Video for stateside/Canadian releases): "The Daleks" (1963-64) *[p.74]*, "The Dalek Invasion of Earth" (1964) *[p.74]*, "The Tenth Planet" (1966) *[p.75]*, "The Moonbase" (1967) *[p.75]*, "The Tomb of the Cybermen" (1967) *[p.75]*, "Doctor Who and the Silurians" (1970) *[p.79]*, "Spearhead from Space" (1970) *[p.79]*, "The Dæmons" (1971) *[p.84]*, "The Curse of Peladon" (1972) *[p.91]*, "The Green Death" (1973) *[p.91]* and "Death to the Daleks" (1974) *[p.92]*. The engrossing recent special 'early days' of

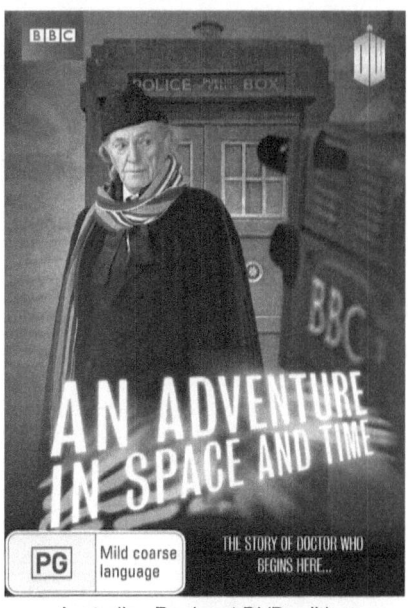

Australian Region 4 DVD edition

DW made-for-TV semi-docudrama feature **AN ADVENTURE IN SPACE AND TIME** (2013) *[p.72]*, showcasing David "Argus Filch" Bradley as aging actor William Hartnell in an incredibly affecting performance as the man who played the first Doctor, can also be picked-up on disc through BBC's video distribution arm. Evidently not concurrently available in any above-board video format (?), in an old video dupe with the digital time-counter visible onscreen throughout, Robert Hardy as *The Incredible Robert Baldick*'s failed pilot episode *[p.88]* (originally broadcast on the BBC showcase series *Drama Playhouse* in 1972) can, as of this writing, be accessed on YouTube at the link entitled "Never Come Night" (@ *https://www.youtube.com/watch?v=FtECxnjbyrA*). A lesser-quality upload with an annoyingly 'herky-jerky' image if sans the counter can be viewed at "The Incredible Robert Baldick: Never Come Night" (@ *https://www.youtube.com/watch?v=HoSi-eE-4ao*); both versions clock-in at the exact same runtime, indicating they might have been ripped from the same 'master' source (possibly a pre-recorded videotape that was released at some point?). As for **THE STONE TAPE** (1972) *[p.89]*, it was simultaneously released separately on both VHS and DVD in 2001 by the British Film Institute (BFI) as part of their Archive Television series, but has since gone OOP. It was later (in 2013) reissued on Region 2 (UK) DVD by 101 Films (in conjunction with The Beeb themselves), whose edition ported-over the same full-length commentary by both the show's writer Nigel Kneale (1922-2006) and film critic Kim Newman that had been included with the BFI's earlier edition from '01. Amidst much fanfare in certain circles at the time, in 2013 BFI also released to disc (Region 2 DVD) the surviving remnants of the largely-'lost' 7-episode series *Dead of Night* (1972) *[p.89]*, their disc gathering together the mere—if a lot better than none at all!—three episodes known to be still in existence: "The Exorcism" (episode #1), "Return Flight" (#2) and "A Woman Sobbing" (#7), variously starring Anna Massey, Peter Barkworth, Edward Petherbridge and Clive Swift. In addition to an illustrated booklet featuring essays and personnel biographies pertaining to the show, BFI's disc edition of *DoN* also includes not only a stills gallery of images from the missing episodes, but even provided links to downloadable copies (on PDF) of their scripts too; so at least the four otherwise long-gone episodes are still extant in some form (although whether those script PDFs are still available online after five years remains to be seen). Another (longer-running) BBC series that is today missing episodes is *Doomwatch* (1970-73) *[p.82]*, starring Simon Oates, Robert Powell and John Paul (as Dr. Spencer Quist). Officially licensed from The Beeb, a 7-disc Region 2 DVD box set entitled "Doomwatch: Series 1-3 – The Remaining Episodes" was issued by Simply Media in 2016. Clocking-in at an exhaustive—and exhausting!—1,030 minutes, it collects together all the show's surviving episodes (a total of 24), including the never-televised-for-censorship-reasons episode "Sex and Violence" *[p.82]*, plus the set also includes an additional documentary special feature coming courtesy of BBC Scotland entitled *The Cult of Doomwatch* (2006, D: Tony Followell).

***Godzilla* Movies: "The Showa Era"** (1954-75) *[pp.207-233]* – Since it would take at least a ten-year-long blog to properly catalogue every Big G home video release known to peoplekind, and we really don't have either the time or the space for that here—not to mention the fact that every single 'Zilla flick is a cinch to come by in umpteen versions all around the globe these days anyway, so why be anal about it?—we're just gonna narrow things down to the absolute basics (i.e., domestic, as in stateside, releases only) here. Hence, we're simply going to list a recent, decent-quality disc source (or sources) for each following title directly after its year of production in parenthesis hereunder: **GODZILLA** (1954; The Criterion Collection, Genius Entertainment) *[p.210]*, **GODZILLA RAIDS AGAIN** (1955; Sony Pictures Home Entertainment [SPHE], Classic Media [CM]) *[p.214]*, **KING KONG VS. GODZILLA** (1962; GoodTimes Home Video [GTHV]) *[p.215]*, **RODAN, THE FLYING MONSTER** (1956; CM) *[p.217]*, **MOTHRA** (1961; SPHE, Mill Creek Entertainment) *[p.218]*, **MOTHRA VS. GODZILLA** (1964; SPHE) *[p.218]*, **GHIDRAH THE THREE-HEADED MONSTER** (1964; Something Weird Video, GTHV) *[p.220]*, **INVASION OF THE ASTRO-MONSTERS** (1965; Simitar Video) *[p.222]*, **EBIRAH, HORROR OF THE DEEP** (1966; Section 23 Films, SPHE) *[p.223]*, **SON OF GODZILLA** (1967; Columbia TriStar Home Video [CTHV]) *[p.224]*, **DESTROY ALL MONSTERS** (1968; ADV Films, Media Blasters [MB]) *[p.225]*, **GODZILLA'S REVENGE** (1969; SPHE, CM) *[p.226]*, **GODZILLA VS. THE SMOG MONSTER** (1971; CTHV) *[p.227]*, **GODZILLA VS. GIGAN** (1972; CTHV) *[p.227]*, **GODZILLA VS. MEGALON** (1972; Rhino Home Video, MB) *[p.229]*, **GODZILLA VS. MECHAGODZILLA** (1974; CTHV) *[p.231]* and **TERROR OF MECHAGODZILLA** (1975; SPHE) *[p.232]*. In closing, I just have to say I'm rather amazed that a seasoned rocker/skin-thumper like our Big G arti-

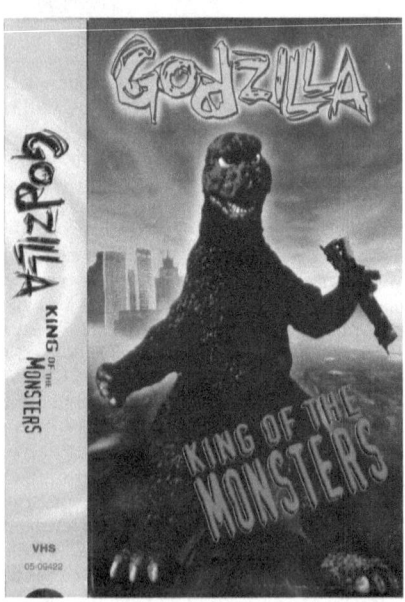

Complain as we might about the inaccuracies of German posters and lobby cards for various Godzilla films, the US VHS company Goodtimes was notorious for their oft-goofy covers!

cle's author Christos M., considering said article *is* entitled "Godzilla A Go-Go" and all, didn't think to hiply namedrop/shoehorn-in Blue Öyster Cult's classic hard rock city-stomper "Godzilla" (*"Oh no, there goes Tokey-yoh / Go-go Godzilla!"*) somewhere along the way, so consider that oversight now rectified. But I'm not even going to bring up the fact he neglected to mention that bikey black leather Norwegian scunge-deathpunkers Turbonegro recorded a track called "Destroy All Monsters" (for the *Age of Conan* [2008] series soundtrack), or that there was an influential Motor City ambient / avant-garde / experimental slash proto-noize / pre-post-prog-punk act of the same name from 1973-1985 co-founded by sultry frontwoman / vocalist / performance artiste Niagara and later (in 1977) joined by once-and-future Stooge axman Ron Asheton either. Promise. (Just razzin' yuz, Chris! I knew you knew. :-D) BTW, for those interested in picking-up a 145m DVD all about that seminal lattermost Detroit band, there's one entitled *Destroy All Monsters – Grow Live Monsters* available online via the MVD Visual/Book Beat label (orderable @ *https://www.sea-urchin.net/audio-video/book-beat-cds/destroy-all-monsters-grow-live-monsters-dvd/*), a compilation of short films made by the members plus archival and live performance footage, et cetera (ad-quote: *"a selection of 8mm, super-8, and 16 mm film phantasies from the period 1971-76"* [do bear in mind that these were the pre-Asheton years, though, Iggy and the Stooges fans! Although chances are the average Igster in-crowder is also a DAM fan anyway [I know I am!], so they won't mind). Coming in a box whose cover art juxtaposes a shot of the band with a detail of the original US one-sheet poster art for Big G's **DESTROY ALL MONSTERS**—which was indeed DAM's namesake, and from which they weren't unknown to sample dialogue and audio FX from time to time in their recordings, or dabbling in horror themes (e.g., *"Like a vampire / I'm gonna bite your vein..."*)— the disc can be acquired for the more-than-reasonable price of €15.00 at the above-cited URL addy; postage not included. It can also be ordered in US dollars rather than euros (@ *www.thebookbeat.com*).

Universal's *Mummy* Series (1932-59) *[pp.11-34]* – **THE MUMMY** (1932) *[p.12]*, **THE MUMMY'S HAND** (1940) *[p.18]*, **THE MUMMY'S TOMB** (1942) *[p.20]*, **THE MUMMY'S GHOST** *[p.22]* and **THE MUMMY'S CURSE** (both 1944) *[p.24]*, as well as **ABBOTT AND COSTELLO MEET THE MUMMY** (1955) *[p.26]* all originated at Universal Studios, which, as long-time fixtures of that company's "Universal Monsters" series, is where their copyrights firmly remain to this day. As for **THE MUMMY**

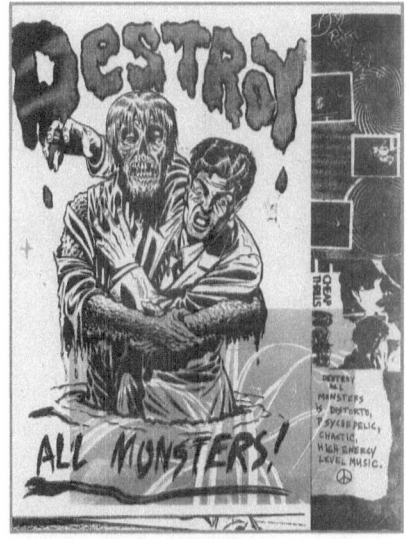

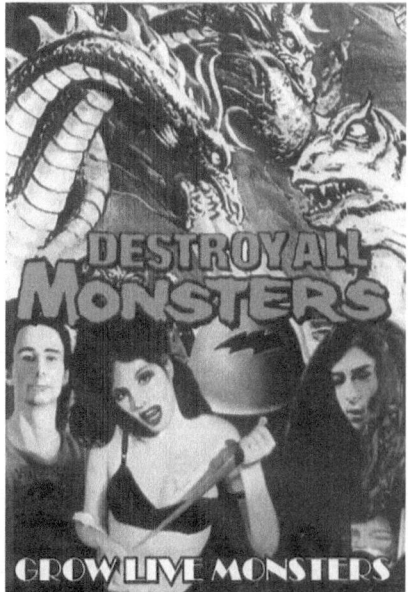

Top: *Destroy All Monsters* fanzine #1 (1976). **Above:** Their 2007 *Grow Live Monsters* compilation DVD (note sexy singer Niagara with long knife!)

(1959, UK) *[p.29]*, while first and foremost a Hammer Production, it nevertheless still fits onto the very tail-end of the 'first' Universal *Mummy* wave by simple virtue of the fact that its principal characters were officially licensed from / authorized for the British studio's usage by Unipix themselves (unlike any of Hammer's subsequent 100% homegrown series entries featuring mum-

Video Availability Information

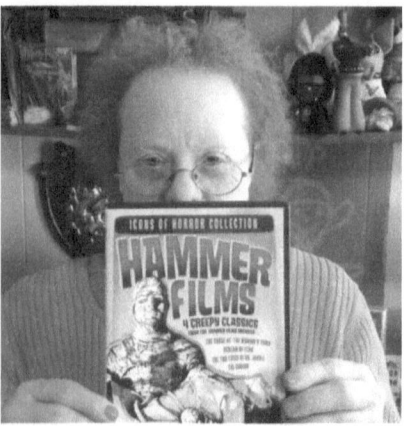

Heather P. just popped-in to remind us of this cool discount Hammer DVD 4-pack she has, featuring the studio's 2nd *Mummy* entry

mies, of which they made three more; just for the record, those are **THE CURSE OF THE MUMMY'S TOMB** [1964] *{p.31}*, **THE MUMMY'S SHROUD** [1967] *{p.32}* and **BLOOD FROM THE MUMMY'S TOMB** [1971] *{p.32}*, none of which featured **MUMMY '59** co-stars Lee and Cushing). All of the first six 100% Uni titles listed off the top of this entry are readily available in about a trillion-gazillion incarnations and formats—starting many decades ago with 8mm film reels, on through Betamax/VHS videocassettes, RCA SelectaVision discs, laserdiscs, then DVDs and now all the way up to Blu-rays—from

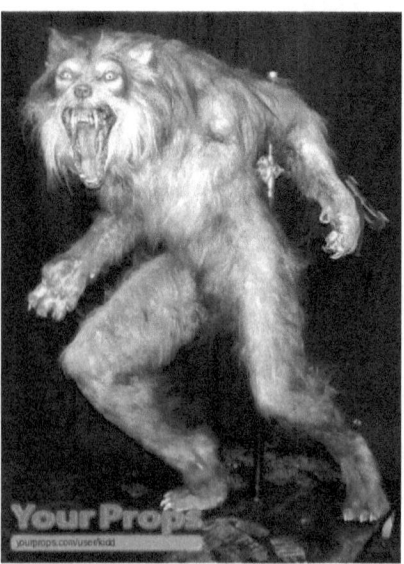

The actual full-scale **BAD MOON** werewolf figure built by Steve Johnson's XFX!

their originating studio (currently under their video wing Universal Pictures Home Entertainment), while the aforementioned belated late '50s Hammer/Universal *Kharis* series rebooter is extant in about as many editions as Unipix's '32 Karloff-as-Imhotep originator is, albeit from a different distribution company (namely its long-time rights holder, Warner Home Video. Incidentally, I [i.e., SF] once shelled-out a whopping $99.99 [Canadian] for Warner's oversized clamshell-box VHS edition of **M** '59 back in about 1988 or so through a mail order club—pan-and-scan/fullscreen, yet!—and was more than happy to do it). Again just for the record, the three final Hammer *Mummy* entries listed above are either currently or have most-recently been made domestically available on disc (DVD and/or Blu) via Mill Creek Entertainment (**TCOTMT**) and Anchor Bay Entertainment (**TMS** and **BFTMT**). We won't bother dwelling on—or barely even mentioning, for that matter—Uni's most-recent 'second' and 'third' wave *Mummy* revivals, the latter of which (starring a virtually mummified Tom Cruise), having done a resounding box-office belly-flop, seems to have stopped dead in its tracks without even properly kick-starting a whole new franchise, unlike what happened with the previous three-film wave toplining Brendan Fraser (which spanned 1999-2008 and spawned numerous spinoffs/rip-offs worldwide). However, being as Troy Howarth does give his, um, 'less-than-fond', let's say, appraisal of **THE MUMMY** (2017) this ish *[p.322]*, we would be remiss not to at least inform any readers who might wish to subject themselves to it that, since flopping so badly, it's currently—and likely for at least the next 300 centuries, assuming the world lasts that long—readily viewable in innumerable forms via whatever secondary subsidiary of Universal it's been unceremoniously consigned to and who are desperately trying to recoup their losses by flogging it to death and beyond at about forty-billion streaming sites across the solar system. The mere fact that it's so damn easy to see makes it a whole lot easier not to bother, but we'll undoubtedly get around to checking it out sooner or later (accent on the latter).

BAD MOON (1996) *[p.260]* – After a rather disastrous theatrical opening in the US, which Warner Brothers neglected to properly promote, this film received its first release via VHS videocassette the following year in 1997. Heavily-cropped from its original 2.35:1 aspect ratio, the reduced image left a lot to be desired. When DVD started to dominate the market, Warner revisited the film in 2000 for one of their customary 'snapcase' releases, and thankfully, the film was now properly presented in its intended 2.35:1 aspect ratio with 16x9 enhancement but, as expected, the disc was bare-bones in the extras department, save for the rather crummy trailer. Warner continued to release the film on DVD both as part of their *4-Film Favorites: Horror* set from 2007 (a real mixed bag which also included Michael Crichton's **COMA** [1978, USA], Michael Wadleigh's **WOLFEN** [1981, USA] and Abel Ferrara's **BODY SNATCHERS** [1993, USA]), and also as part of the Warner Archive Collection, their long-running, Made-On-Demand program in 2010. Licensing the film from Warner, Shout! Factory (through their *highly*-popular Scream Factory line) premiered the film on Blu-ray in 2016 in a downright *flawless* transfer. Detail is superb, with deep, dark blacks and a very healthy, far-from-anemic color palette; it probably couldn't *ever* look any better than it does here! Audio includes a new DTS-HD MA 5.1 audio track and a DTS-HD MA 2.0 audio track, and both sound terrific, especially during the many werewolf attack scenes. Extras include an audio commentary with director Eric Red, which, although very detailed, sounds like he's simply reading from a ready-made script. Some of the topics discussed include his intro to the project through the William Morris agency; a ton of technical aspects, the various stunt-work, and choreographing all of the monster mayhem (which he refers to as [quote] "ripper moments"!), including the attention-grabbing opening. He goes on to praise Steve Johnson's top-notch werewolf design and some of the film's other unused casting choices, including Michael Biehn and Robert Patrick; he also discusses the difference between the film's original theatrical cut (79m51s) and his new director's cut (79m25s), which merely cuts out some laughable CGI effects work. Thank goodness for that! In the second audio commentary, which isn't even listed on the package, director Red returns with star Michael Paré and Arrow in the Head's John Fallon, latter of whose foul-mouthed enthusiasm becomes increasingly grating over the course of the track. I'm no prude or anything, but it all comes across as very juvenile indeed, but Red and Paré still offer plenty of interesting tidbits nonetheless, including about Mariel Hemingway's difficult nature on set. It's definitely worth a listen, but be forewarned: Fallon's rather crude giddiness may be annoying to some. In *Nature of the Beast: The Making of Bad Moon* (35m17s), this nicely-produced extra features interviews with Red, Paré, actor Mason Gamble and SPFX artist Steve Johnson, but much of what is said is also covered in both the audio commentaries, so if you don't have the time to go through those, this'll do just fine. Other extras include the "Unrated Opening Sequence" (6m07s), which is sourced from VHS and features extra nudity and even more gore; too bad decent elements

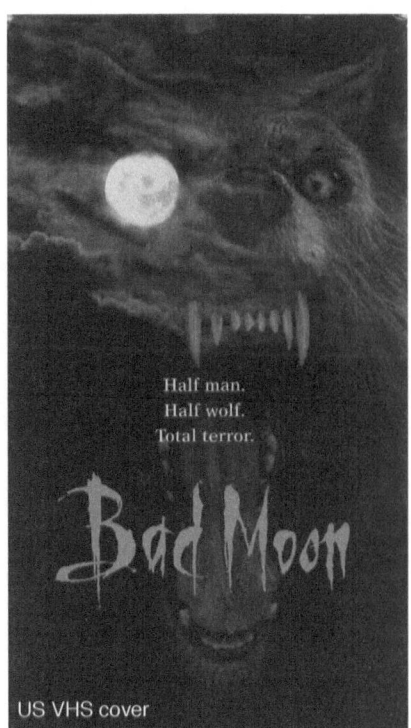

US VHS cover

couldn't be located and integrated back into the main feature, though. A few—if very extensive—storyboard galleries and the frankly lousy theatrical trailer (*"It doesn't have to be Halloween to be this scary!"* indeed!) complete the extras. – **Dennis Capicik**

THE BODY SHOP (1972) *[p.290]* – United's '80s domestic videotape tagline: *"The Meating Place For DISMEMBERS ONLY!"* Image/SWV's DVD ad-lines: *"Welcome to THE BODY SHOP! A Love Story... With Blood And Guts! The Doctor Is Out... Of His Mind!"* Put out on DVD by Image Entertainment in conjunction with Something Weird Video as a Special Edition in 2002, under its notorious mid-'80s Beta/VHS release title of **DOCTOR GORE** (which was released by Tulsa, Oklahoma's United Entertainment simultaneously with [quote] *"The first made-for-home-video movie"*, the infamous splatter-shitter **BLOOD CULT** [1985]). The Image/SWV edition came with an audio commentary by co-producer Jeffrey C. Hogue, but, while he discusses his career in general a *lot*, he disappointingly says very little about **THE BODY SHOP** itself. The film was also reportedly released on at least one American vid label (we don't know which one) as **SHRIEKS IN THE NIGHT**. Strangely enough, to illustrate an 'optical illusion' horror gag using mirrors called "The Operating Table", a still from this film showing J.G. "Pat" Patterson standing alongside 'topless/armless' ingénue Jan Benfield unexpectedly turned-up in Philip Morris' and Dennis Phillips' small press book *How to Operate a Financially Successful Haunted House* (1985). Seen/heard performed in the film live at a local honkytonk by Bill Hicks (backed by The Reignbeaux), for those that want it, the endearingly hokey, verging-on-comatose C&W ballad "A Heart Dies Every Minute"—which, if you happen to dig old school country music as much as I do, is a quite respectable specimen of its kind, and is pretty catchy in its own way—can be viewed on YT (at an obscure channel called Heliogabby) via the link bearing the song's title (@ https://www.youtube.com/watch?v=qnJN-Vul2Tn0). A comment posted under the poorly-attended—1,129 views, 150 subscribers and only 13 likes (but at least no down-votes!) since June 2012—video clip five years ago by one zyphoid666 (i.e., "Whoah, Gregory moonlights as a country lounge crooner") lends further weight to my theory that the song's singer Mr. Hicks and Roy Mehaffey, the player of Greg the hunchback, are one in the same dude, if done-up to look as wildly dissimilar from one another as possible in hopes no one will notice. (Although zyphoid666 goes on to add, "And featuring the reverend Jim Jones on lead guitar, ladies and gentlemen!" so maybe he was just making like a wiseacre and playing-up the similarity between the two [or is it really only *one*] portly beardos? It remains to be seen, monsterphiles!). Incidentally, at the end of his review of the film herein where he listed some related trivia, the normally studious-to-a-fault Les Moore overlooked mentioning a horror magician named Dr. Gore who appeared on a 2007 episode of the UK telly show *Britain's Got Talent*, much to Piers Morgan's amusement. A sort of combination of the present film's maniacal medic, as well as Montag the Magnificent (Ray Sager) from Herschell Gordon Lewis' **THE WIZARD OF GORE** (1970, USA) and Larry Hankin as the reincarnation of the mesmerist Svengali from the funky Luciferian sexy shocker **LUCIFER'S WOMEN** (1974, USA, D: Paul Aratow), this 'new' TV Dr. Gore's novelty magic act—heavily-influenced by *grand guignol* theatre—involved one of his Goth chick assistants having her tongue scissored in half lengthwise and another getting thrown onto a tabletop and sawn 'in two' (!) by an electric jigsaw; both of which scenes, ironically enough, appeared to have been significantly chopped by censors prior to airing.

BONE TOMAHAWK (2015) *[p.264]* – Available in all media in both the USA and Canada from RLJ Entertainment, plus on Australian DVD via Transmission Films.

CURSE OF THE BLUE LIGHTS (1988) *[p.270]* – Formerly (in '89) made available stateside on Beta/VHS videocassette by Magnum Entertainment. A couple of years back there was a fairly decent upload of a rip made from Magnum's full-frame old domestic VHS tape version up on YouTube, which since appears to have been taken down. However, as of this writing, there are uploads of a pretty decent quality Hungarian-dubbed print called **KÉK LIDÉRCEK** ("Blue Curse" [?]), as well as a much fuzzier/ murkier Portuguese-subbed version with muddy English audio and a badly-distorted (as in *stre-e-e-etched*) aspect ratio, entitled **A NOITE DO HORROR** ("Night of Horror") there too, for those who want them. Although a quite convincingly authentic-looking if unofficial, fan-made mock-up of a DVD jacket for the film—it nearly fooled me!—was available to members via the torrent site Cinemageddon *circa* 2009, **COTBL** has evidently never received any legit North American disc release to date, but you can bet it's out there on 'grey' market DVD-R somewhere or other though. What's the odds that Vinegar Syndrome or another similar specialist label—hell, even a bigger outfit like Scream Factory maybe, for that matter—are planning to put out a deluxe Blu-ray edition of it in the not-so-distant future? Pretty good, I'd say! I wouldn't hold my breath if I was you, but don't write the idea off as an impossibility either.

DRY BONES (2013) *[p.273]* – As reported at HNN (*horrornews.net*) in mid-January of 2013, "We're excited and lucky to have Kevin *[Van Hentenryck, of* Basket Case *series fame]* on board," says *[co-director Greg]* Lamberson. "Michael *[O'Hear, his co-director]* and I conceived this film as a horror comedy in the spirit of 1980s films like **FRIGHT NIGHT** and **HOUSE**, and Kevin starred in one of the most twisted horror films of all time. Our roots reach down to the same primordial New York City ooze". This is currently available for a rental (starting at $3.99) on YouTube, and it was issued on domestic DVD in 2014 by Entertainment One.

THE FLESH EATERS (1962 [1964]) *[p.276]* – Dark Sky DVD tagline: *"There's Something In The Water That Eats Flesh!"* Available wayback-when on Betamax/VHS videocassette from both Birmingham's Knockout Video (1981) in the UK—with a severely-censored runtime of a mere 67m32s; hence, *not* much of a video nasty, despite its "X" rating!—and on Monterey Home Video (1985) in the USA. A good way to go for this gritty '60s B-grade doozy these days would be Dark Sky Films' 87-minute (near-as-dammit to uncut as we're ever likely to get) domestic disc release from 2005 as part of their "Monsters" line, which came widescreen (@ 1.85:1). However, their edition *doesn't* include the brief color (i.e., bright blood-red!) tinted insert that originally (?) appeared close to the end of the film in some prints—***ATTENTION: SPOILER ALERT!***—when the hero injects an XL hypodermic into the giant cyclopean monster's eyeball causing it to self-destruct, or the extra footage showing female victims in the Nazi laboratory (mentioned by Les Moore in his review) either. That latter sequence is included as a separate special feature on the Dark Sky disc, and it rather sticks out like a sore thumb when viewed edited into the narrative. Both it and the red-colored insert with the syringe were included in Sinister Cinema's (*was* it SC?) old Beta/VHS transfer print, but we can't remember whether that one was otherwise cut elsewhere or not. According to reports, Fred Olen Ray's Retromedia outfit was at some point hoping to release this flick on disc, featuring an audio commentary by genre expert Tom Weaver, only it didn't pan-out, possibly due to copyrights conflicts (?), although certain advance screener copies of it seem to have gotten sent out somewhere along the line. For a detailed breakdown of its specs by one Charles Phelpson, a knowledgeable, dedicated fan of the film, check out his lengthy customer review on Amazon (entitled "This is NOT the edited TV version" and dated all the way back from October 31st, 2005). It'll give you all the dope you need on this flick's current disc incarnations, until a better option comes along… which may well happen in these days of so many unexpected surprises in the digital disc medium. In fact, due to its well-known rep in psychotronic cult flick circles, it'd be a natural for a fully-loaded Blu-ray release at some point (maybe even as part of The Criterion Collection, as happened with the splattery brainsucker classic **FIEND WITHOUT A FACE** [1958, UK, D: Arthur Crabtree] and a number of other formerly considered 'too-lowbrow/low-grade' monster/horror/sci-fi B flicks that have been put out by them since the dawn of DVD technology). We can only hope!

FRANKENSTEIN '80 (1972) *[p.285]* – This was formerly extant on domestic NTSC Betamax/VHS from Gorgon Video/MPI Home, in a claustrophobic pan-and-scan print contained in an oversized clamshell box (ad-line: *"He Had A Bone To Pick..."*) whose insert artwork looked like it was done by a negligibly-talented kindergartener. It was also issued under the title **FRANKENSTEIN 2000** (not to be confused with the title of our next entry) in France on SECAM Beta/VHS by both Ciné Vidéo Distribution (in 1985) and Space Video (year unknown). At some point or other during the '80s it was put out on tape in Germany by VPS Video under the Anglo title **MIDNIGHT HORROR**.

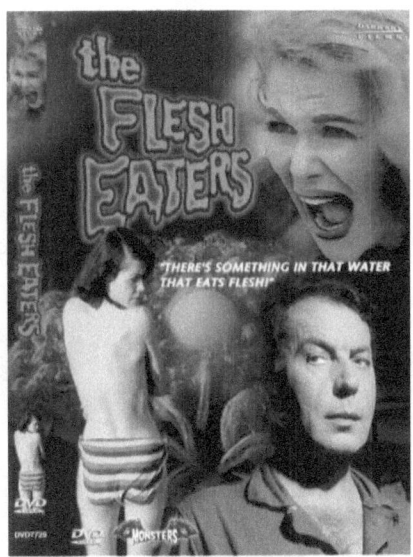

The rather slipshod quickie cover to Dark Sky's otherwise decent DVD edition

The following paragraph of additional video info about **F '80** comes courtesy of our valued pal and contrib Dennis Capicik via his review of the film at his cool Canuck trash/cult movie website Unpopped Cinema (@ *unpoppedcinema. blogspot.ca*). Beginning with a disclaimer about the film's new HD transfer, some (quote) "short scenes were no longer available on 35mm film and had to be inserted from an inferior source", which in this case was a grainy VHS videocassette. Apart from these thankfully-only-brief inserted scenes (including longer-lingering extra bits of nudity and gore), which jar quite noticeably with the bulk of the film's transfer print proper, '84 Entertainment's Blu-ray is most definitely worth the upgrade. Miles better than any other version on the market, all of **FRANKENSTEIN '80**'s previously problematic day-for-night scenes come through just fine here, and will serve as a real revelation to anyone familiar with Gorgon's long-out-of-print, badly pan-and-scanned fullscreen VHS tape. Detail on the Blu is excellent, with stable, robust colors, an aspect which only helps better accentuate all the glistening viscera and stage blood on display. This is also the first time (at least to English-language viewers) that the film has been made available in its original widescreen aspect ratio, which makes for a far-less-confining and claustrophobically constricting viewing experience all-round. The LPCM 2.0 audio is also available in both German and English language options, although the English track does feature some audible hiss, but overall it sounds just fine in light of the film's obvious relatively primitive technical attributes,

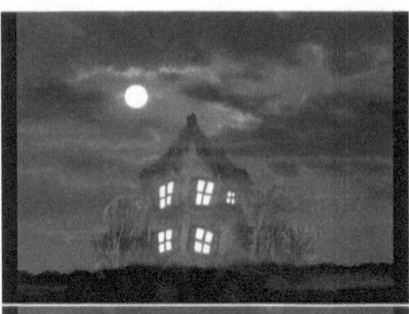
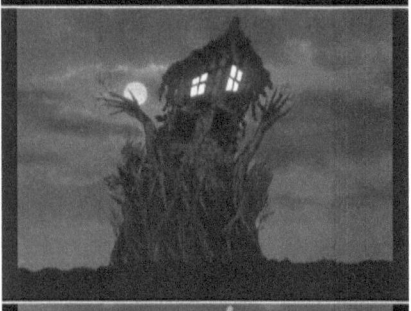
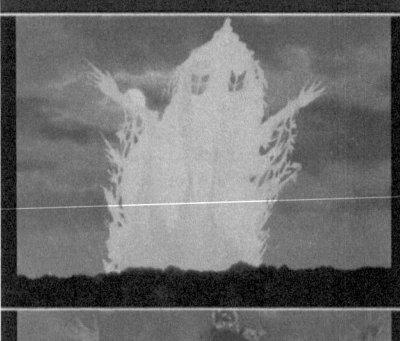
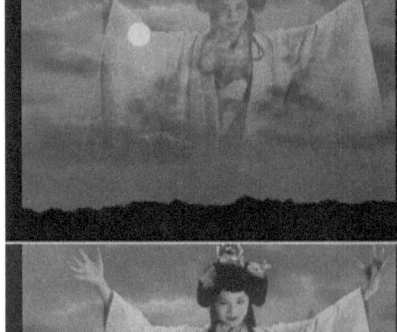

whose shortcomings would have been apparent enough (perhaps more-so) even on the film's original theatrical release. Extras include a fairly beat-up, but most-welcome original trailer, with some brief German narration; alternate opening credits from the US and German (as **MIDNIGHT HORROR**) VHS versions (3m30s), which really makes you appreciate just how fine this new transfer is; a brief gallery (1m07s) of the entire set of Italian *fotobuste* (see pic on p.285); plus 'lost film scenes', which are all the extra inserted scenes, including surrounding context (3m55s). Apart from one extra brief artwork gallery (57s) of video and promotional art present only on the DVD, both discs include the same transfer and extras. Available in three separate Mediabook editions, Cover A (limited to 333 copies) features a nice, retro-styled rendition of the film's original German VPS (Video Program Service) VHS videocassette, while Covers B (222 copies) and Cover C (250 copies) feature, respectively, the French Mike Hunter VHS artwork and French theatrical poster art. – **Dennis Capicik** (Thanks, Denzo! ☺)

FRANKENSTEIN 2000: AFTER DEATH (1991) *[p.281]* – Released on domestic (?) DVD in a Limited Edition by No Fear Video under the title **FRANKENSTEIN 2000: RETURN FROM DEATH**, this was formerly also extant on DVD from Laser Universe in Germany under the shortened title of simply **FRANKENSTEIN 2000**, in grossly deceptive cover art, and that so-called "Red Edition" came with both German and English audio track options. The film's up for grabs on YouTube at the link "Frankenstein 2000 - Return from Death (1991)" (@ *https://www.youtube.com/watch?v=hizXAg8MtY0*), and there are recent-vintage on-camera interviews clips with the movie's uncredited co-writer at the link "Return to death Frankenstein 2000 di Joe D'amato Intervista ad Antonio Tentori" (@ *https://www.youtube.com/watch?v=yQ0QzO2PtCU*) to be found on the excellent Italocentric channel Film&Clips, which legitimately posts SHITLOADS of Italian (s)exploitation movie material on YT (by no means only horror or monster fare, but sometimes), oftentimes either in English-dubbed versions, or with English subs, but sometimes even un-dubbed/un-subbed in other languages too. You never know what you might stumble upon there. So by all means become a subscriber! (But don't bother telling 'em we sent

Home Is Where The Horror Is! A strip of consecutive screen captures from Criterion's lovely Blu-ray of **HOUSE**, depicting the title barmy building's metamorphosis into something formed of a whole lot more than merely bricks and mortar you though, cuz they won't have a fuckin' clue who we are! ☺) NB. Rather than being freebies like most of F&C's content, I've noticed that a small percentage of their Anglo-friendly postings can only be rented VOD for a small fee though, so consider yourself warned.

HOUSE (1977) *[pp.306-321]* – Available in a deluxe edition with all the fixings from The Criterion Collection, either in the Blu-ray or DVD formats (albeit only in its original aspect ratio of 1.37:1 rather than widescreen). So what you waiting for?! It's a mega-monsterpiece of truly unique and unforgettable proportions, and you can't help but love it. If you *don't*, we'll revoke your damn *M!* subscription… assuming we *had* any. ☺ Officially licensed from Toho Co. Ltd., this film was released on British/Irish Region 2 DVD in 2010 by Eureka! as part of their The Masters of Cinema Series. Their edition included a number of the special features that also appeared on Criterion's edition. Their back cover hype imaginatively described **HOUSE** as *"An unforgettable mixture of bubblegum teen melodrama and grisly phantasmagoria."* At the Amazon.com link entitled "House (English Subtitled) 1976", the film can be either rented in SD/HD (for $2.99/$3.99) or purchased in SD/HD (for $14.99/$19.99).

THE INTRUDER WITHIN (1981) *[p.303]* – TWE's rather unimaginative back cover tagline for their '84 domestic videotape release: *"Terror And Death Strike As Monster Preys Upon Trapped Victims"*. Victim's dialogue: *"I think it's inside me!"* Nope, time's been none-too-kind to this one, which didn't have much going for it the first time round, and doesn't even have any real cred as throwback 'retro' fare nowadays either, what with all the competition that's still being dredged up from the depths of the pop cultural barrel on a regular basis. Among the earliest wannabe **ALIEN** (1979, UK/USA) clones, I remember watching this first-run on its initial ABC-TV airing back in '81 and being far from impressed by it; quite the opposite, in fact (to put it mildly!). Rather than on a massive intergalactic space vessel—a much-too-costly milieu by far for a modest-budgeted telly production such as this to pull off, so why even try?!—the setting is instead an extraterrestrial offshore oilrig (owned by the unlikely-sounding Zortron mega-corporation) situated somewhere in the Antarctic Ocean. It should be said that the atypical and authentic milieu, while a potentially interesting one, is utilized with virtually no verve or imagination whatsoever, so the action might just as well have been set in a shopping mall (or even a library) and nobody would know the difference. After drilling close to 20,000 feet into the seabed, the rig ("Zortron

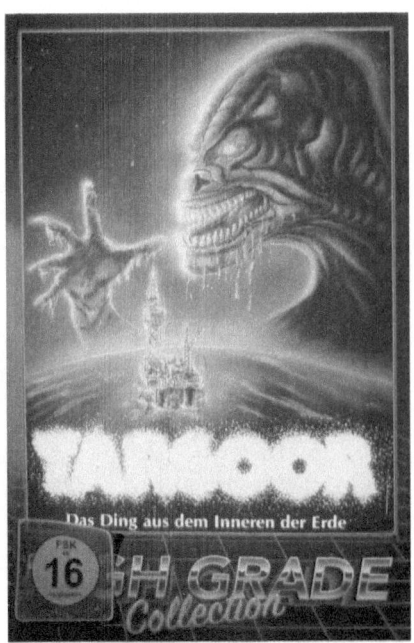

THE INTRUDER WITHIN German DVD 1

101") unleashes a whole lot more—in this case, less *isn't* more, unfortunately—than just crude oil up on the surface. The roughnecks (led by seasoned veterans Chad Everett and Rockne Tarkington) first become aware that something is amiss when a roaring oversized pollywog—"sea lamprey of some sort", my ass!—with teeth fatally chomps ahold of one of their co-workers, to get curtly blasted dead by a Very pistol. Before you know it, the chestnut-shell-like eggs (pedantically described by way-too-young in-house 'expert' Joseph Bottoms—who wildly under- and overacts by turns—as "carapaces") of "idiomorphic lifeforms" begin cracking open… In retrospect, it's not *quite* the all-out stinker/sinker I originally summarily dismissed it as with a contemptuous snort way back when, but it's still not much to get excited about nonetheless, registering as little more than an often shrilly-overacted, insincere and opportunistic quickie cash-in that was thrown together in way too much of a hurry for any of it to register with much conviction and largely just comes across as shallow and insincere. Without shitting all over the present one too much, let's just say that there were some far-more-enjoyable, if even lower-budgeted **ALIEN** imitations that received actual theatrical releases during the same period, and they were much more worthy of a monster maven's time (and disposable income): for instance, Bill Malone's **SCARED TO DEATH** (1980), Allan Holzman's **FORBIDDEN WORLD** (1982) and

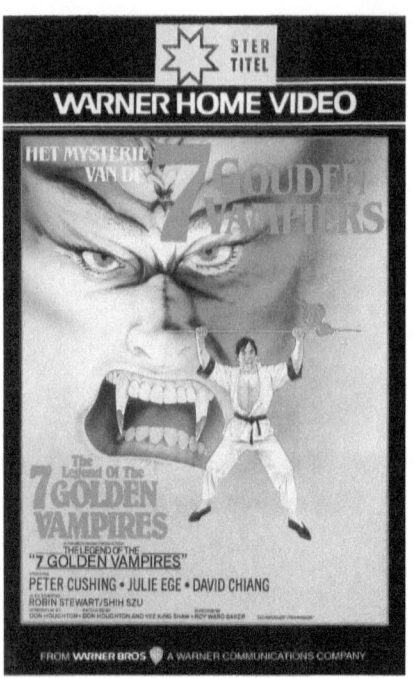

THE LEGEND OF THE 7 GOLDEN VAMPIRES Dutch VHS cover

Jackie Kong's **THE BEING** (1983, all USA), to name only three. And, yep, as is so typical of its type, **TIW**'s supposedly constantly-morphing main monster takes positively *forever* to show up, and when it finally does—about a mere six minutes before the end, FFS!—it's barely worth the wait (although the Gigeresque suit [worn by seasoned stuntman Joe Finnegan] does look pretty cool, what we can see of it, and should have gotten more screen-time in better light). For a low-grade, soon-forgotten American made-for-TV movie that garnered only fair-to-middling ratings (if that) on its original broadcast, however, **THE INTRUDER WITHIN** (a.k.a. **THE LUCIFER RIG** or **ALIEN RIG**) received a surprisingly broad home video release. It was initially issued domestically on Betamax/VHS videocassette in an oversized clamshell-box edition by the stateside wing of Trans World Entertainment (TWE) in 1984. Licensed through TWE U.S.A. during the same period, it was put out in the same cassette formats in Australia (and presumably New Zealand too?) by Video Classics as part of their "Gold" series, hyped with the unimaginative ad-blurb *"An Alien Experience"* so as to better emphasize and exploit the already obvious allusions to Ridley Scott's **ALIEN**. Formerly available on Beta/VHS in the Netherlands via TWE, Inc., with English dialogue and Dutch subtitles, and in Japan from Toshiba Video, in English with Japanese subs, it was also released on tape in Italy by De Laurentiis Ricordi Video under the title **IL TERRORE VIENE DAL PASSATO** ("Terror from Out of the Past"). Coming solely with a native audio track with no subs of any kind, the film was issued on DVD in Germany as part of NUM's High Grade Collection under the typically fanciful German retitle of **TARGOOR – DAS DING AUS DEM INNEREN DER ERDE** ("Targoor – The Thing from Within the Earth"), hyped with the tagline *"Ein Science-Fiction-Horror der Extraklasse"* (no translation needed!). It was also put out with the same specs by the same label as the top half of a "2for1" double-bill DVD, paired-up with **WINDIGO – DIE NACHT DES GRAUENS** (the Germanic title for Jim Makichuk's cheap-but-effective, aboriginal folklore-themed Canuck horror flick **GHOSTKEEPER** [1981]). A Spanish-dubbed clamshell edition of **TIW** was released on tape in Spain under the title **EL INTRUSO** ("The Intruder") by TWE/Videostar. For those who have trouble scoring a legit copy of this film—don't bother expending too much energy (or dough!) trying to do so, as chances are you'll be disappointed!—as of this writing a fairly decent rip/upload of TWE's old videotape version was available for viewing gratis on YouTube at the link entitled "The Intruder Within (1981)" (@ *https://www.youtube.com/watch?v=-08gvh-JG2Yk*).

LAPACHHAPI (2017) *[pp.201-206]* – As of this writing, this still-fairly-recent theatrical release hasn't yet been released on disc in its country of origin (India), but a page for it on the Induna retail site (@ *www.induna.com*) says that an All-Region DVD of it is (quote) "Coming Soon".

THE LEGEND OF THE 7 GOLDEN VAMPIRES (1974) *[p.255]* – Trailer hype for the film (under its US alternate release title **THE 7 BROTHERS MEET DRACULA** [a.k.a. **THE 7 BROTHERS AND THEIR ONE SISTER MEET DRACULA**]): *"Black Belt Against Black Magic... in the Greatest Battle of All Time as The 7 Brothers and Their One Sister Meet Dracula! While vampires drink the blood of the virgins and turn them into zombies! You haven't seen kung fu until you've seen the seven brothers and their one sister in action against Dracula! ...Die, Dracula, die! See the ten-thousand-year-old monster disintegrate before your eyes as the seven brothers and their one sister meet Dracula!"* Shaws character actor Chan Shen appears as Kah, a wandering Chinese pilgrim who visits the Count (John Forbes-Robertson) at Castle Dracula in the Carpathians looking to become his disciple, only to have the racist Drac—shades of the prologue to **BLACULA** (1972, USA, D: William

Crain)—contemptuously dismiss him as an inferior before then assuming the Chinaman's identity as his own for a cover, then relocating to Mainland China to spread the plague of vampirism throughout Asia. Formidable MA mama Shi Szu co-stars as "little sister" Mai Kwei (pronounced "May Kway"—as in "Make way, boys, cuz I'm comin' through, ready or not!"). Her white colonialist BF Leyland Van Helsing (Robin Stewart), a man of heroic mettle who is far from a slouch himself, says to her at one point in adoring admiration, "You're like a beautiful porcelain kitten. Then suddenly you're a fighting tigress. It's *incredible*!" (Talk about place her on a pedestal there, buddy!) Playing a character who is equal parts femininely ladylike and tomboyishly tough and feisty when needed—the BEST kinda female known to Man! (*Hubba-hubba!*)—sex bomb Scandinavian 'Seventies scream queen Julie Ege (1943-2008) is suitably delish as Chiang's cuddlesomely comely *gweilo*/roundeye love interest. Much in the manner of a Filipino *aswang*, against which it is has long been a tried-and-trusted offensive/defensive weapon, a sharpened bamboo spear (known in Tagalog as *bagacay* or *sibat*) is used to do-in the sixth and penultimate vampire. MA sequences were staged by highly prolific long-time Shaw Brothers employees Tang Chia (1937-) and Liu Chia-liang (1936-2013), whose credits within the *wuxia* genre are too numerous to count. In one memorably realistic moment in the present hybrid one, either by accident or design (i.e., as per the script [though it looks purely accidental to me]), Cushing momentarily stumbles and falls into a flaming campfire, only to immediately leap to his feet again and wade back into the fray swinging like the total trouper he was. Not only did this one-of-a-kind prototype spawn a number of variations / imitations in the Hong Kong (and especially Taiwanese) film industry, it also provides a neat forerunner to the HK "hopping vampire" (殭屍 / *jiangshi*) craze that really got started about a decade later and got some pretty good mileage. More recently (in 2013) made available on DVD stateside via Millennium Entertainment, **TLOT7GV** was first issued domestically on disc in a pretty nice widescreen (2.35:1) edition by Starz / Anchor Bay Entertainment back in the embryonic period of the DVD era in 1999 (the year previous, the same outfit had put it out on VHS). Before that, it was released on Beta/VHS cassette on North American shores by both American Video and Media Home Entertainment, as well as the 'cheapie' label Genesis Home Video. Something Weird Video (SWV) were also offering a tape edition somewhere along the line. Fascinatingly enough, following this their first and only Asian-set horror co-production, Hammer Films was planning to produce a follow-up project—first proposed prior to **7 GOLDEN VAMPIRES** as far back as 1970—to be called "DRACULA AND THE BLOODLUST OF KALI" (also announced in '76 as "KALI, DEVIL BRIDE OF

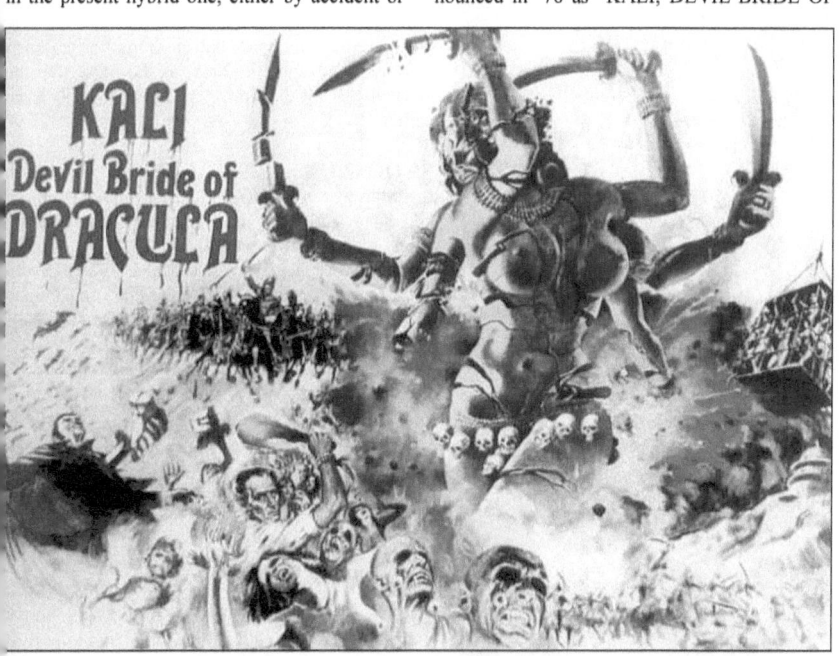

Concept art by Tom Chantrell for the aborted English-Asian follow-up to **THE LEGEND OF THE 7 GOLDEN VAMPIRES**, with yet another flavour of the UK's colonial period gone weird

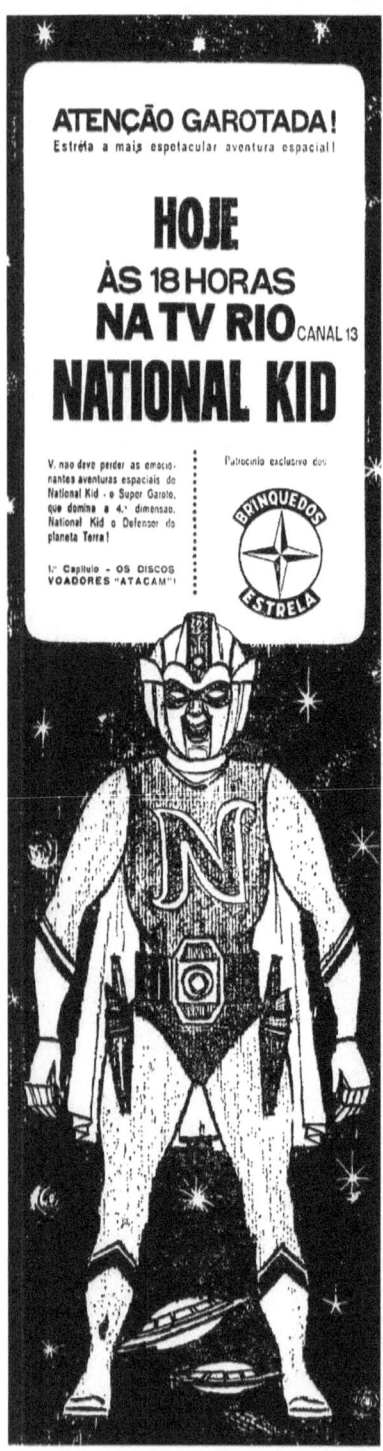

National Kid Brazilian TV guide ad

DRACULA"), which would be set in India rather than China. The studio's frequent conceptual poster artist Tom Chantrell (who is equally famous for his wraparound cover to Denis Gifford's seminal genre tome *A Pictorial History of Horror Movies* [UK: Hamlyn, 1973] as he is for his many, many painterly renderings for British movie posters) even went so far as to render artwork for the film's advertising campaign (see p.343), and his spectacular surviving illustrations clearly depict a likeness of Peter Cushing in the thick of their action, indicating that the star was hoped to return for seconds with/against Drac in another exotic Asiatic scenario. I'd imagine Tim P. would be most interested indeed in seeing this sadly unrealized proposition reach completion. I know I sure wish it'd gotten made! ☻ *That could have been a very cool film, and it would have been interestung to see who they would have teamed up with in the possible Anglo-Indian production, considering so very few horror films were made by Indian directors at the time. - Tim P.*

MIGHTY JOE YOUNG (1949) *[pp.235-247]* – As far as I'm (i.e., SF) concerned, I'm more than happy with the 'bonus' copy of **MJY** that came included in my DVD multi-pack box set entitled "The King Kong Collection", a 3-disc steal-of-a-deal put out in a nice-looking slipcase back in 2005 by Warner Home Video / Turner Entertainment Co. that also includes both **KING KONG** '33 and its same-year quickie sequel **SON OF KONG**, plus scads upon scads of extra features (including reconstructions of **KK**'s famous missing sequences). But for those that want it, **MJY** did come out on domestic Region A Blu-ray via Warners in 2015, as did **SOK** too (the original **KK** hit that format in 2010, possibly even earlier).

NATIONAL KID (1960) *[pp.97-125]* – Though there have been various VHS iterations of *National Kid*, its producer Toei did not get around to releasing a long-overdue DVD set of it until 2015. It is a 5-disc set of very decent quality quality (see p.125 pic, center & bottom), despite some persistent scratches and other unavoidable artifacts of aging. The set comes with a booklet which includes introductory info, character bios and descriptions for every episode. As is typical of Japanese DVDs, the cost of the set is very high, with an MSRP of ¥ 25,920 (about $233.00 US!). On *Amazon.jp* it goes for about 25% off, and can be found on aftermarket sites like *yahoo.jp* for even less. I got mine for about $80. It is still in print, and easy to find online. Be forewarned, though: the set does NOT come with subtitles of any kind! As for the Brazilian edition of *NK*—which had debuted on the TV Rio network on May 8th, 1964—Brazil has had a notorious history of putting out sub-par and oddball DVD collections, and *National Kid* is no different. Though, as I mentioned in my article elsewhere herein, beating Japan to getting the series

Video Availability Information

out on DVD by several years, the various versions were based on old VHS copies, and did *not* look good. One set claimed to contain new prints, with both Portuguese and Japanese audio and with Portuguese subtitles—but actually *didn't*, on any of those counts. But then in 2010, Focus Filmes put out a set which may well stand as the definitive one; a large tin box set with seven discs that even included a National Kid baseball cap! While the first two discs (the "Attack of the Incas" story) have restored individual episodes in Japanese with Portuguese subtitles, the next two discs ("Deep Sea Devil Nelkon" [a.k.a. "Deepsea Devil Nerukon"] and "Underground Demon Castle" stories) are in the Portuguese language only, with Portuguese subtitles. Both storylines were edited-down into two feature-length movies rather than being left in individual episodes. Then the last two discs of the series go back to individual, restored episodes again, in Japanese- and Portuguese-language, with subtitles. The seventh disc is a fan-edit of the Venusian Incas story into a fast-paced movie, plus comes with other extras besides. There's good news and bad news about getting ahold of the Brazilian DVD set, though. It is very cheap by US standards at R80 (Brazilian Real), which equals only about $25.00 US. But it's no easy task to either find or buy! None of the aftermarket sellers ship outside of Brazil, and because it is OOP, none of the big online retail stores have it in stock. What I had to do was contact someone in Brazil who was willing to ship it to me in California. International shipping from Brazil (which was around $60) is where most of the costs were incurred. Once again, just so you know, there are NO English subtitles! Luckily enough, if your only (or primary) language is English, there is a fansub version of the series (@ *nationalkid.blogspot.com*), which seems to be based off of the Portuguese DVDs, since the language and episode lengths/movie versions are exactly as those described above in the Focus Filmes box set. – **Dan Ross**

THE OUTER LIMITS (1963-65) *[pp.35-69]* – Just last month (March), Kino Classics issued Season 1 (all 32 episodes) of this seminal, monster-filled, must-have SF/horror show on Blu-ray, with Season 2 to follow. As for its DVD availability, *TOL* has long been out domestically in that format, and is frequently available at very reasonable prices (I [SF] got my copy of S1 in a clamshell box edition for a mere 20 bucks Canuck at a Toronto area Walmart back in about 2005 or so, and was elated to find it). However, in 2015 an Australian edition was released that unexpectedly proved to be All-Region and is playable on North American machines as well, despite the slipcover's claim that it is formatted for "PAL Region 4" only (reportedly, copies come with stickers attached to the shrink-wrap that correct this bit of misinformation). And not only that, but, unlike the stateside boxed sets—which are burned to inferior dual-sided discs (7

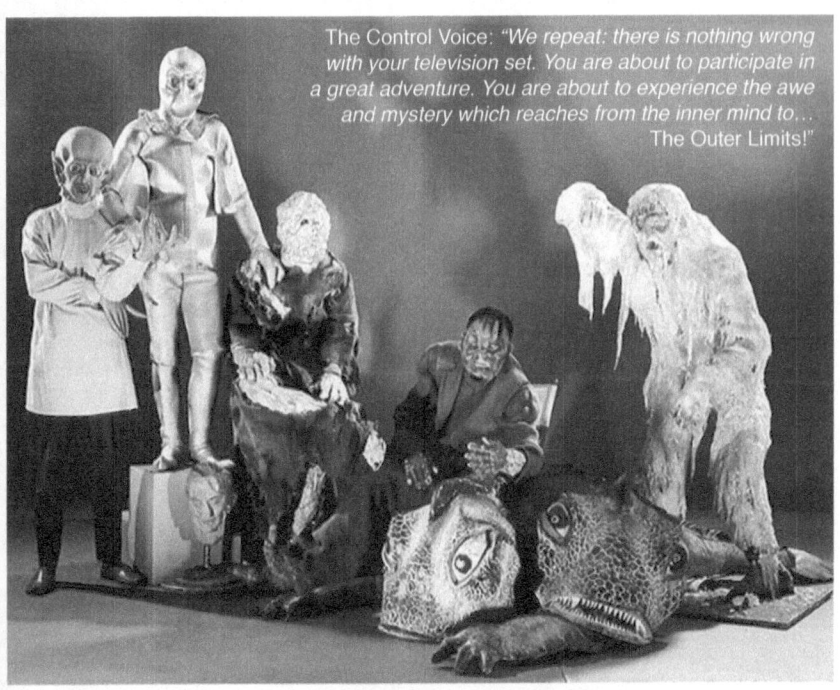

The Control Voice: *"We repeat: there is nothing wrong with your television set. You are about to participate in a great adventure. You are about to experience the awe and mystery which reaches from the inner mind to... The Outer Limits!"*

in total) which can be problematic—the Aussie edition is contained on 14 *single*-sided DVDs instead, and the quality is all the better for it. Most of the customer reviews we scanned-over at Amazon had nothing but glowing things to say about the Australian set, although we did notice one person complaining that one of the discs in theirs wouldn't play in their PS3, while the others did (the same person also says that all the discs played fine in their Blu-ray player, though). So basically, you pays your money and you takes your chances, but it sounds like a pretty good deal to us!

THE SECRET OF THE MUMMY (1982) *[p.298]* – Your guess is as good as ours where to get your hands on an original legit disc or tape copy of this bit of brazen Brazilian bizarrity, but it was previously released on Latin-American (and/or Spanish, as in Spain?) viddy cassette by Video Amanacer (VA) under the title **EL SECRETO DE LA MOMIA** (the direct Hispanic translation of its original Portuguese title, **O SEGREDO DA MÚMIA**), and there is a very nice English-subbed (*YAYYYYYY!!!*) rip of it currently uploaded to YouTube at the link entitled "O segredo da múmia (Ivan Cardoso, 1983)" (@ *https://www.youtube.com/watch?v=uU-9ff-N8_6I*), on the Filmoteca Zé do Caixão—of all places!—channel for those who want it ("Zé do Caixão" a.k.a. José Mojica Marins guest-stars in the film). In 1987, **TSOTM** was put out on Beta and VHS cassette in Japan under the Anglo title **NIGHT OF THE LIVING MUMMY** (plus its equivalent in Japanese *kanji*) by Sony Video Software International/Mount Light Corp., with its original Portuguese audio and Japanese subtitles. For those who are interested in checking-out more of Brazilian filmmaker Ivan Cardoso's work—and there's absolutely no reason why you shouldn't be!—a decent-quality upload of his fun, fast-paced flick **THE SCARLET SCORPION** (*O Escorpião Escarlate*, 1990, Brazil), which—*BONUS!*—again comes with nice clear English subs, can also be found on YT at the link entitled "O Escorpiao Escarlate 1990" (@ *https://www.youtube.com/watch?v=FekELDtq4aU*). It's a zany, anything-goes superhero spoof—with gratuitous T&A!—done in a camped-up old-Hollywood serialesque style, that contains no actual monsters but comes with all sorts of other vintage sci-fi and horror movie trappings and tropes nonetheless, so it's well-worth a *Monster!* reader's time. Albeit only in Portuguese without subs of any kind, there is also a nice widescreen—if severely-edited, only 77m—rip of Cardoso's saucy bloodsucker spoof **THE 7 VAMPIRES** (*As Sete Vampiras*, 1986, Brazil)—no relation to **THE LEGEND OF THE 7 GOLDEN VAMPIRES** (see separate entry above), needless to say!—up on YT too, at the link titled "As Sete Vampiras - O Filme" (@ *https://www.youtube.com/watch?v=8M5gejBc020*). Even better, there is a much longer (nearly 90m)—AND English-subbed—print of the film on the PD ("public domain") website the Internet Archive at the link "As Sete Vampiras (The 7 Vampires) (English Subtitles)" (@ *https://archive.org/details/AsSeteVampiras*). While full-length prints reportedly run 100m (?), the latter option of **THE 7 VAMPIRES** (a.k.a. **LITTLE SHOP OF TERRORS**) is by far the preferable of the two, despite its considerably lesser image quality. But you could always just watch the subbed version first to get a handle on the plot, then follow up by viewing the copy with the much clearer picture and nicer color (the fuzzier, duller, more anemic IA copy looks to have been struck from an old videotape, while the YT one seems to have come from a newer digital source. I downloaded both!). Guest-starring none other than late Spanish horror king "Paul Naschy"/Jacinto Molina—keep your eyeballs peeled for Troy Howarth / WK Books' career-spanning, lavishly-illustrated tome *Human Beasts: The Films of Paul Naschy* in the very near future!—among Cardoso's more recent genre offerings is **A WEREWOLF IN THE AMAZON** (*Um Lobisomem na Amazônia*, 2005, Brazil), a copy of which is uploaded to YouTube at the link "Filme Um Lobisomem Na Amazônia 2005" (@ *https://www.youtube.com/watch?v=0JgT_52pdGA*). If you use a YT-compatible downloader to download that video rip off the site, you can then d-load English subs (i.e., in the standard ".srt" file format) that match-up perfectly with it at Moviesubtitles.org (@ *http://all4divx.com-www.moviesubtitles.org/subtitle-93336.html*). All you'll need in order to watch both the movie and subs combined in-synch is VLC Media Player, but you'll first need to make sure that both the separate video and subtitles files are identically-named in order for them to work together.

SILVER HERMIT FROM SHAOLIN TEMPLE (1979) *[p.250]* – In the original typically sub-par Saturn videotape version, their transfer print was laterally 'squished' from a wider-screen aspect ratio down to just 1.33:1 ("full-frame"), resulting in a noticeably vertically-elongated image that makes everyone and everything look taller/skinnier than they should be. The handy thing about that is, being as a not-bad-quality rip of Saturn's old 'scrunched' copy of **SHFST** has been uploaded to YouTube (@ *https://www.youtube.com/watch?v=q_PChqM6qbI*), if you happen to have a YT downloader (such as SaveFromNetHelper, say) and are a user of the ever-handy-dandy and versatile VLC Media Player ("The Swiss Knife")—if you don't have either of these generally highly-reliable shareware programs, they're easy enough to get via free d-loads online—all you then need to do is download the copy of **SHFST** at said site then open it in VLC and set its aspect ratio to "16:9" in the scroll-down video setup menu, and—*VOILA!*—you get to watch it in a ratio much closer to its original theatrical one. While apparently still not at its full widescreen dimensions (?), things are a lot less claustrophobically cramped/crunched and everything appears considerably more properly proportionate. There. How's *that* for a useful tip c/o of we ye considerate *Monster!* eds, eh?!

TICKS (1996) *[p.267]* – According to director Tony Randel, this film—which represented a real 'step backward' for him not so many years on after directing his best-known effort, the bigger-budgeted / higher-profile **HELLBOUND: HELLRAISER II** (1988, UK/USA)—did receive a very limited theatrical screening, but since it was produced during the time when (quote) "things were changing", it was made more with the home video market in mind. Upon debuting on Beta/VHS videocassette in 1996 courtesy of Republic Pictures Home Video, **TICKS** managed to find a small-but-loyal fanbase, no doubt due in large part to its many gooey, gory F/X. The film also sold well all around the world, and has seen releases in such faraway places as Argentina, entitled **GARRAPATAS ASESINAS** ("Killer Ticks"), and in Hungary as **BOGÁRINVÁZIÓ** ("Beetle Invasion"). Not first made available on disc until its simultaneous DVD-slash-Blu-ray release in 2013 through the equally surprising Olive Films, **TICKS** really looks *immaculate* in this MPEG-4 AVC-encoded 1080p transfer, which is also presented in a nice spacious 1.78:1 aspect ratio. The glistening, gelatinous goo really 'pops' off the screen, while the added granular clarity of the transfer even reveals some heretofore-less-apparent shortcomings of the enthusiastic if out-of-necessity economical FX. The DTS-MA mono audio also sounds clear and free of any distortion, which is particularly active during the climactic massed tick siege. As with most Olive releases, extras are sparse, but this disc includes a lively audio commentary from director Randel and actor Clint Howard, which is nicely moderated by Mondo Digital's Nathaniel Thompson. Some of the subjects they touch on include the genesis of the project, which came to Randel via producer Jack Murphy; the film's original title, "INFESTED" (which was ad-libbed by Howard in the film when, his whole face distorted by ticks that have burrowed beneath his skin, laughs maniacally, "I'm *infested*! HAHAHAHAHAHA-HA!!!" [see top pic, p.269]); the large amount of post-production work and reshoots of the film to (quote) "better fill-out the story"; the various special effects work and technicians whom Randel amusingly refers to as "the goo guys"; the changing climate for low-budget films of the time; and also guest star Howard's contribution to the film, which amounted to a mere single day's work. For some strange reason, considering Olive's large and ever-expanding catalogue of titles (which includes many *film noir* classics), **TICKS** (along with four of their other titles) is currently out-of-print, and it now fetches some very high prices on both Amazon and eBay. – **Dennis Capicik**

WOLF GUY: ENRAGED LYCANTHROPE (1975) *[p.294]* – First made available in May of 2017 on both dual format Region A/1 + B/2 Blu-ray and DVD from Arrow Video (order in the UK @ http://bit.ly/2rmhFUu and in the USA @ http://bit.ly/2rm1FCe). Arrow's first-time-ever Anglo edition of this funky/flaky flick, which still succeeds in entertaining despite its complete lack of any werewolf makeup whatsoever, comes with some noteworthy extras (including on-camera interviews with director Kazuhiko Yamaguchi and producer Toru Yoshida, as well as a reversible jacket with the optional original Japanese B2 poster art [seen on p.298] or Wes Benscoter's newly-commissioned original artwork), and their all-new trailer for the disc release—loudly accompanied by a blistering instrumental excerpt from Goblin's raucously rockin' track "The Quick and the Dead" (from Argento's **PHENOMENA** [1985, Italy]), of all things!—can be viewed on YT at the link entitled "Wolf Guy - The Arrow Video Story" (@ https://www.youtube.com/watch?v=EzsJaqmZua4).

YOUNG-GOO AND DINOSAUR ZUZU (1993) *[p.275]* – There are a pair of viewing options on YT for this kooky Korean kiddie kaiju novelty item, neither of which—perhaps unsurprisingly—come with any subtitles (or few *subtleties* either, for that matter!). So who needs subs anyway?). You can access either a three-part upload (starting at the link "Young Gu And The Dinosaur Zuzu part 1" [@ https://www.youtube.com/watch?v=1erA8pDTSb8] and proceeding from there), or else choose a somewhat nicer-quality, only two-part alternate upload of same at the link "영구와 땡칠이 1탄 (1부) Yong Gu And Daeng Chiri (1989)" (@ https://www.youtube.com/watch?v=Vv_xkabbEec). Luckily, simply keying-in the English characters of that latter title is enough to take you right to it without needing to resort to finding the Korean ones as well. For some reason or other, however, as of this writing there are two otherwise identically-titled links to uploads of different-length versions of Part 1 at the site (one at a runtime of 40:55, the other at 39:07)... but we're sure you can figure it out.

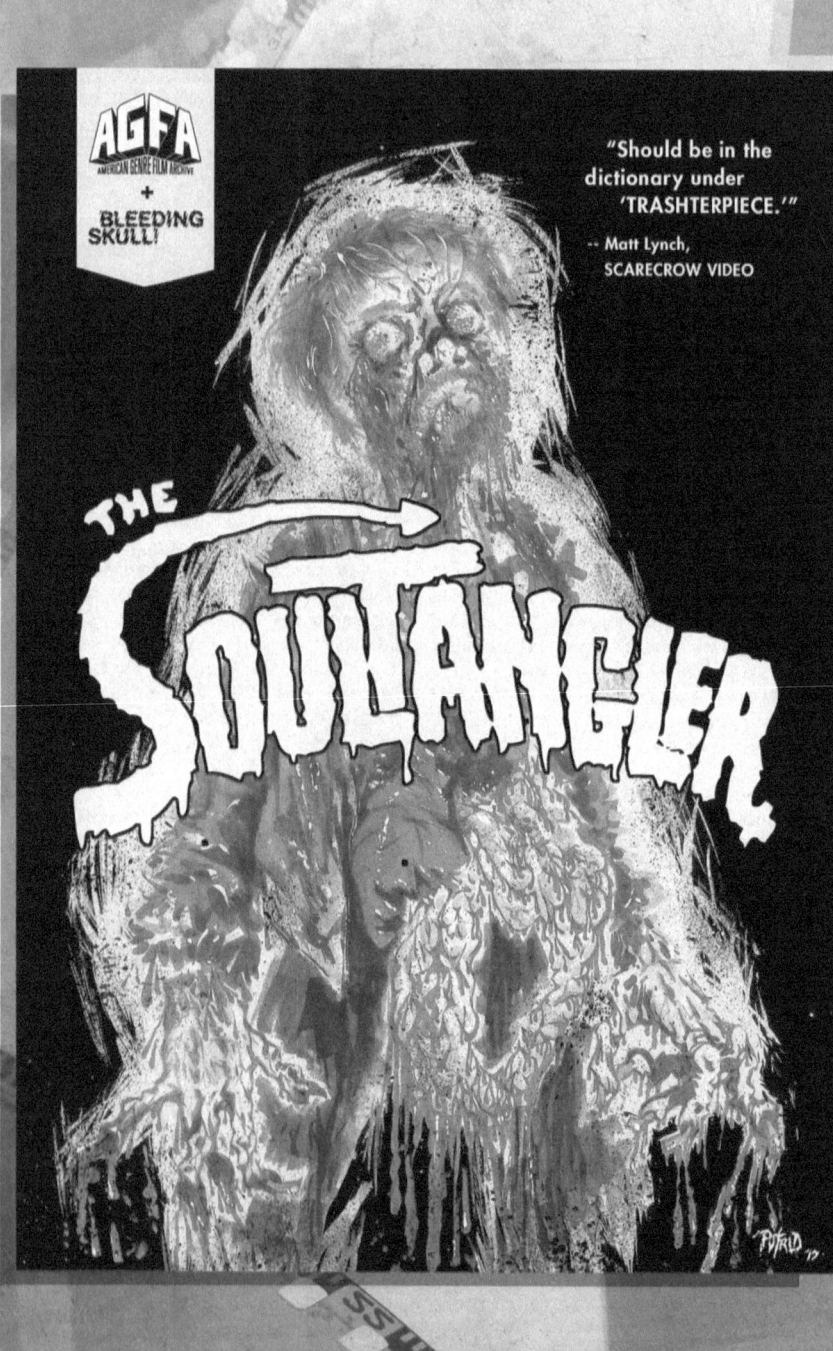

NEW FEATURE!!!
MIDNIGHT SNACKS

Editor's Note: *This ish sees the genesis—if that's not too grandiose a term!—of a brand-new (if far-from-innovative) regular section here in* Monster! *(by* **SF***) that shall cover, in more capsule form than our longer reviews found elsewhere in these pages, various movies we've (i.e., I've ☺) recently viewed in various media formats which pertain to our main theme, but are not otherwise individually covered elsewhere in the mag anyplace. This allows us (= ME! ☺☺) to rattle-on a bit about whatever titles have taken our (i.e., MY!! ☺☺☺) fancy of late and which we (= I!!! ☺☺☺☺) felt were deserving of a shout-out, but couldn't be bothered—Oops! Sorry: "didn't have the time", I meant—to do-up full-length reviews for. If this feature generates any extra interest among readers whatsoever (even an iota; that's all it takes!), we will quite likely extend invitations to our stable of regular contributors to do 'guest spots' here in future issues. So if anyone feels up to the challenge, by all means let We Ye Eds know, okay?*

THE BEAST FROM THE BEGINNING OF TIME (1965, USA, D: Tom Leahy, Jr.) – Dialogue clip: *"This beast kills like a wild animal, but it is human...!"* First things first, for all its faults—and these days there are MANY, what with its would-be monopolistic owner/operator Google's increasingly intolerable (and intolerant, ever-more-restrictive) ongoing attempts at censorship, and its demonetization of 'non-PC' channels (etc.) there—YouTube is nevertheless still a great place for dedicated pop culture crawlers like me to surf in hopes of turning-up some heretofore 'unknown' or 'unseen' artifact from a bygone era and/or exotic clime. Although this particular obscurity hails from the good ol' U.S. of A., so it doesn't exactly qualify as 'exotica' by usual standards, it definitely *is* the product of a whole other age and very much of its time. Shot in B&W on actual celluloid and regionally-produced (by/for KARD TV in Wichita, Kansas, of all places, using local talent) in the mid-1960s, **TBFTBOT** not surprisingly harkens back to the preceding decade, as many a '60s creature feature was known to still do at that time. At a rural excavation led by the cantankerous, antisocial and just plain hateful archaeologist Prof. Maury (Dick Welsbacher), the diggers unearth a fossilized prehistoric (i.e., guesstimated at being up to 60,000,000-year-old [!]) human hand projecting from the ground, and the find is dug out in its entirety still encased inside the block of ancient shale in which it was discovered. Superstitious Hispanic laborers employed at the dig suspect the thing in the rock to be "*el diablo*", however the learned gringo scientists are of a different opinion: that the amazingly well-preserved being locked in the rock is some sort of missing link in Man's evolution, vastly predating all other known finds ("Imagine! A man, a perfect Neanderthal type, living right in the middle of the reptilian age! ... This fella knocks every accepted evolutionary theory into a cocked hat!" – "That corpse is going to revise all scientific thinking as to Man's first hour on the evolutionary timetable. Darwin be damned...!"). The boffins further theorize—being rather too unquestioningly certain about it, it should

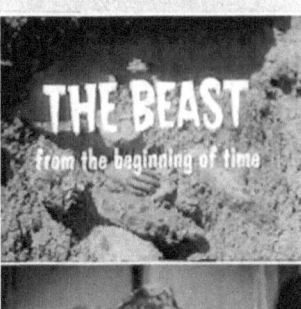

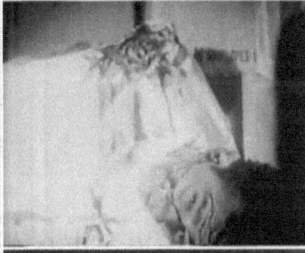

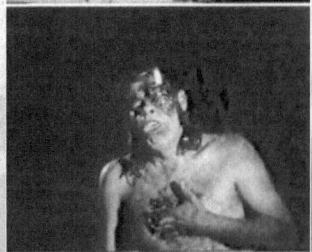

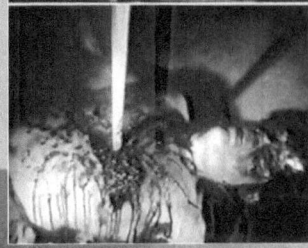

be said—that this missing link may have been struck and killed by a bolt of lightning then fallen into a swamp, which served to preserve his dead body ("...perfectly intact!") for countless millennia. Rather than donate their newly-found priceless artifact to a museum, the amoral Maury instead uses blackmail to force his subordinate Dr. Randall to collaborate with him in making-off with the (quote) "reptile man" (so-called not because it's part-lizard in physiognomy, but rather because it was dug out of geological strata also containing dinosaurs fossils) so that they can make a fortune off touring it on public exhibition. However, before they can do this, the formerly immobile, believed long-dead caveman—which had actually only been in a state of suspended animation due to its freak cause of death, preserved 'bogman'-style—makes off with *itself* by up and absconding in the dead of night, after having evidently been liberated from its shale tomb by first being soaked with rainwater and thus rehydrated then revivified by lightning during a nocturnal torrential downpour. "We never should've taken it from the earth! It's against nature! We gotta *bury* it again, Maury!" rants-'n'-raves the now-gone-hysterical Dr. Crawford, having witnessed *it* ("What does he mean, 'it'?!") go for a little walk, albeit firmly off-screen. Because his explanation of the find's disappearance is disbelieved by his associates, Randall winds up being charged for murdering the dig's labor contractor, Cletus Henderson. This first victim is found bloodily murdered with a shovel stuck in his chest, pinned standing-up to the back of a pickup truck by it, which was a pretty gruesome way to go for a vintage made-for-TV movie. (Indeed, a surprising amount of blood is seen over the course the film; clearly its registering as only jet-black as opposed to bright red on the monochrome film stock was what made this goriness more permissible to be shown on the small screen. Never is the high gore factor more apparent than in the later scene when the now-deceased Dr. Maury is found by his colleagues with one of his arms torn out at the root, complete with jagged, meaty shoulder-stump and blood-streaked white shirt {[see p.349] shades of a shocking scene in the then-recent theatrical release **THE BRAIN THAT WOULDN'T DIE** [1962, USA, D: Joseph Green}.) Institutionalized as criminally insane, Crandall insists that the caveman was the real culprit in the murder for which he got blamed. "It's got to be buried before it storms again!" he explains in one of his more lucid moments. "It...it *feeds* on the lightning! It's its life! *Bury it!*" he persists, thereafter lapsing back into all-out gibbering dementia once more. "That caveman," laughs the jovially skeptical good ol' boy sheriff at one point. "Y'know, that doggone thing looked as much like a *monkey* as it did a man!" As per our expectations, the titular "Beast" is essentially just yer common-and-garden-variety long-haired, hirsute troglodyte in an animal-hide loincloth, albeit with its face horribly disfigured by the lightning bolt that killed it eons ago. While the actor portraying the brute (no less than **TBFTBOT**'s writer-director Leahy himself) really gives the part his all, he quite frankly fails to come across as very intimidating a menace for the most part, and generally just seems more pathetic than terrifying.

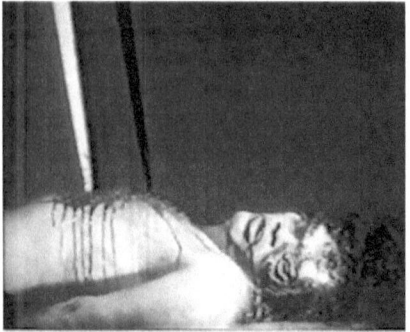

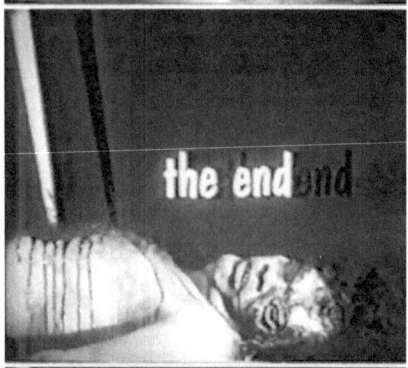

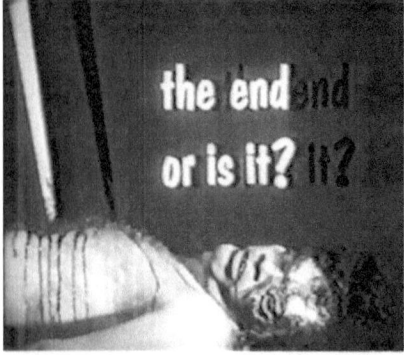

Pages 349-350: Heavily-'ghosted' screen shots from a vid dub of an ancient TV airing of **TBFTBOT**. The 'ghosting' effect was caused by poor antenna reception of the signal (no cable back then!)

ATTENTION: SPOILER ALERT! For the film's goriest scene, unfolding in the paleontology wing of the local museum by night, having been weakened by multiple police gunshots, the ailing beastman is dispatched conclusively when the hero sticks him in the chest—vampire-style!—with one of the sharp spines grabbed from the tail of a (real phony-looking) Stegosaurus skeleton. The oodles of blood (and drool!) seen here must have appeared all the more shocking to contemporaneous audiences, as it's still highly effective today, viscerally speaking. The serviceable script and more-than-tolerable acting are at least on a par with your average "B" or "C"-grade '50s sci-fi/horror outing. In fact, while shot in '65, there is very little on view in it—other than for the excess gruesomeness, of course—to indicate that it mightn't have actually been shot in 1958 instead, that's how snugly this fits into the late '50s Hollywood horror boom in terms of style and tropes, et cetera (a scene showing a teenage couple parked in Lover's Lane making-out in a sports car only to be terrorized by the rampaging monster caveman further cements the '50s connection). **TBFT-BOT**'s post at YT—it's on there broken-up into three separate sections (starting @ *https://www.youtube.com/watch?v=LqSF86QwHwo*)—describes the mostly poor-quality upload (obviously ripped from an old videotape recorded right off the TV 30-odd years ago) thusly: "Very bad reception and even worse recording, but here it is in all its campy, mind-boggling splendor". Here's hoping a much nicer copy surfaces (the film was reportedly released on home video circa 1985), but until then we can be thankful that it's at least viewable at all, even in this rough of a shape. In fact, in this particular case, the copy's audiovisual artifacts (such as surface noise and 'ghost' imagery caused by a weak TV signal) actually serve to enhance the viewing experience in some ways, especially if (like myself) you happen to be a monster kid who remembers staying up late of Friday or Saturday nights in the '70s watching horror host shows—in my case *Count Zappula's Horror House* (hosted by the late Don Melvoin [1922-2002] as the Count), beamed-in to the boonies of Northern Ontario via Traverse City, MI—while constantly desperately readjusting the positioning of your B&W portable TV's rabbit-ears antennae in hopes of improving the shaky picture, which might fade in or out—or sometimes even disappear entirely—at a moment's notice. (Sigh. Those *weren't* the days!) According to Richard Chamberlain's article entitled "The Beast Lives Again As Forgotten Horror Film Resurfaces" at the B Movie Man website (@ *http://www.bmovieman.com/Features/The_Beast/The-Beast_Lives_Again.html*): [...] *in 1980, for reasons unknown, the decision*

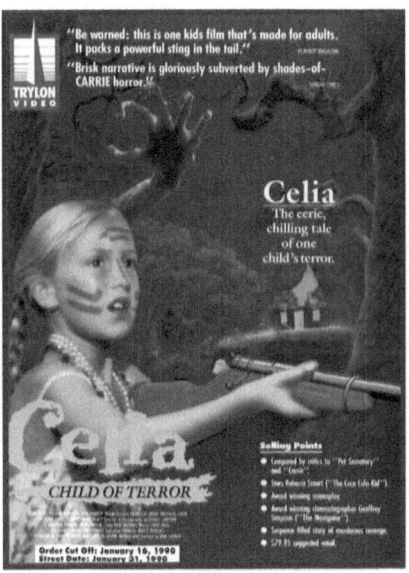

CELIA - CHILD OF TERROR Australasian video trade ad

was made to air the movie as part of a Halloween trick or treat. Many of the cast reminisced about the film in an on screen promo. Leahy would resurrect his character of The Host to introduce the film. A gag rating of NG (Not Good) was played before the movie started. Older viewers enjoyed seeing their local favorites as they appeared 15 years earlier. Young horror movie fans enjoyed watching a movie they'd never seen or even heard about. And as quickly as the hype started, it was over. The movie was returned to the canister and the dust would collect once again. [...] Why not blow the dust off this ancient relic once again and give it a spin on YT tomorrow? I'm real glad *I* discovered it.

CELIA (1989, Australia, D: Ann Turner) – Australasian video tagline: *"The eerie, chilling tale of one child's terror."* Excerpts of a story read to her class by a schoolteacher: *"Through the long grass creep-creep-creeping came the Hobyahs, skip-skip-skipping on the ends of their toes ran the Hobyahs. And the Hobyahs cried, 'Pull down the hemp stalks, eat up the little old man, carry off the little old woman!' Then, little dog Turpie ran out, barking loudly. The Hobyahs were afraid, and ran home as fast as they could go... That night, along came the Hobyahs. Out from the deep woods run-run-running came the Hobyahs..."* Firstly, let me make one thing clear here right at the outset, so there's no misunderstanding: this isn't in any way, shape or form an 'actual' monster movie—nor even a real horror movie either, for that matter—although, albeit they function as purely tertiary characters within the scenario and are little more than symbolic cyphers, it does indeed have monsters in it, which definitely makes it fit this here zine's generally (fairly) rigorous criteria for inclusion herein. How can a movie with creepy creatures in it *not* be a creature feature, you ask? Allow me to explain… Set Down Under during the late 1950s ('57, to be exact), the film is essentially a coming-of-age drama centering around the title alternately angelic/diabolic tomboy preteen female character (perfectly played by expressive then-12-year-old actress Rebecca Smart in twin twisty blonde braids that ideally emphasize her brattiness), who gets up to various exploits and misadventures with members of her peer group (both her friends and enemies); which, in a nutshell, is the main gist of the plot. Factoring quite majorly into the beautifully-written and many-nuanced script is the popular Anglophone/Australasian kids' nonsense story-*cum*-nursery rhyme "The Hobyahs". (Believed to be of "Scotch" *{sic}* [i.e., Scottish] origin, this rather gleefully gruesome, grotesquely comedic tale about titular creepy critters terrorizing elderly country folk by night was originally sourced from the *American Folk-Lore Journal* by a Mr. S.V. Proudfit of Perth and included as tale #69 in editor Joseph Jacobs' folkloric compendium *More English Fairy Tales* [New York and London: G.P. Putnam's Sons, 1894; reprinted in 1922]. Illustrations for the original Putnam edition were rendered by John D. Batten, who downplayed the creatures' more monstrous attributes in favor of a more kid-friendly cartoonishly cutesy look, but artists' conceptions [see below] of the Hobyahs' appearance varied wildly in the many subsequent reprintings of the story, and still do, and they are frequently depicted as considerably more monstrously fearsome in appearance; as, for instance, with their much-scarier-than-usual cinematic counterparts here). Specifically to **CELIA**—and even more specifically to the title character herself, personally—these horrible Hobyahs represent the 'horrors of the unknown' that haunt children's anxieties and terrorize their nightmares the world over. And, yes indeed, the creatures (while not resembling the aforementioned Mr. Batten's artistic conceptions in any way) *are* actually depicted onscreen more than once to varying degrees over the course of the runtime, adding a whole extra layer of watchability to a film that would likely have been every bit as watchable without them, or if they played a far less prominent role in it than they do. Of course, they are in reality nothing more than vividly 'real' figments of Celia's own overactive imagination, but at one key crux of the action—its crescendo, if you will—she actually goes so far as to murder a key local authority figure, mistakenly believing him to be a Hobyah in human guise. It was clearly for this shocking, unexpected scene—and others in which Celia makes like a self-styled priestess of black magic while presiding over voodoo-like rituals and spell-castings with her playmates against their foes—which prompted its video distributor, in hopes of broadening its appeal, to bestow a more immediately exploitative title on the film (namely **CELIA: CHILD OF TERROR**, under which it was released on videotape in Australasia by Trylon Video in 1990 following its critically-acclaimed theatrical run. One of the prime [if debatably inappropriate] selling points of said tape release's promotional push was that it was [quote] *"Compared by critics to PET SEMATARY and CARRIE"*, which well illustrates the tenuous measures the distributor was willing to take in its efforts to pigeon-hole this virtually unclassifiable film as a horror movie, if mostly by simple association). In another of the script's major plot threads, the looming threat of Communism also raises its ugly head when the parents of Celia's best chums from next door begin dabbling in said then-(as now-)'trendy' if utterly indefensible and highly toxic ideology; but not to worry, it's just a passing fad, and they even-

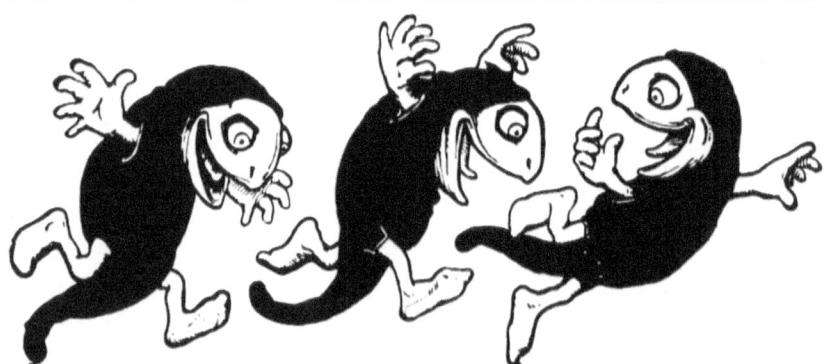

"The Hobyahs", as seen in *More English Fairy Tales* (1894); illustration by John D. Batten

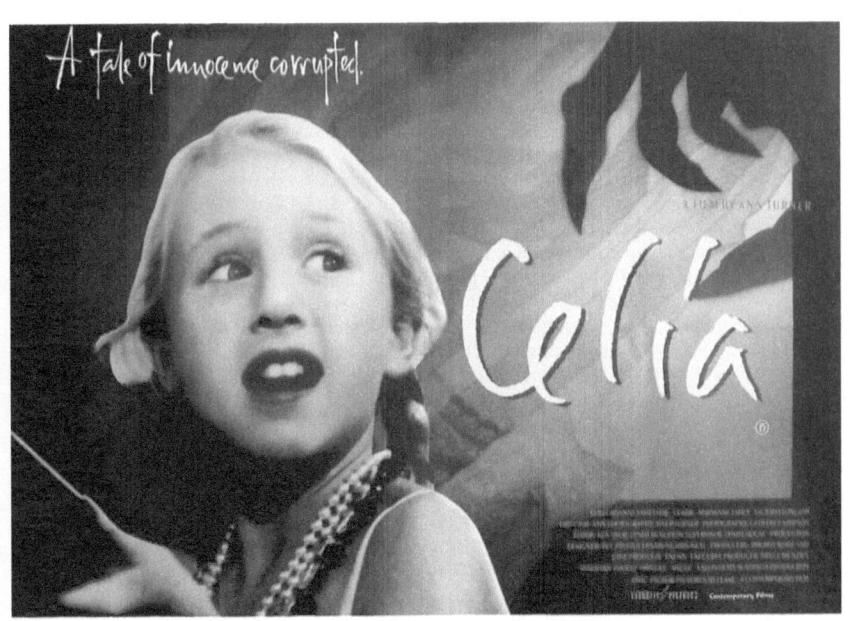

UK quad poster

tually come to realize the error of their ways and get back on the right side of history once again instead of opting to remain Marxist-Leninist scumbags. Celia's pet bunny wabbit and her late beloved kindly—if commie!—grandmother also factor substantially into the plot. Whether you choose to view **CELIA** as a pseudo-monster movie and/or an entry in the 'killer kid' shocker subgenre, or, as was evidently expressly intended by its creators (chiefly writer-director Ms. Turner), as something *more* than that which defies classification without necessarily even trying to, is entirely up to you. But either way, if you're a lover of one-of-a-kind films of any type, it should check all the proper boxes for you and keep you sufficiently engaged from beginning to end. A truly GREAT, unforgettable film, for sure! In more recent years (2009-2010), **CELIA** was made available on DVD Down Under by Umbrella Entertainment (cover blurb: *"A tale of Innocence Corrupted"*) bearing its more truthful and to-the-point original shorter moniker, minus the afore-noted 'technically' truthful if nevertheless still misleading tacked-on qualifier "**CHILD OF EVIL**", which undoubtedly gulled many a horror buff into believing it to be a 'legit' entry in that movie category; which it *is*, somewhat, if not in the ways you might have been expecting. Under the title **CELIA EINE WELT ZERBRICHT** (which loosely translates to something along the lines of "Celia: A Broken World"), it was formerly made available (now-OOP) by Scorpion Releasing on Region 2 DVD in Germany, complete with an English audio option and the ported-over special features from the Anglo edition (presumably with German subs?). Chances are those *Monster!* readers with a predilection for 'something a little bit different' (if with a very definite connection to our usual overlying/unifying theme), may find much of interest in **CELIA** to hold them for its entirety. It sure held me.

THE CHILD (1977, USA, D: Robert Voskanian) – Trailer narration: *"The face of an angel. The heart of a killer. The power of the devil... The child wants to play 'Hide and Go Kill'! ...Her power is unearthly. Her acts, monstrous. Her secret, electrifying... of unspeakable evil!"* I've been on a bit of a '70s kick lately, either re-watching or watching for the very first time movies of various sorts from that classic period of exploitation cinema (including the Apartheid-era South African "Blaxploitation" actioner **JOE BULLET** [1971], the hysterical 'true crime'-based psycho thriller **THE ZODIAC KILLER** [1971], the avant-garde horror weirdie **MALATESTA'S CARNIVAL OF BLOOD** [1973], Duke Mitchell's volcanically-percolating underworld potboiler **MASSACRE MAFIA STYLE** [1974], the grim off-Hollywood/ poverty row survivalist western **APACHE BLOOD** [1975], the speed-crazy, autobatics-filled Peter Fonda/Susan George/Adam Roarke criminal smash-'em-up **DIRTY MARY CRAZY LARRY** [1974], the quirky *Wizard of Oz*-derived glam-age Aussie quasi-rock opera

OZ [1976], the *Walking Tall* vigilante justice trilogy [1973-77], etc). Naturally enough, horror/monster flicks from that time are some of my all-time faves, so it was a given I'd be checking out some of those types; case in point the present title. Produced by American (s)exploitationeer extraordinaire Harry H. Novak and released through his notorious and prolific Boxoffice International Pictures distribco, **THE CHILD** amounts to one of the more lower-profile horror releases of the '70s, and it might very well have remained languishing long-forgotten in limbo if not for the current ongoing retro vogue for rediscovering seemingly every obscure piece of pop cultural detritus from the not-so-distant past, if in this particular instance one well worth saving (and savoring) for posterity. The hoary adage "Everything old becomes new again" has seldom seemed so apt as it does today, especially in regards to the vast amounts of 'previously enjoyed' motion picture product (etc.) that is coming back around again for the entertainment and edification of whole new generations. In this one, an orphaned young woman named Aliciannedel Mar (played by sultry, swarthy straight-haired brunette Laurel Barnett)—a former childhood resident of the area, now returned in adulthood—takes on a job at the out-of-the-way rural home of the Nordon family to serve as live-in caregiver to a (quote) "strange", maladjusted, melancholic and petulantly difficult-to-control tweenage girl named Rosalie (juvenile actress Rosalie Cole, in her only known movie role). Just for maximum spooky atmosphere, the house is located close by to an old cemetery—where Rosalie's recently-deceased mother is buried—on the far side of foreboding, mist-swept woodlands where dimly-viewed grey-skinned ghoulish creatures roam freely by night…and in daytime too, as it happens. Also living at the house are the eccentric, crotchety elderly patriarch Mr. Nordon (Frank Janson) and his 'normie' adult son Len (Richard Hanners), Rosalie's big brother, to whom Aliciannne, as expected, soon finds herself romantically attracted. For the film's first big horror set-piece, Rosalie introduces her (quote) "friends" to a meddling local old biddy / busybody named Mrs. Whitfield (Ruth Ballan) and, just past the stroke of midnight, she is dragged off and bloodily murdered by them.

ATTENTION: SPOILER ALERT! Without giving too much away—the implications have been pretty obvious all along—I'll reveal that Rosalie's secret nighttime playmates are a quintet of (you guessed it!) zombies. "Everyone else is afraid of them, but I'm not. I *like* them!" she proudly proclaims in regards to these creatures, using them as the executors/exactors of her vengeance against those whom she believes caused her mother's death. The special makeup (by one Jay Owens) on these ashen, sunken-eyed, cadaverous, almost mummy/bogman-like crud-encrusted creeps is pretty effective, foreshadowing the familiar brand of Italo-zombie that was waiting to rip out our guts just a couple of years further on down the pike; although the ones seen here tend to move quite a bit swifter than was generally the norm for a zombie back then. The latter third of the action is dominated by a well-done **NOTLD**-style sequence in which the walking corpses besiege Aliciannne and Len inside an old shack. A creepy 'living' scarecrow, an even creepier jack-o'-lantern and a teddy bear that weeps tears of blood also figure in the plot. The periodic gore scenes are nothing if not enthusiastically rendered, with 'one-eyed half-faces' seemingly being makeup artist Owens' forte, as virtually *every* murder victim in the film winds up with one side of their face ripped-off and an eyeball missing! Rob Wallace's exceptional experimental/avant-garde score—which periodically utilizes unnerving distorted sound effects and amelodic, dirge-like out-of-tune piano

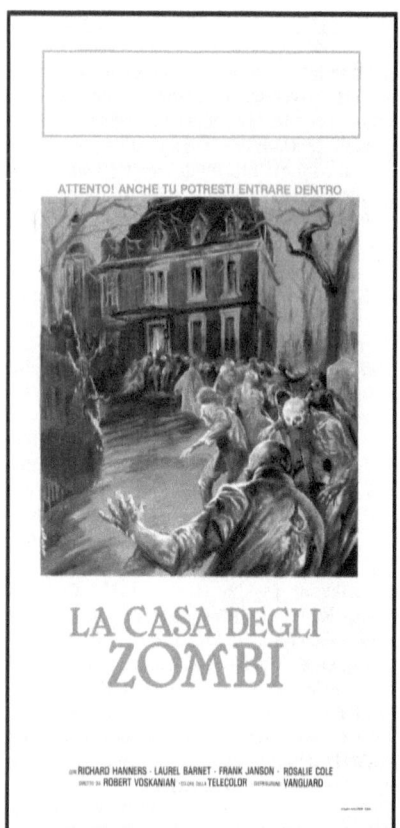

THE CHILD's Italian *locandina* (art by Mafè)

lonking in amidst its more neo-classical instrumentations—at times whips-up suitably discordant cacophonies that accentuate the often dreamlike and at times nightmarish ambience (extra eeriness provided by Detroit, MI-based keyboardist-songwriter Michael Quatro on his Polymoog synthesizer. And yes, he *is* indeed related [he's her big bro] to Joan Jett's self-professed main professional role model, badass black leather-clad '70s grrrl rocker Suzi Quatro!). The cinematography by one Mori Alavi is uniformly fine, amounting to one of **THE CHILD**'s strongest suits (DP Alavi evidently never shot another film [?]; then again, his name hereon sounds like it might be a pseudonym, so perhaps he did do more 'legit' work under a different handle?). Further adding to the dreamy otherworldly nature of the proceedings, actors' lines were evidently dubbed-in after the fact, upon occasion making interlocutors' dialogue sound a tad bit 'off' (i.e., flat and disconnected) in relation to the visual performances. In terms of theme, milieu and mood, this would make an ideal double-bill with Richard Blackburn's macabre adult fairytale **LEMORA: A Child's Tale of the Supernatural** (1973, USA). The present film was released on Beta/VHS tape in Canada back in the day by CIC Video under the more exploitative title of **ZOMBIE CHILD**, but I somehow managed to overlook it at the time. In the USA it was put out in the same formats by both Paragon Video Productions and Monterey Home Video. Also releasing it on VHS, Something Weird Video (SWV) released a "Special Edition" DVD of the film in 2001.

CRYPT OF DARK SECRETS (1976, USA, D: Jack Weis) |– Dialogue: *"Go! Seek the voodoo woman! GO!! Seek the voodoo woman!! Go and seek the voodoo woman!!!"* Another remarkably and wonderfully *odd* download purchase I made from Something Weird Video, I'd been aware of this film's existence for a good long while (via seeing a sexy excerpt from it on SWV's *Extra Weird Sampler* trailer/clip compilation DVD from 2002), but only finally got around to acquiring a copy just recently. Yep, you betcha: this here's another case of 'better late than never' all the way! This 71½-minute-long shot-in-Louisiana marvel is an erotically-charged sexy shocker which deals with a kind of female supernatural creature that is a lot more commonly seen in Asian cinema and only comparatively rarely appears in Western movie fare: namely, a serpent-woman. A local swampers' folk tale tells "…about the woman who lives in the lake and turns into a snake" (of the water moccasin species, I do believe), an immortal being named Damballa (no relation to the similarly-named male voodoo entity!), who is said to reside on fog-enshrouded Haunted Island deep within the bayou. As the local folklore-savvy law officer Lt. Harrigan (Wayne Mack) explains: "I looked it up in the encyclopedia. The Aztecs believed that Damballa is the link between this world and the next. They believe

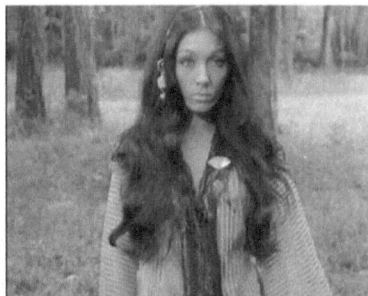

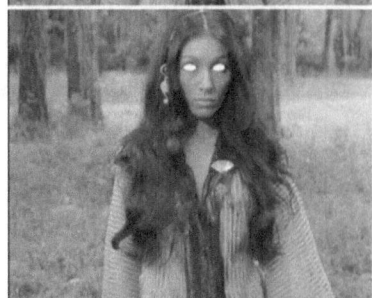

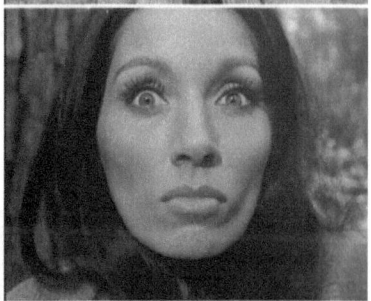

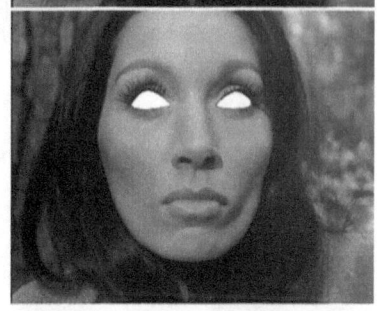

Not Only The Eyes Have It! Honestly, not to sound like a dirty chauvinist pig or anything, but, thanks to her primal pulchritude (literally all over!) combined with her sexy-as-hell 'toffee-nosed' accent, IMO Angloid—if far from *angular*!—stripper-*cum*-um, 'actress' Maureen Ridley is one of *THE* sexiest mamas ever to be seen in a '70s sexploitation flick…or one from any other era either, for that matter!
- **SF** (*blushes*)

it's a rainbow that turns into a snake, and in order to cross over into the next world, you have to walk over this rainbow, or snake, or whatever-the-hell". So there you have it, such as it is! Played by a total knockout name of Maureen Ridley (who is either/and/or of Aussie/Kiwi/Limey [possibly even South African?] origin, judging by her indeterminate 'upper crust' Anglo accent), Damballa can shape-shift from shapely human female to slithery serpent and back again literally in a puff of smoke (those expecting any elaborate time-lapse transformation scenes, fancy dissolves or practical/prosthetic makeup will be left sorely wanting, but the effortless simplicity via how she transforms somehow seems apt to the sensual, dreamy mood). Gleamingly baby-oiled from top-to-bottom/stem-to-stern, the stacked hardbody exotic dancer/actress (who is a *lot* more convincing in that former role than the latter!) performs more than one sexy full-frontal bump-'n'-grind routine with sinuously uninhibited abandon.

For all **CODS**' overall amateurishness of execution, there is a great sense of the primeval rawness and vibrancy of nature, largely evoked by the oftentimes quite beautiful cinematography, which really captures and enhances the otherworldliness of the steamy, sweaty swampland setting. Naturalistic ambient sounds include the chittering of crickets and cicadas, which at times as-good-as drown out the audio track, such is their volume. For much of the runtime, Damballa, rather like a wood nymph, slinks through the forest or skinnydips in the waters of the bayou while from a detached, disdainful distance constantly keeping a watchful eye on the antics of the various mere mortals who intrude on her domain. The hero, Ted Watkins (Ronald Tanet) is a retired, now-pacified and mellow colonel of Rangers who served in Vietnam but got willingly pensioned-off following being wounded and left disabled by shrapnel and now lives upon the spooky isle, although, because he chooses to live at one with nature in peace, Damballa isn't bothered a bit by his presence on her turf. After Earl (Butch Benit) and Max (Harry Uher), a couple of penniless petty criminals from the vicinity, learn (no thanks to *the* most dunderheaded if unwitting bank manager ever! [You'll know what I mean when you see it]) of the secret stash of cash Watkins keeps—fittingly enough—in the breadbox of his out-of-the-way new pad in the swamp, the two miscreants, along with Max's ol' lady Louise (Barbara Hager), case the place before making their big move, doing away with Watkins (or so they think!) before making off with his loot. "You're...you're the girl that swims in the lake", says our hero to the dusky Damballa, without registering any surprise (or other emotion) whatsoever after being given 'the kiss of life' (with lots of tongue!) by her following his being accidentally drowned in the bayou by the overzealous baddies. "The one that... that turns into a snake". In reply she hisses sensually while slinkily sliding all over him in the total nude (*her*, not him!), "*Yesssss!* And now, you exist in the world of the living dead!" Gee, simple as that, eh? We shortly learn that the delectable Damballa is (quote) "The Chosen One" of an ancient tribal sect of dimension-hopping mystical beings, an immortal goddess who exists in-between two worlds at once ("This one and the next", explains her equally-scrumptious high priestess [Susie Sirmen] during a flashback sequence depicting Damballa's backstory), and who is appointed as "The Oracle, The Spirit of Good" to watch over Haunted Island and keep it from harm by encroaching outsiders. Essentially then, her character is much akin to an elemental forest spirit (*à la*, say, the enchanted *engkanto* faerie folk who populate Filipino folklore in vast numbers and serve as guardians of Nature and the environment against the trespasses of humankind). "You can take on any shape you like, or no shape at all", her 3,000-year-old and ready-to-retire predecessor—who doesn't look a day over 30something—casually informs her. "You will find that the cool body of the reptile will be your favorite resting-place, as it was mine". Part of the prophecy she is set to bring to fruition is that she

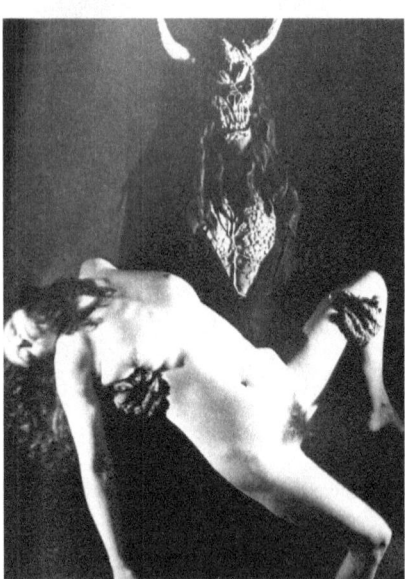

Hellishly Horny: Which part of the above saucy promo photo for **THE DEMON LOVER** did you notice first, I wonder? Robert Skotak's wickedly wonderful devil costume, I bet! *(Wink)*

must form a pair-bond and mate with a mortal human…yep, you guessed it: the lucky fella is Watkins, our laidback, soft-voiced, sleepy-eyed, bushy-bearded, blue-denimed ex-serviceman hunk hero (who, despite all his facial hair, appears *way* too young to have served in both the Vietnam and Korean Wars, as he claims!). As per instructions—"From this cup, drink the juice of the Flower of Forgetfulness, that you may fulfill your destiny"—Watkins does indeed get to hook-up with the dreamily dishy Damballa for all eternity, but, rather than end on a high note of action, **CODS** simply gradually winds down to an easygoing close, ending on an enigmatic if optimistic note that somehow suits the context before the film then simply blows away like a cool breeze back into the enigmatic wilderness whence it came.

For some strange reason, Ms. Ridley, the stunningly-endowed actress playing Damballa, somehow comes across as all-the-sexier despite her nonexistent acting chops and awkward readings of her lines, for the simple reason that her coffee-complexioned, all-natural (indeed, *primordial*) sex appeal succeeds in shining clearly through such comparatively trivial concerns as technical ability, actually somehow becoming part-and-parcel of her sexiness, strangely enough. In an entirely gratuitous—and again, totally *nudo*!—scene that comes from right out of nowhere, in a symbolic act of necrophilia staged inside a mystic circle in a woodland clearing, she languorously dry-humps (!?!?) an ornate metallic sarcophagus (with a glass faceplate that reveals a shriveled, mummy-like cadaver within it). Bearing virtually no relation, if any, to anything else in the narrative—but who cares?!—this is the strikingly provocative sequence contained in the *Extra Weird Sampler* DVD that sold me on much-too-belatedly picking-up a copy of the full film. Still another magical mama, a local 'elderly' (note quotes!) seeress with flour in her hair and bronzer on her face known as The Voodoo Lady (actress uncredited), puts in memorably kooky appearances here and there elsewhere. The presence of a fallen meteorite on the island is mentioned in passing by the hero, adding a potential science-fictional slant to the proceedings, although nothing more is ever made of this particular detail (come to think of it, perhaps it might provide a clue as to the potential extraterrestrial origin of Damballa's people?). The fabled treasure-stash—or rather, cheap chest filled with five-and-dime costume jewelry—of legendary pirate Jean Lafitte has a bigger part to play in the jumbled script, but it's mainly nothing more than a minor subplot intended to pad-out the svelte proceedings to somewhere a bit closer to full feature length (not even close!). Seriously, while

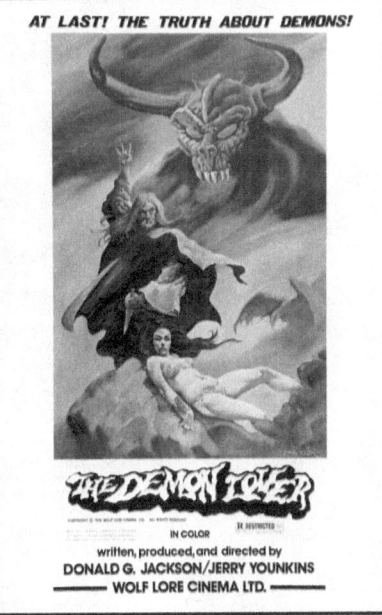

US one-sheet; art by the film's co-star, usual comic artist Val Mayerik

the ridiculously ravishing Ridley is the only one who does the nood thang (a *LOT*!), **CODS** boasts some of the absolute *sexiest* starlets ever to be seen in '70s sexploitation cinema, and that's sure saying something, and they look all the more gorgeous in SWV's pristinely-preserved, flawless print, which is still so crystal-clear and possesses such vibrantly vivid colors that it might have only been shot last week rather than 40+ years ago (it'd look all-the-more spectacular on Blu-ray). Nosirreebob, they sure don't make 'em like they used to; not superbabes like that, nor movies like this either. More's the pity. But no, we're not gonna show you a single nudie shot from the movie here—and there are *many*—so you'll have to buy yourself a copy from SWV if you want to see 'em.

THE DEMON LOVER (1976, USA, Ds: Donald G. Jackson, Jerry Younkins) – Dialogue: *"We've entered the gates of Hell!"* Made earlier in the same year I emigrated to Canada from the UK as a teen with my folks and two kid brothers, while beloved—or at the very least *liked*—by some, this perennial / seminal regional American cult fave of so-called 'D.I.Y.' zee-grade cinema (shot in Jackson, MI) is loathed for its cheapness and not-wrongfully-perceived ineptitude by countless more modern-day horror hipsters, who couldn't 'get' it if their lives depended on it; and that's just fine by me, y'all. It's your loss! Whilst

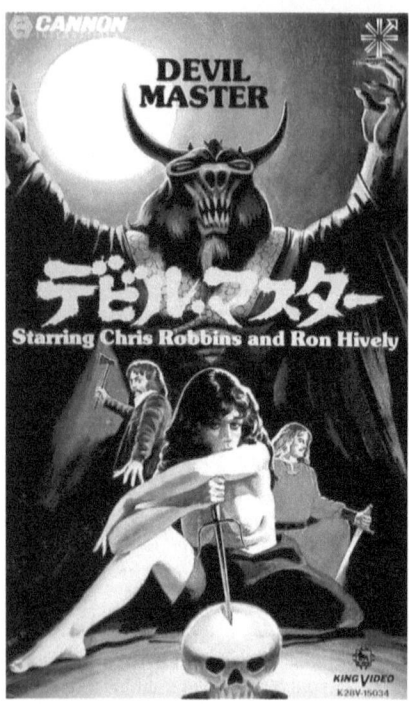

THE DEMON LOVER's Japanese VHS

tossing-and-turning fitfully in the midst of a bad dream caused by a telepathic summons ("Rise! Rise!!") from longhaired, one-black-gloved self-styled satanic high priest Laval Blessing (as played by the even-more-fancifully-named Christmas Robbins, making his only known film appearance), wispy-negligee'd restless sleeper Pamela (Kyra Nash) awakes in the dead of night and, in a somnambulistic trance, drives out into the country—in a lowly AMC Gremlin, yet!—to be unceremoniously brutally dispatched then dragged off into the woods by a roaring beast-thing with razor-sharp claws. Wouldn't you know it, her murder turns out to be merely another part of Pamela's nightmare, however… or *is* it? We subsequently learn that, operating from his stone castle keep on the outskirts of town, evil megalomaniacal hippy-dippy control freak—with faint echoes of Charles Manson—Laval has set his frizzy-banged sights on making a sacrificial neophyte out of Pamela, who is the virginal (?) potential GF of nice guy Damian Kaluta (played by Marvel penciler Val "*Howard the Duck*" Mayerik [who also did the movie's Frazettaesque poster art], whose character herein is surnamed after fellow comics illustrator Mike "*The Shadow*" Kaluta). However, other members of their formed-just-for-laughs coven—consisting of college students into the occult—take exception to self-appointed leader Laval's bossiness and ever-increasing demands of them, so split the scene following an altercation with him, rightly believing he's started taking things way too seriously by far. Having needed the group in order to better channel their collective energy for the purposes of conjuring some major magick (of the darkest *black* kind, natch), Laval shortly consoles himself for his thwarted plans by offering up a token nude woman as a sacrifice-by-sword inside a mystic circle, only to have this ritual interrupted in-progress by the advent of a shadowy, shaggy demonic figure that speaks in a stentorian otherworldly voice ("Bound to serve by magic you invoke!" [sic?] is one of its few intelligible lines, such is the level of audio distortion). Staunchly standing his ground in the demon's presence, Laval promptly commands it to exact violent revenge on his rebellious former co-cultists. Thereafter, Pamela's bloodied corpse is discovered dumped at a local garbage tip, indicating that her presumed dream from the opening sequence was actually merely a premonition of her all-too-real murder, for which Detective Tom "Fritz" Frazetta (Tom Hutton)—driving one of the coolest '70s Yank-made cars, a macho two-door Chevy Monte Carlo sedan!—gets on the case by getting on Laval's case, much to his annoyance. Various other characters are named after an assortment of 'hip' pop cultural personalities, including comic artists and horror filmmakers (e.g., "Janis Romero", "Jane Corben", "Susan Ackerman", "Alex Redondo", "Elaine Ormsby"), and this amounts to one of the very first films to use this since-become-standard means of targeting knowing nudge-nudge/wink-wink in-jokes at specific fanbases, virtually ensuring it some sort of built-in cult following. Before you know it, still more supernaturally-committed homicides presided over by Laval using the demon (played by David J. Howard in a way-cool Robert Skotak-designed-and-constructed big-horned/fanged/clawed hirsute monster suit) as the vessel of his vengeance. "Two girls have been ripped apart as if by wild animals!" exclaims Det. Frazetta in the aftermath of the latest killings, so he consults with occultist/paranormal phenomena specialist Prof. Peckinpah (once-and-future "Leatherface" Gunnar Hansen, onscreen for just one scene) for some pointers. Ron Hively, meanwhile, plays a top-hatted, platform-shoed passable Frank Zappa lookalike who winds up getting shot in the crotch with a crossbow bolt… YOWCH! Retitled **THE DEVIL MASTER**, this funky fright flick was put out on domestic Beta/VHS cassette in abridged form (i.e., from 83 to just 71½ minutes) by the low-end Regal Video outfit back in the early/mid-'80s, and I used to have a copy of that prerecord I scored dirt-cheap someplace. Subsequent stateside videotape reeases by a plethora of different labels bore an assortment of Anglo alternate titles, including **COVEN**, **DEMON TOWER** and **MASTER OF EVIL**; via such video companies as BFP, New Horizons, Premier, Troma Team and Unicorn. As **DEVIL MASTER**, it was released on videotape in Japan by Cannon International/King Video, in English with Japanese subtitles. It was issued on domestic DVD in 2007 by Televista. Although Georgia, USA-based indie horror filmmaker James Sizemore's THE DEMON'S ROOK (2013) is mainly regarded as a loving *homage* to more 'Eighties-style horror fare, I like to think that he was at least in some way influenced by the present film, which is stoned-out 'satanic panic' 'Seventies all the way.

DON'T LET THE RIVERBEAST GET YOU! (2012, USA, D: Charles Roxburgh) – With an epical, epochal title like that, it was inevitable I'd be getting around to watching this bugger sooner or later. In the fictional, generic rural community of "River Town, U.S.A." (represented by locations shot in Manchester, NH, Salem, MA and Seymour, CT), an amphibious monster ("…half ape, half reptile, half I-don't-know-what!") periodically emerges from the local main waterway to off any unwary humans who cross its path. While it kills its victims with nary a dribble of blood nor even any real violence being shown throughout, it does make some mildly gross slobbering noises upon occasion, if that's any sort of consolation. Playfully emphasizing the intentional complete lack of any actual horror or scares to be had herein, a bright red 'fear-flasher' gimmick—shades of the one used in **CHAMBER OF HORRORS** (1966, USA, D: Hy Averback); if not any "Horror Horn", as was also featured in that film—heralds the monster's appearances each and every time it shows up, adding a further self-consciously silly wrinkle to things. Youthful producer/co-writer Matt Farley also self-'stars' as Neil Stuart, the meek milquetoast private tutor hero of the piece, who has long been shunned as a nutball by certain surly town residents for asserting that the supposedly-only-legendary title critter does indeed exist. In a cast consisting entirely of amateur actors—whose amateurishness of delivery is by no means a liability, but actually adds to the naturalistic, easygoing charm of it all (and no, I'm not in any way being condescending by saying that!)—the middle-aged male character nicknamed "Milly" (played by one Millhouse G.) gets the riverbeast's share of the best lines (e.g., "There's nothing out in those woods but the *picnic babes*!") and delivers them with just the right amount of deadpan-if-knowingly-ironic chutzpah. For the movie's most-unforgettable line, with a completely straight face, he actually manages to get out the following profoundly philosophical observation all in one go: "It's as if all that was and all that will be is all mixed-up in one pungent porridge!" I literally had to replay this line three more times after I first heard it, that was how much it cracked me up (I guess you had to be there!). Another hilarious moment comes when slimy, opportunistic town tabloid journalist Sparky Watts exclaims in horror just before he meets his maker after the flubbery monster (suit designed by Gregory Kochan) clambers out of a glorified mud-puddle and comes a-clawin' for him, while he squeals like a little girl, "Heavens to Betsy! The riverbeast *exists*!" Another amusing character is renowned so-called ladies' man and big game hunter ("He's better-known for hunting ladies than hunting beasts!") Ito Hootkins (Jim Farley), who blows—okay, *tootles*—way-out-of-tune blues harp solos at the trees while out communing with the great outdoors by his lonesome and spies on cavorting, giggling "picnic babes" at every opportunity. Dressed in a sandy-colored Desert Storm camo vest, Hootkins gets bloodlessly speared on a sharp stick for his troubles when he gets too close to the beast while snapping its photo. Because, being amphibious in nature, the creature needs to periodically re-wet itself so as to avoid drying-out and expiring, thanks to a bossy freeloading hippie chick his buddy picks up while out busking and allows to platonically move in with him, the hero hits upon the brainstorm of using—wait for it (***ATTENTION: MAJOR SPOILER ALERT!***)—*kitty litter* to absorb all its vital bodily fluids, thus putting paid to the rampaging horror in what

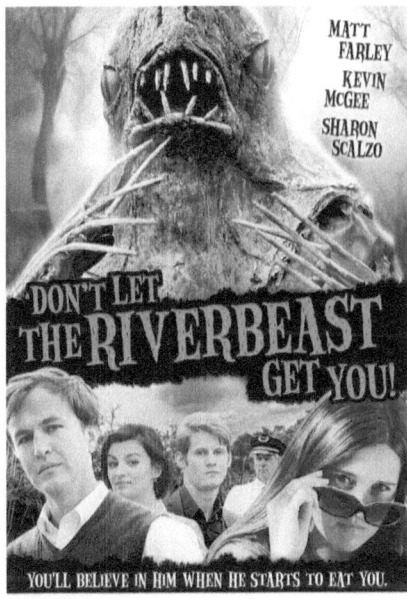

US poster

River Town's pricelessly-named, silver-haired Sheriff Paultique Hanson (Jim McHugh) mildly if wildly overstates at the end "...shall go down in history as possibly *the* greatest aquatic beast-battle mankind has ever waged!" ("If it hadn't been stopped, this beast might have devoured America!"). Made with an endearing sense of playfulness and loads of love despite its many obvious technical shortcomings—whaddaya want on a budget of about $9.99?!—**DLTRGY!** is a highly-likeable D.I.Y. creature feature indeed. No campy, mean-spirited piss-taking at the expense of beloved genre clichés here! Just good old-fashioned, wholesomely down-home F-U-N. And not only that, but The Dying Elk Herd's end-theme ditty ("Don't Let the Riverbeast Get You!" natch) is infectiously catchy-as-fuck in a melodic poppy/punky garage style much in the vein of The Dead Milkmen, which closes things on a suitably jauntily jolly note. There's a legitimately-viewable upload of **DLTRGY!** on YouTube at the prolific and popular Kings of Horror's channel, which currently has close to 500K subscribers and specializes in all kinds of low-to-no-budget indie genre fare and periodically posts content that might be of interest to *M!* readers, so by all means go do some surfin' there.

GODMONSTER OF INDIAN FLATS (1973, USA, D: Fredric Hobbs) – Part modern-day western, part pseudo-social drama (!!) and *ALL* strange, with a totally fucked-up monster, I first became acquainted with this for-the-longest-while-unseen, wild-'n'-wooly wonderama of weirdity (my words!) via a clip included on Something Weird Video's cram-packed 2002 *Extra Weird Sampler* DVD (*"Over 100 of the Most Amazing Movies Ever Made!"*), a trailer/movie excerpt compilation I (i.e., SF) picked-up back in the early 2000s from a Toronto video joint on the express recommendation of Dennis Capicik, who really knows his shit (and Shinola). At long last, as a special self-treat just in time for Christmas 2017, I ordered a copy of **GOIF** (downloaded direct from SWV's website for a mere $9.99) and finally got to see the full flick. Let's just say it was well worth the long wait, and if I'd known it was gonna be as thoroughly demented as it turned out to be—I should've guessed that would be the case by the utter lunacy of the excerpt I saw!—I would've grabbed myself a copy that much sooner. "I say it's a damaged, mongoloid beast!"—So says a duly alarmed representative of the authorities in this seriously brain-damaged regional American ultra-obscurity (shot largely in desolate mountainous terrain in and around Virginia City, Nevada). While he's specifically referring to the mutated bipedal sheep-beast (identified as a "hybrid") in it, his exclamation might just as easily have been used by me to describe the film itself, which I can honestly say is one of the most supremely *bizarro* creepy-cheapies I've yet laid my disbelieving eyeballs upon…and that's sure saying something, cuz I've seen more than my share of weirdities in my time! When first seen angrily busting-loose from its basement laboratory incubator, it must be said that the shaggy woolen mutant monstrosity appears quite impressive and almost lifelike in its appearance and movements. However, when later shown for lengthier stretches out in broad daylight, it comes across as a much more pitifully pathetic thing as it hobbles and wobbles about awkwardly on its stunted, stumpy hind-legs with its misshapen, disproportionate 'arms' (i.e., uh, forelegs) dangling floppily before it like Justine Turdeau's withered, perpetually-flaccid preteen peenie, emitting bobcat-like snarls/roars and porcine snorts/grunts. "Feast your eyes on the Eighth Wonder of the World!" proclaims the (very) poor man's Carl Denham/Max O'Hara who has the sheepozoid creeper captured (= lassoed by a posse of cowpokes, Mighty Joe Young / Gwangi-style!) and puts it on degrading public display, all-caged-up…for less than two minutes anyway, before the ungainly-gaited beastie again busts loose and waddles off wonkily to commit some more small-scale carnage before ultimately going the way of the dodo. Fittingly enough, it all ends amidst raucous maniacal laughter and anarchic chaos down at the local garbage tip. Is **GODMONSTER** godawful? Actually, I prefer to think of it more as *awe*-ful, that's how slack-jawed in amazement and disbelief it periodically—quite often, actually—left me. And yes indeed, you better believe it was worth *every last penny* of the puny ten-buck outlay I made to get it! Oh, and it makes an ideal second feature to watch back-to-back with Jonathan King's far-from-sheepish 2006 Kiwi monster parody/satire **BLACK SHEEP** (see my co-co-editor/shepherd Tony Strauss' witty review of same in *Monster!* #30 [June-July 2016], p.98). Okay, time to flock off to the next entry now…

LATE PHASES (2014, USA, D: Adrián García Bogliano) – I was drawn-in and held by this volcanic slow-burner of a film right from the get-go, and there are some interesting and unusual things going on in it that distinguish it from the typical werewolf tale (which you'd never guess in advance even *was* one, judging by its non-self-explanatory title; its **NIGHT OF THE LONE WOLF** a.k.a. makes the content a bit more clear up front for those who prefer things to be spelled-out for them). Nick Damici (also seen the same year in the decent backwoods demonic shocker **DARK WAS THE NIGHT** [2014, USA, D: Jack Heller], and also in the sci-fi/vampire adventure **STAKE LAND** [2010, USA, D: Jim

Mickle] and its sequel **THE STAKELANDER** [2016, USA, Ds: Dan Berk, Robert Olsen], both of the latter on which Damici also served double-duty as screenwriter) stars to fine downbeat effect as lone wolf Ambrose McKinley, an aging 'Nam vet who suffered severe eye trauma during combat and was left permanently blinded as a result. Haunted by the horrors of his war years and PTSD and having become fatalistic to the point of being suicidal ("The only thing precious about life is it *ends*"), he is convinced by his p-whipped son (the expressive if mumblingly too-emo Ethan Embry)—largely due to the latter's nagging shrew of a wife (Erin Cummings)—to move to an idyllic rural retirement community called Crescent Bay to live-out the rest of his days on his pension as tranquilly and frugally as possible. However, shortly after his arrival, Ambrose is attacked during the night by a murderous beast that has of late been slaughtering local residents in a series of vicious killings that, it being the country and all, the authorities logically attribute to being the work of natural wild animals; Shadow, his loyal seeing-eye German Shepherd, gets mortally wounded whilst attempting to defend his master from the bestially monstrous attacker. Thereafter, the sightless veteran arms himself in constant readiness for another potential attack from the killer, which strikes only nocturnally, during the cycle of the full moon. He begins using his old Army-issue entrenching tool—which can double as a handy ax-like or stabbing weapon, if necessary—as a 'walking cane'. The all-practical, '80s-style transformation sequence (a throwback to the likes of those seen in **AN AMERICAN WEREWOLF IN LONDON** and **THE HOWLING**) is quite the sight to see, while the resultant shaggy-haired, jackal-faced monster is atypical enough to stand out from the rest of the lycanthropic pack. Tom Noonan fills a solid character part as Father Rogers, a chain-smoking local priest who receives an alarming wake-up call as to the true nature of evil forces at work in the world—his parish in particular—when he witnesses the werewolf transforming right before his eyes. And while we're on the topic of transformations here, guest star Tina Louise, the ex-"Ginger" from *Gilligan's Island*, appears to be suffering from the cumulative effects of way too much bad plastic surgery. Just sayin'. I was originally going to say that **LATE PHASES** isn't *quite* in the same league as Eric Red's 1996er **BAD MOON** (see separate entry above [p.336]), but it comes pretty damn close. However, thanks to a couple of startling developments coming late into the narrative—which I'll keep my lip zipped about—I'm pleased to announce that **LP** can quite easily rate being placed atop the same plateau with it to stand proudly shoulder-to-shoulder with **BM**, that's how well it

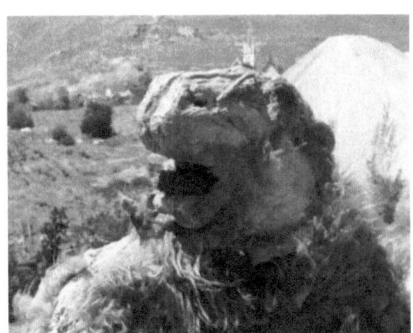

Shari Lewis & "Lamb Chop", Eat Ya Hearts Out: *Mutant sheep alert!* (Fire-up the barbie and break out the mint sauce…)

gets its shit together in the final quarter. ☺ This is a slow-burning volcano that knows just when to blow its top, and does just that in rousing fashion when the time comes before ending on a poetically poignant note. **LP** is out on domestic DVD from Dark Sky Films, and special features-wise their edition comes with all the basics (i.e., commentary, making-of and SFX featurettes, plus a trailer). As **NIGHT OF THE WOLF: LATE PHASES**, Metrodome released it on Region 2 DVD in the UK, with much the same (possibly even identical) bonus features.

THE MONSTER OF CAMP SUNSHINE (1964, USA, D: Ferenc Leroget) – Opening title proclamation: *"The motion picture that follows is a fable. In it there are many nudists but only one monster. In life, it is generally the other way around"*. Incredulous dubbed-on exclamation: *"A* monster*?! In a* noodist *camp!?"* Subtitled **"Or How I Learned to Stop Worrying and Love Nature"** in direct parodic reference to a certain critically-acclaimed Cold War era black comedy of its day, despite also being shot in glorious B&W like **DR. STRANGELOVE** was (albeit much more for budgetary reasons rather than aesthetic ones), the present slice of skid-row sleaze/cheeze is about as far removed from Kubrick as you can get! Yet another Something Weird special. Credited to a certain "S. Eek", the bizarre minimalistically-animated title sequence using pictorial cutouts foreshadows Terry Gilliam's future trademark style with the Monty Python crew (the photography/editing credit goes to one "Motley Crue"!). While periodically—if not very often—featuring post-synched dialogue that matches-up fairly closely with actors' lip movements, much of the plot exposition is also propelled by voiceover narration, as was such a commonplace cost-cutting technique on these kinds of vintage hand-to-mouth poverty row productions. The two heavy-smoking youthful female protagonists, IBM computer-matched

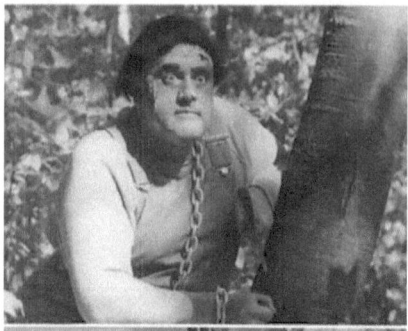
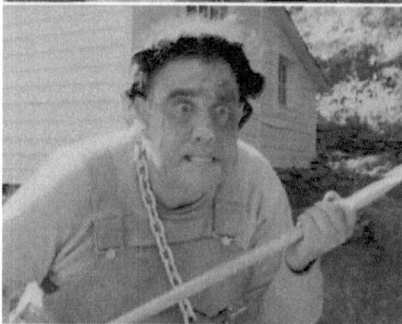
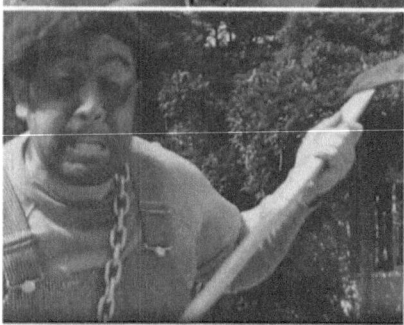

You Axed For It! As the chopper-swinging alleged "monster" of (nudist) Camp Sunshine, for the duration of his entirely mute, er, performance, non-actor Harrison Pebbles halfheartedly pulls 'frightful' faces; this evidently in hopes of making his gawdawful, virtually nonexistent 'special' (facial-only) makeup look even slightly frightening — good luck to that!

(!) roommates Claire (Deborah Spray) and Marta (Sally Parfait), a pro $50-per-hour photographic 'glamor' model and registered nurse respectively, are undoubtedly highly easy on the eye—make that *both* of 'em! In fact, this being a post-nudie cutie / pre-roughie sexploitation outing, **TMOCS** is chockablock/wall-to-wall with a whole bevy of bounteous bouffant ingénues in various stages of undress; it being only '64 (= the P.P. ["Pre-Pubes"] era) and all, however, there's zero pubic hair on view, so no need to get your hairy palms all in a sweat, you pervs!). Key to the plot, such as it is, Nurse Marta works at a hospital testing facility where medical experiments are performed on rodents (the real-life laboratory used for a set really adds some authenticity here, for what it's worth). After experiencing an uneasy premonition of danger prior to heading off to work that day, during her shift poor Marta is beset and terrorized by some escaped experimental lab rats ("HELP!" shrieks a silent movie-style intertitle card), resulting in her very nearly falling to her death out a window of the high-rise building. It is later revealed that Marta's researcher boss Dr. Harrison (James Gatsby) had irresponsibly disposed of the dangerous combination of chemicals and hormones that turned the rats vicious in the East River, whereafter the jar containing the toxic concoction drifts upstream... Prior to this, left severely stressed-out by the rat attack, Marta—a closet nudist who keeps naturism magazines secretly stashed-away in her smalls drawer under her undies—opts to take some time off to recuperate. Sure enough, she and her swingin' roomie Claire (grudgingly, despite her inhibitions regarding public [to use Bart Simpson's word] nakidity) promptly ditch the hustle-'n'-bustle of downtown NYC to go off on an idyllic boonies getaway together... at—yep, you guessed it!—the eponymous Camp Sunshine, a nudist colony ("A place where people could actually go and take off their clothes together outdoors" [*GASP! SHOCK!! HORROR!!!*]). Much titivating ado is made of the disrobing ritual and nudists letting it (almost) all hang out in scenes which reveal strictly boobs and bums, nothing more, often set to jaunty silent movie era-type ragtime or folksy bluegrass music (evidently stock rented tracks?). Not that I was going out of my way to spot them, you understand, but in one group long shot I couldn't help noticing that at least one (1) (flaccid) male reproductive organ can be fleetingly glimpsed. Despite what I said to the contrary above, millisecond glimpses of pubic regions can be spotted here and there...which must have driven the most prudishly puritanical of the censors nuts!

The gals' initial idyll nestled cozily in Mother Nature's nurturing bosom goes without a hitch. Their return visit, on the other hand, goes all pear-shaped when the to-this-point easygoing narrative finally gets down to the nitty-gritty... well, *sorta*, anyway. To cut a long story short, after the carelessly-discarded container of serum is fished out of the water by an incompetent angler with his rod and reel, some of the spilled contents wind up being unwittingly sipped from a freshwater spring by Camp Sunshine's hulking—thankfully fully-clothed!—woman-hating

Midnight Snack Reviews

gardener Hugo, a (quote) "rather simple fellow" (Harrison Pebbles, giving a truly spastic 'performance' while making virtually no effort whatsoever to appear fearsome). As a result, he undergoes an, uh, transformation c/o about 50¢'s worth of silly putty and greasepaint to become the so-called "monster" of the title (which is an overstatement if ever there was one). Having been kept tenuously bound with chains in the interim since the heroines' previous visit, upon their return Hugo busts loose of his bonds, grabs up an axe, then lumbers off into the woods looking for something—or someone—to chop with it. Unfortunately, the clumsy great galoot steps into a bear trap, which snaps shut on his leg, thus ensuring that his chopper remains dry on this his inaugural monster foray. Pushing coinkydink to an even more unbelievable extreme than earlier in the aimlessly meandering narrative, Doc Harrison 'just happens' to discover an antidote to the transformative serum and proceeds to bomb to the rescue by motorbike and light aircraft, parachuting into the camp just in time to administer a curative injection to Hugo before he can cause anything more than a minor flesh wound, only to then have the monster up and perish in a military bombardment anyway (the editor had a real field day here splicing together plentiful war movie/newsreel footage, often from totally anachronistic historical time periods, just to further emphasize the glaring mismatch of film stocks). What started out fairly promisingly ultimately degenerates and disintegrates into an inept mess, but I suppose that's just another part of its, um, 'rough-around-the-edges' charm. Adding to the overall jovial silliness of the affair, a (fictitious) horror movie double-feature is at one point mentioned in passing: "THE MONSTER FROM HAIRY PLANET" billed with "DRACULA MEETS THE BEATLES"! Paired-up as the second feature with **THE BEAST THAT KILLED WOMEN** (1965, USA, D: Barry Mahon) on disc, **TMOCS** is also available via SWV individually either as a DVD-R or direct download (the latter being my preferred option, but to each their own).

PANDORUM (2009, Germany/UK/USA, D: Christian Alvart) – While the story gets a bit murky to follow sometimes (stick with it though, cuz it all [kinda] comes together in the end), this here's one myghty fyne slice of over-the-top monsterrific sci-fi indeed, which Yorz Drooly only finally first got around to very belatedly viewing in early March of '18, for some strange reason. The rudiments of the milieu are this: a gigantic intergalactic terrestrial spaceship, the Elysium, is ferrying many thousands of Earthlings (in a state of cryogenic suspension) to some far-flung new world that has been proven habitable by human beings. However, en route some sort of catastrophic technical failure occurs which sees certain members of the crew—including Dennis Quaid as the senior officer and Ben Foster as a junior crewman—becoming prematurely awoken from suspended animation. We (and they!) shortly learn that a number of other passengers aboard the ship got de-iced too early while still in-transit and, over the course of presumably many millennia, subsequently somehow devolved/degenerated into a fast-breeding, swift-moving new species of feral, carnivorous so-called "Hunters", bearing only the slightest semblance to "Us"; pasty-faced, sightless/noseless horrors often facially resembling a combination of the *Lord of the Rings* franchise's Orcs and *Harry Potter*'s Lord Voldemort, but sometimes with quite a lot of variation in their individual looks, as though their devolution ran randomly amok amongst their physiognomies to come up with endless variations of sheer unadulterated ugliness. Tribal in culture and cannibalistic (towards humans, their distant ancestors) in nature—*if* these so-different-from-us abominations of humanity can even be classified as cannibals at all, being as how, zoologically speaking, a cannibal is an organism that takes sustenance via eating the flesh of its own kind—the Hunters infest a rundown out-of-the-way subsection of the spaceship, constantly multiplying in numbers. And there, in a nutshell, you have the main thrust and antagonists of the story. Oh, and by the way, the "pandorum" of the title refers to a delusory mental ailment suffered by astronauts after spending too long in deep space at zero gravity which causes them to experience

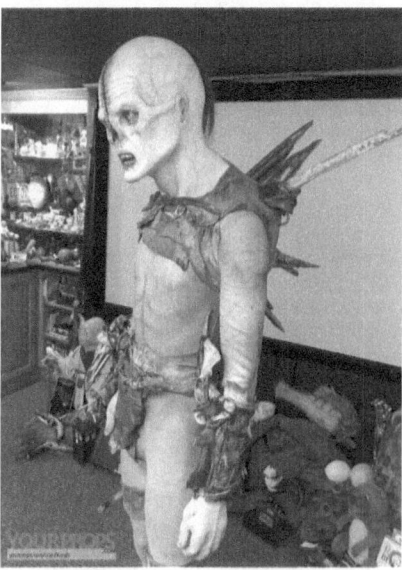

A "Hunter" dummy from **PANDORUM**, made by the Stan Winston Studio

paranoid hallucinations that ultimately turn them homicidal…an angle which also factors into the plot in a big way. But not to worry: the 'orrible ooglies infesting a section of the Elysium are *not* merely figments of any of the protagonists' brain-addled delusions! Yes indeed, it's normal humans versus abnormal subhumanoids for much of the runtime, with plenty of in-fighting among the former group along the way.

But come on, guys, not to go all cultural Marxist-style politically correct and play divisive, tribalistic intersectional identity politics on your asses here or anything, but couldn't you at least have let either the token (cannibal [*YIKES!*]) person of color (the late Eddie Rouse [1954-2014]) or the token martial arts expert (*natch!*) Asian dude (real-life Vietnamese-American MA master, 2008 Strikeforce Middleweight Champion Cung Le) survive at the end, instead of killing 'em both off in such a ruthlessly perfunctory fashion, just because you couldn't be bothered to think of anything better to do with them? But then, in all fairness, you *did* go above and beyond the call of duty by not only meeting but actually voluntarily exceeding the mandatory, SJW-approved PC quota in the 'superultramega-badass-shitkickin'-chick-who-don't-need-no-man-no-way-no-how' department, including not just one but *TWO* furiously ferocious fearsome female freedom-fighters (FFFFF)—Well, in spirit, anyway. There's actually only *one* such chick (angular-featured Teutonic actress Antje Traue, whose apparently phonetically-delivered English reading of her lines is sometimes pretty sketchy); but she's TWICE as kickassly badassish as yer usual token tough chick, so she might as well be twins—that make(s) Imperator Furiosa look like your typical trigger warning / safe space-craving weakling university student (of either sex or any gender, be it feminazi, mangina, attack helicopter, otherkin or whatever). So I guess it all evens out... um, at least until she gets her shapely ass humiliatingly handed to her by an old straight white cisgender alpha male (the top-billed Quaid [of **ENEMY MINE** fame], who definitely doesn't look his age one bit) during the climactic concatenation, anyway. But then that's equality for ya. Welcome to the New Millennium, grrrls! No one ever said it was gonna be a chivalrous Utopia! :-D Then again, the movie *was* made the better part of a decade ago, so perhaps that explains its less-than-textbook (i.e., *Little Red Book*) adherence to the current even-ever-more-puritanical/tyrannical requirements of out-of-control PCness run riot. Incidentally, alternative heartthrob Norman Reedus appears in a bit part herein a year prior to finding international superstardom as the antiheroic co-lead of the AMC TV mega-phenom *The Walking Dead* (2010-). Great action choreography and stuntwork combined with kinetic cutting, fine special makeup FX, and more than one effectively startling plot-twist all add-up to quite the exhilarating rollercoaster ride; although, in this cynical day and age and all, where SF movies often come with downer endings, during the final scene when—***ATTENTION: SPOILER ALERT!***—those hundreds of jettisoned emergency escape-pods start bobbing to the surface of the alien planet's ocean, I was SO expecting (and hoping) a horde of Hunters to come bursting out of 'em to not only further spoil the surviving heroes' day but also royally fuck up their future as well. Oh well, we can't have everything! Having said that, I can't help wondering if maybe some sort of obligatory "feel-good" ending might have been tacked-on in place of such a more downbeat one at the producers' behest, for commercial purposes? Even with its optimistic resolution instead of a darkly despairing one, however, **PANDORUM** really delivers the goods and comes highly recommended. In closing, all I can say is: why the *hell* did I wait so long before ever getting around to watch this??!! Reportedly, Neill "**DISTRICT 9**" Blomkamp's way-bigger-budgeted SF action epic **ELYSIUM** (2013, USA), starring Matt Damon, borrowed both its title from the name of the spaceship in the present film, as well as certain trace elements of its plot too—albeit minus any monsters other than those of the (in)human (and biomechanical) kind.

SATAN'S BLACK WEDDING (1975, USA, D: "Philip Miller"/Nick Millard) – Ad-line: *"A Blood Marriage of Ghouls!"* Trailer narration: *"An abomination in the eyes of God! ...Evil so frightening, so ghastly that it is beyond human endurance! ...Blood-fiends raised from the dead by Satan himself to do his horrible bidding! ...An aura of death and chilling terror will engulf you as you enter a supernatural world of Satanists! ...Terror that will grip your heart in its icy, death-like fingers! ...You are invited to a wedding: SATAN'S BLACK WEDDING. The most diabolical ritual imaginable!"* For some reason, I can still recall where and when I first saw the title of this movie listed: in the 'upcoming releases' column of an early issue of the UK's *House of Hammer* magazine, back when I was still living in Wales as a teen in the 1970s. But a lurid title like that was bound to stick in my memory, I suppose, being as how up till that point I had been exposed to very little in the way of actual, bona fide exploitation flicks, the horror kind least of all. It was a title that greatly titillated me then, but it would be more than half a lifetime more before I would at long last get to see it, having not really been in that much of a hurry to track it down in the interim (I'm pretty casual and easy come/easy go about that sort of thing;

if it happens, it happens. If it doesn't..."*C'est la vie!*" as some Frenchman once said. There are always plenty of other things to stimulate my interest in the meantime!). That said, perhaps if I'd gotten a load of the trailer for it way back when, its imagery and classically-overstated if relatively soft-spoken narrated hyperbole would likely have made me want to see **SBW** a whole lot sooner! As for the film itself, a stylish opening credits sequence depicts grotesquely nightmarish paintings accompanied by a delicately-tinkled piano piece. The striking visual style continues on into the opening scene, wherein a leering male vampire psychically compels a young authoress named Nina Gray (Lisa Milano), who had been writing a shockingly sensationalistic occult novel—involving diabolic nuns and clergy, horrific child sacrifices, etc.—to commit suicide by repeatedly slashing her wrist with a razorblade in surprisingly gruesome fashion (although little in the way of actual abrasions are shown, plenty of thick, paint-like fake blood is slathered around). The vampire proves to be one Father Dakin a.k.a. Daken (the sinister if well-spoken Ray Myles), a satanic priest—possibly a defrocked Roman Catholic one?—who revealingly wears a black dog collar instead of a white one, a particularly conspicuous fashion choice which curiously never raises the eyebrow of anyone who meets him. It is further revealed to us that Nina the suicide has been summoned to hell by Satan and then returns to Earth as one of the undead, cursed to take the lives of all her well-to-do Monterey, CA-based family members. Her inaugural victim is Estella the Italian housemaid, immediately followed by the Gray siblings' bedridden aunt, both of whom she savagely puts the fangy fright-bite on set to the gentle strains of Beethoven's Piano Sonata No. 14, a.k.a. "Moonlight Sonata" (1801), which adds to the overall elegiac mood (the rest of the sparse score is also played mainly on piano, with a few scritchy-scratchy strings heard here and there [possibly those of a piano?]). Once again, plentiful red stuff is poured-on for this initial vamp attack, but nary any actual wounding is shown. Complete with plastic novelty Halloween costume vampire fangs that are only about one step up from those found in Cracker Jack boxes, there is often a detectable 'Euro' ambience to the proceedings, sometimes akin to a French or Italian (or even Mexican or Filipino) vampire movie—which is perfectly fine by me.

Along with her friend and co-writer Jean Holt (actress unknown, although she plays a quite substantial part), Nina had visited a centuries-old unconsecrated church that was said to have been the site of atrocities committed by vampires, where the latter woman fell deeply under the evil influence of the place ("Did you know that Sa-

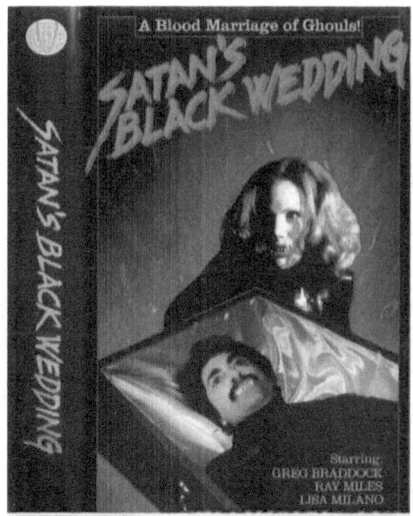

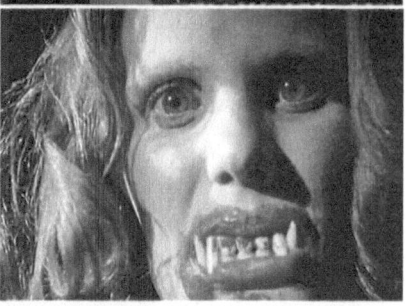

World Video Pictures' 1980s US VHS cover for SBW [top] clearly printed its mere 61m runtime right on its back cover. Above: Lisa Milano bares her cheap plastic vamp fangs!

tan himself once appeared here in this crypt to a group of nuns?" Fr. Dakin/Daken later informs the late Nina's brother Mark [Greg Braddock], who is investigating her suspicious death). By a process of auto-suggestion, she had begun committing to paper the horrors that occurred on the premises close to 150 years earlier, and she and Jean parted ways after Nina began to act more and more strangely in the weeks leading up to her demise. Dimly-viewed down in the dark shadows of the debased church's crypt, a single vampire nun appears for a grand total of about three seconds, and that's *that* for the 'nunsploitation' angle (although the community of satanic sisters and their ungodly antics are alluded to sight-unseen in the dialogue more than once). Considering that Ken Russell's **THE DEVILS** (1971, UK) had only just come out a few years earlier, whipping-up great controversy virtually globally, there's a good chance that **SBW**'s vampiric ex-brides of Christ were inspired by it, while the 'suicidal-sinner-sent-back-to-Earth-by-Satan'

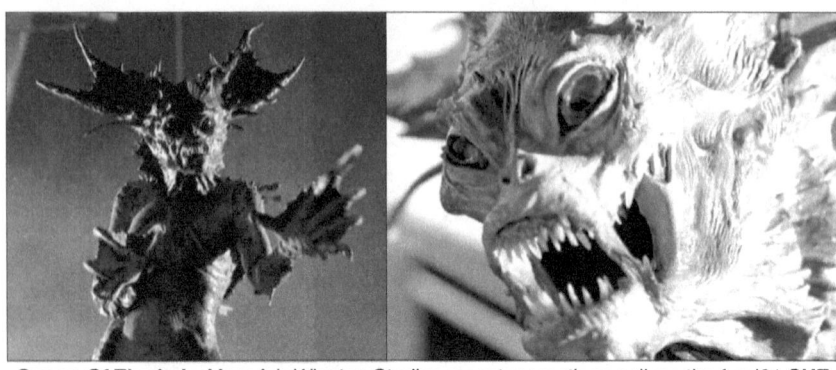

Queen Of The Lair: More fab Winston Studios monster creations enliven the fun '01 **SHE CREATURE** "remake"

angle was likely pinched from Gerardo Damiano/Georgina Spelvin's seminal occult-themed porno chic hit **THE DEVIL IN MISS JONES** (1973, USA). Getting from A to B with no time for any shilly-shallying around, **SBW** is a real *short* feature even by '70s second-feature standards at just over 61½ minutes (which was more like the average running length of a '30s or '40s "B" or "C" programmer), whose acting ranges from not bad to quite good, while its cinematography is at times very strikingly composed/lighted indeed. Because of the atypically brief runtime and since I spotted a couple of edit-points during the film that were conspicuously choppy, I'm tempted to surmise that X number minutes of footage got the chop somewhere along the line, either for censorial reasons or due to simple severe print damage (?); but that's just my take on it. Sporting a subdued pseudo-'50s cool cat haircut and sideburns, affable leading man Braddock has a likeable enough, vaguely John Ashley-via-Elvis quality about him, but despite his good looks and passable acting chops—ironically enough, since in **SBW** he plays a Hollywood actor on leave—this was apparently his only screen acting stint, as with most of the rest of the cast. Here playing the wholly unholy holyman, while Myles also filled supporting parts in both Ted V. Mikels' **BLOOD ORGY OF THE SHE-DEVILS** (1973) and William A. Levey's lowbrow, sexed-up schlock sci-fi'er (about a randy E.T.) **WHAM-BAM-THANK YOU, SPACEMAN** (1975), even his filmography, although longer than most of his cast-mates', is none-too-extensive itself. While there's blood aplenty on view in the present title under review, only very little of a sexploitative nature is included. For instance, during a romantic fireside lovemaking interlude between the hero and heroine, precisely one (1) blurry female nipple is only fleetingly glimpsed in profile, so those attracted by the more erotic implications of the title looking for all sorts of demonic debauchery going on are bound to be sorely disappointed. But those with a jones to see an old-school bloodsucker flick with a lot going for it despite its modest means and brevity might wanna give it a look-see. Like me, you may be pleasantly surprised.

SHE CREATURE (2001, USA, D: Sebastian Gutierrez) – Director Gutierrez in the DVD's mere 2½-minute behind-the-scenes/making-of featurette: *"Our story's about a mermaid... but it's not **SPLASH**!"* Domestic DVD tagline: *"Beautiful, Seductive and Totally Deadly."* Much ado was made in the fan press at the turn of the millennium about the series of 'remakes'—actually, barring their soundalike if not always identical titles, total reimaginings (i.e., 'inspired by')—of '50s AIP "B"-monster movie classics by Creature Features Productions under the official auspices of former American International Pictures co-boss (with the late James H. Nicholson [1916-1972]), executive producer Samuel Z. Arkoff (1918-2001), who outlived his similar-aged late partner by three decades but passed away while the short-lived Creature Features project (hyped as *"The next generation of horror!"*) was still in the offing. For my money—trust me, I bought 'em *all* on DVD when they first came out in the early 2000s—this present title was the best of the bunch, although most of the others have at least a few things going for 'em. They are as follows: **THE DAY THE WORLD ENDED** (2001, D: Terence Gross), **EARTH VS. THE SPIDER** (2001, D: Scott Ziehl) and **HOW TO MAKE A MONSTER** (2001, D: George Huang); the most worthless (i.e., pretentious piece of crap) of the lot being the execrable **TEENAGE CAVEMAN** (2002), directed by Larry Clark, who made that 'controversial' (i.e., scummy) flick about modern teenagers, **KIDS** (1995, USA). As for Gutierrez's **SHE CREATURE**, it's thankfully a whole other kettle of fish by far. The series' only period piece (set at the turn of the 20th Century), its director endeavored to model it along the lines of an Edgar Allan Poe-type tale in a Hammer Films style, and the film stands apart and registers more favorably than its contemporary-set companion pieces largely by virtue of the fact that its costumes and production design have a classier air that can't help but increase its production values. In fact, **SC** even opens with a familiar stock shot showing a windswept clifftop mansion that was 'borrowed' (with AIP's official approval) from Roger Corman's series of '60s Poe adaptations. Opening "Somewhere in Ireland" in 1905, we are soon introduced to silver-tongued if rather sketchy carny sideshow impresario Angus Shaw (as entertainingly played with a convincingly-affected 'Oirish' accent by Rufus Sewell, who always reminds me of the great Ian McShane's kid brother), whose sensational roster of attractions include a starey-eyed Darby "**I WALKED WITH A ZOMBIE**" Jones-like 'walking dead' dude from the Caribbean (Reno Wilson). When the zombie—actually a fake played by a performer in disguise—starts to get out-of-hand after being baited by a mock-heckler planted in the audience for that very purpose, it is shortly lulled into passive submission by the siren song of the show's in-house *faux* 'mermaid' (played by cute English actress Carla Cugino, playing an actress named Lily), who is for some reason billed on the hand-painted poster as "The Colossal Beast" (AIP in-joke alert! ☺). Of course, all this 'drama' is soon revealed to be just part of the show, specially-staged for the punters' entertainment. Frequent genre scene-stealer, long-time character actor Aubrey Morris ([1926-2015] of **THE NIGHT CALLER** [a.k.a. **BLOOD BEAST FROM OUTER SPACE**, 1965, UK, D: John Gilling], **BLOOD FROM THE MUMMY'S TOMB** [1971, UK, Ds: Seth Holt, Michael Carreras], **LIFEFORCE** [1985, UK/USA, D: Tobe Hooper], **BORDELLO OF BLOOD** [1996, USA, D: Gilbert Adler] *et al*) puts in a welcome supporting appearance as an eccentric elderly gent named Woolrich, a former sea captain who pegs Cugino's entanked mermaid act as a sham right from the get-go. It is subsequently revealed that, in another tank at his mansion, Woolrich keeps an all-too-*genuine* mermaid held captive. Played by the suitably alluring Rya Kihlstedt, this redheaded, web-fingered, spiny-finbacked and fishtailed semi-human/semi-piscine female creature had murdered the old man's wife then devoured her (as the trailer narration tells us *"...this beauty has an ugly appetite for human flesh!"*), yet he nonetheless cannot get over his unhealthy infatuation with the beautiful-but-deadly siren in his possession. After Woolrich accidentally up and kicks the bucket under duress, Angus and his cohorts spirit away the late ex-seaman's mermaid in the middle of the night, then ship her out in secret on a slow clipper—called the "Mary Celeste", no less (*uh-oh!*)—bound for America. Mid-Atlantic, the plot thickens all the more… The sultry she-creature ("…that beast…") forges a psychic link with Lily, for whom she feels a strange attraction, and the feeling is mutual. Before you can say "Let's eat sushi tonight", we learn that the fishgirl has somehow managed to impregnate Lily with a fetus. The siren subsequently—if only temporarily—sprouts human legs during the cycle of the full moon, only to later still turn into something a whole lot less human and much more monstrous than before (digital animation is awkwardly intermixed with good ol' practical animatronics during her transformation scene). Now that the beast within her has been unleashed, the, er, mermaid begins slaughtering the ship's crew as part of a horrifying scheme… Sewell's and Cugino's topnotch, committed performances really help sell the story. As with all the other titles in the unfortunately short-lived *Creature Features* series—each of which bear the closing tribute "Dedicated to the Memory of James H. Nicholson"—this was put out on domestic disc by Columbia Tristar Home Entertainment. The present title's special features included an audio commentary by FX artists Stan Winston (1946-2008) and Shane Mahan, supervisor of effects (under the auspices of the Stan Winston Studio), including for the memorable "Queen of the Lair" monster. Rather than in the capacity of FX tech, Winston instead served as one of the many co-producers on the five *CF* flicks, as did his subordinate Mahan, who also did effects work hereon, as well as on a couple of

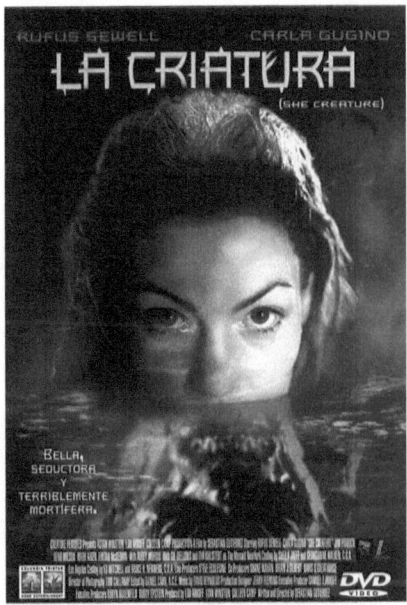

Spanish DVD of **SHE CREATURE**

Midnight Snack Reviews

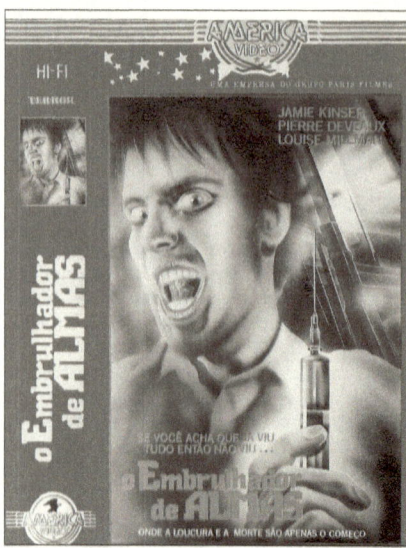

Portuguese-language jacket for the incredibly scarce Brazilian VHS edition of **THE SOULTANGLER**. The same unsigned art appeared on the US release too

the other *CF* entries too, and he would eventually go on to co-design the exquisitely-rendered gill-man seen in Guillermo del Toro's **THE SHAPE OF WATER** (2017, USA [see p.4]).

THE SOULTANGLER (1987, USA, D: Pat Bishow) – Original US VHS trailer narration: *"Run, Kim, run! Scream for your life! From every corner emerges total terror! The most unearthly evils are born! His power permeates the living and controls the dead!"* Original US VHS box taglines: *"All He Wants Is Your Soul. When Madness and Death Are Only the Beginning."* The title character Dr. Anton Lupesky (as played by the so-called Pierre Deveaux [an obvious alias if ever there was one!]) unleashes one of his several epic monologues/rants: *"It's your soul I'm after. I'm a master of souls. I possess many souls, but periodically I need to enrich myself with the soul of a young woman... a beautiful young woman who secretes the magnificent essence that I need to tangle-up with the web of my soul!"* As Dennis Capicik explains in the attendant paragraph of video details immediately following this one, the 'general release' version of this originally-shot-on-16mm film-to-video (at 1.33:1) effort is the better part of a half-hour longer than the hour-plus 'director's cut', the latter of which is a lot easier to take due to being more, um, tightly edited...or at least is mercifully a whole lot *shorter*, anyways. So it's the version of the two included in Mondo Video / Bleeding Skull's homegrown disc edition that we're gonna go with. It clocks-in at just over 62½ minutes (a mere minute more than **SATAN'S BLACK WEDDING** [1975]; see separate entry above), and very nearly *three* of these are taken up by the opening credits alone, which leaves just a 59+-minute timeframe in which to tell its story...minus still *another* three minutes of end credits, that is, so the total narrative only runs around 56m, all-told. As added 'bonuses', the print even comes complete with occasional video dropouts on the master transfer and that dully hollow, out-of-synch sound common to sixteen-mill, whose audio tracks often had to be dubbed-on after the fact rather than taped live simultaneously (although, that said, some scenes were obviously shot with direct sound, cuz nobody could possibly lip-synch *that* well!). Looking for her breakout big scoop in hopes of making an instant name for herself and scoring her very own weekly column on the rag, the beaky Ms.—accent on *Mizz*—Kim Castle (Jamie Kinser), an 'ace' reporter for a (quote) "neighborhood sleaze tabloid", sniffs-out a bizarre story involving nocturnal abductions of young women by homicidal hooded perpetrators, devil worship...and even *weirder* things besides (such as a freshly de-skulled, snail-like crawling human brain with its eyeballs still attached by stalks, for instance!). World-renowned (!?) scientist Doc Lupesky's special serum, called Anphorium, can either transpose people's souls into others' bodies through their eyes (a.k.a. the windows to the soul)... or else potentially leaves those treated with it reduced to gibbering, dribbling undead loons. Plenty of cut-price if fast-moving grease-paint-and-rags zombies—presumably Doc's failed 'soultangling' experimental subjects?—show up, while another specimen seen elsewhere wears much-more-elaborate prosthetic makeup and looks like it stepped right out of the pages of an EC comic. In one of the loonier moments, still another male zombie with dangling entrails attempts to strangle a man with its own intestines while grotesquely waggling its tongue around like crazy. Gruesome eye violence is a recurrent motif, as per the script's specification about how 'soultangled' victims can only be killed via destroying their eyeballs (essentially a variation of the "shoot-'em-in-the-head" zombie-killing credo). A random clip of witches lining-up to kiss the Devil's ass—a notorious satanic rite known in Latin as the *osculum infame*—is at one point edited-in from Benjamin Christensen's silent masterpiece **WITCHCRAFT THROUGH THE AGES** (*Häxan*, 1922, Sweden), as are other brief snippets from the same film, which by simple aesthetic contrast frankly seem jarringly out-of-place in the present, er, 'humble' context. This flaky flick would make for an ideal co-feature on the bottom half of a double bill with "N.G.

Mount"/Norbert Moutier's wacked-out *escargot* splatterfest **TREPANATOR** (1992, France; see *Monster!* #32 [p.217]), which is admittedly more consistently entertaining. Previously only ever available in severely limited numbers on videocassette—including, of all places, in Brazil from the so-called America Video label under the Portuguese retitle **O EMBRULHADOR DE ALMAS** (a literal translation of the original English title)—the present interesting and at times economically inventive zip-budge oddity saw its first-ever DVD release anywhere just this past March. As writer Sheri White opined about the then-forthcoming release earlier this year at the horror website Hellnotes (@ *https://hellnotes.com/the-soultangler-from-agfa-and-bleeding-skull-coming-in-march/*): "If **RE-ANIMATOR** was shot on Long Island for the price of a used car, **THE SOULTANGLER** would be the result. Insane genius *[...]* has developed a drug that allows users to inhabit corpses and transform into rabid maniacs! *[...]* This epic of outsider filmmaking is a dream-like wasteland that's punctuated with severed heads, evil beasties, and hooded slashers." (More follows directly below about the brand-new disc edition's specs…)

Once again (as with our **FRANKENSTEIN '80** entry listing above), the following paragraph of vid info comes courtesy of Dennis C. via his review of the film at his website Unpopped Cinema (@ *unpoppedcinema.blogspot.ca*). Shot in 16mm then edited on video, American Genre Film Archive (AGFA) / Bleeding Skull Video's fully-loaded DVD was transferred from the original one-inch master tapes, and the results are about what you'd expect from such a hand-to-mouth endeavor. The film is also presented in its original 1.33:1 ratio, and while the picture quality is limited by its less-than-optimal source material, it all looks reasonably sharp, with relatively stable colours (which are especially evident during some of the more outlandishly-shot moments). The Dolby Digital audio is also free of both distortion or an overabundance of hiss, with HypnoLoveWheel (i.e., Jim Cook, Griffin Dickerman and Chris Xefos)'s decent electronic score sounding just fine. Unlike Mondo/AGFA's earlier retro big-box VHS edition from 2014 or the once even-harder-to-find Canadian VHS from Astral Video, which housed the standard (89m42s) edition of the film, AGFA have this time round also included a (quote) "previously unseen 62-minute director's cut", which plays far more effectively. In director Pat Bishow's feature-length audio commentary, he goes on to discuss how the distributor forced him to (quote) "pad it out to 90 minutes" because it was simply too short. So, much to his dismay, using previously-discarded takes and extra footage, Bishow went on to (quote) "explain Anphorium" and also add in all those unnecessary filler scenes of people walking and driving, which he equates to (quote) "torture". He also goes on to talk about the trials of shooting a low-budget film such as this, as well as discussing many of the Long Island locations (including that filthy basement!); how much of it was (quote) "done on-the-fly"; plus he also mentions the uncooperative nature of Kinser, who (quote) "wasn't very nice." While Bishow begins his commentary by exclaiming "I can't believe *anybody* is actually listening to this!" he goes on to fill the 90 minutes with ease. Other extras include *The Making of The Soultangler* (12m13s), with plentiful behind-the-scenes footage shot in May of 1985; the film's original video trailer (*"From every corner emerges total terror!"*), still another video trailer from Bishow's earlier film, **THE DEAD OF NIGHT TOWN** (1983); and also a music video shot by Bishow for HypnoLoveWheel's "Wow!" In addition to including the film's very rare Canadian VHS release, the disc also comes with reversible cover art featuring new—and wholly appropriate—art by Matt "Putrid" Carr. – **Dennis Capicik** (Thanks again, Denzo! ☺☺) *[*NB. An upload of Bleeding Skull's earlier VHS version of* **THE SOULTANGLER** *is available to stream for free, with the caveat of an add-on subscription (whatever that means), on Amazon (@ https:// www.amazon.com/Soultangler-Bill-Bernhard/dp/B01N06M51R).]*

NEXT ISSUE:

More Indian monster movie reportage by Tim P; Chris M's "(Second) Son of My Monster Movie Marathon Diary: Godzilla A Go-Go II"; the 2nd and final instalment of Stephen Jilks' "Channel of Darkness" article; "The House That Josh Built", Troy H's new interview with D.I.Y. filmmaker Joshua Kennedy; Pt. 4 of Steve B's career-spanning Brett Piper i-v/article, "Anarchy & Monsters"; an overhauled reprint of Steve F's 27-year-old i-v with Jack Taylor, Spain's second-most-famous horror movie icon; plus MORE!, **MORE!!**, *MORE!!!* & **MORE!!!!**

Midnight Snack Reviews

www.ingramcontent.com/pod-product-compliance
Lightning Source LLC
Chambersburg PA
CBHW031606210526
45464CB00004B/1449